Fodor's 2000

Paris

D0406573

Fodor's Travel Publications, Inc. • New York, Toronto, London, Sydney, Auckland

CONTENTS

MAPS

Circled letters in text correspond to letters on the photographs. For more information on the sights pictured, turn to the indicated page number Ⓐ⟩ on each photograph.

DESTINATION
PARIS

Stroll along formal footpaths in the Jardin du Luxembourg and lose yourself in the halls of the Louvre. Meander through Montmartre and promenade down broad boulevards off the Arc de Triomphe. Master métro lines and river curves. Immerse yourself in the city's patchwork of villages. Linger in a Left Bank café and indulge in gastronomic delights. Admire the architectural filigree—the woven metal of the Eiffel Tower and the plastic tubing encasing the Pompidou Center. Listen to vendors hawking the season's produce in the markets of Montorgueil and Mouffetard. At every turn Paris envelops you in its spell of history, proportion, harmony, and visual delights and compels you to return.

ARCHITECTURE

Ⓐ 45

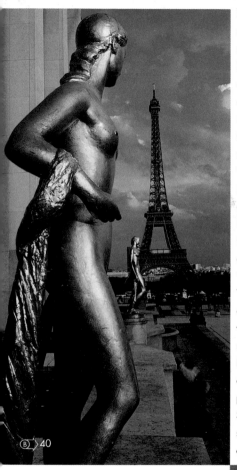

Ⓑ 40

It may be a heightened sense of aesthetics or just Gallic disdain, but Parisians seem to have always greeted the architectural innovations that are continually rising in their midst with skepticism—all the while assembling the most beautiful city on earth. "C'est magnifique," say some Parisians of the grandiose glass pyramid by architect I. M. Pei that sprouted in 1989 from the Cour Napoléon at their beloved Ⓓ**Louvre.** "C'est horrible," say others. The Ⓐ**Grand Palais** was tolerated only as a frothy oddity when it went up as a temporary pavilion for the World's Fair of 1900, but it's still there, a reassuring glass and iron presence on the banks of the Seine. And some Parisians sniffingly refer to the high-rise complex of Ⓔ**La Défense**

as "Houston on the Seine," though this futuristic area and such other glassy creations as the Ⓒ**Institut du Monde Arabe**, completed in 1988, continue to provide the visual theatrics with which Paris astonishes. Even the Ⓑ**Eiffel Tower** wasn't spared Parisian scorn: When the city's grace-

Ⓒ 91

ful icon first appeared above the rooftops in 1889, naysayers quipped that they enjoyed ascending to the top because it was the only place they didn't have to look at the damned thing.

The mansard-roofed buildings lining the grand boulevards that Baron Haussmann sliced through the medieval city in the 19th century are as emblematic of Paris as the Art Nouveau entryways to métro stops such as ⓗ**Porte Dauphine,** which have a playful elegance that you can find only in Paris. But over centuries, other familiar sights have come to represent not only the city but also all things French—the Eiffel Tower, of course, but

also the Arc de Triomphe and ⓖ**Notre-Dame.** Perhaps the world's most famous cathedral, Notre-Dame is the symbolic center of France and, quite literally, the nation's ground zero—it sits at the point from which all distances to the capital are measured. Still, the memories you cherish most may be of small jewels like the Palais de Chaillot, St-Sulpice, or ⓕ**Ste-Chapelle.** More glass than stone, the latter was the Middle Ages' supreme achievement, and its heavenly light has not dimmed over the ages.

A CITY FOR WALKING

"It was always a pleasure crossing bridges in Paris," Ernest Hemingway once wrote. Had he deigned to effuse beyond his characteristically succinct style, he might have added that it's best to make these crossings on foot, stopping midway to regard the monuments along the quais and perhaps ponder the meaning of life as one of the Ⓑ**Bateaux Mouches** slips beneath your feet. On the age-old cobblestones of fabled boulevards such as the rue de Rivoli and twisting medieval streets that fan out from the banks of the Seine, Paris hides all sorts

Ⓑ 38

of secret treasures that can be discovered only on foot. In your random wanderings you may come upon a thrilling street market or old men playing boules, perhaps on ⒟**rue de La Tour Maubourg** in front of the Hôtel des Invalides, delightfully unaware that they are fulfilling a cliché of how French men of a certain age should pass their time. Or you might amble into a street market like the one at ⒠**Bir Hakeim,**

where the shoppers prove that Parisians do spend much of the day in pursuit of gastronomic pleasures. The ⒶⒸ**Marais** still resembles the neighborhood in which Molière and La Fontaine scurried along narrow streets to the salons of 17th-century aristocrats, who built the quarter's magnificent *hôtels particuliers,* as its mansions are known. No doubt these enlightened gentlemen of letters paused a moment or two to take stock of the urbane beauty all around. Few can resist the urge.

MUSEUMS

Not just repositories of masterworks, the museums of Paris also reveal the endlessly fascinating nuances of French culture. It is fitting that the Ⓓ**Musée d'Orsay,** a Belle Epoque former train station, houses the city's legacy of art from 1848 to 1914: Railroads and other everyday phenomena were—shockingly so at the time—favorite subjects of the period's artists, especially the Impressionists, who enjoy pride of place under the glass-vaulted roof. Art has always flourished in Paris; now the city benefits from French government efforts to keep its citizens' masterpieces perpetually within its borders. Near the Musée d'Orsay, the Ⓐ**Musée Rodin** bears testimony to the sculptor who, with the admirable shrewdness that Parisians have elevated to an art form, arranged to live and work at state expense in the 18th-century Hôtel Biron in return for leaving his work behind in its airy rooms and lovely gardens. The

Ⓐ 106

Ⓑ 46

Ⓔ**Musée Picasso,** occupying the 17th-century home of a financier who made his fortune collecting salt taxes, also arose from a compromise—Picasso's heirs gave France 230 paintings, 1,500 drawings, 1,700 prints, and many sculptures in lieu of paying death duties. And it was the French Revolution that opened the Ⓑ**Louvre** to the masses, so that all can now view the extraordinary collection amassed in good part by seven centuries of monarchs, while imagining the history-shaping intrigues that once fermented in these same salons. A proletarian spirit also holds sway at the Ⓕ**Centre Pompidou,** where the world's largest collection of modern art is displayed; though opened in 1977, it has been so popular that it has already needed renovating, and will go into the new millennium looking better than ever. At the futuristic Ⓒ**Parc de La Villette,** with its interactive science and musical-instrument museums and its shining spherical Géode theater, you can look into the city's future. And if the surroundings are any indication, its future will be every bit as fascinating as its past.

Quotidian activities are elevated to high art in Paris, and shopping is no exception. Sophisticated city dwellers that they are, Parisians approach this exercise as a ritual, and an elaborate ritual at that. Pick-

Ⓐ⟩220

ing produce at the open-air markets on rue Mouffetard or rue Montorgueil or at the Ⓐ**Marché d'Aligre**, or searching for haute couture at Jean-Paul Gaultier, Sonia Rykiel, or Ⓕ**Christian Dior**, they cast a discerning eye on the smallest detail and demand the highest quality—which may explain why

SHOPPING
AND MARKETS

Ⓑ⟩219

Ⓒ⟩219

Ⓓ⟩77

the city's shopkeepers are so famously grouchy. Browsing through old books and maps in the stalls of *bouquinistes* (booksellers) on Ⓓ**Quai de l'Hôtel de Ville** along the Seine, or prowling through castoffs at the Ⓔ**Marché aux Puces St-Ouen**, Parisians show their practicality, their sense of economy, and their ability to turn even a piece of junk into an inventively chic treasure. The city's lairs of consumerism are celebrated—the fashion salons, venerable antiques shops, august fashion

showrooms, and *grands magasins* such as Bon Marché, Au Printemps, and the Ⓑ Ⓒ **Galeries Lafayette,** which flaunt Belle Epoque extravagance and trendy designers. Though a short visit

Ⓕ 225

may not give you time to develop a Parisian's innate sense of taste and style, you are sure to be indoctrinated into the pleasures of worldly goods and to come home with some glittering prizes.

15

"Animals feed, men eat, but only wise men know the art of dining," wrote the French gastronome Anthelme Brillat-Savarin. Join them as they pursue their art, and abide by their rules—over a picnic of Camembert on a baguette in the Bois de Boulogne; at a meal created by the brilliant ⑧**Pierre Gagnaire** at his eponymous temple of gastronomy; on such hallowed ground as ©**Restaurant Alain Ducasse**; or when eating one of the same chef's groundbreaking and utterly delicious creations in his less

DINING OUT

Ⓐ▷ 157

expensive bistro-annex Ⓐ**Le Relais du Parc.** Wherever you go in this world capital of good eating, one essential requirement is to toss caloric caution aside (after all, Parisians appear capable of consuming

croissants by the basketful without gaining an ounce) and throw yourself into creations that are nothing short of poetic. Another is to follow the age-old routine: End any proper meal with a cheese course, then dessert (the more decadent and creamy the better), then an *express* (taken black, with sugar). As to the wine: as Monsieur Brillat-Savarin memorably noted, "A meal without wine is like a day without sunshine." A visit to this city without partaking of all the pleasures of the table would be more dire than that.

PARKS AND GARDENS

A⟩104

Every once in a while it's pleasant to regard Paris from the comfort of a chair in one of the city's parks. The experience is all the finer if it's springtime, if you're with someone you love, and if the park is as idyllic as the Ⓐ**Jardin du Luxembourg.** This Left Bank retreat and the Ⓓ**Jardin des Tuileries** across the river provide amusements that are resolutely genteel and satisfy a uniquely French craving to enjoy the great outdoors amid gravel paths, statuary, and manicured flower

Ⓓ 45

beds. In contrast, and not by accident, the surroundings are uncharacteristically rusticated in the Ⓑ**Parc Montsouris**—this expanse of copses and lawns on the city's southern periphery is the only Parisian park in the English style. Understandably, King Henri IV favored a French design when commissioning the pink-brick mansions and central garden that grace the Ⓒ**Place des Vosges,** once the favored in-town address of nobility (known as Place Royale until the Revolution prompted a name change), but in these democratic times the gates are open so that all may enjoy the prettiest square in Paris. As for the city's most poignantly liberating outing, it's to the Ⓔ**Parc André-Citroën,** on the site of one of the famous car maker's former factories, an oasis of greenery and dancing fountains.

Ⓕ 130

LITERARY PARIS

Over the centuries Paris has fueled the genius of no small number of men and women of letters. You are likely to encounter the ghosts of many of them in the Ⓐ**Cimetière du Montparnasse,** where Baudelaire may well be exchanging bons mots with Maupassant, Sartre, and Beckett amid the riot of statuary that honors them, or in the Cimetière du Père-Lachaise, where rocker Jim Morrison rests alongside such luminaries as Gertrude Stein. Oscar Wilde, one of many foreign writers to have sought refuge in Paris, complained of his hotel on Ⓓ**13 rue des Beaux-Arts** in St-Germain-des-Prés, "I am dying beyond my means." A plaque commemorates his passing, shortly

Ⓐ 111

Ⓑ 222

ⓒ 98

ⓓ 113

before which he eyed the wallpaper and uttered one last quip: "One of us has to go." He would be pleased that the surrounding quarter still draws literati, who work in publishing houses or frequent the small bookshops such as ⓑ**Shakespeare and Company,** the city's noted outpost of expat, bookish bohemia. The nearby ⓒ**Sorbonne,** one of Europe's oldest universities, has been the nerve center of Parisian intellectual life since 1253, and any number of landmarks around the city have inspired some of the world's most noted works of literature. The 19th-century realist novelist Emile Zola found his muse in Les Halles, referring to this marketplace and gathering spot for riffraff as the "Belly of Paris." Pedestrian zones and shopping malls have since replaced the stalls of butchers and fishmongers, and one of the few vestiges of the neighborhood Zola would recognize is the church of ⓔ**St-Eustache.** Even there, new statuary looks out at the ever-changing city from an unusual point of view, offering hope that novelty, and the genius it fosters, will continue to be one of Paris's most precious commodities.

ⓔ 58

Parisians can sit for hours in the many wonderful neighborhood cafés like Le Vieux Colombier, Le Sancerre, and Ⓓ**Au Père Tranquille** in the heart of Les Halles, and any true Paris experience requires joining them. Cafés are perfect for a break and for people-watching. The ⒶⒸ**Café de Flore** on boulevard St-Germain is still

CAFÉS

Ⓑ 102

redolent of the 1940s and 1950s, when Jean-Paul Sartre and Simone de Beauvoir held court for a cadre of other iconoclastic writers and artists. You can't help feeling that something profound is being uttered at the next table, any more than you can resist the ultra-rich hot chocolate being served. Only Paris can muster settings as impossibly pretty as the Jardins du Palais-Royal, the Galerie Vivienne, and the Ⓑ**Cour de Rohan**; before you abandon yourself to romance at a café here, remember that the guillotine was invented nearby. Most typical of Paris is the *café du coin*, where, for the price of a cup of coffee or a glass of beer or wine, you can catch up on gossip and observe everyday life passing by—which is always a lot more interesting in Paris than elsewhere.

C ▷ 163

D ▷ 162

PERFORMING ARTS AND NIGHTLIFE

Although Paris has always been a place to abandon inhibitions and sow wild oats, the city has lost the reputation for naughtiness it had back in the days when artist Toulouse-Lautrec painted the Ⓓ**Moulin Rouge** and, later, when the creatively dissolute writers of the Lost Generation drank until dawn in Montparnasse. Still, the shows in this celebrated nightclub and a few others are as formidable as ever. And

though the Lost Generation is long gone, along with most of the smoke-filled *boîtes de nuit* they frequented, succeeding generations of night owls have found new venues. Clubs like Le Petit Opportun and Le Sunset in Les Halles and Ⓑ**New Morning** in the 10ᵉ arrondissement have earned Paris a reputation as one of the world's serious jazz cities, and the Ⓕ**Divan du Monde** in Pigalle is a major stop on the international rock circuit. The Ⓐ**Opéra Garnier** in the 9ᵉ arrondissement has been upstaged by the new Ⓒ**Opéra de la Bastille,** which pays homage to its address by providing grand opera at (somewhat) proletarian prices; but Garnier's sumptuous hall, built with upper-class tastes in mind, is not entirely out of fashion—it's now the home of the illustrious Paris Ballet. If you yearn

to dance in the moonlit streets like Maurice Chevalier and Leslie Caron, visit on July 13th. All Paris turns out in neighborhoods like the Marais for the Ⓔ**Bals des Sapeurs-Pompiers** (Firemen's Balls), late-night, outdoor dance parties that usher in Bastille Day on the 14th, but more than that, simply to enjoy a balmy summer evening in this most beautiful of cities.

GREAT ITINERARIES

Paris in 5 Days

A visit to Paris is never quite as simple as a quick look at a few landmarks. Each neighborhood has its own treasures, so be ready to explore—a pleasant prospect in this most elegant of cities.
☉ So that you don't show up somewhere and find the doors locked, shuffle the itinerary segments with closing days in mind. To avoid crowds, go to museums and major sights early in the day. Note, too, that some museums and major sights have reduced entrance fees on Sunday and that many museums are closed early in the week (on Monday your best bet is the Day 2 itinerary).

Paris, a superb modern art museum. Or take a tour of the Seine on the Bateaux Mouches; these boats depart regularly from Place de l'Alma. From here, walk or take the métro to the Arc de Triomphe; from the top there's a great view of the boule-

Ⓐ 56

DAY 1

Head first to the Eiffel Tower: morning (or late evening) is the best time to avoid the crowds. The most thrilling approach is via the Champ de Mars. Afterwards consider visiting the Art Deco Palais de Chaillot, with its numerous museums. Also in the area is the Musée Guimet, with Asian art, and the Musée d'Art Moderne de la Ville de

vards emanating from L'Étoile and the noble vistas extending to the Louvre and La Défense. Then work your way along the Champs-Élysées, across Place de la Concorde and the Jardin des Tuileries (with a visit, perhaps, to the notable Orangerie or Jeu de Paume museums) to the Louvre. Don't visit the museum now—wait until the next morning, when it will be less crowded.
☉ Don't do this on a Monday if you plan to go to the Musée d'Art Moderne, because it's closed then. The Jeu de Paume is closed Monday, the Orangerie on Tuesday.

Ⓑ 46

DAY 2

Get to the Ⓑ Louvre early to avoid the crowds; in a morning you'll be able to see only part of the museum—it's that big. After lunch, wander along the ritzy rue St-Honoré. Here you'll find the French president's home, the Palais de l'Élysée, and the Neoclassical Ⓐ Église de la Madeleine. For good shopping and a look at Haussmann's 19th-century Paris and the famous Opéra Garnier, join up with the Grand Boulevards. Spend the late afternoon getting a sense

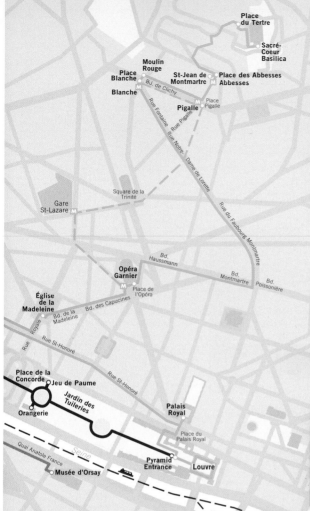

☺ 105

⊙ This is fine any day but Tuesday, when the Louvre is closed.

DAY 3

Start the morning admiring the Impressionists in the ©Musée d'Orsay; arrive early to avoid the crowds. Then head west to the Palais Bourbon, home of the Assemblée Nationale (the French parliament), and the Hôtel des Invalides, with its impressive Église du Dôme. If you're up for another museum, visit the Musée Rodin; if not, see its rose garden, filled with Rodin's sculptures. Continue east toward the enormous church of St-Sulpice. From here it's just three stops to the Vavin métro station in Montparnasse.

⊙ This won't work on Sunday, when the Hôtel des Invalides is closed, or on Monday, when the Musée d'Orsay and the Musée Rodin are closed.

of Paris's villagelike character by exploring Montmartre. Either walk (north along rue du Faubourg Montmartre to rue Notre-Dame de Lorette to rue Fontaine to Place Blanche) or take the métro to the Pigalle or Blanche stop. On boulevard de Clichy you'll find the famous Moulin Rouge. Continue up into Montmartre, via Place des Abbesses. On this square are two Art Nouveau gems: the church of St-Jean de Montmartre, and the Art Nouveau Guimard entrance to the Abbesses métro station. From here walk through the winding, hilly streets to Place du Tertre, and then on to Sacré-Coeur, where there's a tremendous view of the city below.

DAY 4

Begin by visiting Notre-Dame Cathedral and Ste-Chapelle on Ile de la Cité. Then head over to the neighboring Ile St-Louis and wander the narrow streets. Cross over the Seine to explore the Latin Quarter, using the Panthéon dome as a landmark. Set aside more time if you plan to see the Musée National du Moyen-Age or the Institut du Monde Arabe, relax in the Jardin du Luxembourg, or sip coffee in a neighborhood café. In the afternoon visit the Centre Pompidou and explore the winding streets of the Marais. The Musée Picasso is in one of this old neighborhood's hôtels particuliers (mansions).

27

L'Étoile
Place Charles
de Gaulle
Arc de Triomphe

Av. des Champs-Élysées

Marionettes des Champs-Élyseés

Rond Point des Champs-Élysées

Av. des Champs-Élysées

Palais de la Découverte

Place de la Concorde

Jardin des Tuileries

Seine

Place de l'Alma

Pont d'Alma

Place de la Résistance

Place du Trocadéro

Palais de Chaillot

Place de Varsovie

Pont d'Iéna

Eiffel Tower

Seine

To Bois de Boulogne

To Parc André-Citroën

The elegant Place des Vosges is pleasant for a break.
☉ Closings make this a problem on Monday (Institut du Monde Arabe), Tuesday (Musée du Moyen-Age, Centre Pompidou, Musée Picasso), and Wednesday (Musée Picasso).

DAY 5

To get a sense of the splendor in which French royalty lived, spend most of the day visiting Versailles.
☉ This is fine any day but Monday.

If You Have More Time

You can attack the smaller museums like the Maillol and the Marmottan and explore the funky Bastille, elegant Passy, and up-and-coming Bercy neighborhoods. Or take the métro to see attractions on the edge of the city: Père-Lachaise Cemetery, the Parc de la Villette, or the Bois de Boulogne or Bois de Vincennes, Paris's two largest parks. Or take a day trip to Fontainebleau, Chartres, or other points of interest around Paris.

If You Have 3 Days

On a first visit, start by following the suggestions for the first two days of the 5-day itinerary above: See the Eiffel Tower, the Arc de Triomphe, Champs-Élysées, and the Jardin des Tuileries on the first day; and tour the Louvre, the Faubourg St-Honoré, the Grand Boulevards, and Montmartre on the second day. On the third day visit the Musée d'Orsay and then Ⓕ Notre-Dame; in the afternoon explore the Latin Quarter.

Paris with Kids

Paris's major museums, like the Louvre and the Musée d'Orsay, can be as engaging as they are educational—as long as you keep your visits short. Many activities and museums are designed especially for children, and some museums even have children's programs.
☉ Note that many museums are closed on Monday or Tuesday. You may need to shuffle the itinerary around according to museum closings.

DAY 1

Give your kids an idea of how Paris was planned by climbing to the top of the Ⓓ Arc de Triomphe. From here work your way down the Champs-Élysées toward Place de la Concorde. Stop for a puppet show at the Marionettes des Champs-Élysées, at avenues Matignon and Gabriel, halfway down the Champs. Or head to the Palais de la Découverte, just off the Champs, to catch a planetarium show. Continue walking down the Champs, to the Jardin des Tuileries, where kids can sail boats on a small pond. For an afternoon treat, head for Angélina (on rue de Rivoli), a tearoom famous for its thick hot chocolate.
☉ If you want to see the puppet show, do this on a Wednesday, Saturday, or Sunday. Skip this on Monday when the Palais de la Découverte is closed.

DAY 2

In the morning head to the Ⓔ Eiffel Tower for a bird's-eye view of the city. After you descend, either ride on one of the Bateaux Mouches at Place de l'Alma, nearby; or brave Les Égouts, the Paris sewers (the tour takes about an hour and departs from Place de la Résistance, across the Seine). Next take the métro to the Parc André-Citroën, where there's a computerized "dancing fountain," or to the Bois de

Boulogne, where you'll find a zoo (the Jardin d'Acclimatation), rowboats, and plenty of wide-open space.

⊘ *This won't work on Thursday or Friday, when Les Égouts are closed.*

DAY 3

Introduce your kids to Notre-Dame Cathedral; go early so you don't have to wait to get in. Have lunch in the area, and then head nearby, then continue on foot or by bus to the Arènes de Lutèce, one of the few vestiges of the former Roman city. Not far on foot or by métro is the Jardin des Plantes, a botanical garden with the state-of-the-art Grande Galerie de l'Évolution, a museum exhibiting a collection of taxidermy of all kinds of animals. Also just a métro ride away in Montparnasse are the Catacombs, Roman quarries that served as headquarters for the and catch a magic show. Or take in the Centre Pompidou; either see an exhibit (often there are special kids' programs related to the shows) or simply ride the escalator to the top (free) for a great view of Paris. Around the corner, on the Square Igor-Stravinsky, watch the imaginative, moving sculptures in the fountain. Another option is to take the métro from Châtelet–Les-Halles to the Porte de la Villette; in the whimsical park of the same name are an interactive science museum, a museum of musical instruments, an IMAX theater, and

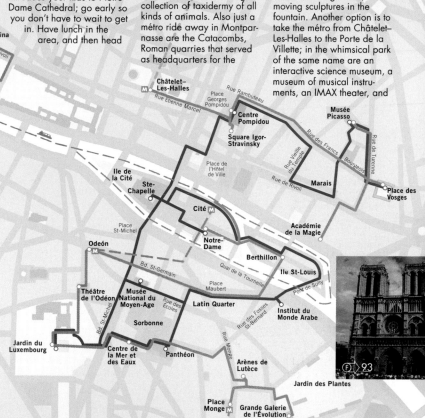

93

to Berthillon on the Ile St-Louis for some of the city's best ice cream. Afterward cross the Seine and walk or take the métro to the Odéon stop. From here walk around the colonnaded Théâtre de l'Odéon to the Jardin du Luxembourg, where there's a playground, a pond where kids can rent miniature boats, a café, and plenty of places to sit. Ready for more? Walk to the Centre de la Mer et des Eaux, an aquarium French Resistance during World War II.

⊘ *Don't try to see the Catacombs on Monday or the Grande Galerie de l'Évolution on Tuesday, when they're closed.*

DAY 4

On Day 4, at the Musée Picasso in the Marais, show your kids the paintings and sculptures of one of France's finest artists. Nearby, pick up a sandwich to eat on a bench in the Place des Vosges. If your children are up for another museum, one that's more child-oriented, head for the Académie de la Magie various innovative structures to play on and in.

⊘ *Because of closings, do this between Thursday and Sunday: The Parc de la Villette is closed Monday, the Centre Pompidou Tuesday, the Musée Picasso Tuesday and Wednesday, and the Académie de la Magie every day except Wednesday and weekends.*

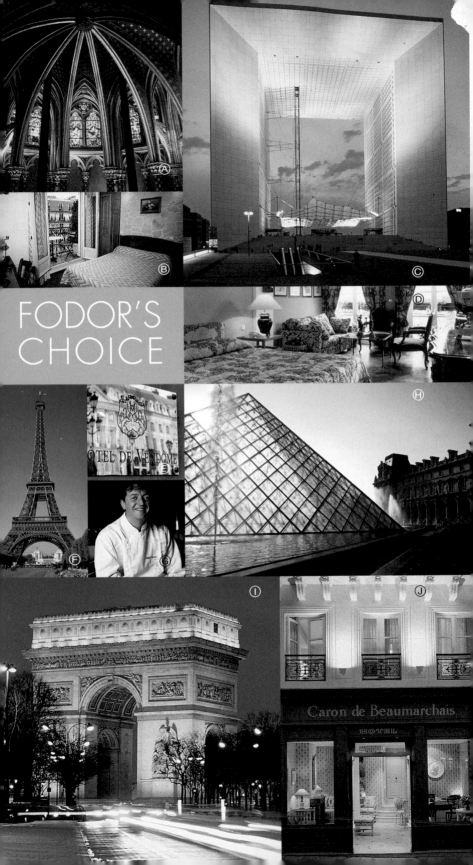

FODOR'S
CHOICE

Caron de Beaumarchais

Even with so many special places in Paris, Fodor's writers and editors have their favorites. Here are a few that stand out.

CHURCHES

Basilique de St-Denis. This cathedral-size Gothic church in the northern suburb of St-Denis contains the elaborately carved tombs of the French kings. ☞ p. 128

Église du Dôme. Under the dome of this commanding Baroque church, part of Les Invalides, Napoléon rests in imperial splendor. ☞ p. 103

Notre-Dame Cathedral. At this historic church, climb to the towers for a glimpse of the gargoyles and for wonderful views of Paris. ☞ p. 93

Ⓐ **Ste-Chapelle.** Built by Louis IX to house what he believed to be the Crown of Thorns from Christ's crucifixion and fragments of the True Cross, Ste-Chapelle shimmers with stained glass. ☞ p. 96

FLAVORS

Guy Savoy. At his handsome luxury restaurant, chef Guy Savoy creates contemporary classics. $$$$ ☞ p. 158

Pierre Gagnaire. Legendary chef Pierre Gagnaire brings together at least three different tastes and textures in each sensational dish. $$$$ ☞ p. 149

Au Trou Gascon. Feast on first-rate Southwestern specialties—such as superb cassoulet—in a pretty Belle Epoque setting. $$$ ☞ p. 153

Le Violon d'Ingres. Chef Christian Constant has a hit on his hands with this stylish spot serving excellent contemporary bistro fare. $$–$$$ ☞ p. 147

Chardenoux. This cozy restaurant with tile floors and a long zinc bar stands out for its traditional bistro menu. $$ ☞ p. 152

Ⓖ **Philippe Detourbe.** Detourbe's contemporary cuisine is simply spectacular. $$ ☞ p. 155

Le Relais du Parc. This bistro annex is run by renowned chef Alain Ducasse, who understands how and what people want to eat today. $$ ☞ p. 157

Au Bon Accueil. The excellent, reasonably priced *cuisine du marché* (a menu based on what's in the markets) has made this bistro a hit. $–$$ ☞ p. 147

Le Petit Troquet. This minuscule bistro serves a very good menu based on what's fresh in the markets. $$ ☞ p. 148

COMFORTS

Ⓔ **Vendôme.** The Second Empire–style rooms are simply sumptuous. $$$–$$$$ ☞ p. 172

Ⓓ **Relais St-Germain.** Rooms in this hotel are named for French literary heroes and are at least twice the size of those you'll find elsewhere at this price level. $$$ ☞ p. 177

Le Tourville. Here is a rare find: a cozy, stylish hotel that doesn't cost a fortune. $$–$$$ ☞ p. 179

Ⓙ **Caron de Beaumarchais.** Beaumarchais's work is the theme of this hotel in the heart of the Marais. $$ ☞ p. 174

Grand Hôtel de Besançon. This hotel, with its very Parisian cream-color facade and wrought-iron balconies, has it all—intimacy, comfort, affordability, and a delightful location. $$ ☞ p. 173

Ⓑ **Familia.** The hospitable Gaucheron family bends over backward for you at this pleasant Latin Quarter hotel. $ ☞ p. 176

MONUMENTS

Ⓘ **Arc de Triomphe.** Commissioned by Napoléon I as a monument to his military might, this is the world's largest triumphal arch. ☞ p. 44

Ⓕ **Eiffel Tower.** The 10,000-ton result of a contest held to design a tower for the 1889 World Exposition, the Eiffel Tower is the most-recognized landmark in Paris. ☞ p. 40

July Column. The bronze column on Place de la Bastille, the site of the infamous Bastille prison destroyed on July 14, 1789, commemo-rates the 1830 and 1848 uprisings. ☞ p. 74

Ⓗ **The Louvre's glass pyramid.** This modern glass structure, I. M. Pei's new entrance to the museum, was extremely controversial when first unveiled. ☞ p. 46

VIEWS TO REMEMBER

The Eiffel Tower from Trocadéro. This view of the Eiffel Tower is unsurpassed and is particularly pretty when the fountains in Trocadéro plaza are on. ☞ p. 40

Ⓒ **The Grande Arche from Esplanade de la Défense.** The colossally elegant triumphal arch, shaped like a hollow cube, towers above an immense flight of white marble steps. It's even better at night. ☞ p. 129

The Ile de la Cité from the Pont des Arts. The footbridge across the Seine between the Louvre and the Institut de France offers a romantic vantage point of the towers of Notre-Dame climbing above the roofs of Ile de la Cité, with the Hôtel de Ville and Tour St-Jacques piercing the skyline to the left. ☞ p. 108

Notre-Dame from the Pont de l'Archevêché. Standing on the bridge behind Notre-Dame, you get breathtaking views of the east end of the cathedral ringed by flying buttresses, surmounted by the spire. ☞ p. 93

Paris spread out beneath Sacré-Coeur in Montmartre. The basilica is set on the highest hill in Paris, providing extensive views of the city. ☞ p. 120

St-Gervais–St-Protais from the bottom of rue des Barres. The charming view of the flying buttresses above the roofs and cobbles of this pedestrian street is quintessential Paris. ☞ p. 86

1 EXPLORING PARIS

Bearing the marks of 2,000 years of history and a rich cultural heritage, Paris overwhelms, astonishes, and surprises. From the heights of the Arc de Triomphe, the city swaggers with the knowledge that it is at the pinnacle of architectural beauty, artistic development, and culinary delight. On its narrow, rambling streets, the city invites unhurried exploration.

Revised and
updated by
Simon Hewitt

A CITY OF VAST, NOBLE PERSPECTIVES and winding, hidden streets, Paris remains a combination of the pompous and the intimate. Whether you've come looking for sheer physical beauty, cultural and artistic diversions, world-famous dining and shopping, history, or simply local color, you will find it here in abundance.

The French capital is also a practical city for visitors: It is relatively small as capitals go, with many of its major sights and museums within walking distance of one another. The city's principal tourist axis is less than 6½ km (4 mi) long, running parallel to the north bank of the Seine from the Arc de Triomphe to the Bastille. In fact, the best way to get to know Paris is on foot, although public transportation—particularly the métro subway system—is excellent. Buy a *Plan de Paris* booklet: a city map-guide with a street-name index that also shows métro stations. Note that all métro stations have a detailed neighborhood map just inside the entrance.

Paris owes both its development and much of its visual appeal to the Seine River, which weaves through its heart. Each bank of the Seine has its own personality; the *Rive Droite* (Right Bank), with its spacious boulevards and formal buildings, generally has a more sober and genteel feeling than the more carefree and bohemian *Rive Gauche* (Left Bank) to the south. The historical and geographical heart of the city is Notre-Dame Cathedral on the Ile de la Cité, the larger of the Seine's two islands (the other is the Ile St-Louis).

Our coverage of Paris is divided into 12 neighborhood walks. There are several "musts" that you don't want to miss, especially if this is your first time in Paris: the Eiffel Tower, the Arc de Triomphe, the Louvre, and Notre-Dame. Note that a few monuments and museums close for lunch, between noon and 2, and that admission prices listed are for adults, but often there are special rates for students, children, and senior citizens. If you are weary and in need of a break, keep in mind that cafés are a great boon; *boulangeries* (bakeries), too, are good spots for a snack.

It must also be said that a visit to Paris will never be quite as simple as a quick look at a few landmarks. Every *quartier* (neighborhood) has its own treasures, and you should be ready to explore—a very pleasant prospect in this most elegant of cities. Follow our suggested "good walks" or use them as a guide to create your own. Sights that are "off the beaten path" are noted: You might want to make a brief excursion to one of these places in conjunction with a walk or visit them on another day when you have more time.

FROM THE EIFFEL TOWER TO PONT DE L'ALMA

The Eiffel Tower lords it over southwest Paris and, wherever you are on this walk, you can see it looming overhead. Water is the second theme: fountains playing beneath Place du Trocadéro; tours along the Seine on the Bateaux Mouches; and an underground prowl through the city's sewers, if you can stand it. Museums are the third: The area around Trocadéro is full of them. And style is the fourth: not just because the buildings here are overwhelmingly elegant, but also because, with the Champs-Élysées a brief walk to the north, the top names in world fashion are all congregated around avenue Montaigne.

Numbers in the text correspond to numbers in the margin and on the Eiffel Tower to Pont de l'Alma map.

A Good Walk

The verdant expanse of the **Champ de Mars** ①, once used as a parade ground by the **École Militaire** ② (still in use as a military academy and therefore not open to the public), then as site of the World Exhibitions, provides a thrilling approach to the iron symbol of Paris, the **Tour Eiffel** ③. As you get nearer, the Eiffel Tower's colossal bulk (it's far bigger and sturdier than pictures suggest) becomes increasingly evident. (If you want to skip this walk through the parade grounds, just take the métro directly to the Eiffel Tower.)

Across the Seine from the Eiffel Tower, above stylish gardens and fountains on the heights of Place du Trocadéro, is the Art Deco **Palais de Chaillot** ④, a cultural center containing numerous museums. Pause on the piazza, lined by gold statues, to admire the view of the Eiffel Tower and—until January 1, 2000—its giant digital clock ticking off the days to the Millennium. The left wing of the Palais houses the **Musée de l'Homme** ⑤, an anthropology museum, and the **Musée de la Marine** ⑥, a maritime museum. The right wing was badly damaged by fire in 1997 and its **Musée des Monuments Français** ⑦, with copies of statues, columns, and archways, was set to reopen in late 1999.

The area around Place du Trocadéro is a feast for museum lovers. The **Musée Guimet** ⑧, on Place d'Iéna, contains three floors of Indo-Chinese and Far Eastern art, and is slated to reopen in early 2000 after extensive renovation. Farther down the avenue du Président-Wilson is the **Palais Galliéra** ⑨, where you can see exhibits on clothing design and fashion. Across the street, the **Musée d'Art Moderne de la Ville de Paris** ⑩ has temporary exhibits as well as a permanent collection of modern art.

Continue down to Place de l'Alma, where a giant golden torch appears to be saluting the memory of Diana, Princess of Wales, who died in a car crash in the tunnel below in August 1997. Across the **Pont de l'Alma** ⑪ (to the left) is the entrance to **Les Égouts** ⑫, Paris's sewers. If you prefer a less malodorous tour of the city, stay on the Right Bank and head down the sloping side road to the left of the bridge to the embarkation point of the **Bateaux Mouches** ⑬ and their tours of Paris by water.

Stylish avenue Montaigne, home to many of the leading Paris fashion houses (☞ Chapter 6), runs up from Place de l'Alma toward the Champs-Élysées. The 1913 facade of the Théâtre des Champs-Élysées (☞ Chapter 4), 100 yards up avenue Montaigne on the left, is a forerunner of the Art Deco style. Farther along this street is the plush Hôtel Plaza-Athénée. The distinctively slender spire of the neo-Gothic **American Cathedral of the Holy Trinity** ⑭ is visible up avenue George-V from Place de l'Alma. Turn left after the cathedral to reach avenue Marceau and the church of **St-Pierre de Chaillot** ⑮, with its handsome carved facade.

TIMING

You can probably cover this 3½-km (just over 2-mi) walk in a couple of hours, but if you wish to ascend the Eiffel Tower, take a trip along the Seine, or visit any of the plethora of museums along the way, you'd be best off allowing most of the day.

Sights to See

⑭ **American Cathedral of the Holy Trinity.** This slender-spired, neo-Gothic church was built by architect G. S. Street between 1885 and 1888. ⊠ *23 av. George-V,* ☎ *01–47–20–17–92.* ⊙ *Weekdays 9–12:30 and 2–5, Sat. 9–noon. Services: weekdays 9 AM, Sun. 9 and 11 AM. Guided tours Sun. and Wed. 12:30. Métro: Alma-Marceau.*

Paris Exploring

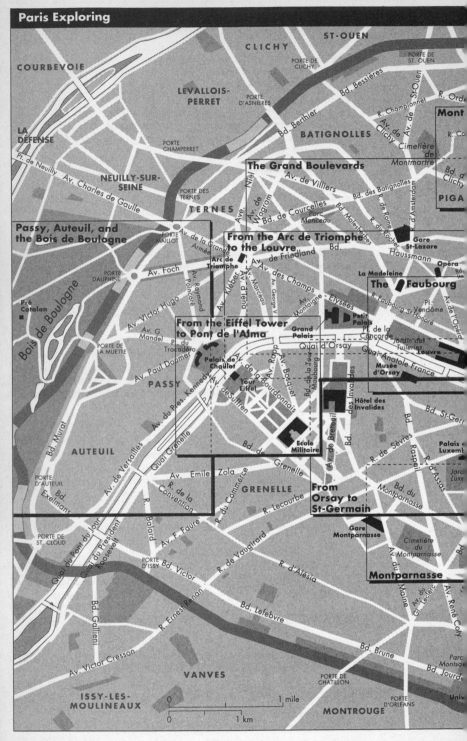

COURBEVOIE

ST-OUEN

CLICHY

PORTE DE
CLICHY

PORTE DE
ST. OUEN

R. Orde

LEVALLOIS-
PERRET

Bd. Berthier

BATIGNOLLES

R. Ce

Mont

PORTE
D'ASNIÈRES

Bd. Bessières

Av. de St-Ouen

Cimetière
de
Montmartre

R. Championnet

LA
DÉFENSE

PORTE
CHAMPERRET

Av. de
Clichy

Bd. d
Clichy

Pt. de Neuilly

NEUILLY-SUR-
SEINE

Av. Charles de Gaulle

PORTE DES
TERNES

TERNES

Av. de Villiers

Bd. des Batignolles

R. de Rome

R. d'Amsterdam

PIGA

The Grand Boulevards

Av. Niel

Av. de
Wagram

Av. de Courcelles

Bd. Malesherbes

Gare
St-Lazare

Parc
Monceau

Bd. Haussmann

Opéra

**Passy, Auteuil, and
the Bois de Boulogne**

PORTE
MAILLOT

Av. de la Grande
Armée

**From the Arc de Triomphe
to the Louvre**

Arc de
Triomphe

Av. de Friedland

Bd.

La Madeleine

The Faubourg

PORTE
DAUPHINE

Av. Foch

Av. Kléber

Av. d'Iéna

Av. Marceau

Av. des Champs

R. Faubourg St-Honoré

Pl.
Vendôme

Av. de l'Opéra

Pré
Catalan

Av. Victor Hugo

Av. Raymond
Poincaré

Av. George V

Av.
Montaigne - Élysées

**From the Eiffel Tower
to Pont de l'Alma**

Petit
Palais

Pl. de la
Concorde

Jardin des
Tuileries

Louvre

Bois de Boulogne

Av. G
Mandel

du
Trocadéro

Grand
Palais

Quai d'Orsay

Quai Anatole France

PORTE DE
LA MUETTE

Av. Paul Doumer

Palais de
Chaillot

Musée
d'Orsay

PASSY

Tour
Eiffel

Av. de la Bourdonnais

Av. de Suffren

Av. Bosquet

Bd. de la Tour Maubourg

Hôtel des
Invalides

Bd. St-Ger

Bd. Murat

Av. du Prés. Kennedy

Quai de Grenelle

École
Militaire

Av. de Breteuil

Bd.

R. de Sèvres

Palais d
Luxemb

AUTEUIL

Bd.
Exelmans

PORTE
D'AUTEUIL

Av. de Versailles

Av. Emile Zola

R. de la
Convention

R. du Commerce

GRENELLE

Grenelle

R. Lecourbe

**From
Orsay to
St-Germain**

Bd. de
Montparnasse

Raspail

Jard
Luxe

PORTE DE
ST. CLOUD

Quai du Pont du Jour

Quai du Président
Roosevelt

R. Balard

Av. F. Faure

PORTE
D'ISSY

Bd. Victor

R. de Vaugirard

R. d'Alésia

Gare
Montparnasse

Cimetière
du
Montparnasse

Av. du
Montparnasse

Montparnasse

Av. du Maine

Bd. Galliéni

R. Ernest Renan

Bd. Lefebvre

Bd. Brune

Parc
Montsou
Bd. Jourde

Av. Victor Cresson

VANVES

PORTE DE
CHÂTILLON

PORTE
D'ORLÉANS

MONTROUGE

Univ

ISSY-LES-
MOULINEAUX

0   1 mile

0   1 km

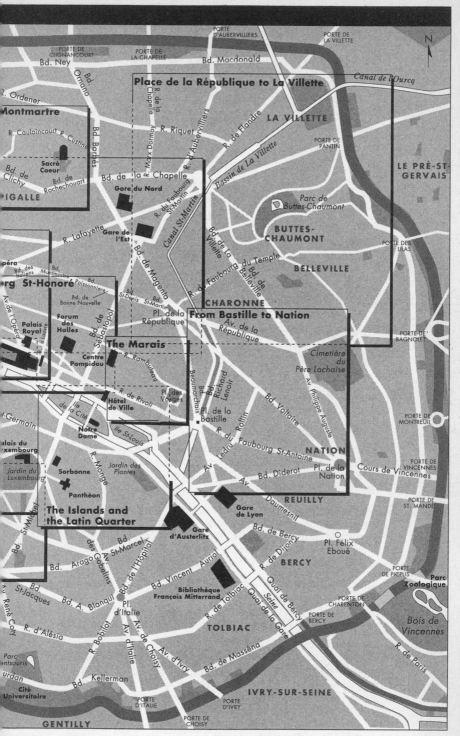

Place de la République to La Villette

From Bastille to Nation

The Marais

The Islands and
the Latin Quarter

Montmartre

PORTE DE
CLIGNANCOURT
Bd. Ney

PORTE DE
LA CHAPELLE

PORTE
D'AUBERVILLIERS

Bd. Macdonald

PORTE DE
LA VILLETTE

N

Canal de l'Ourcq

R. Ordener

Bd. Ornano

PORTE DE
LA CHAPELLE

R. de la Chapelle

R. d'Aubervilliers

R. de Flandre

LA VILLETTE

LE PRÉ-ST-
GERVAIS

R. Caulaincourt

R. Custine

Bd. Barbès

R. Riquet

R. de Flandre

Bassin de La Villette

PORTE DE
PANTIN

Sacré
Coeur

Bd. de
Clichy

Bd. de
Rochechouart

Bd. de la Chapelle

Gare du Nord

R. du Faubourg
St-Martin

Canal St-Martin

Parc de
Buttes-Chaumont

PORTE DES
LILAS

PIGALLE

R. Lafayette

Gare de
l'Est

Bd. de Magenta

Bd. de la Villette

BUTTES-
CHAUMONT

BELLEVILLE

Opéra

Bd. des
Italiens

Bd.
Montmartre

Bd.
Poissonnière

Bd. de
Bonne Nouvelle

Bd.
St-Denis

Bd.
St-Martin

R. du Faubourg du Temple

Bd. de
Belleville

Fg St-Honoré

Forum
des
Halles

Bd. de Sébastopol

Pl. de la
République

CHARONNE

Av. de l'Opéra

Palais
Royal

R. Rambuteau

Centre
Pompidou

Beaumarchais

Bd. Richard
Lenoir

Cimetière
du
Père Lachaise

PORTE DE
BAGNOLET

St-Germain

de la Cité

R. de Rivoli

Hôtel
de Ville

Pl. des
Vosges

Pl. de la
Bastille

Bd. Voltaire

Av. Philippe Auguste

Palais du
Luxembourg

Notre
Dame

Île St-Louis

R. du Faubourg St-Antoine

NATION

PORTE DE
MONTREUIL

Jardin du
Luxembourg

Sorbonne

R. Monge

Jardin des
Plantes

Av. Ledru Rollin

R. du Rollin

Bd. Diderot

Pl. de la
Nation

Cours de Vincennes

PORTE DE
VINCENNES

Panthéon

Gare
de Lyon

Av. Daumesnil

REUILLY

PORTE DE
ST. MANDÉ

Bd. St-Michel

Gare
d'Austerlitz

Bd. de Bercy

Pl. Félix
Eboué

PORTE DE
PICPUS

Parc
Zoologique

Bd.
St-Jacques

Bd. Arago

Bd. des Gobelins

Av. St-Marcel

Bd. de l'Hôpital

Bd. Vincent Auriol

BERCY

Bois de
Vincennes

René Coty

Bd. A. Blanqui

Bibliothèque
François Mitterrand

R. de Tolbiac

Quai de Bercy

Quai de la Gare

Saône

R. de Dijon

PORTE DE
CHARENTON

PORTE DE
BERCY

R. de Paris

Parc
Montsouris

Jourdan

R. d'Alésia

R. Bobillot

Pl.
d'Italie

Av. de Choisy

Av. d'Italie

Av. d'Ivry

Bd. de Masséna

TOLBIAC

Cité
Universitaire

Bd. Kellerman

PORTE
D'ITALIE

PORTE
D'IVRY

IVRY-SUR-SEINE

GENTILLY

PORTE DE
CHOISY

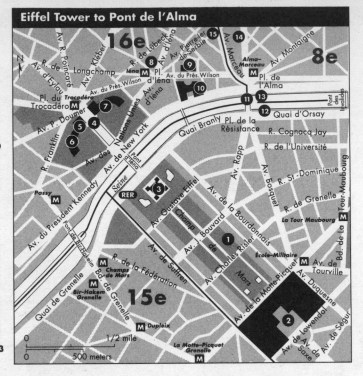

Eiffel Tower to Pont de l'Alma

(🖐) ⑬ **Bateaux Mouches.** These popular motorboats set off on their hour-long
tours of Paris waters regularly (every half hour in summer) from Place
de l'Alma, heading east to the Ile St-Louis and then back west, past
the Eiffel Tower, as far as the Allée des Cygnes and its miniature version of the Statue of Liberty. *Bateaux mouches* translates, misleadingly,
as "fly boats"; the name mouche actually refers to a district of Lyon
where the boats were originally manufactured. ⊠ *Pl. de l'Alma,* ☎ *01–
40–76–99–99.* 🎟 *40 frs. Métro: Alma-Marceau.*

(🖐) ① **Champ de Mars.** This long, formal garden, landscaped at the start of
the century, lies between the Eiffel Tower and École Militaire. It was
previously used as a parade ground and was the site of the World Exhibitions of 1867, 1889 (date of the construction of the Eiffel Tower),
and 1900. *Métro: École Militaire; RER: Champ-de-Mars.*

② **École Militaire** (Military Academy). This harmonious 18th-century military academy, facing the Eiffel Tower across the Champ de Mars, is
still in use for army training and is not open to the public. ⊠ *Pl. du
Maréchal-Joffre. Métro: École Militaire.*

⑫ **Les Égouts** (The Sewers). Brave the unpleasant—though tolerable—smell
of the Paris sewers to follow an underground city of banks, passages,
and footbridges. Name signs indicate the streets above you, and detailed panels and displays illuminate the history of waste disposal in
Paris, whose sewer system is the largest in the world after Chicago's.
The tour takes about an hour. ⊠ *Opposite 93 quai d'Orsay,* ☎ *01–
47–05–10–29.* 🎟 *25 frs.* 🕐 *Sat.–Wed. 11–5 (Sept.–Easter 11–4).
Closed Jan. Métro: Alma-Marceau; RER: Pont de l'Alma.*

OFF THE
BEATEN PATH

AMERICAN CHURCH – This Left Bank neo-Gothic church, built 1927–31, offers help and advice to English-speaking foreigners. ✉ *65 quai d'Orsay,* ☎ *01–47–05–07–99. Métro: Alma-Marceau; RER: Pont de l'Alma.*

⑩ **Musée d'Art Moderne de la Ville de Paris** (Paris Museum of Modern Art). Both temporary exhibits and a permanent collection of top-quality 20th-century art can be found at this modern art museum. It takes over, chronologically speaking, where the Musée d'Orsay leaves off: Among the earliest works are Fauve paintings by Vlaminck and Derain, followed by Picasso's early experiments in Cubism. Its vast, unobtrusive, white-walled galleries provide an ideal backdrop for the bold statements of 20th-century art. Loudest and largest are the canvases of Robert Delaunay. Other highlights include works by Braque, Rouault, Gleizes, Da Silva, Gromaire, and Modigliani. There is also a large room devoted to Art Deco furniture and screens, where Jean Dunand's gilt and lacquered panels consume oceans of wall space. There is a pleasant, if expensive, museum café and an excellent bookshop specializing in 19th- and 20th-century art and architecture, with many books in English. ✉ *11 av. du Président-Wilson,* ☎ *01–53–67–40–00.* 🖽 *27 frs.* ⊙ *Tues.–Fri. 10–5:30, weekends 10–6:45. Métro: Iéna.*

⑧ **Musée Guimet.** This Belle Epoque museum was founded by Lyonnais industrialist Émile Guimet, who traveled around the world in the late 19th century amassing priceless Indo-Chinese and Far Eastern objets d'art, plus the largest collection of Cambodian art this side of Cambodia. After a massive renovation and extensive scheme, the museum was due to reopen in early 2000. ✉ *6 Pl. d'Iéna,* ☎ *01–45–05–00–98.* 🖽 *Admission details uncertain at press time. Métro: Iéna.*

⑤ **Musée de l'Homme** (Museum of Mankind). Artifacts, costumes, and domestic tools from around the world, dating from prehistoric times, make up this earnest anthropological museum on the second and third floors of the Palais de Chaillot. ✉ *17 Pl. du Trocadéro,* ☎ *01–44–05–72–72.* 🖽 *30 frs.* ⊙ *Wed.–Mon. 9:45–5:15. Métro: Trocadéro.*

NEED A
BREAK?

Get a tremendous view of the Eiffel Tower and the Invalides dome with your ice cream, cocktail, or 129-franc lunch at **Le Totem** (☎ 01–44–05–90–00), an elegant bar and restaurant in the south wing of the Palais de Chaillot.

⑥ **Musée de la Marine** (Maritime Museum). In the west wing of the Palais de Chaillot, this museum contains ship models and seafaring paraphernalia illustrating French naval history up to the age of the nuclear submarine. ✉ *17 Pl. du Trocadéro,* ☎ *01–53–65–69–69.* 🖽 *38 frs.* ⊙ *Wed.–Mon. 10–6. Métro: Trocadéro.*

⑦ **Musée des Monuments Français** (French Monuments Museum). This museum was founded in 1879 by architect-restorer Viollet-le-Duc (the man mainly responsible for the extensive renovation of Notre-Dame and countless other Gothic cathedrals). Its tribute to French buildings of the Romanesque and Gothic periods (roughly 1000–1500) takes the form of painstaking copies of statues, columns, archways, and frescoes—an excellent introduction to French medieval architecture. It is easy to imagine yourself strolling among ruins as you pass through the first-floor gallery. Substantial sections of a number of French churches and cathedrals are represented here, notably Chartres and Vézelay. Mural and ceiling paintings—copies of works in churches around the country—dominate the other three floors. The value of these paintings has become increasingly evident as many of the originals continue to deteriorate. On the ceiling of a circular room is a reproduction of the painted dome of Cahors cathedral, which gives a more vivid sense of the skills of the medieval painter than the original itself. A fire in 1997 temporarily closed the museum; it was due to reopen by late 1999. ⊠ *1 Pl. du Trocadéro,* ☎ *01–44–05–39–10. Métro: Trocadéro.*

❹ Palais de Chaillot (Chaillot Palace). This honey-color Art Deco cultural center was built in the 1930s to replace a Moorish-style building constructed for the World Exhibition of 1878. It contains four large museums: the **Musée de l'Homme,** the **Musée de la Marine,** the **Musée des Monuments Français,** and the **Musée du Cinéma Henri-Langlois** (☞ individual museum listings, *above*). The tumbling gardens leading to the Seine contain sculptures and some dramatic fountains. The palace terrace, flanked by gilded statuettes (and often invaded by roller skaters and skateboarders), offers a wonderful, picture-postcard view of the Eiffel Tower. ⊠ *Pl. du Trocadéro. Métro: Trocadéro.*

❾ Palais Galliéra. This luxurious mansion, built in 1888 for the Duchesse de Galliéra, houses rotating exhibits on costumery and clothing design. ⊠ *10 av. Pierre-1ᵉʳ-de-Serbie,* ☎ *01–47–20–85–23.* ▧ *45 frs.* ☉ *Tues.– Sun. 10–5:40. Métro: Iéna.*

⑪ Pont de l'Alma (Alma Bridge). This bridge is best known for the chunky stone "Zouave" statue carved into one of the pillars. Zouaves were Algerian infantrymen recruited into the French army who were famous for their bravura and colorful uniforms. (The term came to be used for volunteers in the Union army during the American Civil War.) There is nothing quite so glamorous, or colorful, about the Alma Zouave, however, whose hour of glory comes in times of watery distress: Parisians use him to judge the level of the Seine during heavy rains. In 1995, for instance, the Zouave was submerged up to his waist, and the roads running along the riverbanks were under several feet of water. *Métro: Alma-Marceau.*

⑮ St-Pierre de Chaillot. A sturdy 210-ft tower signals this neo-Romanesque church, built in 1937 between the Seine and the Champs-Élysées. Henri Bouchard's monumental frieze above the entrance depicts scenes from the life of St. Peter. ⊠ *av. Marceau. Métro: Alma-Marceau.*

★ ⟲ **❸ Tour Eiffel** (Eiffel Tower). Paris's most famous landmark was built by Gustave Eiffel for the World Exhibition of 1889, the centennial of the French Revolution, and was still in good shape to celebrate its own 100th birthday. Such was Eiffel's engineering wizardry that even in the strongest winds his tower never sways more than 4½ inches. Its colossal bulk exudes a feeling of mighty permanence. You may have trouble believing that it nearly became 7,000 tons of scrap iron when its concession expired in 1909. Only its potential use as a radio antenna saved the day; it now bristles with a forest of radio and television transmitters. Restoration in the late 1980s didn't make the elevators any faster (lines are inevitable), but the nocturnal illumination is fantastic—every girder highlighted in glorious detail. If you're full of energy, stride up the stairs as far as the third deck. If you want to go to the top, you'll have to take the elevator. The view at 1,000 ft may not beat that from the Tour Montparnasse (☞ Montparnasse, *below*), but the setting makes it considerably more romantic. ⊠ *Quai Branly,* ☎ *01– 44–11–23–23.* ▧ *By elevator: 2nd floor, 20 frs; 3rd floor, 42 frs; 4th floor, 59 frs. By foot: 2nd and 3rd floors only, 14 frs.* ☉ *July–Aug., daily 9 AM–midnight; Sept.–June, daily 9 AM–11 PM. Métro: Bir-Hakeim; RER: Champ-de-Mars.*

FROM THE ARC DE TRIOMPHE TO THE LOUVRE

The Arc de Triomphe stands foursquare at the top of the city's most famous avenue: the Champs-Élysées. Site of most French national celebrations, the Champs-Élysées is the last leg of the Tour de France bicycle race on the third or fourth Sunday in July and the site of vast ceremonies on Bastille Day (July 14) and Armistice Day (November 11). Its trees are often decked with the French *tricolor* and foreign flags to mark visits from heads of state. Explore both its commercial upper half and its verdant lower section, sloping down gracefully to Place de la Concorde, with its Egyptian obelisk. Beyond lie the Tuileries Gardens and the gleaming glass pyramid of the world's largest museum, the Louvre. Local charm is not a feature of this exclusive sector of western Paris; it's beautiful, grand—and a little impersonal. The French moan that it's losing its character, and, as you notice the number of fast-food joints along the Champs-Élysées, you'll know what they mean—though renovation has gone some way to restoring the street's legendary elegance.

Numbers in the text correspond to numbers in the margin and on the Arc de Triomphe to Louvre map.

A Good Walk

The colossal, 164-ft **Arc de Triomphe** ① sits on Place Charles-de-Gaulle, known to Parisians as L'Étoile, or The Star—a reference to the streets that fan out from it. This is Europe's most chaotic traffic circle: Short of a death-defying dash, your only way of getting to the Arc de Triomphe in the middle is to take an underground passage from the top right of avenue des Champs-Élysées. The view from the top of the Arc de Triomphe illustrates the star effect of the 12 radiating avenues and enables you to admire the vista down the **Champs-Élysées** ②, as the avenue is known, toward Place de la Concorde and the distant Louvre. West of the Champs-Élysées, and visible from the Arc de Triomphe, are the beautiful Bois de Boulogne (☞ Passy, Auteuil, and the Bois de Boulogne, *above*); the posh suburb of Neuilly; and the towering office buildings and ultramodern arch of La Défense (☞ Off the Beaten Path, *below*). Visible to the east is the Louvre. (The Charles de Gaulle–Étoile métro and RER station, which sprawls underground beneath the Étoile, provides quick access to the western suburbs, if you want to make the excursion now.)

Walk down the Champs-Élysées and stop by the **Office de Tourisme de la Ville de Paris** ③ (the main city tourist office) at No. 127, on the right-hand side as you arrive from L'Étoile. Three hundred yards down on the left, at 116 bis, is the famous **Lido** ④ nightclub, opposite the venerable Le Fouquet's restaurant-café, once frequented by Orson Welles and James Joyce (☞ Chapter 4).

Continue to the Rond-Point and turn right onto spacious avenue Franklin-D.-Roosevelt. Some 200 yards down is the **Palais de la Découverte** ⑤, with exhibits on science and technology. It occupies the rear half of the glass-roofed **Grand Palais** ⑥, which forms an attractive duo with the **Petit Palais** ⑦ on the other side of avenue Winston-Churchill. In 1998, the Queen of England unveiled a 10-ft statue of Churchill himself, gazing toward the Seine and the **Pont Alexandre-III** ⑧, the exuberant bridge that leads to the gilt-domed Hôtel des Invalides.

A statue of French World War I hero Georges Clemenceau, scarf blowing in the wind, guards the leafy lower reaches of the Champs-Élysées, with well-tended gardens off to the left, leading to the broad, airy **Place de la Concorde** ⑨. Beyond the Obelisk with its newly gilded top, two

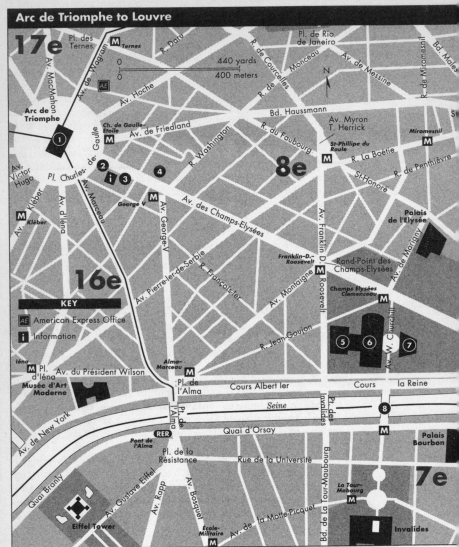

R. du Rocher
R. des Londres
Av. de Clichy
Ste-Trinité
R. d'Aumale
St-Augustin
Gare St-Lazare
R. d'Amsterdam
Trinité-d'Est-d'Orves
R. de Châteaudun
Notre-Dame-de-Lorette
Bd. Malesherbes
Pl. St-Augustin
R. St-Lazare
St-Lazare
R. de Mogador
R. Chaussée d'Antin
9e
R. Taitbout
Le Peletier
St-Augustin
Bd. Haussmann
Roquepine
Bd. Malesherbes
R. Pasquier
R. Mathurins
R. Tranchet
R. Auber
Auber
R. Drouot
R. d'Aguesseau
R. Faubourg
R. Bassy d'Anglas
R. Royale
Église de la Madeleine
Havre-Caumartin
RER
R. Scribe
Opéra
Pl. de l'Opéra
Richelieu-Drouot
Bd. de la Madeleine
AE
Bd. des Capucines
Opéra
Bd. des Italiens
Pl. de la Madeleine
Madeleine
R. Cambon
R. des Capucines
R. de la Paix
R. du Quatre Septembre
Concorde
St-Honoré
R. de Castiglione
Pl. Vendôme
Pl. St-Honoré
Pyramide
Av. de l'Opéra
4 Septembre
Bibliothèque National
2e
R. des Petits Champs
Banque de France
9
10
R. de Rivoli
Tuileries
Jardin des Tuileries
1er
Palais Royal
R. de Richelieu
Jardin du Palais Royal
11
12
Pl. de la Concorde
Quai des Tuileries
Louvre
Palais Royal
13
Bd. St-Germain
Quai
RER
Anatole France
14
15
16
Jardin du Carrousel
Musée d'Orsay

smallish buildings stand sentinel to the Jardin des Tuileries or Tuileries Gardens. Nearest the rue de Rivoli is the **Musée du Jeu de Paume** ⑩, host to outstanding exhibits of contemporary art. An identical building, nearer the Seine, is the **Musée de l'Orangerie** ⑪, containing some early 20th-century paintings by Monet, Renoir, and other Impressionists.

Stroll through the grounds of the grand **Jardin des Tuileries** ⑫ and survey the surrounding cityscape. To the north is the disciplined, arcaded rue de Rivoli; to the south, the Seine and the gold-hued Musée d'Orsay with its enormous clocks; to the west, the Champs-Élysées and Arc de Triomphe; to the east, the Arc du Carrousel and the Louvre. Manicured lawns and eccentric diagonal hedges lead on toward the **Arc du Carrousel** ⑬, a small relation of the distant Arc de Triomphe. Steps lead down here to the **Carrousel du Louvre** ⑭, a posh underground shopping mall. But you'll probably want to stay above ground and cross the paved esplanade, passing Louis XIV on his rearing bronze steed, to reach I. M. Pei's famous glass pyramid entry to the **Louvre** ⑮. Before plunging into the depths of the world's largest museum, pause to admire the statue-lined 19th-century facades of the giant forecourt and the elegant **Cour Carrée** ⑯ beyond. Then turn to assess the vista—aligned almost perfectly—that leads through the Arc du Carrousel to the Concorde obelisk, then up the Champs-Élysées to the Arc de Triomphe, with the shadowy towers of La Défense beyond.

TIMING

This 4-km (2½-mi) walk will probably take you a morning or afternoon to complete. It makes sense to do this walk on one of your first few days in Paris: The city's tourist office is here, and the view from the top of the Arc de Triomphe is like a short course in the city's geography. Sunny weather is a must, when the tour's vistas and photogenic moments are best. At night, head elsewhere in search of Parisian ambience and an affordable meal.

Sights to See

⑬ **Arc du Carrousel.** This small triumphal arch between the Louvre and the Tuileries was erected by Napoléon from 1806 to 1808. The four bronze horses on top were originally the famous gilded horses that Napoléon looted from Venice; when these were returned in 1815, Bosio designed four new ones harnessed to a chariot, driven by a goddess symbolizing the Restoration (of the monarchy). *Métro: Palais-Royal.*

★ ❶ **Arc de Triomphe.** This colossal, 164-ft triumphal arch was planned by Napoléon—who believed himself to be the direct heir to the Roman emperors—to celebrate his military successes. Unfortunately, Napoléon's strategic and architectural visions were not entirely on the same plane, and the Arc de Triomphe proved something of an embarrassment. Although the emperor wanted the monument completed in time for an 1810 parade in honor of his new bride, Marie-Louise, the arch was still only a few feet high, and a dummy arch of painted canvas was strung up to save face.

Empires come and go, and Napoléon's had been gone for more than 20 years before the Arc de Triomphe was finally finished, in 1836. It has some magnificent sculpture by François Rude, such as the *Departure of the Volunteers,* better known as *La Marseillaise,* to the right of the arch when viewed from the Champs-Élysées. After showing alarming signs of decay, the structure received a thorough overhaul in 1989 and is once again neo-Napoleonic in its splendor. There is a small museum halfway up the arch devoted to its history. France's Unknown Soldier is buried beneath the archway; the flame is rekindled every evening at 6:30. ⊠ *Pl. Charles-de-Gaulle,* ☎ *01–43–80–31–31.* ≋ *35 frs.* ⊙ *Daily 9:30–11; winter, daily 10–10:30. Métro or RER: Étoile.*

OFF THE BEATEN PATH **MUSÉE DAPPER** – African art is beautifully displayed in this tranquil four-story *hôtel particulier* (town house). It's one métro stop from L'Étoile or a 10-minute walk along avenue Victor-Hugo. ⊠ *50 av. Victor-Hugo,* ☎ *01–45–00–01–50.* ≋ *20 frs, Wed. free.* ⊙ *Daily 11–7. Métro: Victor-Hugo.*

⑭ **Carrousel du Louvre.** Part of the early '90s Louvre renovation program, this subterranean shopping complex is centered on an inverted glass pyramid and contains a wide range of stores, spaces for fashion shows, an auditorium, and a huge parking garage. At lunchtime, museum visitors rush to the mall-style food court where fast food goes international. Note that you can get into the museum (and avoid some lines) by entering through the mall. ⊠ *Entrances on rue de Rivoli or by the Arc du Carrousel. Métro: Palais-Royal.*

❷ **Champs-Élysées.** The 2-km (1¼-mi) Champs-Élysées was originally laid out in the 1660s by the landscape gardener Le Nôtre as a park sweeping away from the Tuileries. You won't see many signs of those pastoral origins today as you stroll past the cafés, restaurants, airline offices, car showrooms, movie theaters, and shopping arcades that occupy its upper half. In an attempt to reestablish this thoroughfare as one of the world's most beautiful avenues, the city planted extra trees, broadened sidewalks, added coordinated designer street-furniture (everything from benches and lighting to traffic lights, telephone booths, and trash cans), refurbished Art Nouveau newsstands, built underground parking to alleviate congestion, and clamped down on garish storefronts. *Métro: George-V, Franklin-D.-Roosevelt, Étoile.*

⑯ **Cour Carrée.** Don't let the Louvre's main court and I. M. Pei's pyramids tempt you away from the second, more architecturally sophisticated courtyard. Louis XIII's harmoniously imposing Cour Carrée, with its assured feel of an Oxford quadrangle, was one of the supreme architectural achievements of his reign. It has been painstakingly restored, with thousands of cobblestones laid in place of tarmac. Its eastern front takes the form of a giant colonnade, designed by Claude Perrault in the 1660s; the balcony, overlooking the former royal church of St-Germain-l'Auxerrois, has only been open to visitors since 1998. *Métro: Louvre-Rivoli.*

❻ **Grand Palais.** With its curved glass roof, the Grand Palais is unmistakable when approached from either the Seine or the Champs-Élysées and forms an attractive duo with the Petit Palais on the other side of avenue Winston-Churchill. Both these stone buildings, adorned with mosaics and sculpted friezes, were built for the world's fair of 1900, and, as with the Eiffel Tower, there was never any intention that they would be permanent additions to the city. But once they were up, no one seemed inclined to take them down. Today, the atmospheric iron-and-glass interior of the Grand Palais plays host to major exhibitions but was closed for renovation in 1994 and is unlikely to reopen before 2002. ⊠ *av. Winston-Churchill. Métro: Champs-Élysées-Clemenceau.*

☞ ⑫ **Jardin des Tuileries** (Tuileries Garden). This impressive garden—really more of a lengthy park—is typically French: formal and neatly patterned, with statues, rows of trees, and gravel paths. It's a charming place to stroll and survey the surrounding cityscape; you may see a string quartet or jugglers entertaining large crowds on weekends. A fair, with a small skating rink, sets up here between December and February. *Métro: Tuileries.*

④ Lido. Free-flowing champagne, foot-stomping melodies in French and English, and topless razzmatazz pack in the crowds (of mostly tourists) every night for the show at this famous nightclub, which has been around since 1946. ⊠ *116 av. des Champs-Élysées. Métro: George-V.*

⑮ Louvre. Although it is now a coherent, unified structure, the Louvre—the world's largest museum and one of its most stunning at night when illuminated by 70,000 discreet lightbulbs—is the product of centuries. Originally built by Philippe-Auguste in the 13th century as a fortress, it was not until the reign of pleasure-loving François I, 300 years later, that today's Louvre gradually began to take shape. Through the years, Henri IV (1589–1610), Louis XIII (1610–43), Louis XIV (1643–1715), Napoléon I (1804–14), and Napoléon III (1852–70) all contributed to its construction. Before rampaging revolutionaries burned part of it down during the bloody Paris Commune of 1871, the building was even larger. The open section facing the Tuileries Gardens was originally the Palais des Tuileries, the main Paris residence of the royal family.

The uses to which the building has been put have been almost equally varied. Though Charles V (1364–80) made the Louvre his residence—parts of the original medieval fortress have been excavated and can be seen during your visit—later French kings preferred to live elsewhere, mainly in the Loire Valley. Even after François I decided to make the Louvre his permanent home, and accordingly embarked on an ambitious rebuilding program (most of which came to nothing), the Louvre never became more than a secondary palace.

When, in 1682, Louis XIV decided to move the French court out of the city to Versailles, despite having initiated a major program of rebuilding at the Louvre, it seemed that the Louvre would never be more than a home for minor courtiers. Indeed, during the remainder of Louis's reign, the palace underwent a rapid decline. Its empty apartments were taken over by a rabble of artists; little shacklike shops were set up against the walls; and chimneys sprouted higgledy-piggledy from the severe lines of the facades. Louis XV (1715–74), thanks in large measure to the financial shrewdness of his chief minister, Marigny, inaugurated long-overdue renovations, though he, too, preferred to live at Versailles.

The Louvre's association with the French crown did not last much longer. It was from the Tuileries Palace that Louis XVI and Marie-Antoinette fled in 1791 (they had been under house arrest), two years after being forced back to Paris from Versailles. They got as far as Varennes, in Lorraine, only to be arrested and returned again to Paris for trial and, ultimately, execution. The palace was taken over by the Revolutionary leaders—the Convention first, then the Directory. At the very end of the century, Napoléon, initially as first consul, subsequently as emperor, initiated further renovations and made the Louvre into a museum. This did not, however, prevent the three remaining French kings—Louis XVIII (1814–24), who has the dubious distinction of having been the only French monarch to die in the Louvre; Charles X (1824–30); and Louis-Philippe (1830–48)—from making the Louvre their home. The latter two suffered the indignity of expulsion at the hands of the dreaded Paris mob in the uprisings of 1830 and 1848.

★ The Louvre's recent history centers on I. M. Pei's **glass pyramid,** surrounded by three smaller pyramids in the Cour Napoléon. Unveiled in March of 1989, it's more than just a grandiloquent gesture, a desire on the part of the late president François Mitterrand, who commissioned it, to make his mark on the city. The pyramid provided a new, and much needed, entrance to the Louvre; it also tops a large mu-

Louvre

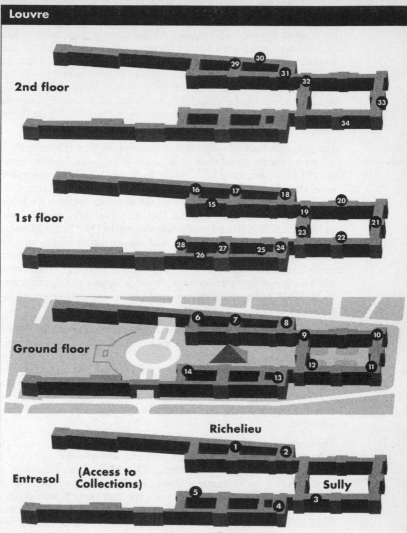

2nd floor

1st floor

Ground floor

Richelieu

Entresol (Access to Collections)

Sully

Denon

Egyptian Antiquities: 11, 21

French Paintings:
14th–17th cent., 31
18th–19th cent., 33
19th cent. (large), 25, 34

French Sculptures:
17th–18th cent., 1
17th–19th cent., 7
Middle Ages, Renaissance, 6

Greek, Etruscan and Roman Antiquities:
Bronzes and Precious Objects, 23
Ceramics and Terracotta, 22
Greek Antiquities, 4, 12

Etruscan and Roman Antiquities, 13
Venus de Milo, 12

Islamic and Asia Minor Antiquities:
Arab Antiquities, 10
Iranian Antiquities, 9
Islamic Art, 2
Mesopotamia, 8

Italian Paintings: 26
Mona Lisa, 27

Italian Sculptures:
11th–15th cent., 5
16th–19th cent., 14
Michelangelo's The Dying Slave, 14

Medieval Louvre: 3

Northern School Paintings:
Holland, Flanders, Germany, 29

Northern Sculptures:
17th–19th cent., 14

Objets d'Art:
17th–18th cent., 18, 20
Galerie d'Apollon (Crown Jewels), 24
Middle Ages, Renaissance, 17
Napoléon III Apartments, 15
19th cent., 16, 19

Prints and Drawings:
French 17th cent., 32
Italian School, 28
Northern Schools, 30

seum shop, café, and restaurant. Moreover, it acts as the terminal point for the most celebrated city view in Europe, a majestic vista stretching through the Arc du Carrousel, the Tuileries Gardens, across Place de la Concorde, up the Champs-Élysées to the towering Arc de Triomphe, and ending at the giant modern arch at La Défense, 4 km (2½ mi) more to the west. Needless to say, the architectural collision between the classical stone blocks of the courtyard surrounding the pyramid and the pseudo-Egyptian glass panels caused a furor. But, as time has passed, initial outrage has faded—as it once did for the Eiffel Tower.

The pyramids marked only the first phase of the Grand Louvre Project, a plan for the restoration of the museum launched by Mitterrand in 1981 for an estimated $1.3 billion. In November 1993, exactly 200 years after the Louvre first opened its doors to the public, Mitterrand cut the ribbon on the second phase: the renovation of the **Richelieu wing** on the north side of the Cour Napoléon. Built between 1852 and 1857 by Napoléon III and grudgingly vacated in 1989 by the Ministry of Finance, the wing was gutted and reconstructed by Pei and his French associates and reopened to house more than 12,000 artworks, nearly a third from storage. The wing contains principally the Islamic and Mesopotamian art collections, French sculpture and painting, and Napoléon III's sumptuous apartments lovingly restored to their full ostentatious glory.

The third phase of the Grand Louvre project is ongoing. By 1996 a much-needed improvement of lighting and air-conditioning had been carried out; the remaining exterior facades had been cleaned; and the adjacent Tuileries Gardens had been restored to their original splendor. By 1998, the museum had 11 new rooms of Persian and Arab antiquities; extra space for Greek, Roman, and Egyptian art; and first-time-ever public access to the balcony of the east wing's mighty colonnade.

The Louvre's extraordinary collections encompass paintings, drawings, antiquities, sculpture, furniture, coins, and jewelry—the quality and the sheer variety are overwhelming. The number-one attraction is Leonardo da Vinci's enigmatic **Mona Lisa** (*La Joconde* to the French). The picture is smaller than you might expect and kept behind protective glass; it is invariably surrounded by a crowd of worshipers. But there are numerous other works of equal quality. The collections are divided into seven areas: Asian antiquities, Egyptian antiquities, Greek and Roman antiquities, sculpture, objets d'art, paintings, and prints and drawings. What follows is no more than a selection of favorites, chosen to act as key points for your exploration.

PAINTINGS

French paintings dominate the picture collection. Following are the highlights, in chronological order:

Shepherds in Arcadia, by Poussin (1594–1665), is a sturdy example of the Rome-based painter's fascination with the classical world and of the precision of his draftsmanship. His colors, by contrast, are surprisingly vivid, almost Venetian.

Cleopatra Landing, by Claude (1600–82), presents an altogether more poetic vision of the ancient world as delicately atmospheric, with the emphasis on light and space rather than on the nominal subject matter.

Embarkation for the Island of Cythera, by Watteau (1684–1721), concentrates on creating an equally poetic mood, but there is an extra layer of emotion: The gallant gentlemen and courtly women seem drugged by the pleasures about to be enjoyed but disturbingly aware of their transitory nature, too.

Oath of the Horatii, by David (1748–1825), takes a much sterner view of classical Rome; this is neoclassicism—severe, uncompromising, and austere. The moral content of the painting takes precedence over purely painterly qualities; it also held an important political message for contemporaries, championing the cause of Republicanism.

La Grande Odalisque, by Ingres (1780–1867), is one of the supreme achievements of this habitually staid "academic" artist; sensuous yet remote and controlled. Here, exoticism and the French classical tradition gel to produce a strikingly elegant image.

Raft of the Medusa, by Géricault (1791–1824), conveys a gloomily Romantic view of the human state, nightmarish despite its heroism and grand scale.

Liberty Guiding the People, by Delacroix (1798–1863), in sharp contrast to the conservative classical paintings of the 19th century, celebrates the courageous spirit of revolutionary idealism. While Liberty evokes a classical reference, she symbolizes the heroism of the bloody uprising on July 27–29, 1830.

Among works by non-French painters, pride of place must go to the **Mona Lisa,** if only by virtue of its fame. The Italian Renaissance is also strongly represented by Fra Angelico, Mantegna, Raphael, Titian, and Veronese. Holbein, Van Eyck, Rembrandt, Hals, Brueghel, and Rubens—whose giant Maria de Médicis canvases have an entire hall to themselves—underline the achievements of northern European painting. The Spanish painters El Greco, Murillo, and Goya are also represented.

SCULPTURE

Three-dimensional attractions start with marvels of ancient Greek sculpture, such as the soaring *Victory of Samothrace,* from the 3rd century BC, and the *Venus de Milo,* from the 2nd century BC. The strikingly realistic *Seated Scribe* dates from around 2000 BC. One of the best-loved exhibits is Michelangelo's *Slaves,* intended for the unfinished tomb of Pope Julius II. These can be admired in the Denon Wing, where the sculpture section is housed partly in the brick-vaulted former imperial stables. Other highlights include a 12th-century Crucifixion from Bavaria, Gregor Erhart's sensuous 15th-century colored wooden statue of *Mary Magdalene,* and a 17th-century walnut *Death of St. Francis* from Spain.

FURNITURE AND OBJETS D'ART

The number-one attraction is the French crown jewels, a glittering display of extravagant jewelry, including the 186-carat Regent diamond. Among the collections of French furniture, don't miss the grandiose 17th- and 18th-century productions of Boulle and Riesener, marvels of intricate craftsmanship and elegant luxury. The series of immense Gobelins tapestries are for those with a fondness for opulent decoration.

If you have time for only one visit, these selections give you an idea of the riches of the museum. But try to make repeat visits—the Louvre is about half price on Sunday and after 3 PM on other days. (Unless you plan to go to a number of museums every day, the 1-, 3-, and 5-day tourist museum passes probably aren't worth your money, since you could easily spend a whole day at the Louvre alone.) Study the plans at the entrance to get your bearings and pick up a map to take with you. ⊠ *Palais du Louvre (it's faster to enter through the Carrousel du Louvre mall on rue de Rivoli than through the pyramid),* ☎ *01–40–20–51–51 for information.* 🖃 *45 frs; 26 frs after 3 PM and all day Sun.;*

THE SUN PRESIDENT

FRANCE'S HEAVILY CENTRALIZED political system breeds big budgets and big egos. And no French leader since Louis XIV was as big a builder as François Mitterrand, under whose 14-year Presidential reign (1981–95) new structures rose at breakneck pace.

Mitterrand's presidential predecessors were no hard act to follow. The de Gaulle era was synonymous with high-rise housing projects; Georges Pompidou demolished the beloved iron-and-glass market halls of Les Halles, though he did leave his name to the popular Pompidou Center.

Mitterrand thumbed his nose at them both by choosing four outlandish skyscrapers for his last grand project: the new Bibliothèque Nationale. Just after its inauguration he died, ensuring it would be named after him—now it's called the **Bibliothèque François-Mitterrand.**

Mitterrand's most famous legacy is the glass **Pyramid** designed by I. M. Pei to crown the new entry to the **Louvre.** The choice of a pyramid was no coincidence: Mitterrand, nicknamed the Sphinx, derived a mystical thrill from all things Egyptian.

Most of Mitterrand's buildings exude the same geometric simplicity. Among them: the sphere—witness the **Géode** cinema at La Villette, covered in polished metal like a gleaming giant ball; and the cube—in hollowed form at **La Défense,** where a colossal arch closes a five-mi vista, via the Champs-Élysées and Napoleon's (smaller) Arc de Triomphe, to the Louvre pyramid.

Much of Mitterrand's efforts centered on run-down East Paris. The graceless **Opéra de la Bastille** has proved the least popular of his projects, at least externally; but

the auditorium is spectacular, and it rejuvenated the whole district. **La Villette** was granted a new science museum by Adrien Fainsilber at one end, and a music academy and concert hall by Christian de Portzamparc at the other; the former slaughterhouse in between escaped the fate of Les Halles to become an exhibition center.

JEAN NOUVEL, arguably France's foremost contemporary architect, built the **Fondation Cartier** in Montparnasse, and the **Institut du Monde Arabe** on the Left Bank. Farther upstream, the elephantine **Finance Ministry** dips its trunk into the Seine alongside the **Bercy Sports Center,** which is shaped like a pyramid with grass walls.

As with Louis XIV, stone, water, and greenery invariably went together in the Mitterrand scheme. **Bercy** is surrounded by trim gardens in the formal French tradition; the Canal St-Denis and Canal de l'Ourcq intersect, like the arms of the Versailles Grand Canal, at **La Villette;** modern sculptures and a giant fountain adorn the concourse at La Défense, recalling Versailles. Like the Sun King with his secret groves, Mitterrand liked to surprise, as with the forest of trees lurking within the national library's sunken courtyard, hidden by a towering wooden staircase 300 yards wide.

Jacques Chirac, Mitterrand's successor, is a more prosaic fellow. As Mayor of Paris, he was content to repave **Place Vendôme** and the plaza in front of the **Hôtel de Ville,** and widen the sidewalks on the **Champs-Élysées.** Chirac's only pyramid will probably remain the canvas **teepee** that was strung up in front of the Pompidou Center from 1997 to 1999 explaining why it was closed.

free 1st Sun. of month. ⊙ *Thurs.–Sun. 9–6, Mon. and Wed. 9* AM–*9:45* PM. *Some sections open limited days. Métro: Palais-Royal.*

⑩ **Musée du Jeu de Paume.** Renovations transformed this museum, at the entrance to the Tuileries Garden, into an ultramodern, white-walled showcase for excellent temporary exhibits of bold contemporary art. The building was once the spot of jeu de paume games (literally, palm game—a forerunner of tennis). ⊠ *Pl. de la Concorde,* ☎ *01–42–60–69–69.* 🎫 *38 frs.* ⊙ *Tues. noon–9:30, Wed.–Fri. noon–7, weekends 10–7. Métro: Concorde.*

⑪ **Musée de l'Orangerie.** Several of Claude Monet's *Water Lily* series head the choice array of early 20th-century paintings in this museum in the Tuileries Garden. Works by Renoir, Cézanne, Matisse, and Marie Laurencin, the "Popess of Cubism," are also on display. ⊠ *Pl. de la Concorde,* ☎ *01–42–97–48–16.* 🎫 *30 frs.* ⊙ *Wed.–Mon. 9:45–5:15. Métro: Concorde.*

❸ **Office de Tourisme de la Ville de Paris** (Paris Tourist Office). The modern, spacious Paris Tourist Office, near the Arc de Triomphe, is worth a visit at the start of your stay to pick up free maps, leaflets, and information on upcoming events. Most of the staff speak English and can also help book accommodations or tickets for shows. You can also exchange money here and buy métro tickets and souvenirs. ⊠ *127 av. des Champs-Élysées,* ☎ *01–49–52–53–54 (01–49–52–53–56 for recorded information in English).* ⊙ *Daily 9–8. Métro: Charles-de-Gaulle–Étoile.*

⌣ ❺ **Palais de la Découverte** (Palace of Discovery). A planetarium, working models, and scientific and technological exhibits on such topics as optics, biology, nuclear physics, and electricity make up this science museum behind the Grand Palais. ⊠ *av. Franklin-D.-Roosevelt,* ☎ *01–40–74–81–73.* 🎫 *27 frs, 13 frs extra for planetarium.* ⊙ *Tues.–Sat. 9:30–6, Sun. 10–7. Métro: Champs-Élysées–Clemenceau.*

❼ **Petit Palais.** The smaller counterpart to the Grand Palais, just off the Champs-Élysées, beautifully presents a permanent collection of French painting and furniture, with splendid canvases by Courbet and Bouguereau. Temporary exhibits are often held here, too. The sprawling entrance gallery contains several enormous turn-of-the-century paintings on its walls and ceilings. Outside, take time to admire two fine statues near each corner of the building: French World War I hero Georges Clemenceau, facing the Champs-Élysées, was joined in 1998 by Jean Cardot's resolute image of Winston Churchill facing the Seine. ⊠ *av. Winston-Churchill,* ☎ *01–42–65–12–73.* 🎫 *27 frs.* ⊙ *Tues.–Sun. 10–5:40. Métro: Champs-Élysées–Clemenceau.*

❾ **Place de la Concorde.** This majestic square at the foot of the Champs-Élysées was laid out in the 1770s, but there was nothing in the way of peace or concord about its early years. Between 1793 and 1795, it was the scene of more than 1,000 deaths by guillotine; victims included Louis XVI, Marie-Antoinette, Danton, and Robespierre. The 107-ft Obelisk, originally built in the 8th century BC, was a present from the viceroy of Egypt and erected here in 1833; it received its gilded cap in 1998. Among the handsome, symmetrical 18th-century buildings facing the square is the deluxe Hôtel Crillon (☞ Chapter 3), identified by a discreet marble plaque. At the near end of high-walled rue Royale is the legendary Maxim's restaurant. Unless you choose to eat here, you won't be able to see the riot of crimson velvets and florid Art Nouveau furniture inside. *Métro: Concorde.*

8 **Pont Alexandre-III.** No other bridge over the Seine epitomizes the fin de siècle frivolity of the Belle Epoque like the exuberant, bronze-lamp-lined Pont Alexandre-III. The bridge was built, like the Grand and Petit Palais nearby, for the 1900 world's fair, and ingratiatingly named in honor of the visiting Russian czar. *Métro: Invalides.*

THE FAUBOURG ST-HONORÉ

The Faubourg St-Honoré—the area just north of the Champs-Élysées and the Tuileries—is synonymous with style, as you will see as you progress from the President's Palace, past a wealth of art galleries and the Neoclassical Madeleine church, to stately Place Vendôme. Leading names in fashion can be found farther east on Place des Victoires, close to what was, for centuries, the gastronomic heart of Paris: Les Halles (pronounced *lay al*), once the city's main market. These giant glass-and-iron market halls were once replenished nightly by an army of wagons, then trucks, which caused astounding traffic jams in the city's already congested streets. The market was closed in 1969 and replaced by a park and a modern shopping mall, the Forum des Halles. The surrounding streets underwent a transformation and are now filled with shops, cafés, restaurants, and chic apartment buildings. The brash modernity of the mall stands in contrast to the august church of St-Eustache nearby. Similarly, the incongruous black-and-white columns in the classical courtyard of Richelieu's neighboring Palais-Royal present a further case of daring modernity—or architectural vandalism, depending on your point of view. Parisians may delight in their role as custodians of a glorious heritage, but, as this walk shows, they are not content to remain mere guardians of the past.

Numbers in the text correspond to numbers in the margin and on the Faubourg St-Honoré map.

A Good Walk

Start your walk in front of the most important home in France: the **Palais de l'Élysée** ①, the Presidential Palace; crash barriers and gold-braided guards keep visitors at bay. There's more to see in the plethora of art galleries and luxury fashion boutiques lining rue du Faubourg St-Honoré, where you will also see Sotheby's auction house and the British Embassy. From rue du Faubourg St-Honoré, turn left onto rue Boissy-d'Anglas and cut right through an archway into Cité Berryer, a newly restored courtyard with several trendy shops. It leads to rue Royale, a classy street lined with jewelry stores. Looming to the left is the sturdy **Église de la Madeleine** ②.

Cross boulevard de la Madeleine and take rue Duphot down to rue St-Honoré, where you'll find **Notre-Dame de l'Assomption** ③, noted for its huge dome and solemn interior. Continue to rue de Castiglione, then head left to one of the world's most opulent squares, **Place Vendôme** ④, ringed with jewelers. That's Napoléon standing at the top of the square's bronze central column—and that's the Ritz, fronted by those Rolls-Royces, halfway down on the left. Return to rue St-Honoré and continue to the mighty church of **St-Roch** ⑤. It's worth having a look inside to see the bombastically Baroque altarpiece in the circular Lady Chapel at the far end.

Take the next right onto rue des Pyramides and cross Place des Pyramides, with its gilded statue of Joan of Arc on horseback, to the northernmost wing of the Louvre: home to the **Musée de la Mode** ⑥, dedicated to costumes and fashion. Stay on arcaded rue de Rivoli to Place du Palais-Royal. On the far side of the square is the **Louvre des Antiquaires** ⑦, a chic shopping mall housing upscale antiques stores.

Opposite, beyond the exuberant fountains of Place André-Malraux, Garnier's 19th-century Opéra (☞ The Grand Boulevards, *below*) beckons at the far end of the avenue of the same name.

On the corner of rue de Richelieu and rue de Rivoli is the **Comédie Française** ⑧, the time-honored setting for performances of classical French drama. To the right of the theater is the unobtrusive entrance to the **Palais-Royal** ⑨; its courtyard is a surprising oasis in the heart of the city, and a study in both classical and contemporary French landscape architecture. Walk down to the far end of the garden and peek into the glassy Belle Epoque interior of Le Grand Véfour (☞ Chapter 2), one of the swankiest restaurants in the city.

One block north of here, on rue de Richelieu, stands what used to be France's main national library, the **Bibliothèque Nationale Richelieu** ⑩. Rue des Petits-Champs heads east to the circular **Place des Victoires** ⑪: That's Louis XIV riding the plunging steed in the center of the square. You'll find some of the city's most upscale fashion shops here and on the surrounding streets, along with the 17th-century church of **Notre-Dame des Victoires** ⑫. Head south down rue Croix-des-Petits-Champs, past the nondescript Banque de France on your right, and take the second street on the left to the circular **Bourse du Commerce** ⑬, the Commercial Exchange. Alongside it is a 100-ft-high fluted column, the **Colonne de Ruggieri.**

You don't need to scale Ruggieri's Column to spot the bulky outline of the church of **St-Eustache** ⑭, a curious architectural hybrid of Gothic and classical styles. Today most of the market area that once sat on this site is occupied by the **Jardin des Halles** ⑮, and a modern, multilevel shopping mall, the **Forum des Halles** ⑯. Rue Berger leads to the square des Innocents, with its handsome 16th-century Renaissance fountain. Farther east you can see the futuristic funnels of the Centre Pompidou (☞ The Marais, *below*) jutting above the surrounding buildings.

From the far end of the square des Innocents, rue St-Denis leads to Place du Châtelet, with its theaters, fountain, and the **Tour St-Jacques** ⑰ looming up to your left—all that remains of a church that once stood here. Turning right on quai de la Mégisserie, you can divide your attention between the exotic array of caged birds for sale along the sidewalk and the view across the Seine toward the turreted Conciergerie (☞ The Islands and the Latin Quarter, *below*). As you cross rue du Pont-Neuf, the birds give way to the Art Deco Samaritaine department store with its panoramic rooftop café. Turn right on rue de l'Arbre-Sec, then the first left on to rue des Prêtres to reach **St-Germain l'Auxerrois** ⑱, once the French royal family's parish church. Opposite is the colonnaded eastern facade of the Louvre (☞ From the Arc de Triomphe to the Louvre, *above*).

TIMING

With brief visits to churches and monuments, this 5½-km (3½-mi) walk should take about three to four hours. On a nice day, linger in the gardens of the Palais-Royal; on a cold day, indulge in an unbelievably thick hot chocolate at the Angélina tearoom on rue de Rivoli.

Sights to See

⑩ **Bibliothèque Nationale Richelieu** (Richelieu National Library). France's longtime national library used to contain more than 7 million printed volumes; many have been removed to the giant new Bibliothèque François-Mitterrand (☞ From Bastille to Nation, *below*), though original manuscripts and prints are still here. You can admire Robert de Cotte's 18th-century courtyard, and peep into the magnificent 19th-century reading room, but you cannot enter (it's only open to re-

KEY

AE American Express Office

0   220 yards
0   200 meters

Bourse
La Bourse

R. de Cléry
Rue Réaumur

R. Vivienne
R. N.-D. des Victoires
R. du Mail
Rue d'Aboukir
R. Montmartre

2e

R. St-Sauveur
Reaumur
Sébastopol

R. Grene
R. St-Denis

Banque
de France

R. Coquillère
R. Etienne Marcel

R. de Turbigo

Bd. de Sébastopol

14

1er

Etienne
Marcel

Les Halles

R. Pierre
Lescot

R. St-Denis

3e

R. Croix des Petits-Champs
R. du Louvre
R. du Faubourg-St-Honoré

15

R. Berger

16

Châtelet-
Les Halles

Sq. des
Innocents

R. Rambuteau

Centre Pompidou

Louvre

R. de Rivoli

R. des Halles

R. St-Denis

R. de l'Amiral
de Coligny
R. de Prêtres
R. de l'Arbre-Sec
R. du Pont Neuf

18

Pl. Igor
Stravinsky

R. St-Martin

R. du Renard

Châtelet

17

R. de Rivoli

4e

Pont Neuf

Quai de la Mégisserie

Hôtel de Ville

Pont
des Arts

stitut
France

Pont Neuf

Châtelet

Conciergerie

Pont
au Change

Pl. du
Châtelet

du
ais
al

7

9

10

11

12

13

searchers). The collections are on exhibit from time to time in the library's galleries. ⊠ *58 rue de Richelieu.* ⊙ *Daily 9–8. Métro: Bourse.*

⑬ **Bourse du Commerce** (Commercial Exchange). The circular, shallow-domed, 18th-century Commercial Exchange building near Les Halles began life as the Corn Exchange; Victor Hugo waggishly likened it to a jockey's cap without the peak. ⊠ *rue de Viarmes. Métro or RER: Les Halles.*

Colonne de Ruggieri (Ruggieri's Column). The 100-ft-high fluted column, behind the Bourse du Commerce, is all that remains of a mansion built here in 1572 for Catherine de Médicis. The column is said to have been used as a platform for stargazing by her astrologer, Ruggieri. *Métro: Les Halles.*

⑧ **Comédie Française.** This theater is the setting for performances of classical French drama, with tragedies by Racine and Corneille and comedies by Molière regularly on the bill. The building itself dates from 1790, but the Comédie Française company was created by that most theatrical of French monarchs, Louis XIV, back in 1680. If you understand French and have a taste for the mannered, declamatory style of French acting—it's a far cry from method acting—you'll appreciate an evening here (☞ Chapter 4). ⊠ *Pl. André-Malraux,* ☎ *01–44–58–15–15. Métro: Palais-Royal.*

❷ **Église de la Madeleine.** With its rows of uncompromising columns, this sturdy Neoclassical edifice—designed in 1814 but not consecrated until 1842—looks more like a Greek temple than a Christian church. In fact, La Madeleine, as it is known, was nearly selected as Paris's first train station (the site of the Gare St-Lazare, just up the road, was chosen instead). Inside, the only natural light comes from three shallow domes. The walls are richly and harmoniously decorated; gold glints through the murk. The portico's majestic Corinthian colonnade supports a gigantic pediment with a frieze of the Last Judgment. From the top of the church's steps, you can see down rue Royale across Place de la Concorde to the Palais Bourbon (parliament building). From the bottom of the steps, another vista extends up boulevard Malesherbes to the domed church of St-Augustin. ⊠ *Pl. de la Madeleine.* ⊙ *Mon.–Sat. 7:30–7, Sun. 8–7. Métro: Madeleine.*

NEED A BREAK? **L'Écluse** (⊠ 15 Pl. de la Madeleine), a cozy wine bar on the square to the west of the Église de la Madeleine, serves stylish snacks, such as foie gras and carpaccio, and a range of Bordeaux wines.

⑯ **Forum des Halles.** Les Halles, the iron-and-glass halls of the central Paris food market, were closed in 1969 and replaced in the late '70s by the Forum des Halles, a characterless, modern shopping mall. Nothing remains of either the market or the rambunctious atmosphere that led 19th-century novelist Emile Zola to dub Les Halles *le ventre de Paris* ("the belly of Paris"), although rue Montorgueil, behind St-Eustache, retains something of its original bustle. Unfortunately, much of the plastic, concrete, glass, and mock-marble facade of the multi-level shopping mall is already showing signs of wear and tear. This state of affairs is not much helped by the hordes of teenagers and down-and-outs who invade it toward dusk. Nonetheless, if you are a serious shopper, you might want to check out the French chain stores, the few small boutiques, and the weekly fashion shows by up-and-coming young designers held here (☞ Chapter 6). ⊠ *Main entrance: rue Pierre-Lescot. Métro: Les Halles; RER: Châtelet–Les Halles.*

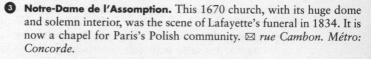 **Jardin des Halles** (Les Halles Garden). This garden, crisscrossed with paths and alleyways flanked by bushes, flower beds, and trim little lawns, takes up much of the site once occupied by Les Halles, the city's central market. Children love the bush shaped like a rhinoceros. *Métro: Les Halles; RER: Châtelet–Les Halles.*

Louvre des Antiquaires. This shopping mall, off Place du Palais-Royal opposite the Louvre, is a minimuseum in itself. Its stylish, glass-walled corridors, lined with upscale antiques dealers, deserve a browse whether you intend to buy or not (☞ Chapter 6). ⊠ *Main entrance: Pl. du Palais-Royal.* ☉ *Tues.–Sun. 11–7. Métro: Palais-Royal.*

Musée de la Mode (Fashion Museum). This museum, housed in the northwestern wing of the Louvre building, has a glittering array of costumes and fashion accessories dating back to the 18th century. ⊠ *107 rue de Rivoli,* ☎ *01–44–55–57–50.* ⊠ *40 frs.* ☉ *Tues.–Sun. 11–6. Métro: Palais-Royal.*

NEED A
BREAK?
Founded in 1903, **Angélina** (⊠ 226 rue de Rivoli, ☎ 01–42–60–82–00) is an elegant *salon de thé* (tearoom), famous for a cup of hot chocolate so thick you'll need a fork to eat it (irresistible even in summer).

Notre-Dame de l'Assomption. This 1670 church, with its huge dome and solemn interior, was the scene of Lafayette's funeral in 1834. It is now a chapel for Paris's Polish community. ⊠ *rue Cambon. Métro: Concorde.*

Notre-Dame des Victoires. Visit this central Paris church, built from 1666 to 1740, to see the 30,000 ex-voto tablets that adorn its walls. ⊠ *Pl. des Petits-Pères. Métro: Sentier.*

Palais de l'Élysée. This "palace," where the French president lives, works, and receives official visitors, was originally constructed as a private mansion in 1718. (Incidentally, when Parisians talk about "L'Élysée," they mean the president's palace; the Champs-Élysées is known simply as "Les Champs," the fields.) The Élysée has housed presidents only since 1873; before then, Madame de Pompadour (Louis XV's influential mistress), Napoléon, Joséphine, the Duke of Wellington, and Queen Victoria all stayed here. President Félix Faure died here in 1899 in the arms of his mistress, so it is said. Although you can catch a glimpse of the palace forecourt and facade through the Faubourg St-Honoré gateway, it is difficult to get much idea of the building's size, or of the extensive gardens that stretch back to the Champs-Élysées, because it is closed to the public. ⊠ *55 rue du Faubourg-St-Honoré. Métro: Miromesnil.*

OFF THE
BEATEN PATH
ST. MICHAEL'S ENGLISH CHURCH – Down the street from the Palais de l'Élysée, this modern church is an architectural disaster. But it's worth the trip for the warm welcome offered visitors, English-speaking ones in particular. ⊠ *5 rue d'Aguesseau,* ☎ *01–47–42–70–88. Services Thurs. 12:45 and Sun. 10:30 (with Sun. school) and 6:30. Métro: Miromesnil.*

Palais-Royal (Royal Palace). The buildings of this former palace—royal only in that all-powerful Cardinal Richelieu (1585–1642) magnanimously bequeathed them to Louis XIII—date from the 1630s. In his early days as king, Louis XIV preferred the relative intimacy of the Palais-Royal to the intimidating splendor of the Louvre. He soon decided, though, that his own intimidating splendor warranted a more majestic setting; hence, of course, Versailles. Today, the Palais-Royal is home to the French Ministry of Culture, and its buildings are not open to the public. They overlook a colonnaded courtyard with black-and-white striped half-columns and revolving silver spheres that slither around in two fountains, the controversial work of architect Daniel Buren. The splendid gardens beyond are bordered by arcades harboring discreet boutiques and divided by rows of perfectly trimmed little trees. This was once the haunt of prostitutes and gamblers: a veritable sink of vice. These days it's hard to imagine anywhere more hoity-toity. ⊠ *Pl. du Palais-Royal. Métro: Palais-Royal.*

④ Place Vendôme. With its granite pavement and Second Empire street lamps, Mansart's rhythmic, perfectly proportioned example of 17th-century urban architecture shines in all its golden-stoned splendor. The square is a fitting showcase for the deluxe Ritz Hotel and the cluster of jewelry display windows found here. Napoléon had the square's central column made from the melted bronze of 1,200 cannons captured at the battle of Austerlitz in 1805. That's him standing vigilantly at the top. Painter Gustave Courbet headed the Revolutionary hooligans who, in 1871, toppled the column and shattered it into thousands of metallic pieces. The Third Republic stuck them together again and sent him the bill. A plaque at No. 8 states that the St-Jacques Resistance group established its first radio link with Charles de Gaulle in London from here in April 1941. *Métro: Opéra.*

⑪ Place des Victoires. This circular square, now home to many of the city's top fashion boutiques, was laid out in 1685 by Jules-Hardouin Mansart in honor of the military victories of Louis XIV, that indefatigable warrior whose nearly continuous battles may have brought much prestige to his country but came perilously close to bringing it to bankruptcy, too. Louis is shown galloping along on a bronze horse in the middle; his statue dates from 1822 and replaced one destroyed during the Revolution. *Métro: Sentier.*

⑭ St-Eustache. Since the demolition of the 19th-century iron-and-glass market halls at the beginning of the '70s, St-Eustache has reemerged as a dominant element on the central Paris skyline. It is a huge church, the "cathedral" of Les Halles, built as the market people's Right Bank reply to Notre-Dame on the Ile de la Cité. St-Eustache dates from a couple of hundred years later than Notre-Dame. With the exception of the feeble west front, added between 1754 and 1788, construction lasted from 1532 to 1637, spanning the decline of the Gothic style and the emergence of the Renaissance. As a consequence, the church is a curious architectural hybrid. Its exterior flying buttresses are Gothic, but its column orders, rounded arches, and thick, comparatively simple window tracery are unmistakably classical. Few buildings bear such eloquent witness to stylistic transition. St-Eustache also hosts occasional organ concerts. ⊠ *2 rue du Jour,* ☎ *01–46–27–89–21 for concert information.* ☉ *Daily 8–7. Métro: Les Halles; RER: Châtelet–Les Halles.*

⑱ St-Germain l'Auxerrois. Until 1789, this church was used by the French royal family as their Paris parish church, in the days when the adjacent Louvre was a palace rather than a museum. The fluid stonework of the facade reveals the influence of 15th-century Flamboyant Gothic style, enjoying its final shrieks before the classical takeover of the Renaissance. Notice the unusually wide windows in the nave and the equally unusual double aisles. The triumph of classicism is evident, however, in the fluted columns around the choir, the area surrounding the altar. These were added in the 18th century and are characteristic of the desire of 18th-century clerics to dress up medieval buildings in the architectural raiment of their own day. ⊠ *Pl. du Louvre. Métro: Louvre-Rivoli.*

⑤ St-Roch. This huge church, designed by Lemercier in 1653 but completed only in the 1730s, is almost as long as Notre-Dame (138 yards) thanks to Hardouin-Mansart's domed Lady Chapel at the far end, with its elaborate Baroque altarpiece. Classical playwright Pierre Corneille (1606–84) is buried here; a commemorative plaque honors him at the left of the entrance. ⊠ *rue St-Honoré. Métro: Tuileries.*

⑰ Tour St-Jacques. This ornate 170-ft stump tower (now used for meteorological purposes and not open to the public) belonged to a 16th-century church destroyed in 1797. ⊠ *Pl. du Châtelet. Métro: Châtelet.*

NEED A BREAK?	Twenty different international beers are available on draft, and more than 180 in bottles, at **Le Trappiste** (⊠ 4 rue St-Denis, ☎ 01–42–33–08–50), just north of Place du Châtelet. Mussels and french fries are the traditional accompaniment, although various other snacks (hot dogs, sandwiches) are also available.

THE GRAND BOULEVARDS

The focal point of this walk is the avenue that runs west to east from St-Augustin, the city's grandest Second Empire church, to Place de la République, whose very name symbolizes the ultimate downfall of the imperial regime. The avenue's name changes six times along the way, which is why Parisians refer to it, in plural, as "Les Grands Boulevards."

The makeup of the neighborhoods along the Grand Boulevards changes steadily as you head east from the posh 8ᵉ *arrondissement* toward working-class east Paris. The *Grands Magasins* (department stores) at the start of the walk epitomize upscale Paris shopping. They stand on boulevard Haussmann, named in honor of the regional prefect who oversaw the reconstruction of the city in the 1850s and 1860s. The opulent Opéra Garnier, just past the Grands Magasins, is the architectural showpiece of the period (often termed the Second Empire and corresponding to the rule of Napoléon III).

Haussmann's concept of urban planning proved grand enough to ward off the postwar skyscrapers and property sharks that bedevil so many other European cities (Paris's urban planners relegated them to the outskirts). Though lined with the seven-story blocks typical of Haussmann's time, the boulevards date from the 1670s, when they were created on the site of the city's medieval fortifications. These were razed when Louis XIV's military triumphs appeared to render their raison d'être obsolete, and replaced by leafy promenades known from the outset as "boulevards."

This walk takes in some of the older sights on both sides of the boulevard, including the city's traditional auction house, the colonnaded stock exchange, and the Sentier district with its busy fabric traders. It ends on the tranquil banks of the little-known Canal St-Martin.

Numbers in the text correspond to numbers in the margin and on The Grand Boulevards map.

A Good Walk

Take the Métro to Monceau in the tony 8ᵉ arrondissement and step through gold-topped iron gates to enter the **Parc Monceau** ①. At the middle of the park, head left to avenue Velasquez, past the **Musée Cernuschi** ②—home to Chinese art from Neolithic pottery to contemporary paintings. Continue on to boulevard Malesherbes and turn right, then right again onto rue de Monceau, to reach the **Musée Nissim de Camondo** ③, whose aristocratic interior reflects the upbeat tone of this posh part of Paris.

Take a left down rue de Téhéran, left along avenue de Messine, and left again on rue de Laborde to reach the innovative iron-and-stone church of **St-Augustin** ④. Cross the square in front and turn left along boulevard Haussmann to get to the leafy, intimate Square Louis XVI with its **Chapelle Expiatoire** ⑤ dedicated to Louis XVI and Marie-Antoinette. Be sure to take a look at the amusing stone carvings on the gleaming 1930s-style facade of the bank at the corner of rue Pasquier and rue Mathurins. Some 300 yards farther down boulevard Haussmann are the Grands Magasins: Paris's most renowned department stores. First comes **Au Printemps** ⑥, then **Galeries Lafayette** ⑦. Marks & Spencer, across the street, provides an outpost for British goods like ginger biscuits and bacon rashers. Opposite the Galeries Lafayette is the massive bulk of the **Opéra Garnier** ⑧. Before venturing around to inspect its extravagant facade, you might like to take in a multiscreen overview of Paris and its history at the **Paristoric** ⑨ movie venue at No. 7 rue Scribe.

Boulevard des Capucines, lined with cinemas and restaurants, heads left from the Opéra, becoming boulevard des Italiens. Turn left onto rue Laffitte for a startling view of the Sacré-Coeur looming above the porticoed church of Notre-Dame-de-Lorette. Turn right on boulevard Haussmann, then left down rue Drouot to the **Hôtel Drouot** ⑩, Paris's central auction house. Rue Rossini leads from Drouot, as it is known, to rue de la Grange-Batelière. Halfway along on the right is the **Passage Jouffroy** ⑪, one of the many covered galleries that honeycomb the center of Paris. At the far end of the passage is the **Musée Grévin** ⑫, a waxworks museum. Cross boulevard Montmartre to the passage des Panoramas, leading to rue St-Marc. Turn right, then left down rue Vivienne, to find the foresquare, colonnaded **Bourse** ⑬, the Paris Stock Exchange.

If you wish, you can continue down rue Vivienne from the Bourse and join the Faubourg St-Honoré (☞ *above*) walk at the Bibliothèque Nationale. If you're feeling adventurous, head east along rue Réaumur, whose huge-windowed buildings once formed the heart of the French newspaper industry—stationery shops still abound—and cross rue Montmartre. You can catch sight of the St-Eustache church to your right; the distant spires of St-Ambroise emerge on the horizon. Take the second left up rue de Cléry: a narrow street that is the exclusive domain of fabric wholesalers, and often crammed with vans, palettes, and delivery people creating colorful chaos. The lopsided building at the corner of rue Poissonnière looks as if it is struggling to stay upright on the district's drunken slopes. Continue up rue de Cléry as far as rue des Degrés—not a street at all, but a 14-step stairway—then look for the clock and crooked turnip tower of **Notre-Dame de Bonne-Nouvelle** ⑭, hemmed in by rickety housing that looks straight out of Balzac. You can enter via No. 19 bis and cross through the church to emerge beneath the front portico on rue de la Lune. Head left as far as rue Poissonnière, then turn right to return to the Grand Boulevards, by now going under the name of boulevard de Bonne-Nouvelle.

On the near corner of the boulevard stands the **Rex** ⑮, an Art Deco movie theater where you can take a backstage tour. Cross the boulevard for a view of its wedding-cake tower, then head up boulevard de Bonne-Nouvelle to the **Porte St-Denis** ⑯, a newly cleaned triumphal arch dating from the reign of Louis XIV. A little farther on is the smaller but similar **Porte St-Martin** ⑰. From here take rue St-Martin south to the **Conservatoire National des Techniques** ⑱, an industrial museum housed partly in the former church of St-Martin. A lengthy restoration had still not been completed at press time, so you may have to

The Grand Boulevards

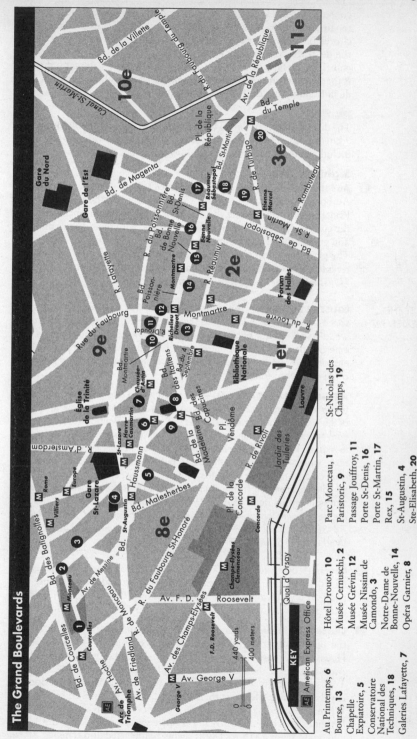

console yourself with a glimpse of the solemn domed forecourt and repair to the leafy square opposite, or to the high, narrow, late-Gothic church of **St-Nicolas des Champs** ⑲ across rue Réaumur. Head left on rue de Turbigo, past the cloister ruins and Renaissance gateway that embellish the far side of St-Nicolas. Some 400 yards along on the right is the Baroque church of **Ste-Elisabeth** ⑳, shortly after you reach Place de la République (☞ From République to La Villette, *below*).

TIMING

The distance between Parc Monceau and Place de la République is about 7 km (4½ mi), which will probably take you at least four hours to walk, including coffee breaks and window-shopping.

Sights to See

⑥ **Au Printemps.** Founded in 1865 by Jules Jaluzot—former employee of Au Bon Marché, which opened 13 years earlier on the Left Bank—Au Printemps swiftly became the mecca of Right Bank shoppers, enabling the current opulent Belle Epoque buildings, with their domes and gold and green mosaic name signs, to be erected by the turn of the century. The glass cupola in Café Flo dates from 1923; and the rooftop cafeteria has a splendid view of the Paris skyline (☞ Chapter 6). ⊠ *64 bd. Haussmann. Métro: Havre-Caumartin.*

OFF THE
BEATEN PATH

ÉGLISE DE LA TRINITÉ – This church, a worthy 1860s essay in neo-Renaissance, is fronted by a lawn and fountains, and crowned by a central wedding-cake tower of dubious aesthetic merit that has nonetheless emerged as a landmark feature of the Right Bank skyline. It's at the far end of rue Mogador, opposite the back of the Opéra. ⊠ *Pl. d'Estienne-d'Orves. Métro: Trinité.*

ATELIER DE GUSTAVE MOREAU – This town house and studio of painter Gustave Moreau (1826–98), doyen of the Symbolist movement, is one of the strangest artistic experiences in Paris. The Symbolists strove to convey ideas through images, but many of the ideas Moreau was trying to express were so obscure that the artist had to provide explanatory texts, which rather defeats the point. But it's easy to admire his extravagant colors and flights of fantasy, influenced by Persian and Indian miniatures. From the Trinité church, take rue Blanche to the right, then turn right on rue de la Tour-des-Dames; the museum is at the far end of rue de la Rochefoucauld. ⊠ *14 rue de la Rochefoucauld,* ☎ *01-48-74-38-50.* ☜ *22 frs.* ☉ *Thurs.–Sun. 10–12:45 and 2–5:15, Mon. and Wed. 11–5:15. Métro: Trinité.*

⑬ **Bourse** (Stock Exchange). The Paris Stock Exchange, a serene, colonnaded 19th-century building, is a far cry from Wall Street. Bring your passport if you want to tour it. ⊠ *rue Vivienne.* ☜ *30 frs. Guided tours only (in French), weekdays every ½ hr 1:15–3:45. Métro: Bourse.*

⑤ **Chapelle Expiatoire.** This unkempt mausoleum emerges defiantly from the lush undergrowth of verdant square Louis-XVI off boulevard Haussmann, marking the initial burial site of Louis XVI and Marie-Antoinette after their turns at the guillotine on Place de la Concorde. Two stone tablets are inscribed with the last missives of the doomed royals: touching pleas for their Revolutionary enemies to be forgiven. When compared to the pomp and glory of Napoleon's memorial at the Invalides, this tribute to royalty (France was ruled by kings until 1792 and again from 1815 to 1848) seems halfhearted and trite. ⊠ *29 rue Pasquier,* ☎ *01-44-32-18-00.* ☜ *15 frs.* ☉ *Thurs.–Sat. 1–5. Métro: St-Augustin.*

⑱ **Conservatoire National des Techniques** (National Technical Museum). The former church and priory of St-Martin des Champs was built between the 11th and 13th centuries. Confiscated during the Revolution, it was used first as an educational institution, then as an arms factory, before becoming, in 1799, the Conservatoire des Arts et Métiers. Today the church forms the south wing of the National Technical Museum, an industrial museum with a varied collection of models (locomotives, vehicles, and agricultural machinery), astronomical instruments, looms, and glass, together with displays on printing, photography, and the history of television. The splendid 13th-century refectory, a large hall supported by central columns, is now used as a library. The museum was set to reopen in late 1999 after major renovations. ⊠ *292 rue St-Martin,* ☎ *01–40–27–23–31. Métro: Arts et Métiers.*

❼ **Galeries Lafayette.** This turn-of-the-century department store has a vast, shimmering, Belle Epoque glass dome that can only be seen if you venture inside (☞ Chapter 6). ⊠ *40 bd. Haussmann. Métro: Chaussée d'Antin; RER: Auber.*

❿ **Hôtel Drouot.** Hidden away in a grid of narrow streets not far from the Opéra is Paris's central auction house, where everything from stamps and toy soldiers to Renoirs and 18th-century commodes is sold. The 16 salesrooms make for fascinating browsing, and there's no obligation to bid. The mix of ladies in fur coats with money to burn, penniless art lovers desperate to unearth an unidentified masterpiece, and scruffy dealers trying to look anonymous makes up Drouot's unusually rich social fabric. Sales are held most weekdays, with viewings in the morning; anyone can attend. ⊠ *9 rue Drouot,* ☎ *01–48–00–20–00.* ⊙ *Viewings Mon.–Sat. 11–noon and 2–6, with auctions starting at 2. Closed mid-July–mid-Sept. Métro: Richelieu-Drouot.*

OFF THE
BEATEN PATH

NOTRE-DAME DE LORETTE – This little-known church was built from 1823 to 1836 in the Neoclassical style popular at the time. Of principal interest is the array of religious wall paintings; they are of varying quality but have been successfully restored. From the Hôtel Drouot turn right onto rue Rossini, then take the third right onto rue Laffitte; the church is at the far end. ⊠ *rue de Châteaudun. Métro: Notre-Dame-de-Lorette.*

❷ **Musée Cernuschi.** The collection includes Chinese art from Neolithic pottery (3rd century BC) to funeral statuary, painted 8th-century silks, and contemporary paintings, as well as ancient Persian bronze objects. ⊠ *7 av. Velasquez,* ☎ *01–45–63–50–75.* ⊠ *17 frs.* ⊙ *Tues.–Sun. 10–5:40. Métro: Monceau.*

☺ ⑫ **Musée Grévin.** Founded in 1882, this waxworks museum, around the corner from the Hôtel Drouot, ranks in scope and ingenuity with Madame Tussaud's in London. Dozens of wax renderings of historical and contemporary celebrities are on display. ⊠ *10 bd. Montmartre,* ☎ *01–42–46–13–26.* ⊠ *55 frs.* ⊙ *Daily 1–6:30; Christmas, Easter, July–Aug. 10–7. Métro: Grands Boulevards.*

❸ **Musée Nissim de Camondo.** The elegant decadence of the last days of the regal Ancien Régime (1770–90) is fully reflected in the lavish interior of this aristocratic Parisian mansion, built in the style of Louis XVI. ⊠ *63 rue de Monceau,* ☎ *01–53–59–06–40.* ⊠ *27 frs.* ⊙ *Wed.–Sun. 10–5. Métro: Monceau.*

⑭ **Notre-Dame de Bonne-Nouvelle.** This wide, soberly Neoclassical church is tucked away off the Grand Boulevards. The previous church (the second) on the spot was ransacked during the Revolution, and the current one, built 1823–29 after the restoration of the French monarchy, was ransacked by Communard hooligans in May 1871. The highlight is the semicircular apse behind the altar, featuring some fine 17th-century paintings beneath a three-dimensional, 19th-century grisaille composition by Abel de Pujol. A wide variety of pictures, statues, and works of religious art can be found in the side chapels. ⊠ *rue de la Lune. Métro: Bonne-Nouvelle.*

OFF THE
BEATEN PATH **ST-VINCENT DE PAUL** – Flanked by two foursquare towers, this early 19th-century church (built 1824–44) stands out amid the undistinguished streets surrounding the Gare du Nord. The facade is lent drama by the pedimented portico and the majestic flight of steps leading up from the square. Inside, Hippolyte Flandrin's glittering gold fresco, high up the nave walls, depicts an endless procession of religious worthies. From Notre-Dame de Bonne-Nouvelle, cross the boulevard and follow rue d'Hauteville to the end. ⊠ *Pl. Franz-Liszt. Métro: Poissonnière.*

⑧ Opéra Garnier. The original Paris Opera, begun in 1862 by Charles Garnier at the behest of Napoléon III, was not completed until 1875, five years after the emperor's abdication. It is said that it typifies Second Empire architecture, which is to say that it is a pompous hodgepodge of styles, imbued with as much subtlety as the crash of cymbals. After paying the entry fee, you can stroll around at leisure. The monumental foyer and staircase are impressive—a stage in their own right—where, on opening nights, celebrities preen and prance. If the lavishly upholstered auditorium seems small, it is only because the stage is the largest in the world—more than 11,000 square yards, with room for up to 450 performers. Marc Chagall painted the ceiling in 1964. The **Opera Museum,** containing a few paintings and theatrical mementos, is unremarkable. ⊠ *Pl. de l'Opéra,* ☎ *01–40–01–22–63.* 🎫 *30 frs.* ⊙ *Daily 10–5:30; closed occasionally for rehearsals; call 01–47–42–57–50 to check. Guided tours in English at 3 PM (60 frs). Métro: Opéra.*

NEED A
BREAK? Few cafés are as grand as the Belle Epoque **Café de la Paix** (⊠ 5 Pl. de l'Opéra, ☎ 01–40–07–30–10). Once described as "the center of the civilized world," it was a regular meeting place for the glitterati of 19th- and 20th-century Paris; the prices are as grand as the setting.

① Parc Monceau. The most picturesque gardens on the Right Bank were laid out as a private park in 1778 and retain some of the fanciful elements then in vogue, including mock ruins and a phony pyramid. In 1797 André Garnerin, the world's first-recorded parachutist, staged a landing in the park. The rotunda—known as the Chartres Pavilion—is surely the city's grandest public rest room; it started life as a tollhouse. ⊠ *Entrances on bd. de Courcelles, av. Velasquez, av. Ruysdaël, av. van Dyck. Métro: Monceau.*

OFF THE
BEATEN PATH **MUSÉE JEAN-JACQUES HENNER** – At this museum you can see the work of Jean-Jacques Henner (1829–1905), a nearly forgotten Alsatian artist whose obsessive fondness for milky-skinned, auburn-haired female nudes distinguishes his work. ⊠ *43 av. de Villiers,* ☎ *01–47–63–42–73.* 🎫 *21 frs.* ⊙ *Tues.–Sun. 10–noon and 2–5. Métro: Malesherbes.*

ST-ALEXANDRE NEVSKY – The gilt onion domes of this Russian Orthodox cathedral erected in neo-Byzantine style in 1860 provide an exotic addition to the city's roof line. Inside, the wall of icons that divides the church in two creates a mystical atmosphere. From Parc Monceau, turn left onto boulevard Courcelles, then take the third left onto rue Pierre-le-Grand. ⊠ *12 rue Daru. Métro: Courcelles.*

MUSÉE JACQUEMART-ANDRE – Art from the Italian Renaissance and 18th-century France compete for attention in this sumptuous late-19th-century mansion, which you can visit with an English audio-guide. Note the freshly restored Tiepolo frescoes in the staircase and on the dining-room ceiling. To get here from Parc Monceau, leave by the avenue Van Dyck exit, turn left down rue de Courcelles, and then take a left on boulevard Haussman. ⊠ *158 bd. Haussmann,* ☎ *01–42–89–04–91.* ⊡ *47 frs.* ☉ *Daily 10–6. Métro: St-Philippe-du-Roule.*

STE-ODILE – The colossal dark-brick tower of this modern church (built 1938–46) surges into the northern Paris skyline like a stumpy rocket, reminiscent of something out of Soviet Russia. The inside smacks more of Scandinavia, with its simple lines, splendid stained glass, and decorative restraint. Take the métro at Villiers to Porte de Champerret: The church is off Place Stuart-Merrill on avenue Stéphane-Mallarmé. ⊠ *av. Stéphane-Mallarmé. Métro: Porte de Champerret.*

ST-PHILIPPE-DU-ROULE – The best part about this dimly lit church, built by Chalgrin between 1769 and 1784, is the 19th-century fresco by Théodore Chassériau above the altar, featuring the *Descent from the Cross.* From Parc Monceau, leave by the avenue Van Dyck exit and turn left down rue de Courcelles, cross boulevard Haussmann, then take a right on avenue Myron-T-Herrick. ⊠ *Pl. Chassaigne-Goyon. Métro: St-Philippe-du-Roule.*

- ⑨ **Paristoric.** This 40-minute split-screen presentation of Paris and its history is pricey and sometimes hard to follow, but the spectacular photography and tasteful musical accompaniment, with St-Saëns's Organ Symphony employed to majestic effect, are enjoyable. Be sure to get headphones to hear the English translation. ⊠ *11 bis rue Scribe,* ☎ *01–42–66–62–06.* ⊡ *50 frs.* ☉ *Apr.–Oct., daily 9–8, Nov.–Mar., daily 9–6. Métro: Opéra.*

- ⑪ **Passage Jouffroy.** Built in 1846, as its giant clock will tell you, this shop-filled *passage* (gallery) was one of the first precursors to the modern-day shopping mall. ⊠ *Entrance on bd. Montmartre, rue de la Grange-Batelière. Métro: Richelieu-Drouot.*

- ⑯ **Porte St-Denis.** This 76-ft triumphal arch, which is slightly larger and older than the neighboring Porte St-Martin, was erected by François Blondel in 1672 to celebrate the victories of *Ludovico Magno* (as Louis XIV is here styled) on the Rhine. The bas reliefs by François Girardon include campaign scenes and military attributes stacked on shallow, slender pyramids. The arch, superbly cleaned in 1998, faces rue St-Denis—formerly the royal processional route into Paris from the north (last so used by Queen Victoria in 1855), but now better known for activity along the sidewalk. ⊠ *bd. St-Denis. Métro: Strasbourg–St-Denis.*

- ⑰ **Porte St-Martin.** This 56-ft triumphal arch, which is slightly smaller and younger than the neighboring Porte St-Denis, was designed by Blondel's pupil Pierre Bullet in 1674, and also cleaned in 1998. Louis XIV's victories at Limburg (in Flanders) and Besançon in Franche-Comté get bas-relief coverage from Martin Desjardins. ⊠ *bd. St-Denis. Métro: Strasbourg–St-Denis.*

- ☾ ⑮ **Rex.** If you're a movie buff, you may want to inspect Europe's self-styled "Grandest Cinema," built in 1932—although the 50-minute backscreen tour, full of special effects and loudspeaker commentary (available in English), gives only a tantalizing glimpse of the 2,700-seat auditorium, with its star-spangled roof and onstage fountains. You're surreptitiously filmed as you go around, with an individualized souvenir video (40 francs) available as you leave. If you still want more, see a movie here. ⊠ *1 bd. Poissonnière,* ☎ *08–36–68–05–96.* 🎫 *40 frs.* ⊙ *Wed.–Sun. 11–5. Métro: Bonne-Nouvelle.*

④ St-Augustin. This domed church was dexterously constructed in the 1860s within the confines of an awkward, V-shape site. It represented a breakthrough in ecclesiastical engineering, insofar as the use of metal pillars and girders obviated the need for exterior buttressing. The dome is bulky but well proportioned and contains some grimy but competent frescoes by the popular 19th-century French artist William Bouguereau. ⊠ *Pl. St-Augustin. Métro: St-Augustin.*

㉑ Ste-Elisabeth. This studied essay in Baroque (built 1628–46) is pleasantly unpretentious; there's no soaring bombast here. The church has brightly restored wall paintings and a wide, semicircular apse around the choir, where biblical scenes are carved into stupendous 17th-century wood paneling transferred from an abbey in Arras in northern France. ⊠ *rue du Temple. Métro: Temple.*

⑲ St-Nicolas des Champs. The rounded-arch, fluted Doric capitals in the chancel of this church date from 1560 to 1587, a full century later than the pointed-arch nave (1420–80). There is a majestic mid-17th-century organ and a fine *Assumption of the Virgin* (1629) by Simon Vouet above the high altar. The south door (1576) on rue au Maire is gloriously carved and surrounded by a small but unexpectedly well-tended lawn complete with rosebushes. ⊠ *rue St-Martin. Métro: Arts et Métiers.*

FROM RÉPUBLIQUE TO LA VILLETTE

Place de la République is the gateway to northeast Paris, a largely residential area that is often underestimated by tourists. The Canal St-Martin forms the focal point of this walk. Today its barges transport mainly tourists and pleasure boats, but it was once a busy thoroughfare linking the Seine to the city's central slaughterhouse at La Villette. The Mitterrand era saw La Villette landscaped beyond recognition, with science and music museums and a concert hall up amidst a wittily designed postmodern park. Nearby, 19th-century city planner Baron Haussmann let his hair down at the tumbling Buttes-Chaumont Park, going to town with a lake, a waterfall, a grotto, and phony cliffs.

Numbers in the text correspond to numbers in the margin and on the Place de la République to La Villette map.

A Good Walk

Begin your walk at **Place de la République** ①. Cross the square and take rue du Faubourg-du-Temple to the **Canal St-Martin** ②, whose locks and pale-green footbridges conjure up an unexpected flavor of Amsterdam. You arrive as the canal emerges from a 2½-km (1½-mi) tunnel that starts beyond the Bastille. Follow it left, then take the second right up avenue Richerand to the **Hôpital St-Louis** ③, Paris's oldest hospital, with its serene courtyard and chapel still intact. Leave the hospital on rue de la Grange-aux-Belles, and turn left, then right down rue Bichat, to find the Canal St-Martin bending beneath the unassuming white facade of the **Hôtel du Nord** ④, made famous by the film of the same name. The canal continues north to the circular **Rotonde de La Villette** ⑤. It surveys both the elevated métro line and the unruffled sheen of the Bassin de La Villette, where boats leave on a mile-long trip to the **Parc de La Villette** ⑥, with its postmodern science and music museums. If you prefer the 30-minute walk along the canal to the park, take the left bank of quai de la Seine, past the tiny, 18th-century Portuguese Jewish cemetery at No. 44. Cross over the canal on the Pont de Crimée, near the church of St-Jacques–St-Christophe, before continuing up quai de la Marne. Yet another option is to follow avenue Secrétan southeast from the Rotonde to the picturesque **Parc des Buttes-Chaumont** ⑦. Wend your way left around this tumbling park—once a quarry—and skirt the lake before climbing to the top of the man-made cliff for a panoramic view of the city.

Leave the park from the eastern corner. Turn left on rue Botzaris, and then right up rue de Crimée. Take the first left up a flight of stairs to the dowdy little street called villa Albert-Robida. You're now on the fringe of the **Quartier d'Amérique** ⑧, so called because the stone quarried in the Buttes-Chaumont is said to have been used to build the White House. All the two- and three-story houses around here—originally the quarriers' cottages—are a far cry from the seven-story buildings dominating the rest of Paris. Turn left down rue Arthur-Rozier and continue to rue de Mouzaïa. These days these small houses are very desirable: Some of the prettiest are found in the villas or mews, leading off of rue de Mouzaïa. Venture up quaint, cobbled villa Emile-Lobet on the right—the five grey skyscrapers looming at the far end are a chilling architectural contrast to the colorful paintwork and ivy-covered railings of the houses. Turn left and left again down flag-paved villa de Bellevue and cross to villa du Progrès. Take a left at the bottom of the street, and then a right down rue de la Fraternité to reach **Place du Rhin-et-Danube** ⑨.

More mewsy alleyways can be found on either side of rue Miguel-Hidalgo, with a cute view of the foresquare brick tower of the church of St-Francis d'Assisi at the far end of villa des Boërs. From here, take a right on rue Compans and head up to the **Cimetière de La Villette** ⑩. The entrance is flanked by a grim stone cube that once served as the local morgue. Admire the extrovert windows and roofline of the new school opposite, then take allée Darius-Milhaud along the side of the cemetery. This promenade curves through the heart of this district, which was totally rebuilt in the 1990s; cross rue Petit and continue to the flight of stairs leading up to the bulky silhouette of the Cité de la Musique, a modern concert hall. The entry to the Parc de La Villette is down to the left.

TIMING

The stretch along the Canal St-Martin from Place to la République to the Bassin de La Villette, via the Hôpital St-Louis, is approximately 2 km (1 mi). You may even want to allot a whole morning or afternoon to exploring the Parc des Buttes-Chaumont or the Parc de La Villette. Or you might want to return to one of these on another day.

Sights to See

② **Canal St-Martin.** The canal was built at the behest of Napoleon from 1802 to 1825, with the aim of providing the city with drinking water. It was not assigned to navigable traffic until the 1850s and was partly covered (between Bastille and République) by Haussmann in 1862. With its quiet banks, locks, and footbridges, the canal is much loved by novelists and film directors; Simenon's famous inspector Maigret solved many a mystery along its deceptively sleepy banks. Major development has transformed the northern end of the canal, around Place de Stalingrad and its 18th-century rotunda, and there are 10-franc boat trips (⊠ Embarkation at 13 quai de la Loire) along the once industrial Bassin de La Villette to the nearby Parc de La Villette. *Métro: Jacques-Bonsergent, Jaurès.*

⑩ **Cimetière de La Villette** (La Villette Cemetery). One of Paris's smallest cemeteries, it is reserved for residents of the 19th arrondissement. ⊠ *Entrance on rue d'Hautpoul. Métro: Ourcq.*

Place de la République to La Villette

0 — 400 yards
0 — 400 meters

Corentin Cariou
6

R. Riquet
R. d'Aubervilliers
R. de Flandre
R. de Crimée
Crimée
Canal de l'Ourcq

R. Riquet
R. de Flandre
Riquet
Bassin de La Villette

Av. Jean Jaurès
Porte de Pantin

19e

R. Watin
Ourcq
10

Av. Chapelle
Stalingrad
5
Laumière
Danube
9

R. du Chateau Landon
Av. Jean Jaurès
Jaurès
R. de Meaux
Bolivar
Mouzaia
8

R. du Faubourg St-Martin
La Fayette
Louis Blanc
Bd. de La Villette
Av. Simon Bolivar
Manin
R. de Crimée
Botzaris
R. de

10e
Canal St-Martin
Colonel Fabien
7
Buttes-Chaumont
Pl. des Fêtes

Gare de l'Est
R. de la Grange aux Belles
Bd. de La Villette
Av. Simon Bolivar
R. de Belleville

4
3
Jourdain

R. de Lancry
Boncourt
R. des Pyrénées
Pyrénées
N

2
du Temple
R. de Belleville
Bd. de Belleville

Jacques-Bonsergent
Belleville

Pl. de la République
R. du Faubourg
Av. Parmentier
R. St-Maur
Couronnes
R. de Ménilmontant
R. des Pyrénées

1
République
20e

Temple
Av. de la République
R. Oberkampf
Ménilmontant
Bd. de Ménilmontant
Gambetta
Pl. Gambetta

Bd. St-Martin
Bd. du Temple
Oberkampf
Parmentier
R. Oberkampf
St-Maur
Père Lachaise
Av. Gambetta
Cimetière du Père Lachaise

3e
Filles du Calvaire

❸ Hôpital St-Louis (St. Louis Hospital). Though it's not, technically speaking, a tourist sight, no one will begrudge you a discreet visit to Paris's first hospital, erected in 1607–10, at the same time as the Place des Vosges (☞ The Marais, *below*). The main courtyard, known as the Quadrilatère Historique, with its steep roofs and corner pavilions, has been remarkably preserved. The chapel, tucked away along rue de la Grange-des-Belles, needs some renovation, but shelters *Suffer Little Children to Come Unto Me,* a painting by Charles de La Fosse (1636–1716), and the handsome wood balcony carved with trumpeting angels and the monograms of hospital founders Henry IV and Maria de Médicis. ⊠ *Entrances on av. Richerand, rue de la Grange-aux-Belles, av. Claude-Vellefaux.* ☉ *Daily 5AM–9PM; chapel open weekday afternoons.*

❹ Hôtel du Nord (North Hotel). Despite its unassuming white facade, this hotel is famous in France for its starring role in director Marcel Carné's 1938 movie of the same name. Plans to demolish it provoked a public outcry and it was restored to former glory (as a café-restaurant) in 1995. ⊠ *102 quai de Jemmappes,* ☎ *01–40–40–78–78. Métro: Jacques-Bonsergent.*

☺ ❼ Parc des Buttes-Chaumont. This picturesque, steep-sloped park in northeast Paris has a lake, waterfall, and cliff-top folly. Until town planner Baron Haussmann got his hands on it in the 1860s, the area was a garbage dump and quarry—legend has it that the local gypsum was used in the foundation of the White House. ⊠ *rue Botzaris. Métro: Buttes-Chaumont, Botzaris.*

☺ ❻ Parc de La Villette. Until the 1970s this 130-acre site, in an unfashionable corner of northeast Paris commonly known as "La Villette," was home to a cattle market and slaughterhouse (*abattoir*). Only the slaughterhouse, known as **La Grande Halle** (Great Hall), remains: a magnificent iron-and-glass structure ingeniously transformed into an exhibition-cum-concert center. But everything else here—from the science museum and spherical cinema to the music academy, each interconnected by designer gardens with canopied walkways and red cubical follies—is futuristic.

Although La Villette breathes the architectural panache of the Mitterrand era, the late president only oversaw one project himself: the **Cité de la Musique** (☞ Chapter 4), a giant postmodern music academy with a state-of-the-art concert hall. Designed by architect Christian de Portzamparc, it was only completed in 1997 with the opening of the spectacular **Musée de la Musique** (Music Museum). The museum contains a mind-tingling array of 900 instruments; their story is told with wireless headphones (ask for English commentary).

The **park** itself, laid out in the 1980s to the design of Bernard Tschumi, links the academy to the science museum half a mile away. Water and the Grande Halle are the park's focal elements. Two new bridges cross the Canal de l'Ourcq, which bisects the park; one becomes a covered walkway, running parallel to the Canal St-Denis, and continues up to the science museum—itself surrounded by the unruffled sheen of a broad moat, reflecting the spherical outline of **La Géode** (☞ Chapter 4). This looks like a huge silver golf ball but is actually a cinema made of polished steel, with an enormous, 180-degree curved screen.

The pompously styled **Cité des Sciences et de l'Industrie** (Industry and Science Museum) tries to do for science and industry what the Pompidou Center does for modern art. Adrien Fainsilber's rectangular building, also conceived in the 1970s, even looks like the Pompidou Center, minus the gaudy piping. Inside, displays are bright and thought-provoking, though most are in French only. The brave attempt to render technology fun and easy involves 60 do-it-yourself contraptions that make you feel more participant than onlooker. Lines (especially during school holidays) can be intimidating. ⊠ *Science Museum: 30 av. Corentin-Cariou; Music Museum: 221 av. Jean-Jaurès,* ☎ *Science Museum: 01–40–05–80–00; Music Museum: 01–44–84–44–84.* ▨ *Science: 50 frs (planetarium 25 frs); Music: 35 frs.* ◷ *Science: Tues.– Sun. 10–6; Music: Tues.–Thurs. noon–6, Fri. and Sat. noon–7:30, Sun. 10–6. Métro: Porte de La Villette; Porte de Pantin.*

❶ **Place de la République.** This large, oblong square, laid out by Hauss-mann in 1856–65, is dominated by a matronly, Stalin-size statue symbolizing *The Republic* (1883). The square is often used as a rallying point for demonstrations. République has more métro lines than any other station in Paris. *Métro: République.*

❾ **Place du Rhin-et-Danube.** Although seven streets intersect at this square in the Quartier d'Amérique, it retains a rural, unhurried feel. The small white statue of a young girl clutching a sheaf of wheat recalls the area's pastoral origins, before it was absorbed into Paris in the 19th century. The métro station underneath was built in a former quarry. *Métro: Danube.*

❽ **Quartier d'Amérique** (America Quarter). This neighborhood is so named because the gypsum that was once quarried here (mostly on the site that was transformed into the Parc des Buttes-Chaumont in the 1860s) was shipped to America and used, so the story goes, in building the White House. The quartier is made up of a grid of streets and narrow mews (known as "villas") lined with modest, two- and three-story houses and once inhabited by quarriers, but now some of the most sought-after homes in the city. *Métro: Botzaris.*

❺ **Rotonde de La Villette.** This strange, circular building was one of the tollhouses built around the edge of Paris by Nicolas Ledoux in the 1780s. Symbols, to the populace, of taxes and oppression, most of these austere, daunting buildings were promptly dismantled during the Revolution. Luckily, the Rotunda survived to remind us of Ledoux's thrilling architecture. Like Mitterrand, Ledoux was fascinated by masonic symbols such as spheres and pyramids. Although the Rotunda is partly obscured by the aboveground métro as you approach from the south, its clean-cut outlines and honey-color stonework can be admired from the north, where a newly paved courtyard overlooks the Bassin de la Villette and the barges lining up at the lock to reach the Canal St-Martin. ⊠ *Pl. de Stalingrad. Métro: Stalingrad.*

FROM BASTILLE TO NATION

At the center of the Bastille neighborhood is Place de la Bastille, site of the infamous prison stormed on July 14, 1789—an event that came to symbolize the beginning of the French Revolution. Largely in commemoration of the bicentennial of the Revolution, the Bastille area was renovated and soon became one of the liveliest areas in Paris. Galleries, shops, theaters, cafés, restaurants, and bars now fill formerly decrepit buildings and alleys. Southeast of the Bastille are the imposing Place de la Nation and the up-and-coming Bercy neighborhood, as well as the verdant Bois de Vincennes (☞ *below*).

Numbers in the text correspond to numbers in the margin and on the From Bastille to Nation map.

A Good Walk

Start your walk at **Place de la Bastille** ①, which is easily accessible by métro. Today the square is dominated by the Colonne de Juillet and the curving glass facade of the modern **Opéra de la Bastille** ②. Leading away from the square are rue de la Roquette, a street alive with shops and cafés, and rue de Lappe, a vibrant nocturnal street lined with bars, clubs, and restaurants. Both streets are worth exploring—and are especially hopping at night. Turn right at the end of rue de Lappe onto rue de Charonne to reach rue du Faubourg-St-Antoine, famous for its cabinetmakers. You'll see why if you take the unevenly cobbled passage du Chantier, just opposite. Its boutiques sell furniture and nothing else. (Peek into other *passages* as well for more glimpses of the behind-the-scenes life of the Bastille.)

Continue along rue Faubourg-St-Antoine, and then take a right down avenue Ledru-Rollin, crossing rue Charenton and passing the modern church of St-Antoine, to reach avenue Daumesnil. The disused railroad viaduct has been tastefully transformed into a series of designer boutiques with a walkway on top—restyled the **Viaduc des Arts** ③.

Saunter down as far as rue Hector-Malot, then turn right across avenue Daumesnil to the Gare de Lyon métro station. If you'd like to visit the large, new national library, the **Bibliothèque François-Mitterrand** ④, take line 14 from Gare de Lyon for three stops to the Bibliotheque station. Or get off one stop earlier at Cour St-Emilion and explore the revamped **Bercy** ⑤ neighborhood, with its restored wine warehouses and innovative park. The four L-shaped towers of the national library loom across the Seine as you head west toward the grass-covered walls of the Palais Ominsports stadium. Follow rue de Bercy, under the elephantine Ministère des Finances, and then turn right through the tunnel, up to rue de Rambouillet. Here rejoin avenue de Daumesnil and the Viaduc des Arts. Head up the steps to see what's on top of the viaduct: Gone are the tracks, ousted by the Promenade Plantée, a walkway lined with trees and flowers. The walkway continues for another 2½ km (1½ mi). But you might just want to stay on it for about 1 km (½ mi) before turning left on rue de Picpus. Some 350 yards up on the right is the entry to the **Cimetière de Picpus** ⑥, where General Lafayette is buried.

Continue on rue de Picpus for about 250 yards, and then cross rue Fabre-d'Eglantine to reach majestic **Place de la Nation** ⑦, flanked away to the right by two towering columns that once marked the eastern entry to Paris. From here it's a short métro ride to the city's most famous cemetery, the **Cimetière du Père-Lachaise** ⑧, or to the **Bois de Vincennes** ⑨, a large park with lakes, castle, and a zoo.

TIMING

The walk from Place de la Bastille to Place de la Nation, including an excursion to the Bercy neighbhorhood, is about 7 km (4½ mi) long and takes about 3½ hours to complete. Count on more time if you also visit the new national library.

Sights to See

⑤ **Bercy.** Bercy is a testament to the French genius for urban renewal. Tucked away on the Right Bank of the Seine, south of the Gare de Lyon in the 12e arrondissement, this colorful district was for decades filled with warehouses storing wine from the provinces. Now sport and finance set the tone. The first thing you'll see as you emerge from Bercy métro station is the mighty glass wall of the **Ministère des Finances** (Finance Ministry), which moved—grudgingly—to these new quayside offices from the Louvre. To the left is the ingeniously sloping, grass-walled **Palais Omnisports**, a weird-looking stadium that hosts sports and

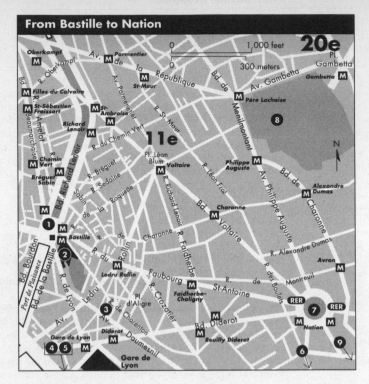

From Bastille to Nation

music events and seats 17,000, approached on all sides by gleaming white steps. Across the Seine, dominating the city's southeast skyline, are the four glass towers of architect Dominique Perrault's new national library, the Bibliothèque François-Mitterrand (☞ *below*). A hundred yards from the Palais Omnisports is a quirky, cubistic building designed by Frank Gehry, who described it as "a dancing figure in the park." It opened as an American Center in 1994 but closed in 1996 due to lack of funds, and is set to reopen sometime in 2000 as a French movie museum, the **Maison du Cinéma.** The **jardin** (garden) opposite is a witty, state-of-the-art designer park with trim lawns, vines, rose-strewn arbors, and cobbled alleys lined by centurion trees providing a ghostly map of the former wineries. At the **Maison du Jardin** (Garden Center; ✉ rue de Bercy) you can get gardening advice and see displays of seasonal vegetables. Curved walkways fly over rue de Dijon to land by a Chinese lily pond near the Cours St-Emilion, where two rows of wine warehouses have been preserved and renovated. *Métro: Bercy, Cours St-Emilion.*

④ Bibliothèque François-Mitterrand (François-Mitterrand Library). As the last of former president Mitterrand's *grands travaux* (grand building projects) before he left office, the *Très Grande Bibliothèque* (Very Big Library, as some facetiously call it) opened in early 1997. The new library subsumes the majority of the collections in the old Bibliothèque Nationale and, with some 11 million volumes between its walls, surpasses the Library of Congress as the largest library in the world. Architect Dominique Perrault's controversial design features four soaring 24-story towers that house most of the books; library goers are relegated to underground reading rooms. A stunning interior courtyard—sunk beneath ground level and invisible as you approach, despite its thicket of full-size evergreens—provides breathing space. You can visit part of the library for free, or pay to inspect one of the temporary exhibits or for the right to consult more than 300,000 books (millions more are available to qualified researchers). ✉ *11 quai François-Mauriac,* ☎ *01–53–79–59–59.* 🎫 *20 frs library, 35 frs exhibitions.* ⊙ *Tues.–Sat. 10–7, Sun. noon–6. Closed public holidays and first half Sept. Métro: Bibliothèque.*

👆 ⑨ **Bois de Vincennes** (Vincennes Woods). Sandwiched between the unexciting suburb of Charenton and the working-class district of Fontenay-sous-Bois, to the southeast of Paris, the Bois de Vincennes is often considered a poor man's Bois de Boulogne. But the comparison is unfair: The Bois de Vincennes is no more difficult to get to (métro to Porte Dorée; Bus 46) and has equally illustrious origins. It, too, was landscaped under Napoléon III, although a park had already been created here by Louis XV in 1731. The park has several lakes, notably **Lac Daumesnil,** with two islands, and **Lac des Minimes,** with three; rowboats can be hired at both. In addition, the park is home to a zoo, a tribal art museum, the **Hippodrome de Vincennes** (a cinder-track racecourse), a castle, a flower garden, and several cafés. In the spring there's an amusement park, the **Foire du Trône.** Bikes can be rented from the Château de Vincennes métro station for 25 frs an hour or 100 frs a day.

Some 600 mammals and 200 species of birds can be seen at the Bois de Vincenne's **Zoo de Vincennes,** the largest zoo in France. One of the most striking features is an artificial rock 236 ft high, inhabited by wild mountain sheep and penguins. The rock, built in 1934 of reinforced concrete, reopened in 1996 after a large-scale restoration program that added a new elevator to the top. ✉ *53 av. de St-Maurice,* ☎ *01–44–75–20–10.* 🎫 *40 frs.* ⊙ *Apr.–Oct., daily 9–6; Nov.–Mar., daily 9–5. Métro: Porte Dorée.*

The **Musée des Arts d'Afrique et d'Océanie** (Museum of the Arts of Africa and Oceania) is at the Porte Dorée entrance to the Bois de Vincennes. It's housed in an Art-Deco building whose awesome facade is covered with a sculpted frieze depicting sites and attractions of France's erstwhile overseas empire. Inside, headdresses, bronzes, jewelry, masks, statues, and pottery from former French colonies are spaciously displayed under subtle spotlighting. Look out for the ominous Hakenkreuz set in the patterned mosaic floor of the huge reception hall; the sinister overtones it was soon to acquire, as the Nazi swastika emblem, were unsuspected when the building opened for the Colonial Exhibition in 1931. There is also a tropical aquarium (open from 10 AM weekends) in the basement, with rows of tanks filled with colorful tropical fish. ✉ *293 av. Daumesnil,* ☎ *01–44–74–85–01.* 🎫 *30 frs.* ⊙ *Mon. and Wed.–Fri. 10–noon and 1:30–5:30, weekends 12:30–6. Métro: Porte Dorée.*

The historic **Château de Vincennes** is on the northern edge of the Bois de Vincennes. Built in the 15th century by various French kings, the castle is France's medieval Versailles, an imposing, high-walled castle surrounded by a dry moat and dominated by a 170-ft keep. The sprawling castle grounds also contain a replica of Ste-Chapelle (built 1379–1552) on the Ile de la Cité and two elegant, classical wings designed by Louis Le Vau in the mid-17th century, now used for naval-military administration and closed to the public. ✉ *av. de Paris,* ☎ *01–48–08–31–20.* 🎫 *32 frs.* ⊙ *Daily 10–6; winter, daily 10–5; guided tours of chapel every 45 min. Métro: Château de Vincennes.*

The **Parc Floral de Paris** (Paris Floral Park) is the Bois de Vincennes's 70-acre flower garden. It includes a lake and water garden and is renowned for its seasonal displays of blooms. It also contains a miniature train, a game area, and an "exotarium" with tropical fish and reptiles. ⊠ *Rte. de la Pyramide.* 🎫 *5 frs.* ⊙ *Daily 9:30–8 (summer), daily 9:30–5 (winter). Métro: Château de Vincennes.*

❽ Cimetière du Père-Lachaise (Father Lachaise Cemetery). The largest, most interesting, and most prestigious of Paris's cemeteries dates from the start of the 19th century. On the eastern fringe of Paris, it is a veritable necropolis whose tombs compete in grandiosity, originality, and often, alas, dilapidation. Cobbled avenues, steep slopes, and lush vegetation create a powerful atmosphere. Named after the Jesuit father—Louis XIV's confessor—who led the reconstruction of the Jesuit Rest House completed here in 1682, the cemetery houses the tombs of the French author Colette; the composer Chopin; the playwright Molière; the writers Honoré Balzac, Marcel Proust, Paul Eluard, Oscar Wilde, and Gertrude Stein and Alice B. Toklas (buried in the same grave); the popular French actress Simone Signoret and her husband, singer-actor Yves Montand; and Edith Piaf. Perhaps the most popular shrine is to rock star Jim Morrison, where dozens of faithful fans, following the trail of spray-painted graffiti, come to pay homage to the songwriter. (Now, along with the fans, there's a guard who makes sure you don't stay too long.) Of less dubious taste is the sculpted tomb of Romantic artist Théodore Géricault, shown brush in hand above a bronze relief plaque replicating his *Raft of the Medusa*. The cemetery was the site of the Paris Commune's final battle, on May 28, 1871, when the rebel troops were rounded up, lined against the Mur des Fédérés (Federalists' Wall) in the southeast corner, and shot. Get hold of a map at the entrance—Père Lachaise is an easy place to get lost in. ⊠ *Entrances on rue des Rondeaux, bd. de Ménilmontant, and rue de la Réunion.* ⊙ *Daily 8–6; Oct.–Easter, daily 8–dusk. Métro: Gambetta, Philippe-Auguste, Père Lachaise.*

❻ Cimetière de Picpus. Most of those 1,300 executed at the guillotine on Place de la Nation in 1794 were buried in a mass grave at the nearby Picpus Cemetery. Also buried here is General Lafayette, whose gravesite can be identified by its U.S. flag. ⊠ *Entrance at 35 rue Picpus (once inside, ring bell of caretaker's home for access to cemetery),* ☎ *01–43–44–18–54.* 🎫 *15 frs.* ⊙ *Oct.–Easter, Tues.–Sat. 2–4; Easter–Sept., Tues.–Sat. 2–6. Guided visits, Tues.–Sun. at 2:30 and 4. Métro or RER: Nation.*

❷ Opéra de la Bastille (Bastille Opera). Designed by Argentine-born architect Carlos Ott, the state-of-the-art Bastille Opera, on the south side of Place de la Bastille, opened July 14, 1989, in commemoration of the bicentennial of the French Revolution. The steep-climbing auditorium seats more than 3,000 and has earned more plaudits than the curving glass facade, which strikes Parisians as depressingly like that of yet another modern office building. For information about tickets to peformances, *see* Chapter 4. ⊠ *Pl. de la Bastille,* ☎ *01–44–73–13–00.* 🎫 *Guided tours 50 frs. Métro: Bastille.*

❶ Place de la Bastille. Nothing remains of the infamous Bastille prison destroyed at the beginning of the French Revolution. Until 1988, there ★ was little more to see here than a huge traffic circle and the **Colonne de Juillet** (July Column). As part of the countrywide celebrations for July 1989, the bicentennial of the French Revolution, the Opéra de la Bastille was erected, inspiring substantial redevelopment on the surrounding streets, especially along rue de Lappe—once a haunt of Edith Piaf—and rue de la Roquette. What was formerly a humdrum neighborhood rapidly became one of the most sparkling and attractive in the city. Streamlined art galleries, funky jazz clubs, and Spanish-style tapas bars set the tone.

The Bastille, or, more properly, the Bastille St-Antoine, was a massive building, protected by eight immense towers and a wide moat (its ground plan is marked by paving stones set into the modern square). It was built by Charles V in the late 14th century. He intended it not as a prison but as a fortress to guard the eastern entrance to the city. By the reign of Louis XIII (1610–43), however, the Bastille was used almost exclusively to house political prisoners. Voltaire, the Marquis de Sade, and the mysterious Man in the Iron Mask were all incarcerated here, along with many other unfortunates. It was this obviously political role—specifically, the fact that the prisoners were nearly always held by order of the king—that led the "furious mob" (in all probability no more than a largely unarmed rabble) to break into the prison on July 14, 1789, kill the governor, steal what firearms they could find, and free the seven remaining prisoners.

Later in 1789, the prison was knocked down. A number of the original stones were carved into facsimiles of the Bastille and sent to each of the provinces as a memento of royal oppression. The key to the prison was given by Lafayette to George Washington, and it has remained at Mount Vernon ever since. The power of legend being what it is, what soon became known as the Storming of the Bastille was elevated to the status of a pivotal event in the course of the French Revolution, demonstrating the newfound power of a long-suffering population. Thus it was that July 14 became the French national day, an event now celebrated with patriotic fervor throughout the country.

The July Column actually commemorates a more substantial political event: the July uprising of 1830 when the repressive Charles X, the Bourbon king about whom it was said that "the Bourbons learnt nothing, and forgot nothing," was overthrown. It's sometimes hard to imagine the turmoil that was a feature of French political life from the Revolution of 1789 through the 19th century (and, arguably, well into the 20th). After the fall of Napoléon in 1815, the restoration of a bone-headed monarchy, personified first by Louis XVIII, then by Charles X, virtually guaranteed that further trouble was in store. Matters came to a head in July 1830 with the St-Cloud Decrees, restricting the franchise—the right to vote—to a handful of landowners. Charles was duly toppled in three days of fighting at the end of the month—the Three Glorious Days—and a new, constitutionally elected monarch, Louis-Philippe, took the throne.

Louis-Philippe's reign was hardly more distinguished, despite attempts to curry favor among the populace. Nor was it noticeably more liberal. Louis-Philippe did, nonetheless, have the July Column built as a memorial, stipulating that 500 of those killed in the fighting of 1830 were to be buried under it. When, in 1848, Louis-Philippe himself was ousted, the names of a handful of the Parisians killed in the fighting of 1848 were then added to those already on the column. Meanwhile Louis-Philippe and his wife, disguised as Mr. and Mrs. William Smith, fled to Britain and threw themselves at the mercy of Queen Victoria. Mr. Smith died in England two years later. *Métro: Bastille.*

7 Place de la Nation. The towering, early 19th-century, statue-topped columns on majestic Place de la Nation stand sentinel at the Gates of Paris—the eastern sector's equivalent of the Arc de Triomphe, with the bustling but unpretentious Cours de Vincennes providing a down-to-earth echo of the Champs-Élysées. Place de la Nation (known as Place du Trône—Throne Square—until the Revolution) was the scene of 1,300 executions at the guillotine in 1794. Most were buried in a mass grave at the nearby Cimetière de Picpus (☞ *above*). *Métro or RER: Nation.*

VANISHED REVOLUTION

PARISIANS HAD A rebellious reputation long before the French Revolution. Such was Louis XIV's disdain for the Paris mob that he moved his court out to **Versailles,** which remained the capital of France until 1789.

But the writing was on Louis's garden wall. On June 20, 1789, the Third Estate met in Versailles and swore to end absolute monarchy at the **Jeu de Paume** (which still stands). Then, three months later, a horde of half-starved citizens stomped 10 mi from Paris to force the royal family to return to the city.

That was after the storming of the Bastille. Nothing remains of the fortress-cum-prison whose name is synonymous with the outbreak of the Revolution—the huge pillar in the middle of today's **Place de la Bastille** hails the rebels who ousted Charles X in 1830.

Louis XVI and Marie-Antoinette were ensconced in the **Tuileries Palace,** which blocked off the west wing of the Louvre (facing the Tuileries Gardens) until revolutionaries burnt it down during the Paris Commune of 1871. It was from the Tuileries that the royal family made their ill-fated flight on June 20, 1791. But they were hauled back and jailed in the **Prison du Temple,** on the site of the Carreau de Temple on rue Perrée, just south of what is now Place de la République. The prison was razed in 1808 to put an end to royalist pilgrimages.

Louis XVI went to the scaffold in the northwest corner of **Place de la Concorde,** near today's Hôtel Crillon, on January 21, 1793. The guillotine was later moved to the Tuileries gates, and another 1342 peo-ple subjected to it over the next two years. Marie-Antoinette, who spent the last two months of her life in **La Conciergerie** on Ile de la Cité, was slain on October 16, 1793. Danton (April 5, 1794) and Robespierre (July 28, 1794) followed her; their cells can still be seen.

Meanwhile, on July 13, 1793, revolutionary firebrand Jean-Paul Marat was stabbed to death in his bath by Charlotte Corday at his home on **rue des Cordeliers.** Marat's journal L'Ami du Peuple, a vociferous advocate of the death penalty, was printed in the nearby **cour de Commerce St-André** (at No. 8)—just opposite the house (No. 9) where Dr. Joseph Guillotin is said to have dreamt up his penal machine.

PERHAPS THE MOST poignant epitaph to all the bloodshed is the little mausoleum erected in **Square Louis-XVI,** the garden just off boulevard Haussmann, where the bones of Louis XVI and Marie-Antoinette sojourned for 20 years before joining those of their ancestors at St-Denis.

By then, the Revolution had joined them in the trashcan of history, its republican ideals buried when Napoleon crowned himself Emperor of the French on December 2, 1804, in the erstwhile Temple of Reason—henceforth known once more as **Notre-Dame Cathedral.**

A giant painting of that ceremony by artist Louis David, who orchestrated the revolutionary pageants on the **Champ de Mars,** can be seen in the **Louvre,** along with his famous icon to bathtub victim Marat. Period mementos can be admired in the **Musée Carnavalet** in the Marais.

③ **Viaduc des Arts** (Arts Viaduct). With typical panache, Paris planners have converted this redbrick viaduct—originally, the last mile of the suburban railroad that led to Place de la Bastille (the site of the Bastille Opéra was once a station)—into a stylish promenade. Upscale art, crafts, and furniture shops occupy the archways below, and a walkway, with shrubs, flowers, and benches, has replaced the tracks up above (☞ Chapter 6). ⊠ *av. Daumesnil. Métro: Gare de Lyon.*

THE MARAIS

The Marais is one of Paris's oldest, most historic, and most sought-after residential districts. Renovation is the keynote; well into the '70s this was one of the poorest areas, filled with dilapidated tenements and squalid courtyards. The area's regeneration was sparked by the building of the Pompidou Center (known to Parisians as Beaubourg)—until Frank Gehry's Guggenheim Museum opened in Bilbao, Spain, in 1997, it was unquestionably Europe's most architecturally whimsical museum. The gracious architecture of the 17th and early 18th centuries, however, sets the tone for the rest of the Marais. Today, most of the Marais's spectacular *hôtels particuliers*—loosely, "mansions," onetime residences of aristocratic families—have been restored and many are now museums. There are trendy boutiques and cafés among the kosher shops of the traditionally Jewish neighborhood around rue des Rosiers.

The history of the Marais—the word, incidentally, means marsh or swamp—goes back to when Charles V, king of France in the 14th century, moved his court here from the Ile de la Cité. However, it wasn't until Henri IV laid out Place Royale, today the Place des Vosges, in the early 17th century, that the Marais became *the* place to live. Aristocratic dwellings began to dot the neighborhood, and their salons filled with the beau monde. But following the French Revolution, the Marais rapidly became one of the most deprived, dissolute areas in Paris.

Thus it was spared the attentions of Baron Haussmann, the man who rebuilt so much of Paris in the mid-19th century—so, though crumbling, the Marais's ancient golden-hued buildings and squares remained intact. You won't be able to get into many of the historic homes that spangle the neighborhood—the private hôtels particuliers—but this shouldn't stop you from admiring their handsome facades or trying to push through the heavy formal doors (*portes cochères*) to glimpse the discreet courtyards that lurk behind them.

Jewish heritage is also an important part of the Marais's history. Jewish immigrants began settling in this area in the 13th century, though the main wave of immigrants (from Russia and Central Europe) came in the 19th century. Another wave—of Sephardic Jews from North Africa—arrived here in the 1960s following Algerian independence. Today there are still many kosher shops and restaurants among the trendy, newer arrivals.

Numbers in the text correspond to numbers in the margin and on the Marais map.

A Good Walk

Begin this walk in front of the **Hôtel de Ville** ①. You can't inspect the lavish interior, but head left to the traffic-free square, with its fountains and forest of street lamps, to admire the exuberant facade. Turn left along quai de l'Hôtel de Ville; *bouquinistes* (booksellers) line the Seine, and you may catch a glimpse of the towers of Notre-Dame through the trees. Take the next left up picturesque rue des Barres to the church of **St-Gervais–St-Protais** ②, one of the last Gothic constructions in the country

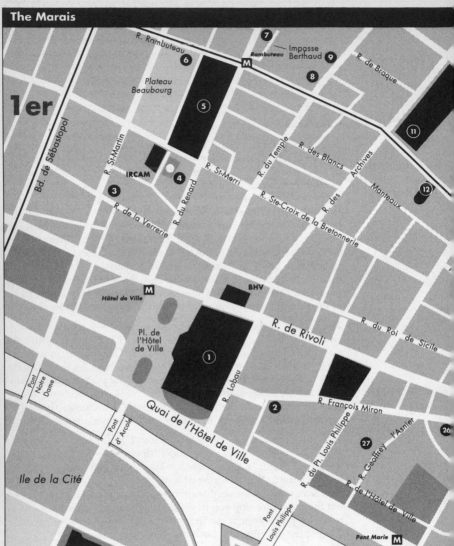

Académie de la
Magie, **23**

Archives
Nationales, **11**

Atelier Brancusi, **6**

Centre Pompidou, **5**

Hôtel de Beauvais, **26**

Hôtel de Montmor, **9**

Hôtel de Sens, **24**

Hôtel de Sully, **21**

Hôtel de Ville, **1**

Maison Européenne
de la
Photographie, **25** .

Maison de Victor
Hugo, **19**

Mémorial du Martyr
Inconnu, **27**

Musée d'Art Juif, **8**

Musée Bricard, **13**

Musée Carnavalet, **17**

Musée de la Chasse et
de la Nature, **10**

Musée Cognacq-
Jay, **16**

Musée Picasso, **14**

Musée de la Poupée, **7**

Notre-Dame des
Blancs-Manteaux, **12**

Place des Vosges, **18**

St-Denis-du-St-
Sacrement, **15**

St-Gervais–
St-Protais, **2**

St-Merri, **3**

St-Paul–St-Louis, **22**

Ste-Marie, **20**

Square Igor-
Stravinsky, **4**

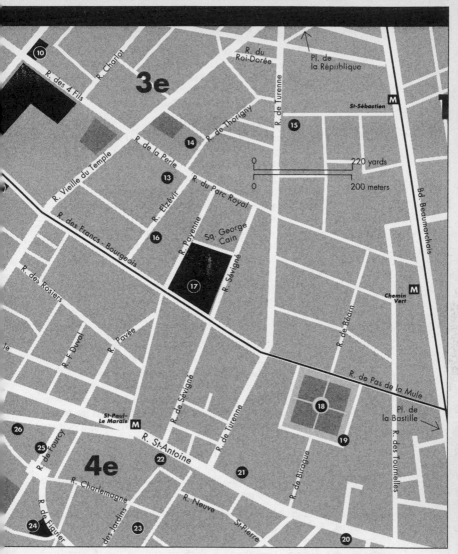

R. du
Roi-Dorée

Pl. de
la République

R. Charlot

R. des 4 Fils

3e

R. de Thorigny

R. de Turenne

St-Sébastien

M

10

15

14

R. de la Perle

R. Vieille du Temple

13

R. du Parc Royal

220 yards

200 meters

Bd. Beaumarchais

R. Elzévir

R. des Francs - Bourgeois

16

R. Payenne

Sq. George
Cain

R. des Rosiers

17

R. Sévigné

Chemin
Vert

M

R. de Béarn

R. F. Duval

R. Pavée

R. de Pas de la Mule

Pl. de
la Bastille

St-Paul-
Le Marais

M

26

R. de Sévigné

18

R. de Turenne

19

R. des Tournelles

25

R. de Fourcy

R. St-Antoine

4e

22

R. de Birague

21

R. Charlemagne

R. Neuve

24

R. de Figuier

des Jardins

23

St-Pierre

20

and a newly cleaned riot of Flamboyant decoration. From the church, head up to rue de Rivoli and take a left to get to rue du Temple. On your way, you'll pass one of the city's most popular department stores, the Bazar de l'Hôtel de Ville, or BHV, as it's known (☞ Chapter 6). Take rue de la Verrerie, the first street on your left, and pause as you cross rue du Renard to take in an impressive clash of architectural styles: to your left, the medieval silhouette of Notre-Dame; to the right, the gaudy colored pipes of the Centre Pompidou.

Cross rue du Renard and take the second right to the ornate 16th-century church of **St-Merri** ③. Rue St-Martin, full of stores, restaurants, and galleries, leads past the designer Café Beaubourg. Turn right to reach **Square Igor-Stravinsky** ④ with its unusual fountain; on one side of the square is IRCAM, where you can hear performances of contemporary classical music (☞ Chapter 4). Up ahead looms the newly renovated **Centre Pompidou** ⑤, overlooking a sloping piazza that is often aswarm with musicians, mimes, dancers, and fire-eaters. On the far side you can visit the **Atelier Brancusi** ⑥ before crossing rue Rambuteau to the Quartier de l'Horloge; take pedestrian rue de Brantôme and turn left into rue Bernard-de-Clairvaux to admire Le Défenseur du Temps, a modern mechanical clock that whirs into action on the hour as St. George defends Time against a dragon, an eagle, or a crab (symbols of fire, air, and water). At noon, 6 PM, and 10 PM he takes on all three at once.

Return to rue Rambuteau, turn left, and cross rue Beaubourg. If you're with children, duck into impasse Berthaud to visit the **Musée de la Poupée** ⑦. Otherwise, stay on rue Rambuteau and turn left onto rue du Temple, where the **Musée d'Art et d'Histoire du Judaïsme** ⑧ is in the stately Hôtel de St-Aignan at No. 71. The **Hôtel de Montmor** ⑨ at No. 79 is another splendid 17th-century mansion. Take a right onto rue des Haudriettes; just off to the left at the next corner is the **Musée de la Chasse et de la Nature** ⑩, the Museum of Hunting and Nature, housed in one of the Marais's most stately mansions. Head right on rue des Archives, crossing rue des Haudriettes, and admire the medieval gateway with two fairy-tale towers, now part of the **Archives Nationales** ⑪, the archives museum entered from rue des Francs-Bourgeois (Street of the Free Citizens) around to the left.

Continue past the Crédit Municipal (the city's grandiose pawnbroking concern), the Dôme du Marais restaurant (housed in a circular 18th-century chamber originally used for auctions), and the church of **Notre-Dame des Blancs-Manteaux** ⑫, with its superb inlaid pulpit. A corner-turret signals rue Vieille-du-Temple: Turn left past the palatial Hôtel de Rohan (now part of the Archives Nationales), then right onto rue de la Perle to the **Musée Bricard** ⑬, occupying a mansion as impressive as the assembly of locks and keys within. From here it is a step down rue de Thorigny (opposite) to the palatial 17th-century Hôtel Salé, now the **Musée Picasso** ⑭. Church-lovers may wish to detour up rue de Thorigny and along rue du Roi-Doré to admire the severe neoclassical portico of **St-Denis-du-St-Sacrement** ⑮ and the *Deposition* by Delacroix inside.

Backtrack along rue de Thorigny and turn left onto rue du Parc-Royal. Halfway down rue Elzévir is the **Musée Cognacq-Jay** ⑯, a must if you are interested in 18th-century furniture, porcelain, and paintings. If you can't face another museum, take the next right, rue Payenne, instead, and tarry in the sunken garden at square Georges-Cain, opposite the 16th-century Hôtel de Marle, now used as a Swedish culture center. Next door you can enjoy a rear view of the steep-roofed Cognacq-Jay building. Rue Payenne becomes rue Pavée as you pass beneath a lookout turret. Peek into the next courtyard on the left at the cheerfully askew facade of the Bibliothèque Historique de la Ville de Paris. Continuing on rue Pavée takes you to rue des Rosiers, with its excellent Jewish bakeries and falafel shops. Back on rue des Francs-Bourgeois is the **Musée Carnavalet** ⑰, the Paris History Museum, in perhaps the swankiest edifice in the Marais. A short walk along rue des Francs-Bourgeois takes you to large, pink-brick **Place des Vosges** ⑱, lined with covered arcades. At No. 6, you can visit the **Maison de Victor Hugo** ⑲, where the workaholic French author once lived.

Exit the square to rue St-Antoine: To the left is the church of **Ste-Marie** ⑳; to the right is the **Hôtel de Sully** ㉑, home to the Caisse Nationale des Monuments Historiques (Historic Monuments Trust) at No. 62. Across rue St-Antoine, pause to admire the mighty Baroque church of **St-Paul–St-Louis** ㉒. Take the left-hand side door out of the church into narrow passage St-Paul, then turn right onto rue St-Paul, past the grid of courtyards that make up the Village St-Paul antiques-shops complex. Children enjoy the **Académie de la Magie** ㉓ farther down at No. 11. At rue de l'Ave-Maria, turn right to reach the painstakingly restored **Hôtel de Sens** ㉔, a strange mixture of defensive stronghold and fairy-tale château. If you are a photography fan, head up rue Figuier, then down rue de Fourcy to the **Maison Européenne de la Photographie** ㉕. Back down rue Figuier, turn left on rue de Jouy past two 17th-century mansions: the Hôtel d'Aumont on your left and the **Hôtel de Beauvais** ㉖ on your right (entry round the corner in rue François-Miron). The next left, rue Geoffroy-l'Asnier, leads past the stark **Mémorial du Martyr Inconnu** ㉗: a huge bronze memorial to those who died in Nazi concentration camps.

TIMING

At just over 5-km (3-mi) long, this walk will comfortably take a whole morning or afternoon. If you choose to spend an hour or two in any of the museums along the way, allow a full day. Be prepared to wait in line at the Picasso Museum. Note that some of the museums don't open until the afternoon and that most shops in the Marais don't open until the late morning.

Sights to See

Ⓒ ㉓ **Académie de la Magie** (Museum of Magic). Housed in a 16th-century cellar, this museum contains antique magic paraphernalia, including some from Houdini's bag of tricks. There's a magic show every hour. ⊠ *11 rue St-Paul,* ☎ *01–42–72–13–26.* ⊑ *45 frs.* ☉ *Wed. and weekends 2–7. Métro: St-Paul.*

⑪ **Archives Nationales** (National Archives). If you're a serious history buff, you will be fascinated by the thousands of intricate historical documents, dating from the Merovingian period to the 20th century, at the National Archives (also known as the Musée de l'Histoire de France) in the palatial Hôtel de Soubise. The highlights are the Edict of Nantes (1598), the Treaty of Westphalia (1648), the wills of Louis XIV and Napoléon, and the Declaration of Human Rights (1789). Louis XVI's diary is also in the collection, containing his sadly ignorant entry for July 14, 1789, the day the Bastille was stormed and, for all intents and purposes, the French Revolution began: *"Rien"* ("Nothing"). You can also visit the apartments of the prince and princess de Soubise; don't miss them if you have any interest in the lifestyles of 18th-century French aristocrats.

The buildings housing the Archives have external charm, too: The **Hôtel de Soubise** and the **Hôtel de Rohan** (originally built for the archbishop of Strasbourg), across the lawn facing rue Vieille-du-Temple, both display the cool, column-fronted elegance of the early 18th century; the Porte de Clisson, a turreted gateway on rue des Archives, was erected in 1380 for the Hôtel de Clisson, the Paris base of the Duke of Bedford (regent of France during the English occupation from 1420 to 1435). ⊠ *60 rue des Francs-Bourgeois,* ☎ *01–40–27–60–96.* ▦ *20 frs.* ☉ *Mon., Wed.–Fri. noon–5:45, weekends 1:45–5:45. Métro: Rambuteau.*

⑥ Atelier Brancusi (Brancusi Studio). Romanian-born sculptor Constantin Brancusi settled in Paris in 1898 at age 22. This light, airy museum in front of the Pompidou Center, designed by Renzo Piano, contains four glass-fronted rooms that reconstitute Brancusi's working studios, crammed with smooth, stylized works from all periods of his career. ⊠ *11 rue St-Paul,* ☎ *01–44–78–12–33.* ▦ *20 frs.* ☉ *Wed.–Mon. noon–10. Métro: Rambuteau, Châtelet–Les Halles, Hôtel de Ville.*

⑤ Centre Pompidou (Pompidou Center). The Centre National d'Art et de Culture Georges-Pompidou is its full name, although it is known to Parisians simply as Beaubourg (for the neighborhood). Georges Pompidou (1911–74) was the president of France who launched the project. Unveiled in 1977, three years after his death, the Pompidou Center was soon attracting over 8 million visitors a year—five times more than intended. Hardly surprising, then, that it was soon showing signs of fatigue: The much-vaunted, gaudily painted service pipes snaking up the exterior (painted the same colors that were used to identify them on the architects' plans) needed continual repainting, while the plastic tubing enclosing the exterior escalators was cracked and grimy. In 1996 the government stepped in and took drastic action, shutting the Center until the end of 1999 and embarking on top-to-bottom renovation.

You approach the center across **Place Georges-Pompidou,** a substantial, gently sloping piazza, home to the **Atelier Brancusi** (☞ *above*). The center is most famous for its **Musée National d'Art Moderne** (Modern Art Museum). The emphasis here is largely on French works, from Fauvism and Cubism to postwar abstract art. Also look for rotating exhibits of contemporary art. In addition, there's a public reference library, a language laboratory, an industrial design center, a cinema, a café, a restaurant, and a gift shop. ⊠ *Pl. Georges-Pompidou,* ☎ *01–44–78–12–33.* ▦ *Admission prices were unavailable at press time.* ☉ *Wed.–Mon. noon–10. Métro: Rambuteau, Châtelet–Les Halles, Hôtel de Ville.*

....

NEED A   Stop in for coffee at the ultramodern **Café Beaubourg** (⊠ 43 rue St-
BREAK?   Merri, ☎ 01–48–87–63–96), on the corner of Place Georges-Pompidou. The high-tech design is lightened by the little glass-top tables, several of which are covered with artists' paintings.

....

㉖ Hôtel de Beauvais. Dating from 1655, this is one of the finest mansions in the Marais. It was built for Pierre de Beauvais with surprisingly generous funding from the normally parsimonious Louis XIV. The reason for the Sun King's unwonted largesse: a reward for de Beauvais's willingness to turn a blind eye to the activities of his wife, Catherine-Henriette Bellier, in educating the young monarch in matters sexual. Louis, who came to the throne in 1643 at the age of 4, was 14 when Catherine first gave him the benefit of her expertise; she was 40. It's being renovated until 2001. ⊠ *68 rue François-Miron. Métro: St-Paul.*

⑨ Hôtel de Montmor. This 17th-century mansion was once home to M. Montmor, Louis XIII's financial adviser. His son ran a salon here frequented by such luminaries as philosopher and mathematician Pierre Gassend, physicist Gilles de Roberval, writer and professor of medicine Gui Patin, and Dutch astronomer Christian Huygens. This informal gathering of the "Boffins" prompted the creation of the Académie des

Sciences in 1666. Note the huge windows and intricate ironwork on the second-floor balcony. ⊠ *79 rue de Temple. Métro: Rambuteau.*

㉔ Hôtel de Sens. One of a handful of civil buildings in Paris to have survived from the Middle Ages—witness the pointed corner towers, Gothic porch, and richly carved decorative details—this sumptuous Marais mansion was built in 1474 for the archbishop of Sens. Its best-known occupants were Henri IV and his queen, Marguérite, philanderers both. While Henri dallied with his mistresses—he is said to have had 56—at a series of royal palaces, Marguérite entertained her almost equally large number of lovers here. Today the building houses occasional exhibits and a fine-arts library, the **Bibliothèque Forney.** ⊠ *1 rue du Figuier,* ☎ *01–42–78–14–60.* ▧ *20 frs for exhibitions.* ☉ *Tues.–Sat. 1:30–8. Métro: Pont-Marie.*

㉑ Hôtel de Sully. This late-Renaissance mansion, begun in 1624, has a stately garden and a majestic courtyard with statues, richly carved pediments, and dormer windows. It is the headquarters of the **Caisse Nationale des Monuments Historiques,** responsible for administering France's historic monuments. Guided visits to Paris sites and buildings begin here, though all are conducted in French. The excellent bookshop, just inside the gate, has a wide range of publications on Paris, many of them in English. The bookshop is open daily 10–12:45 and 1:45–6. ⊠ *62 rue St-Antoine,* ☎ *01–44–61–20–00. Métro: St-Paul.*

❶ Hôtel de Ville (City Hall). Overlooking the Seine, the City Hall is something of a symbol for the regeneration of the surrounding Marais district, since much of the finance and direction for the restoration of the area has been provided by municipal authorities. As the area has been successfully redeveloped, the prestige of the mayor of Paris has grown. In fact, until 1977, Paris was the only city in France without a mayor; with the creation of the post and the election of Jacques Chirac (now president of France), leader of the right-of-center Gaullist party, the position has become pivotal in both Parisian and French politics. It comes as no surprise, therefore, that Chirac oversaw a thorough restoration of the Hôtel de Ville, both inside and out.

The square in front of the Hôtel de Ville was relaid in the 1980s and equipped with fancy lamps and fountains. In the Middle Ages it was the site of public executions. Most victims were hanged, drawn, and quartered; the lucky ones were burned at the stake. Following the short-lived restoration of the Bourbon monarchy in 1830, the building became the seat of the French government, a role that came to a sudden end with the uprisings in 1848. During the Commune of 1871, the Hôtel de Ville was burned to the ground. Today's exuberant building, based closely on the 16th-century Renaissance original, went up between 1874 and 1884. In 1944, following the liberation of Paris from Nazi rule, General de Gaulle took over the leadership of France from here. ⊠ *Pl. de l'Hôtel-de-Ville.* ☉ *For special exhibitions only. Métro: Hôtel-de-Ville.*

㉕ Maison Européenne de la Photographie (European Photography Center). This museum, unveiled in 1996, combines spacious modern galleries with the original stonework of a venerable hôtel particulier. Despite its name, the museum has an impressive collection of both European and American photography, and stages up to four different exhibitions every three months. ⊠ *5 rue Fourcy,* ☎ *01–44–78–75–00.* ▧ *30 frs. Free Wed. after 5 PM.* ☉ *Wed.–Sun. 11–8. Métro: St-Paul.*

⓳ Maison de Victor Hugo (Victor Hugo's House). The workaholic French author, famed for *Les Misérables* and the *Hunchback of Notre-Dame,* lived in a corner of Place des Vosges between 1832 and 1848. The memorabilia here include several of his atmospheric, Gothic-horror-movie ink sketches, tribute to Hugo's unsuspected talent as an artist. ✉ *6 Pl. des Vosges,* ☎ *01–42–72–10–16.* 💳 *27 frs.* ☉ *Tues.–Sun. 10–5:45. Métro: St-Paul.*

㉗ Mémorial du Martyr Inconnu (Memorial of the Unknown Martyr). In March 1992, this memorial was erected at the **Center for Contemporary Jewish Documentation**—50 years after the first French Jews were deported from France—to honor the memory of the 6 million Jews who died "without graves" at the hands of the Nazis. The basement crypt has a dramatic, black marble Star of David containing the ashes of victims from Nazi death camps in Poland and Austria. The center has archives, a library, and a gallery that hosts temporary exhibitions. ✉ *17 rue Geoffroy-l'Asnier,* ☎ *01–42–77–44–72.* 💳 *15 frs.* ☉ *Sun.–Fri. 10–1 and 2–5:30. Métro: Pont-Marie.*

⑧ Musée d'Art et d'Histoire du Judaïsme (Museum of Jewish Art and History). With its clifflike courtyard ringed by giant pilasters, the Hôtel St-Aignan, completed in 1650 to the design of Pierre le Muet, is one of the most awesome sights in the Marais. It opened as the city's Jewish museum in late 1998 after a 20-year restoration. The interior has been renovated to the point of blandness, but the exhibits have good explanatory English texts on Jewish history and practice. Highlights include an array of 13th-century tombstones excavated in Paris; wooden models of destroyed East European synagogues; a roomful of early Chagalls; and Christian Boltanski's stark, two-part tribute to Shoah victims, in the form of plaques on an outer wall naming the (mainly Jewish) inhabitants of the Hôtel St-Aignan in 1939, and canvas hangings with the personal data of the 13 residents who were deported and died in concentration camps. Jewish people settled in France in the Rhône Valley as early as the 1st century BC; a synagogue existed in Paris by 582; an expulsion order was issued by Charles VI in 1394, but fitfully enforced; and 40,000 French Jews were granted full citizenship by the Revolution in 1791. France's Jewish population went from 300,000 to 180,000 with the deportation and departure during World War II, but has since grown to around 700,000. ✉ *71 rue du Temple,* ☎ *01–53–01–86–53.* 💳 *40 frs.* ☉ *Sun.–Fri. 11–6. Métro: Rambuteau, Hôtel de Ville.*

☕ ⑬ Musée Bricard. Also called the Musée de la Serrure (Lock Museum), this museum is housed in a sober Baroque mansion designed in 1685 by the architect of Les Invalides, Libéral Bruand, for himself. Anyone with a taste for fine craftsmanship will appreciate the intricacy and ingenuity of many of the older locks displayed here. One represents an early security system—it would shoot anyone who tried to open it with the wrong key. Another was made in the 17th century by a master locksmith who was himself held under lock and key while he labored over it—the task took him four years. ✉ *1 rue de la Perle,* ☎ *01–42–77–79–62.* 💳 *30 frs.* ☉ *Weekdays 2–5. Métro: St-Paul.*

⑰ Musée Carnavalet. Two adjacent mansions in the heart of the Marais house this museum of Paris history. Material dating from the city's origins until 1789 is in the Hôtel Carnavalet, and material from 1789 to the present is in the Hôtel Peletier St-Fargeau. In the late 17th century, the Hôtel Carnavalet was home to the most brilliant salon in Paris, presided over by Madame de Sévigné, best known for the hundreds of letters she wrote to her daughter; they've become one of the most enduring chronicles of French high society in the 17th century. The Hôtel Carnavalet, transformed into a museum in 1880, is full of maps and plans, furniture, and busts and portraits of Parisian worthies down the ages. The section on the Revolution includes riveting models of guillotines and objects associated with the royal family's final days, including the king's razor, and the chess set used by the royal prisoners at the approach of their own endgame. ⊠ *23 rue de Sévigné,* ☎ *01–42–72–21–13.* 🎟 *27 frs.* ⊙ *Tues.–Sun. 10–5:30. Métro: St-Paul.*

NEED A BREAK? **Marais Plus** (⊠ 20 rue des Francs-Bourgeois, ☎ 01–48–87–01–40), on the corner of rue Elzévir and rue des Francs-Bourgeois, is a delightful, artsy gift shop with a cozy salon de thé in the back.

⑩ Musée de la Chasse et de la Nature (Museum of Hunting and Nature). This museum is housed in the Hôtel de Guénégaud, designed around 1650 by François Mansart and one of the Marais's most stately mansions. There's an extensive collection of hunting paraphernalia, including a series of immense 17th- and 18th-century still lifes (notably by Desportes and Oudry) of dead animals and a wide variety of swords, guns, muskets, and taxidermy. ⊠ *60 rue des Archives,* ☎ *01–42–72–86–42.* 🎟 *30 frs.* ⊙ *Wed.–Mon. 10–12:30 and 1:30–5:30. Métro: Rambuteau.*

⑯ Musée Cognacq-Jay. Devoted to the arts of the 18th century, this museum contains an outstanding collection of furniture, porcelain, and paintings (notably by Watteau, Boucher, and Tiepolo). ⊠ *8 rue Elzévir,* ☎ *01–40–27–07–21.* 🎟 *17 frs.* ⊙ *Tues.–Sun. 10–5:40. Métro: St-Paul.*

⑭ Musée Picasso. The Picasso Museum opened in the fall of 1985 and shows no signs of losing its immense popularity. The building itself, put up between 1656 and 1660 for financier Aubert de Fontenay, quickly became known as the Hôtel Salé—*salé* meaning, literally, salted—as a result of the enormous profits made by de Fontenay as the sole appointed collector of the salt tax. The mansion was luxuriously restored by the French government as a permanent home for the pictures, sculptures, drawings, prints, ceramics, and assorted works of art given to the government by Picasso's heirs after the painter's death in 1973 in lieu of death duties. It's the largest collection of works by Picasso in the world—no masterpieces, but all works kept by Picasso himself; in other words, works that he especially valued. There are pictures from every period of his life: a grand total of 230 paintings, 1,500 drawings, and nearly 1,700 prints, as well as works by Cézanne, Miró, Renoir, Braque, Degas, and Matisse. The palatial surroundings of the Hôtel Salé add to the pleasures of a visit. ⊠ *5 rue de Thorigny,* ☎ *01–42–71–25–21.* 🎟 *30 frs, Sun. 20 frs.* ⊙ *Thurs.–Mon. 9:30–5:30. Métro: St-Sébastien.*

☝ ⑦ Musée de la Poupée (Doll Museum). If you love dolls, make a detour to this quaint, low-ceilinged house in a cul-de-sac behind the Pompidou Center to admire the rarefied collection of 300 French dolls dating back to the 1850s—many wearing their original costumes. Bisque-head dolls with enamel eyes were the Paris specialty, with Steiner, Bru, and Jumeau among the leading makers represented here. Two of the museum's six rooms are devoted to temporary exhibits, and there's a well-stocked gift shop. ⊠ *Impasse Berthaud,* ☎ *01–42–72–73–11.* 🎟 *35 frs.* ⊙ *Tues.–Sun. 10–6. Métro: Rambuteau.*

⑫ Notre-Dame des Blancs-Manteaux. The Blancs Manteaux were white-robed 13th-century mendicant monks whose monastery once stood on this spot. For the last 100 years, this late-17th-century church has had an imposing 18th-century facade that belonged to a now-destroyed church on the Ile de la Cité. Unfortunately, the narrow streets of the Marais leave little room to step back and admire it. The inside has fine woodwork and a Flemish-style Rococo pulpit whose marquetry panels are inlaid with pewter and ivory. ⊠ *rue des Blancs-Manteaux. Métro: Rambuteau.*

⑱ Place des Vosges. Laid out by Henri IV at the start of the 17th century, and originally known as Place Royale, this square is the oldest in Paris. It stands on the site of a former royal palace, the Palais des Tournelles, which was abandoned by the Italian-born queen of France, Catherine de Médicis, when her husband, Henri II, was killed in a tournament here in 1559. It was always a highly desirable address, reaching a peak of glamour in the early years of Louis XIV's reign, when the nobility were falling over themselves for the privilege of living here. Its buildings have been softened by time, their pale pink brick crumbling slightly in the harsh Parisian air and the darker stone facings pitted with age. The two larger buildings on either side of the square were originally the king's and queen's pavilions. The statue in the center is of Louis XIII. It's not the original; that was melted down in the Revolution, the same period when the square's name was changed in honor of the French département of the Vosges, the first in the country to pay the new revolutionary taxes. With its arcades, symmetrical pink-brick town houses, and trim green garden, bisected in the center by gravel paths and edged with plane trees, the square achieves harmony and balance: It's a pleasant place to tarry on a sultry summer afternoon. *Métro: Chemin-Vert.*

⑮ St-Denis-du-St-Sacrement. This severely Neoclassical edifice dates from the 1830s. It is a formidable example of architectural discipline, oozing restraint and monumental dignity (or banality, according to taste). The grisaille frieze and gilt fresco above the semicircular apse have clout if not subtlety; the Delacroix *Deposition* (1844), in the front right-hand chapel as you enter, has both. ⊠ *rue de Turenne. Métro: St-Sébastien.*

❷ St-Gervais–St-Protais. This imposing church near the Hôtel de Ville is named after two Roman soldiers martyred by the emperor Nero in the 1st century AD. The original church—no trace remains of it now—was built in the 7th century. The present church, a riot of Flamboyant-style decoration, went up between 1494 and 1598, making it one of the last Gothic constructions in the country. Pause to look at the facade, constructed between 1616 and 1621. It's an early example of French architects' use of the classical orders of decoration on the capitals (topmost sections) of the columns. Those on the first floor are plain and sturdy Doric; the more elaborate Ionic is used on the second floor; and the most ornate of all—Corinthian—is used on the third floor. The church hosts occasional organ and choral concerts. ⊠ *Pl. St-Gervais,* ☎ *01–47–26–78–38 for concert information.* ☉ *Tues.–Sun. 6:30 AM– 8 PM. Métro: Hôtel de Ville.*

❸ St-Merri. This church near the Pompidou Center, completed in 1552, has a turret containing the oldest bell in Paris (cast in 1331) and an 18th-century pulpit supported on carved palm trees. ⊠ *rue de la Verrerie. Métro: Hôtel de Ville.*

㉒ St-Paul–St-Louis. The leading Baroque church in the Marais, with its elegant dome rising 180 ft above the crossing, was begun in 1627 by the Jesuits and partly modeled on their Gesu church in Rome. Look out for Delacroix's dramatic *Christ in the Mount of Olives* high up in the transept, and the two huge shells, used as fonts, presented by Victor Hugo when he lived on nearby Place des Vosges. ⊠ *rue St-Antoine. Métro: St-Paul.*

⑳ Ste-Marie. Constructed 1632–34 by François Mansart as the chapel of the Convent of the Visitation, this is now a Protestant "reformed" church. The large dome above the distinctive nave rotunda is one of the earliest in Paris. ⊠ *rue St-Antoine. Métro: Bastille.*

④ Square Igor-Stravinsky. The café-lined square, next to the Pompidou Center and backed by the church of St-Merri, has a fountain animated by the colorful and imaginative sculptures of French artist Niki de St-Phalle, together with the aquatic mechanisms of her Swiss partner Jean Tinguely. The fountain (sculptures and all) was erected in 1980. It is not part of the Pompidou Center, but it fits right in. *Métro: Rambuteau.*

THE ISLANDS AND THE LATIN QUARTER

Of the two islands in the Seine—the Ile St-Louis and the Ile de la Cité—it is the Ile de la Cité that forms the historic heart of Paris. It was here, for obvious reasons of defense, and in the hope of controlling the trade that passed along the Seine, that the earliest inhabitants of Paris, the Gaulish tribe of the Parisii, settled in about 250 BC. They called their little home Lutetia, meaning "settlement surrounded by water." Whereas the Ile St-Louis is today largely residential, the Ile de la Cité remains deeply historic. It has been inhabited for more than 2,000 years and is the site of one of the most beautiful churches in France—the great, brooding cathedral of Notre-Dame. Most of the island's other medieval buildings fell victim to town planner Baron Haussmann's ambitious rebuilding program of the 1860s. Among the rare survivors are the jewel-like Ste-Chapelle, a vision of shimmering stained glass, and the Conciergerie, the former city prison.

South of Ile de la Cité on the Left Bank of the Seine is the bohemian Quartier Latin, with its warren of steep sloping streets, populated largely by Sorbonne students and academics who fill the air of the cafés with their ideas—and tobacco smoke. The name Latin Quarter comes from the university tradition of studying and speaking in Latin, a tradition that disappeared during the Revolution. The university began as a theological school in the Middle Ages and later became the headquarters of the University of Paris; in 1968, the student revolution here had an explosive effect on French politics, resulting in major reforms in the education system.

A grim modern skyscraper at the Jussieu campus, the science division of the University of Paris, reiterates the area's yen for learning, yet fails to outgun the mighty dome of the Panthéon in its challenge for skyline supremacy. Most of the district's appeal is less emphatic: Roman ruins, tumbling street markets, the two oldest trees in Paris, and chance glimpses of Notre-Dame all await your discovery.

Numbers in the text correspond to numbers in the margin and on the Islands and the Latin Quarter map.

A Good Walk

The oldest bridge in Paris, confusingly called the **Pont Neuf** ①, or New Bridge, is built across the western tip of Ile de la Cité. Find your way to the middle of the bridge and the **Square du Vert-Galant** ② below, with its proud equestrian statue of Henri IV. On the quay side of the square, vedette motorboats start their tours along the Seine.

Opposite the square, on the other side of the bridge, is Place Dauphine, completed the same year as the Pont Neuf (although much altered since). Cross Place Dauphine and head left, then right along quai de l'Horloge. The street is named for the oldest clock (*horloge*) in Paris—marking time since 1370 from high up on the **Conciergerie** ③, the prison where Marie-Antoinette was kept during the French Revolution. Take a right on boulevard du Palais to reach the imposing **Palais de Justice** ④, the 19th-century Law Courts; you can wander around the buildings amongst the black-robed lawyers or attend a court hearing. But the real interest here is the medieval **Ste-Chapelle** ⑤, tucked away to the left of the main courtyard. Rue de Lutèce, opposite the Law Courts, leads to the extensive flower market 150 yards down on the left. Turn right on rue de la Cité to come face to face with the serene, golden facade of **Notre-Dame** ⑥. The cathedral is at the geographic and historic heart of Paris, and its dark, solemn interior feels suitably reverential.

Cross the Seine along the pont au Double to square René-Viviani, where you'll find a battered acacia—which vies with a specimen in the Jardin des Plantes for the title of oldest tree in Paris—and a spectacular view of Notre-Dame. Behind the square lies the church of **St-Julien-le-Pauvre** ⑦, built at the same time as Notre-Dame, and the tiny, elegant streets of the Maubert district. Turn left out of the church and cross rue St-Jacques to the elegantly proportioned church of **St-Séverin** ⑧. The surrounding streets are for pedestrians only and crammed with cheap restaurants fronted by suave waiters touting customers at most hours of the day and night. Take rue St-Séverin, a right on rue Xavier-Privas, and a left on rue de la Huchette—home to Paris's smallest theater and oldest jazz club—to reach **Place St-Michel** ⑨. The grandiose fountain, depicting St. Michael slaying the dragon, is a popular meeting spot at the nerve center of the Left Bank.

Turn left up boulevard St-Michel and cross boulevard St-Germain. To your left, behind some forbidding railings, lurks a garden with ruins that date from Roman times. These belong to the **Musée National du Moyen-Age** ⑩, the National Museum of the Middle Ages. The entrance is down rue Sommerard, the next street on the left. Cross Place Paul-Painlevé, in front of the museum, up toward the **Sorbonne** ⑪ university, fronted by a small plaza where the Left Bank's student population congregates after classes. Continue uphill until you are confronted, up rue Soufflot on your left, by the menacing domed bulk of the **Panthéon** ⑫, originally built as a church but now a monument to France's most glorious historical figures. On the far left corner of Place du Panthéon stands **St-Etienne-du-Mont** ⑬, a church whose facade is a mishmash of architectural styles. Explore the top of quaint rue de la Montagne-Ste-Geneviève alongside, then turn right onto rue Descartes to reach **Place de la Contrescarpe** ⑭. This square looks almost provincial during the day as Parisians flock to the daily market on rue Mouffetard.

Duck into the old church of **St-Médard** ⑮ at the foot of rue Mouffetard, then head left for 250 yards along rue Censier and turn left again into rue Georges-Desplas to discover the beautiful white **Mosquée** ⑯, complete with minaret. Blink twice and you'll be convinced you've left Paris behind. On the far side of the Mosque extends the **Jardin des Plantes** ⑰, spacious botanical gardens; the first building you'll come to is the **Grande Galerie de l'Evolution** ⑱, a museum with a startling collection of taxidermy, many of extinct or endangered animals. The museums of entomology, paleontology, and mineralogy are on the south side of the park along rue Buffon; an old-fashioned zoo is on the other.

Although it's a bit out of the way, **St-Louis de la Salpêtrière** ⑲, the church of the Salpêtrière Hospital, is in walking distance from the Jardin des Plantes: Take boulevard de l'Hôpital, at the east end of the park; the church is between the Gare d'Austerlitz and the hospital. Farther upriver, via quai d'Austerlitz and quai de la Gare, is the new Bibliothèque François-Mitterrand (☞ From Bastille to Nation, *above*), the French National Library, with its four huge shiny glass towers.

If you forego the distant pleasures of southeast Paris, take the northwest exit from the Jardin des Plantes up rue Lacépède then rue de Navarre to the **Arènes de Lutèce** ⑳, the remains of a Roman amphitheater. Rue

The Islands and the Latin Quarter

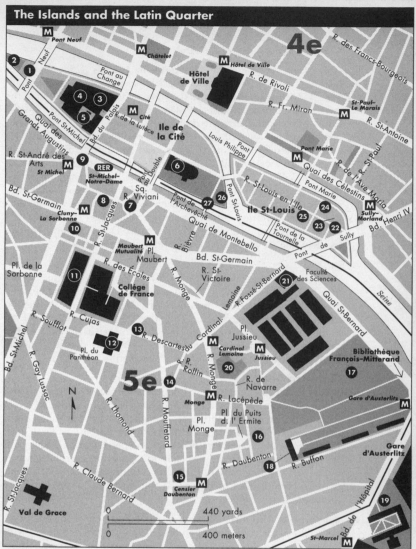

des Arènes and rue Limé lead to Place Jussieu and its hideous 1960s concrete campus; there's greater refinement around the corner down rue des Fossés-St-Bernard at the glass-facaded **Institut du Monde Arabe** ㉑, a center devoted to Arab culture.

Cross the Seine on Pont de Sully to the **Ile St-Louis** ㉒, the smaller of the city's two islands; it's an ideal place for strolling and window-shopping. The **Hôtel Lambert** ㉓ and the **Hôtel de Lauzun** ㉔ are two of the most majestic mansions on the island. Rue St-Louis-en-l'Ile runs the length of the island, dividing it in two. Walk down the street and admire the strange, pierced spire of **St-Louis-en-l'Ile** ㉕; stop off for an ice cream at Berthillon at No. 31. Then head down to the Pont St-Louis at the island's western tip to admire the views of Notre-Dame, and the Hôtel de Ville and St-Gervais church on the Right Bank. Just across the bridge on Ile de la Cité lies the **Mémorial de la Déportation** ㉖, a starkly moving modern crypt dedicated to the French Jews who died in Nazi concentration camps. You may wish to linger in the quiet garden above before savoring the view of Notre-Dame from the **Pont de l'Archevêché** ㉗, which links the island to the Left Bank.

TIMING

At just under 6 km (about 3½ mi), this walk can be done in a morning or afternoon, or serve as the basis for a leisurely day's exploring—given that several sites, notably Notre-Dame and the Musée de Cluny—deserve a lengthy visit. Note that the Grande Galerie d'Évolution stays open until 10 PM on Thursday. You can easily make a brief excursion to St-Louis de la Salpêtrière as well as the Bibliothèque François-Mitterrand (☞ From Bastille to Nation, *above*).

Sights to See

☾ ⑳ **Arènes de Lutèce** (Lutèce Arena). This Roman arena was only discovered in 1869 and has since been excavated and landscaped to reveal parts of the original amphitheater. Designed as a theater and circus, the arena was almost totally destroyed by the barbarians in AD 280, though you can still see part of the stage and tiered seating. Along with the remains of the baths at the Cluny, this constitutes rare evidence of the powerful Roman city of Lutetia that flourished on the Left Bank in the 3rd century. ⊠ *Enter by rue Monge or rue de Navarre.* ⊘ *Daily 8–sunset. Métro: Monge.*

❸ **Conciergerie.** This turreted medieval building by the Seine was originally part of the royal palace on Ile de la Cité. Most people know it, however, as a prison, the place of confinement for Danton, Robespierre, and, most famously, Marie-Antoinette during the French Revolution. From here, all three—and countless others who fell foul of the Revolutionary leaders—were bundled off to the guillotine. Marie-Antoinette's cell can still be seen, as can objects connected with the ill-fated queen. A chapel, embellished with the initials M. A., occupies the true site of her confinement. You can also visit the guardroom, complete with hefty Gothic vaulting and intricately carved columns, and the monumental Salle des Gens d'Armes, where a short corridor leads to the kitchen, with its four vast fireplaces. The building's name derives from the governor, or *concierge,* of the palace, whose considerable income was swollen by the privilege he enjoyed of renting out shops and workshops. ⊠ *1 quai de l'Horloge,* ☎ *01–53–73–78–50.* ⌸ *32 frs; joint ticket with Ste-Chapelle 50 frs.* ⊘ *Daily 9:30–6:30; winter, daily 10–5. Métro: Cité.*

☾ ⑱ **Grande Galerie de l'Evolution** (Great Hall of Evolution). This vast, handsome glass-and-iron structure in the Jardin des Plantes (☞ *below*) was built, like the Eiffel Tower, in 1889 but abandoned in the 1960s. It reopened amid popular acclaim in 1994 and now contains one of the world's finest collections of taxidermy, including a section devoted to extinct and endangered species. There's a reconstituted dodo—only a foot actually remains of this clumsy, flightless bird from Mauritius—and a miniature South African zebra, the quagga, which disappeared earlier this century. Stunning lighting effects include push-button spot-lighting and a ceiling that changes color to suggest storms, twilight, or hot savannah sun. ⊠ *36 rue Geoffroy-St-Hilaire,* ☎ *01–40–79–39–39.* ☞ *40 frs.* ☉ *Wed.–Mon. 10–6, Thurs. 10–10. Métro: Monge.*

㉓ Hôtel Lambert. Leading Baroque architect Louis Le Vau (1612–70) designed this majestic mansion on the eastern end of the Ile St-Louis. The interior decor is by Eustache Le Sueur and Charles Le Brun. Voltaire was its most illustrious inhabitant; unfortunately, you can only admire it from outside. ⊠ *2 rue St-Louis-en-l'Ile. Métro: Pont-Marie.*

㉔ Hôtel de Lauzun. There is rich history to this Ile St-Louis mansion, built in about 1650 for Charles Gruyn, a supplier of goods to the French army who accumulated an immense fortune, then landed in jail before the house was even completed. In the 19th century, the revolutionary critic and visionary poet Charles Baudelaire (1821–67) had an apartment here, where he kept a cache of stuffed snakes and crocodiles. In 1848, the poet Théophile Gautier (1811–72) moved in, making it the meeting place of the Club des Haschischines, the Hashish Eaters' Club; novelist Alexandre Dumas and painter Eugène Delacroix were both members. The club came to represent more than just a den of drug takers and gossips, for these men believed passionately in the purity of art and the crucial role of the artist as sole interpreter of the chaos of life. Art for Art's Sake—the more refined and exotic the better—was their creed. Anything that helped the artist reach heightened states of perception was applauded. Now the building is used for more decorous receptions by the mayor of Paris. ⊠ *17 quai d'Anjou,* ☎ *01–43–54–27–14.* ☞ *25 frs.* ☉ *Easter–Oct., weekends 10–5:30. Métro: Pont-Marie.*

㉒ Ile St-Louis. The smaller of the two Paris islands is linked to the Ile de la Cité by Pont St-Louis. The contrast between the islands is striking: Whereas the Ile de la Cité is steeped in history and dotted with dignified public buildings, the Ile St-Louis is a discreet residential district. The island's most striking feature is its architectural unity, which stems from the efforts of a group of early 17th-century property speculators. At that time, there were two islands here, the Ile Notre-Dame and Ile aux Vaches—Cow Island, a reference to its use as grazing land. The speculators, led by an energetic engineer named Christophe Marie (after whom the Pont Marie was named), bought the two islands, joined them together, and divided the newly formed Ile St-Louis into building plots. Baroque architect Louis Le Vau (1612–70) was commissioned to erect a series of imposing town houses, and by 1664 the project was largely complete. People still talk about the quaint, village-street feel of rue St-Louis-en-l'Ile, which runs the length of the island, dividing it neatly in two. From quai de Bourbon at the western end, facing the Ile de la Cité, there are attractive views of Notre-Dame, the Hôtel de Ville, and the church of St-Gervais. In summer, rows of baking bodies attest to the quai's enduring popularity as the city's favorite sunbathing spot. *Métro: Pont-Marie.*

㉑ Institut du Monde Arabe (Institute of the Arab World). Jean Nouvel's striking glass-and-steel edifice adroitly fuses Arabic and European styles and was greeted with enthusiasm when it opened in 1988. Note the 240 shutterlike apertures that open and close to regulate light exposure. Inside, the Institute tries to do for Arab culture what the Pompidou Center does for modern art, with the help of a sound-and-image center; a vast library and documentation center; and an art museum containing an array of Arab-Islamic art, textiles, and ceramics, plus exhibits on Arabic mathematics, astronomy, and medicine. Glass elevators whisk you to the ninth floor, where you can sip mint tea at the rooftop café and enjoy a memorable view of the Seine and Notre-Dame. ⊠ *1 rue des Fossés-St-Bernard,* ☎ *01–40–51–38–38.* ☞ *40 frs.* ☉ *Tues.– Sun. 10–6. Métro: Cardinal-Lemoine.*

✆ **⑰** **Jardin des Plantes** (Botanical Gardens). Bordered by the Seine, the drab Gare d'Austerlitz, and the utilitarian Jussieu (a branch of the Paris University system), this enormous swath of greenery contains botanical gardens, the Grande Galerie de l'Evolution, and three other natural history museums, which celebrated their centenary with a six-month renovation program in 1998. The **Grande Galerie de l'Evolution** (☞ *above*) is devoted to stuffed animals; the **Musée Entomologique** to insects; the **Musée Paléontologique** to fossils and skeletons dating back to prehistoric times; and the **Musée Minéralogique** to rocks and minerals. The stock of plants in the botanical gardens, dating from the first collections from the 17th century, has been enhanced by subsequent generations of devoted French botanists. The garden shelters what is claimed to be Paris's oldest tree, an *acacia robinia,* planted in 1636. There is also an alpine garden, an aquarium, a maze, a number of hothouses, and one of the world's oldest zoos, started by Napoleon. ⊠ *Entrances on rue Geoffroy-St-Hilaire, rue Civier and rue Buffon.* ☎ *Museums and zoo 20–30 frs.* ☉ *Museums Wed.–Mon. 10–5; zoo daily 9–6 (June–Aug.), 9–5 (Sept.–May); garden daily 7:30–sunset. Métro: Monge.*

㉖ **Mémorial de la Déportation** (Memorial of the Deportation). On the eastern tip of the Ile de la Cité, in what was once the city morgue, lies a starkly moving modern crypt, dedicated to all the French men, women, and children who died in Nazi concentration camps. ☎ *Free.* ☉ *Daily 9–6; winter, daily 9–dusk. Métro: Maubert-Mutualité.*

⑯ **Mosquée** (Mosque). This beautiful white mosque was built from 1922 to 1925, complete with arcades and minaret, and decorated in the style of Moorish Spain. Students from the nearby Jussieu and Censier universities pack themselves into the tea salon, for cups of sweet mint tea at the café, and restaurant, for copious quantities of couscous. The sunken garden and tiled patios are also open to the public (the prayer rooms are not) as are the *hammams,* or Turkish baths. ⊠ *2 Pl. du Puits-de-l'Ermite,* ☎ *01–45–35–97–33.* ☎ *15 frs for guided tour, 85 frs for Turkish baths.* ☉ *Baths daily 10–9; Tues. and Sun. men only; Mon., Wed.– Sat. women only. Guided tours of mosque Sat.–Thurs. 10–noon and 2–6. Métro: Monge.*

OFF THE BEATEN PATH   **CHINATOWN** – If China, rather than Arabia, is your cup of tea, take the métro at nearby Censier-Daubenton to Paris's Chinatown. Although not as ornamental as San Francisco's or New York's, Paris's Chinatown nevertheless has myriad electronics and clothing stores and dozens of restaurants with an exciting array of Chinese *comestibles* (foods). Tang-Frères Chinese supermarket (⊠ 48 av. d'Ivry) packs in a serious crowd of shoppers on weekends. The Temple de l'Association des Résidents d'Origine Chinoise (⊠ 37 rue du Disque) is a small Buddhist temple that looks like a cross between a school cafeteria and an exotic Asian enclave filled with Buddha figures, fruit, and incense. For a more upscale version of Chinese culture, head out to **Chinagora** in the eastern suburbs (☞ Off the Beaten Path, *below*). *Métro: Tolbiac.*

⑩ Musée National du Moyen-Age (National Museum of the Middle Ages). This museum is housed in the 15th-century Hôtel de Cluny. The mansion has an intricately vaulted chapel and a cloistered courtyard with mullioned windows that originally belonged to monks of the Cluny Abbey in Burgundy, hence the museum's former name, the Musée de Cluny. A stunning array of tapestries heads its vast exhibition of medieval decorative arts; don't miss the graceful *Dame à la Licorne* (Lady and the Unicorn) series, woven in the 15th or 16th century, probably in the southern Netherlands. Alongside the mansion are the city's Roman baths—both hot (*Caldarium*) and cold (*Frigidarium*), the latter containing the *Boatmen's Pillar,* Paris's oldest sculpture. ⊠ *6 Pl. Paul-Painlevé,* ☎ *01–53–73–78–00.* ⊡ *30 frs, Sun. 20 frs.* ⊘ *Wed.– Mon. 9:15–5:45. Métro: Cluny–La Sorbonne.*

★ **⑥ Notre-Dame.** Looming above the large, pedestrian Place du Parvis on the Ile de la Cité is the Cathédrale de Notre-Dame, the most enduring symbol of Paris. The square (*kilomètre zéro* to the French, the spot from which all distances to and from the city are officially measured) is the perfect place to assess the facade. The cathedral was begun in 1163, with an army of stonemasons, carpenters, and sculptors working on a site that had previously seen a Roman temple, an early Christian basilica, and a Romanesque church. The chancel and altar were consecrated in 1182, but the magnificent sculptures surrounding the main doors were not put into position until 1240. The north tower was finished 10 years later.

Despite various changes in the 17th century, the cathedral remained substantially unaltered until the French Revolution. Then, the statues of the kings of Israel were hacked down by the mob, chiefly because they were thought to represent the despised royal line of France, and everything inside and out that was deemed "anti-Republican" was stripped away. An interesting postscript to this destruction occurred in 1977, when some of the heads of these statues were discovered salted away in a bank vault on boulevard Haussmann. They'd apparently been hidden there by an ardent royalist who owned the small mansion that now forms part of the bank. (The restored heads are now on display in the Musée National du Moyen-Age.)

By the early 19th century, the excesses of the Revolution were over, and the cathedral went back to fulfilling its religious functions again. Napoléon crowned himself emperor here in May 1804 (David's heroic painting of the lavish ceremony can be seen in the Louvre). Full-scale restoration started in the middle of the century, the most conspicuous result of which was the reconstruction of the spire. It was then, too, that Haussmann demolished the warren of little buildings in front of the cathedral, creating Place du Parvis.

The facade divides neatly into three levels. At the first-floor level are the three main entrances, or portals: the Portal of the Virgin on the left, the Portal of the Last Judgment in the center, and the Portal of St. Anne on the right. All three are surmounted by magnificent carvings— most of them 19th-century copies of the originals—of figures, foliage, and biblical scenes. Above these are the restored statues of the kings of Israel, the Galerie des Rois. Above the gallery is the great rose window and, above that, the Grand Galerie, at the base of the twin towers. The south tower houses the great bell of Notre-Dame, as tolled by Quasimodo, Victor Hugo's fictional hunchback. The 387-step climb to the top of the towers is worth the effort for a close-up of the famous gargoyles—most of them added in the 19th century—and the expansive view of the city.

Notre-Dame (Interior)

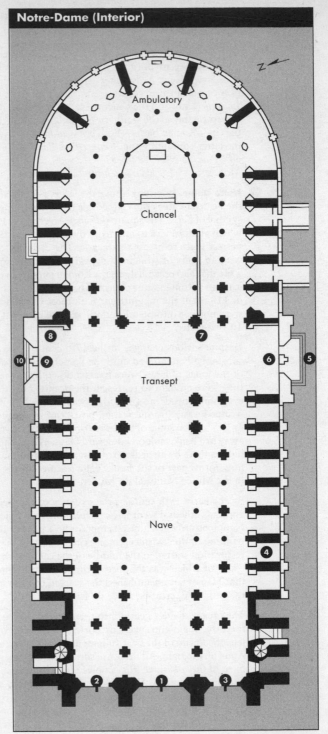

Ambulatory

Chancel

Transept

Nave

The cathedral interior, with its vast proportions, soaring nave, and soft, multicolor light filtering through the stained-glass windows, inspires awe, despite the inevitable throngs of tourists. The best time to visit is early in the morning, when the cathedral is at its lightest and least crowded. At the entrance are the massive 12th-century columns supporting the twin towers. Look down the nave to the transepts—the arms of the church—where, at the south (right) entrance to the chancel, you'll glimpse the haunting 12th-century statue of Notre-Dame de Paris, Our Lady of Paris. The chancel itself owes parts of its decoration to a vow taken by Louis XIII in 1638. Still without an heir after 23 years of marriage, he promised to dedicate the entire country to the Virgin Mary if his queen produced a son. When the longed-for event came to pass, Louis set about redecorating the chancel and choir. On the south side of the chancel is the Trésor (treasury), with a collection of garments, reliquaries, and silver and gold plate.

Under the square in front of the cathedral is the **Crypte Archéologique,** Notre-Dame's archaeological museum. It contains remains of previous churches on the site, scale models charting the district's development, and relics and artifacts dating from the Parisii who lived here 2000 years ago, unearthed during excavations here in the 1960s. Slides and models detail the history of the Ile de la Cité. The foundations of the 3rd-century Gallo-Roman rampart and of the 6th-century Merovingian church can also be seen.

If your interest in the cathedral is not yet sated, duck into the **Musée Notre-Dame** (✉ 10 rue du Cloître-Notre-Dame), across the street opposite the North Door. The museum's paintings, engravings, medallions, and other objects and documents chart the history of Notre-Dame cathedral. ✉ *Pl. du Parvis,* ☎ *01–44–32–16–72.* 🎫 *Towers: 32 frs; towers and crypt: 50 frs; treasury: 15 frs; museum: 15 frs.* ☉ *Cathedral: 8–7; towers: Apr.–Sept., daily 9:30–7:30; Oct.–Mar., daily 10–5; treasury: weekdays 9:30–6:30; crypt: Apr.–Sept., daily 9:30–6; Oct.–Mar., daily 10–4:30; museum: Wed. and weekends 2:30–6. Métro: Cité.*

4 **Palais de Justice** (Law Courts). The city's courts were built by Baron Haussmann in his characteristically weighty neoclassical style in about 1860. You can wander around the buildings, watch the bustle of the lawyers, or attend a court hearing. But the real interest here is the medieval part of the complex, spared by Haussmann: La Conciergerie and Ste-Chapelle (☞ *above* and *below*). ✉ *bd. du Palais. Métro: Cité.*

12 **Panthéon.** Originally commissioned by Louis XV to mark his recovery from illness in 1744, Germain Soufflot's mighty domed church was not begun until 1764, or completed until 1790—whereupon godless Revolutionary supremos had its windows blocked and ordered it transformed into a national shrine. Puvis de Chavannes's giant frescoes in the nave, retracing the life of Ste-Geneviève, warrant appraisal, along with a model of Foucault's pendulum, first hoisted in 1851 to prove the earth's rotation on its axis. Today the Panthéon is a monument to France's most glorious historical figures; the crypt holds the remains of Voltaire, Zola, Rousseau, and dozens of other national heroes. Nobel prize–winning scientist Marie Curie became the first woman to join their ranks in 1995. ✉ *Pl. du Panthéon,* ☎ *01–44–32–18–00.* 🎫 *32 frs.* ☉ *Apr.–Sept., daily 9:30–6:30; Oct.–Mar., daily 10–6:15. Métro: Cardinal-Lemoine; RER: Luxembourg.*

OFF THE BEATEN PATH **LYCÉE LOUIS-LE-GRAND –** Molière, Voltaire, and Robespierre studied at this venerable school, founded in 1530 by François I as the College of Three Languages. Students learned High Latin, Greek, and Hebrew as well as many other subjects eschewed by academics at the Sorbonne.

Today's buildings, dating from the 17th century, are still part of a school. From the Panthéon, follow rue Soufflot, then take the first right onto rue St-Jacques. ⊠ *123 rue St-Jacques. RER: Luxembourg.*

....

⑭ **Place de la Contrescarpe.** This intimate square behind the Panthéon doesn't start to swing until after dusk, when its cafés and bars fill up. During the day, the square looks almost provincial as Parisians flock to the daily market at the bottom of rue Mouffetard, a steeply sloping street that retains much of its bygone charm. *Métro: Monge.*

⑨ **Place St-Michel.** This square on the Seine was named for Gabriel Davioud's grandiose 1860 fountain, depicting St. Michael slaying the dragon. *Métro, RER: St-Michel.*

㉗ **Pont de l'Archevêché** (Archbishop's Bridge). This bridge, built in 1828, links Ile St-Louis to the Left Bank. The bridge offers a breathtaking view of the east end of the cathedral, ringed by flying buttresses, floating above the Seine like some vast stone ship. *Métro: Maubert-Mutualité.*

❶ **Pont Neuf** (New Bridge). Crossing the Ile de la Cité, just behind square du Vert-Galant, is the oldest bridge in Paris, confusingly called the New Bridge. It was completed in 1607 and was the first bridge in the city to be built without houses lining either side. *Métro: Pont-Neuf.*

❺ **Ste-Chapelle** (Holy Chapel). This chapel was built by the genial and pious Louis IX (1226–70), whose good works ensured his subsequent canonization. It was conceived as home for what Louis believed to be the crown of thorns from Christ's crucifixion and fragments of the true cross; he acquired these from the impoverished Emperor Baldwin of Constantinople at phenomenal expense. Architecturally, for all its delicate and ornate exterior decoration—notice the open latticework of the pencil-like *flèche,* or spire, on the roof—the design of the building is simplicity itself. In essence, it's no more than a thin, rectangular box, much taller than it is wide. But think of it first and foremost as an oversize reliquary, an ornate medieval casket designed to house holy relics. The building is actually two chapels in one. The plainer, first-floor chapel, made gloomy by insensitive mid-19th-century restorations (which could do with restoration themselves), was for servants and lowly members of the court. The infinitely more spectacular upper chapel, up a dark spiral staircase, was for the king and important members of the court. The chapel walls, consisting mainly of stained glass, constitute a technical tour de force. Here, again, some clumsy 19th-century work has added a deadening touch, but the glory of the chapel—the stained glass—is spectacularly intact. The chapel is airy and diaphanous, the walls glowing and sparkling as light plays on the windows. Notice how the walls, in fact, consist of at least twice as much glass as masonry: The entire aim of the architects was to provide the maximum amount of window space. Ste-Chapelle is one of the supreme achievements of the Middle Ages and is a highlight of Paris. Come early in the day to avoid the dutiful crowds that trudge around it. Better still, try to attend one of the regular, candlelit concerts. ⊠ *4 bd. du Palais,* ☎ *01-43-54-30-09 for concert information.* ⊠ *32 frs; joint ticket with Conciergerie 50 frs.* ☉ *Daily 9:30–6:30; winter, daily 10–5. Métro: Cité.*

⑬ **St-Etienne-du-Mont.** The ornate facade of this mainly 16th-century church combines Gothic, Baroque, and Renaissance elements. Inside, the curly, carved rood screen (1525–35), separating nave and chancel, is the only one of its kind in Paris. Note the uneven-floored chapel behind the choir, which can be reached via a cloister containing exquisite 17th-century stained glass. ⊠ *Pl. de l'Abbé-Basset. Métro: Cardinal-Lemoine.*

❼ St-Julien-le-Pauvre. This tiny church was built at the same time as Notre-Dame (1165–1220), on a site where a succession of chapels once stood. The church belongs to a Greek Orthodox order today, but was originally named for St. Julian, bishop of Le Mans, who was nicknamed Le Pauvre after he gave all his money away. ⊠ *rue St-Julien-le-Pauvre. Métro: St-Michel.*

OFF THE
BEATEN PATH

ST-NICOLAS DU CHARDONNET – The first church on the site was apparently built in a field of *chardons* (thistles), and, more recently, St-Nicolas has been a thorn in the side of the Catholic Church by refusing to abandon Latin mass. Stubborn priests are not, however, the most visible attraction of this pleasant Baroque edifice (1656–1709) just off Place Maubert. There is a Corot study for the *Baptism of Christ* in the first chapel on the right and a *Crucifixion* by Brueghel the Younger in the sacristy. To get there from St-Julien, cross the garden behind the church and take rue Lagrange, which turns into rue Monge and leads to this square. ⊠ *Sq. de la Mutualité. Métro: Maubert-Mutualité.*

⑲ St-Louis de la Salpêtrière. The church of the Salpêtrière Hospital stands next to the Gare d'Austerlitz, which it dominates with its unmistakable, lantern-topped octagonal dome. It was built (1670–77) in the shape of a Greek cross from the designs of Libéral Bruant. ⊠ *bd. de l'Hôpital. Métro: Gare d'Austerlitz.*

㉕ St-Louis-en-l'Ile. The only church on the Ile St-Louis, built from 1664 to 1726 to the Baroque designs of architect Louis Le Vau, is lavishly furnished and has two unusual exterior features: its original pierced spire, holy in every sense, and an iron clock added in 1741. ⊠ *rue St-Louis-en-l'Ile. Métro: Pont-Marie.*

NEED A
BREAK?

Cafés all over sell the haute couture of ice cream, but **Berthillon** (⊠ 31 rue St-Louis-en-l'Ile, ☎ 01–43–54–31–61) itself is the place to come. More than 30 flavors are served; expect to wait in line. The shop is open Wednesday–Sunday.

⑮ St-Médard. This church at the bottom of rue Mouffetard contains the painting *St. Joseph with the Christ Child* by Spanish master Zurbarán. The nave and facade, with its large late-Gothic window, date from the late 15th century. The 17th-century choir is in contrasting classical style. ⊠ *rue Mouffetard. Métro: Censier-Daubenton.*

OFF THE
BEATEN PATH

MANUFACTURE DES GOBELINS – Tapestries have been woven on this spot in southeastern Paris, on the banks of the long-covered Bièvre river that once flowed into the Seine, since 1662. Guided tours—in French only—combine historical explanation with the chance to admire both old tapestries and today's weavers at work in their airy workshops. ⊠ *42 av. des Gobelins,* ☎ *01–44–08–52–00.* ▦ *45 frs.* ☉ *Tues.–Thurs., guided tours only at 2 and 2:45. Métro: Gobelins.*

❽ St-Séverin. This unusually wide Flamboyant Gothic church dominates the Left Bank neighborhood filled with squares and pedestrian streets. In the 11th century, the church that stood here was the parish church for the entire Left Bank. Louis XIV's cousin, a capricious woman known simply as the Grande Mademoiselle, adopted St-Séverin when she tired of St-Sulpice; she then spent vast sums getting court decorator Le Brun to modernize the chancel in the 17th century. Note the splendidly deviant spiraling column in the forest of pillars behind the altar. ⊠ *rue des Prêtres St-Séverin.* ☉ *Weekdays 11–5:30, Sat. 11–10. Métro: St-Michel.*

⑪ **Sorbonne.** Named after Robert de Sorbon, a medieval canon who founded a theological college here in 1253 for 16 students, the Sorbonne is one of the oldest universities in Europe. For centuries it has been one of France's principal institutions of higher learning, as well as the hub of the Latin Quarter and nerve center of Paris's student population. The church and university buildings were restored by Cardinal Richelieu in the 17th century, and the maze of amphitheaters, lecture rooms, and laboratories, and the surrounding courtyards and narrow streets, retain a hallowed air. You can visit the main courtyard on rue de la Sorbonne and peek into the main lecture hall, a major meeting point during the tumultuous student upheavals of 1968 and also of interest for a giant mural by Puvis de Chavannes, the *Sacred Wood* (1880–89). The square is dominated by the university church, the noble **Église de la Sorbonne,** whose outstanding exterior features are its cupola and Corinthian columns. Inside is the white marble tomb of that ultimate crafty cleric, Cardinal Richelieu himself. ✉ *rue de la Sorbonne. Métro: Cluny–La Sorbonne.*

OFF THE **CENTRE DE LA MER ET DES EAUX** – A spell of fish-gazing is a soothing,
BEATEN PATH mesmerizing experience for young and old. The Center of Sea and Waters is one of the principal aquariums in Paris. From the Sorbonne, go up rue de la Sorbonne, then take the first left on rue Cujas, and a right on rue St-Jacques. ✉ *195 rue St-Jacques.* ▨ *30 frs.* ☉ *Tues.–Fri. 10–12:30 and 1:15–5:30, weekends 10–5:30. RER: Luxembourg.*

❷ **Square du Vert-Galant.** The equine statue of the Vert Galant himself—amorous adventurer Henri IV—surveys this leafy square at the western end of the Ile de la Cité. Henri, king of France from 1589 until his assassination in 1610, was something of a dashing figure, by turns ruthless and charming, a stern upholder of the absolute rights of monarchy, and a notorious womanizer. He is probably best remembered for his cynical remark that *"Paris vaut bien une messe"* ("Paris is worth a mass"), a reference to his readiness to renounce Protestantism to gain the throne of predominantly Catholic France and, indeed, be allowed to enter the city. To ease his conscience he issued the Edict of Nantes in 1598, according French Protestants (almost) equal rights with their Catholic counterparts. It was Louis XIV's renunciation of the edict nearly 100 years later that led to the massive Huguenot exodus from France—an economic catastrophe for the country. The square itself is a fine spot to linger on a sunny afternoon, and is the departure point for the glass-topped vedette tour boats on the Seine (at the bottom of the steps to the right). *Métro: Pont-Neuf.*

FROM ORSAY TO ST-GERMAIN

This walk covers the western half of the Left Bank, from the Musée d'Orsay in the stately 7ᵉ arrondissement, to the Faubourg St-Germain, a lively and colorful area in the 6ᵉ arrondissement. The Musée d'Orsay houses a superb array of Impressionist paintings in a spectacularly converted Belle Epoque rail station on the Seine. Farther along the river, the 18th-century Palais Bourbon, home to the National Assembly, sets the tone. Luxurious ministries and embassies—including the Hôtel Matignon, residence of the French prime minister—line the surrounding streets, their majestic scale completely in keeping with the Hôtel des Invalides, whose gold-leafed dome climbs heavenward above the regal tomb of Napoléon. The splendid Rodin Museum is only a short walk away.

To the east, the boulevard St-Michel slices the Left Bank in two: on one side, the Latin Quarter (☞ The Islands and the Latin Quarter, *above*);

on the other, the Faubourg St-Germain, named for St-Germain-des-Prés, the oldest church in Paris. The venerable church tower has long acted as a beacon for intellectuals, most famously during the 1950s when Albert Camus, Jean-Paul Sartre, and Simone de Beauvoir ate and drank existentialism in the neighborhood cafés. Today most of the philosophizing is done by tourists, yet a wealth of bookshops, art stores, and antiques galleries ensure that "St-Germain," as the area is known, retains its highbrow appeal. A highlight of St-Germain is the Jardin du Luxembourg, the city's most famous and colorful park. The 17th-century palace overlooking the gardens houses the French Senate.

Numbers in the text correspond to numbers in the margin and on the Orsay to St-Germain map.

A Good Walk

Arrive at the **Musée d'Orsay** ① early to avoid the crowds that flock to see the museum's outstanding works of art. A good meeting point is the pedestrian square outside the museum, where huge bronze statues of an elephant and a rhinoceros disprove the notion that the French take their art *too* seriously. Across the square stands the **Musée de la Légion d'Honneur** ②, where you can find an array of French and foreign decorations. From here, if you're short on time, you can cut south down rue de Bellechasse to the Hôtel Matignon (☞ *below*). Otherwise, head west along rue de Lille to the **Palais Bourbon** ③, home of the Assemblée Nationale (the French Parliament). There's a fine view across the Seine to Place de la Concorde and the church of the Madeleine.

Rue de l'Université leads from the Assemblée to the grassy Esplanade des Invalides and an encounter with the **Hôtel des Invalides** ④, founded by Louis XIV to house wounded (*invalid*) veterans. The most impressive dome in Paris towers over the church at the back of the Invalides— the Église du Dôme. From the church, turn left, then left again into boulevard des Invalides, then right on rue de Varenne to reach the Hôtel Biron, better known as the **Musée Rodin** ⑤. Here you can see a fine collection of Auguste Rodin's emotionally charged statues. The quiet, distinguished 18th-century streets between the Rodin Museum and the Parliament are filled with embassies and ministries. The most famous, farther along rue de Varenne, is the **Hôtel Matignon** ⑥, residence of the French prime minister. Just before, at No. 51, is one of Paris's handful of private cul-de-sacs. Next door at No. 53 you can pay your respects to American novelist Edith Wharton, who lived and worked here from 1910 to 1920. Take the next left into rue du Bac, then right onto rue de Grenelle, past the **Musée Maillol** ⑦, dedicated to the work of sculptor Aristide Maillol, and Bouchardon's monumental **Fontaine des Quatre Saisons** ⑧.

Turn left down boulevard Raspail and cross to rue de Luynes. Carry on across boulevard St-Germain to inspect the stately 17th-century church of **St-Thomas d'Aquin** ⑨, then double back and head east along boulevard St-Germain for 400 yards to the **Café de Flore** ⑩, one of the principal haunts of the intelligentsia after World War II. Another popular café, two doors down, is **Les Deux Magots** ⑪; politicians and showbiz types still wine and dine at the pricey Brasserie Lipp (☞ Chapter 2) across the street. Looming above cobbled Place St-Germain-des-Prés stands **St-Germain-des-Prés** ⑫, Paris's oldest church.

Follow rue de l'Abbaye, along the far side of the church, to rue de Furstenberg. The street opens out into a quiet square, bedecked with white globe lamps and catalpa trees, where you'll find Eugène Delacroix's studio, the **Atelier Delacroix** ⑬. Take a left on rue Jacob and turn right down rue Bonaparte to the **École Nationale des Beaux-Arts** ⑭, whose

Orsay to St-Germain

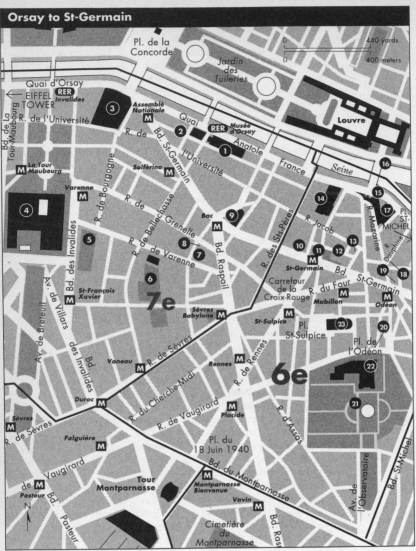

Atelier Delacroix, **13**

Café de Flore, **10**

Carrefour de Buci, **18**

Les Deux Magots, **11**

École Nationale des Beaux-Arts, **14**

Fontaine de Quatre Saisons, **8**

Hôtel des Invalides, **4**

Hôtel Matignon, **6**

Hôtel des Monnaies, **17**

Institut de France, **15**

Jardin du Luxembourg, **21**

Musée de la Légion d'Honneur, **2**

Musée Maillol, **7**

Musée d'Orsay, **1**

Musée Rodin, **5**

Palais Bourbon, **3**

Palais du Luxembourg, **22**

Pont des Arts, **16**

Le Procope, **19**

St-Germain-des-Prés, **12**

St-Sulpice, **23**

St-Thomas d'Aquin, **9**

Théâtre de l'Odéon, **20**

students can often be seen painting and sketching on the nearby quays and bridges. Wander into the courtyard and galleries of the school to see the casts and copies of the statues stored here for safekeeping during the Revolution.

Continue down to the Seine and turn right along the quai, past the **Institut de France** ⑮. With its distinctive dome and commanding position overlooking the **Pont des Arts** ⑯—a footbridge affording delightful views of the Louvre and Ile de la Cité—the Institute is one of the city's most impressive waterside sights. Farther along, on quai de Conti, you pass the **Hôtel des Monnaies** ⑰, the national mint.

Head up rue Dauphine, the street that singer Juliet Greco put on the map when she opened the erstwhile Tabou jazz club here in the '50s. It's linked 150 yards up by the open-air passage Dauphine to rue Mazarine, which leads left to the **Carrefour de Buci** ⑱, a busy crossroad. Fanning out from the Carrefour are lively rue de Buci, with one of the best morning food markets in Paris; rue de l'Ancienne-Comédie, so named because it was the first home of the legendary Comédie Française, cutting through to busy Place de l'Odéon; and rue St-André des Arts, which leads swiftly to the historic **Cour du Commerce St-André** (opposite No. 66), a cobbled pedestrian street. Halfway down on the left—opposite the oldest café in Paris, **Le Procope** ⑲—stands one of the few remaining towers of the 12th-century fortress wall built by Philippe-Auguste, overlooking a tiny courtyard, the **Cour de Rohan.** (From here it's a short walk to Place St-Michel; ☞ The Islands and the Latin Quarter, *above*.)

Head to the end of cour du Commerce St-André, cross boulevard St-Germain, and climb rue de l'Odéon to the colonnaded **Théâtre de l'Odéon** ⑳. Behind the theater, across rue de Vaugirard, lies the spacious **Jardin du Luxembourg** ㉑, one of the most stylish parks in the city. The large pond, usually animated by an armada of toy boats that can be hired alongside, enjoys the scenic backdrop of the rusticated **Palais du Luxembourg** ㉒. Today the palace houses the French Senate and is not open to the public.

Return to rue de Vaugirard and head west before turning right down pretty rue Férou to Place St-Sulpice, a spacious square ringed with cafés; Yves St-Laurent's famous Rive Gauche store is at No. 6. Looming over the square is the enormous church of **St-Sulpice** ㉓. If you wish to now explore Montparnasse (☞ *below*), walk west down rue du Vieux-Colombier and take the métro three stops to Vavin.

TIMING

Depending on how long you spend in the plethora of museums and shops along the way, this 6½-km (4-mi) walk could take four hours to a couple of days. Aim for an early start—that way you can hit the Musée d'Orsay early, when crowds are smaller, then get to the rue de Buci street market in full swing, in the late afternoon (the stalls are generally closed for lunch until 3 PM). Note that the Hôtel des Invalides is open daily, but Orsay is closed Monday. You might consider returning to one or more museums on another day or night—Orsay is open late on Thursday evenings.

Sights to See

⑬ **Atelier Delacroix.** The studio of artist Eugène Delacroix (1798–1863) contains only a small collection of his sketches and drawings, but if you want to pay homage to France's foremost Romantic painter, it's a good place to visit. ✉ *6 rue Furstenberg,* ☎ *01-43-54-04-87.* ✉ *22 frs.* ☉ *Wed.–Mon. 9:30–5:30. Métro: St-Germain-des-Prés.*

⑩ Café de Flore. In the postwar years, Jean-Paul Sartre and Simone de Beauvoir would meet their friends and followers at this popular café (☞ Chapter 2). These days it's mostly filled with tourists. ⊠ *172 bd. St-Germain. Métro: St-Germain-des-Prés.*

⑱ Carrefour de Buci. This crossroads was once a notorious Left Bank landmark: During the 18th century, it contained a gallows, an execution stake, and an iron collar for punishing troublemakers. In September 1792 the revolutionary army used this daunting site to enroll its first volunteers, and many Royalists and priests lost their heads here during the bloody course of the Revolution. There's nothing sinister, however, about the carrefour today, as brightly colored flowers spill onto the sidewalk at the flower shop on the corner of rue Grégoire-de-Tours. A couple of the small streets fanning out from the carrefour are of interest. **Rue de Buci** has a good outdoor food market (⊘ Tues.–Sat. 8–1 and 4–7, Sun. 9–1). **Rue de l'Ancienne-Comédie** got its name because it was the first home of the Comédie Française. *Métro: Mabillon.*

....

NEED A
BREAK?
If you happen to arrive when the market on rue de Buci is closed, **La Vieille France** (⊠ 14 rue de Buci, ☎ 01–43–26–55–13) patisserie may help fill the gap.

Cour du Commerce St-André. Revolutionary Jean-Paul Marat printed his newspaper, *L'Ami du Peuple,* at No. 8; and at No. 9, Dr. Guillotin conceived the idea for a new, "humane" method of execution—it was rumored that he practiced it on sheep first—that remained in force for murderers until 1981. *Métro: Odéon.*

....

Cour de Rohan (Rohan Courtyard). This series of cloistered courtyards and passageways was once part of the home of the archbishops of Rouen (over the years the name was transformed into Rohan). It's now lined with cafés and shops. ⊠ *Entrance on cour du Commerce St-André. Métro: Odéon.*

⑪ Les Deux Magots. This old-fashioned St-Germain café, named after the two Chinese figures, or *magots,* inside, still thrives on its post–World War II reputation as one of the Left Bank's prime meeting places for the intelligentsia. It remains crowded day and night, but these days you're more likely to rub shoulders with tourists than with philosophers. Still, if you are in search of the mysterious glamour of the Left Bank you can do no better than to station yourself at one of the sidewalk tables—or at a window table on a wintry day—to watch the passing parade. ⊠ *6 Pl. St-Germain-des-Prés,* ☎ *01–45–48–55–25. Métro: St-Germain-des-Prés.*

⑭ École Nationale des Beaux-Arts (National Fine Arts College). Occupying three large mansions near the Seine, this school—today the breeding ground for painters, sculptors, and architects—was once the site of a convent, founded in 1608 by Marguerite de Valois, the first wife of Henri IV. During the Revolution, the convent was turned into a depot for works of art salvaged from the monuments that were under threat of destruction by impassioned mobs. Only the church and cloister remained by the time the Beaux-Arts school was established in 1816. ⊠ *14 rue Bonaparte.* ⊘ *Daily 1–7. Métro: St-Germain-des-Prés.*

....

NEED A
BREAK?
The popular **La Palette** café (⊠ 43 rue de Seine, ☎ 01–43–26–68–15), on the corner of rue de Seine and rue Callot, has long been a favorite haunt of Beaux-Arts students. One of them painted the ungainly portrait of the patron, François, that presides with mock authority.

....

⑧ Fontaine des Quatre Saisons (Four Seasons Fountain). This allegorical fountain, designed by Edmé Bouchardon in 1739 to help boost the district's water supply, has a wealth of sculpted detail. Flanked by a majestic curved screen, the seated figure of *Paris,* framed by Ionic columns, surveys the rivers *Seine* and *Marne,* while bas-reliefs peopled by industrious cupids represent the seasons. ⊠ *57–59 rue de Grenelle. Métro: Rue du Bac.*

④ Hôtel des Invalides. Les Invalides, as it is widely known, is an outstanding monumental Baroque ensemble, designed by architect Libéral Bruand in the 1670s at the behest of Louis XIV to house wounded (*invalid*) soldiers. Although no more than a handful of old soldiers live at the Invalides today, the military link remains in the form of the **Musée de l'Armée** (Army Museum), one of the world's foremost military museums, with a vast, albeit musty, collection of arms, armor, uniforms, banners, and military pictures down through the ages. In the same space as the Army Museum, the **Musée des Plans-Reliefs** (Model Museum) contains a fascinating collection of old scale models of French towns; the largest and most impressive is Strasbourg, which takes up an entire room. The main, cobbled courtyard is a fitting scene for the parades and ceremonies still occasionally held at the Invalides.

The 17th-century **Église St-Louis des Invalides**, the Invalides's original church, was the site of the first performance of Berlioz's *Requiem,* in 1837. The most impressive dome in Paris towers over Jules Hardouin-
★ Mansart's **Église du Dôme** (Dome Church), built onto the end of Église St-Louis but blocked off from it in 1793—no great pity, perhaps, as the two buildings are vastly different in style and scale. The remains of Napoléon are here, in a series of no fewer than six coffins, one inside the next, within a bombastic tomb of red porphyry, ringed by low reliefs and a dozen statues symbolizing Napoléon's campaigns. Among others commemorated in the church are French World War I hero Marshal Foch; Napoléon's brother Joseph, erstwhile king of Spain; and fortification builder Vauban.

Some 200 display cabinets in the west wing of the Invalides, at the **Musée de l'Ordre de la Libération** (Order of Liberation Museum), evoke various episodes of World War II: De Gaulle's Free France organization, the Resistance, the Deportation, and the 1944 Liberation. The Order of the Liberation was created by General de Gaulle after the fall of France in 1940 to honor those who made outstanding contributions to the Allied victory in World War II (Churchill and Eisenhower figure among the rare foreign recipients). ⊠ *Pl. des Invalides; Liberation Museum entrance: 51 bis bd. de La Tour-Maubourg.* ☎ *01–44–42–37–67 Army and Model museums; 01–47–05–35–15 Liberation Museum.* ▨ *Dome Church: 37 frs; Army and Model museums: 38 frs; Liberation Museum: 10 frs.* ☉ *Dome Church: daily 10–5:45, winter, daily 10–4:45; Army and Model museums: daily 10–5:45 (to 4:45 in winter); Liberation Museum: Mon.–Sat. 2–5. Métro: La Tour-Maubourg.*

NEED A BREAK? A short trek down boulevard des Invalides to rue de Babylone is the **Pagode** (⊠ 57 bis rue de Babylone), a movie theater and small tearoom, which offers an exotic environment for sipping hot tea and cooling your heels. It's open Monday–Saturday 4–10 and Sunday 2–8.

⑥ Hôtel Matignon. The residence of the French prime minister is the Left Bank counterpart to the president's Élysée Palace. "Matignon" was built in 1721, but only since 1958 has it housed heads of state. From 1888 to 1914, it was the embassy of the Austro-Hungarian Empire. ⊠ *57 rue de Varenne.* ☉ *Not open to the public. Métro: Varenne.*

⑰ **Hôtel des Monnaies** (Mint). Louis XVI transferred the Royal Mint to this imposing mansion in the late 18th century. Although the mint was moved again, to Pessac, near Bordeaux, in 1973, weights and measures, medals, and limited-edition coins are still made here. The **Musée de la Monnaie** (Coin Museum) has an extensive collection of coins, documents, engravings, and paintings. On Tuesday and Friday at 2 PM you can catch the coin metal craftsmen at work in their ateliers overlooking the Seine. ✉ *11 quai de Conti,* ☎ *01–40–46–55–35.* 🎫 *20 frs.* ☉ *Tues.–Fri. 11–5:30, weekends noon–5:30. Métro: Pont-Neuf.*

⑮ **Institut de France** (French Institute). The Institute is one of France's most revered cultural institutions, and its curved, dome-topped facade is one of the Left Bank's most impressive waterside sights. The Tour de Nesle, which formed part of Philippe-Auguste's wall fortifications along the Seine, used to stand here and, in its time, had many royal occupants, including Henry V of England. The French novelist Alexandre Dumas (1824–95) featured the stormy history of the Tour de Nesle—during which the lovers of a number of French queens were tossed from its windows—in a melodrama of the same name. In 1661 the wealthy Cardinal Mazarin left 2 million French *livres* (pounds) in his will for construction of a college that would be dedicated to educating students from Piedmont, Alsace, Artois, and Roussillon, provinces that had been annexed to France during the years of his ministry. Mazarin's coat of arms is sculpted on the dome, and the public library in the east wing, which holds more than 350,000 volumes, still bears his name.

At the beginning of the 19th century, Napoleon stipulated that the Institute be transferred here from the Louvre. The Académie Française, the oldest of the five academies that compose the Institute, was created by Cardinal Richelieu in 1635. Its first major task was to edit the definitive French dictionary (which still isn't finished); it is also charged with safeguarding the purity of the French language. Election to its ranks, subject to approval by the French head of state, is the highest literary honor in the land—there can only be 40 "immortal" lifelong members at any one time. The appointment of historian and author Marguerite Yourcenar to the Académie in 1986 broke the centuries-old tradition of the academy as a male bastion. The Institute also embraces the Académie des Beaux-Arts, the Académie des Sciences, the Académie des Inscriptions et Belles Lettres, and the Académie des Sciences Morales et Politiques. ✉ *Pl. de l'Institut.* ☉ *Guided visits reserved for cultural associations only. Métro: Pont-Neuf.*

㉑ **Jardin du Luxembourg** (Luxembourg Garden). One of the prettiest of Paris's few large parks, the Luxembourg Garden has fountains, ponds, trim hedges, precisely planted rows of trees, and gravel walks that are typical of the French fondness for formal gardens. The 17th-century Palais du Luxembourg (☞ *below*) provides an imposing backdrop. *Métro: Odéon; RER: Luxembourg.*

② **Musée de la Légion d'Honneur** (Legion of Honor Museum). French and foreign decorations are displayed in this elegant mansion by the Seine, officially known as the Hôtel de Salm. The original building, constructed in 1786, burned down during the Commune in 1871 and was rebuilt in 1878. ✉ *2 rue de Bellechasse,* ☎ *01–40–62–84–25.* 🎫 *25 frs.* ☉ *Tues.–Sun. 2–5. Métro: Solférino; RER: Musée d'Orsay.*

⑦ **Musée Maillol.** Bronzes by Art Deco sculptor Aristide Maillol (1861–1944), whose sleek, stylized nudes adorn the Tuileries Garden, can be admired at this handsome town house lovingly restored by his former muse, Dina Vierny. Maillol's drawings, paintings, and tapestries are also on show. Works by other artists include a roomful of Poliakoff abstractions and two sensuous Zitman nudes in the barrel-vaulted cellar café. ⊠ *61 rue de Grenelle,* ☏ *01–42–22–59–58.* 🎟 *40 frs.* ☉ *Wed.–Mon. 11–6. Métro: Rue du Bac.*

❶ Musée d'Orsay. Since opening in December 1986, the Musée d'Orsay—devoted to the arts (mainly French) spanning the period 1848–1914—has become one of the city's most popular museums. Beginning in 1900, the building was used as a train station for routes between Paris and the southwest of France. By 1939, the Gare d'Orsay had become too small for mainline travel, and intercity trains were transferred to the Gare d'Austerlitz. Gare d'Orsay became a suburban terminus until it closed in the 1960s. The building was temporarily used as a theater, an auction house, and a setting for Orson Welles's movie *The Trial,* based on Kafka's novel, before it was finally slated for demolition. However, the destruction of the 19th-century Les Halles (market halls) across the Seine provoked a furor among conservationists, and in the late 1970s, former president Giscard d'Estaing ordered Orsay to be transformed into a museum. Architects Pierre Colboc, Renaud Bardou, and Jean-Paul Philippon were commissioned to remodel the building; Gae Aulenti, known for her renovation of the Palazzo Grassi in Venice, was hired to reshape the interior. Aulenti's modern design in a building almost a century old provoked much controversy, but the museum's attributes soon outweighed any criticism.

The museum sets out to form a bridge between the classical collections of the Louvre and the modern collections of the Pompidou Center. Exhibits take up three floors, but the immediate impression is of a single, vast, stationlike hall. The chief artistic attraction is the Impressionists, whose works are displayed under the roof. Renoir, Sisley, Pissarro, and Monet arc all well represented. Highlights include Monet's *Les Coquelicots* (*Poppy Fields*) and Renoir's *Le Moulin de la Galette* (*Biscuit Windmill*), which differs from many other Impressionist paintings in that Renoir worked from numerous studies and completed it in his studio rather than painting it in the open air. Nonetheless, its focus on the activities of a group of ordinary Parisians amusing themselves in the sun on a Montmartre afternoon is typical of the spontaneity and fleeting sense of moment that are the essence of Impressionism. Whereas Monet, the only one of the group to adhere faithfully to the tenets of Impressionism throughout his career, strove to catch the effects of light, Renoir was more interested in the human figure.

The post-Impressionists—Cézanne, van Gogh, Gauguin, and Toulouse-Lautrec—are also represented on the top floor. You may find the intense, almost classical serenity of Cézanne the dominant presence here; witness his magnificent Mont Ste-Victoire series, in which he paints and repaints the same subject, in the process dissolving form until the step to cubism and abstract painting seems an inevitability. Or you may be drawn by the vivid simplicity and passion of van Gogh or by the psychedelic, pagan rhythms of Gauguin.

On the first floor are the works of Manet and the delicate nuances of Degas. Be sure to see Manet's *Déjeuner sur l'Herbe* (*Lunch on the Grass*), the painting that scandalized Paris in 1863 at the Salon des Refusés, an exhibit organized by artists refused permission to show their work at the Academy's official annual salon. The painting shows a nude woman and two clothed men picnicking in a park. In the background, another girl bathes in a stream. Manet took the subject, poses and all, from a little-known Renaissance print in the Louvre but updated the clothing to mid-19th century France. What would otherwise have been thought a respectable "academic" painting thus became deeply shocking: two clothed men with a naked woman in 19th-century

France! The loose, bold brushwork, a far cry from the polished styles of the Renaissance, added insult to artistic injury. Another reworking by Manet of a classical motif is his reclining nude, *Olympia*. Gazing boldly out from the canvas, she was more than respectable 19th-century Parisian proprieties could stand.

If you prefer more academic paintings, look at Puvis de Chavannes's larger-than-life classical canvases. The pale, limpid beauty of his figures is enjoying considerable attention after years of neglect. If you are excited by more modern developments, look for the early 20th-century Fauves (meaning wild beasts, the name given them by an outraged critic in 1905)—particularly Matisse, Derain, and Vlaminck. Thought-provoking sculptures also litter the museum at every turn. Two further highlights are the faithfully restored Belle Epoque restaurant and the model of the entire Opéra quarter, displayed beneath a glass floor. ⊠ *1 rue de la Légion d'Honneur,* ☎ *01–40–49–48–14.* ⌻ *40 frs, Sun. 30 frs.* ☉ *Tues.–Sat. 10–6, Thurs. 10–9:45, Sun. 9–6. Métro: Solférino; RER: Musée d'Orsay.*

NEED A BREAK?   Find respite from the overwhelming collection of art in the **Musée d'Or-say Café,** in the Musée d'Orsay behind one of the giant station clocks, close to the Impressionist galleries on the top floor. From the rooftop terrace alongside there is a panoramic view across the Seine toward Montmartre and Sacré-Coeur.

---

❺ Musée Rodin. The splendid Hôtel Biron, with its spacious vestibule, broad staircase, and light, airy rooms, retains much of its 18th-century atmosphere and makes a gracious setting for the sculpture of Auguste Rodin (1840–1917). You'll doubtless recognize the seated *Le Penseur* (*The Thinker*), with his elbow resting on his knee, and the passionate *Le Baiser* (*The Kiss*). There is also an outstanding white marble bust of Austrian composer Gustav Mahler, as well as numerous examples of Rodin's obsession with hands and erotic subjects. From the second-floor rooms, which contain some fine if murky paintings by Rodin's friend Eugène Carrière (1849–1906), you can see the large garden behind the house. Don't skip the garden: It is exceptional both for its rosebushes (more than 2,000 of them, representing 100 varieties) and for its sculpture, including a powerful statue of the novelist Balzac and the despairing group of medieval city fathers known as the *Burghers of Calais.* ⊠ *77 rue de Varenne,* ☎ *01–44–18–61–10.* ⌻ *28 frs, Sun. 18 frs, gardens only 5 frs.* ☉ *Easter–Oct., Tues.–Sun. 10–5:45; Nov.–Easter, Tues.–Sun. 10–4:45. Métro: Varenne.*

❸ Palais Bourbon. The most prominent feature of the home of the Palais Bourbon—home of the Assemblée Nationale, the French Parliament since 1798—is its colonnaded facade, commissioned by Napoléon to match that of the Madeleine. Cortot's sculpted pediment portrays France holding the tablets of law, flanked by Force and Justice. ⊠ *Pl. du Palais-Bourbon.* ☉ *During temporary exhibits only. Métro: Assemblée Nationale.*

OFF THE BEATEN PATH   **STE-CLOTILDE –** This neo-Gothic church (built 1846–58) is notable for its imposing twin spires, visible from across the Seine. French classical composer César Franck was organist here from 1858 to 1890. From the Palais Bourbon, take rue Bourgogne south, then take a left on rue Las-Cases. ⊠ *rue Las-Cases. Métro: Solférino.*

㉒ Palais du Luxembourg (Luxembourg Palace). The gray, imposing, rusticated Luxembourg Palace was built, like the surrounding Luxembourg Gardens, for Maria de Médicis, widow of Henri IV, at the beginning

Musée d'Orsay

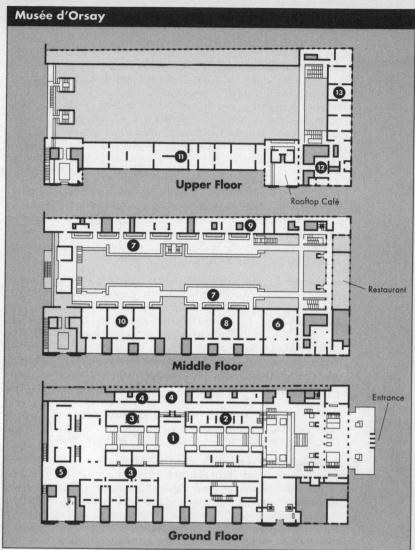

Upper Floor

Rooftop Café

Restaurant

Middle Floor

Entrance

Ground Floor

Architecture
1850–1900, **5**

Art Nouveau, **10**

Decorative Arts
1850–1880, **4**

Decorative Arts and
Interiors of the Third
Republic, **6**

History of Painting
and the Portrait
1850–1880, **2**

Impressionism
and Post-
Impressionism, **11**

Neo-
Impressionism, **12**

Painting before
1870, **3**

Painting
1880–1900, **8**

Painting after 1900, **9**

Rousseau; the
Pont-Aven School;
the Nabis, **13**

Sculpture, **7**

Sculpture
1850–1870, **1**

of the 17th century. Maria was born and raised in Florence's Pitti Palace, and, having languished in the Louvre after the death of her husband, she was eager to build herself a new palace, where she could recapture something of the lively, carefree atmosphere of her childhood. In 1612, she bought the Paris mansion of the Duke of Luxembourg, tore it down, and built her palace. It was not completed until 1627, and Marie was to live there for just five years. In 1632, Cardinal Richelieu had her expelled from France, and she saw out her declining years in Cologne, Germany, dying there almost penniless in 1642. The palace remained royal property until the Revolution, when the state took it over and used it as a prison. Danton, the painter David, and Thomas Paine were all detained here. Today the French Senate meets here, so the building is not open to the public. ⊠ *15 rue de Vaugirard. Métro: Odéon; RER: Luxembourg.*

🟢 **Pont des Arts** (Bridge of Arts). This elegant iron-and-wood footbridge linking the Louvre to the Institut de France is a favorite with painters, art students, and misty-eyed romantics moved by the delightful views of the Ile de la Cité. The bridge got its name because the Louvre was once called the Palais des Arts. *Métro: Pont-Neuf.*

🟢 **Le Procope.** The oldest café in Paris was opened in 1686 by an Italian named Francesco Procopio. Many of Paris's most famous literary sons and daughters have imbibed here through the centuries, ranging from erudite academics like Denis Diderot to debauchees like Oscar Wilde, as well as Voltaire, Balzac, George Sand, Victor Hugo, and even Benjamin Franklin, who popped in whenever business brought him to Paris. The fomenters of the French Revolution met at the Procope, too, so old Ben may have rubbed shoulders with Marat, Danton, Robespierre, and company. In 1988 a large restaurant group bought the Procope, aiming to give it a "new lease on life and a renewed literary and cultural vocation." They have succeeded in resuscitating it as a restaurant, but it's now filled with tourists, not writers. ⊠ *13 rue de l'Ancienne-Comédie,* ☎ *01–43–26–99–20. Métro: Odéon.*

🟢 **St-Germain-des-Prés.** Paris's oldest church was first built to shelter a relic of the true cross, brought back from Spain in AD 542. The chancel was enlarged and the church then consecrated by Pope Alexander III in 1163; the tall, sturdy tower—a Left Bank landmark—dates from this period. The colorful 19th-century frescoes in the nave by Hippolyte Flandrin, a pupil of the classical painter Ingres, depict vivid scenes from the Old Testament. The church stages superb organ concerts and recitals. ⊠ *Pl. St-Germain-des-Prés.* ☉ *Weekdays 8–7:30; weekends 8–9. Métro: St-Germain-des-Prés.*

🟢 **St-Sulpice.** Dubbed the Cathedral of the Left Bank, this enormous 17th-century church has entertained some unlikely christenings—the Marquis de Sade's and Charles Baudelaire's, for instance—and the nuptials of irreverent wordsmith Victor Hugo. The 18th-century facade was never finished, and its unequal towers add a playful touch to an otherwise sober design. The interior is baldly impersonal, despite the magnificent Delacroix frescoes—notably *Jacob Luttant avec l'Ange* (*Jacob Wrestling with the Angel*)—in the first chapel on your right. ⊠ *Pl. St-Sulpice. Métro: St-Sulpice.*

🟢 **St-Thomas d'Aquin.** This elegant, domed church, designed by Pierre Bulet in 1683, was originally dedicated to St-Dominique and flanked by a convent—whose buildings now belong to the Army. The east-end chapel was added in 1722 and the two-tiered facade in 1768. Pope Pius VII popped in during his trip to Paris for Napoleon's coronation in December 1804. ⊠ *Pl. St-Thomas-d'Aquin. Métro: Rue du Bac.*

㉑ **Théâtre de l'Odéon.** At the north end of the Luxembourg Gardens, on Place de l'Odéon, sits the colonnaded Odéon Theater. It was established in 1792 to house the Comédie Française troupe; the original building was destroyed by fire in 1807. Since World War II it has specialized in 20th-century productions and was the base for Jean-Louis Barrault's and Madeleine Renaud's theater company, the Théâtre de France, until they fell out of favor with the authorities for their alleged role in spurring on student revolutionaries in May 1968. Today, the theater is the French home of the Theater of Europe and stages excellent productions by major foreign companies, sometimes in English (☞ Chapter 4). ⊠ *Pl. de l'Odéon,* ☎ *01–44–41–36–36. Métro: Odéon.*

MONTPARNASSE

A mile to the south of the Seine lies the Montparnasse district, named after Mount Parnassus, the Greek mountain associated with the worship of Apollo and the Muses. Montparnasse's cultural heyday came in the first four decades of the 20th century, when it replaced Montmartre as *the* place for painters and poets to live. Pablo Picasso, Amedeo Modigliani, Ernest Hemingway, Jean Cocteau, and Leon Trotsky were among the luminaries who spawned an intellectual café society—later to be found at St-Germain (☞ From Orsay to St-Germain, *above*)—and prompted the launch of a string of arty brasseries along the district's main thoroughfare, the broad boulevard du Montparnasse.

The boulevard may lack poetic charm these days, but nightlife stays the pace as bars, clubs, restaurants, and cinemas crackle with energy beneath continental Europe's tallest high-rise: the 59-story Tour Montparnasse. Although the Tower itself is a typically bland product of the early 1970s, of note only for the view from the top, several more adventurous buildings have risen in its wake. Ricardo Bofil's semicircular Amphithéâtre housing complex, with its whimsical postmodernist quotations of classical detail, is the most famous. The glass-cubed Cartier center for contemporary art, and the Montparnasse train station with its giant glass facade and designer garden above the tracks, are other outstanding examples.

If you have a deeper feel for history, you may prefer the sumptuous Baroque church of Val-de-Grâce or the quiet earth of Montparnasse cemetery, where Baudelaire, Sartre, Bartholdi (who designed the Statue of Liberty), and actress Jean Seberg slumber. The Paris underground had its headquarters nearby—in the Roman catacombs—during the Nazi occupation. After ignoring Hitler's orders to blow up the city, it was in Montparnasse that Governor von Choltitz signed the German surrender in August 1944.

Numbers in the text correspond to numbers in the margin and on the Montparnasse map.

A Good Walk

Take the métro or walk to the Vavin station (only three stops from St-Sulpice; ☞ From Orsay to St-Germain, *above*), beneath Rodin's 10-ft statue of Balzac and alongside the round-ended café La Rotonde at the corner of boulevards Raspail and Montparnasse. Three other cafés, famous since Montparnasse's interwar heyday, are all within a stone's throw on boulevard du Montparnasse: Le Sélect at No. 99 and, across the street, the Café du Dôme (No. 108) and **La Coupole** ①, with its painted columns and restored Art Deco interior (No. 102) (☞ Chapter 2). Head west along boulevard du Montparnasse to **Place du 18-Juin-1940** ②. Towering above the square is the **Tour Montparnasse** ③. Behind the building is the huge, gleaming glass facade of Gare Montparnasse, the train station that is home to the 200-mph *TGV Atlantique,* serving western France.

Cross Place Bienvenüe, to the right of Tour Montparnasse, then take avenue Maine, then your first left into rue Antoine-Bourdelle. The sharp brick outlines of the **Musée Bourdelle** ④, full of the powerful sculpture of Antoine Bourdelle, loom halfway along. Continue to the end of the street and turn left into rue Armand-Moissant; note the elegant beige and green brick facade of the Ecole Commerciale on your left before turning right onto boulevard de Vaugirard. There's a fine view from here of Tour Montparnasse away to your left. A short way along the boulevard is the **Musée de la Poste** ⑤, a must if you're a stamp collector. Cross the boulevard and take the elevator by No. 25 to reach the **Jardin Atlantique** ⑥, a modern park laid over the rail tracks of Montparnasse station. Memories of World War II—notably the French Resistance and the Liberation of Paris—are evoked in a modern museum at the park entrance.

Cross the Jardin Atlantique at the far end and turn left down to **Place de Catalogne** ⑦, dominated by the monumental curves of the postmodern Amphithéâtre housing complex. Explore its arcades and circular forecourts, and compare its impersonal grandeur with the cozy charm of the small church of Notre-Dame du Travail behind. Rue Jean-Zay leads from Place de Catalogne to the corner of the high-walled **Cimetière du Montparnasse** ⑧. Enter the cemetery down rue Froidevaux if you wish to pay homage to local and foreign worthies. Rue Froidevaux continues to Place Denfert-Rochereau, where you can admire the huge bronze *Lion of Belfort* by Frédéric-Auguste Bartholdi, the sculptor of the Statue of Liberty (he, too, is buried in Montparnasse cemetery), and visit the extensive underground labyrinth of the **Catacombs** ⑨, which tunnel under much of the Left Bank and the suburbs.

Walk up boulevard Raspail, past the eye-catching glass cube that houses the **Fondation Cartier** ⑩. Take the third right onto rue Campagne-Première, a handsome street once inhabited by Picasso, Miró, Kandinsky, and Modigliani. Note the tiled facade on the artists' residence at No. 31. Turn right at the bottom of the street onto boulevard du Montparnasse. At avenue de l'Observatoire stands perhaps the most famous bastion of Left Bank café culture, the **Closerie des Lilas** ⑪. Up avenue de l'Observatoire is the **Observatoire de Paris** ⑫, Louis XIV's astronomical observatory. In the other direction, the tree-lined avenue sweeps past the **Fontaine de l'Observatoire** ⑬. To the right of the fountain, at the bottom of rue du Val-de-Grâce, is the imposing Baroque dome of **Val de Grâce** ⑭. Straight ahead is the Jardin du Luxembourg (☞ From Orsay to St-Germain, *above*).

TIMING

This walk around Montparnasse is just under 5-km (3-mi) long and should comfortably take a morning or an afternoon if you choose to check out one of the historic cafés, the cemetery, and the catacombs along the way.

Sights to See

⑨ Catacombs. Enter the Paris catacombs, originally built by the Romans to quarry stone, from Place Denfert-Rochereau. The square was named after General Denfert-Rochereau (d. 1878) in 1879, the heroic Governor of Belfort during the Prussian invasion of 1870. The square had been known as Place d'Enfer (Hell Square) until it was punningly renamed after the general. The catacombs, which tunnel under much of the Left Bank, were used to store millions of skeletons from disused graveyards; during World War II, they were the headquarters of the French

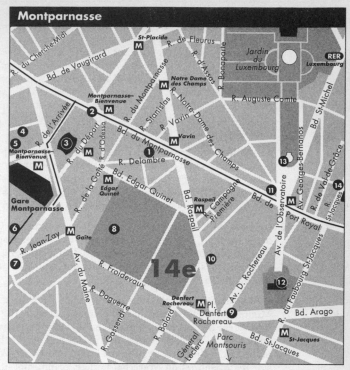

Resistance. Bring a flashlight. ⊠ *1 Pl. Denfert-Rochereau,* ☏ *01–43–22–47–63.* 🎟 *27 frs.* ☉ *Tues.–Fri. 2–4, weekends 9–11 and 2–4. Guided tours on Wed. at 2:45; 20 frs extra. Métro and RER: Denfert-Rochereau.*

⑧ Cimetière du Montparnasse (Montparnasse Cemetery). High walls encircle this cemetery, a haven of peace in one of Paris's busiest shopping and business areas. It is not picturesque (with the exception of the towered rump of an old windmill that used to be a student tavern) but contains many of the quarter's most illustrious residents, buried only a stone's throw away from where they lived and loved: Charles Baudelaire, Auguste Bartholdi (who designed the Statue of Liberty), Alfred Dreyfus, Guy de Maupassant, Camille Saint-Saëns, Jean-Paul Sartre, Tristan Tzara, and, more recently, photographer Man Ray, playwright Samuel Beckett, actress Jean Seberg, and singer-songwriter Serge Gainsbourg. ⊠ *Entrances on rue Froidevaux, bd. Edgar-Quinet. Métro: Raspail, Gaîté.*

⑪ Closerie des Lilas. Now a pricey bar-restaurant, the Closerie remains a staple of all literary tours of Paris. Commemorative plaques fastened to the bar mark the places where literati like Baudelaire, Verlaine, Hemingway, and Apollinaire used to station themselves. Although the lilacs (*lilas*) have gone from the terrace, it still opens onto a garden wall of luxuriant evergreen foliage, and is as crowded in the summer as it ever was in the '30s. ⊠ *171 bd. du Montparnasse,* ☏ *01–43–26–70–50. Métro: Vavin; RER: Port-Royal.*

OFF THE BEATEN PATH   **MUSÉE ZADKINE** - Russian-born sculptor Ossip Zadkine (1890–1967) trained in London before setting up in Paris in 1909. The works on exhibit at this museum, in Zadkine's former house and studio, reveal the influences of Rodin, African art, and Cubism. ⊠ *100 bis rue d'Assas,* ☏ *01–43–26–91–90.* 🎟 *27 frs.* ☉ *Tues.–Sun. 10–5:30. Métro: Vavin.*

① **La Coupole.** One of Montparnasse's most famous brasseries, La Coupole opened in 1927 as a bar–restaurant–dance hall and soon became a home-away-from-home for Apollinaire, Max Jacob, Cocteau, Satie, Stravinsky, and Hemingway. It may not be quite the same mecca these days, but it still pulls in a classy crowd. The columns painted by a host of Parisian artists, including Chagall and Brancusi, which lend La Coupole its Art Deco panache, were restored in the late '80s, along with the mosaic floor and original citronwood furniture (☞ Chapter 2). ⊠ *102 bd. du Montparnasse,* ☎ *01–43–20–14–20.* ☉ *Daily 7:30 AM–2 AM. Métro: Vavin.*

⑩ **Fondation Cartier** (Cartier Foundation). Architect Jean Nouvel's eye-catching giant glass cube is a suitable setting for the temporary, thought-provoking shows of contemporary art organized here by jewelry giant Cartier. ⊠ *261 bd. Raspail,* ☎ *01–42–18–56–50.* ⊠ *30 frs.* ☉ *Tues.–Sun. noon–8. Métro: Raspail.*

⑬ **Fontaine de l'Observatoire** (Observatory Fountain). Gabriel Davioud's fountain, built in 1873, is topped by Jean-Baptiste Carpeaux's four bronze statues of female nudes holding a globe, representing Les Quatre Parties du Monde (The Four Continents). ⊠ *av. de l'Observatoire. RER: Port-Royal.*

⑥ **Jardin Atlantique** (Atlantic Garden). Built over the tracks of Gare Montparnasse, this smart designer park, opened in 1994, features an assortment of trees and plants found in coastal regions near the Atlantic Ocean—thus the name. A museum building at the station end of the garden houses souvenirs and video coverage of World War II inside the **Mémorial du Maréchal-Leclerc**, commemorating the liberator of Paris, and the **Musée Jean-Moulin** (☎ 01–40–64–39–44, ⊠ 17 frs, ☉ Tues.–Sun. 10–5:40), devoted to the leader of the French Resistance. In the center of the park, what looks like a quirky piece of metallic sculpture is actually a meteorological center, with a battery of flickering lights reflecting temperature, wind speed, and monthly rainfall. ⊠ *Pont des Cinq-Martyrs-du-Lycée-Buffon. Métro: Montparnasse-Bienvenüe.*

④ **Musée Bourdelle** (Bourdelle Museum). Opened in 1949 in the studios and gardens where Rodin's pupil Antoine Bourdelle (1861–1929) lived and worked, and extended by Christian de Portzamparc in 1992, this spacious brick museum houses 500 works in plaster, marble, and bronze, including castings of Bourdelle's landmark works, *Heracles the Archer* and the *Dying Centaur.* ⊠ *18 rue Antoine-Bourdelle,* ☎ *01–49–54–73–73.* ⊠ *27 frs.* ☉ *Tues.–Sun. 10–5:40. Métro: Falguière.*

⑤ **Musée de la Poste** (Postal Museum). On display at this multistory museum of postal history are international and French stamps (dating as far back as 1849), postal carriers' uniforms and mailboxes, sorting and stamp-printing machines, and one of the balloons used to send mail out of Paris during the Prussian siege of 1870. Top-to-bottom renovation was expected to be finished by late 1999. ⊠ *24 bd. de Vaugirard,* ☎ *01–42–79–23–45.* ⊠ *25 frs.* ☉ *Mon.–Sat. 10–6. Métro: Montparnasse-Bienvenüe.*

⑫ **Observatoire de Paris** (Paris Observatory). The Observatory was constructed in 1667 for Louis XIV by architect Claude Perrault. Its four facades are aligned with the four cardinal points—north, south, east, and west—and its southern wall is the determining point for Paris's official latitude, 48° 50′11″N. French time was based on this Paris meridian until 1911, when the country decided to adopt the international Greenwich Meridian. ⊠ *av. de l'Observatoire. RER: Port-Royal.*

ARTISTS, WRITERS, AND EXILES

FOR THREE-QUARTERS OF a century—roughly from the 1880s to the 1950s—Paris enjoyed a reputation as Europe's most creative and bohemian capital, acting as a magnet for the international avant-garde.

The decades before World War I saw the slopes of **Montmartre,** in north Paris, alive with the sound of Belle Epoque music. Whirling windmills and swirling petticoats set the tone, no more so than at the Moulin Rouge cabaret, whose dancers doing the Can-Can were immortalized in posters and paintings by Toulouse-Lautrec. Femmes fatales? Lautrec drank and drugged himself to premature death.

Artists had moved into the district as early as the 1860s, when Monet and Manet pursued their interest in steam and rail at the Gare St-Lazare. New boulevards meant easier access to nearby Montmartre: Cheap and pretty, with an abundance of shady nightlife, it was an artist's dream. Van Gogh, Cézanne, Seurat, Signac, Degas, Vuillard, and Dufy all followed. Renoir painted his *Moulin de la Galette*; Picasso and Braque sighted Cubism in the Bateau Lavoir on Place Emile-Godeau.

Montmartre lost its luster after World War I; Utrillo remained, his repetitive street-scenes a weak postscript to the powerful austerity of his youthful White Period.

The Roaring Twenties saw the Paris art scene shift south to another hill: **Montparnasse.** Picasso and Modigliani decamped to rue Campagne-Première, joined by Miro and Kandinsky; Braque worked nearby in rue du Douanier-Rousseau.

Belle Epoque cabarets lost out to Art Deco bars and brasseries, a whole string of them along boulevard du Montparnasse: the Coupole, Dôme, Select, Rotonde, and the Closerie des Lilas, most of them assiduously frequented by Ernest Hemingway. Gertrude Stein held court for her "Lost Generation" near the Luxembourg Garden, hosting Picasso and writers like Ezra Pound, Henry Miller, and Zelda and F. Scott Fitzgerald. Redevelopment, epitomized by the Tour Montparnasse, has long since exiled aesthetes.

After World War II the literati went north to **St-Germain-des-Prés,** whose own cluster of cafés—Flore (where Sartre and de Beauvoir preached existentialism), Lipp, Les Deux Magots (once favored by Rimbaud and Gide)—became the beacon for left-wing intellectuals in the 1950s and 1960s.

Picture and antiques dealers crowd the streets of St-Germain, rubbing shoulders with the publishing houses that have been here since before Joyce first published *Ulysses* at Shakespeare & Company on rue de l'Odéon in 1922. Baudelaire, Voltaire, and Oscar Wilde (as well as Delacroix, Sibelius, and Wagner) all lived in the area; Voltaire died there in 1788, and Wilde expired round the corner at 13 rue des Beaux-Arts—a plaque on the building commemorates the spot and the street is still home to a fine-arts school.

THESE DAYS, HOWEVER, once they finish school, few art students stick around: Paris is no longer the thriving center for contemporary art that it once was. But intellectual ghosts still haunt the Left Bank: at the bouquinistes by the Seine, along the creaking floorboards of Shakespeare & Co., or in the tiny Théâtre de la Huchette, where Ionesco's Bald Soprano sings nightly for her supper to full houses.

7 Place de Catalogne (Catalonia Square). This circular square is dominated by the monumental **Amphithéâtre**, a housing complex built in the 1980s by architect Ricardo Boffil. Its chunky reinvention of classical detail may strike you as witty—or as overkill. Behind is the turn-of-the-century **Notre-Dame du Travail** church, which made a powerful statement when it was built: Its riveted iron-and-steel framework was meant to symbolize the work ethos enshrouded in the church's name. The Sebastopol Bell above the facade is a trophy from the Crimean War. ⊠ *Pl. de Catalogne. Métro: Gaîté.*

2 Place du 18-Juin-1940. This square beneath the Tour Montparnasse is named for the date of the radio speech Charles de Gaulle broadcast from London, urging the French to resist the Germans after the Nazi invasion of May 1940. It was here that German military governor Dietrich von Choltitz surrendered to the Allies in August 1944, ignoring Hitler's orders to destroy the city as he withdrew. A plaque on the wall of what is now a shopping center—originally the Montparnasse train station extended this far—commemorates the event. *Métro: Montparnasse-Bienvenue.*

3 Tour Montparnasse (Montparnasse Tower). As continental Europe's tallest skyscraper, completed in 1973, this 685-ft building offers a stupendous view of Paris from its open-air roof terrace. It attracts 800,000 visitors each year; on a clear day, you can see for 40 km (25 mi). A glossy brochure, "Paris Vu d'en Haut," explains just what to look for. It is also supposed to have the fastest elevator in Europe. Fifty-two of the 59 stories are taken up by offices, and a vast commercial complex, including a Galeries Lafayette department store, spreads over the first floor. Banal by day, the tower becomes Montparnasse's neon-lit beacon at night. ⊠ *33 av. du Maine.* ☎ *46 frs.* ⊘ *Apr.–Sept., daily 9:30 AM–11:30 PM; Oct.–Mar., Sun.–Thurs. 9:30 AM–10:30 PM, Fri.–Sat. 9:30 AM–11 PM. Métro: Montparnasse-Bienvenüe.*

14 Val de Grâce. This imposing 17th-century Left Bank church, extensively restored in the early 1990s, was commissioned by Anne of Austria and designed by François Mansart. Its powerfully rhythmic two-story facade rivals the Dôme Church at the Invalides as the city's most striking example of Italianate Baroque. Pierre Mignard's 1663 cupola fresco features more than 200 sky-climbing figures. The church's original abbey buildings are now a military army hospital, with a small museum of army medical history. ⊠ *1 Pl. Alphonse-Laveran,* ☎ *01–40-51-51-94.* ▦ *Museum 30 frs.* ⊘ *Museum Tues.–Wed. noon–6, weekends 1:30–5. RER: Port-Royal.*

MONTMARTRE

On a dramatic rise above the city is Montmartre, site of the Sacré-Coeur Basilica and home to a once-thriving artistic community. Although the fabled nightlife of old Montmartre has fizzled down to some glitzy nightclubs and porn shows, Montmartre still exudes a sense of history, a timeless quality infused with that hard-to-define Gallic charm.

Windmills once dotted Montmartre (often referred to by Parisians as *La Butte,* meaning "the mound"). They were set up here not just because the hill was a good place to catch the wind—at more than 300 ft, it's the highest point in the city—but because Montmartre was covered with wheat fields and quarries right up to the end of the 19th century. Today, only two of the original 20 windmills remain.

Visiting Montmartre means negotiating a lot of steep streets and flights of steps. The crown atop this urban peak, Sacré-Coeur, is something of an architectural oddity. It has been called everything from grotesque to sublime; its silhouette, viewed from afar at dusk or sunrise, looks more like a mosque than a cathedral.

There is a disputed story of how Montmartre got its name. Some say the name comes from the Roman temple to Mercury that was once here, called the Mound of Mercury, or *Mons Mercurii*. Others contend that it was an adaptation of *Mons Martyrum,* a name inspired by the burial here of Paris's first bishop, St. Denis. The popular version of his martyrdom is that he was beheaded by the Romans in AD 250 but arose to carry his severed head from rue Yvonne-Le-Tac to a place 6½ km (4 mi) to the north, an area now known as St-Denis. A final twist on the name controversy is that Montmartre briefly came to be known as Mont-Marat during the French Revolution. Marat was a leading Revolutionary figure who was stabbed to death in his bath.

Numbers in the text correspond to numbers in the margin and on the Montmartre map.

A Good Walk

Take the métro to the Blanche stop and start your tour at one of Paris's least-known but most atmospheric cemeteries, the tumbling **Cimetière de Montmartre** ① at the end of avenue Rachel (off boulevard de Clichy). Return to **Place Blanche,** home to the famous **Moulin Rouge** ②, the windmill-turned-dance-hall immortalized by Toulouse-Lautrec. The Café Cyrano, next door to the Moulin Rouge, was once the haunt of Salvador Dali and his fellow Surrealists. A few steps along the boulevard is the **Musée de l'Erotisme** ③, whose collection of erotic artifacts from around the world pays fulsome tribute to Montmartre's Sin City image.

Walk up lively rue Lepic from Place Blanche. The tiny Lux Bar at No. 12 has a 1910 mosaic showing Place Blanche at the beginning of the century. Wind your way up to the **Moulin de la Galette** ④, on your left, atop its leafy hillock opposite rue Tholozé, once a path over the hill. Then turn right down rue Tholozé, past **Studio 28** ⑤, the first cinema built expressly for experimental films.

Continue down rue Tholozé to rue des Abbesses, and turn left toward the triangular **Place des Abbesses** ⑥. Note the austere, redbrick **St-Jean l'Evangéliste** ⑦ on the square. Tiny rue André-Antoine, to the right of the popular Café St-Jean, leads to what was originally the **Théâtre Libre** ⑧, or Free Theater, at No. 37. Return to the square and take rue Yvonne-Le-Tac, off to the right. Paris's first bishop, St-Denis, is commemorated by the 19th-century **Chapelle du Martyre** ⑨ at No. 9, built on the spot where he is said to have been beheaded.

Return to the square and follow rue Ravignan as it climbs, via Place Emile-Goudeau, an enchanting little cobbled square, to the **Bateau-Lavoir** ⑩, or "Boat Wash House," at its northern edge. Painters Picasso and Braque had studios in the original building; this drab concrete building was built in its place. Continue up the hill via rue de la Mire to **Place Jean-Baptiste-Clément** ⑪, where Modigliani had a studio.

The upper reaches of rue Lepic lead to rue Norvins, formerly rue des Moulins (Windmill Street). At the end of the street, to the left, is stylish avenue Junot, site of the Cité Internationale des Arts (International Residence of the Arts), where the city authorities rent out studios to artists from all over the world. Continue right past the bars and tourist shops until you reach famous **Place du Tertre** ⑫. Check out the restaurant **La Mère Catherine** ⑬, a favorite with the Russian Cossacks when they occupied Paris. Fight your way through to the southern end of the square for a breathtaking view of the city. Around the corner on rue Poulbot,

Montmartre

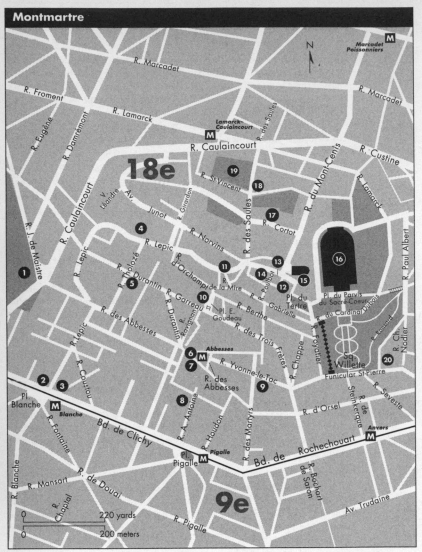

Bateau-Lavoir, **10**
Chapelle du
Martyre, **9**
Cimetière de
Montmartre, **1**
Cimetière
St-Vincent, **19**
Espace Dali, **14**

Halle St-Pierre, **20**
Lapin Agile, **18**
La Mère
Catherine, **13**
Moulin de la
Galette, **4**
Moulin Rouge, **2**

Musée de
l'Erotisme, **3**
Musée de
Montmartre, **17**
Place des Abbesses, **6**
Place Jean-Baptiste
Clément, **11**
Place du Tertre, **12**

Sacré-Coeur, **16**
St-Jean
l'Evangéliste, **7**
St-Pierre de
Montmartre, **15**
Studio 28, **5**
Théâtre Libre, **8**

the **Espace Dali** ⑭ houses works by Salvador Dali, who once had a studio in the area.

Return to Place du Tertre. Just off the square is the tiny church of **St-Pierre de Montmartre** ⑮. Looming menacingly behind is the scaly white dome of the Basilique du **Sacré-Coeur** ⑯. The cavernous interior is worth visiting for its golden mosaics; climb to the top of the dome for the view of Paris.

Walk back toward Place du Tertre. Turn right onto rue du Mont-Cenis and left onto rue Cortot, site of the **Musée de Montmartre** ⑰, which, like the Bateau-Lavoir, once sheltered an illustrious group of painters, writers, and assorted cabaret artists. One of the best things about the museum, however, is its view of the tiny vineyard on neighboring rue des Saules. Another famous Montmartre landmark is at No. 22: the bar-cabaret **Lapin Agile** ⑱, originally one of the raunchiest haunts in Montmartre. Opposite the Lapin Agile is the tiny **Cimetière St-Vincent** ⑲.

Return to Sacré-Coeur and head down the cascading staircases to Place St-Pierre. On the corner to the left is the **Halle St-Pierre** ⑳, site of the Museum of Naive Art. The neighboring streets teem with fabric shops, which are good places to find inexpensive materials. From the top of rue de Steinkerque, one of the busiest shopping streets, you can take in the archetypal view of Sacré-Coeur soaring skyward atop its grassy mound, with the funicular railway to the left. Turn right at the bottom of rue de Steinkerque and head toward Place Pigalle, notorious as a center of sleazy nightlife, although recently classier bars and nightclubs have been springing up in their places.

If, after you've walked around Montmartre, you still have the energy to see another illustrious church, make the excursion to the Gothic **Basilique de St-Denis** (☞ Off the Beaten Path, *below*) in the nearby suburb of St-Denis. Take the métro at Place de Clichy to St-Denis–Basilique. Or get on at Anvers (near the Halle St-Pierre) and transfer at Place de Clichy.

TIMING

Reserve four to five hours for this 4-km (2½-mi) walk: Many of the streets are steep and slow going. Include half an hour each at Sacré-Coeur and the museums (the Dali museum is open daily, but the Montmartre museum is closed Monday). Leave about 1½ hours for the excursion to St-Denis, including the métro ride there. From Easter through September, Montmartre is besieged by tourists. Two hints to avoid the worst of the rush: Come on a gray day, when Montmartre's sullen-tone facades suffer less than most in the city; or during the afternoon, and return to Place du Tertre (maybe via the funicular) by the early evening, once the tourist buses have departed. More festive times of the year are June 24, when fireworks and street concerts are staged around Montmartre, or on the first weekend of October for the revelry that accompanies the wine harvest at the vineyard on rue des Saules.

Sights to See

⑩ **Bateau-Lavoir** (Boat Wash House). Montmartre poet Max Jacob coined the name for the original building on this site, which burned down in 1970. He said it resembled a boat and that the warren of artists' studios within was perpetually paint-splattered and in need of a good hosing down. It was in the original Bateau-Lavoir that, early this century, Pablo Picasso and Georges Braque made their first bold stabs at the concept of Cubism—a move that paved the way for abstract painting. The poet Guillaume Apollinaire also had a studio here; his book *Les Peintures du Cubisme* (1913) set the seal on the movement's historical acceptance. The new building also contains art studios, but, if you didn't know its history, you'd probably walk right past it; it is the epitome of poured concrete drabness. ⊠ *13 Pl. Emile-Goudeau. Métro: Abbesses.*

❾ Chapelle du Martyre (Martyr's Chapel). It was in the crypt of the original chapel—built over the spot where St-Denis is said to have been martyred around AD 250—that Ignatius of Loyola, Francis Xavier, and five other companions swore an oath of poverty, chastity, and service to the Church in 1534. This led to the founding of the Society of Jesus (the Jesuits) in Rome six years later: a decisive step in the efforts of the Catholic Church to reassert its authority in the face of the Protestant Reformation. ⊠ *9 rue Yvonne-Le-Tac. Métro: Abbesses.*

❶ Cimetière de Montmartre (Montmartre Cemetery). Although not as large as the better-known Père Lachaise, this leafy, split-level cemetery is just as moving and evocative. Incumbents include painters Jean-Baptiste Greuze, Honoré Fragonard and Edgar Degas; Adolphe Sax, inventor of the saxophone; composers Hector Berlioz and Jacques Offenbach; and La Goulue, the Belle Epoque cabaret dancer who devised the French Cancan. The florid Art Nouveau tomb of novelist Emile Zola (1840–1902), who died in nearby rue de Clichy, lords it over a lawn near the entrance—though Zola's mortal remains were removed to the Panthéon in 1908. ⊠ *av. Rachel. Métro: Blanche.*

❶❾ Cimetière St-Vincent (St. Vincent Cemetery). It's a small graveyard, but if you're a serious student of Montmartre you may want to visit painter Maurice Utrillo's burial place. ⊠ *Entrance on rue Lucien-Gaulard (via rue St-Vincent), behind the Lapin Agile. Métro: Lamarck-Caulaincourt.*

❶❹ Espace Dali (Dali Center). Some of Salvador Dali's less familiar works are among the 25 sculptures and 300 prints housed in this museum. The atmosphere is meant to approximate the surreal experience, with black walls, low lighting, and a New Agey musical score—punctuated by recordings of Dali's own voice. ⊠ *11 rue Poulbot,* ☎ *01–42–64–40–10.* ▩ *35 frs.* ☉ *Daily 10–6; summer, daily 10–8. Métro: Abbesses.*

☝ ❷⓪ Halle St-Pierre (St. Peter's Market Hall). This elegant iron-and-glass 19th-century market hall, at the foot of Sacré-Coeur, houses a children's play area, a café, and the **Musée de l'Art Naïf Max-Fourny** (Museum of Naive Art) with its psychedelic collection of contemporary international Naive painters. ⊠ *2 rue Ronsard,* ☎ *01–42–58–72–89.* ▩ *Museum: 40 frs.* ☉ *Daily 10–6. Métro: Anvers.*

❶❽ Lapin Agile. This bar-cabaret was originally one of the raunchiest haunts in Montmartre. It got its curious name—the Nimble Rabbit—when the owner, André Gill, hung up a sign (now in the Musée du Vieux Montmartre) of a laughing rabbit jumping out of a saucepan clutching a bottle of wine. In those days, the place was still tamely called La Campagne (The Countryside). Once the sign went up, locals rechristened it the Lapin à Gill, meaning Gill's Rabbit. When, in 1886, it was sold to cabaret singer Jules Jouy, he called it the Lapin Agile, which has the same pronunciation in French as Lapin à Gill. In 1903, the premises were bought by the most celebrated cabaret entrepreneur of them all, Aristide Bruand, portrayed by Toulouse-Lautrec in a series of famous posters. Today, it manages to preserve at least something of its earlier flavor, unlike the Moulin Rouge. ⊠ *22 rue des Saules,* ☎ *01–46–06–85–87. Métro: Lamarck-Caulaincourt.*

❶❸ La Mère Catherine. This restaurant was a favorite with the Russian Cossacks who occupied Paris in 1814. Little did they know that when they banged on the tables and shouted *"bistro,"* the Russian word for "quickly," they were inventing a new breed of French restaurant. ✉ *6 Pl. du Tertre. Métro: Abbesses.*

4 **Moulin de la Galette** (Biscuit Windmill). This windmill, on a hillock shrouded by shrubbery, is one of the remaining two in Montmartre. It was once the focal point of an open-air cabaret (made famous in a painting by Renoir), and rumor has it that the miller, Debray, was strung up on its sails and spun to death after striving vainly to defend it against invading Cossacks in 1814. Unfortunately, it is now privately owned and can only be admired from the street below. ✉ *rue Tholozé. Métro: Abbesses.*

2 **Moulin Rouge** (Red Windmill). Built in 1885 as a windmill, this world-famous cabaret was transformed into a dance hall in 1900. Those wild, early days were immortalized by Toulouse-Lautrec in his posters and paintings. It still trades shamelessly on the notion of Paris as a city of sin: If you fancy a Vegas-style night out, with computerized light shows and troupes of bare-breasted women sporting feather headdresses, this is the place to go (☞ Chapter 4). The cancan, by the way—still a regular feature here—was considerably raunchier when Toulouse-Lautrec was around. ✉ *82 bd. de Clichy,* ☎ *01–53–09–82–82. Métro: Blanche.*

3 **Musée de l'Erotisme** (Erotic Museum). Opened in 1997, this seven-story museum at the foot of Montmartre claims to provide "a prestigious showcase for every kind of erotic fantasy." Its 2,000 works of art—you may find that this term is used rather loosely—include Peruvian potteries, African carvings, Indian miniatures, Nepalese bronzes, Chinese ivories, and Japanese prints. Three floors are devoted to temporary exhibitions of painting and photography. ✉ *72 bd. de Clichy,* ☎ *01–42–58–28–73.* 🎫 *40 frs.* ☉ *Daily 10 AM–2 AM. Métro: Blanche.*

17 **Musée de Montmartre** (Montmartre Museum). In its turn-of-the-century heyday, Montmartre's historical museum was home to an illustrious group of painters, writers, and assorted cabaret artists. Foremost among them were Renoir—he painted the *Moulin de la Galette,* an archetypal Parisian scene of sun-drenched revelers, while he lived here—and Maurice Utrillo, Montmartre painter par excellence. Utrillo was encouraged to paint by his mother, Suzanne Valadon, a model of Renoir's and a major painter in her own right. Utrillo's life was anything but happy, despite the considerable success his paintings enjoyed. He was an alcoholic continually in trouble with the police and spent most of his declining years in hospitals. He took the gray, crumbling streets of Montmartre as his subject matter, working more effectively from postcards than from the streets themselves. For all that, almost all his best works—from his "White Period"—were produced before 1916 (he died in 1955). They evoke the atmosphere of old Montmartre hauntingly: To help convey the decaying buildings of the area, he mixed plaster and sand with his paints. The museum also provides a view of the tiny **vineyard**—the only one in Paris—on neighboring rue des Saules. A token 125 gallons of wine are still produced every year. It's hardly *grand cru* stuff, but there are predictably bacchanalian celebrations during the harvest on the first weekend of October. ✉ *12 rue Cortot,* ☎ *01–46–06–61–11.* 🎫 *25 frs.* ☉ *Tues.–Sun. 11–6. Métro: Lamarck-Caulaincourt.*

6 **Place des Abbesses.** This triangular square is typical of the picturesque, slightly countrified style that has made Montmartre famous. The entrance to the Abbesses métro station, a curving, sensuous mass of delicate iron, is one of the two original Art Nouveau entrance canopies left in Paris. *Métro: Abbesses.*

Place Blanche. The name Place Blanche—White Square—comes from the clouds of chalky dust that used to be churned up by the carts that carried wheat and crushed flour from the nearby windmills, including the Moulin Rouge. *Métro: Blanche.*

OFF THE BEATEN PATH	**MUSÉE DE LA VIE ROMANTIQUE –** For many years this tranquil, countrified town house at the foot of Montmartre was the site of Friday-evening salons hosted by the Dutch-born painter Ary Scheffer and including the likes of Ingres, Delacroix, Turgenev, Chopin, and Sand. The memory of author George Sand (1804–76)—real name Aurore Dudevant—haunts the museum. Portraits, furniture, and household possessions, right down to her cigarette box, have been moved here from her house in Nohant in the Loire Valley. There's also a selection of Scheffer's competent artistic output on the first floor. Head down rue Blanche from Place Blanche; the third left is rue Chaptal. ⌧ *16 rue Chaptal,* ☎ *01–48–74–95–38.* ⌧ *18 frs.* ☉ *Tues.–Sun. 10–5:40. Métro: St-Georges.*

⑪ **Place Jean-Baptiste-Clément.** Painter Amedeo Modigliani (1884–1920) had a studio here at No. 7. Some say he was the greatest Italian artist of the 20th century, fusing the genius of the Renaissance with the modernity of Cézanne and Picasso. He claimed that he would drink himself to death—he eventually did—and chose the right part of town to do it in. Look for the octagonal tower at the north end of the square; it's all that's left of Montmartre's first water tower, built around 1840 to boost the area's feeble water supply. ⌧ *Pl. Jean-Baptiste-Clément. Métro: Abbesses.*

⑫ **Place du Tertre** (Mound Square). This tumbling square (*tertre* means hillock) regains its village atmosphere only in the winter, when the branches of the plane-trees sketch traceries against the sky. At any other time of year you'll be confronted by a swarm of artists clamoring to do your portrait and crowds of tourists. If one produces a picture of you without your permission, you're under no obligation to buy. *Métro: Abbesses.*

NEED A BREAK?	**Patachou** (⌧ 9 Pl. du Tertre, ☎ 01–42–51–06–06) sounds the one classy note on Place du Tertre, serving exquisite, if expensive, cakes and teas.

⑯ **Sacré-Coeur** (Sacred Heart Basilica). The white domes of this basilica patrol the Paris skyline from the top of Montmartre. The French government decided to erect Sacré-Coeur in 1873, as a sort of national guilt offering in expiation for the blood shed during the Commune and Franco-Prussian War in 1870–71. It was to symbolize the return of self-confidence to late-19th-century Paris. Even so, the building was to some extent a reflection of political divisions within the country: It was largely financed by French Catholics fearful of an anticlerical backlash and determined to make a grandiloquent statement on behalf of the Church. Building lasted until World War I; the basilica was not consecrated until 1919. Stylistically, the Sacré-Coeur borrows elements from Romanesque and Byzantine models. Built on a grand scale, the effect is strangely disjointed and unsettling; architect Paul Abadie (who died in 1884, long before the church was finished) had made his name by sticking similar scaly, pointed domes onto the medieval cathedrals of Angoulême and Périgueux in southern France. The gloomy, cavernous interior is worth visiting for its golden mosaics; climb to the top of the dome for the view of Paris. ⌧ *Pl. du Parvis-du-Sacré-Coeur. Métro: Anvers.*

❼ **St-Jean l'Evangéliste.** This redbrick church, built in 1904, was one of the first concrete buildings in France; despite its sinuous Art Nouveau curves, the bricks had to be added later to soothe offended locals. ⊠ *Pl. des Abbesses. Métro: Abbesses.*

NEED A
BREAK? **Le St-Jean** (⊠ 23 rue des Abbesses) is an intimate, large-windowed café, popular with locals on account of its authentic 1950s decor—neon lighting, vast bar, and mosaic-tile floor. The tables outside offer a good vantage point over busy Place des Abbesses.

⑮ St-Pierre de Montmartre. Sitting awkwardly beneath the brooding silhouette of Sacré-Coeur, just off Place du Tertre, is this church—one of the oldest in Paris. Built in the 12th century as the abbey church of a substantial Benedictine monastery, it's been remodeled on a number of occasions through the years; thus the 18th-century facade, built under Louis XIV, clashes with the mostly medieval interior. ⊠ *Off Pl. du Tertre. Métro: Anvers.*

❺ Studio 28. What looks like no more than a generic little movie theater has a distinguished dramatic history: When it opened in 1928, it was the first purposely built for *art et essai,* or experimental theater, in the world. Over the years, the movies of directors like Jean Cocteau, François Truffaut, and Orson Welles have been shown here before their official premieres. ⊠ *10 rue Tholozé,* ☎ *01–46–06–36–07. Métro: Abbesses.*

❽ Théâtre Libre (Free Theater). Founded in 1887 by director André Antoine (1858–1943), this theater was immensely influential in popularizing the work of iconoclastic young playwrights such as Ibsen and Strindberg. Antoine later became the director of the Odéon Theater in 1906. ⊠ *37 rue André-Antoine. Métro: Abbesses.*

PASSY, AUTEUIL, AND THE BOIS DE BOULOGNE

Passy and Auteuil were independent villages until Baron Haussman soldered them together in 1860 and annexed them to Paris under the mundane title of the 16ᵉ Arrondissement. Tumbling alleys and countrified cul-de-sacs recall those bygone days, colliding with some of the city's finest 20th-century architecture by Guimard, Perret, Le Corbusier, and Mallet-Stevens.

Away to the west is the sprawling Bois de Boulogne—an enormous park that also assumed its present form during the days of Haussmann and Napoléon III, when it became Parisians' favorite day trip. The 16ᵉ is the largest arrondissement in Paris, and the Bois, as it is known, is almost of equal size. Public transportation to the Bois is poor, and few Parisians and even fewer visitors ever get to know all its glades and pathways. The photogenic Lac Supérieur, however, which anchors the Bois's eastern sector, is easy to reach by foot and métro.

Numbers in the text correspond to numbers in the margin and on the Passy, Auteuil, and the Bois de Boulogne map.

A Good Walk

Start at the **Cimetière de Passy** ① above Place du Trocadéro. A map to the left of the entrance charts the tombs of the famous buried here. Leaving the cemetery, cross avenue Paul-Doumer, and veer left to a small garden (Square Yorktown) where there is a statue of Benjamin Franklin. Turn right down rue Benjamin-Franklin. Verdant gardens flank the curved wing of the Palais de Chaillot to your left (☞ From the Eiffel Tower to Pont de l'Alma, *above*). On the right, at No. 25 bis, note the huge-windowed Immeuble Perret—an innovative building for its time

(1903), with a reinforced-concrete facade clad in floral-patterned ceramic tiles. Auguste Perret, then just 29, was to become one of the century's leading architects.

Cross Place Costa-Rica, with its plummeting view of the overground métro as it shoots across the Seine, and take rue Raynouard. Just past No. 9, spear left down the Passage des Eaux, a sinister-looking stone staircase flanked by barbed wire: the nearest Paris gets to urban hell, straight out of Dickens, and duly depositing you in rue Charles-Dickens at the bottom. You reemerge into daylight to be confronted by a templelike town house with huge Greek columns and, to your left, the quaint **Musée du Vin** ②, with exhibits on wine in its medieval cellars. After an excursion through pastures bacchanalian, big-city reality hits again as you retrace your steps along rue Charles-Dickens and venture through a metal grille toward a vast building site. Turn right to reach avenue Marcel-Proust, in search of the time when the fortresslike walls on the right supported some of the fanciest flats in Paris, and the majestic double-staircase halfway along once led down to the grand entrance of the Ministry of Public Works (relocated to La Défense) rather than a gap in the building-site fence.

A policeman generally lurks a hundred yards on, barring the leafy driveway to the Turkish Embassy. You might have to consult him for advice as you search for rue Bertin, a cobbled, ivy-clad alley that sneaks off right, undisturbed by traffic, to a flight of stairs that leads back to rue Raynouard and the **Maison de Balzac** ③: a dachalike bungalow with trim lawns, once home to France's own Dickens. Rue Benjamin-Franklin returns at the corner of rues Raynouard and Singer where— says a tall, tapering plaque—the great man invented the lightning-conductor between 1777 and 1785. Rue Raynouard tumbles down past the circular bulk of **Maison de Radio France** ④, the headquarters of state radio and television. If you'd like to see a miniversion of the **Statue of Liberty** ⑤, head left toward the Seine; it's at the end of the Allée des Cygnes, a striplike artificial island backed by the skyscrapers of the 1970s Front de Seine complex that cynical Parisians dub their mini-Manhattan.

Continue on rue Raynouard, which becomes rue La Fontaine, to inspect the **Castel-Béranger** ⑥ at No. 14, one of the city's earliest Art Nouveau buildings. If you're a fan of sculptor Auguste Rodin you may want to make a detour up avenue du Recteur-Poincaré to **Place Rodin** ⑦ to see a small bronze casting of his male nude, *L'Age d'Airain*. Otherwise stay on rue La Fontaine, pass the **Orphelins d'Auteuil** ⑧—a still-functioning orphanage. Pause at No. 60, the **Hôtel Mezzara** ⑨, another fine Guimard mansion. Some 150 yards along, turn left onto rue des Perchamps. Note the bay-windowed, stripey-tiled Studio Building at No. 20—it looks contemporary, but was built by Henri Sauvage in 1927. Also note the funky white mansion at the corner of rue Leconte-de-l'Isle, with its heavy, outsized triglyphs. Some beefy Baroque caryatids on loan from Vienna are visible across the street at No. 33, incongrously supporting a row of wafer-thin balconies.

Continue along rue des Perchamps to **rue d'Auteuil** ⑩. To the left is the elongated dome of the Église d'Auteuil, modeled on the papal tiara. Head right along this old, crooked shopping street to sloping Place Jean-Lorrain, home to a crowded market on Wednesday and Saturday mornings, then turn right down rue La Fontaine toward the chunky Crédit Lyonnais bank. Veer left up avenue Mozart and pause at No. 122; the elongated doorway and sinuous window frames again pay tribute to Guimard. Around the corner in Villa Flore, a tiny cul-de-sac, you can see the odd-shaped site Guimard had to contend with: The

Passy, Auteuil, and the Bois de Boulogne

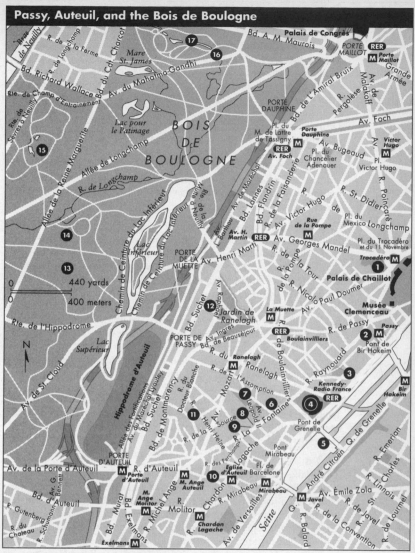

Bois de Boulogne, **13**

Castel-Béranger, **6**

Cimetière de Passy, **1**

Fondation
Le Corbusier, **11**

Hôtel Mezzara, **9**

Jardin
d'Acclimatation, **17**

Maison de Balzac, **3**

Maison de Radio
France, **4**

Musée
Marmottan, **12**

Musée National des
Arts et Traditions
Populaires, **16**

Musée du Vin, **2**

Orphelins
d'Auteuil, **8**

Parc de Bagatelle, **15**

Place Rodin, **7**

Pré Catalan, **14**

Rue d'Auteuil, **10**

Statue of Liberty, **5**

building ends in a narrow point, with jagged brickwork vainly beckoning an addition.

Take the next left up rue Henri-Heine, with its row of elegant town houses, then turn left onto rue du Dr-Blanche, and left again to get to square du Dr-Blanche, a leafy cul-de-sac. At the far end is the **Fondation Le Corbusier** ⑪. If you like such spartan interwar architecture and want to see more, explore rue Mallet-Stevens, a mews lined with sturdy evergreens and elegant houses from the late '20s, farther along rue du Dr-Blanche to the right. Turn left onto rue de l'Assomption, then right and, opposite the end of rue du Ranelagh, cross the disused St-Lazare-Auteuil rail line. Take a right on avenue Raphaël, which overlooks the elegant Jardin du Ranelagh—site of the world's first hot-air balloon launch in 1783. At the corner of rue Louis-Boilly is the **Musée Marmottan** ⑫, famed for its collection of Impressionist pictures and illuminated manuscripts.

Continue on avenue Raphaël and cross boulevard Suchet to sprawling Place de Colombie. Turn left down avenue de St-Cloud to reach the large **Bois de Boulogne** ⑬. Straight ahead is the bigger of the park's two lakes, the Lac Inférieur; you can cross to the island in the middle on a little ferry for a picnic or café lunch. When you're done, skirt south around the lake to check out the less picturesque Lac Supérieur, then take the chemin de Ceinture/route de la Grande-Cascade to the **Pré Catalan** ⑭, home to the Shakespeare Garden, trim lawns and stately trees. Cross the Pré Catalan and exit from its north side. If you're short on time or energy, head right via the Lac Inférieur and return to civilization at Porte Dauphine; otherwise head left along route des Lacs to the **Parc de Bagatelle** ⑮, with its magnificent flower garden and 18th-century château. A good walk east from here will take you along avenue du Mahatma-Gandhi, past the **Musée National des Arts et Traditions Populaires** ⑯ and the children's playground, the **Jardin d'Acclimatation** ⑰, to Porte Maillot, where you can get a métro back to central Paris.

TIMING

This walk, which divides neatly into two—town (Paris) and country (Bois de Boulogne)—will probably take you a full day. (You may want to save the Bois de Boulogne for another day.) The Lac Inférieur is a good midway spot to stop for lunch. By then you'll have covered 5–6 km (3–3½ mi), depending on whether you detour to the Statue of Liberty and Place Rodin. The second half of the tour covers just under 4 km (2½ mi) if you return from the Pré Catalan to Porte Dauphine, or just under 6 km (3½ mi) if you take in the Parc de Bagatelle and return to Porte Maillot. Sturdy, comfortable footwear is a must to negotiate the slopes and steps of the Paris sector and the gravelly pathways of the Bois de Boulogne.

Sights to See

🐾 ⑬ **Bois de Boulogne.** Class and style have been associated with this 2,200-acre wood—known to Parisians as "Le Bois"—ever since it was landscaped into an upper-class playground by Baron Haussmann in the 1850s. Emphasizing that onetime glamour is Haussmann's approach road from the Arc de Triomphe: avenue Foch, Paris's widest boulevard (120 yards across), originally named avenue de l'Impératrice in honor of Empress Eugénie (wife of Napoléon III). The Porte Dauphine métro station at the bottom of avenue Foch retains its original Art Nouveau iron-and-glass entrance canopy, designed by Hector Guimard.

The wood is crisscrossed by broad, leafy roads, home to rowers, joggers, strollers, riders, *pétanque* (boules) players, picnickers, and lovers.

Meetings at **Longchamp** and **Auteuil** racetracks are high up the social calendar and re-create something of a Belle Epoque atmosphere. The French Open tennis tournament at the beautiful **Roland Garros** stadium in late May is another occasion when Parisian style and elegance are on full display.

The manifold attractions of Le Bois include cafés, restaurants, lakes, waterfalls, gardens, and museums. Rowboats can be rented at both **Lac Inférieur** and **Lac Supérieur**. A cheap and frequent ferry crosses to the idyllic island in the middle of Lac Inférieur. The **Fête à Neu-Neu**, a giant carnival, takes place every September and October around the two lakes. Buses traverse the Bois de Boulogne during the day (take Bus 244 from Porte Maillot), but Le Bois becomes a distinctly adult playground after dark, when prostitutes of various genders come prowling for clients. *Main entrance at bottom of ave. Foch. Métro: Porte Maillot, Porte Dauphine, or Porte d'Auteuil; Bus 244.*

6 **Castel-Béranger.** Dreamt up in 1895 by Hector Guimard (of métro fame) when he was 28, this building is considered the city's first Art Nouveau structure. The apartment building once housed Postimpressionist Paul Signac as well as Guimard himself. Today, the place looks a little dowdy and its occupants are less illustrious—though this hasn't stopped them from posting a menacing sign on the assymetrical iron doorway warning you to keep out. Rust-streaked pale green paintwork, however, fails to detract from the florid appeal of the iron doors and balconies, nor from the eccentric use of colored brick. Cross the street to admire the mask-fronted iron balconies and quilt-patterned brown, red, and turquoise brickwork, then venture around the side into Hameau Béranger to see rampant ivy obliterating the original fancy iron fencing, beneath the dismayed gaze of stylized seahorses halfway up the walls. There's a cleaner, subtler display of Art Nouveau at the corner of rue Lafontaine and rue Gros, where a finely carved stone apartment building segues into the dainty rue Agar. Tucked away at the corner of rue Gros is a tiny café-bar with Art Nouveau glass front and interior furnishings. ⊠ *14 rue la Fontaine. Métro: Ranelagh; RER: Maison de Radio-France.*

NEED A BREAK? It seats just 15, but the **Café-Bar Antoine** (⊠ 17 rue la Fontaine, ☎ 01–40–50–14–30) warrants a visit for its Art Nouveau facade, floor tiles, and carved wooden bar. Count on 200 francs for a meal or stick to a snack and coffee.

1 **Cimetière de Passy** (Passy Cemetery). Perched on a spur above Place du Trocadéro in the shadow of the Eiffel Tower and Palais de Chaillot, this cemetery was opened in 1820 when Passy was a country village. Its handsome entrance—two sturdy pavilions linked by a colonnade—is a 1930s Art Deco cousin to the nearby Palais de Chaillot. Precocious painter-poetess Marie Baskirtseff's tomb, with its pinnacles and stone Byzantine dome, dominates the cemetery; a plexiglassed Pietà mourns Hungarian peer Pierre Perenyi nearby. Just left of the main crossroads is a weathered bust of Impressionist Edouard Manet, buried with his wife, Berthe Morisot, next to the poignant figure of a girl in a hat—calling to mind Zola's novel *Une Page d'Amour*, which ends with the burial of the young heroine Jeanne in Passy Cemetery, "alone, facing Paris, forever." Claude Debussy is also among the incumbents. ⊠ *rue du Commandant-Schloesing.* ◷ *Daily 9–8 or dusk. Métro: Trocadéro.*

11 **Fondation Le Corbusier** (Le Corbusier Foundation). This center is less of a museum in honor of Swiss architect Charles-Edouard Jeanneret, better known as Le Corbusier (1887–1965), than a well-preserved 1923 example of his innovative construction techniques, based on geometric forms, recherché color schemes, and unblushing recourse to iron and concrete. The sloping ramp that replaces the traditional staircase is one of the most eye-catching features. ⊠ *10 sq. du Dr-Blanche,* ☎ *01–42–88–41–53.* 🎫 *15 frs.* ☉ *Weekdays 10–12:30, 1:30–6. Métro: Jasmin.*

⑨ Hôtel Mezzara. With its sumptuous wrought-iron staircase, Art Nouveau windows, and plaster molding, this Hector Guimard mansion, built in 1911 as a workshop for textile designer Paul Mezzara, has one of the finest interiors in Paris. Unfortunately, it is only open during exhibitions, though a bit of curiosity and perseverance might get you through the door. ⊠ *60 rue la Fontaine,* ☎ *01–45–27–02–29. Métro: Jasmin.*

⑰ Jardin d'Acclimatation (Zoo). At this children's zoo and amusement park on the northern edge of the Bois de Boulogne (*above*), you see a mix of exotic and familiar animals, take a boat trip along an "enchanted river," ride a miniature railway, and enjoy various fairground booths that keep young and old entertained. The zoo and amusement park can be reached via the miniature railway—a surefire hit with children—that runs from Porte Maillot on Wednesdays and weekends, beginning at 1:30; tickets cost 6 francs. Many of the attractions have separate entry fees (except the zoo, which is spread throughout the park), notably the child-oriented art museum and workshop center, the **Musée en Herbe** (literally, "museum in the grass"); admission is 16 francs. ⊠ *bd. des Sablons,* ☎ *01–40–67–97–66.* 🎫 *12 frs.* ☉ *Daily 10–6. Métro: Les Sablons.*

③ Maison de Balzac (Balzac's House). The Paris home of the great French 19th-century novelist Honoré de Balzac (1799–1850) contains a wide range of exhibits charting his tempestuous life. ⊠ *47 rue Raynouard,* ☎ *01–42–24–56–38.* 🎫 *17 frs.* ☉ *Feb.–Dec., Tues.–Sun. 10–5:40. Métro: Passy.*

④ Maison de Radio France (Radio France Building). The home to state radio and television, completed in 1962, is a monstrous circular building—over 500 yards in circumference and said to be the largest in France in terms of floor space—with a 200-ft tower overlooking the Seine. You can explore the foyer, obtain tickets to attend recordings, or join a guided tour (in French) of the studios and the museum, with its notable array of old radios. ⊠ *116 av. du Président-Kennedy,* ☎ *01–42–30–15–16.* 🎫 *Guided tours 18 frs.* ☉ *Mon.–Sat. 10:30–4:30. Métro: Ranelagh; RER: Maison de Radio-France.*

⑫ Musée Marmottan. Paris's "other" Impressionist museum (after the Musée d'Orsay)—one of the most underestimated museums in Paris—is in a 19th-century mansion. The Marmottan Museum has an extensive collection of works by Claude Monet (including *Impression-Sunrise,* from which the term Impressionist derives). There are also fine works by other Impressionists, including Pissarro, Renoir, and Sisley. Displayed on the first and second floors are some magnificent medieval illuminated manuscripts and the original furnishings of a sumptuous early 19th-century Empire mansion. ⊠ *2 rue Louis-Boilly,* ☎ *01–42–24–07–02.* 🎫 *40 frs.* ☉ *Tues.–Sun. 10–5:30. Métro: La Muette.*

⑯ Musée National des Arts et Traditions Populaires (National Museum of Folk Arts and Traditions). In a nondescript modern building next to the Jardin d'Acclimatation, this museum contains an impressive variety of artifacts related principally to preindustrial rural life. Many exhibits have buttons to press and knobs to twirl; however, there are no descriptions in English. The museum is a favorite destination for school field trips, so avoid weekday afternoons. ⊠ *6 av. du Mahatma-*

Gandhi, ☎ *01–44–17–60–00.* 🖼 *22 frs, Sun. 15 frs.* ☉ *Wed.–Mon. 9:30–5:15. Métro: Les Sablons.*

② **Musée du Vin** (Wine Museum). In the vaulted cellars of a former 13th-century abbey, this small museum is devoted to traditional wine-making artifacts. The premises double as a wine bar and the visit includes a wine-tasting. ⊠ *5 sq. Charles-Dickens,* ☎ *01–45–25–63–26.* 🖼 *35 frs.* ☉ *Tues.–Sun. 10–6. Métro: Passy.*

❽ **Orphelins d'Auteuil** (Auteuil Orphanage). This still-functioning orphanage, founded in 1866 by Abbé Roussel, has pretty, sloping gardens, a redbrick cloister, a craft shop, and a tasteful Neo-Gothic chapel (built 1927). ⊠ *40 rue La Fontaine,* ☎ *01–44–14–75–20. Métro: Jasmin.*

⑮ **Parc de Bagatelle.** This beautiful floral garden counts irises, roses, tulips, and water lilies among its showstoppers; it is at its most colorful between April and June. The velvet green lawns and majestic 18th-century buildings (sometimes hosts to art exhibitions) are fronted by a terrace with attractive views of the Seine. ⊠ *Rte. de Sèvres–Neuilly or rte. Lacs-à-Bagatelle,* ☎ *01–40–67–97–00.* 🖼 *10 frs gardens only; 30 frs park and château buildings.* ☉ *Daily 9–8 or dusk. Métro: Pont de Neuilly.*

❼ **Place Rodin.** A half-sized bronze casting of Rodin's virile *Bronze Age* nude (*L'Age d'Airain*), created in 1874, emerges unblushingly from rose-bushes at the heart of this minor roundabout. *Métro: Ranelagh.*

⑭ **Pré Catalan.** This garden in the Bois de Boulogne (☞ *above*) contains one of Paris's largest trees: a copper beech more than 200 years old. The **Shakespeare Garden** on the west side has flowers, herbs, and trees mentioned in Shakespeare's plays. ⊠ *Rte. de la Grande-Cascade.* ☉ *Shakespeare Garden daily 3–3:30 and 4:30–5.* 🖼 *5 frs. Métro: Porte Dauphine.*

⑩ **Rue d'Auteuil.** This narrow, crooked, shopping street escaped the attentions of Baron Haussmann and retains a country feel. Molière once lived on the site of No. 2; Racine was on nearby rue du Buis; the pair met up to clink glasses and exchange drama notes at the Mouton Blanc Inn, now a brasserie at No. 40. Note some genuinely old buildings dating from the 17th and 18th centuries at Nos. 19, 21, 25, and 29; the elegant courtyard of the school at No. 11 bis; and the scaly dome of the **Église d'Auteuil** (built in the 1880s), an unmistakable small-time cousin of the Sacré Coeur. Rue d'Auteuil is at its liveliest on Wednesday and Saturday mornings when a much-loved street market crams onto Place Jean-Barraud. *Métro: Michel-Ange–Auteuil or Église d'Auteuil.*

OFF THE BEATEN PATH

MUSÉE NATIONAL DE LA CÉRAMIQUE – Hundreds of the finest creations of the world-famous Sèvres porcelain works are displayed "on premises" in the National Ceramics Museum, at the southern end of the tumbling, wooded Parc de St-Cloud, a short métro ride from the Michel-Ange–Auteuil stop. ⊠ *Pl. de la Manufacture, Sèvres,* ☎ *01–41–14–04–20.* 🖼 *22 frs.* ☉ *Wed.–Mon. 10–5:15. Métro: Pont de Sèvres; Tramway: Musée de Sèvres.*

SERRES D'AUTEUIL – Tropical and exotic plants sweat it out in mighty hothouses just off Place de la Porte-d'Auteuil, on the southern fringe of the Bois de Boulogne. A bewildering variety of plants and flowers are grown here for use in Paris's municipal parks and for displays on official occasions. The surrounding gardens' leafy paths and well-tended lawns offer cooler places to admire floral virtuosity. ⊠ *3 av. de la Porte-d'Auteuil.* 🖼 *5 frs.* ☉ *Daily 10–5:30. Métro: Porte d'Auteuil.*

⑤ **Statue of Liberty.** Just in case you'd forgotten that the enduring symbol of the American dream is actually French, a reduced version of Frédéric-Auguste Bartholdi's matriarch brandishes her torch at the southern tip of the Allée des Cygnes. To Bartholdi's dismay, she originally faced the city, and was only turned around to gaze east (toward the New World) in 1937. The best view of her can be had during a Bateau-Mouche river tour: Boats usually make an obliging U-turn right in front. The original statue—the one in New York City—is known in French as *La Liberté Éclairant le Monde* (Liberty Lighting Up the World); it was made in Paris in 1886 with the help of a giant steel framework designed by Gustave Eiffel. ⊠ *Allée des Cygnes.* *Métro: Javel; RER: Maison de Radio-France.*

OFF THE BEATEN PATH

If you're in search of wide-open green spaces, skyscrapers, the church where Gothic architecture made its first appearance, or small, unique museums, make a brief excursion to the city's peripheries. Unlike New York or London, most of Paris's largest parks (with the notable exception of the Tuileries and Luxembourg Gardens) are found on the fringes of the city and in its nearby banlieues (suburbs). Parks and small museums are scattered throughout the fringes of the city; soaring steel and glass have been banished to the outskirts at La Défense; and the Gothic Basilique de St-Denis is in the nearby, northern suburb of St-Denis.

Thanks to France's spectacular victory over Brazil in the 1998 Soccer World Cup Final at the Stade de France in St-Denis, the name of this suburb is now known around the world. Along with a visit to the futuristic stadium, St-Denis's Art and History Museum, and the burial place of the French kings offer other reasons to make the brief jaunt by métro to this working-class suburb, whose nascent prosperity is reflected in Oscar Niemeyer's gleaming headquarters of Communist daily *L'Humanité* on rue de Strasbourg.

Another suburb worth visiting, just south of the Bois de Boulogne, is Boulogne-Billancourt. This area rose to prominence between the wars as the center of the French movie and automobile industries. A rich legacy of Art Deco buildings remain; these can be seen along the "Parcours des Années Trente" (1930s Trail). More Art Deco works can be found at the 1930s Museum, also in Boulogne-Billancourt.

TIMING
Although none of these sights are more than 25 minutes from central Paris by métro or RER (with a 10-minute walk from the station in some instances), set aside at least a couple hours, if not a whole morning or afternoon, to visit them. Late spring is a particularly good time to explore any of the parks, which are at their most colorful between April and June.

Sights to See

★ **Basilique de St-Denis.** Built between 1136 and 1286, the St. Denis Basilica is in some ways the most important Gothic church in the Paris region. It was here, under dynamic prelate Abbé Suger, that Gothic architecture (typified by pointed arches and rib vaults) arguably made its first appearance. Suger's writings also show the medieval fascination with the bright, shiny colors that appear in stained glass. The kings of France soon chose St-Denis as their final resting place, and their richly sculpted tombs—along with what remains of Suger's church—can be seen in the choir area at the east end of the church. The vast 13th-century nave is a brilliant example of structural logic; its columns, capitals, and vault are a model of architectural harmony. The facade, retaining the rounded arches of the Romanesque style that preceded the

In case you want to see the world.

At American Express, we're here to make your journey a smooth one. So we have over 1,700 travel service locations in over 130 countries ready to help. What else would you expect from the world's largest travel agency?

do more   AMERICAN EXPRESS

Travel

Call 1 800 AXP-3429 or visit www.americanexpress.com/travel

In case you want to be welcomed there.

We're here to see that you're always welcomed at establishments everywhere. That's why millions of people carry the American Express® Card — for peace of mind, confidence, and security, around the world or just around the corner.

do more

Cards

In case you're running low.

We're here to help with more than 190,000 Express Cash locations around the world. In order to enroll, just call American Express at 1 800 CASH-NOW before you start your vacation.

do more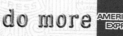

Express Cash

And in case you'd rather be safe than sorry.

We're here with American Express® Travelers Cheques. They're the safe way to carry money on your vacation, because if they're ever lost or stolen you can get a refund, practically anywhere or anytime. To find the nearest place to buy Travelers Cheques, call 1 800 495-1153. Another way we help you do more.

do more

AMERICAN
EXPRESS

**Travelers
Cheques**

Gothic style, is set off by a small rose window, reputedly the earliest in France. ✉ *1 rue de la Légion d'Honneur.* 🎟 *Choir and tombs: 32 frs.* 🕑 *Mon.–Sat. 10–7, Sun. noon–7; Oct.–Easter, Mon.–Sat. 10–5, Sun. noon–5. Guided tours daily at 1:15 and 3. Métro: St-Denis–Basilique.*

Chinagora. In the near eastern suburb of Alfortville, at the confluence of the Marne and Seine rivers, the Chinese "village" (really more of a complex) of Chinagora offers an upscale look at Chinese culture. Hong Kong architect Liang Kunhao's glitzy complex includes everything from restaurants and a hotel to an emporium, an exhibition center, and a tearoom. Some 400,000 green-and-ochre glazed tiles, imported from China, make up the pagoda roofscape. Stop off near the métro at the high-towered church of **Ste-Agnès** (✉ rue Nordling, Maisons-Alfort), an Art Deco jewel from the 1930s. ✉ *1 Pl. du Confluent, Alfortville,* ☎ *01–43–96–37–38. Métro: Alfort–École Vétérinaire.*

La Défense. You may be pleasantly surprised by the absence of high-rise buildings and concrete towers in central Paris; one of the reasons for this is that French planners, with their usual desire to rationalize, ordained that modern high-rise development be expelled to the outskirts. Over the last 20 years, La Défense, just west of Paris across the Seine from Neuilly, has been transformed into a futuristic showcase for state-of-the-art engineering and architectural design. Few people actually live amid all this glass and concrete; most just come to work. The soaring high-rises are mainly taken up by offices—often the French headquarters of multinational companies—with no expense spared in the pursuit of visual ingenuity. Outlines, shadows, reflections, plays of light, and swirling underpasses make for a stimulating, but slightly terrifying, cityscape. Highlights include the spherical IMAX cinema, **Musée de l'Automobile** for car fans, and, crowning the plaza, the **Grande Arche de La Défense,** an enormous open cube aligned with avenue de la Grande-Armée, the Arc de Triomphe, the Champs-Élysées, and the Louvre. Tubular glass elevators whisk you 360 ft to the top. ✉ *Parvis de La Défense,* ☎ *01–49–07–27–57.* 🎟 *Arch 40 frs; auto museum 35 frs.* 🕑 *Arch daily 10–7; auto museum daily 12:30–7:30. Métro, RER: Grande Arche de La Défense.*

Expo-Musée Renault. Until the closure of its factory by the Seine in the 1990s, car-giant Renault was the main employer in the suburb of Boulogne-Billancourt. This turn-of-the-century brick mansion, near the Musée Albert Kahn (☞ *below*), pays tribute to Renault with models, posters, photographs, and souvenirs. ✉ *27 rue des Abondances, Boulogne-Billancourt.* ☎ *01–46–05–21–58.* 🎟 *Free.* 🕑 *Sept.–July, Tues. 2–6, Thurs. noon–6. Métro: Boulogne–Pont de St-Cloud.*

Musée Albert Kahn. The 72,000 photographs of places and people from around the world, amassed by banker Albert Kahn between 1909 and 1931, form the basis for the nostalgic travel exhibitions staged here. Around the museum, a delightful 8-acre park contains fruit trees, rose bushes, and French-, English-, and Japanese-style gardens. ✉ *14 rue du Port, Boulogne-Billancourt,* ☎ *01–46–04–52–80.* 🎟 *15 frs.* 🕑 *Tues.–Sun. 11–6. Métro: Boulogne–Pont-St-Cloud.*

Musée d'Art et d'Histoire (Art and History Museum). This museum in St-Denis is housed in a former convent with a notable porticoed 18th-century chapel. The collections include local archaeological finds, medieval ceramics, and souvenirs from the Paris Commune of 1870–71, when Paris was besieged by the Prussians and cut off from the outside world. ✉ *22 bis rue Gabriel-Péri, St-Denis,* ☎ *01–42–43–05–10.* 🎟 *35 frs.* 🕑 *Wed.–Sat. and Mon., 10–5:30; Sun. 2–6:30. Métro: Porte de Paris.*

Musée-Jardin Paul Landowski (Landowski Museum and Garden). One of the sculptors featured at the 1930s Museum (☞ *below*) is Paul Landowski (1875–1961), and more of his vigorously expressive bronze and marble statues can be admired here on the site of his former studio. ⊠ *14 rue Max-Blondat, Boulogne-Billancourt,* ☎ *01–55–18– 46–41.* ☒ *15 frs.* ⊙ *Wed. and weekends 10–noon and 2–5. Métro: Boulogne–Jean-Jaurès.*

🐾 **Parc Andre-Citroën** (Andre-Citroën Park). This innovative and lovely park in southwest Paris was built on the site of the former Citroën automobile factory. Now it has lawns, Japanese rock gardens, rambling wildflowers, and elegant greenhouses full of exotic plants and flowers. There's also a delightful, computer-programmed "dancing fountain" that you can play in. On a sunny day, it's a great place to take a break from sightseeing. ⊠ *Entrances on rue St-Charles and rue de la Montagne de l'Esperou. Métro, RER: Javel.*

🐾 **Parc Montsouris and Cité Universitaire** (Montsouris Park and University City). The picturesque, English-style Montsouris Park and the University "City," or campus, are in the residential 14ᵉ arrondissement, south of Montparnasse. Parc Montsouris has cascades, a lake, and a meteorological observatory disguised as a Tunisian Palace. The Cité Universitaire, opposite Parc Montsouris and next to the futuristic Stade Charléty athletics stadium, houses 5,000 international students in buildings that date mainly from the 1930s and reflect the architecture of different countries. Le Corbusier designed the Swiss and Brazilian houses; John D. Rockefeller funded the Maison Internationale; and the Sacré-Coeur church recalls the simple, muscular confidence of buildings erected in Mussolini's Italy. ⊠ *Parc Montsouris: entrances on av. Reille, bd. Jourdan, and rue Gazan; Cité Universitaire: entrance at 19 bd. Jourdan,* ☎ *Cité Universitaire information: 01–44–16–64– 00. RER: Cité Universitaire.*

Parcours des Années Trente and Musée des Années 30 (1930s Trail and 1930s Museum). For a look at outstanding Art Deco buildings by such architects as Le Corbusier, Auguste Perret, Raymond Fisher, and Robert Mallet-Stevens, follow the "1930s Trail" in the suburb of Boulogne-Billancourt. The route is outlined in an illustrated booklet available at the magnificent Hôtel de Ville (⊠ av. André-Morizet), built by Tony Garnier in 1934. More Art Deco is to be found at the Musée des Années 30 (1930s Museum), next to the Hôtel de Ville. This museum has a wealth of beautifully presented paintings and sculpture produced in France during the interwar period. There's also an intriguing section on "colonial art," which borders between the naïve and the patronizing. The collection of furniture and objects is disappointingly sparse. ⊠ *28 av. André-Morizet, Boulogne-Billancourt,* ☎ *01–55–18–53–70.* ☒ *20 frs.* ⊙ *Tues.–Sun. 2–6. Métro: Marcel-Sembat.*

Stade de France (National Stadium). This 80,000-seat stadium was built especially for the 1998 Soccer World Cup. Its flat glass roof, supported on slender pointed masts, is often likened to a flying saucer. Behind-the-scene tours take in the dressing rooms, reception areas, and a vertiginous view of the pitch—with the Basilique St-Denis visible to the north and the Sacré-Coëur away to the south. ⊠ *av. Jules-Rimet (Porte H), St-Denis,* ☎ *01–55–93–00–45.* ☒ *35 frs, guided tours 90 frs.* ⊙ *Apr.–Sept., daily 10–6; guided tours at 10, 2, and 4. Métro: Porte de Paris.*

2   DINING

If you dream of savoring truffle-studded foie gras from Limoges china, breaking the crust of a steaming cassoulet in a thick crockery bowl, or dining on a simple but delicious steak with fries, Paris is the ultimate gourmet destination. It's still a bastion of classic French cooking, but Paris's culinary landscape is nonetheless changing with a new generation of chefs who are bringing exciting innovations to French cuisine.

Revised and
updated by
Alexander
Lobrano

PARIS IS ONE OF THE WORLD'S GREAT food capitals
and a stronghold of classic French cuisine. Nonetheless, if you are coming from New York, London,
or Los Angeles, where innovative restaurants abound, you may find
the French capital a little staid. In fact, a battle is currently being
waged between the traditionalists and a remarkable new generation
of chefs who are modernizing French cooking—and changing the
French culinary landscape.

Tellingly, the trendiest new brasserie in town, Alcazar, is run by En-
glishman Sir Terence Conran. On top of that, the menu at superstar
chef Alain Ducasse's new bistro, Spoon, Food and Wine, is substantially inspired by Asian and American cooking (over half the wine list
is American, too). These new bistros and brasseries are very popular,
so it's a good idea to make reservations as soon as you get to town (or
even beforehand). Many serve a seasonal menu, which means that the
chef shops daily and buys according to what's fresh, in season, and
well-priced in the markets. Since dishes change frequently, those mentioned are cited more to give you an idea of a restaurant's cooking style
than as specific recommendations.

Facing an increasingly penny-wise public, many Paris restaurants now
offer excellent, fixed-price menus. Still, it's not unusual to hear tales
of outrageous prices, mediocre food, and haughty waiters; it's certainly
possible to have a bad meal in Paris. Yet the city's restaurants exist principally for the demanding Parisians themselves, for whom every meal
is, if not a way of life, certainly an event worthy of their undivided attention. To dine well, therefore, look for restaurants where the French
go—even if they are off the beaten path. Keep in mind, however, that
world-famous restaurants are bound to be frequented by foreigners as
well as Parisians and that an American at the next table is not always
a bad sign.

Included in this listing are a variety of restaurants and price ranges.
More than half are in the 1er–8^e *arrondissements,* within easy reach of
hotels and sights; many others are in the 14^e and 16^e, also popular visitor areas; and some are in the 11^e–20^e, outlying, often residential
neighborhoods where the rents are cheaper and young chefs can af-
ford to strike out on their own. Recognizing that even in Paris you may
not want to eat French food at every meal, several ethnic restaurants
are also listed. (One area worth exploring—especially at lunchtime—
is Paris's Chinatown in the 13^e arrondissement; the main streets are
avenue d'Ivry and avenue du Choisy.)

Mealtimes
Generally, Paris restaurants are open from noon to about 2 and from
7:30 or 8 to 10 or 10:30. Brasseries have longer hours and often serve
all day and late into the evening; some are open 24 hours. The iconoclastic wine bars do as they want, frequently serving hot food only
through lunch and cold assortments of charcuterie and cheese until a
late-afternoon or early evening close. Assume a restaurant is open
every day unless otherwise indicated. Surprisingly, many restaurants
close on Saturday as well as Sunday. July and August are the most common months for annual closings, but Paris in August is no longer quite
the wasteland it used to be.

Menus
All establishments must post their menus outside, so study them carefully before deciding to enter. Most restaurants have two basic types

of menu: à la carte and fixed price (prix fixe, or *un menu*). The prix-fixe menu is usually the best value, though choices are more limited. Most menus begin with a first course (*une entrée*), often subdivided into cold and hot starters, followed by fish and poultry, then meat; it's rare today that anyone orders something from all three. However, outside of brasseries, wine bars, and other simple places, it's inappropriate to order just one dish, as you'll understand when you see the waiter's expression. In recent years, the *menu dégustation* (tasting menu) has become popular; consisting of numerous small courses, it allows for a wide sampling of the chef's offerings. In general, consider the season when ordering; daily specials are usually based on what's freshest in the market that day.

See the Menu Guide at the end of the book for guidance with menu items that appear frequently on French menus and throughout the reviews that follow.

Prices

Although prices are high, we have made an effort to include a number of lower-priced establishments. By French law, prices must include tax and tip (*service compris* or *prix nets*), but pocket change left on the table in basic places, or an additional 5% in better restaurants, is always appreciated. Beware of bills stamped "Service Not Included" in English or restaurants slyly using American-style credit-card slips, hoping that you'll be confused and add the habitual 15% tip. In neither case should you tip beyond the guidelines suggested above.

CATEGORY	COST*
$$$$	over 550 frs
$$$	300 frs–550 frs
$$	175 frs–300 frs
$	under 175 frs

per person for a three-course meal, including tax and service but not drinks

Reservations

In the reviews below, we have only indicated where reservations are essential (and when booking weeks or months in advance is necessary) and where reservations are not accepted. Because restaurants are open for only a few hours for lunch and dinner, and because meals are long affairs here, we urge you to make reservations. Most wine bars do not take reservations; reservations are also unnecessary for brasserie and café meals at odd hours.

Restaurant Types

What's the difference between a bistro and a brasserie? Can you order food at a café? Can you go to a restaurant just for a snack? The following definitions should help.

A **restaurant** traditionally serves a three-course meal (first, main, and dessert) at both lunch and dinner. Although this category includes the most formal, three-star establishments, it also applies to humble neighborhood spots. Don't expect to grab a quick snack. In general, restaurants are what you choose when you want a complete meal and when you have the time to linger over it. Wine is typical with restaurant meals. Hours are fairly consistent (☞ Mealtimes, *above*).

Many say that **bistros** served the world's first fast food. After the fall of Napoléon, the Russian soldiers who occupied Paris were known to bang on zinc-topped café bars, crying *"bistro"*—"quickly" in Russian. In the past, bistros were simple places with minimal decor and service. Although many nowadays are quite upscale, with beautiful interiors and chic clientele, most remain cozy establishments serving straight-forward, frequently gutsy cooking, a wide variety of meats, and long-simmered dishes such as pot-au-feu and veal blanquette.

Brasseries—ideal places for quick, one-dish meals—originated when Alsatians fleeing German occupiers after the Franco-Prussian War came to Paris and opened restaurants serving specialties from home. Pork-based dishes, *choucroute* (sauerkraut and sausages), and beer (*brasserie* also means brewery) were—and still are—mainstays here. The typical brasserie is convivial and keeps late hours. Some are open 24 hours a day—a good thing to know, since many restaurants stop serving at 10:30 PM.

Like bistros and brasseries, **cafés** come in a confusing variety. Often informal neighborhood hangouts, cafés may also be veritable show-places attracting chic, well-heeled crowds. At most cafés, regulars congregate at the bar, where coffee and drinks are cheaper than at tables. At lunch, tables are set and a limited menu is served. Sandwiches, usually with *jambon* (ham), *fromage* (cheese, often Gruyère or Camembert), or *mixte* (ham and cheese), are served throughout the day. Cafés are for lingering, for people-watching, and for daydreaming; they are listed separately below.

Wine bars, or bistros *à vins,* are a newer phenomenon. These informal places often serve very limited menus, perhaps no more than open-face sandwiches (*tartines*) and selections of cheeses and cold cuts (*charcuterie*). Owners concentrate on their wine lists, which often include less well-known, regional selections, many of them available by the glass. Like today's bistros and brasseries, some wine bars are very upscale indeed, with full menus and costly wine lists. Still, most remain friendly and unassuming places for sampling wines you might otherwise never try.

Smoking
You can count on it: Parisians smoke before, during, and after meals. Restaurants are supposed to have no-smoking sections—if you want to sit in one, make this very clear—though these areas are often limited to a very few tables and are generally not strictly enforced.

What to Wear
Casual dress is acceptable at all but the fanciest restaurants. Be aware that in Paris, however, casual usually means more dressed up than you may be used to. When in doubt, leave the blue jeans and sneakers behind. Most of all, use your judgment. In the reviews below, we have indicated where a jacket and/or tie are required.

Wine
The wine that suits your meal is the wine you like. The traditional rule of white with fish and red with meat no longer applies. If the restaurant has a sommelier, let him help you. Most sommeliers are knowledgeable about their lists and will suggest what is appropriate after you've made your tastes and budget known. In addition to the wine list, informal restaurants will have a *vin de la maison* (house wine) that is less expensive. Simpler spots will have wines *en carafe* (in a carafe) or *en pichet* (in a pitcher). Except for wine bars and brasseries, most restaurants do not sell wine by the glass. If you'd like something before the meal, consider ordering your wine for the meal ahead of time, or sample a typical French *apéritif,* such as a *kir,* chilled white wine with black-currant liqueur.

Restaurants by Arrondissement

1er Arrondissement (Louvre/Les Halles)
See Right Bank Dining map.

FRENCH

$$$$ ✕ **Gérard Besson.** Chef Besson has mastered a superb classical repertoire, subtly enlivened by his creative touches. The terrine of Bresse
chicken with foie gras and the oyster flan are delicious. In season, experience the *lièvre à la royale*, braised hare in a luscious brown sauce.
For dessert, sample the unusual confit of fennel with vanilla ice cream.
The setting is attractive and intimate, with pale pink fabrics and carved
wood panels. There is an excellent wine cellar and a good-value 280-
franc lunch menu. ✉ *5 rue du Coq-Héron,* ☎ *01–42–33–14–74. AE,
DC, MC, V. Closed Sun. No lunch Sat. Jan.–Sept. Métro: Les Halles.*

$$$$ ✕ **Le Grand Véfour.** Luminaries from Napoléon to Colette to Jean
Cocteau frequented this intimate address under the arcades of the
Palais-Royal; you can request to be seated at their preferred tables. A
sumptuously decorated restaurant, with mirrored ceiling and painted
glass panels, it is perhaps the prettiest in Paris, and its 18th-century
origins make it one of the oldest. Chef Guy Martin impresses with his
unique blend of sophisticated yet rustic dishes, including foie gras–stuffed
ravioli and truffled veal sweetbreads. ✉ *17 rue Beaujolais,* ☎ *01–42–
96–56–27. Reservations essential 1 wk in advance. Jacket and tie. AE,
DC, MC, V. Closed weekends and Aug. Métro: Palais-Royal.*

$$–$$$ ✕ **Chez Pauline.** For a dressy night out in a chic but comfortable
restaurant where irreproachable traditional French food is served,
head to this venerable bistro. The doorman in livery sets the tone—
service is solicitous and unfailingly correct. Indulge in classic luxury
foods like foie gras, truffles, and fine seafood. If you're a fan of crème
brûlée, take note of Chez Pauline's version: four different individual
portions in little china ramekins. ✉ *5 rue Villedo,* ☎ *01–42–96–20–
70. Reservations essential. AE, DC, MC, V. Closed Sun. No lunch Sat.
Métro: Pyramides.*

$$ ✕ **Au Pied de Cochon.** The menu at this lively, landmark, 24-hour
brasserie in Les Halles is classic French: shellfish, onion soup, *steak
frites* (steak and fries), and, of course, the eponymous pig's feet. The
decor is Busby Berkleyesque—with wall sconces adorned with giant
bunches of frosted glass grapes. Popular since its founding in 1946,
today it's mostly filled with tourists. But a frisky crowd of noctam-
bulists can be found here, and the terrace is a good spot for people-
watching in nice weather. ✉ *6 rue Coquillière,* ☎ *01–40–13–77–00.
AE, DC, MC, V. Métro: Les Halles.*

$$ ✕ **Le Fumoir.** This handsome café-restaurant by the Louvre is one of
the city's trendiest new addresses—it's usually filled with media stars,
young artistes, and fashion types. The large, airy space has bare wood
floors, a big, wood bar, and a book-lined library stocked with international magazines and papers. The menu features simple fare such as
salads, pasta dishes, grilled chicken and veal, and carrot cake. There's
also a great selection of single-malt whiskies. *6 rue de l'Amiral-Col-
igny,* ☎ *01–42–92–00–24. AE, MC, V. Métro: Louvre.*

$$ ✕ **Le Poquelin.** The theaterlike scenery gives this welcoming little
restaurant an atmosphere that's both elegant and relaxed. Owners Mag-
gie and Michel Guillaumin proudly serve classic French cooking with
a twist—like an Asian-influenced garnish of ground sesame seeds on
a generous serving of shrimp and mixed greens, and free-range chicken
with a preserved-lemon sauce. The wine list is also good and fairly priced.
✉ *17 rue Molière,* ☎ *01–42–96–22–19. AE, DC, MC, V. Closed
weekends. Métro: Palais-Royal.*

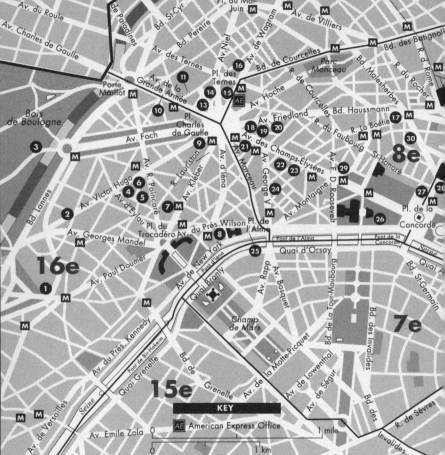

À la Cloche
des Halles, **39**

Alain Ducasse, **6**

Les Allobroges, **66**

Les Ambassadeurs, **27**

L'Ambroisie, **76**

Androuët, **48**

Astier, **63**

L'Astor, **30**

Au Bascou, **61**

Au Bourguignon du
Marais, **80**

Au Camelot, **68**

Au Petit
Colombier, **14**

Au Pied
de Cochon, **40**

Au Pressoir, **88**

Au Trou Gascon, **86**

Au Vieux Bistrot, **53**

Aux Crus de
Bourgogne, **41**

Aux Négociants, **51**

Baracane, **82**

Bistrot des Deux
Théâtres, **47**

Le Bistrot du
Cochon d'Or, **57**

Le Bistrot du
Sommelier, **17**

Bofinger, **83**

Brasserie Flo, **55**

La Butte Chaillot, **7**

Café Runtz, **45**

Chardenoux, **84**

Chartier, **46**

Les Chauffeurs, **1**

Chez Casimir, **54**

Chez Georges, **43**

Chez Jenny, **62**

Chez Michel, **52**

Chez Nenesse, **70**

Chez Omar, **69**

Chez Pauline, **35**

Chez Tante
Louise, **29**

Les Élysées, **21**

Fellini, **75**

La Fermette
Marbeuf, **24**

Les Fernandises, **60**

Le Fumoir, **90**

Gaya, **31**

Gérard Besson, **42**

Le Graindorge, **13**

Le Grand Véfour, **36**

Le Grizzli, **73**

Guy Savoy, **15**

L'Huitrier, **16**
Jacques Mélac, **65**
Jamin, **8**
Julien, **56**
Langevin, **50**
Ledoyen, **26**
Lucas-Carton, **28**
Le Moulin à Vins, **49**
L'Oulette, **89**
Le Passage, **81**
Le Pavillon
Puebla, **58**
Le Petit Rétro, **4**
Pierre au Palais
Royal, **33**

Pierre Gagnaire, **25**
Le Poquelin, **34**
Port Alma, **19**
Le Pré Catalan, **3**
Prunier, **9**
Le Reconfort, **71**
Le Relais du Parc, **5**
Le Repaire de
Cartouche, **67**
Le Restaurant d'Eric
Frechon, **59**
Restaurant du Palais-
Royal, **37**
La Rôtisserie
d'Armaillé, **11**

Le Rubis, **32**
Saudade, **74**
Sébillon, **22**
Spoon, Food and
Wine, **23**
Le Square
Trousseau, **85**
Stella Maris, **18**
La Table
de Pierre, **12**
Taillevent, **20**
Le Timgad, **10**
La Tour du
Montlhéry, **72**
Trumilou, **79**

Le Vaudeville, **44**
Il Vicolo, **78**
Le Vieux Bistro, **77**
Le Villaret, **64**
Le Vivarois, **2**
Willi's Wine Bar, **38**
Les Zygomates, **87**

Left Bank Dining

$$ ✕ **Pierre au Palais-Royal.** Locals fretted over the transformation of one of the city's most venerable traditional tables into this restaurant, but have since flocked to this place created by Jean-Paul Arabian, husband of chef Ghislaine Arabian, formerly of Ledoyen (☞ 8ᵉ arrondissement, *below*). Arabian retained the old-fashioned decor but hired a young chef who had been at some of the best restaurants in Italy. His style is judiciously modern—he has retained classics like *boeuf á la ficelle* (poached beef), but added a superb salad garnished with raw tuna and lemon, and a shepherd's pie made with duck. Dress up to be well received in this very Parisian, clubby-feeling spot. ⊠ *10 rue de Richelieu,* ☎ *01–42–96–09–17. Reservations essential. AE, DC, MC, V. Closed Sun. Métro: Palais-Royal.*

$$ ✕ **Restaurant du Palais-Royal.** Tucked away in the northern corner of the magnificent Palais-Royal garden, this pleasant bistro has a lovely terrace and good food. A salad of baby scallops and mushrooms in a balsamic vinaigrette is among the interesting contemporary dishes. Find a perfect wine to match from the appealing list. It's a wonderful spot for a romantic tête-à-tête. ⊠ *Jardins du Palais-Royal, 110 Galerie Valois,* ☎ *01–40–20–00–27. AE, MC, V. Closed Sun. No lunch Sat. Métro: Palais-Royal.*

$–$$ ✕ **Aux Crus de Bourgogne.** This delightfully old-fashioned bistro, with its bright lights and red-checker tablecloths, attracts a happy, lively crowd. It opened in 1932 and quickly became popular by serving two luxury items—foie gras and cold lobster with homemade mayonnaise—at surprisingly low prices, a tradition that happily continues. Among the bistro classics on the menu, the *boeuf au gros sel* (beef boiled in bouillon with vegetables and garnished with rock salt) and *confit de canard* (duck confit) are very satisfying. ⊠ *3 rue Bachaumont,* ☎ *01–42–33–48–24. V. Closed weekends and Aug. Métro: Sentier.*

$–$$ ✕ **La Tour du Montlhéry.** When the centuries-old Les Halles marketplace became an aseptic shopping mall, many neighborhood bistros closed or went upscale. The Montlhéry managed to hang on to the old-market feel, with its sagging wood-beam ceilings, red-checker tablecloths, and exposed brick walls lined with imaginative portraits. If you don't mind passing under hanging samples of your future meal (sausages, etc.) on your way into the dining room, then you can enjoy the simple grilled food served by jovial waiters. Go for the *côte de boeuf* (prime rib) and wash it down with a good Beaujolais. ⊠ *5 rue des Prouvaires,* ☎ *01–42–36–21–82. MC, V. Closed weekends and July 14–Aug. 15. Métro: Les Halles.*

$–$$ ✕ **Willi's Wine Bar.** This English-owned wine bar is a renowned haunt for Anglophiles as well as chic Parisians. The simple, often original menu changes to reflect the market's offerings and might include chicken liver terrine, sea trout with lemon butter, and crème brûlée. The wine list includes more than 250 listings with an emphasis on Rhônes. The quality of the service can vary. ⊠ *13 rue des Petits-Champs,* ☎ *01–42–61–05–09. MC, V. Closed Sun. Métro: Bourse.*

$ ✕ **A la Cloche des Halles.** Forgive the tacky decor and enjoy quiches, omelets, and assortments of high-quality cheeses and charcuterie at this small, popular, crowded wine bar. Served by the glass or bottle, wines include some good Beaujolais. Get here by 12:30 PM for lunch—even better, make a reservation. The simple menu is served until 10 PM. ⊠ *28 rue Coquillière,* ☎ *01–42–36–93–89. No credit cards. Closed Sun. Métro: Les Halles.*

$ ✕ **Le Rubis.** This humble neighborhood wine bar enjoys tremendous popularity with everyone from executives to construction workers. One or two hearty plats du jour, such as *petit salé* (salted, slow-cooked pork ribs) with lentils and *boudin noir* (blood sausage), plus omelets, cheeses, and charcuterie make up the menu. And there's an eclectic selection of adequate wines by the glass or bottle. ✉ *10 rue du Marché St-Honoré,* ☎ *01–42–61–03–34. Reservations not accepted. No credit cards. Closed Sun. and mid-Aug. No dinner Sat. Métro: Tuileries.*

ITALIAN

$–$$ ✕ **Fellini.** This friendly Italian restaurant with exposed stone walls and pink napery has two locations. At both, the antipasto buffet is wonderfully varied, the spaghetti with baby clams delicious, and the veal dishes are good, too. Offbeat wines from Sardinia or Ischia complete the meal. ✉ *47 rue de l'Arbre Sec,* ☎ *01–42–60–90–66, Métro: Louvre; 58 rue de la Croix-Nivert,* ☎ *01–45–77–40–77, Métro: Commerce. MC, V. Closed Sun. No lunch Sat. at Croix-Nivert.*

PORTUGUESE

$$ ✕ **Saudade.** At this charming Portuguese restaurant, *fado* (traditional music), *azulejos* (decorative tiles), and superb *caldo verde* (a delicate soup of bouillon, potatoes, kale, and chorizo sausage) set the tone. You can also choose from 20 different cod dishes: The *bacalhau à bras,* for instance, is a delicious combination of salt cod, potatoes, onions, and eggs. The Portuguese wines are excellent, as is the service. ✉ *34 rue des Bourdonnais,* ☎ *01–42–36–30–71. AE, DC, MC, V. Closed Sun. Métro: Les Halles.*

SEAFOOD

$$ ✕ **Gaya.** Come here for seafood in all its guises, from marinated anchovies to fish soup to grilled sole—much of it with a Mediterranean accent. The colorful Portuguese tiles on the ground floor are delightful; upstairs is less attractive. ✉ *17 rue Duphot,* ☎ *01–42–60–43–03. AE, MC, V. Closed Sun. Métro: Madeleine.*

2e Arrondissement (La Bourse)
See Right Bank Dining map.

FRENCH

$$ ✕ **Chez Georges.** The traditional bistro cooking is good—herring, sole, kidneys, steaks, and *frites* (fries)—and the atmosphere is better. A wood-paneled entry leads you to an elegant and unpretentious dining room where one long, white-clothed stretch of table lines the mirrored walls, and attentive waiters sweep efficiently along the entire length. ✉ *1 rue du Mail,* ☎ *01–42–60–07–11. AE, DC, MC, V. Closed Sun. and Aug. Métro: Sentier.*

$$ ✕ **Le Vaudeville.** One of Jean-Paul Bucher's seven Parisian brasseries, Le Vaudeville is filled with well-dressed Parisians (many of them from the Stock Exchange across the street) and is a good value, thanks to its assortment of prix-fixe menus. Shellfish, house-smoked salmon, and desserts such as profiteroles are particularly fine. Enjoy the handsome 1930s decor and joyful dining until 2 AM daily. ✉ *29 rue Vivienne,* ☎ *01–40–20–04–62. AE, DC, MC, V. Closed Dec. 24. Métro: Bourse.*

$ ✕ **Café Runtz.** Next to the Salle Favart, in a neighborhood once filled with theaters, this friendly bistro has been given an overhaul by star decorator Jacques Grange. Old brass gas lamps on each table and rich *boiseries* (woodwork) create a cozy but elegant atmosphere. Tasty, hearty Alsatian dishes include Gruyère salad, onion tart, choucroute, and fresh fruit tarts. Order a pitcher of Riesling or other Alsatian wine to go along. The two prix-fixe menus are a good value; one of them, the "Salé-Sucré," includes quiche with green salad, a fruit tart, and a glass of wine or mineral water and is served all afternoon. ✉ *16 rue Favart,* ☎ *01–42–96–69–86. AE, MC, V. Closed Sat. lunch and Sun. and Aug. Métro: Richelieu-Drouot.*

3ᵉ Arrondissement (Beaubourg/Marais)

See Right Bank Dining map.

FRENCH

$$　✕ Chez Nenesse. On a quiet corner on the northernmost edge of the Marais, this pleasant, old-fashioned neighborhood bistro draws a stylish crowd of fashion and media types and local regulars. They come for chef Alain Le Meur's delicious fare: Before setting out on his own, he worked at a variety of esteemed restaurants and his experience shows in precise cooking, original side dishes, and attractively garnished plates. Start with artichoke hearts in walnut-oil vinaigrette or a sautée of wild mushrooms and snails, and then try game (in season), roasted veal kidney, or fricassee of chicken in vinegar sauce. Desserts are excellent. Go with the Gigondas or Cahors from the slightly pricey wine list. ⊠ *17 rue Saintonge,* ☎ *01–42–78–46–49. MC, V. Closed weekends and Aug. Métro: Filles du Calvaire.*

$$　✕ Le Reconfort. This bistro on the northern edge of the Marais scores big with the fashion crowd, giving the place a definite buzz. But even if this isn't your scene, you can still enjoy the traditional French food, with North African and Italian touches. Start with the *compote de legumes* (vegetable and chickpea cake with Moroccan spices), and continue with confit de canard with crispy potatoes. The brief wine list has several good buys, like the house Côtes du Rhône. ⊠ *37 rue Poitou,* ☎ *01–42–76–06–36. Reservations essential. MC, V. Closed Sun., Mon. Métro: St-Sebastian Froissart.*

$　✕ Au Bascou. Gregarious proprietor Jean-Guy Lousteau enthusiastically shares his knowledge of the wines of southwest France at this fashionable little bistro (the mosaics made of broken mirrors are an especially nice touch.) The sturdy, savory cuisine of the Basque country stars on the menu, and the country ham, cod with broccoli puree, and sautéed baby squid are particularly flavorful. ⊠ *38 rue Réaumur,* ☎ *01–42–72–69–25. MC, V. Closed weekends. Métro: Arts et Métiers.*

$　✕ Chez Jenny. Since the installation of a rotisserie grill, this restaurant has become *the* place for some of the best choucroute in the capital. The sauerkraut, delivered weekly by a private supplier in Alsace, is garnished with a variety of charcuterie and a big grilled ham knuckle. For dessert, the perfectly aged Muenster cheese and homemade blueberry tart are good choices. The ambience is lively. ⊠ *39 bd. du Temple,* ☎ *01–42–74–75–75. AE, DC, MC, V. Métro: République.*

NORTH AFRICAN

$　✕ Chez Omar. Whether you're a die-hard couscous fan or have never tried it before, Omar's is the place for this signature North African dish. Order it with grilled skewered lamb, spicy *merguez* sausage, a lamb shank, or chicken—portions are generous. The restaurant, in a former turn-of-the-century bistro, is popular with a fashionable crowd. Proprietor Omar Guerida, who speaks English, is famously friendly. ⊠ *47 rue de Bretagne,* ☎ *01–42–72–36–26. MC, V. No lunch Sun. Métro: Filles du Calvaire.*

4ᵉ Arrondissement (Marais/Ile St-Louis)

See Right Bank Dining map.

FRENCH

$$$$　✕ L'Ambroisie. At this tiny, romantic restaurant on Place des Vosges, chef-owner Bernard Pacaud serves refined, oft-imitated cuisine, such as red bell pepper mousse, and braised oxtail. The jewellike Italianate setting of flowers, tapestries, and subdued lighting adds to the pleasure of eating here. ⊠ *9 pl. des Vosges,* ☎ *01–42–78–51–45. Reservations essential 1 month in advance. MC, V. Closed Sun., Mon., Aug., and mid-Feb. Métro: St-Paul.*

$$ ✕ **Au Bourguignon du Marais.** The handsome, contemporary look of
★ this Marais bistro and wine bar is the perfect backdrop for the good,
traditional fare and excellent Burgundies served by the glass and bot-
tle. Especially good choices are the smoked salmon, the fricasee of cèpe
and girolles mushrooms, the reasonably priced escargots, and the
nicely seasoned steak tartare. ⊠ *19 rue de Jouy,* ☎ *01–48–87–15–40.
MC, V. Closed Sun. Métro: St-Paul.*

$$ ✕ **Le Grizzli.** It's said that this turn-of-the-century bistro used to have
dancing bears out front—thus the name. The owner gets many of his
ingredients—especially the wonderful ham and cheeses—from his native Auvergne. Several dishes are cooked on a hot slate, including the
salmon and the lamb. There's an interesting selection of wines from
southwest France. ⊠ *7 rue St-Martin,* ☎ *01–48–87–77–56. MC, V.
Closed Sun. Métro: Châtelet.*

$$ ✕ **Le Vieux Bistro.** Overlook the touristy location next to Notre-Dame
and the corny name, "the old bistro." This place really *is* generations
old, and its menu is full of bistro classics, such as beef fillet with mar-
row, éclairs, and tart Tatin. The decor is nondescript, but the fre-
quently fancy crowd doesn't seem to notice. ⊠ *14 rue du
Cloître-Notre-Dame,* ☎ *01–43–54–18–95. MC, V. Métro: Hôtel de Ville.*

$–$$ ✕ **Bofinger.** One of the oldest, most beautiful, and most popular
brasseries in Paris has generally improved since brasserie maestro Jean-
Paul Bucher took over. Settle in to one of the tables dressed in crisp
white linens, under the gorgeous Art Nouveau glass cupola, and enjoy
fine classic brasserie fare, such as oysters, grilled sole, or fillet of lamb.
The house Muscadet is a good white wine, the Fleurie is a pleasant red.
Note that the no-smoking section here is not only enforced, but is also
in the prettiest part of the restaurant. ⊠ *5–7 rue de la Bastille,* ☎ *01–
42–72–87–82. AE, DC, MC, V. Métro: Bastille.*

$ ✕ **Baracane.** The owner of this small, simple place oversees the menu
of robust specialties from his native southwest France—roast lamb with
thyme, cassoulet, and madeleine cookies with stewed rhubarb. The reasonable dinner menu and the even cheaper lunch menu keep the Baracane solidly affordable and one of the best values in the Marais. ⊠ *38
rue des Tournelles,* ☎ *01–42–71–43–33. MC, V. Closed Sun. No lunch
Sat. Métro: Bastille.*

$ ✕ **Trumilou.** Crowds of students, artist types, and others on a budget
come here to eat bistro cuisine, such as leg of lamb and apple tarts.
The nondecor is somehow homey, the staff is friendly, and the location facing the Seine and the Ile St-Louis is especially pleasant in nice
weather, when you can sit on the narrow terrace under the trees. ⊠
84 quai de l'Hôtel de Ville, ☎ *01–42–77–63–98. MC, V. Closed Mon.
Métro: Pont-Marie.*

ITALIAN

$$ ✕ **Il Vicolo.** Low-key but stylish, with a trendy, young crowd, this restau-
rant serves authentic and very good contemporary Italian cuisine—it's
ideal for a night off from French food. The spicy chickpea soup is de-
licious, as is the Livorno-style red mullet, served in a sauce of wine and
herbs. Delicious desserts and a nice Italian wine list finish off the
evening. ⊠ *8 rue de Jouy,* ☎ *01–42–78–38–86. MC, V. Closed Sun.,
Mon. Métro: St-Paul.*

5e Arrondissement (Latin Quarter)
See Left Bank Dining map.

CHINESE

$ ✕ **Mirama.** Regulars at this popular and rather chaotic Chinese restau-
rant order the soup, a rich broth with a nest of thick noodles garnished
with dumplings, barbecued pork, or smoked duck. Main courses are

generous—the best are made with shellfish; the Peking duck is also excellent. Service is brisk, so plan on coffee in a nearby café. For dining alone, it's a good place to eat. ⊠ *17 rue St-Jacques,* ☎ *01–43–29–66–58. V. Métro: St-Michel.*

FRENCH

$$$$ ✕ **La Tour d'Argent.** Dining at this temple to haute cuisine is an event—from apéritifs in the ground-floor bar to dinner in the top-floor dining room, with its breathtaking view of Notre-Dame. The food, however, though often good, rarely reaches the same heights as the setting. La Tour classics such as *caneton Tour d'Argent* (pressed duck) have been lightened and contemporary creations added, including *canard de l'an 2000* (duck for the year 2000)—tender slices of duck breast in a rich wine sauce—and scallop salad with truffles. The wine list is one of the greatest in the world. The lunch menu is somewhat more affordable. ⊠ *15 quai de la Tournelle,* ☎ *01–43–54–23–31. Reservations essential at least 1 wk in advance. Jacket and tie at dinner. AE, DC, MC, V. Closed Mon. Métro: Cardinal Lemoine.*

$$–$$$ ✕ **La Timonerie.** Only a few steps along the quai from La Tour d'Argent is this elegant little restaurant with fine cooking and no theatrics. Philippe de Givenchy works with a small staff, and his creations are consistently interesting and well executed. Typical of his inventive style are risotto with pig's feet, roasted turbot with apricots, and sublime chocolate tart. ⊠ *35 quai de la Tournelle,* ☎ *01–43–25–44–42. Jacket and tie. MC, V. Closed Sun. and Mon. Métro: Maubert-Mutualité.*

$$ ✕ **Campagne et Provence.** On the quai across from Notre-Dame, this very pleasant little restaurant has a rustic Provençal look and a menu to match that includes grilled John Dory with preserved fennel, and peppers stuffed with cod and eggplant. In season, have the roasted figs with shortbread and black-currant sauce, an outstanding dessert. The interesting, well-priced list of regional wines adds to the dining experience. ⊠ *25 quai de la Tournelle,* ☎ *01–43–54–05–17. MC, V. Closed Sun. No lunch Sat., Mon. Métro: Maubert-Mutualité.*

$$ ✕ **Chez René.** This reliable address at the eastern end of boulevard St-Germain has satisfied three generations of Parisians, who count on finding dishes from Burgundy, such as *boeuf Bourguignon* (beef stewed in wine) and coq au vin, along with the wines of the Maconnais and Beaujolais. The dining rooms are cozy, with red leatherette banquettes and white honeycomb tile floors. ⊠ *14 bd. St-Germain,* ☎ *01–43–54–30–23. MC, V. Closed Sat. lunch and Sun., Aug., and late Dec.–early Jan. Métro: Cardinal Lemoine.*

$ ✕ **Chantairelle.** Delicious south-central Auvergne cuisine is the highlight of this friendly, good-value restaurant. The owners want you to fully experience the region, hence the recycled barn timbers, little stone fountain, and oils diffusing scents from the Auvergne. The copious main courses—you may not want to order an appetizer—include stuffed cabbage and *potée,* a casserole of pork and vegetables in broth. Try a bottle of Châteauguy, a regional red, and finish up with blueberry tart. ⊠ *17 rue Laplace,* ☎ *01–46–33–18–59. MC, V. Closed Sun. No lunch Sat. Métro: Maubert-Mutualité.*

$ ✕ **Le Reminet.** The atmosphere is relaxed at this unusually good bistro
★ in a small, narrow room with stone walls, though chandeliers and mirrors add an unexpected note of elegance. The menu changes regularly and displays the young chef's talent with dishes like a salad of scallops, greens, and sesame seeds, and roasted guinea hen with buttered Savoy cabbage. If available, try the luscious caramelized pears with cream. The lower-priced wines have been carefully chosen and are a good value. ⊠ *3 rue des Grands-Degrés,* ☎ *01–44–07–04–24. AE, MC, V. Closed Mon. and Tues. Métro: Maubert-Mutualité.*

SPANISH

$ ✕ **Fogon St-Julien.** On one of Paris's oldest streets, this intimate, friendly restaurant serves outstanding Spanish food. Start with a selection of delicious tapas and continue with the superb paella. It's made, like in Valencia, with short grain rice, broth, and saffron and studded with a generous and varied array of shellfish. Finish up with a Catalan-style crème caramel, accompanied by a glass of Muscatel, and splurge on one of their excellent Riojas. *10 St-Julien-le-Pauvre,* ☎ *01–43–54–31–33. Reservations essential. MC, V. Closed Sun. and last 3 wks Aug. Métro: St-Michel.*

6ᵉ Arrondissement (St-Germain-des-Prés)
See Left Bank Dining map.

FRENCH

$$ ✕ **Alcazar.** Englishman Sir Terence Conran's stunning new brasserie is one of the chicest and liveliest spots in town. In a former, legendary cabaret of the same name, this place seats three hundred under the skylight roof. Above, on the mezzanine, a long, brushed steel bar gives you a view of the scene. Young French chef Guillaume Lutard, formerly at Taillevent and Prunier, has created a regularly changing, appealingly classic menu: Besides the platters of oysters and shellfish, there's sea bass with fennel roast, duckling in honey and spices, and even vegetarian options. Desserts, such as fruit tarts and roasted pears in caramel, are simple but good. Note that there's a separate and less expensive bar menu—a good option for a quick, casual bite, especially if you like fish and chips—they're state of the art here. ⊠ *62 rue Mazarine,* ☎ *01–53–10–19–99. Reservations essential. AE, DC, MC, V. Métro: Odéon.*

$$ ✕ **La Bastide Odéon.** This little corner of Provence in Paris is just a
★ few steps from the Luxembourg Gardens. A sunny yellow restaurant with old oak tables and chairs, it's one of the best places to sample Mediterranean cuisine. Chef Gilles Ajuelos cooks fine fish dishes; wonderful pastas, such as tagliatelle in *pistou* (basil and pine nuts) with wild mushrooms; and delightful main courses, like roast suckling pig, and cod with capers. The best bet on the slightly pricey wine.list is the red Côteaux du Tricastin. ⊠ *7 rue Corneille,* ☎ *01–43–26–03–65. MC, V. Closed Sun., Mon. Métro: Odéon; RER: Luxembourg.*

$$ ✕ **Les Bookinistes.** Talented chef Guy Savoy's successful, fifth bistro is a cheery postmodern place that's painted peach, with red, blue, and yellow wall sconces, and looks out on the Seine. The menu of French country cooking changes seasonally and might include a mussel and pumpkin soup or baby chicken roasted in a casserole with root vegetables. The somewhat pricey wine list contrasts with the reasonable food prices. Service is friendly, if erratic. ⊠ *53 quai des Grands-Augustins,* ☎ *01–43–25–45–94. AE, DC, MC, V. No lunch weekends. Métro: St-Michel.*

$$ ✕ **Les Brezolles.** Ivory and mocha make an ideal backdrop for the well-heeled, mostly local clientele at this little restaurant on a corner in St-Germain. Well-known chef Jean-Paul Duquesnoy, who formerly had an eponymous place in the 7th, now offers more affordable upscale dining with his prix-fixe menus and well-chosen, well-priced wine list. Zucchini flowers stuffed with crab mousse are a signature starter; the appealing main courses include freshly smoked salmon steak with a garnish of julienned apple, and veal shank with chestnuts. The star dessert is a caramelized pastry with rice pudding and apricot sauce. ⊠ *5 rue Mabillon,* ☎ *01–43–26–73–70. Reservations essential. AE, DC, MC, V. Closed Sun., Mon. Métro: Mabillon.*

$$ ✕ **Chez Dumonet-Josephine.** Stylish and convivial, this venerable bistro with ambered walls, moleskin banquettes, and frosted glass lamps is popular with theater people and politicians. Generous portions of

classic French cuisine are served· typical are the very good boeuf Bourguignon and the roasted saddle of lamb with artichokes. The wine list is excellent but expensive. ⊠ *117 rue du Cherche-Midi,* ☎ *01–45 19 52–40. AE, DC, MC, V. Closed weekends. Métro: Duroc.*

$$ ✕ **L'Épi Dupin.** Half-timbered walls, sisal carpeting, and crisp white table linens are the backdrop for this pocket-size bistro that draws a loyal business crowd at noon and chic locals at night. The menu of delicious and reasonably priced French classics is revised regularly and might include mixed greens garnished with foie gras, and fillet of lamb with ratatouille. Bread and pastries are baked on premises. The prix-fixe menu is an excellent option, and the service is efficient if occasionally brusque. ⊠ *11 rue Dupin,* ☎ *01–42–22–64–56. Reservations essential. MC, V. Closed Sun. Métro: Sèvres-Babylone.*

$–$$ ✕ **Le Bouillon Racine.** Originally a *bouillon,* a Parisian soup restaurant popular at the turn of the century, this two-story place is now a delightfully renovated Belle Epoque oasis with a good Belgian menu. The terrine of leeks and the ham mousse are fine starters; the *waterzooie,* Belgian stewed chicken and vegetables, and the roast cod with white beans are excellent main dishes. The mocha-beer mousse with malt sauce is one of the many superb desserts. In honor of Belgium's some 400 different brews, it has a wonderful selection of beers. ⊠ *3 rue Racine,* ☎ *01–44–32–15–60. Reservations essential. AE, MC, V. Closed Sun. Métro: Odéon.*

$ ✕ **Bistro Mazarin.** Leave the tourists on boulevard St-Germain and join the locals at this casual, bustling bistro for good house wines and sturdy food that's especially satisfying given the prices. Lentil salad, a steak with frîtes, and a pitcher of the house red make for a pleasant meal. When the weather is good, food is served on the terrace. ⊠ *42 rue Mazarine,* ☎ *01–43–29–99–01. MC, V. Closed Sun. Métro: Mabillon.*

$ ✕ **Chez Maître Paul.** This calm, comfortable little restaurant a few steps from the Odéon is a great place to discover the little-known cooking of the Jura and Franche-Comté regions of eastern France. Though sturdy, this cuisine appeals to modern palates, too; start with the *montbéliard,* a smoked sausage served with potato salad—ample enough for two— then try one of the succulent free-range chicken dishes, either in a sauce of *vin jaune,* a dry wine from the region that resembles sherry, or baked with cream and cheese. The walnut meringue and chocolate cake are delicious, and the regional Arbois wines are worth trying. ⊠ *12 rue Monsieur-le-Prince,* ☎ *01–43–54–74–59. AE, DC, MC, V. Metro: Odéon.*

$ ✕ **Claude Sainlouis.** This cheerful spot has served the same dependable food for a very long time: inexpensive steak, fries, and salad. There's not much variety, but all of Paris—professionals, tourists, lovers—crowds boisterously into the dark, red dining room for lunch and dinner. ⊠ *27 rue du Dragon,* ☎ *01–45–48–29–68. No credit cards. Closed Sun., Aug., and 15 days at Easter and Christmas. No dinner Sat. Métro: St-Germain-des-Prés.*

$ **Le Montagnard.** This rustic little spot—"The Mountaineer" —has a jolly crowd who come to dine on fondue and *raclette* (cheese melted on potatoes). Split an *assiette montagnard,* an appetizing assortment of Savoyard cold cuts such as *viande de Grisons* (air-dried beef), and then go for the cheese or beef fondus. End your meal with such regional desserts as blueberry tart and vacherin cheese. And bear in mind a little tip from the mountains: fresh black pepper makes a cheese meal much more digestible. *24 rue des Canettes,* ☎ *01–43–26–47–15. AE, MC, V. Closed Sun. Métro: Mabillon.*

SEAFOOD

$$ ✕ **L'Espadon Bleu.** Chef Jacques Cagna's moderately priced seafood restaurant is a good place to drop anchor in St-Germain. Yellow walls,

blue beams, and attractive mosaic tables featuring the restaurant's namesake (a blue swordfish) make it stylishly nautical. Try the ravioli stuffed with tiny scallops or the grilled swordfish steak. For dessert, don't skip the Baba au Rhum, three tiny rum-soaked cakes with whipped cream and fruit. The prix-fixe menu is a great deal. *25 rue des Grands Augustins,* ☎ *01–46–33–00–85. Reservations essential. AE, MC, V. Closed Mon. No lunch weekends. Métro: Odéon.*

7° Arrondissement (Invalides)
See Left Bank Dining map.

FRENCH

$$$$ ✕ **L'Arpège.** One block from the Rodin Museum is this unusually minimalist restaurant with curving, handcrafted wood panels and wrought-iron window frames. Chef-owner Alain Passard's cuisine is both original (strips of lobster in vin jaune sauce and a dessert of stuffed sweet tomato) and classic (lamb in pepper cream sauce). Passard is a very talented chef, but this restaurant doesn't quite deliver the same streamlined haute cuisine experience found elsewhere, mainly because the service is often cold and bumbling. Brave it, though, for some splendid food. The prix-fixe lunch seems like a bargain at 390 francs. ⊠ *84 rue de Varenne,* ☎ *01–45–51–47–33. AE, DC, MC, V. Closed weekends and Aug. Métro: Varenne.*

$$$$ ✕ **Jules Verne.** Distinctive all-black decor and top-ranked chef Alain Reix's cuisine—not to mention a location at 400 ft up, on the second level of the Eiffel Tower—make the Jules Verne one of the hardest dinner reservations to get in Paris. Sautéed baby squid with duck foie gras and filet mignon of veal cooked with preserved lemon and dried fruits are examples of Reix's cooking, which, like the service, has its ups and downs. Come for lunch—a table is easier to snag. ⊠ *Eiffel Tower,* ☎ *01–45–55–61–44. Reservations essential. Jacket and tie. AE, DC, MC, V. Métro: Bir-Hakeim.*

$$$ ✕ **Le Violon d'Ingres.** Christian Constant, former head chef of the Hôtel
★ Crillon, has created a hit with his own well-heeled bistro in one of the quieter but most fashionable parts of the city. A suit-beclad crowd comes to sample the regularly revised menu, which may include such dishes as cream of pumpkin soup with sheep's cheese, risotto with boned chicken wings, and guinea hen on a bed of diced turnips. It's the perfect place for dressing up and making a night of dinner out on the town. ⊠ *135 rue St-Dominique,* ☎ *01–45–44–15–05. Reservations essential. AE, DC, MC, V. Closed Sun., Mon. Métro: École-Militaire.*

$–$$ ✕ **Au Bon Accueil.** If you want to see what well-heeled Parisians like
★ to eat these days, book a table at this extremely popular bistro as soon as you get to town. The excellent, reasonably priced *cuisine du marché* (daily menu based on what's in the markets) has made it a hit. Desserts are homemade and delicious, from the fruit tarts to the superb *pistache,* a pastry curl filled with homemade pistachio ice cream. The Château Mont Redon Côtes du Rhône is a standout on the wine list. ⊠ *14 rue de Montessuy,* ☎ *01–47–05–46–11. Reservations essential. MC, V. Closed Sun. Métro, RER: Pont l'Alma.*

$–$$ ✕ **L'Oeillade.** The food—such as shrimp tempura, and calf's liver in a raspberry vinegar sauce—is generally very good (except when the chef has an occasional off night) and the prices are unbeatable. Watch out for the wines, however—they will intoxicate your bill. The blond-wood paneling and interesting 20th-century paintings are unpretentious—the same cannot always be said about the clientele. ⊠ *10 rue de St-Simon,* ☎ *01–42–22–01–60. MC, V. Closed Sun. No lunch Sat. Métro: Rue du Bac.*

$-$$ ✕ **Les Olivades.** Excellent Provençal cuisine is served by a cheerful staff in this brightly decorated former storefront café. Start with ravioli stuffed with goat cheese; follow with scallops with vegetables; the melted chocolate cake with lavender ice cream makes a fine finale. The three-course dinner and two-course lunch menus are a good value. ✉ *41 av. Ségur,* ☎ *01–47–83–70–09. Reservations essential. MC, V. Closed Sun. No lunch Sat. Métro: Ségur, École Militaire.*

$-$$ ✕ **Le Petit Troquet.** In the shadow of the Eiffel Tower is this tiny, pleasant bistro filled with homey antiques like metal signs for detergents, old clocks, and soda siphons. The prix-fixe menu of very good bistro fare changes daily, but may include such dishes as goat-cheese mousse with smoked salmon, roast chicken, and fruit crumble for dessert. It's very popular with locals, so book ahead. ✉ *28 rue de l'Exposition,* ☎ *01–47–05–80–39. MC, V. Reservations essential. Closed Sun., Mon. Métro: École Militaire.*

$ ✕ **Chez l'Ami Jean.** Neighborhood families compose a large portion of the clientele at this welcoming, homey Basque restaurant. The haphazard decor includes banners, baskets, and photos of the staff and regulars. Enjoy the *piperade* (eggs with ham, tomatoes, and green peppers), duck or goose confits, and the nutty *gâteau Basque* for dessert. ✉ *27 rue Malar,* ☎ *01–47–05–86–89. MC, V. Closed Sun. and Aug. Métro: La Tour–Maubourg.*

$ ✕ **Thoumieux.** Budget prices for decent food like rillettes, duck confit, and cassoulet make this place—owned by the same family for three generations—popular. Don't come with gourmet expectations, but for a solid, gently priced meal. The red velour banquettes, yellow walls, and bustling waiters in long, white aprons are delightfully Parisian. ✉ *79 rue St-Dominique,* ☎ *01–47–05–49–75. MC, V. Métro: Invalides.*

SEAFOOD

$$$-$$$$ ✕ **Paul Minchelli.** Minchelli is a minimalist who believes that seasonings should not distract from the taste of his impeccably fresh—and very expensive—catch of the day. The baby clams with garlic and fiery espelette peppers as well as the sea bass drizzled with lemon and olive oil are just two of his wonderful dishes. The dressy dining room with gentle lighting and witty trompe l'oeil "views" out of "portholes" is the backdrop for a very stylish crowd, often sprinkled with celebrities. ✉ *54 bd. de La Tour-Maubourg,* ☎ *01–47–05–89–86. MC, V. Closed Sun., Mon. Métro: École Militaire.*

8ᵉ Arrondissement (Champs-Élysées)
See Right Bank Dining map.

FRENCH

$$$$ ✕ **Les Ambassadeurs.** In the opulent Hôtel Crillon, this restaurant is undoubtedly one of the finest in Paris. Respected chef Dominique Bouchet has an absolute mastery of classical French cooking, which he tempers with an awareness of modern tastes. Typical of his sophisticated cooking are the potato pancake topped with smoked salmon and caviar-flecked, and the scallops wrapped in bacon with tomato and basil. You may find the all-marble dining room, with its crystal chandeliers, mirrors, and heavy blue draperies, overbearing, but it's beautiful nonetheless. And it's hard to fault the view of place de la Concorde, the distinguished service, or the memorable wine list. Lunch is more affordable, though still expensive; there's also a good brunch. ✉ *10 pl. de la Concorde,* ☎ *01–44–71–16–16. Reservations essential. Jacket and tie at dinner. AE, DC, MC, V. Métro: Concorde.*

$$$$ ✕ **Les Élysées.** Chef Alain Solivères is a passionate cook whose repu-
★ tation continues to grow in Paris gourmet circles. Come here when you want to treat yourself, since not only is the food exquisite, but service

is also impeccable and the intimate dining room, under a beautiful turn-of-the-century *verrière* (glass ceiling), is the kind of place where you want to linger. Note, though, that it's very busy at midday, so unless you're coming for the good-value lunch menu, dinner is a calmer option. Soliveres' menu changes seasonally and draws inspiration from southern France, Basque country, Bordeaux, and Languedoc. Dishes include a "risotto" of wheat grains cooked in squid's ink, and a roasted duck liver served with baby artichokes and arugula. There's also superb wine service. ☒ *In the Hôtel Vernet, 25 rue Vernet,* ☎ *01–47–23–43–10. AE, DC, MC, V. Reservations essential. Closed weekends. Métro: George V.*

$$$$ ✗ **Ledoyen.** Whether you want to eat light or hearty, young chef Christian Le Squer's elegant, beautifully realized menu is a treat. He uses superb produce, as seen in the wonderful first course called *les coquillages* (the shellfish), a delicious dish of risotto, made bright green by herbs and topped with lobster, langoustine, scallops, and grilled ham. The turbot with truffled mashed potatoes is excellent, too, and don't skip the first-rate cheese trolley. The elegant restaurant has gilded ceilings and walls, plush armchairs, and tables with candelabra. It's off the Champs-Élysées near place de la Concorde. ☒ *1 av. Dutuit, on the Carré des Champs-Élysées,* ☎ *01–47–42–23–23. Reservations essential. AE, DC, MC, V. Closed weekends. Métro: Place de la Concorde, Champs-Élysées–Clemenceau.*

$$$$ ✗ **Lucas-Carton.** Foie gras wrapped in cabbage, a spicy duck Apicius, and red mullet with preserved lemons and olives are examples of chef Alain Senderens's provocative blend of creative and traditional cuisine. If you love wine, Senderens has the perfect menu: Each course is accompanied by a precisely chosen wine. The beautiful dining rooms glow with Belle Epoque splendor, and the international crowd is one of the dressiest in Paris. ☒ *9 pl. de la Madeleine,* ☎ *01–42–65–22–90. Reservations essential at least 3 wks in advance. Jacket and tie at dinner. MC, V. Closed Sun., Aug., and late Dec. No lunch Sat. Métro: Madeleine.*

$$$$ ✗ **Pierre Gagnaire.** Legendary chef Pierre Gagnaire's cooking is at once ★ intellectual and poetic—in a single dish at least three or four often unexpected tastes and textures are brought together in a sensational experience. Two intriguing dishes from a recent menu—it changes seasonally—included duck foie gras wrapped in bacon and lacquered like a Chinese duck, and sea bass smothered in herbs with tiny clams. The *Grand Dessert,* a five-course presentation of different desserts, is not to be missed. The only drawbacks are the uneven service and the scanty wine list. ☒ *6 rue de Balzac,* ☎ *01–44–35–18–25. Reservations essential. AE, DC, MC, V. Closed Sat. No lunch Sun. Métro: Charles-de-Gaulle–Étoile.*

$$$$ ✗ **Taillevent.** Many say this is the best restaurant in Paris—and dining in the paneled rooms of this mid-19th-century mansion is certainly a sublime experience. Service is exceptional, the wine list remarkable, and the classical French cuisine usually perfect. Among the signature dishes are cream of watercress soup with caviar, and truffled tart of game. Desserts are also superb, especially the creamy chocolate tart served with thyme ice cream. ☒ *15 rue Lamennais,* ☎ *01–45–63–39–94. Reservations essential 3–4 wks in advance. Jacket and tie. AE, MC, V. Closed weekends and Aug. Métro: Charles de Gaulle–Étoile.*

$$$ ✗ **L'Astor.** Chef Eric Lecerf pays homage to his mentor, Joël Robuchon, by offering some classic Robuchon dishes like cauliflower cream with caviar and spiced roasted lobster. But he also shows his own talent with sophisticated offerings like sole with baby squid and artichokes. The service and wine list are superb. Trendy interior designer Frederique Mechiche is responsible for the spacious and attractive dining room, which takes a cue from the '30s with star appliqués on the walls and

a checkerboard carpet. ⊠ *In the Hôtel Astor, 11 rue d'Astorg,* ☎ *01–53–05–05–20. AE, DC, MC, V. Métro: Madeleine.*

$$$ ✕ **Stella Maris.** The pretty Art Deco front window is the centerpiece at this minimalist spot near the Arc de Triomphe. An expense-account crowd mixes with serious French gourmets to dine on the very subtle cuisine of Japanese chef Taderu Yoshino, who trained with Joël Robuchon. You'll find only a nuance or two of Japan, however, in such delicious dishes as langoustines in a "cappuccino" of green lentils, a terrine of savoy cabbage with truffles, and scallops with caramel sauce. ⊠ *4 rue Arsène-Houssaye,* ☎ *01–42–89–16–22. Reservations essential. AE, DC, MC, V. Closed Sun. No lunch Sat. Métro: Etoile.*

$$–$$$ ✕ **Le Bistrot du Sommelier.** The 30-page wine list is the chief attraction at this restaurant owned by jolly Philippe Faure-Brac, who, in 1992, attained the high achievement of World's Best Sommelier. Wines from the Côtes du Rhône are his specialty and he will often recommend one of these. Harvest-theme tapestries and frescoes create the backdrop for the dishes of ravioli with fresh herbs and cheese as well as the pullet in *vin jaune* (yellow wine from the Jura). ⊠ *97 bd. Haussmann,* ☎ *01–42–65–24–85. Reservations essential. AE, DC, MC, V. Closed weekends and Aug. Métro: St-Augustin.*

$$ ✕ **Androuët.** The ideal address if you're mad for cheese, this restaurant has been proudly serving a vast assortment of beautifully aged *fromages* (cheeses) from all over France for almost a century. If you really want a cheese-filled feast, or just want to learn more about the stuff, order the tasting menu, which takes you through the seven main French types. Also available are a variety of good dishes like lobster with Roquefort and Camembert croquettes. ⊠ *41 rue Arsène-Houssaye,* ☎ *01–42–89–95–00. AE, DC, V. Closed Sun. Métro: Étoile.*

$$ ✕ **Chez Tante Louise.** Chef Bernard Loiseau's new Paris outpost—his original eponymous one is in Saulieu in Burgundy—is an appealing bastion of traditional Burgundian cooking. He has wisely left the vintage '30s decor almost completely untouched. But the food is pleasantly old-fashioned and hearty—like *oeufs en meurette à la bourguignonne* (poached eggs in red wine sauce with bacon) and sole "Tante Louise," in which a filet is served on a bed of *duxelles* (finely chopped mushrooms). Of course, there's a nice selection of Burgundies, and service is prompt and professional for the well-dressed crowd. ⊠ *41 rue Boissy d'Anglas,* ☎ *01–42–65–06–85. Reservations essential. AE, DC, MC, V. Closed weekends. Métro: Madeleine.*

$$ ✕ **La Fermette Marbeuf.** It's a favorite haunt of French TV and movie stars who like the spectacular Belle Epoque mosaics and stained glass and appreciate the solid, updated classic cuisine. Try gâteau of chicken livers and sweetbreads, saddle of lamb with *choron* (a tomato-spiked bearnaise sauce), and bitter chocolate fondant. Prices here are exceptional, considering the quality of the food, the surroundings, and the neighborhood. La Fermette becomes animated around 9 PM. ⊠ *5 rue Marbeuf,* ☎ *01–53–23–08–00. AE, DC, MC, V. Métro: Franklin-D.-Roosevelt.*

$$ ✕ **Sébillon.** The original Sébillon has nurtured chic residents of the fashionable suburb of Neuilly for generations; this elegant, polished branch off the Champs-Élysées continues the tradition. The menu includes lobster salad, lots of shellfish, and—the specialty—roast leg of lamb sliced table-side and served in unlimited quantity. Service is notably friendly. ⊠ *66 rue Pierre Charron,* ☎ *01–43–59–28–15. AE, DC, MC, V. Métro: Franklin-D.-Roosevelt.*

CONTEMPORARY

$$ ✕ **Spoon, Food and Wine.** Star chef Alain Ducasse's blueprint of a bistro for the 21st century has been packed ever since it opened in late 1998.

What draws the trendy crowd is the playful, Asian- and American-inspired menu, the good wines by the glass, and the great decor—at night, the large white linen shades on the walls are rolled up to reveal plum upholstery. Try the Thai soup, the pasta dishes, and the roast salmon with bearnaise sauce. Parisians can't get over the fact that more than half the wines are American (French and other European wines are also served). It's a good address if you're a vegetarian, since there are many salads and vegetable and grain dishes. ☒ *14 rue de Marignan,* ☎ *01–40–76–34–44. Reservations essential. AE, MC, V. Métro: Franklin-D.-Roosevelt.*

9ᵉ Arrondissement (Opéra/Pigalle-Clichy)
See Right Bank Dining map.

FRENCH

$ ✕ **Bistrot des Deux Théâtres.** Quality is high and prices are low at this well-run restaurant in the Pigalle-Clichy area. The prix-fixe menu includes apéritif, first and main dishes, a cheese or dessert course, half a bottle of wine, and coffee. The food—such as foie gras salad, steak with morels, and apple tart flambéed with Calvados—is far from banal. ☒ *18 rue Blanche,* ☎ *01–45–26–41–43. MC, V. Métro: Trinité.*

$ ✕ **Chartier.** People come here more for the bonhomie than the food, which is often rather ordinary. This cavernous turn-of-the-century restaurant enjoys a huge following among budget-minded students, solitary bachelors, and tourists. You may find yourself sharing a table with strangers as you study the long, old-fashioned menu of such favorites as hard-boiled eggs with mayonnaise, steak tartare, and roast chicken with fries. ☒ *7 rue du Faubourg-Montmartre,* ☎ *01–47–70–86–29. Reservations not accepted. No credit cards. Métro: Rue Montmartre.*

10ᵉ Arrondissement (République/Gare du Nord)
See Right Bank Dining map.

FRENCH

$$ ✕ **Brasserie Flo.** The first of brasserie king Jean-Paul Bucher's eight Paris addresses is hard to find down its passageway near Gare de l'Est, but it's worth the effort. The rich wood and stained glass is typically Alsatian, and brasserie standards such as shellfish, steak tartare, and choucroute are savory. Order a carafe of Alsatian wine to go with your meal. It's open until 1:30 AM, with a special night-owl menu from 11 PM. ☒ *7 cour des Petites-Écuries,* ☎ *01–47–70–13–59. AE, DC, MC, V. Métro: Château d'Eau.*

$$ ✕ **Julien.** Another Jean-Paul Bucher brasserie, with dazzling Belle Epoque decor, this one is a kind of poor man's Maxim's. Fare includes smoked salmon, foie gras, cassoulet, and sherbets. Diners are ebullient and lots of fun; this place has a strong following with the fashion crowd, so it's mobbed during the biannual fashion and fabric shows. There's service until 1:30 AM, with a special late-night menu from 11 PM. ☒ *16 rue du Faubourg St-Denis,* ☎ *01–47–70–12–06. AE, DC, MC, V. Métro: Strasbourg–St-Denis.*

$-$$ ✕ **Chez Michel.** Talented young chef Thierry Breton pulls in a stylish
★ crowd of Parisians—despite the neighborhood (near the train station) and the plain decor—with his wonderful cuisine du marché and superb dishes from his native Brittany. Typical of Breton's kitchen are roasted scallops with ribbons of celery root, and preserved guinea hen with a remoulade of beets, which sounds complicated but is deliciously hearty. ☒ *10 rue Belzunce,* ☎ *01–44–53–06–20. Reservations essential. MC, V. Closed Sun., Mon. No lunch Sat. Métro: Gare du Nord.*

$ ✕ **Au Vieux Bistrot.** If you're staying near the Gare du Nord or looking for a meal in the area before taking the train, this pleasant, old-fashioned neighborhood bistro is a good bet. From the big zinc bar to the steak with mushroom sauce and veal in cream, this place delivers a traditional bistro experience. Finish up with the fruit tart. Service is friendly. ⊠ *30 rue Dunkerque,* ☎ *01–48–78–48–01. MC, V. Closed Sun. No dinner Sat. Métro: Gare du Nord.*

$ ✕ **Chez Casimir.** Another project of chef Thierry Breton of Chez Michel (☞ *above*), this easygoing bistro is equally popular with stylish Parisian professionals for whom it serves as a sort of canteen. The menu shows Breton's cooking style with dishes like lentil soup with fresh croutons, braised endive and andouille sausage salad, and roast lamb on a bed of Paimpol beans. Good desserts include *pain perdu,* a version of French toast, eaten for dessert—here it's topped with a roasted pear. ⊠ *6 rue de Belzunce,* ☎ *01–48–78–28–80. MC, V. Closed weekends. Métro: Gare du Nord.*

11° Arrondissement (Bastille/République)
See Right Bank Dining map.

FRENCH

$$ ✕ **Chardenoux.** A bit off the beaten track but well worth the effort, this cozy neighborhood bistro with etched-glass windows, dark bent-wood furniture, and a long zinc bar attracts savvy Parisians and knowing foreigners. The traditional cooking is first-rate: Start with the homemade rabbit terrine or salad of fennel in orange vinaigrette, then sample the veal chop with morels or a game dish. Savory desserts and a nicely chosen wine list with several excellent Côtes du Rhônes complete the meal. ⊠ *1 rue Jules-Valles,* ☎ *01–43–71–49–52. AE, V. Closed Sun. and Aug. No lunch Sat. Métro: Charonne.*

$$ ✕ **Les Fernandises.** The chef-owner of this neighborhood spot near Place de la République is more concerned with his Normandy-inspired cuisine than with his restaurant's inconsequential decor. Fresh foie gras sautéed in cider, and scallops in cream sauce are examples of his varied style. The selection of Camemberts is superb. ⊠ *17 rue Fontaine-au-Roi,* ☎ *01–43–57–46–25. MC, V. Closed Sun., Mon., and Aug. Métro: République.*

$$ ✕ **Le Repaire de Cartouche.** Near the Cirque d'Hiver, in the Bastille,
★ this split-level, '50s-style bistro with dark wood decor offers excellent food for good-value prices. Young chef Rodolphe Paquin is a creative and impeccably trained cook who does a stylish take on earthy French regional dishes. The menu changes regularly, but typical are a salad of *haricots verts* (string beans) topped with tender slices of squid, scallops on a bed of finely diced pumpkin, and old-fashioned desserts like custard with tiny madeleine cookies. The wine list is very good, too, with bargains like a Pernand-Vergelesses (red Burgundy) for $20. *99 rue Amelot,* ☎ *01–47–00–25–86. AE, MC, V. Reservations essential. Closed Sun. No dinner Mon. Métro: Filles du Calvaire.*

$ ✕ **Astier.** The prix-fixe menu (there's no à la carte) at this pleasant restaurant is a remarkable value. Among the high-quality seasonal dishes are baked eggs topped with truffled foie gras, fricassee of *joue de boeuf* (beef cheeks), and plum *clafoutis* (a creamy cake). Service can be rushed, but the enthusiastic crowd does not seem to mind. Study the excellent wine list, which has some surprising buys. ⊠ *44 rue Jean-Pierre Timbaud,* ☎ *01–43–57–16–35. AE, MC, V. Closed weekends and Aug. Métro: Parmentier.*

$ ✕ **Au Camelot.** This minuscule bistro with a single, five-course menu brings in the crowds who come for the excellent home-style cooking. A meal here usually begins with a generous serving of soup, followed by a fish course, a main dish, cheese, and dessert. Along with well-prepared classics, expect creative dishes like crab lasagna alongside classics like chicken in mushroom cream sauce. Though the place is noisy and very crowded, service is friendly, and the house Bordeaux is a treat.

⊠ *50 rue Amelot,* ☎ *01–43–55–54–04. Reservations essential. No credit cards. Closed Sun. No lunch Mon., Sat. Métro: République.*

$ ✕ **Jacques Mélac.** Robust cuisine matches noisy camaraderie at this popular wine bar–restaurant, owned by mustachioed Jacques Mélac. The charcuterie, the salad of preserved duck gizzards, the braised beef, and the cheeses from central France are all good choices. Monsieur Mélac, who has a miniature vineyard out front, hosts a jolly party at harvest time. ⊠ *42 rue Léon Frot,* ☎ *01–43–70–59–27. MC, V. Closed weekends in Aug. No dinner Mon. Métro: Charonne.*

$ ✕ **Le Passage.** Not far from Place de la Bastille, in the obscure Passage de la Bonne Graine, is this friendly spot with a homey ambience. Though it bills itself as a wine bar, it has a full menu, including five kinds of *andouillette* (chitterling sausage). The wine list is excellent. ⊠ *18 Passage de la Bonne Graine (enter by 108 av. Ledru-Rollin),* ☎ *01–47–00–73–30. AE, MC, V. Closed Sun. No lunch Sat. Métro: Ledru-Rollin.*

$ ✕ **Le Villaret.** The owner of this restaurant once ran Astier (☞ *above*), and his experience shows. Salmon tart, hot foie gras salad, duck confit, and seasonal fruit clafoutis are some of the interesting and well-prepared dishes. The exposed stone and half-timbering combines traditional and modern styles. There's no lunch; dinner runs until 1 AM. ⊠ *13 rue Ternaux,* ☎ *01–43–57–89–76. MC, V. Closed Sun. and Aug. No lunch. Métro: Parmentier.*

12e Arrondissement (Bastille/Gare de Lyon)
See Right Bank Dining map.

FRENCH

$$$ ✕ **Au Pressoir.** Chef-owner Henri Séguin's excellent restaurant in the eastern part of Paris deserves more attention than it receives. His menu has such original, exciting choices as fricassee of lobster with morels, pigeon with eggplant blinis, and chocolate soup with brioche. The wine list is tops, and service is friendly and professional. ⊠ *257 av. Daumesnil,* ☎ *01–43–44–38–21. MC, V. Closed weekends, mid-Feb., and Aug. Métro: Michel-Bizot.*

$$$ ✕ **Au Trou Gascon.** At this charming Belle Epoque establishment off Place Daumesnil, owner Alain Dutournier serves his version of the cuisine of Gascony—a region of outstanding ham, foie gras, lamb, and poultry—and his classic white chocolate mousse. The $60 prix-fixe menu, wine included, is an excellent value by Paris standards. ⊠ *40 rue Taine,* ☎ *01–43–44–34–26. AE, DC, MC, V. Closed Sun., Aug., and Christmas wk. No lunch Sat. Métro: Daumesnil.*

$$$ ✕ **L'Oulette.** Chef-owner Marcel Baudis's take on the cuisine of his na-
★ tive southwest France is original and delicious. Recommended dishes include the salmon and Parmesan tart with truffle vinaigrette, pike-perch in a crust of garlic and parsley with a sauce of fresh grape juice, and *pain d'épices* (spice cake). The restaurant, in the rebuilt Bercy district, is a bit hard to find, so bring your map. ⊠ *15 pl. Lachambeaudie,* ☎ *01–40–02–02–12. AE, MC, V. Closed Sun. No lunch Sat. Métro: Dugommier.*

$$ ✕ **Le Square Trousseau.** Since fashion designer Jean-Paul Gaultier moved his headquarters nearby, this charming turn-of-the-century bistro has become fashionable. You might see a supermodel or two while dining on the homemade foie gras and the tender baby chicken with mustard and bread-crumb crust. The house wine is a good value, especially the Morgon, a fruity red. ⊠ *1 rue Antoine Vollon,* ☎ *01–43–43–06–00. MC, V. Métro: Ledru-Rollin.*

$ ✕ **Les Zygomates.** Since it's in a part of the city few tourists venture to, this handsome old butcher's shop converted into a bistro is mostly filled with young locals. They come for the delicious modern bistro food, like a terrine of rabbit with tarragon, chicken in cream with chives, and a very fairly priced catch-of-the-day selection. ⊠ *7 rue Capri,* ☎ *01–40–19–93–04. V. Closed Sun., Sat. June–Sept., 1st 3 wks of Aug. No lunch Sat. Oct.–May. Métro: Michel-Bizot, Daumesnil.*

13ᵉ Arrondissement (Les Gobelins)
See Left Bank Dining map.

FRENCH

$$$ ✕ **Au Petit Marguéry.** Both staff and diners seem to be having a good time in this warm, convivial place run by three brothers. The menu goes beyond the usual bistro classics to include such dishes as cold lobster, cod fillet with spices, and excellent lamb from the Pyrénées. Prices are at the low end of this category. ⊠ *9 bd. de Port Royal,* ☎ *01–43–31–58–59. AE, DC, MC, V. Closed Sun., Mon., Christmas wk, and Aug. Métro: Les Gobelins.*

$$ ✕ **Anacréon.** A former chef from the Tour d'Argent has transformed a neighborhood café into a pleasant new-wave bistro. Inventive dishes such as compressed duck with red peppercorns, and fresh cod with spices have been highlights on the regularly changing menu. Desserts are always good, too, and the St-Joseph is a perfect choice from the wine list. ⊠ *53 bd. St-Marcel,* ☎ *01–43–31–71–18. Reservations essential. MC, V. Closed weekends. Métro: Les Gobelins.*

$ ✕ **L'Avant Gout.** For excellent contemporary French cooking at very reasonable prices, it's worth seeking out this tiny, off-the-beaten-path bistro in this residential part of the city. Though the place can get crowded and noisy, you won't be disappointed by young Chef Christophe Beaufront's appealing and unusual daily prix-fixe chalkboard menu, which might include dishes like sea bass with creamy celery root and almonds, and steak with roasted shallots. Delicious homemade desserts and a good wine list with a fine selection of lower-priced bottles round off the meal. ⊠ *26 rue Bobillot.* ☎ *01–53–80–24–00. MC, V. Reservations essential. Closed Sun., Mon. Métro: Place d'Italie.*

$ ✕ **Le Terroir.** A jolly crowd of regulars makes this little bistro festive. Based on first-rate ingredients from all over France, the menu is solidly classical—salads with chicken livers or fresh marinated anchovies, calves' liver or monkfish with saffron, and pears marinated in wine for dessert, for instance. There's also a well-balanced wine list. ⊠ *11 bd. Arago,* ☎ *01–47–07–36–99. AE, MC, V. Closed Sun. No lunch Sat. Métro: Les Gobelins.*

14ᵉ Arrondissement (Montparnasse)
See Left Bank Dining map.

FRENCH

$$$ ✕ **Louis Landes.** If you're yearning for an excellent meal in a traditional formal French setting with all the trappings, this sophisticated but welcoming restaurant is ideal. Cuisine of southwestern France is the specialty—reflected in the duck-feather motif of the china and wallpaper. Though renowned for the cassoulet and foie gras, the rest of the menu tempts, too, with dishes like grilled bream with potato puree, and homemade cocoa ice cream. The excellent wine list and the bargain, 195-franc prix-fixe menu also add to its appeal. *157 ave. du Maine.* ☎ *01–45–43–08–04. AE, DC, MC, V. Reservations essential. Closed Sun. and Aug. No lunch Sat. Métro: Alésia.*

$$ ✕ **Contre-Allée.** Left Bank students and professors crowd this large restaurant, simply decorated with bullfighting posters. The menu has original selections such as squid salad with mussels and roast cod with Parmesan; homemade fresh pasta accompanies many dishes. A sidewalk terrace enlivens shady avenue Denfert-Rochereau in summer. The restaurant serves until 11:00 PM. ⊠ *83 av. Denfert-Rochereau,* ☎

01–43–54–99–86. *AE, DC, MC, V. No lunch Sat. Métro: Denfert-Rochereau.*

$$ ✕ **La Coupole.** This world-renowned, cavernous address in Montparnasse practically defines the term brasserie (it's owned by Jean-Paul Bucher)—and its murals are famous, too. Many find it too large, too noisy, and too expensive, and no one likes the long wait at the bar before being seated. Still, it has been popular with everyone from Left Bank intellectuals (Jean-Paul Sartre and Simone de Beauvoir were regulars) to bourgeois grandmothers. Expect the usual brasserie menu, including perhaps the largest shellfish presentation in Paris, choucroute, and a wide range of desserts. ✉ *102 bd. du Montparnasse,* ☎ *01–43–20–14–20. AE, DC, MC, V. Métro: Vavin.*

SEAFOOD

$–$$ ✕ **Vin & Marée.** The third, lower-priced annex of the fancy Right Bank fish house La Luna is a welcome addition to Montparnasse. Begin with a tasty bowl of baby clams in a creamy lemon-butter sauce, offered as an hors d'oeuvre, then have a generous plate of fresh red shrimps sautéed in thyme, followed by white tuna in shallot sauce or sautéed red mullets, if available—the menu changes depending on what's in the market that day. Nicely chosen wines come by the bottle, carafe, or glass. ✉ *108 av. du Maine,* ☎ *01–43–20–29–50. AE, MC, V. Métro: Montparnasse, Gaité.*

15ᵉ Arrondissement (Motte-Picquet/Balard)
See Left Bank Dining map.

FRENCH

$$ ✕ **Le Barrail.** A favorite with staff from nearby *Le Monde,* this neighborhood spot has hospitable service and an unassuming setting. Enjoy such dishes as foie gras *aux pommes* (with apples) and the increasingly hard-to-find potatoes *Dauphine,* pureed potatoes added to choux pastry, shaped into balls, and deep-fried. Ordering the prix-fixe menu will lessen the cost of your meal. ✉ *17 rue Falguière,* ☎ *01–43–22–42–61. MC, V. Closed weekends and early Aug. Métro: Pasteur.*

$$ ✕ **Bistrot d'Hubert.** In a studied environment that might have sprung from the pages of *Elle Decor,* this popular bistro—frequented by a stylish crowd—serves food that perfectly expresses the counter-currents of the Parisian culinary landscape. The prix-fixe menu is split into two: "tradition" and "innovation." You might have the crab in a garlic mayonnaise with a pickled cactus garnish, followed by a tuna steak in a "caramel" of Balsamic vinegar, or go for the more classic roast lamb. Don't skip the superb tiramisu with chicory ice cream. Service is very friendly, and the short, well-chosen wine list offers chef Alain Senderen's (of Lucas Carton) Cahors and a lovely Domaine de Mont Redon rosé. ✉ *41 bd. Pasteur,* ☎ *01–47–34–15–50. Reservations essential. AE, DC, MC, V. Métro: Pasteur.*

$$ ✕ **La Dinée.** Young chef Christophe Chabanel's restaurant in a rather remote location at the edge of the 15ᵉ arrondissement is filled noon and night by a crowd of stylish regulars who come to be surprised by his culinary creativity. Signature dishes include suckling pig with salsify, mushrooms and sage and roast lamb with baked eggplant in a vinaigrette of fresh herbs. The dining room, with blue print fabrics and wooden tub chairs, is simple; service is professional if a little fussy. ✉ *85 rue Leblanc,* ☎ *01–45–54–20–49. V. Closed Sun. No lunch Sat. Métro: Balard.*

$$ ✕ **Philippe Detourbe.** With its black-lacquer trim, mirrors, and Bur-
★ gundy velvet upholstery, this place is unexpectedly glamorous. It also serves excellent food for very reasonable prices, so book several days in advance. Detourbe, a self-taught chef, is gifted and very ambitious—

his menu of contemporary French cooking changes with every meal. Dishes may include smoked salmon filled with cabbage *rémoulade* (creamy dressing) or John Dory with baby leeks, fresh almonds, and country ham. Desserts are fantastic. The wine list is brief but well chosen and service is friendly and efficient. ⊠ *8 rue Nicolas Charlet*, ☎ *01–42–19–08–59. Reservations essential. MC, V. Closed Sun. No lunch Sat. Métro: Pasteur.*

$ ✕ **Chez Pierre.** Specializing in Burgundian cooking, this small, old-fashioned restaurant has the ambience of a Doisneau photo, replete with friendly waiters ready with a wry remark. The prix-fixe menu is a great deal and has such classic starters as *oeufs en meurette* (poached eggs in red wine sauce) and *jambon persillé* (parsleyed ham), and main dishes like beef bourguignon and coq au vin. Finish off with a homemade plum tart or a chocolate Bavarois. The short wine list features a good selection of reasonably priced Burgundies. ⊠ *117 rue de Vaugirard*, ☎ *01–47–34–96–12. MC, V. Closed weekends. Métro: Falguière.*

$ ✕ **L'Os à Moelle.** This small, popular bistro has a very good value six-course dinner menu (there's no à la carte) that changes daily; portions are generous. A sample meal might include white-bean soup, bread, sautéed foie gras, *rouget* (red mullet fish), lamb with potato puree, cheese with a small salad, and a delicious roasted pear with cinnamon ice cream. At lunchtime, there's a short à la carte menu that's as good. With an excellent list of fairly priced wines, your bill can stay comfortably low. ⊠ *3 rue Vasco-de-Gama*, ☎ *01–45–57–27–27. Reservations essential. MC, V. Closed Sun., Mon. Métro: Balard.*

$ ✕ **Le Petit Plat.** Though this popular neighborhood bistro is tiny and out of the way, and service can be a bit offhanded, the food is usually very good. The specialty is generous portions of urbanized French country cooking: terrine of rabbit in tarragon aspic, sausage with potato salad in shallot vinaigrette, and roast chicken with sautéed mushrooms. The excellent wine list was selected by Henri Gault of Gault-Millau, the famous French food guide (his daughter is one of the three owners). ⊠ *45 av. Émile-Zola*, ☎ *01–45–78–24–20. V. Closed Sun. and Mon. Métro: Charles-Michel.*

$ ✕ **Le Troquet.** Tucked away on a quiet street in a residential neighborhood near the headquarters of UNESCO, this contemporary modern bistro feeds a crowd of regulars. They come for chef Philippe Etchebest's tasty, constantly changing, prix-fixe menu of dishes from the Basque and Béarn regions of southwestern France. A typical meal might include cream of zucchini soup, hot scallops on a bed of mixed vegetables, pan-roasted dove, sheep's cheese with cherry preserves, and a chocolate macaroon. The Béarn red wine makes for good drinking at a good price. ⊠ *21 rue François-Bonvin*, ☎ *01–45–66–89–00. MC, V. Closed Sun. No lunch Sat. Métro: Segur.*

THAI

$ ✕ **Sawadee.** Once you've tried the delicious Thai food here, you'll understand why this off-the-beaten-path spot is full every night. The place is a bit nondescript, but the atmosphere is casual and the service friendly. Start with the unusual fried-rice salad, or the delicate ravioli of shrimp and pork, and then try the shrimp sautéed with salt and pepper, or the chopped beef with basil. ⊠ *53 av. Emile Zola*, ☎ *01–45–77–68–90. AE, MC, V. Closed Sun. Métro: Charles Michel.*

16ᵉ Arrondissement (Trocadéro/Bois de Boulogne)
See Right Bank Dining map.

FRENCH

$$$$ ✕ **Alain Ducasse.** Alain Ducasse serves some exquisite food in this town house restaurant, formerly the preserve of Joël Robuchon. Opinions

vary widely, however, on whether or not a meal here is worth the investment; given the generally very classical nature of the cooking style—as opposed to Ducasse's splendid creativity in his restaurant in Monte Carlo—some come away feeling let down. If you're a resolute fan of traditional haute cuisine, however, this can be a rapturous meal. Dishes like roast lamb garnished with "crumbs" of dried fruit and duckling roasted with fig leaves are marvelously subtle, though others—sea bass with watercress sauce—are good but underwhelming. There's something vaguely forlorn about the richly decorated rooms—maybe the fact that the whole experience is just too serious—and the service can be distracted and unfriendly. Should you decide on a meal here, be prepared for the unsurprisingly expensive wine list, and consider coming for the 480-franc lunch menu. ⊠ *59 av. Raymond-Poincaré,* ☎ *01–47–27–12–27. Reservations essential several months in advance. AE, DC, MC, V. Closed weekends. Métro: Victor Hugo.*

$$$$ ✗ **Le Pré Catalan.** Dining beneath the chestnut trees on the terrace of this fanciful palace restaurant in the Bois de Boulogne is a Belle Epoque fantasy. Chef Frederic Anton has brought new life to the cuisine of this venerable establishment, with elegant dishes such as spit-roasted baby pigeon in a caramelized sauce, sweetbreads with morels and asparagus tips, and roast pear on a caramelized waffle with bergamot ice cream. The lunch menu is more reasonably priced. ⊠ *Bois de Boulogne, rte. de Surèsnes,* ☎ *01–45–24–55–58. Reservations essential. Jacket and tie. AE, DC, MC, V. Closed Mon. and mid-Feb. No dinner Sun. Métro: Porte Dauphine.*

$$$$ ✗ **Le Vivarois.** Though his vintage '60s dining room never changes, his staff is not always up to par, and his cooking can be uneven, chef-owner Claude Peyrot remains one of the most inspired contemporary French chefs. He's a master with fish and puff pastry; his *bavarois* of red bell pepper (a creamy, molded concoction) is oft imitated, and his original dishes shine: warm oysters with curry, scallops with sesame and ginger, and black currant mousse. ⊠ *192 av. Victor Hugo,* ☎ *01–45–04–04–31. AE, DC, MC, V. Closed weekends and Aug. Métro: Rue de la Pompe.*

$$$ ✗ **Jamin.** At this intimate, elegant restaurant, where Joël Robuchon
★ made his name, you can find excellent haute cuisine at almost half the price of what you'd find elsewhere. Benoit Guichard, Robuchon's second for many years, is a subtle and accomplished chef and a particularly brilliant *saucier* (sauce maker). The menu changes regularly, but Guichard tends toward dishes like sea bass with pistachios in fennel sauce, and braised beef with cumin-scented carrots. The gratin of rhubarb with a red-fruit sauce makes an excellent dessert. ⊠ *32 rue de Longchamp,* ☎ *01–45–53–00–07. Reservations essential. AE, DC, MC, V. Closed Sun. No lunch Sat. Métro: Iéna.*

$$ ✗ **La Butte Chaillot.** A dramatic iron staircase connects two levels in turquoise and earth tones at one of the most popular of chef Guy Savoy's fashionable bistros. Dining here is part theater, as the à la mode clientele demonstrate, but it's not all show: The very good food includes tasty ravioli from the town of Royans, roast chicken with mashed potatoes, and stuffed veal breast with rosemary. A wide sidewalk terrace fronts tree-shaded avenue Kléber. ⊠ *112 av. Kléber,* ☎ *01–47–27–88–88. AE, MC, V. Métro: Trocadéro.*

$$ ✗ **Le Relais du Parc.** This bistro-annex is now run by Alain Ducasse, who understands the way that people want to eat today: His menu allows you to eat as large or light as you like. Two delicious starters— the lobster salad and the baby potatoes with black truffles in a creamy oxtail-stock sauce—make good meals, followed by cheese or dessert. Main courses, such as lamb chops with vegetable lasagna, are excellent. The cheese plate is good, too, but the desserts could be better and the wine list is overpriced. ✉ *55 av. Raymond-Poincaré,* ☎ *01–44–05–66–10. Reservations essential. AE, DC, MC, V. Métro: Victor Hugo.*

$ ✗ **Les Chauffeurs.** Not only is this tranquil bistro in this expensive part of town a favorite address of well-dressed regulars, but it's also the night-off hangout for some of the capital's best-known chefs. What attracts the discerning and the experts is the moderately priced, reliably good classic cooking and the pleasant, relaxed ambience. Try the airy fish terrine or an Alsatian *cervelas* (fine pork sausage) salad, and then, depending on what's on the menu, go for the sole meunière or the roast chicken. Good Beaujolais wines are served by the carafe. *8 chaussée de la Muette,* ☎ *01–42–88–50–05. MC, V. Métro: La Muette.*

$ ✗ **Le Petit Rétro.** Two different clienteles—men in expensive suits at noon and well-dressed locals in the evening—frequent this little bistro with Art Nouveau tiles and bentwood furniture. You can't go wrong with the daily special, which is written on a chalkboard presented by one of the friendly waitresses. Come in some night when you want a good solid meal, like the perfect *pavé de boeuf* (thick steak) in a ruddy red-wine and stock sauce, accompanied by potatoes au gratin and caramelized braised endive. ✉ *5 rue Mesnil,* ☎ *01–44–05–06–05. MC, V. Closed Sun. No lunch Sat. Métro: Victor Hugo.*

SEAFOOD

$$$$ ✗ **Port Alma.** Owner Madame Canal's charming welcome and the nautical-blue and pastel decor make this place festive. Look forward to attentive, polite service. Monsieur Canal, the chef, is from southwest France, near Spain, and his cuisine is bursting with full, sunny flavors. Try the turbot with thyme, the sea bass in a salt crust with fennel gratin, or the bouillabaisse (order ahead). ✉ *10 av. de New York,* ☎ *01–47–23–75–11. AE, DC, MC, V. Closed Sun. and Aug. Métro: Alma-Marceau.*

$$–$$$ ✗ **Prunier.** Founded in 1925, this seafood restaurant is one of the best—and surely the prettiest—in Paris. The famous Art Deco mosaics glitter and the white marble counters shine with the impeccably fresh shellfish displayed like precious jewels. The kitchen not only excels at classic French fish cooking but has added some interesting dishes like a *Saintongeaise* plate—raw oysters with grilled sausages—eaten in Bordeaux. Accompany your meal with wine from the well-balanced list. No reservations are needed for the raw bar on the main level, but book for lunch or dinner in the upstairs dining room. ✉ *16 av. Victor Hugo,* ☎ *01–44–17–35–85. Jacket and tie. AE, DC, MC, V. Closed Sun., Mon. Métro: Étoile.*

17ᵉ Arrondissement (Monceau/Clichy/ Arc de Triomphe)
See Right Bank Dining map.

FRENCH

$$$$ ✗ **Guy Savoy.** Come here for a perfectly measured contemporary
★   haute cuisine experience, since top chef Guy Savoy's other dining rooms have not distracted him from his handsome luxury restaurant near the Arc de Triomphe. The oysters in aspic, sea bass with spices, and poached and grilled pigeon reveal the magnitude of his talent, and his mille-feuille is a contemporary classic. ✉ *18 rue Troyon,* ☎ *01–43–80–40–61. AE, MC, V. Closed Sun. No lunch Sat. Métro: Charles de Gaulle–Étoile.*

$$–$$$ ✗ **Au Petit Colombier.** It's a perennial favorite among Parisians, who come to eat comforting *cuisine bourgeoise* (traditional cuisine) in the warm dining rooms accented with wood and bright copper. Menu standards include milk-fed lamb chop *en cocotte* (in a small, enameled casserole) and coq au vin. Service is friendly and unpretentious. ✉ *42 rue* *des Acacias,* ☎ *01–43–80–28–54. AE, MC, V. Closed Sat. No lunch Sun. Métro: Charles de Gaulle–Étoile.*

\$\$–\$\$\$ ✕ **Le Graindorge.** Formerly at the justly popular Au Trou Gascon, chef-owner Bernard Broux has thrived since he opened his own establishment. He prepares an original mix of the cuisines of southwest France and his native Flanders: Experience the succulent eel terrine in a delicious herb aspic (seasonal), and red mullet with endives in beer sauce. Madame Broux oversees the pleasant dining rooms, which have a decidedly provincial feel, and can help you select one of the many fine beers. ⊠ *15 rue de l'Arc-de-Triomphe,* ☎ *01–47–54–00–28. AE, MC, V. Closed Sun. No lunch Sat. Métro: Charles de Gaulle–Étoile.*

\$ ✕ **La Rôtisserie d'Armaillé.** Admire the handsome oak paneling, cranberry and green upholstery, and the *très* Parisian crowd at star chef Jacques Cagna's fourth restaurant. The prix-fixe menu has many tempting choices, among them *pastilla* (pastry layers) of guinea hen and a terrific chocolate cake. Wines are a little pricey. ⊠ *6 rue d'Armaillé,* ☎ *01–42–27–19–20. AE, MC, V. Closed Sun. No lunch Sat. Métro: Argentine.*

\$ ✕ **La Table de Pierre.** The Louis XVI–style setting is somewhat surprising in one of the best Basque restaurants in Paris. Such dishes as peppers stuffed with *brandade* (salt cod casserole), *émincé* (thin slices) of squid, duck confit, and *gâteau Basque* (a chewy, sweet cake filled with cream) are full of the colors and flavors of the Pays Basque. Owner Pierre Darrieumerlou is an agreeable host. ⊠ *116 bd. Péreire,* ☎ *01–43–80–88–68. AE, MC, V. Closed Sun. No lunch Sat. Métro: Péreire.*

NORTH AFRICAN

\$\$ ✕ **Le Timgad.** For a stylish evening out and a night off from French food, head to this elegant, beautifully decorated North African restaurant. Start with a savory *brick* (crispy parchment pastry filled with meat, eggs, or seafood), followed by tasty couscous or succulent *tagine* (meat or poultry that's slowly braised inside a domed pottery casserole). The lamb tagine with artichokes is especially good. ⊠ *21 rue de Brunel,* ☎ *01–45–74–23–70. MC, V. Métro: Argentine.*

SEAFOOD

\$ ✕ **L'Huitrier.** If you share the Parisians' craving for oysters, this is the place for you. The friendly owner will describe the different kinds available; you can follow these with any of several daily fish specials. The excellent cheeses are from the outstanding shop of Roger Alléosse. Blond wood and cream colors prevail. ⊠ *16 rue Saussier-Leroy,* ☎ *01–40–54–83–44. AE, MC, V. Métro: Ternes.*

18ᵉ Arrondissement (Montmartre)
See Right Bank Dining map.

FRENCH

\$\$ ✕ **Langevin.** Engravings of old Montmartre and discreet lighting create a relaxed, comfortable atmosphere at this tiny, popular neighborhood restaurant. Working in a mostly traditional register, able chef Paul Langevin creates dishes like escargots on artichoke hearts, and roast duckling with turnips. The *sablé* (a shortbread pastry) with raspberries is a treat. There's a well-chosen wine list and several good-buy prix-fixe menus. ⊠ *39 rue Lamarck,* ☎ *01–46–06–86–00. AE, MC, V. No dinner Sun. Métro: Lamarck-Caulaincourt.*

\$ ✕ **Aux Négociants.** This wine bar in Montmartre has zero decor, but the neighborhood regulars and well-heeled clientele find it welcoming. One or two hot plates are offered daily; otherwise, enjoy the terrines, cheeses, and other simple choices, served with affordable wines by the glass or bottle. ⊠ *27 rue Lambert,* ☎ *01–46–06–15–11. No credit cards. Closed weekends and Mon. No dinner Fri. Métro: Château Rouge.*

$ ✕ **Le Moulin à Vins.** The atmosphere at this popular wine bar–bistro is sepia-toned, since both the place itself and surrounding neighborhood evoke pre-modern Paris. It's perfect for a lunch of salad or a cold-meat-and-cheese plate while touring Montmartre. In the evening it's much livelier, when devoted regulars come for the daily short list of hot dishes. If it's available, opt for the delicious rabbit in mustard sauce with tagliatelle. Standards like the country terrine and quiche Lorraine are excellent, too, and the wine list is outstanding, especially the Côtes du Rhone. ⊠ *6 rue Burq,* ☎ *01–45–52–81–27. MC, V. Closed Sun., Mon., and Aug. Métro: Abbesses.*

19ᵉ Arrondissement (Buttes-Chaumont/La Villette)
See Right Bank Dining map.

FRENCH

$$$ ✕ **Le Pavillon Puebla.** A bucolic setting and original, flavorful cuisine, such as squid sautéed in saffron, and boned pigeon with chorizo-stuffed cabbage are the draw at this turn-of-the-century building in the spectacular Parc des Buttes-Chaumont. The elegant dining rooms are a romantic cold-weather setting, and the large terrace is extremely popular in summer. The restaurant feels wonderfully removed from the bustle of the city, but it's a bit hard to find. ⊠ *In the Parc Buttes-Chaumont (entrance on rue Botzaris),* ☎ *01–42–08–92–62. MC, V. Closed Sun., Mon. Métro: Buttes-Chaumont.*

$$ ✕ **Le Bistrot du Cochon d'Or.** A great spot if you're a real carnivore, this bistro annex is more appealing than the venerable steak house of the same name, which has become absurdly expensive. If you're visiting the Cité de la Musique or La Villette, take a trip across the street for first-rate French specialty cuts, including *pied du cochon* (pig's feet) and *tête de veau* (calf's head). ⊠ *192 av. Jean Jaurès,* ☎ *01–42–45–46–46. AE, DC, MC, V. Métro: Porte de Pantin.*

$$ ✕ **Le Restaurant d'Eric Frechon.** This simply decorated little place is a
★   sterling example of a price-conscious, market-menu bistro. Chef Eric Frechon worked with Christian Constant at the Hôtel Crillon, which means his cooking is more adventurous and elegant than most classic bistro fare. Examples of his dishes include cod sautéed with chestnuts in morel mushroom juice, and scallops with green asparagus, bacon, and truffles. Desserts are equally creative. ⊠ *10 rue du Général-Brunet,* ☎ *01–40–40–03–30. V. Closed Sun. and Mon. Métro: Danube.*

20ᵉ Arrondissement (Père Lachaise)
See Right Bank Dining map.

FRENCH

$ ✕ **Les Allobroges.** If you're intrepid, you'll be rewarded with this charming, chic restaurant in one of the city's more remote neighborhoods. Chef Olivier Pateyron offers several excellent prix-fixe menus at prices that would be nearly impossible in a city-center location. Surrounded by wood-print wallpaper, framed prints of farm animals, and arrangements of dried flowers, you can feast on a delicious ragout of vegetables in veal stock with cubes of foie gras, lamb braised with garlic, and chocolate soup with vanilla ice cream. ⊠ *71 rue des Grand-Champs,* ☎ *01–43–73–40–00. AE, MC, V. Closed Sun., Mon. Métro: Maraîchers.*

Cafés and Salons de Thé

Following is a list of cafés and *salons de thé* (tea shops) that will give you a feel for Paris's best. (☞ Chapter 1 for more cafés, listed as suggested spots to take a break from sightseeing.)

LUNCH BOX

IF YOU'RE A BUDGETWISE GOURMET, the chimes of noon should be music to your ears. Many of Paris's best restaurants have prix-fixe lunch menus that are dramatically more affordable than dinner from their á la carte menus. At elegant Ledoyen, for example, the $50 lunch menu is less than half of what an average á la carte meal would cost (about $125 per person). To be sure to enjoy these midday feasts, it is essential that you make reservations.

Keep in mind that you may have to ask for the lunch menu, for obvious reasons— most restaurants would prefer that you order à la carte. Also note that the prix-fixe lunch menus often have a more limited selection—you usually get a choice of only a few appetizers, main courses, and desserts. These menus are usually designed to have broad appeal, but you might see scrumptious looking dishes from the à la carte menu en route to other tables—this is one possible drawback to the prix-fixe lunch, and, unfortunately, substitutions are rarely allowed.

To keep a lid on costs, skip the cocktail before your meal, ask for a carafe of water instead of bottled water (even if you do get some nasty stares from waiters), go with the house wine, and be aware that coffee is often extra and can run 30–35 francs for an espresso (find a nice café nearby instead). Note, too, that many more modest restaurants have excellent value prix-fixe menus at midday, such as the 135-franc lunch at L'Épi Dupin and Le Grizzli bistros. Also look out for chalkboards announcing the modestly priced plat du jour at restaurants and cafés.

Following is a list of outstanding noon-time buys from the restaurants listed in this chapter: Alain Ducasse, 540 francs; Les Ambassadeurs, 340 francs; L'Arpège, 450 francs; L'Astor, 360 francs; Au Bon Accueil, 185 francs; Au Trou Gascon, 240 francs; Campagne et Provence, 150 francs; Chantairelle, 120 francs; Les Élysées, 330 francs; Fellini, 120 francs; Gérard Besson, 275 francs; Jamin, 325 francs; Jules Verne, 350 francs; Lucas-Carton, 400 francs; Pierre Gagnaire, 500 francs; Port Alma, 225 francs; Le Pré Catalan, 360 francs; Saudade, 170 francs; La Tour d'Argent, 400 francs. And to put things in final perspective, if 500 francs per person at Pierre Gagnaire sounds stiff, keep in mind that the average price for an à la carte meal there is 1,200 francs.

ANOTHER OPTION is to put your own meal together. Paris has many open-air markets (☞ Chapter 6) as well as a medley of specialty shops—including *boulangeries* (bakeries, which also sell pre-made sandwiches), *fromageries* (cheese shops), *pâtisseries* (pastry shops), and *supermarchés* (supermarkets). Also look out for *épiceries* (food shops) or *charcuteries* (French delis); the pâtés and meat products that once filled the shelves have moved over to make room for prepared salads, quiches, breads, and desserts. Choose what appeals to you most and take it to one of the city's parks for your own *déjeuner sur l'herbe* (picnic or, literally, "lunch on the grass").

Three sandwich shops worth looking out for—if you have too much sightseeing to do, and want to eat in a hurry—are **Au Pain Quotidien** (⊠ 18 Pl. du Marché St-Honoré, 1er); **Cosi** (⊠ 54 rue de Seine, 6e); and **Lina's** (⊠ 4 rue Cambon, 1er; 7 av. de l'Opéra, 1er; 27 rue St-Sulpice, 6e; 23 av. de Wagram, 17e), where you can get American-style sandwiches with such items as roast beef and smoked salmon, and excellent brownies.

1er and 2e Arrondissements (Les Halles/Palais-Royal)

A Priori Thé. Stop in for tea while browsing through the lovely Galerie Vivienne shopping arcade. ⊠ *35–37 Galerie Vivienne, at 66 rue Vivienne,* ☎ *01–42–97–48–75. Métro: Bourse.*

Au Père Tranquille. One of the best places in Paris for people-watching, this café also offers free entertainment from street artists and local performers. ⊠ *16 rue Pierre Lescot,* ☎ *01–45–08–00–34. Métro: Les Halles.*

Bernardaud. Decorated by interior-design star, Olivier Gagnère, this quiet spot in a covered atrium serves good snacks on the company's own china. ⊠ *11 rue Royale,* ☎ *01–42–66–22–55. Métro: Concorde.*

Café Marly. Run by the Costes brothers, this café overlooking the main courtyard of the Louvre and I. M. Pei's glass pyramid is one of the chicest places in Paris to meet for a drink or a coffee. Note that ordinary café service shuts down during meal hours when overpriced, mediocre food is served. *Cour Napoleon du Louvre (enter from the Louvre courtyard), 93 rue de Rivoli,* ☎ *01–49–26–06–60. Métro: Palais-Royal.*

Café Verlet. Many Parisians think this compact spot serves the best coffee in town. You can also get sandwiches and delicious tarts. ⊠ *256 rue St-Honoré,* ☎ *01–42–60–67–39. Métro: Tuileries.*

Le Ruc Univers. Actors from the Comédie Française and young hipsters hang out at this sleekly modern café near the Louvre. ⊠ *1 pl. André Malraux,* ☎ *01–42–60–31–57. Métro: Palais-Royal.*

Salon de Thé du Palais-Royal. Have tea here on the terrace overlooking the gardens of the Palais-Royal. ⊠ *Jardins du Palais-Royal, 110 Galérie de Valois,* ☎ *01–40–20–00–27. Métro: Palais-Royal.*

4e Arrondissement (Marais/Beaubourg/Ile St-Louis)

Brasserie de l'Ile St-Louis. In one of the most picturesque parts of the city, this brasserie serves good food on a great terrace. ⊠ *55 quai de Bourbon,* ☎ *01–43–54–02–59. Métro: Pont Marie.*

Café Beaubourg. Near the Pompidou Center, this slick, modern café, designed by architect Christian de Portzamparc, is one of the trendiest spots to rendezvous for fashion and art types. Omelets and decent salads are served if you've missed lunch or want a light dinner. ⊠ *43 rue St-Merri,* ☎ *01–48–87–63–96. Métro: Hôtel-de-Ville.*

Dame Tartine. Enjoy a delicious tartine as you watch the moving sculptures in the Stravinsky fountain next to the Pompidou Center. ⊠ *2 rue Brisemiche,* ☎ *01–42–77–32–22. Métro: Rambuteau, Les Halles.*

Le Flore en l'Ile. At this café on the Ile St-Louis you can find renowned Berthillon ice cream and a magnificent view of the Seine. ⊠ *42 quai d'Orléans,* ☎ *01–43–29–88–27. Métro: Pont Marie.*

Le Loir dans la Théière. This wonderful tea shop in the heart of the Marais has comfortable armchairs and delicious patisseries. ⊠ *3 rue des Rosiers,* ☎ *01–42–72–90–61. Métro: St-Paul.*

Ma Bourgogne. On the exquisite Place des Vosges, this is a calm oasis for a coffee or a light lunch away from the noisy streets. ⊠ *19 pl. des Vosges,* ☎ *01–42–78–44–64. Métro: St-Paul.*

Mariage Frères. This elegant salon de thé serves 500 kinds of tea, along with delicious tarts. ⊠ *30 rue du Bourg-Tibourg,* ☎ *01–42–72–28–11. Métro: Hôtel de Ville.*

Petit Fer à Cheval. Great coffee is served in the perfect setting for watching the fashionable Marais locals saunter by. ⊠ *30 rue Vieille-du-Temple,* ☎ *01–42–72–47–47. Métro: St-Paul.*

6e Arrondissement (St-Germain/Montparnasse)

Brasserie Lipp. This brasserie, with its turn-of-the-century decor, was a favorite spot of Hemingway's; today television celebrities, journalists, and politicians come here for coffee on the small glassed-in terrace off the main restaurant. ☒ *151 bd. St-Germain,* ☏ *01–45–48–53–91. Métro: St-Germain-des-Prés.*

Café de Flore. Picasso, Chagall, Sartre, and de Beauvoir, attracted by the luxury of a heated café, worked and wrote here in the early 20th century. Today you'll find more tourists than intellectuals, but its outdoor terrace is still a popular spot (☞ Chapter 1). ☒ *172 bd. St-Germain,* ☏ *01–45–48–55–26. Métro: St-Germain-des-Prés.*

Café de la Mairie. Preferred by Henry Miller and Saul Bellow to those on the noisy boulevard St-Germain, this place still retains the quiet and unpretentious air of a local café. ☒ *8 pl. St-Sulpice,* ☏ *01–43–26–67–82. Métro: St-Sulpice.*

Café Orbital. Have a snack while you access your E-mail or the Internet. ☒ *13 rue de Médicis,* ☏ *01–43–25–76–77. RER: Luxembourg.*

Les Deux Magots. Dubbed the second home of the *"élite intellectuelle,"* this café counted Rimbaud, Verlaine, Mallarmé, Wilde, and the Surrealists among its regulars (☞ Chapter 1). These days it's overpriced and mostly filled with tourists. ☒ *170 bd. St-Germain,* ☏ *01–45–48–55–25. Métro: St-Germain-des-Prés.*

La Palette. In good weather, the terrace is as popular with local art students and gallery owners as it is with tourists. On a rainy afternoon, the interior, too, is cozy—it's decorated with works of art by its habituées. ☒ *43 rue de Seine,* ☏ *01–43–26–68–15. Métro: Odéon.*

La Rotonde. Once a second home to foreign artists and political exiles in the '20s and '30s, the café's clientele isn't as exotic today. But it's still a pleasant place to have a coffee on the sunny terrace. ☒ *105 bd. Montparnasse,* ☏ *01–43–26–68–84. Métro: Montparnasse.*

Le Sélect. Isadora Duncan and Hart Crane used to hang out here; now it's a popular spot for a post-cinema beer. ☒ *99 bd. Montparnasse,* ☏ *01–45–48–38–24. Métro: Vavin.*

Le Vieux Colombier. Take a seat on the lovely wicker furniture in front of one of the big windows in this café just around the corner from St-Sulpice and the Vieux Colombier theater. ☒ *65 rue de Rennes,* ☏ *01–45–48–53–81. Métro: St-Sulpice.*

8ᵉ Arrondissement (Champs-Élysées)

Ladurée. This new branch of the famous salon de thé founded in 1862 looks like it has been around since the turn of the century (the original on rue Royale has). Be sure to try the macaroons or the little tea sandwiches for which this place is famous. ☒ *75 av. des Champs-Élysées,* ☏ *01–42–89–11–11. Métro: Concorde.*

11ᵉ Arrondissement (Bastille)

Café de l'Industrie. Have a late-afternoon coffee or beer in the warm yellow rooms of this Bastille hangout where the walls are covered with photos of movie stars. ☒ *16 rue St-Sabin,* ☏ *01–47–00–13–53. Métro: Bastille.*

Pause Cafe. This hip Bastille spot attracts a chic, arty crowd for coffee, cheap beer, and tasty, inexpensive chili and quiche at its red-and-yellow Formica tables. ☒ *41 rue de Charonne,* ☏ *01–48–06–80–33. Métro: Ledru-Rollin.*

14ᵉ Arrondissement (Montparnasse)

Café du Dôme. Now a fancy brasserie—though you can still just have a cup of coffee or a drink here—this place began as a dingy meeting place for exiled artists and intellectuals such as Lenin, Picasso, and Chaim Soutine. ☒ *108 bd. Montparnasse,* ☏ *01–43–35–25–81. Métro: Vavin.*

Café de la Place. This café is a charming, wood-paneled spot that is perfect for watching the activity inside and out. ☒ *23 rue d'Odessa,* ☏ *01–42–18–01–55. Métro: Montparnasse.*

18ᵉ Arrondissement (Montmartre)

La Crémaillère. Alphonse Mucha frescoes decorate the walls at this veritable monument to fin-de-siècle art in Monmartre. ⊠ *15 pl. du Tertre,* ☎ *01–46–06–58–59. Métro: Anvers.*

Le Sancerre. Sit on the terrace sipping a coffee or a beer and watch the artists, hipsters, and tourists all pass by on their way through Montmartre. ⊠ *35 rue des Abbesses,* ☎ *01–45–58–08–20. Métro: Abbesses.*

19ᵉ Arrondissement (Buttes-Chaumont/La Villette)

Café de la Musique. This vast, stylishly postmodern café is adjacent to the Cité de la Musique in the Parc de La Villette. In the evenings it's primarily filled with people attending concerts, but the free jazz on Wednesday night and the interesting crowd make it worth the excursion. ⊠ *214 av. Jean-Jaurès,* ☎ *01–48–03–15–91. Métro: Porte de Pantin.*

Wine Bars

Paris wine bars are the perfect place to enjoy a glass (or bottle) of wine with a plate of cheese, charcuterie, or a simple but delicious hot meal. Bar owners are often true wine enthusiasts ready to dispense expert advice. Hours vary widely, so it's best to check ahead if your heart is set on a particular place; many, however, close around 10 PM.

Aux Bons Crus. This cramped, narrow venue has an authentic Parisian feel (it dates from 1905). ⊠ *7 rue des Petits-Champs, 1ᵉʳ,* ☎ *01–42–60–06–45. Métro: Bourse.*

Au Sauvignon. A stylish but jolly Left Bank crowd frequents this homey, friendly spot with an ideally placed terrace. Delicious *tartines* (open-face sandwiches) are served. *80 rue des Sts-Pères, 7ᵉ,* ☎ *01–45–48–49–02. Métro: Sèvres-Babylone.*

Le Baron Rouge. At this noisy, convivial haunt, wine spills from the barrels. ⊠ *1 rue Théophile-Roussel, 12ᵉ,* ☎ *01–43–43–14–32. Métro: Ledru-Rollin.*

Le Comptoir. Glasses of Burgundy and Bordeaux, as well as more unusual selections such as wines from Corsica are served. ⊠ *5 rue Monsieur-Le-Prince, 6ᵉ,* ☎ *01–43–29–12–05. Métro: Odéon.*

Jacques Mélac. This wine bar is named after the jolly owner who harvests grapes from the vine outside and bottles several of his own wines. ⊠ *42 rue Léon-Frot, 11ᵉ,* ☎ *01–43–70–59–27. Métro: Charonne.*

Le Moulin à Vins. Wines from the southwest and the Rhône valley and sturdy bistro cuisine are served. Stop by and elbow your way in among the locals at the bar. ⊠ *6 rue Burq, 18ᵉ,* ☎ *01–42–52–81–27. Métro: Abbesses.*

La Robe et le Palais. Come here for the more than 120 wines from all over France, served *au compteur* (according to the amount consumed), as well as a daily selection of good bistro-style dishes for lunch and dinner. ⊠ *13 rue des Lavandières-Ste-Opportune, 1ᵉʳ,* ☎ *01–45–08–07–41. Métro: Châtelet–Les Halles.*

Le Rubis. This resolutely old-time bar specializes in Burgundies. It's most crowded during the day; from 7 to 9:30 PM it's best to be smoke resistant. ⊠ *10 rue du Marché St-Honoré, 1ᵉʳ,* ☎ *01–42–61–03–34. Métro: Tuileries.*

La Tartine. Inexpensive wine and tartines in a tatty, almost seedy, turn-of-the-century bar has given this place antihero status among the rebel cognoscenti. ⊠ *24 rue de Rivoli, 4ᵉ,* ☎ *01–42–72–76–85. Métro: St-Paul.*

3   LODGING

Whether you favor palatial grandeur or homespun hospitality, there are wonderful hotels for every taste and budget in Paris. Splurge, and you could find yourself in sumptuous digs in a luxurious Right Bank mansion. Search, and you could land a room in one of the city's many stylish good-value hotels.

Revised and
updated by
Christopher
Mooney

WINDING STAIRCASES, flower-filled window
boxes, concierges who seem to have stepped
from a 19th-century novel—all of these still
exist in abundance in Paris hotels. So do grand rooms with marble baths,
Belle Epoque lobbies, and polished staff at your beck and call. In Paris
there are wonderful hotels for every taste and budget.

Our criteria when selecting the hotels reviewed below were quality, location, and character. Few chain hotels are listed, since most (with some
notable exceptions) lack the charm and authenticity found in typical
Parisian lodgings. Similarly, fewer hotels are listed in outlying arrondissements (the 10ᵉ to the 20ᵉ) because these are farther from the
major sights. Generally, there are more hotels on the Right Bank offering luxury—or at any rate formality—than there are on the Left Bank,
where hotels are frequently smaller and richer in old-fashioned ambience. The Right Bank's 1ᵉʳ and 8ᵉ arrondissements are still the most
exclusive and prices here reflect this. Less-expensive alternatives on the
Right Bank are the fashionable Marais quarter (3ᵉ and 4ᵉ arrondissements) and the 11ᵉ and 12ᵉ, near the Opéra Bastille.

Despite the huge choice of hotels, you should always reserve well in advance, especially if you're determined to stay in a specific place. You can
do this by telephoning or faxing ahead, then asking for written or faxed
confirmation. As you will probably be asked to send a deposit, be sure
to discuss refund policies before releasing your credit card number or
mailing your check or money order. During peak seasons, some hotels
require total prepayment. Always demand written confirmation of your
reservation, detailing the duration of your stay, the price, the location
and the type of your room (single or double, twin beds or double), and
the bathroom (shower—*douche*—or bath—*baignoire*, private or shared).

As part of a general upgrade of the city's hotels in recent years, scores
of lackluster, shabby Paris lodgings have been replaced by good-value
establishments in the lower to middle price ranges. Many of these are
family run. Despite widespread improvements, however, many Paris
hotels (especially budget accommodations) still have idiosyncrasies—
some endearing, others less so. Hotel rooms in Paris's oldest quarters
are generally much smaller than their American counterparts. The
standard French double bed is slightly smaller than the American version. Although air-conditioning has become de rigueur in middle- to
higher-priced hotels, it is generally not a prerequisite for comfort nor
is it always available (ask, if you want to be absolutely sure). Reviews
indicate the number of rooms with private bathrooms (which may include a shower or a tub, but not necessarily both). It's rare to find moderately priced places that have shared toilets or bathrooms, but be sure
you know what you are getting when you book a budget hotel.

Almost all Paris hotels charge extra for breakfast, with prices ranging
from 30 francs to more than 200 francs per person in luxury establishments. Though hotels may not automatically add the breakfast charge
to your bill, it's wise to inform the desk staff if you don't plan to have
breakfast at the hotel (you may want to find the nearest café instead).
For anything more than the standard Continental breakfast of café au
lait and baguette or croissants, the price will be higher. Some hotels
have especially pleasant breakfast areas, and we have noted this where
applicable. Luxury hotels often have restaurants, but finding a place
to eat in Paris is rarely a problem.

You'll notice that stars appear on a shield on the facade of most hotels. The French government grades hotels on a scale from one star to

four-star deluxe based on a notoriously complicated evaluation of amenities and services. At the bottom end of the scale are the one-star hotels, where you might have to share a bathroom and do without an elevator. You can expect two- and three-star hotels to have private bathrooms, elevators, and in-room televisions. At the high end are the luxurious four-star hotels, which have excellent amenities and prices to match. The ratings are sometimes misleading, however, since many hotels prefer to be under-starred for tax reasons.

We list hotels by price. Over the past few years luxury hotel prices have risen faster than their more moderate counterparts. Often a hotel in a certain price category will have a few rooms that are less expensive; it's worth asking. Rates must be posted in all rooms (usually on the backs of doors), with all extra charges clearly shown. There is a nominal *séjour* tax of 7 francs per person, per night.

Unless otherwise stated, the hotels reviewed below have elevators, rooms have TVs (many with cable, including CNN), minibars, and telephones, and English is spoken. Additional facilities, such as restaurants and health clubs, are listed at the end of each review.

CATEGORY	COST*
$$$$	over 1750 frs
$$$	1000 frs–1750 frs
$$	600 frs–1000 frs
$	under 600 frs

All prices are for a standard double room, including tax and service.

1ᵉʳ Arrondissement (Louvre)

See Right Bank Lodging map.

$$$$ ☷ **Costes.** Jean-Louis and Gilbert Costes's eponymous hotel is the darling of decorating magazines and a magnet for models and actors. Though converted from an intimate, 19th-century town house, the Costes now conjures up the palaces of Napoléon III. Every room is swathed in rich garnet and bronze tones and contains a luxurious mélange of patterned fabrics, heavy swags, and enough brocade and fringe to blanket the Champs-Élysées. And the bathrooms are truly marvelous affairs. ⊠ *239 rue St-Honoré, 75001,* ☏ *01–42–44–50–50,* 𝖥𝖠𝖷 *01–42–44–50–01. 85 rooms. Restaurant, bar, air-conditioning, in-room modem lines, in-room safes, room service, indoor pool, sauna, exercise room, laundry service. AE, DC, MC, V. Métro: Tuileries.*

$$$$ ☷ **Inter-Continental.** This exquisite late-19th-century hotel, with its restored sumptuous period details, was designed by the architect of the Paris Opéra, Charles Garnier. Three of its gilt and stuccoed public rooms are official historic monuments. Rooms, though more sedate than the public spaces, have Empire-style furnishings and rich period fabrics. The most coveted and spacious guest rooms overlook quiet inner courtyards. In summer, breakfast on the patio is a delicious experience. Service is impeccable. ⊠ *3 rue de Castiglione, 75001,* ☏ *01–44–77–11–11; 800/327–0200 in the U.S.,* 𝖥𝖠𝖷 *01–44–77–14–60. 375 rooms, 70 suites. Restaurant, bar, air-conditioning, in-room safes, no-smoking rooms, room service, laundry service, meeting rooms. AE, DC, MC, V. Métro: Concorde.*

$$$$ ☷ **Meurice.** The Meurice, owned by the Audrey group, is one of the finest hotels in the city. The Louis XVI–style first-floor salons are sumptuous, and the rooms, adorned with Persian carpets, marble mantelpieces, and ormolu clocks, are opulent. Most bathrooms are done in Florentine marble. Book well in advance to land a room or a suite overlooking the Tuileries Gardens. The hotel's restaurant, Le Meurice,

Alexander, **5**
L'Astor, **17**
Axial Beaubourg, **54**
Bradford-Élysées, **14**
Bretonnerie, **52**
Bristol, **16**
Britannique, **55**
Caron de
Beaumarchais, **51**

Castex, **44**
Costes, **30**
Crillon, **19**
Deux-Iles, **48**
Eber-Monceau, **10**
Ermitage, **37**
Étoile-Péreire, **9**
Excelsior, **20**
Garden Hôtel, **40**

Grand Hôtel de
Besançon, **36**
Grand Hôtel
Inter-Continental, **23**
Grand Hôtel
Jeanne-d'Arc, **50**
Hôtel de Noailles, **25**
Hôtel du Jeu de
Paume, **47**
Hôtel du 7e Art, **46**

Hyatt Regency Paris-
Madeleine, **18**
Inter-Continental, **27**
Jardins du
Trocadéro, **3**
Jules-César, **42**
Keppler, **6**
Lancaster, **13**
Le Laumière, **38**

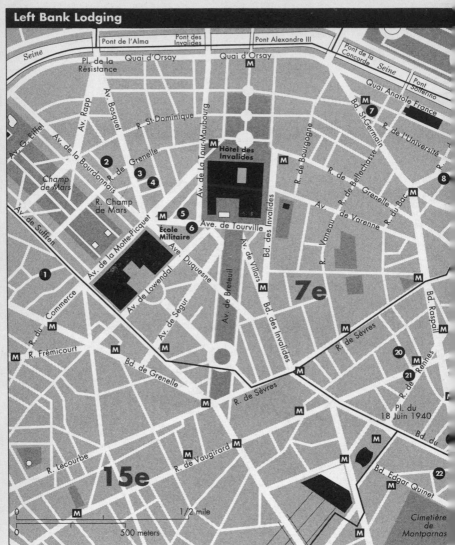

Left Bank Lodging

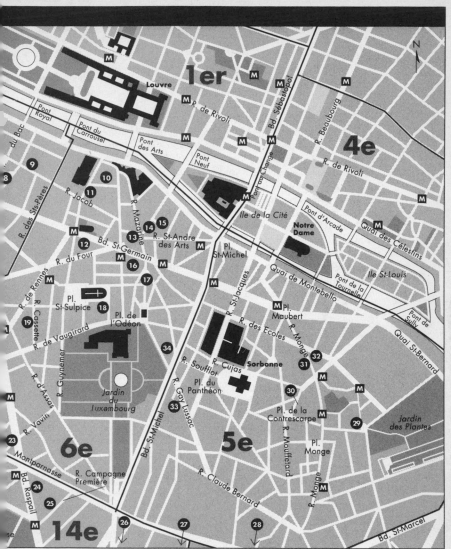

Relais Christine, **15**
Relais St-Germain, **17**
Relais St-Sulpice, **18**
Résidence les
Gobelins, **28**
St-Grégoire, **20**
Solférino, **7**
Le Tourville, **5**

Timhotel Jardin des
Plantes, **29**
Tour Eiffel Dupleix, **1**

is fabled. ✉ *228 rue de Rivoli, 75001,* ☎ *01–44–58–10–10,* FAX *01–44–58–10–15. 180 rooms, 28 suites. Restaurant, bar, air-conditioning, no-smoking rooms, room service, laundry service, business services. AE, DC, MC, V. Métro: Tuileries, Concorde.*

$$$$ 🎬 **Régina.** In the handsome place des Pyramides, this hundred-year-old Art Nouveau gem oozes old-fashioned grandeur in both public spaces and guest rooms. There's a sublime Belle Epoque lounge and fine antiques throughout. Request a room on rue de Rivoli facing the Louvre and the Tuileries Gardens. ✉ *2 rue des Pyramides, 75001,* ☎ *01–42–60–31–10,* FAX *01–40–15–95–16. 129 rooms, 15 suites. Restaurant, bar, air-conditioning, in-room safes, no-smoking rooms, room service, laundry service, meeting rooms. AE, DC, MC, V. Métro: Tuileries.*

$$$$ 🎬 **Ritz.** Festooned with gilt and ormolu, dripping with crystal chandeliers, and swathed in heavy silk and tapestries, this hotel, which opened in 1896, is the epitome of fin-de-siècle Paris. The Ritz has always attracted its share of historical intrigue, most recently as the starting point of Princess Diana's fatal car ride. Yet it's surprisingly intimate. The staff is famous for its ironclad discretion, and the lack of a lobby discourages paparazzi and sightseers who might annoy the privileged clientele. Legendary suites are named after former residents, such as Marcel Proust and Coco Chanel. Don't miss the famous Hemingway Bar (which the writer claimed to have "liberated" in 1944). ✉ *15 pl. Vendôme, 75001,* ☎ *01–43–16–30–30,* FAX *01–43–16–36–68. 142 rooms, 45 suites. 3 restaurants, 2 bars, air-conditioning, in-room modem lines, in-room safes, room service, indoor pool, beauty salon, health club, shops, laundry service, meeting rooms, parking (fee). AE, DC, MC, V. Métro: Opéra.*

$$$–$$$$ 🎬 **Vendôme.** This hotel has the best guest-to-staff ratio in Paris and
★ every luxury perk imaginable. Rooms are in sumptuous, Second Empire style, with walls and furnishings in muted earth torestaurateurnes and hand-carved wood detailing throughout. The bathrooms are over the top: brass, marble and silver bathtubs, waterproof telephones, and a full line of toiletries from Guerlain. Best of all, besides a videophone for checking out visitors at the door, is the fully automated bedside console that controls the lights, curtains, and electronic do-not-disturb sign. ✉ *1 Pl. Vendôme, 75001,* ☎ *01–42–60–32–84,* FAX *01–49–27–97–89. 19 rooms, 11 suites. Restaurant, bar, air-conditioning, room service, baby-sitting, in-room safes, in-room modem lines, laundry service. AE, DC, MC, V. Métro: Concorde, Opéra.*

$$$ 🎬 **Square.** There's little that's "square" about this very hip boutique hotel. Owned by restaurateur Patrick Derderian, it's also home to his trendy Zebra Square café. Rooms are bright and spacious by Paris standards, and decorated in what is best described as an enthusiastic brio of extravagant minimalism. Curved doors, walls, and furniture break up a hard-edged design dominated by stripes and squares, while flowers, designer lamps, and enormous beds help soften the Zen aesthetic. Large desks, plus three phone lines and a fax/answering machine in each room make it ideal for business travel. But the reading room, art gallery, and very sleek bar make it a good choice for pleasure-seekers as well. ✉ *3 rue de Boulainvilliers, 75001,* ☎ *01–44–14–91–90,* FAX *01–44–14–91–99. 16 rooms, 6 suites. Restaurant, bar, air-conditioning, in-room modem lines, in-room safes, conference room, room service, mini-bar, laundry service, parking (fee). AE, DC, MC, V. Métro: Passy.*

$$ 🎬 **Britannique.** Open since 1870, the Britannique blends courteous English service with old-fashioned French elegance. It has a handsome winding staircase and soundproof rooms well-appointed in mahogany and warm tones. During World War I, the hotel served as headquarters for a Quaker mission. ✉ *20 av. Victoria, 75001,* ☎ *01–42–33–74–59,* FAX *01–42–33–82–65. 40 rooms, 31 with bath, 9 with shower.*

Bar, in-room modem lines, in-room safes, no-smoking rooms. AE, DC, MC, V. Métro: Châtelet.

$$ ⊡ **Paris Hôtel des Tuileries.** This remarkably quiet hotel, tucked away in an 18th-century town house on a small side street, is in a superb spot, within walking distance of the Louvre, Tuileries Gardens, and Place Vendôme. Everything, from the creaky cage elevator and wide French windows to the sturdy wooden armoires and gilt mirrors, is quaintly old-fashioned. A tiny lobby lounge and tapestry-covered breakfast room are the only public areas. ⊠ *10 rue St-Hyacinthe, 75001,* ☎ *01–42–61–04–17,* FAX *01–49–27–91–56. 18 rooms, 8 suites. Bar, air-conditioning, in-room safes, room service, laundry service. AE, DC, MC, V. Métro: Tuileries, Concorde.*

$–$$ ⊡ **Régence Opéra.** You can't beat the location—right in the heart of Paris, within a stone's throw of the Opéra Garnier, Palais Royal, and Louvre. Rooms are more spacious than you'd expect for the price, though they are somewhat generic, with pastel hues, floral bedspreads, and standard-issue wooden furnishings. ⊠ *5 rue Thérèse, 75001,* ☎ *01–42–96–10–01; 800/44–UTELL in the U.S.,* FAX *01–42–96–15–22. 43 rooms. Bar, no-smoking floors, room service, baby-sitting, laundry service. AE, DC, MC, V. Métro: Pyramides.*

$ ⊡ **Londres St-Honoré.** An appealing combination of character and comfort distinguishes this small, inexpensive hotel, a five-minute walk from the Louvre. Exposed oak beams, statues in niches, and rustic stone walls give this place old-fashioned charm, while modern pluses include satellite TV. Though rooms have floral bedspreads and standard hotel furniture, they are pleasant and the price is right. Note that the elevator doesn't go to the ground floor. ⊠ *13 rue St-Roch, 75001,* ☎ *01–42–60–15–62,* FAX *01–42–60–16–00. 29 rooms. AE, DC, MC, V. Métro: Pyramides.*

$ ⊡ **Louvre Forum.** This hotel is a find: Smack in the center of Paris, it has extremely reasonably priced, clean, comfortable, well-equipped rooms, and a friendly feel. What it lacks in old world appeal, it makes up for in location, amenities, and price. Breakfast is served in a homey vaulted cellar. ⊠ *25 rue du Bouloi, 75001,* ☎ *01–42–36–54–19,* FAX *01–42–33–66–31. 27 rooms. Bar. AE, DC, MC, V. Métro: Louvre.*

2ᵉ Arrondissement (La Bourse)

See Right Bank Lodging map.

$$$$ ⊡ **Westminster.** This former private mansion on an elegant street between the Opéra and Place Vendôme was built in the mid-19th century. It preserves its gracious atmosphere with marble fireplaces, crystal chandeliers, and parquet floors. The pleasant piano bar is a popular rendezvous, and the hotel's restaurant, Le Céladon, serves outstanding French cuisine. ⊠ *13 rue de la Paix, 75002,* ☎ *01–42–61–57–46; 800/203–3232 in the U.S.,* FAX *01–42–60–30–66. 83 rooms, 18 suites. Restaurant, bar, air-conditioning, in-room safes, no-smoking rooms, room service, baby-sitting, laundry service, meeting rooms, parking (fee). AE, DC, MC, V. Métro: Opéra.*

$$ ⊡ **Grand Hôtel de Besançon.** This terrific hotel, with its very Parisian cream-colored facade and wrought-iron balconies, has it all—intimacy, comfort, affordability, and a location on a delightful, pedestrian market street near Les Halles, the Pompidou Center, and the Marais. Rooms are classically decorated with French upholsteries and period reproductions, and despite the busy area nearby, they are quiet. ⊠ *56 rue Montorgueil, 75002,* ☎ *01–42–36–41–08,* FAX *01–45–08–08–79. 11 rooms, 14 suites. In-room modem lines, in-room safes, laundry service. AE, DC, MC, V. Métro: Etienne-Marcel, Les Halles.*

$$ ⊞ **Hôtel de Noailles.** With a nod to the work of postmodern designers like Putman and Starck, this new-wave inn (part of the Tulip Inn group) is a star among Paris's new crop of well-priced, hip, style-driven boutique hotels. Though not to everyone's taste, rooms are imaginatively decorated with funky furnishings and contemporary details like rubbery curtains; the look is fun and very hip. A young, cosmopolitan clientele has made this one their own. ⊠ *9 rue de Michodière, 75002,* ☎ *01–47–42–92–90,* FAX *01–49–24–92–71. 58 rooms. Bar, air-conditioning, laundry service. AE, DC, MC, V. Métro: Opéra.*

3ᵉ Arrondissement (Marais)

See Right Bank Lodging map.

$$$$ ⊞ **Pavillon de la Reine.** On the 17th-century place des Vosges, this mag-
★   nificent mansion was reconstructed from original plans. It's filled with Louis XIII–style antiques, rich-toned fabrics, and fireplaces. For an absolutely royal feeling, ask for a duplex with French windows overlooking the first of two flower-filled courtyards behind the historic Queen's Pavilion. Breakfast is served in a vaulted cellar. ⊠ *28 Pl. des Vosges, 75003,* ☎ *01–40–29–19–19; 800/447–7462 in the U.S.,* FAX *01–40–29–19–20. 30 rooms, 25 suites. Bar, breakfast room, air-conditioning, room service, laundry service, free parking. AE, DC, MC, V. Métro: Bastille, St-Paul.*

4ᵉ Arrondissement (Marais/Ile St-Louis)

See Right Bank Lodging map.

$$$ ⊞ **Hôtel du Jeu de Paume.** The showpiece of this lovely 17th-century hotel on the Ile St-Louis is the stone-walled, vaulted lobby–cum–breakfast room. It stands on an erstwhile court where French aristocrats once played *jeu de paume,* an early version of tennis using palm fronds. Rooms are on the small side, but nicely done up in butter-yellow, with rustic antiques, beamed ceilings, and damask upholsteries. ⊠ *54 rue St-Louis-en-l'Ile, 75004,* ☎ *01–43–26–14–18,* FAX *01–40–46–02–76. 30 rooms, 1 junior suite. Bar, baby-sitting, laundry service. AE, DC, MC, V. Métro: Pont-Marie.*

$$ ⊞ **Axial Beaubourg.** A solid bet in the Marais, this hotel in a 16th-century building has beamed ceilings in the lobby and in the six first-floor rooms. Most have pleasant if functional decor and all have satellite TV. The Pompidou Center and the Picasso Museum are five minutes away. ⊠ *11 rue du Temple, 75004,* ☎ *01–42–72–72–22,* FAX *01–42–72–03–53. 39 rooms. Air-conditioning, in-room modem lines, in-room safes, no-smoking rooms. AE, DC, MC, V. Métro: Hôtel de Ville.*

$$ ⊞ **Bretonnerie.** This small hotel is in a 17th-century *hôtel particulier* (town house) on a tiny street in the Marais, a few minutes' walk from the Pompidou Center. The Louis XIII–style rooms come complete with upholstered walls, antiques, beamed ceilings, four-poster beds, and marble-clad bathrooms, or some combination thereof. Their size varies considerably from spacious to cramped; the larger ones are pricier. Breakfast is served in the vaulted cellar. ⊠ *22 rue Ste-Croix-de-la-Bretonnerie, 75004,* ☎ *01–48–87–77–63,* FAX *01–42–77–26–78. 27 rooms, 3 suites. In-room safes, parking (fee). MC, V. Métro: Hôtel de Ville.*

$$ ⊞ **Caron de Beaumarchais.** The theme of this intimate hotel is the work
★   of Caron de Beaumarchais, who wrote *The Marriage of Figaro* in 1778. First-edition copies of his books adorn the public spaces. Rooms faithfully reflect the taste of 18th-century French nobility, right down to the reproduction wallpapers and upholsteries. Fresh flowers and fluffy bathrobes are a bonus for the price. Bathrooms feature heavy antique mirrors and hand-painted tiles. Streetside rooms on the second through

fifth floors are the largest, while the slightly smaller sixth-floor gar-rets under the mansard roof have beguiling views across Right Bank rooftops. ☒ *12 rue Vieille-du-Temple, 75004,* ☎ *01–42–72–34–12,* FAX *01–42–72–34–63. 19 rooms. Air-conditioning, laundry service. AE, DC, MC, V. Métro: Hôtel de Ville.*

$$ ⊞ **Deux-Iles.** This converted 17th-century mansion on the Ile St-Louis has long won plaudits for charm and comfort. Flowers and plants are scattered throughout the large, stunning main hall and tapestries cover the exposed stone walls. The delightfully old-fashioned rooms, blessed with exposed beams, are small but airy and sunny. Ask for one over-looking the little garden courtyard. In winter, a roaring fire warms the lounge. ☒ *59 rue St-Louis-en-l'Ile, 75004,* ☎ *01–43–26–13–35,* FAX *01–43–29–60–25. 17 rooms. Air-conditioning, in-room safes, baby-sitting. AE, MC, V. Métro: Pont-Marie.*

$$ ⊞ **St-Louis.** Louis XIII–style furniture and oil paintings set the tone in the public areas in this 17th-century town house on the Ile St-Louis. Rooms are much simpler and more standard, but exposed beams and stone walls make them appealing as well. Breakfast is served in the at-mospheric cellar. ☒ *75 rue St-Louis-en-l'Ile, 75004,* ☎ *01–46–34–04–80,* FAX *01–46–34–02–13. 21 rooms. In-room safes, in-room modem lines. MC, V. Métro: Pont-Marie.*

$–$$ ⊞ **Hôtel du 7ᵉ Art.** The theme of this hip Marais hotel fits its name ("Seventh Art" is what the French call filmmaking): Hollywood from the '40s to the '60s. Posters of James Cagney, Marilyn Monroe, Char-lie Chaplin, and other stars cover the walls throughout. Rooms are small and spartan, but clean, quiet, and equipped with cable TV. There's no elevator. Breakfast is served in the handsome wood-paneled lounge or in the rustic cellar room; there's also an inviting bar. The clientele is young, trendy, and primarily American. ☒ *20 rue St-Paul, 75004,* ☎ *01–44–54–85–00,* FAX *01–42–77–69–10. 23 rooms. Bar, in-room safes. AE, DC, MC, V. Métro: St-Paul.*

$ ⊞ **Castex.** This Marais hotel in a Revolution-era building is a bargain-hunter's dream. Rooms are low on frills but squeaky clean, the own-ers are extremely friendly, and the prices are rock-bottom, which ensures that the hotel is often booked months ahead by a largely young, American clientele. There's no elevator, and the only TV is in the ground-floor salon. ☒ *5 rue Castex, 75004,* ☎ *01–42–72–31–52,* FAX *01–42–72–57–91. 27 rooms. In-room modem lines. MC, V. Métro: Bastille.*

$ ⊞ **Grand Hôtel Jeanne-d'Arc.** If you're on a budget, you're sure to get your money's worth at this hotel near Place des Vosges in the Marais. Though rooms are on the spartan side, they are clean, well-main-tained, and fairly spacious (some have a couch). Doubles start at just over 300 frs and, for families or groups, there are triples or quadru-ples for under 600 frs. The staff, too, is friendly. ☒ *3 rue de Jarente, 75004,* ☎ *01–48–87–62–11,* FAX *01–48–87–37–31. 36 rooms. MC, V. Métro: St-Paul.*

$ ⊞ **Place des Vosges.** A loyal, eclectic clientele swears by this small, his-toric Marais hotel on a delightful street just off Place des Vosges. The Louis XIII–style reception area and rooms with oak-beamed ceilings, rough-hewn stone, and a mix of rustic finds from secondhand shops evoke old Marais. Ask for the top-floor room, the hotel's largest, for its view over Right Bank rooftops; others are the size of walk-in clos-ets and are less expensive. ☒ *12 rue de Birague, 75004,* ☎ *01–42–72–60–46,* FAX *01–42–72–02–64. 16 rooms. Breakfast room. AE, DC, MC, V. Métro: Bastille.*

$ ⊞ **Vieux Marais.** This pleasingly old-fashioned hotel with a turn-of-the-century facade is on a quiet street in the heart of the Marais. Rooms are bright, impeccably clean, and equipped with satellite TV;

try to get one overlooking the courtyard. Breakfast is served in a pretty lounge. The staff is exceptionally courteous. ⊠ *8 rue du Plâtre, 75004,* ☎ *01–42–78–47–22,* ℻ *01–42–78–34–32. 30 rooms. Air-conditioning, in-room safes. MC, V. Métro: Hôtel de Ville.*

5ᵉ Arrondissement (Latin Quarter)

See Left Bank Lodging map.

$$ ⛫ **Jardin du Luxembourg.** Blessed with a personable staff and a smart,
★ stylish look, this hotel, on a calm side street just a block from the Luxembourg Gardens, is one of the most sought-after in the Latin Quarter. Rooms are small (common for this neighborhood) but intelligently furnished to optimize space; the rustic pieces and warm ocher, rust, and indigo give them a Provençal feel. Ask for one with a balcony overlooking the street; the best, No. 25, has dormer windows and a peekaboo view of the Eiffel Tower. ⊠ *5 Impasse Royer-Collard, 75005,* ☎ *01–40–46–08–88,* ℻ *01–40–46–02–28. 27 rooms. Air-conditioning, no-smoking rooms, in-room safes, sauna. AE, DC, MC, V. Métro: Luxembourg.*

$$ ⛫ **Libertel Quartier Latin.** The new flagship of the Libertel chain combines sleek design with intellectual rigor. Interior decorator Didier Gomez took his cues from the nearby Sorbonne university, turning the downstairs lounge into an elegant reading room and lining the walls with photos and portraits of celebrated writers. Rooms, furnished with ebony furniture and quilted bedcovers, emphasize sculpted lines and quiet comfort. Ask for one on the sixth floor, preferably No. 602 or 603, which have a beautiful view of Notre Dame from their balconies. If this doesn't inspire you to finally write that novel, maybe the carpets will: They're inscribed with quotations from Balzac and Baudelaire. ⊠ *9 rue des Ecoles, 75005,* ☎ *01–44–27–06–45,* ℻ *01–43–25–36–70. 24 rooms, 5 suites. Air-conditioning, in-room safes, room service. AE, DC, MC, V. Métro: Cardinal Lemoine.*

$ ⛫ **Familia.** It's hard to beat the price or this level of homespun com-
★ fort—the hospitable Gaucheron family, the hotel's owners, bend over backward for you. About half the rooms have sepia frescoes of celebrated Paris scenes painted by an artist from the Beaux Arts school; some are appointed with exquisite Louis XV–style furnishings, others have nice mahogany pieces. Those overlooking the animated Latin Quarter street have double-glazed windows; book a month ahead for one with a walk-out balcony on the second or fifth floor. ⊠ *11 rue des Écoles, 75005,* ☎ *01–43–54–55–27,* ℻ *01–43–29–61–77. 30 rooms. AE, MC, V. Métro: Cardinal Lemoine.*

$ ⛫ **Grandes Écoles.** This delightfully intimate hotel looks and feels like a country cottage dropped smack in the middle of the Latin Quarter. It is off the street and occupies three buildings on a beautiful leafy garden, where breakfast is served in summer. Parquet floors, Louis-Philippe furnishings, lace bedspreads, and the absence of TV all add to the rustic ambience. ⊠ *75 rue du Cardinal Lemoine, 75005,* ☎ *01–43–26–79–23,* ℻ *01–43–25–28–15. 51 rooms. Parking (fee). MC, V. Métro: Cardinal Lemoine.*

$ ⛫ **Timhotel Jardin des Plantes.** Across the street from the lovely Jardin des Plantes, this pleasant, modern hotel—part of the Timhotel chain—has very reasonable prices and perfectly suitable rooms with blond-wood furnishings and floral upholsteries. There's a fifth-floor terrace where you can breakfast or sunbathe in summer, and a sauna in the cellar. ⊠ *5 rue Linné, 75005,* ☎ *01–47–07–06–20,* ℻ *01–47–07–62–74. 33 rooms. Restaurant, bar, sauna. AE, DC, MC, V. Métro: Jussieu.*

6e Arrondissement (St-Germain/Montparnasse)

See Left Bank Lodging map.

$$$$ ⊞ **Relais Christine.** On a quiet street between the Seine and boulevard St-Germain, this luxurious and popular hotel, occupying 16th-century abbey cloisters, oozes romantic ambience. Rooms are spacious (particularly the duplexes on the upper floors) and well appointed in the old Parisian style (rich upholsteries, mahogany pieces); the best have exposed ceiling beams and overlook the garden. The breakfast room is an erstwhile stone chapel. ⊠ *3 rue Christine, 75006,* ☎ *01–40–51–60–80; 800/447–7462 in the U.S.,* FAX *01–40–51–60–81. 31 rooms, 18 suites. Bar, air-conditioning, no-smoking rooms, room service, baby-sitting, laundry service, meeting rooms, free parking. AE, DC, MC, V. Métro: Odéon.*

$$$–$$$$ ⊞ **L'Hôtel.** Rock idols and movie stars adore this expensive and eccentric Left Bank hotel. Oscar Wilde died here in Room 16. The decor is over the top at times; one small double is decorated entirely in leopard skin; another handsome suite features the mirrored, Art Deco boudoir furniture of vaudeville star Mistinguett. Many rooms are extremely small. The hotel bar, which sports a live tree and a gurgling fountain, is popular with a well-heeled international crowd. ⊠ *13 rue des Beaux-Arts, 75006,* ☎ *01–44–41–99–00,* FAX *01–43–25–64–81. 25 rooms, 2 suites. Bar, air-conditioning, in-room safes, baby-sitting. AE, DC, MC, V. Métro: St-Germain-des-Prés.*

$$$ ⊞ **Buci Latin.** Modern artwork on the walls and zebra-upholstered chairs
★ in the lobby set the tone at this funky, upscale hotel. Each room's door is inspired by the work of a famous artist—Magritte, Léger, Monet, or Basquiat—done by local painters. Rooms are small, but the Santa-Fe decor, ochre walls, exposed beams, arty, contoured tables give them a quirky feel. The more spacious duplex suite on the top floor, right under the roof, has a small bathroom loft with a shower, make-up table, and free-standing bathtub. ⊠ *34 rue de Buci, 75006,* ☎ *01–43–29–07–20,* FAX *01–43–29–67–44. 26 rooms, 2 suites. Air-conditioning, in-room modem lines, room service, mini-bar, laundry service. AE, DC, MC, V. Métro: Mabillon.*

$$$ ⊞ **Hôtel de l'Abbaye.** Once a convent, this delightful hotel near St-Sulpice features a stone-vaulted entrance and a lovely flower-filled back garden with a stone fountain. The blend of stylishly rustic antiques and earthy apricot and ocher tones makes for a calm, cozy atmosphere. The first-floor rooms open onto the garden; most of those on the upper floors have oak beams and sitting alcoves. The four duplexes with private terraces are more expensive. Breakfast is included. ⊠ *10 rue Cassette, 75006,* ☎ *01–45–44–38–11,* FAX *01–45–48–07–86. 42 rooms, 4 suites. Bar, air-conditioning, room service, baby-sitting, laundry service. AE, MC, V. Métro: St-Sulpice.*

$$$ ⊞ **Relais St-Germain.** The interior-designer owners of this outstanding hotel in the heart of St-Germain-des-Prés have exquisite taste and a superb respect for tradition and detail. Moreover, rooms are at least twice the size of what you find at other hotels in the area for the same price. Much of the furniture was selected with a knowledgeable eye from the city's *brocantes* (secondhand dealers) and every room has its own unique treasures. Doubles have separate sitting areas; four have kitchenettes. Breakfast is included. ⊠ *9 carrefour de l'Odéon, 75006,* ☎ *01–43–29–12–05,* FAX *01–46–33–45–30. 21 rooms and 1 suite, all with bath. Bar, air-conditioning, in-room safes, room service, baby-sitting, laundry service. AE, DC, MC, V. Métro: Odéon.*

$$–$$$ ⊞ **Le Clos Médicis.** Contemporary style meets Provençal tradition at this classy little hotel in St-Germain-des-Prés. Warm colors, and a mix of modern pieces, painted country furnishings, and wrought-iron items set the tone. Rooms are small (except for the duplex) but laden with comforts, such as minibars and crisp terry-cloth robes. ⊠ *56 rue Monsieur-le-Prince, 75006,* ☎ *01–43–29–10–80,* 𝔽𝔸𝕏 *01–43–54–26–90. 37 rooms, 1 duplex suite. Bar, air-conditioning, in-room modem lines, no-smoking rooms. AE, DC, MC, V. Métro: Luxembourg.*

$$–$$$ 🖬 **Fleurie.** On a quiet side street near place de l'Odéon, this spiffy, family-run hotel has pretty, pastel-color rooms and many modern luxury amenities, including marble-clad bathrooms with heated towel racks. Antiques, Oriental rugs, and rich upholsteries fill the 18th-century building. The staff is helpful. ⊠ *32–34 rue Grégoire-de-Tours, 75006,* ☎ *01–53–73–70–70,* 𝔽𝔸𝕏 *01–53–73–70–20. 29 rooms. Bar, air-conditioning, in-room modem lines, in-room safes, baby-sitting, laundry service. AE, DC, MC, V. Métro: Odéon.*

$$–$$$ 🖬 **Hôtel d'Aubusson.** Prices are kept in check for what you get at this
★ hotel: original Aubusson tapestries, Versailles-style parquet floors, a chiseled stone fireplace, and restored antiques. Even the smallest rooms are good-sized by Paris standards, and all are decked out in rich burgundies, greens, or blues. The 10 best rooms have canopied beds and ceiling beams. In summer, you can have your breakfast or pre-dinner drink in the paved courtyard. ⊠ *33 rue Dauphine, 75006,* ☎ *01–43–29–43–43,* 𝔽𝔸𝕏 *01–43–29–12–62. 49 rooms with bath. Bar, air-conditioning, in-room safes, baby-sitting, laundry service. AE, MC, V. Métro: Odéon.*

$$–$$$ 🖬 **Hôtel de Buci.** The eager-to-please staff adds to the luxurious feeling of this small hotel on the lively rue de Buci market street. Rooms, which vary in size from cozy to good-sized, have armoires and reproductions of 18th-century fabrics in warm, regal patterns; bathrooms are done in marble. Ask for a room overlooking the back for a quieter night's sleep, or one in front for a glimpse of Paris. The lobby, filled with club chairs and fresh flowers, and the cellar breakfast room are good spots to rendezvous. ⊠ *22 rue de Buci, 75006,* ☎ *01–55–42–74–74,* 𝔽𝔸𝕏 *01–55–42–74–44. 24 rooms. Breakfast room, in-room modem lines, minibars, business services, meeting room. AE, DC, MC, V. Métro: Odéon.*

$$–$$$ 🖬 **Manoir de St-Germain-des-Prés.** This stylish hotel is right next to the Brasserie Lipp and across from the Café de Flore. Rooms are done up in traditional 18th-century luxe, with wainscoting and rich upholsteries. Amenities promote genuine R&R, from Jacuzzis and sound-proof rooms to thirsty terry robes and well-stocked minibars; and breakfast is included. ⊠ *153 bd. St-Germain-des-Prés, 75006,* ☎ *01–42–22–21–65,* 𝔽𝔸𝕏 *01–45–48–22–25. 32 rooms. Bar, air-conditioning, in-room modem lines, in-room safes, hot tubs, laundry service. AE, DC, MC, V. Métro: St-Germain-des-Prés.*

$$–$$$ 🖬 **Relais St-Sulpice.** A savvy clientele of discerning taste frequents this fashionable little hotel. It's a stylish blend of various periods and regions—African artworks line the hallways; Provençal tiles adorn the bathrooms; Chinese engravings wink to Parisians' penchant for the Orient in the 1930s; heavy fabrics drape the windows; and thick, cotton-piqué downy comforters envelop wrought-iron beds. There's a sauna downstairs, right off the atrium breakfast salon. Room 11 has a terrific view of St-Sulpice. ⊠ *3 rue Garancière, 75006,* ☎ *01–46–33–99–00,* 𝔽𝔸𝕏 *01–46–33–00–10. 26 rooms. Air-conditioning, in-room safes, no-smoking rooms, sauna, baby-sitting, laundry service, meeting rooms, parking (fee). AE, DC, MC, V. Métro: St-Germain-des-Prés, St-Sulpice.*

$$ 🖬 **Atelier Montparnasse.** This Art Deco–inspired gem was designed with style and comfort in mind. Rooms are tastefully done and all the bathrooms feature unique mosaic reproductions of famous French paintings. The hotel is across the street from the famous brasseries Le Select and La Coupole, and within walking distance of the Luxembourg Gardens and St-Germain-des-Prés. Art lovers take note: The hotel hosts monthly exhibits of the works of local painters. ⊠ *49 rue Vavin, 75006,* ☎ *01–46–33–60–00,* FAX *01–40–51–04–21. 16 rooms, 1 triple. Bar, room service, baby-sitting, laundry service. AE, DC, MC, V. Métro: Vavin.*

$$ ⊡ **Bonaparte.** The congenial staff only makes staying in this intimate place more of a treat. Old-fashioned upholsteries, 19th-century furnishings, and paintings create a quaint feel in the relatively spacious rooms. And the location in the heart of St-Germain is nothing short of fabulous. ⊠ *61 rue Bonaparte, 75006,* ☎ *01–43–26–97–37,* FAX *01–46–33–57–67. 29 rooms. Air-conditioning, in-room safes, laundry service, refrigerators. MC, V. Métro: St-Germain-des-Prés.*

$$ ⊡ **St-Grégoire.** On a calm street off bustling rue de Rennes, this dis-
★ creet little hotel offers quiet and comfortable refuge from the hectic pace of Paris. Rooms, in muted pinks, yellows, and beiges, have simple antique furniture and bucolic prints on the walls. The sitting room/lobby is especially cozy, with its rustic fireplace and flowery wallpaper. Particularly romantic are Rooms 14 and 16, which have enclosed, ivy-covered terraces. ⊠ *43 rue de l'Abbé Grégoire, 75006,* ☎ *01–45–48–23–23,* FAX *01–45–48–33–95. 20 rooms, 1 suite. Air-conditioning, baby-sitting. AE, DC, MC, V. Métro: St-Placide.*

$–$$ ⊡ **Aramis-St-Germain.** Get great value for your money at this hotel, which, surprisingly, is part of the Best Western chain. It's understated, yet classically French. Rooms have damask bedspreads and sturdy cherry-wood armoires. All are soundproof and equipped with cable TV; about half have air-conditioning; and nine have whirlpool baths. Harvey's Piano Bar, on the ground floor, is popular with a smart business set. ⊠ *124 rue de Rennes, 75006,* ☎ *01–45–48–03–75; 800/528-1234 in the U.S.,* FAX *01–45–44–99–29. 42 rooms. Bar, minibars, laundry service. AE, DC, MC, V. Métro: St-Placide.*

7ᵉ Arrondissement (Invalides/École Militaire)

See Left Bank Lodging map.

$$$$ ⊡ **Montalembert.** Created by hotel goddess Grace Leo-Andrieu, this
★ is one of Paris's most originally voguish boutique accommodations. Whether appointed with traditional or contemporary furnishings, rooms are all about simple lines and chic luxury. A host of signature elements were designed especially for the hotel by the world's hippest designers: quilts in bold navy-and-white stripes, Frette linens and fabrics, Cascais marble bathrooms, and cast-bronze door handles. Ask about special packages if you're staying for more than three nights. ⊠ *3 rue de Montalembert, 75007,* ☎ *01–45–49–68–68; 800/628-8929 in the U.S.,* FAX *01–45–49–69–49. 50 rooms, 6 suites. Restaurant, bar, air-conditioning, in-room modem lines, in-room safes, room service, in-room VCRs, massage, baby-sitting, meeting rooms. AE, DC, MC, V. Métro: Rue du Bac.*

$$–$$$ ⊡ **Le Tourville.** Here is a rare find: a cozy, upscale hotel that doesn't cost a fortune. Each room has crisp, virgin-white damask upholstery set against pastel or ocher walls, a smattering of antique bureaus and lamps, original artwork, and fabulous old mirrors. Though smaller doubles are priced at the low end of the $$ category, the four doubles with walk-out terraces nip into the $$$ bracket. The junior suites have Jacuzzis. The staff couldn't be more helpful. ⊠ *16 av. de Tourville, 75007,* ☎ *01–47–05–62–62; 800/528-3549 in the U.S.,* FAX *01–47–05–43–90. 27 rooms, 3 junior suites. Bar, air-conditioning, laundry service. AE, DC, MC, V. Métro: École Militaire.*

$$ ⊡ **Hôtel du Cadran.** Colorful window boxes lend a welcoming touch to this cheerful hotel in a handsome corner building near the market on rue Cler. The charming Madame Chaine and her gracious staff go out of their way to ensure that you enjoy your stay, from recommending a bistro to booking theater tickets. Rooms have coordinating drapes and bedspreads in cheery colors, and are very comfortable. Ask about special weekend rates. ✉ *10 rue du Champ de Mars, 75007,* ☎ *01–40–62–67–00,* FAX *01–40–62–67–13. 42 rooms. Bar, air-conditioning, in-room modem lines, in-room safes, no-smoking rooms, baby-sitting, laundry service, meeting rooms, travel services. AE, DC, MC, V. Métro: École Militaire.*

$$ 🔲 **Hôtel de l'Université.** Staying at this hotel in a 17th-century town house between boulevard St-Germain and the Seine feels like going back in time. Rooms have English and French antiques and their original fireplaces. Ask for one with a terrace on the fifth floor. Those with showers are more moderately priced. ✉ *22 rue de l'Université, 75007,* ☎ *01–42–61–09–39,* FAX *01–42–60–40–84. 27 rooms. Air-conditioning, in-room modem lines, in-room safes, room service. AE, MC, V. Métro: Rue du Bac.*

$$ 🔲 **Latour Maubourg.** In the heart of the elegant 7ᵉ arrondissement, a stone's throw from the Invalides and the Prime Minister's residence, is this small hotel where personalized service is emphasized. The place is homey and unpretentious, from its very helpful staff to its simply furnished rooms with their appealing mix of mismatched finds. ✉ *150 rue de Grenelle, 75007,* ☎ *01–47–05–16–16,* FAX *01–47–05–16–14. 9 rooms, 1 suite. MC, V. Métro: Latour Maubourg.*

$–$$ 🔲 **Solférino.** Across the street from the Musée d'Orsay, the Solférino is a cheerful little hotel. The look is upbeat, with bright color schemes and flower-filled window boxes; rooms have satellite TV. The skylighted breakfast room is a pleasant place to greet the day. ✉ *91 rue de Lille, 75007,* ☎ *01–47–05–85–54,* FAX *01–45–55–51–16. 52 rooms, 46 with bath, 6 with shower and shared bath. AE, MC, V.* ☉ *Closed Dec. 25–Jan. 1. Métro: Solférino.*

$ 🔲 **Champ de Mars.** Françoise and Stéphane Gourdal's comfortable hotel
★ has an appealing blue-and-yellow French country-house style. Rooms are equipped with satellite TV and CNN; the two on the ground floor open onto a leafy courtyard. The neighborhood—near the Eiffel Tower and Invalides—is difficult to beat. ✉ *7 rue du Champ de Mars, 75007,* ☎ *01–45–51–52–30,* FAX *01–45–51–64–36. 25 rooms. AE, MC, V. Métro: École Militaire.*

$ 🔲 **Eiffel Rive Gauche.** On a quiet side street just a couple blocks from the Eiffel Tower, this modern hotel with a leafy patio is a great budget find. The look is functional but rooms are spacious and comfortable. The owner, Mr. Chicheportiche, is a multilingual, walking encyclopedia of Paris. One caveat: A steep phone surcharge is added if you make a collect call. ✉ *6 rue du Gros Caillou, 75007,* ☎ *01–45–51–24–56,* FAX *01–45–51–11–77. 30 rooms. AE, MC, V. Métro: École Militaire.*

8ᵉ Arrondissement (Champs-Élysées)

See Right Bank Lodging map.

$$$$ 🔲 **L'Astor.** Part of the Westin-Demeure hotel group, L'Astor is a bastion of highly stylized, civilized chic. The Art Deco lobby is decked out in boldly patterned armchairs, huge mirrors, and clever ceiling frescoes. There's also a cozy bar; a small, neoclassic-inspired library; and a stunning trompe l'oeil dining room. Guest rooms are testimonials to the sober Regency style, with weighty marble fireplaces and mahogany furnishings. Several suites have walk-out balconies with superb vistas. The hotel's restaurant is supervised by the celebrated chef Joël Robuchon. ✉ *11 rue d'Astorg, 75008,* ☎ *01–53–05–05–05; 800/WESTIN1* *in the U.S.,* 𝐅𝐀𝐗 *01–53–05–05–30. 134 rooms, 5 suites. Restaurant, bar, air-conditioning, in-room modem lines, in-room safes, no-smoking rooms, room service, beauty salon, health club, laundry service. AE, DC, MC, V. Métro: Miromesnil, St-Augustin.*

$$$$ ⊞ **Bristol.** The understated facade on rue du Faubourg St-Honoré might mislead the unknowing, but the Bristol ranks among Paris's top four hotels and has the prices to prove it (doubles start at 3,250 frs). Some of the spaciously elegant rooms have authentic Louis XV and Louis XVI furniture and magnificent marble bathrooms; others have a less flamboyant 19th-century style. The public areas are filled with Old Master paintings, sculptures, sumptuous carpets, and tapestries. ✉ *112 rue du Faubourg St-Honoré, 75008,* ☎ *01–53–43–43–00,* 𝐅𝐀𝐗 *01–53–43–43–01. 154 rooms, 41 suites. Restaurant, bar, air-conditioning, in-room modem lines, in-room safes, room service, indoor pool, sauna, health club, laundry service, meeting rooms, free parking. AE, DC, MC, V. Métro: Miromesnil.*

$$$$ ⊞ **Crillon.** One of Paris's most famous "palace" hotels, the Crillon comprises two 18th-century town houses on place de la Concorde. Marie-Antoinette took singing lessons here; one of the original *grands appartements,* now protected as national treasures, has been named after her. Rooms are lavishly decorated with Rococo and Directoire antiques, crystal and gilt wall sconces, and gold fittings. The sheer quantity of marble downstairs—especially in Les Ambassadeurs restaurant—is staggering. ✉ *10 Pl. de la Concorde, 75008,* ☎ *01–44–71–15–00; 800/888–4747 in the U.S.,* 𝐅𝐀𝐗 *01–44–71–15–02. 118 rooms and 45 suites. 2 restaurants, 2 bars, tea shop, air-conditioning, in-room safes, no-smoking rooms, room service, exercise room, baby-sitting, laundry service, meeting rooms. AE, DC, MC, V. Métro: Concorde.*

$$$$ ⊞ **Hyatt Regency Paris-Madeleine.** This Haussmannesque building near the Opéra Garnier feels more like a boutique hotel than an international chain, thanks to stylized details like cherry paneling and mismatched bedside tables. You can also expect the usual plush carpeting and luxurious upholsteries. Book a room on the seventh or eighth floor facing boulevard Malesherbes for a view of the Eiffel Tower. ✉ *24 bd. Malesherbes, 75008,* ☎ *01–55–27–12–34; 800/223–1234 in the U.S.,* 𝐅𝐀𝐗 *01–55–27–12–35. 81 rooms, 5 suites. Restaurant, bar, air-conditioning, in-room modem lines, in-room safes, no-smoking floors, room service, sauna, exercise room, laundry service, business services, meeting rooms. AE, DC, MC, V. Métro: St-Augustin.*

$$$$ ⊞ **Lancaster.** The Lancaster—one of Paris's most venerable institutions—
★ has been meticulously transformed into one of the city's most modish luxury hotels. Seamlessly blending the traditional with the contemporary, the overall feel is one of timeless elegance. Every detail speaks of quality, from the hotel's own line of bath products to the Porthault linens. Many of the suites pay homage to the hotel's colorful regulars, from Garbo to Huston to Sir Alec Guinness. Marlene Dietrich's is decorated in lilac (her favorite color) and features a superb Louis XV desk. ✉ *7 rue de Berri, 75008,* ☎ *01–40–76–40–76; 800/63-SAVOY in the U.S.,* 𝐅𝐀𝐗 *01–40–76–40–00. 50 rooms, 10 suites. Restaurant, bar, air-conditioning, in-room modem lines, in-room safes, room service, in-room VCRs, sauna, exercise room, baby-sitting, laundry service, meeting rooms. AE, DC, MC, V. Métro: George-V.*

$$$$ ⊞ **Paris Marriott Champs-Élysées.** Take a ground-zero locale, a stylish atrium lobby, and a chic, 19th-century style, and you've got the Paris Marriott. Ebony furnishings and antique prints are some of the nice touches that make you forget this is a chain, and state-of-the-art soundproofing shuts out the cacophonic Champs. ✉ *70 av. Champs-Élysées, 75008,* ☎ *01–53–93–55–00; 800/228–9290 in the U.S.,* 𝐅𝐀𝐗 *01–53–93–55–01. 174 rooms, 18 suites. Restaurant, 2 bars, air-conditioning,* *in-room modem lines, in-room safes, no-smoking floors, room service, sauna, exercise room, baby-sitting, laundry service, business services, meeting rooms. AE, DC, MC, V. Métro: George V.*

$$-$$$ 🛏 **Bradford-Élysées.** This turn-of-the-century hotel conserves its old-fashioned feel while providing modern amenities. An old wooden elevator carries you from the flower-filled lobby to the spacious, luxurious rooms equipped with Louis XVI–style furniture, brass beds, and fireplaces. ⊠ *10 rue St-Philippe-du-Roule, 75008,* ☎ *01-45-63-20-20,* FAX *01-45-63-20-07. 50 rooms. Bar, air-conditioning, in-room modem lines, in-room safes, no-smoking rooms, baby-sitting, laundry service. AE, DC, MC, V. Métro: St-Philippe-du-Roule.*

$$ 🛏 **Résidence Monceau.** Within a stone's throw of the Parc Monceau, this friendly, fashionable hotel is a calm oasis of refined tranquility. Warm tones make rooms cozy; the efficient and professional staff makes your stay easy. The breakfast garden, surrounded by ivy-covered trellises, is a lovely place to start the day. ⊠ *85 rue du Rocher, 75008,* ☎ *01-45-22-75-11,* FAX *01-45-22-30-88. 50 rooms, 1 suite. Bar, no-smoking rooms, travel services. AE, DC, MC, V. Métro: Villiers.*

9e Arrondissement (Opéra)

See Right Bank Lodging map.

$$$$ 🛏 **Grand Hôtel Inter-Continental.** Open since 1862, Paris's biggest luxury hotel has a facade that seems as long as the Louvre. The grand salon's Art Deco dome and the restaurant's painted ceilings are registered landmarks. The truly Art Deco rooms are spacious and light. The famed Café de la Paix is one of the city's great people-watching spots. ⊠ *2 rue Scribe, 75009,* ☎ *01-40-07-32-32; 800/327-0200 in the U.S.,* FAX *01-42-66-12-51. 475 rooms and 39 suites. 3 restaurants, 2 bars, air-conditioning, in-room modem lines, in-room safes, no-smoking rooms, room service, in-room VCRs, sauna, health club, laundry service, business center, meeting rooms. AE, DC, MC, V. Métro: Opéra.*

11e Arrondissement (Bastille)

See Right Bank Lodging map.

$ 🛏 **Garden Hôtel.** This family-run hotel is on a pretty garden square in a quiet residential neighborhood 10 minutes from Père Lachaise cemetery. Rooms are functional but spotless; those in front have lovely views of the verdant square. All have double-glazed windows to ensure quiet. The staff speaks little English. Bathtubs are half size. ⊠ *1 rue du Général-Blaise, 75011,* ☎ *01-47-00-57-93,* FAX *01-47-00-45-29. 42 rooms. AE, MC, V. Métro: St-Ambroise.*

$ 🛏 **Résidence Alhambra.** The white facade, back garden, and flower-filled window boxes brighten an otherwise lackluster neighborhood. Inside, the look is more spartan, with smallish, modernly appointed rooms; all have satellite TV. The best reason to stay here is that prices are rock-bottom and the hotel is near the Marais and is accessible to five métro lines at Place de la République. ⊠ *13 rue de Malte, 75011,* ☎ *01-47-00-35-52,* FAX *01-43-57-98-75. 58 rooms. MC, V. Métro: Oberkampf.*

12e Arrondissement (Bastille/Gare de Lyon)

See Right Bank Lodging map.

$$–$$$ 🛏 **Le Pavillon Bastille.** Here's a smart address (across from the Opéra Bastille) for savvy travelers who appreciate getting perks for less. The transformation of this 19th-century hôtel particulier into a colorful, high-design hotel garnered architectural awards. A fiercely loyal, hip

clientele loves its bright blue and yellow interior and whimsical touches. Every detail is pitch perfect from the friendly staff right down to the 17th-century fountain in the garden. ⊠ *65 rue de Lyon, 75012,* ☎ *01–43–43–65–65; 800/233–2552 in the U.S.,* FAX *01–43–43–96–52. 24 rooms, 1 suite. Bar, air-conditioning, in-room safes, minibars, room service. AE, DC, MC, V. Métro: Bastille.*

$$ ⊡ **Modern Hôtel-Lyon.** Just a block from the Gare de Lyon is this cozy, congenial, family-run hotel, open since 1903. With its rooms in blues and lavenders, the feel is French country. ⊠ *3 rue Parrot, 75012,* ☎ *01–43–43–41–52,* FAX *01–43–43–81–16. 47 rooms, 1 suite. In-room safes. AE, DC, MC, V. Métro: Gare de Lyon.*

$ ⊡ **Jules-César.** This hotel near the Gare de Lyon and the Opéra Bastille opened in 1930. It has a rather glitzy lobby with an abundance of marble. Rooms are more subdued, with simple furnishings and chenille bedspreads. Ask for one facing the street—they are larger and brighter than those in the back. ⊠ *52 av. Ledru-Rollin, 75012,* ☎ *01–43–43–15–88,* FAX *01–43–43–53–60. 48 rooms. AE, MC, V. Métro: Gare de Lyon.*

13e Arrondissement (Gobelins)

See Left Bank Lodging map.

$ ⊡ **Résidence les Gobelins.** Wicker furniture and warm colors create a cozy feel at this small, simple hotel on a quiet side street between Place d'Italie and the Latin Quarter. Some rooms overlook a small flower-filled garden, as does the lounge where breakfast is served. ⊠ *9 rue des Gobelins, 75013,* ☎ *01–47–07–26–90,* FAX *01–43–31–44–05. 32 rooms. In-room modem lines. AE, DC, MC, V. Métro: Gobelins.*

14e Arrondissement (Montparnasse)

See Left Bank Lodging map.

$$ ⊡ **Raspail-Montparnasse.** Rooms are named after the artists who made Montparnasse the art capital of the world in the '20s and '30s—Picasso, Chagall, and Modigliani, to name a few. Pastels, however, are the dominant colors, complemented by contemporary blond-wood furniture and crisp cotton upholsteries. Most rooms are at the low end of this price category; five have spectacular panoramic views of Montparnasse and the Eiffel Tower. ⊠ *203 bd. Raspail, 75014,* ☎ *01–43–20–62–86; 800/44–UTELL in the U.S.,* FAX *01–43–20–50–79. 38 rooms. Bar, air-conditioning, in-room safes, meeting rooms. AE, DC, MC, V. Métro: Vavin.*

$–$$ ⊡ **Istria.** This small, family-run hotel on a quiet side street was a Montparnasse artists' hangout in the '20s and '30s. It has a flower-filled courtyard and simple, clean, comfortable rooms with soft, pastel-toned Japanese wallpaper and light-wood furnishings. ⊠ *29 rue Campagne-Première, 75014,* ☎ *01–43–20–91–82,* FAX *01–43–22–48–45. 26 rooms. In-room safes, meeting rooms. AE, DC, MC, V. Métro: Raspail.*

$–$$ ⊡ **Lenox-Montparnasse.** The hotel may be modern, '60s-era, but it's in the heart of Montparnasse, just around the corner from the famous Dôme and Coupole brasseries, and close to the Luxembourg Gardens. The best rooms have fireplaces, old mirrors, and exposed beams; others have more of a functional, contemporary style. ⊠ *15 rue Delambre, 75014,* ☎ *01–43–35–34–50,* FAX *01–43–20–46–64. 52 rooms, 6 suites. Bar, no-smoking rooms, in-room modem lines, meeting rooms, laundry service, parking (fee). AE, DC, MC, V. Métro: Vavin.*

$ ⊡ **Midi.** Don't be put off by the facade and the reception area, which might make you think you're in a chain hotel. Rooms are French-provincial style—rich colors, stenciled furniture, and lots of wrought iron—and have large floor-to-ceiling windows. Some have air-conditioning, others have whirlpool baths, and those facing the street are quite spacious. ⊠ *4 av. Réné-Coty, 75014,* ☎ *01–43–27–23–25,* FAX *01–43–21–24–58. 46 rooms. AE, DC, MC, V. Métro and RER: Denfert-Rochereau.*

$ 🔲 **Parc Montsouris.** This modest hotel in a 1930s villa is on a quiet residential street next to the lovely Parc Montsouris. Attractive oak pieces and high-quality French fabrics embellish the small but clean rooms; satellite TV is another plus. Those with showers are very inexpensive; suites sleep four. ⊠ *4 rue du Parc-Montsouris, 75014,* ☎ *01–45–89–09–72,* FAX *01–45–80–92–72. 28 rooms, 7 suites. Air-conditioning, no-smoking rooms, laundry service. AE, MC, V. Métro: Montparnasse-Bienvenue.*

15ᵉ Arrondissement (Champ de Mars)

See Left Bank Lodging map.

$ 🔲 **Tour Eiffel Dupleix.** Inside this '70s-era hotel, within walking distance of the Eiffel Tower, are inexpensive, comfortable rooms with modern bathrooms, cable TV with CNN, and double-glazed windows that block out the street noise. The light-wood furniture and crisp damask give rooms a clean if simple feel; some have great views of the Eiffel Tower. The buffet breakfast is one of the city's least expensive. ⊠ *11 rue Juge, 75015,* ☎ *01–45–78–29–29,* FAX *01–45–78–60–00. 40 rooms. No-smoking floors, laundry service, travel services, parking (fee). AE, DC, MC, V. Métro: Dupleix.*

16ᵉ Arrondissement (Trocadéro/Bois de Boulogne)

See Right Bank Lodging map.

$$$$ 🔲 **Saint James Paris.** Called the "only château-hôtel in Paris," this gra-
★   cious late-19th-century neoclassical mansion is surrounded by a lush private park. Ten rooms on the third floor open onto a winter garden; the poshest option is booking one of the two duplex gatehouses. The magnificent bar-library is lined with floor-to-ceiling oak bookcases. The restaurant is reserved for guests; in warm weather, meals are served in the garden. ⊠ *43 av. Bugeaud, 75116,* ☎ *01–44–05–81–81, 800/447–7462 in the U.S.,* FAX *01–44–05–81–82. 24 rooms, 24 suites. Restaurant, bar, air-conditioning, in-room modem lines, in-room safes, no-smoking rooms, room service, sauna, health club, baby-sitting, laundry service, meeting rooms, free parking. AE, DC, MC, V. Métro: Porte Dauphine.*

$$$ 🔲 **Alexander.** Everything about this hotel smacks of Old Europe, from the old-fashioned cage elevator to the 20-ft corniced ceilings and period wall sconces (which bathe all in warm, rosy hues). It's also on one of Paris's finest shopping avenues. Note that there's air-conditioning on the sixth floor only. ⊠ *102 av. Victor Hugo, 75116,* ☎ *01–45–53–64–65, 800/843–3311 in the U.S.,* FAX *01–45–53–12–51. 60 rooms, 2 suites. Laundry service, parking (fee). AE, DC, MC, V. Métro: Victor Hugo.*

$$–$$$ 🔲 **Jardins du Trocadéro.** This good-value hotel near the Trocadéro and the Eiffel Tower seamlessly blends old-style French elegance (period antiques, Napoléon draperies) with modern conveniences (soundproofing, satellite TV, VCRs, modem lines). Marble bathrooms feature terry robes and whirlpool baths. ⊠ *35 rue Benjamin Franklin, 75116,* ☎ *01–53–70–17–70, 800/246–0041 in the U.S.,* FAX *01–53–70–17–80. 18 rooms, 5 suites. Bar, air-conditioning, in-room modem lines, in-room safes, no-smoking rooms, room service, hot tubs, laundry service, meeting rooms, parking (fee). AE, DC, MC, V. Métro: Trocadéro.*

$ 🔲 **Keppler.** On the edge of the 8th and 16th arrondissements, near the Champs-Élysées, is this small hotel in a 19th-century building. The spacious, airy rooms have simple teak furnishings and floral upholsteries and some nice amenities (like satellite TV and room service) for the price. ⊠ *12 rue Keppler, 75116,* ☎ *01–47–20–65–05,* ℻ *01–47–23–02–29. 49 rooms. Bar, in-room safes, no-smoking rooms, room service. AE, MC, V. Métro: George V.*

$ ★ ⚏ **Queen's Hotel.** One of only a handful of hotels in the tony residential district near the Bois de Boulogne, Queen's is a small, comfortable, old-fashioned hotel with a high standard of service. Each room focuses on a different 20th-century French artist. The rooms with baths have Jacuzzis. ⊠ *4 rue Bastien-Lepage, 75016,* ☎ *01–42–88–89–85,* ℻ *01–40–50–67–52. 22 rooms. Air-conditioning, in-room safes, refrigerators, no-smoking rooms. AE, DC, MC, V. Métro: Michel-Ange–Auteuil.*

17ᵉ Arrondissement (Monceau/Clichy)

See Right Bank Lodging map.

$$ ★ ⚏ **Étoile-Péreire.** The extremely congenial owner has created a unique, intimate hotel, behind a quiet, leafy courtyard in a chic residential district. It consists of two parts: a fin-de-siècle building on the street and a 1920s annex overlooking an interior courtyard. Rooms and duplexes—in deep shades of roses or blues with crisp, white damask upholstery—have a very tailored, very finished look. Only the suites have air-conditioning. The copious breakfast is legendary, featuring 40 assorted jams and jellies. ⊠ *146 bd. Péreire, 75017,* ☎ *01–42–67–60–00,* ℻ *01–42–67–02–90. 21 rooms, 5 duplex suites. Bar, in-room safes, no-smoking rooms, laundry service. AE, DC, MC, V. Métro: Péreire.*

$$ ⚏ **Regent's Garden.** Built in the mid-19th century by Napoléon III for his doctor, this hotel near the Arc de Triomphe is adorned, as you would imagine, with marble fireplaces, mirrors, gilt furniture, and cornicing. Ask for a room overlooking the gorgeous garden, where breakfast is served in summer. ⊠ *6 rue Pierre-Demours, 75017,* ☎ *01–45–74–07–30,* ℻ *01–40–55–01–42. 39 rooms. Air-conditioning, lobby lounge, parking (fee). AE, DC, MC, V. Métro: Charles-de-Gaulle-Étoile, Ternes.*

$–$$ ⚏ **Eber-Monceau.** This small hotel—part of the Relais du Silence group—is just one block from the Parc Monceau. It attracts a stylish media and fashion set, though the engaging owner, Jean-Marc Eber, is always delighted to welcome first-time guests. Rooms are tastefully done in bright, cheerful colors; ask for one overlooking the courtyard. ⊠ *18 rue Léon Jost, 75017,* ☎ *01–46–22–60–70,* ℻ *01–47–63–01–01. 13 rooms, 8 with bath, 5 with shower, 5 suites. Bar, air-conditioning, no-smoking floors, laundry service, parking (fee). AE, DC, MC, V. Métro: Courcelles.*

$ ⚏ **Excelsior.** Only a five-minute walk from Montmartre and near more than a dozen bus and métro lines is this tiny, endearing place. Rustic antiques and heavy armoires in the small, spotless rooms give them a warm, cozy feel. Request one overlooking the little garden. ⊠ *16 rue Caroline, 75017,* ☎ *01–45–22–50–95,* ℻ *01–45–22–59–88. 22 rooms. Laundry service. AE, DC, MC, V. Métro: Place de Clichy.*

$ ⚏ **L'Ouest.** Although this unpretentious hotel overlooks the railroad near Pont-Cardinet station, you can be sure of a restful sleep, since all rooms are soundproof. Some get more light and are more spacious than others, so be sure to ask for one of these. All have simple yet pleasant wood furniture and striped cotton bedspreads. The area isn't sight-filled, but Montmartre, Parc Monceau, and the *grands magasins* (department stores) are all within easy reach. ⊠ *165 rue de Rome, 75017,* ☎ *01–42–27–50–29,* ℻ *01–42–27–27–40. 48 rooms. In-room modem lines, parking (fee). AE, DC, MC, V. Métro: Rome.*

$ ⚏ **Palma.** This modest hotel in a small, 19th-century building between the Arc de Triomphe and Porte Maillot is one of the best deals in the city. Cheerful and homey, if not luxurious, rooms have basic wood furnishings and bright floral wallpaper; ask for one on the top floor with a view across Right Bank rooftops. There's air-conditioning on the sixth (top) floor only. ⊠ *46 rue Brunel, 75017,* ☎ *01–45–74–74–51,* FAX *01–45–74–40–90. 37 rooms. AE, MC, V. Métro: Argentine.*

18ᵉ Arrondissement (Montmartre)

See Right Bank Lodging map.

$ 🖬 **Ermitage.** This elfin, family-run hotel dates from Napoléon III's time and is filled with antiques of the period. Rooms have a feeling of old-fashioned elegance. The building is only two stories high, but the hilly Montmartre neighborhood ensures that some rooms have a nice view of Paris. ⊠ *24 rue Lamarck, 75018,* ☎ *01–42–64–79–22,* FAX *01–42–64–10–33. 12 rooms. No credit cards. Métro: Lamarck-Caulaincourt.*

$ 🖬 **Regyn's Montmartre.** Despite the small rooms, this owner-run hotel on Montmartre's evocative place des Abbesses provides comfortable accommodations. Each floor is dedicated to a Montmartre artist; poetic homages by local writers are featured in the hallways and reproductions of works hang in rooms. Otherwise, rooms are spotless but functional. Ask for one on the top two floors for great views of either the Eiffel Tower or Sacré-Coeur; those on the lower floors are darker and less inviting. Overall, courteous service and a relaxed atmosphere make this an attractive choice. ⊠ *18 Pl. des Abbesses, 75018,* ☎ *01–42–54–45–21,* FAX *01–42–23–76–69. 22 rooms. In-room safes. AE, MC, V. Métro: Abbesses.*

$ 🖬 **Utrillo.** This very likeable hotel is on a quiet side street at the foot of Montmartre, near colorful rue Lepic. Reproduction prints and marble-top breakfast tables in every room make them feel charmingly old-fashioned, while the white and pastel color scheme makes them feel brighter and more spacious than they actually are. Two rooms (Nos. 61 and 63) have views of the Eiffel Tower. ⊠ *7 rue Aristide-Bruant, 75018,* ☎ *01–42–58–13–44,* FAX *01–42–23–93–88. 30 rooms. Sauna. AE, DC, MC, V. Métro: Abbesses.*

19ᵉ Arrondissement (Buttes-Chaumont)

See Right Bank Lodging map.

$ 🖬 **Le Laumière.** Though it's some distance from the city center, the rock-bottom rates of this family-run hotel near the rambling Buttes-Chaumont park make it hard to resist. The staff, too, is exceptionally helpful. Unfortunately, the modern, modular furniture is less inspiring, though some of the larger rooms overlook a garden. Ask about special rates. ⊠ *4 rue Petit, 75019,* ☎ *01–42–06–10–77,* FAX *01–42–06–72–50. 54 rooms. MC, V. Métro: Laumière.*

Apartment Rentals

If you will be staying longer than a week, want to do your own cooking, or need a base large enough for a family, consider a furnished rental. Policies differ from company to company, but you can generally expect a minimum required stay of one week; a refundable deposit (expect $200–$500), payable on arrival; and weekly or biweekly maid service.

Following is a list of good-value residence hotels, each with multiple properties in Paris. **Citadines Résidences Hôtelières** (⊠ 18 rue Favart, 75002, ☎ 01–41–05–79–04, FAX 01–44–50–23–50). **Mercure** (⊠ 20 esplanade Charles-de-Gaulle, 92000, Nanterre, ☎ 01–46–69–79–00, FAX 01–47–25–46–48). **Orion** (⊠ 30 Pl. d'Italie, 75013, ☎ 01–40–78–54–54; 800/546–4777, 212/688–9538 in the U.S., FAX 01–40–78–54–55;

212/688–9467 in the U.S.). **Paris Appartements Services** (✉ 69 rue d'Argout, 75002, ☎ 01–40–28–01–28, FAX 01–40–28–92–01).

The **Rothray** agency (✉ 10 rue Nicolas Flamel, 74004, ☎ 01–48–87–13–37 or 01–40–28–91–84, FAX 01–42–78–17–72 or 01–40–26–34–33) has pretty apartments for for short- or long-term rental in stylish neighborhoods like the Marais. U.S.–based agencies also rent apartments in Paris; for information about these, ☞ Lodging *in* Smart Travel tips.

4 NIGHTLIFE AND THE ARTS

Whether you love dancing the night away at a fashionable club, sipping Pernod at a crowded bar, or listening to music in a state-of-the-art concert hall, Paris has it all. From gilded opera houses to low-key jazz clubs, trendy discos, and Art Deco cinemas, the City of Light lights up the night.

THE ARTS

Revised and
updated by
Ian Phillips

WITHOUT A DOUBT, PARIS has been the 20th-century's capital of the arts. In 1909, Serge Diaghilev arrived in the city with his Ballets Russes. In the '20s, Josephine Baker charmed audiences at the Théâtre des Champs-Élysées. And in the '40s, Jean-Paul Sartre and Simone de Beauvoir wrote masterpieces at the Café de Flore. Nowadays, artistic life may not quite be what it once was, but Parisians are still proud of being intellectual and passionate about all things cultural. The city has an impressive number of venues and regularly attracts international theater, dance, and opera companies. In addition, the phenomenal number of movie theaters makes Paris a cinephile's heaven.

The music and theater season runs from September through June; in summer, most productions are found at festivals elsewhere in France. Detailed entertainment listings can be found in the weekly magazines **Pariscope** (which has an English-language section), **L'Officiel des Spectacles,** and **Figaroscope** (a supplement to *Le Figaro* newspaper). The **Paris Tourist Office's 24-hour hot line** in English (☎ 08–36–68–31–12) and its Web site (www.paris-touristoffice.com) are other good sources of information about activities in the city.

Tickets can be purchased at the theater itself (try to get them in advance, as many of the more popular performances sell out quickly). Your hotel or a travel agency such as **Paris-Vision** (✉ 1 rue Auber, 9ᵉ, ☎ 01–40–06–01–00, métro Opéra) may also be able to help you. Tickets can also be purchased at **FNAC** stores, especially the on in the Forum des Halles (✉ 1–5 rue Pierre Lescot, 3rd level down, 1ᵉ, ☎ 01–49–87–50–50, métro Châtelet–Les Halles). **Virgin Megastore** (✉ 52 av. des Champs-Élysées, 8ᵉ, ☎ 08–03–02–30–24, métro Franklin-D.-Roosevelt) also sells theater and concert tickets. Half-price tickets for same-day theater performances are available at the **Kiosques Théâtre** (✉ across from 15 Pl. de la Madeleine, métro Montparnasse-Bienvenue; and outside the Gare Montparnasse, Pl. Raoul Dautry, 15ᵉ, métro Montparnasse-Bienvenue), open Tuesday–Saturday 12:30–8, and Sunday 12:30–4. Expect to pay a 16-franc commission per ticket, and a line.

Circus

You don't need to know French to enjoy the circus. Venues change frequently, so it is best to check one of the weekly guides; tickets range from 40 to 180 frs. From tigers to yaks, dogs, and clowns, **Cirque Diana Moreno Bormann** (✉ Jardin d'Acclimatation, Bois de Boulogne, ☎ 01–45–00–23–01, métro Sablons) is good for all ages; performances are on Saturday and Wednesday at 3 PM and on Saturday afternoon at 2:30 and 5. **Cirque Alexis Gruss** (no fixed address, ☎ 01–44–17–96–22 for information) remains an avowedly old-fashioned production with showy horsemen. **Cirque de Paris** (✉ 115 bd. Charles de Gaulle, Villeneuve-la-Garenne, ☎ 01–47–99–40–40, métro Porte de Clignancourt, then Bus 137) offers "A Day at the Circus": a peek behind the scenes in the morning, lunch with the artists, and a performance in the afternoon. **Cirque d'Hiver** (✉ 110 rue Amelot, 11ᵉ, ☎ 01–47–00–12–25, métro Filles du Calvaire), constructed in 1852 as a circus hall, is now only occasionally home to the circus; more often fashion shows and parties are held here.

Classical Music

Cité de la Musique (⊠ in the Parc de La Villette, 221 av. Jean-Jaurès, 19ᵉ, ☎ 01–44–84–44–84, métro Porte de Pantin) presents a varied program of classical, experimental, and world music concerts in a postmodern setting.

IRCAM (⊠ 1 Pl. Igor-Stravinsky, 4ᵉ, ☎ 01–44–78–48–43, métro Châtelet–Les Halles, Hôtel de Ville) organizes concerts of contemporary classical music on the premises, at the Pompidou Center next door, or at the Cité de la Musique (☞ *above*).

Maison de Radio France (⊠ 116 av. du Président Kennedy, 16ᵉ, ☎ 01–42–30–15–16, RER Maison de Radio France), the base for countless radio and TV stations, is also home to the Orchestre National de France, which performs in the smallish, modern Salle Olivier Messiaen.

Salle Gaveau (⊠ 45 rue de la Boétie, 8ᵉ, ☎ 01–49–53–05–07, métro Miromesnil) has an old-world atmosphere and plays host to chamber music, piano, and vocal recitals.

Salle Pleyel (⊠ 252 rue du Faubourg St-Honoré, 8ᵉ, ☎ 01–45–61–53–00, métro Ternes) is Paris's principal home of classical music. The Orchestre de Paris and other leading international orchestras play here regularly, and there's a fine series of recitals by international stars.

Théâtre des Champs-Élysées (⊠ 15 av. Montaigne, 8ᵉ, ☎ 01–49–52–50–50, métro Alma-Marceau) is worthy of a visit based solely on architectural merit and ambience, but this elegantly restored, plush Art Deco temple also hosts top-quality concerts and ballet.

Church and Museum Concerts

Paris has a never-ending stream of free or inexpensive lunchtime and evening church concerts, ranging from organ recitals to choral music and orchestral works. Some are scheduled as part of the **Festival d'Art Sacré** (☎ 01–44–70–64–10 for information) between mid-November and Christmas. Check the weekly listings for information; telephone numbers for most church concerts vary with the organizer.

Ste-Chapelle (⊠ 4 bd. du Palais, 1ᵉʳ, ☎ 01–42–77–65–65, métro Cité) holds outstanding candlelit concerts from April until mid-October; make reservations well in advance. Other churches with concerts: **Notre-Dame** (⊠ Ile de la Cité, 4ᵉ, métro Cité). **St-Eustache** (⊠ rue du Jour, 1ᵉʳ, métro Les Halles). **St-Germain-des-Prés** (⊠ Pl. St-Germain-des-Prés, 6ᵉ, métro St-Germain-des-Prés). **St-Julien-Le-Pauvre** (⊠ 23 quai de Montebello, 5ᵉʳ, métro St-Michel). **St-Louis-en-l'Ile** (⊠ 19 bis rue St-Louis-en-l'Ile, 4ᵉ, métro Pont-Marie). **St-Roch** (⊠ 296 rue St-Honoré, 1ᵉʳ, métro Tuileries).

Museums are another good place to find classical concerts. Some of the best are held in the **Auditorium du Louvre** (⊠ Palais du Louvre, ☎ 01–40–20–51–86, métro Palais Royal–Musée du Louvre) on Wednesday evening and Thursday lunchtime. The **Musée d'Orsay** (⊠ 1 rue de Bellechasse, 7ᵉ, ☎ 01–45–49–48–14, RER Musée d'Orsay) regularly holds small-scale concerts (song cycles, piano recitals, or chamber music) at lunchtime or in the early evening. The **Musée du Moyen Age** (⊠ 6 Pl. Paul Painlevé, 5ᵉ, ☎ 01–53–73–78–16, métro Cluny–La Sorbonne) stages early music concerts between March and October.

Dance

As a rule, more avant-garde or up-and-coming choreographers show their works in the smaller performance spaces in the Bastille and the Marais and in theaters in nearby suburbs. Classical ballet is found in places as varied as the opera house and the sports stadium. Check the weekly guides for listings.

Maison des Arts et de la Culture (1 Pl. Salvador Allende, 94000 Créteil, ☎ 01–45–13–19–19) attracts well-known modern dance companies. **Opéra Garnier** (✉ Pl. de l'Opéra, 9ᵉ, ☎ 08–36–69–78–68, métro Opéra) is the sumptuous home of the well-reputed Paris Ballet, as well as host to many major foreign dance troupes. **Théâtre de la Bastille** (✉ 76 rue de la Roquette, 11ᵉ, ☎ 01–43–57–42–14, métro Bastille) merits mention as an example of the innovative activity in the Bastille area; it has an enviable record as a launching pad for tomorrow's modern dance stars. **Théâtre de la Ville** (✉ 2 Pl. du Châtelet, 4ᵉ, métro Châtelet; ✉ 31 rue des Abbesses, 18ᵉ, métro Abbesses, ☎ 01–42–74–22–77 for both) is *the* place for contemporary dance.

Film

Paris has hundreds of cinemas showing contemporary and classic French and American movies, as well as an array of independent, international, and documentary films. A number of theaters, especially in principal tourist areas such as the Champs-Élysées, the boulevard des Italiens near the Opéra, St-Germain-des-Prés, and Les Halles, run English-language films. Check the weekly guides for a movie of your choice. The initials "v.o." mean *version original,* or not dubbed; films that are dubbed are indicated by the initials "v.f." (*version française*). Cinema admission runs 37 to 51 francs; some cinemas have reduced rates on certain days (normally Monday) or for early shows; others offer reductions with the purchase of a multiple entry card. Most theaters post two show times: the *séance,* when the commercials, previews, and, sometimes, short films begin; and the feature presentation, which usually starts 10–25 minutes later.

Paris has a number of big-screen cinemas: **Gaumont Grand Écran** (✉ 30 Pl. d'Italie, 13ᵉ, ☎ 01–45–80–77–00, métro Place d'Italie); **Grand Rex** (✉ 1 bd. Poissonnière, 2ᵉ, ☎ 01–42–36–83–93, métro Bonne Nouvelle); **Kinopanorama** (✉ 60 av. de la Motte-Piquet, 15ᵉ, ☎ 01–43–06–50–50, métro La Motte Picquet Grenelle); **Max Linder Panorama** (✉ 24 bd. Poissonnière, 9ᵉ, ☎ 01–48–24–88–88, métro Grands Boulevards); and **UGC Ciné Cité Les Halles** (✉ Pl. de la Rotonde, Forum des Halles, Level-3, access by the Porte du Jour near the St-Eustache church, 1ᵉʳ, ☎ 08–36–68–68–58, métro Les Halles). **MK2 Quai de Seine** (✉ 14 quai de Seine, 19ᵉ, ☎ 08–36–68–14–07, métro Jaurès), a relatively new complex showing major releases, is well worth a visit for its location on the Bassin de la Villette.

Many small theaters showing classic and independent films are found in the Latin Quarter, with some notable exceptions. Showings are often organized around retrospectives (check "Festivals" in weekly guides). Following is a list of some of the noteworthy independent cinemas: **Action Écoles** (✉ 23 rue des Écoles, 5ᵉ, ☎ 01–43–29–79–89, métro Maubert-Mutualité); **Champo** (✉ 51 rue des Écoles, 5ᵉ, ☎ 01–43–54–51–60, métro Cluny–La Sorbonne); **Grande Action** (✉ 5 rue des Écoles, 5ᵉ, ☎ 01–43–29–44–40, métro Cardinal Lemoine or Jussieu); and **Quartier Latin** (✉ 9 rue Champollion, 5ᵉ, ☎ 01–43–26–84–65, métro Cluny–La Sorbonne).

Cinéma des Cinéastes (✉ 7 av. de Clichy, 17ᵉ, ☎ 01–53–42–40–20, métro Place de Clichy) shows previews of feature films, as well as documentaries, short subjects, and rarely shown movies; it's in an old cabaret transformed into a movie theater and wine bar. **Cinémathèque Française** (✉ 42 bd. de Bonne-Nouvelle, 10ᵉ, ☎ 01–47–04–24–24, métro Bonne Nouvelle and Palais de Chaillot, 7 av. Albert de Mun, 16ᵉ, ☎ 01–55–73–16–80, métro Trocadéro) has classic French and international films daily Wednesday–Sunday. **L'Entrepôt** (⊠ 7 rue Francis-de-Pressensé, 14ᵉ, ☎ 01–45–40–78–38, métro Pernety) screens films and has a café, bar, restaurant, and bookstore. **Le Forum de l'Image** (⊠ Forum des Halles, Porte St-Eustache entrance, 1ᵉʳ, ☎ 01–44–76–62–00, métro Les Halles) organizes thematic viewings of its archives of films and videos on the city of Paris. For 30 francs you can watch up to four films, two hours of video, and surf the Web for 30 minutes.

Dôme Imax (⊠ La Défense, ☎ 08–36–67–06–06, RER La Défense) shows 3-D flicks. **La Géode** (⊠ at the Cité des Sciences et de l'Industrie, Parc de La Villette, 26 av. Corentin-Cariou, 19ᵉ, ☎ 01–40–05–12–12, métro Porte de La Villette) screens wide-angle Omnimax films—usually documentaries—on a 1,000-square-meter spherical surface. In summer at the **Parc de La Villette** (métro Porte de Pantin or Porte de La Villette) movies are shown outdoors on a large screen; check the weekly guides for films.

Galleries

Art galleries are scattered throughout the city, but those focusing on the same period are often clustered in one neighborhood. There are many contemporary art galleries, for instance, near the Pompidou Center, the Picasso Museum, and the Bastille Opera. More recently, several avant-garde galleries have moved to rue Louise Weiss near the Bibliothèque François-Mitterrand in the 13th. (Note that it's not uncommon for galleries to be hidden away in courtyards, with the only sign of their presence a small plaque on the front of the buildings; take these as invitations to push through the doors.) Around St-Germain, the galleries are generally more traditional, and works by old masters and established modern artists dominate the galleries around rue du Faubourg St-Honoré and avenue Matignon. To help you plot your course, get a free copy of the gallery map published by the Association des Galeries; it's available at many of the galleries listed below.

Artcurial (⊠ 61 av. Montaigne, 8ᵉ, ☎ 01–42–99–16–16, métro Franklin-D.-Roosevelt) has the feel of a museum shop. It sells artist-designed decorative objects and exhibits works by such artists as Bram van Velde and Zao Wou-Ki.

Carré Rive Gauche (métro St-Germain-des-Prés or Rue du Bac) is an area sheltering dozens of art and antique galleries on its narrow lanes.
Didier Aaron (⊠ 118 rue Faubourg St-Honoré, 8ᵉ, ☎ 01–47–42–47–34, métro Miromesnil) is probably Paris's best-known antiques dealer; his gallery is filled with sumptuous furniture, paintings, and objects from the 18th and early 19th centuries. Clients include Hubert de Givenchy, the King of Morocco, and Karl Lagerfeld.
Galerie Arnoux (⊠ 27 rue Guénégaud, 6ᵉ, ☎ 01–46–33–04–66, métro Odéon), one of many galleries on this street, specializes in abstract painting of the '50s, as well as in the works of young painters and sculptors.
Galerie Claude Bernard (⊠ 7 rue des Beaux-Arts, 6ᵉ, ☎ 01–43–26–97–07, métro St-Germain-des-Prés) is very well established in the domain of traditional figurative work.
Galerie Dina Vierny (⊠ 36 rue Jacob, 6ᵉ, ☎ 01–42–60–23–18, métro St-Germain-des-Prés) was set up after the war by the former muse of sculptor Aristide Maillol. Since, she has discovered artists such as Serge Poliakoff, Vladimir Yankelevsky, and Ilya Kabakov.
Galerie Laage-Salomon (⊠ 57 rue du Temple, 4ᵉ, ☎ 01–42–78–11–71, métro Hôtel de Ville) shows a well-known, very international group of artists, such as Per Kirkeby, Georg Baselitz, and A. R. Penck.
Galerie Lelong (⊠ 13 rue de Téhéran, 8ᵉ, ☎ 01–45–63–13–19, métro Miromesnil), which also has galleries in New York and Zurich, represents a mix of contemporary artists.

Finally, a travel companion that doesn't snore on the plane or eat all your peanuts.

123 456 7891 2345
J.D. SMITH

When traveling, your MCI WorldCom Card is the best way to keep in touch. Our operators speak your language, so they'll be able to connect you back home—no matter where your travels take you. Plus, your MCI WorldCom Card is easy to use, and even earns you frequent flyer miles every time you use it. When you add in our great rates, you get something even more valuable: peace-of-mind. So go ahead. Travel the world. MCI WorldCom just brought it a whole lot closer.

You can even sign up today at www.mci.com/worldphone or ask your operator to make a collect call to 1-410-314-2938.

EASY TO CALL WORLDWIDE

1 Just dial the WorldPhone access number of the country you're calling from.
2 Dial or give the operator your MCI WorldCom Card number.
3 Dial or give the number you're calling.

France ◆	0-800-99-0019
Germany	0800-888-8000
Ireland	1-800-55-1001
Italy ◆	172-1022
Spain	900-99-0014
Sweden ◆	020-795-922
Switzerland ◆	0800-89-0222
United Kingdom To call using BT To call using CWC	0800-89-0222 0500-89-0222

For your complete WorldPhone calling guide, dial the WorldPhone access number for the country you're in and ask the operator for Customer Service. In the U.S. call 1-800-431-5402.

◆ Public phones may require deposit of coin or phone card for dial tone.

EARN FREQUENT FLYER MILES

AmericanAirlines
AAdvantage

Continental Airlines
OnePass

▲ Delta Air Lines
SkyMiles

MILEAGE PLUS.
United Airlines

U·S AIRWAYS
DIVIDEND MILES

MCI WorldCom, its logo and the names of the products referred to herein are proprietary marks of MCI WorldCom, Inc. All airline names and logos are proprietary marks of the respective airlines. All airline program rules and conditions apply.

MCI WORLDCOM

The first thing you need overseas is the one thing you forget to pack.

FOREIGN CURRENCY DELIVERED OVERNIGHT

Chase Currency To Go® delivers foreign currency to your home by the next business day*

It's easy—before you travel, call 1-888-CHASE84 for delivery of any of 75 currencies

Delivery is free with orders of $500 or more

Competitive rates— without exchange fees

You don't have to be a Chase customer—you can pay by Visa® or MasterCard®

 CHASE

THE RIGHT RELATIONSHIP IS EVERYTHING.®

1•888•CHASE84
www.chase.com

Galerie Louis Carré (⊠ 10 av. de Messine, 8ᵉ, ☎ 01–45–62–57–07, métro Miromesnil) has a long history of promoting French artists, including Bazaine, but it is not lost in the past.

Galerie Maeght (⊠ 42 rue du Bac, 7ᵉ, ☎ 01–45–48–45–15, métro Rue du Bac) is the Paris branch of the Fondation Maeght in St-Paul-de-Vence. You can find paintings, as well as books, prints, and reasonably priced posters.

Galerie Patrick Fourtin (⊠ 6 Pl. de Valois, 1ᵉʳ, ☎ 01–42–60–12–63, métro Palais-Royal) specializes in French furniture from the '40s and '50s, and is an address favored by many of the world's top decorators.

Galerie Templon (⊠ in courtyard of 30 rue Beaubourg, 3ᵉ, ☎ 01–42–72–14–10, métro Rambuteau) was the first to bring American artists to Paris in the '60s; now it represents many artists, including French star Jean-Pierre Raynaud.

Joyce (⊠ Palais Royal, 9 rue de Valois, 1ᵉʳ, ☎ 01–40–15–03–72, métro Palais-Royal) is a gallery and boutique set up by successful Asian retailer Joyce Ma, who regularly invites Asian artists to show their work.

Louvre des Antiquaires (⊠ 2 Pl. du Palais-Royal, 1ᵉʳ, ☎ 01–42–97–27–00, métro Palais-Royal) is an elegant multifloor complex where 250 of Paris's leading dealers showcase their rarest objects, including Louis XV furniture, tapestries, and antique jewelry. The center is open Tuesday–Sunday; it's closed Sunday in July and August.

Opera

Getting tickets to the Opéra de la Bastille or the Opéra Garnier can be difficult on short notice, so it is a good idea to plan ahead. Get a list of performances from the Paris Tourist Office's "Saison de Paris" booklet or by writing to the Opéra de la Bastille (⊠ 120 rue de Lyon, 75576, Paris Cedex 12) well in advance. Make your selection and send back the booking form, giving several choices of nights and performances. If the response is affirmative, just pick up and pay for your tickets before the performance (you can also pay for them by credit card in advance). A word of caution: Buying from a scalper is not recommended, as there have been reports of people selling counterfeit tickets.

Opéra de la Bastille (⊠ Pl. de la Bastille, 12ᵉ, ☎ 08–36–69–78–68, métro Bastille), the ultramodern facility built in 1989, has taken over the role as Paris's main opera house from the Opéra Garnier; tickets range from 45 to 650 francs.

Opéra Comique (⊠ 5 rue Favart, 2ᵉ, ☎ 01–42–44–45–46, métro Richelieu-Drouot) is a lofty old hall that presents excellent comic operas and lightweight musical entertainment.

Opéra Garnier (⊠ Pl. de l'Opéra, 9ᵉ, ☎ 08–36–69–78–68, métro Opéra) still hosts occasional performances of the Paris Opéra.

Théâtre Musical de Paris (⊠ Pl. du Châtelet, 1ᵉʳ, ☎ 01–40–28–28–40, métro Châtelet), better known as the Théâtre du Châtelet, puts on opera productions, classical concerts, dance performances, and the occasional play.

Puppet Shows

On most Wednesday, Saturday, and Sunday afternoons, the Guignol, the French equivalent of Punch and Judy, can be seen going through their ritualistic battles in a number of Paris's parks, including the **Champ de Mars** (☎ 01–48–56–01–44, métro École Militaire) and the **Jardins du Ranelagh** (☎ 01–45–83–51–75, métro La Muette). The **Jardin du Luxembourg** (☎ 01–43–26–46–47, métro Vavin) and the **Jardin d'Acclimatation** (in the Bois de Boulogne, ☎ 01–45–01–53–52, métro Sablons) both have year-round, weatherproof performance spaces.

Theater

A number of theaters line the Grand Boulevards between the Opéra and République, but there is no Paris equivalent to Broadway or the West End. Shows are mostly in French, with a few notable exceptions.

Bouffes du Nord (⊠ 37 bis bd. de la Chapelle, 10ᵉ, ☏ 01–46–07–34–50, métro La Chapelle) is the home of English director Peter Brook who regularly delights with his wonderful experimental productions.

Café de la Gare (⊠ 41 rue du Temple, 4ᵉ, ☏ 01–42–78–52–51, métro Hôtel de Ville) is a fun spot to experience a particularly Parisian form of theater, the *café-théâtre*—a mixture of satirical sketches and variety show riddled with slapstick humor, performed in a café setting. You need a good grasp of French.

La Cartoucherie (⊠ in the Bois de Vincennes, ☏ 01–48–08–39–74 or 01–43–28–36–36, métro Château de Vincennes, then take the shuttle bus), a complex of five theaters in a former munitions factory, turns cast and spectators into an intimate theatrical world. The resident director is the revered Ariane Mnouchkine. Go early for a simple meal; the cast often helps serve.

Comédie Française (⊠ Pl. du Théâtre Français, 1ᵉʳ, ☏ 01–44–58–15–15, métro Palais-Royal) dates back to 1680 and is the most hallowed institution in French theater. It specializes in classical French plays by the likes of Racine, Molière, and Marivaux. Reserve seats in person about two weeks in advance, or turn up an hour beforehand and wait in line for cancellations.

MC93 Bobigny (⊠ 1 bd. Lenine, Bobigny, ☏ 01–41–60–72–72, métro Bobigny–Pablo Picasso), in a suburb northeast of Paris, often stages top-flight English and American productions.

Nouveau Théâtre Mouffetard (⊠ 73 rue Mouffetard, 5ᵉ, ☏ 01–43–31–11–99, métro Monge) is home to inexpensive and popular modern drama productions.

Théâtre Gérard Philippe(⊠ 59 bd. Jules-Guesdes, St-Denis, ☏ 01–48–13–17–00, métro St-Denis–Basilique) is run by one of France's most talented young directors, Stanislas Nardey. For only 50 francs, you can see high-caliber, innovative theater and the occasional contemporary dance performance.

Théâtre de la Huchette (⊠ 23 rue de la Huchette, 5ᵉ, ☏ 01–43–26–38–99, métro St-Michel) is a highlight for Ionesco admirers; this tiny Left Bank theater has been staging his *The Bald Soprano* every night since 1950!

Théâtre Mogador (⊠ 25 rue de Mogador, 9ᵉ, ☏ 01–53–32–32–00, métro Trinité), one of Paris's most sumptuous theaters, is the place for musicals and other productions with popular appeal.

Théâtre de l'Odéon (⊠ Pl. de l'Odéon, 6ᵉ, ☏ 01–44–41–36–36, métro Odéon) has made pan-European theater its primary focus and offers some of the finest productions in Paris.

Théâtre de la Renaissance (⊠ 20 bd. St-Martin, 10ᵉ, ☏ 01–42–08–18–50, métro Strasbourg-St-Denis) was once home to Belle Epoque star Sarah Bernhardt (she was manager from 1893 to 1899). Big French stars often perform in plays here.

NIGHTLIFE

You've immersed yourself in culture all day and you want a night out on the town. The hottest spots are near Menilmontant and Parmentier, the Bastille, and the Marais. The Left Bank is definitely a lot less happening. The Champs-Élysées is making a comeback, though the clientele remains predominantly foreign. On weeknights, people are usually home after closing hours at 2 AM, but weekends mean late-night partying. Take note: The last métro runs between 12:30 and 1 AM (you can take a cab, though they can be hard to find between midnight and 2 AM on weekends); you may just have to stay out until the métro starts running again at 5:30 AM!

Bars

The best of the bars in Paris have character, witty waiters, local color, and inventive cocktails at prices that permit consumption without counting. The variety of bars is also impressive—bars serving light food, moody late-night bars, bars with DJs, and bars with live music. Other options include cafés, many of which turn into bars at night, and wine bars (☞ Cafés and Salons de Thé and Wine Bars *in* Chapter 2).

BASTILLE AND THE EASTERN RIGHT BANK

Café Charbon (✉ 109 rue Oberkampf, 11ᵉ, ☎ 01–43–57–55–13, métro St-Maur, Parmentier) is a beautifully restored 19th-century café, whose trend-setting clientele converses to jazz in the background. The atmosphere gets livelier after 10 PM when a DJ takes over.

Café de la Musique (✉ 213 av. Jean Jaurès, in the Parc de la Villette, 19ᵉ, ☎ 01–48–03–15–91, métro Porte de Pantin) has a large selection of cocktails and limited brasserie offerings in a comfortable setting inspired by the '40s. Varied musical menus include live jazz on Wednesday.

Chez Prune (✉ 36 rue Beaurepaire, 10ᵉ, ☎ 01–42–41–30–47, métro Jacques Bonsergent) is a lively bar with a terrace overlooking one of the footbridges crossing the Canal St-Martin.

China Club (✉ 50 rue de Charenton, 12ᵉ, ☎ 01–43–43–82–02, métro Ledru-Rollin) has three floors of bars and a restaurant with lacquered furnishings and a colonial Orient theme. During happy hour (7–9), all cocktails are 35 fr.

La Fabrique (✉ 53 rue du Faubourg St-Antoine, 11ᵉ, ☎ 01–43–07–67–07, métro Bastille) is a bar and restaurant that brews its own beer (look out for the huge copper vats by the entrance). It really gets going every evening after 9 PM when a DJ hits the turntables

La Favela Chic (✉ 131 rue Oberkampf, 11ᵉ, ☎ 01–43–57–15–47, métro Ménilmontant) is a hip, Brazilian-style bar. The terrace is usually packed with stylishly dressed Parisians drinking *caïpirinhas* or *mojitos,* while the crowd inside chats to a background of Latin rhythms.

Sanz Sans (✉ 49 rue du Faubourg St-Antoine, 11ᵉ, ☎ 01–44–75–78–78, métro Bastille) has added a new twist to bar life—the "actors" on the upstairs lounge's gilt-framed video screen are really the habitués of the downstairs bar.

Le What's Up Bar (✉ 15 rue Daval, 11ᵉ, ☎ 01–48–05–88–33, métro Bastille) is one of Paris's hippest bars: It looks decidedly modern, the clientele is trendy, and the music (from 10:30 PM) is a mixture of house and garage. On Friday and Saturday expect to pay 50 francs to get in (though the amount covers your first drink).

CHAMPS-ÉLYSÉES/OPÉRA/LOUVRE

Buddha Bar (✉ 8 rue Boissy d'Anglas, 8ᵉ, ☎ 01–53–05–90–00, métro Concorde), with its imposing Buddha contemplating the stylish crowd, has a spacious mezzanine bar that overlooks the dining room where cuisines, east and west, meet somewhere in California.

Le Fumoir (✉ 6 rue Amiral de Coligny, 1ᵉʳ, ☎ 01–42–92–00–24, métro Louvre) is a fashionable spot for a late afternoon beer or early evening cocktail (dinner is also served). There's a large bar in front, a library with shelves of books in back, and leather couches throughout.

Harry's New York Bar (⊠ 5 rue Daunou, 2ᵉ, ☎ 01–42–61–71–14, métro Opéra), a cozy, wood-paneled hangout popular with expatriates, is haunted by the ghosts of Ernest Hemingway and F. Scott Fitzgerald. **Man Ray** (⊠ 34 rue Marbeuf, 8ᵉ, ☎ 01–56–88–36–36, métro Franklin-D.-Roosevelt) is one of the hottest places in town, which is not surprising given that it is owned by Johnny Depp, Sean Penn, and Simply Red's Mick Hucknall. The Asian–art deco style is reminiscent of a 1930s supper club. The bar is open until 2 AM and serves cocktails, tapas, and sushi.

LATIN QUARTER

Alcazar (⊠ 62 rue Mazarine, 6ᵉ, ☎ 01–53–10–19–99, métro Odéon), Sir Terence Conran's first Parisian restaurant, has a stylish bar on the first floor, where you can sip a glass of wine under the huge glass roof. **Le Comptoir** (⊠ 5 rue Monsieur-Le-Prince, 6ᵉ, ☎ 01–43–29–12–05, métro Odéon) is a wine bar serving Burgundies and Bordeaux by the glass, as well as more unusual wines, such as ones from Corsica.

MARAIS

Le Café du Trésor (⊠ 5 rue Trésor, 4ᵉ, ☎ 01–44–78–06–60, métro St-Paul) is a lively, sophisticated bar, where DJs spin every night (except Sunday) a mixture of house and funk. There's also a restaurant adjacent. **La Chaise au Plafond** (⊠ 10 rue du Trésor, 4ᵉ, ☎ 01–42–76–03–22, métro St-Paul) has the feel of a traditional bistro with a few offbeat contemporary touches. Never overcrowded, it's the perfect place for an excellent glass of wine. **La Tartine** (⊠ 24 rue de Rivoli, 4ᵉ, ☎ 01–42–72–76–85, métro Saint-Paul) serves inexpensive glasses of wine and *tartines* (open-face sandwiches) in a tatty, almost seedy, turn-of-the-century bar that has earned antihero status among the cognoscenti.

MONTMARTRE

Moloko (⊠ 26 rue Fontaine, 9ᵉ, ☎ 01–48–74–50–26, métro Blanche), a smoky late-night bar with several rooms, a mezzanine, a jukebox, and a small dance floor, is a popular spot with a trendy, fun-loving crowd. **Le Sancerre** (⊠ 35 rue des Abbesses, 18ᵉ, ☎ 01–42–58–08–20, métro Abbesses), a café by day, turns into a lively watering hole for jovial Montmartrois and artist types.

Hotel Bars

Elegant and upscale, with a classic Parisian feel, the city's hotel bars are quiet spots to meet for a drink. Following are some of the best: **Bristol** (⊠ 112 rue du Faubourg St-Honoré, 8ᵉ, ☎ 01–53–43–43–42, métro Miromesnil). **Crillon** (⊠ 10 Pl. de la Concorde, 8ᵉ, ☎ 01–44–71–15–39, métro Concorde). **Intercontinental** (⊠ 3 rue Castiglione, 1ᵉʳ, ☎ 01–44–77–10–47, métro Tuileries). **Lutétia** (⊠ 45 bd. Raspail, 6ᵉ, ☎ 01–49–54–46–09, métro Sèvres-Babylone). **Ritz Hemingway Bar** (⊠ 15 Pl. Vendôme, 1ᵉʳ, ☎ 01–43–16–33–65, métro Opéra), where the writer drank to the Liberation of Paris.

Cabarets

Paris's cabarets are household names, often shunned by Parisians and loved by tourists. You can dine at many of them: Prices range from 200 frs (simple admission plus one drink) to more than 750 frs (dinner plus show). For 400 to 500 frs, you get a seat plus half a bottle of champagne.

L'Ane Rouge (⊠ 3 rue Laugier, 17ᵉ, ☎ 01–43–80–79–97, métro Ternes) is a typical French cabaret playing to a mixed Parisian and foreign crowd, where the emphasis is on laughs and entertainment, with a host of singers, magicians, comedians, and ventriloquists.

Au Lapin Agile (✉ 22 rue des Saules, 18ᵉ, ☎ 01–46–06–85–87, métro Lamarck Caulaincourt), in Montmartre, considers itself the doyen of cabarets. Picasso once paid for a meal with one of his paintings. Prices are lower than elsewhere, as it is more of a large bar than a full-blown cabaret.

Au Pied de la Butte (✉ 62 bd. Rochechouart, 18ᵉ, ☎ 01–46–06–02–86, métro Anvers) played host in the past to Edith Piaf, Jacques Brel, and Maurice Chevalier. Today, it has three shows per evening with modern-day songsters interpreting the traditional French repertoire and magicians performing tricks.

Le Caveau de la Bolée (✉ 25 rue de l'Hirondelle, 6ᵉ, ☎ 01–43–54–62–20, métro St-Michel) was a prison in the 14th century, but these days you are free to sing along to Edith Piaf melodies or be entertained by magicians and mind readers.

Crazy Horse (✉ 12 av. George V, 8ᵉ, ☎ 01–47–23–32–32, métro Alma-Marceau) is one of the best-known clubs for pretty dancers and raunchy routines with lots of humor and few clothes.

Éléphant Bleu (✉ 49 rue de Ponthieu, 8ᵉ, ☎ 01–42–25–17–61, métro Franklin-D.-Roosevelt) is a cabaret-cum-restaurant with an exotic (often Asian) touch to most of its shows.

Lido (✉ 116 bis av. des Champs-Élysées, 8ᵉ, ☎ 01–40–76–56–10, métro George V) stars the famous Bluebell Girls; the owners claim no show this side of Las Vegas can rival it for special effects.

Madame Arthur (✉ 75 bis rue des Martyrs, 18ᵉ, ☎ 01–42–54–40–21, métro Pigalle) stages a wacky, burlesque drag show—men dressed as famous French female vocalists—that's not for the faint-hearted.

Michou (80 rue des Martyrs, 18ᵉ, ☎ 01–46–06–16–04, métro Pigalle) is owned by the always blue-clad Michou, famous in Paris circles. The men on stage wear extravagant drag—high camp and parody are the order of the day.

Moulin Rouge (✉ 82 bd. de Clichy, 18ᵉ, ☎ 01–53–09–82–82, métro Blanche), that old favorite at the foot of Montmartre, mingles the Doriss Girls, the cancan, and a horse in an extravagant spectacle.

Paradis Latin (✉ 28 rue du Cardinal Lemoine, 5ᵉ, ☎ 01–43–25–28–28, métro Cardinal Lemoine) is perhaps the liveliest, busiest, and trendiest cabaret on the Left Bank.

Casino

Casino d'Enghien (✉ 3 av. de Ceinture, ☎ 01–39–34–13–00), the nearest public casino, is by the lake at Enghien-les-Bains, 16 km (10 mi) north of Paris. For admittance, take an ID, put on a jacket and tie, and leave your sports shoes at home.

Clubs

Paris's *boîtes de nuit* (nightclubs) tend to be both expensive and exclusive—if you know someone who is a regular or who knows the ropes it makes it easier to get through the door. The less affluent '90s, however, have been a humbling experience for more than a few clubs: Some have survived by offering club goers more, including meals, theme nights, and special events. Given the fragility of a club's life, it's best to check before going out. Many clubs are closed Monday and some on Tuesday; by Wednesday most are functioning at full swing.

BASTILLE AND THE EASTERN RIGHT BANK

Le Balajo (✉ 9 rue de Lappe, 11ᵉ, ☎ 01–47–00–07–87, métro Bastille), in an old Java ballroom, offers a bit of everything: salsa, techno, retro, even *bal musette*, the accordion music so evocative of Montmartre street balls.

Les Étoiles (⊠ 61 rue Château d'Eau, 10ᵉ, ☎ 01–47–70–60–56, métro Château d'Eau), open Thursday–Saturday, is the place for salsa (with a live band). Dinner, featuring South American specialties, is served from 9 to 11.

La Java (⊠ 105 rue du Faubourg du Temple, 10ᵉ, ☎ 01–42–02–20–52, métro Belleville), where Edith Piaf and Maurice Chevalier made their names, has live Latin music and Cuban jam sessions on Thursday and Friday nights.

CHAMPS-ÉLYSÉES

Le Cabaret (⊠ 68 rue Pierre-Charron, 8ᵉ, ☎ 01–42–89–44–14, métro Franklin-D.-Roosevelt), once just that, still has the original red velvet and flock wallpaper decor. Nowadays it's a hybrid: There are still nightly cabaret acts (such as knife throwers, shadow puppeteers, etc.), as well as a bar area and a dance floor (the music is soul and funk). Princess Caroline of Monaco, Liza Minelli, and Naomi Campbell have all been spotted here.

Niel's (⊠ 27 av. Ternes, 17ᵉ, ☎ 01–47–66–45–00, métro Ternes) attracts a well-off set of regulars, as well as top models and showbiz glitterati. Music runs the gamut from salsa to house.

MONTPARNASSE

Dancing La Coupole (⊠ 100 bd. du Montparnasse, 14ᵉ, ☎ 01–43–27–56–00, métro Vavin) has retro disco on Friday and Saturday nights; and on Tuesday, salsa, preceded at 8:30 by an optional refresher course—an idea that seems to have breathed new life into this monument.

MONTMARTRE

Bus Palladium (⊠ 6 rue Fontaine, 9ᵉ, ☎ 01–53–21–07–33, métro Blanche) invites women free on Tuesday; on other nights it caters to a fashionable but relaxed crowd. Fear no techno; it serves up a mixture of rock, funk, and disco.

L'Élysée Montmartre (⊠ 72 bd. de Rochechouart, 18ᵉ, ☎ 01–44–92–45–45, métro Pigalle) holds extremely popular *bals* (balls) every other Saturday, where the music runs the gamut of hits from the '40s to the '80s and the DJ is backed up by a 10-piece orchestra. Its regular "Scream" parties (with a predominately gay crowd) are on top of every serious clubber's list.

Les Folies Pigalle (⊠ 11 Pl. Pigalle, 9ᵉ, ☎ 01–48–78–25–26, métro Pigalle) is a former cabaret decorated like a '30s bordello. The ambience is decadent, the music varies according to the day of the week (hip-hop on Wednesday and Sunday, a mixture of house and techno at other times), and Saturday nights feature a male strip show (for women only) 9–11 PM.

Gay and Lesbian Bars and Clubs

Gay and lesbian bars and clubs are mostly concentrated in the Marais and include some of the hippest addresses in the city. Keep in mind, however, that clubs fall in and out of favor at lightning speed. The best way to find out what's hot is by picking up a copy of the free weekly *e.m@le* in one of the bars listed below.

For Men and Women

Amnésia Café (⊠ 42 rue Vieille-du-Temple, 4ᵉ, ☎ 01–42–72–16–94, métro Rambuteau, St-Paul) has an underlit bar and Art Deco ceiling paintings that attract a young, professional gay and lesbian crowd.

Banana Café (⊠ 13 rue de la Ferronnerie, 1ᵉʳ, ☎ 01–42–33–35–31, métro Châtelet–Les Halles) has a trendy, energetic, and scantily clad mixed crowd; dancing on the tables is the norm.

Queen (⊠ 102 av. des Champs-Élysées, 8ᵉ, ☎ 01–53–89–08–90, métro George V) is one of the most talked-about nightclubs in Paris: Everyone lines up to get in. Monday is disco night, with house and techno on other days; the "Respect" evening on Wednesday is particularly popular and quite mixed.

Mostly Men

Bar d'Art/Le Duplex (⊠ 25 rue Michel-Le-Comte, 3ᵉ, ☎ 01–42–72–80–86, métro Rambuteau) is frequented by young, tortured-artist types who enjoy the frequent art exhibitions, alternative music, and dim lighting.

Café Cox (⊠ 15 rue des Archives, 4ᵉ, ☎ 01–42–72–08–00, métro Hôtel de Ville) is a prime, gay pick-up joint. Behind the smoked-glass windows, men line the walls and check out the talent.

Café Rude (⊠ 23 rue du Temple, 4ᵉ, ☎ 01–42–74–05–15, métro Hôtel de Ville) has a chic and convivial modernist restaurant and bar upstairs. Downstairs in "The Bunker," the action gets more rambunctious.

Le Dépôt (⊠ 10 rue aux Ours, 3ᵉ, ☎ 01–44–54–96–96, métro Etienne Marcel) is a bar, club, and back room. The ever-popular Gay Tea Dance on Sunday (from 5 PM) is held here.

L'Open Café (⊠ 17 rue des Archives, 4ᵉ, ☎ 01–42–72–26–18, métro Hôtel de Ville) is more convivial than neighboring Café Cox (☞ *above*) with sunny yellow walls. In summer, the crowd spills out onto the street.

Le Scorpion (⊠ 25 bd. Poissonière, 9ᵉ, ☎ 01–40–26–01–50, métro Rue Montmartre) is one of Paris's longest-standing gay nightclubs. Wednesday is disco night, Thursday is devoted to French pop, and weekends to techno and house. From Sunday through Tuesday there are drag shows.

Mostly Women

Champmeslé (⊠ 4 rue Chabanais, 2ᵉ, ☎ 01–42–96–85–20, métro Bourse) is the hub of lesbian nightlife (open until dawn), with a dusky back room reserved for women only. Thursday night (starting at 10) is a cabaret of traditional French songs.

Le Pulp! (⊠ 25 bd. Poissonnière, 2ᵉ, ☎ 01–40–26–01–93, métro Grands Boulevards) is one of the few lesbian-only nightclubs in Paris. Open Wednesday through Saturday, it has regular theme nights such as "Housewife" and "One Night Stand." The music is a mix of disco and house.

Les Scandaleuses (⊠ 8 rue des Ecouffes, 4ᵉ, ☎ 01–48–87–39–26, métro St-Paul) is probably Paris's hippest lesbian hangout. Men are also allowed in (in small numbers) as long as they are accompanied by "scandalous women."

Jazz Clubs

Paris is one of the world's great jazz cities, with plenty of variety, including some fine, distinctive local talent. Most jazz clubs are in the Latin Quarter or around Les Halles. For nightly schedules, consult the specialty magazine *Jazz Hot* or *Jazz Magazine*. Note that nothing gets going until 10 or 11 PM and that entry prices vary widely from about 40 francs to more than 100 francs.

CHAMPS-ÉLYSÉES

Lionel Hampton Jazz Club (⊠ Méridien Hotel, 81 bd. Gouvion-St-Cyr, 17ᵉ, ☎ 01–40–68–30–42, métro Porte Maillot), named for the zingy xylophonist loved by Parisians, hosts a roster of international jazz musicians in a spacious, comfortable atmosphere.

Le Bilboquet (⊠ 13 rue St-Benoît, 6ᵉ, ☎ 01–45–48–81–84, métro St-Germain-des-Prés) is the place to find primarily French musicians playing mainstream jazz in a faded Belle Epoque decor.

Le Petit Journal (⊠ 71 bd. St-Michel, 5ᵉ, ☎ 01–43–26–28–59, métro Montparnasse-Bienvenue; ⊠ 13 rue du Commandant-Mouchotte, 14ᵉ, ☎ 01–43–21–56–70, métro Montparnasse-Bienvenue), with two locations, has long attracted the greatest names in French and international jazz. It now specializes in Dixieland jazz and also serves dinner from 8:30 to midnight.

La Villa (⊠ 29 rue Jacob, 6ᵉ, ☎ 01–43–26–60–00, métro St-Germain-des-Prés) is a stylish hotel with a bar in the basement, attracting serious pianists and jazz musicians to its stylish, ultramodern setting.

Au Duc des Lombards (⊠ 42 rue des Lombards, 1ᵉʳ, ☎ 01–42–33–22–88, métro Châtelet–Les Halles) has modern contemporary jazz in an ill-lit, romantic bebop venue with decor inspired by the Paris métro.

Le Baiser Salé (⊠ 58 rue des Lombards, 1ᵉʳ, ☎ 01–42–33–37–71, métro Châtelet–Les Halles) attracts a younger crowd with salsa, rhythm and blues, fusion, and funk.

New Morning (⊠ 7 rue des Petites-Ecuries, 10ᵉ, ☎ 01–45–23–51–41, métro Château d'Eau) is a premier spot for serious fans of avant-garde jazz, folk, and world music; decor is spartan, the mood reverential.

Le Petit Opportun (⊠ 15 rue des Lavandières-Ste-Opportune, 1ᵉʳ, ☎ 01–42–36–01–36, métro Châtelet–Les Halles), in a converted bistro, always has French artists and sometimes features top-flight American soloists with French backup.

Le Sunset (⊠ 60 rue des Lombards, 1ᵉʳ, ☎ 01–40–26–46–60, métro Châtelet–Les Halles) delivers jazz from both French and American musicians; on Sunday night there's a featured vocalist.

Pubs

Pubs wooing English-speaking clients with a selection of beers are becoming increasingly popular with Parisians. They are also good places to find reasonably priced food at off-hours.

Académie de la Bière (⊠ 88 bis bd. de Port Royal, 5ᵉ, ☎ 01–43–54–66–65, RER Port-Royal) serves 145 brews and good french fries and *moules marinière* (mussels cooked in white wine).

The Auld Alliance (⊠ 80 rue François Miron, 4ᵉ, ☎ 01–48–04–30–40, métro St-Paul) has walls adorned with Scottish shields, bar staff dressed in kilts, and a swear box for anyone who mentions the word "England." There are over 70 malt whiskies to choose from, true Scottish beers, salmon and venison, and even the infamous haggis.

Connolly's Corner (⊠ 12 rue Mirbel, 5ᵉ, ☎ 01–43–31–94–22, métro Place Monge) is a convivial Irish pub with Guinness on tap and traditional Irish music on Tuesday, Thursday, and Sunday. Just make sure you don't wear a tie—it will be snipped off and stuck on the wall (though you'll be compensated with a free pint).

The Cricketer (⊠ 41 rue des Mathurins, 8ᵉ, ☎ 01–40–07–01–45, métro St-Augustin) replies to the virtual Irish monopoly on Paris pubs with amber ales from Adnams of Sussex. Cricket memorabilia adorns the walls.

Finnegans Wake (⊠ 9 rue des Boulangers, 5ᵉ, ☎ 01–46–34–23–65, métro Jussieu) attracts a mixed Franco-British clientele with its Guinness on tap, Irish music, and Gaelic language classes on Wednesday evenings.

The Frog and Rosbif (⊠ 116 rue St-Denis, 2ᵉ, ☎ 01–42–36–34–73, métro Etienne Marcel) has everything you could want from an English "local." Beers are brewed on premises and rugby and football matches are shown on the giant-screen TV.

Kitty O'Shea's (⊠ 10 rue des Capucines, 2ᵉ, ☎ 01–40–15–08–08, métro Opéra) has authentic pub trappings and Guinness on tap.

Rock, Pop, and World Music Venues

Unlike jazz, French rock is generally not considered to be on a par with its American and British cousins. Even so, Paris is a great place to catch some of your favorite groups because concert halls tend to be smaller and tickets can be less expensive. It's also a good spot to see all kinds of world music. Most places charge from 90 to 120 frs and get going around 11 PM. The best way to find out about upcoming concerts is to consult the bulletin boards in FNAC stores (☞ Music *in* Specialty Shops *in* Chapter 6).

Le Bataclan (⊠ 50 bd. Voltaire, 11ᵉ, ☎ 01–48–06–28–12, métro Oberkampf) is a legendary venue for live rock, rap, and reggae in an intimate setting.

Casino de Paris (⊠ 16 rue de Clichy, 9ᵉ, ☎ 01–49–95–99–99, métro Trinité), once a favorite with Serge Gainsbourg, has a horseshoe balcony and a cramped, cozy, music-hall feel.

La Cigale (⊠ 120 bd. Rochechouart, 18ᵉ, ☎ 01–42–23–15–15, métro Pigalle) often plays host to up-and-coming French rock bands.

Divan du Monde (⊠ 75 rue des Martyrs, 18ᵉ, ☎ 01–44–92–77–66, métro Pigalle) attracts a varied crowd, depending on the music of the evening: reggae, soul, funk, or salsa. Most nights after the concert, a DJ takes over.

L'Élysée Montmartre (⊠ 72 bd. Rochechouart, 18ᵉ, ☎ 01–44–92–45–45, métro Anvers) dates from Gustave Eiffel, its builder, who, it's hoped, liked a good concert. It's one of the prime venues for emerging French and international rock groups.

Olympia (⊠ 28 bd. des Capucines, 9ᵉ, ☎ 01–47–42–25–49, métro Madeleine), a legendary venue once favored by Jacques Brel and Edith Piaf, still hosts leading French singers.

L'Opus Café (⊠ 167 quai de Valmy, 10ᵉ, ☎ 01–40–34–70–00, métro Louis Blanc), on the picturesque Canal St-Martin, has jazz and soul concerts.

Palais Omnisports de Paris-Bercy (⊠ 8 bd. de Bercy, 12ᵉ, ☎ 01–44–68–44–68, métro Bercy) is the largest venue in Paris and is where English and American pop stars perform.

Zenith (⊠ Parc de la Villette, 19ᵉ, ☎ 01–42–08–60–00, métro Porte-de-Pantin) is a large concert hall that primarily stages rock shows; check posters and listings for details.

After-Hours Dining

Chances are that some of your nocturnal forays will have you looking for sustenance at an unlikely hour. If so, you might find it handy to know that there are restaurants open round the clock (☞ Chapter 2 for more suggestions).

L'Alsace (⊠ 39 av. des Champs-Élysées, 8ᵉ, ☎ 01–53–93–97–00, métro Franklin-D.-Roosevelt) is a smart, if characterless, brasserie-restaurant, serving seafood and sauerkraut around the clock.

Au Chien Qui Fume (⊠ 33 rue du Pont-Neuf, 1ᵉʳ, ☎ 01–42–36–07–42, métro Les Halles), open until 2 AM, is filled with paintings (in the style of old masters) of smoking dogs. Traditional French cuisine and seafood platters are served.

Au Pied de Cochon (⊠ 6 rue Coquillière, 1ᵉʳ, ☎ 01–40–13–77–00, métro Les Halles), near St-Eustache church, once catered to the all-night workers at the adjacent Paris food market. Its Second Empire decor has been restored, and traditional dishes like pig's trotters and chitterling sausage still grace the menu.

La Cloche d'Or (⊠ 3 rue Mansart, 9ᵉ, ☎ 01–48–74–48–88, métro Place de Clichy) is a Paris institution where the likes of François Mitterrand, Depêche Mode, and the dancers from the Moulin Rouge have all dined on its traditional French cuisine. It's open until 5 AM every day except Sunday.

Les Coulisses (⊠ 5 rue du Mont-Cenis, 18ᵉ, ☎ 01–42–62–89–99, métro Lamarck-Caulaincourt), in Montmartre, near picturesque Place du Tertre, has the most character of all the late-night restaurants: Its red banquettes and 18th-century Venetian mirrors make it look like an Italian theater. The food—traditional French—is served until 4 AM. In the basement is a club, open Thursday–Saturday.

Grand Café des Capucines (⊠ 4 bd. des Capucines, 9ᵉ, ☎ 01–43–12–19–00, métro Opéra), whose exuberant turn-of-the-century dining room matches the mood of the neighboring Opéra, serves excellent oysters, fish, and meat dishes at hefty prices. It's open around the clock.

Hippopotamus (⊠ 5 bd. des Batignolles, 8ᵉ, ☎ 01–43–87–85–15, métro Place de Clichy), open until 5 AM, is part of a chain where you can get hearty meat dishes and other traditional fare.

Le Muniche (⊠ 7 rue St-Benoît, 6ᵉ, ☎ 01–42–61–12–70, métro St-Germain-des-Prés), open until 2 AM, serves seafood and French specialties in a pristine Art Deco setting.

La Tour de Montlhéry (⊠ 5 rue des Prouvaires, 1ᵉ, ☎ 01–42–36–21–82, métro Les Halles) has an old-fashioned feel. It's open 24 hours a day during the week and is closed weekends.

5 OUTDOOR ACTIVITIES AND SPORTS

Parisians are often envied for their ability to stay thin despite their love of buttery foods and chocolate treats and their seeming disdain for exercise. The truth is they do like sports; if they're not walking or bicycling, many Parisians are swimming, playing soccer, and even working out at health clubs. Although facilities in the heart of the city are limited, you can find places to exercise and get outdoors. There are also a number of large stadiums in and around the city where you can see soccer, rugby, and tennis matches.

Revised and
updated by
Ian Phillips

PARISIANS ARE NOT AS FANATICAL about exercising as their counterparts elsewhere; you won't see as many people jogging or find as many health clubs in Paris. Lack of space in the heart of the city is one limit to athletic activities. Nonetheless, given the choice between taking the métro and walking or biking to their destination, many Parisians choose the latter. Also, swimming is very popular; you'll find that public pools are often full. This interest in exercise is growing: Over the last few years the number of health clubs has grown exponentially. It was only in 1997 that laws were passed allowing people to sit, walk, or even play sports on the grass in parks (before it had been strictly forbidden); these days you can enjoy (most) lawns without being reprimanded. One of the best spots for sports in Paris is the Buttes-Chaumont, a park with enough space for soccer and other games. Also good are Paris's two large parks—the Bois de Boulogne on the western fringe of the city and the Bois de Vincennes on the eastern side—where wide-open spaces allow for a variety of activities. (☞ For information on more parks in Paris, *see* Chapter 1.)

The best starting point for finding out about athletic activities in Paris is the booklet *Le Guide du Sport à Paris,* available from the Paris Tourist Office (☞ Visitor Information *in* the Gold Guide). It lists sports facilities in each *arrondissement*, has a map of bike lanes throughout the city, and contains a calendar of big sporting events. Further information can be obtained by calling the **Allô-Sports Service** (☎ 01–42–76–54–54), Monday–Thursday 10:30–5 and Friday 10:30–4:30; it's in French only.

PARTICIPANT SPORTS

Bicycling

Paris's two large parks are the best places for biking: the **Bois de Boulogne** (métro Porte Maillot, Porte Dauphine, or Porte d'Auteuil; Bus 244), on the western side of Paris, and the **Bois de Vincennes** (métro Château de Vincennes or Porte Dorée), on the eastern side.

The city also has over 125 km (78 mi) of **bike lanes** and there are plans to develop even more. Unfortunately, most bike routes are along the main axes of the city, which means that you may find yourself riding in traffic. One particularly agreeable exception is the **Promenade Plantée**, which runs along a former viaduct in the 12e arrondissement. In addition, cars have been banned altogether on Sunday from certain scenic routes, including the banks of the Seine from 9 to 6, mid-March through late autumn, and the picturesque **Canal St-Martin** from 2 to 6 all year long.

The following places rent bikes (for between 70F and 100F per day) and organize guided tours of Paris; hours and routes vary daily, so call for information. **Escapade Nature** (✉ 95 bis rue Rambuteau, 1e, ☎ 01–53–17–03–18, métro Châtelet–Les Halles). **Maison Roue Libre** (✉ 95 bis rue de Rambuteau, ☎ 01–40–28–00–77). **Pariscyclo** (✉ Rond Point de Jardin d'Acclimatation, in the Bois de Boulogne, ☎ 01–47–47–76–50, métro Les Sablons). **Paris à Vélo, C'est Sympa** (✉ 37 bd. Bourdon, 4e, ☎ 01–48–87–60–01, métro Bastille). **Paris Vélo Rent a Bike** (✉ 2 rue Fer à Moulin, 5e, ☎ 01–43–37–59–22, métro Censier-Daubenton).

If you would prefer to go bicycling outside of the city, one of the most pleasant places to do so is in the **Fontainebleau Forest** (for directions there, *see* Chapter 7). A guide to biking in the forest is available for 35 francs from the **Fontainebleau Tourist Office** (4 rue Royale, ☎ 01–60–74–99–99), as are bikes for rent. You can also rent bikes from **Georges Mullot** (☎ 01–64–22–36–14) at the train station in Avon. In Fontainebleau, **La Petite Reine** (32 rue des Sablons, ☎ 01–60–74–57–57) is the source for mountain bikes.

Boating

Rowboats can be rented in the Bois de Boulogne at **Lac Inférieur** and in the Bois de Vincennes at **Lac des Minimes** and **Lac Daumesnil.** The **Base Nautique de La Villette** (✉ 15–17 quai de la Loire, 19ᵉ, ☎ 01–42–40–29–90, métro Jaurès) rents canoes that you can take out on the canal; it's open Saturday 9–noon and 2–5 to adults only, and for 12- to 17-year-olds on Wednesday 2–5.

Boules

The rules of this classic French game (also called *pétanque*), which involves throwing metal balls at a wooden sphere, are fairly fundamental and easy to pick up. All around Paris, you'll see elderly men battling it out; an especially popular spot is on rue de La Tour-Maubourg in front of Les Invalides. Other popular venues for boules include the **Arènes de Lutèce** (the restored Roman amphitheater on rue de Navarre in the 5ᵉ arrondissement, métro Monge) and near the Château de Vincennes in the **Bois de Vincennes.** For lessons, contact the **Association Sportive de la Boule du 12e** (✉ rte. des Fortifications, Bois de Vincennes, ☎ 01–43–46–58–79, métro Porte de Vincennes); it's open daily 2–8. If you get hooked and would like to continue playing once back home, you can buy everything you need for a game of boules at **La Maison du Bouliste** (✉ 85 bd. Richard-Lenoir, 11ᵉ, ☎ 01–47–00–24–37, métro Richard-Lenoir).

Golf

If you just want to keep up your swing, then head to the practice range at **Aquaboulevard** (✉ 4 rue Louis-Armand, 15ᵉ, ☎ 01–53–78–10–79, métro Balard); it costs 70 francs. **Golf Club de L'Étoile** (✉ 10 av. de la Grande-Armée, 17ᵉ, ☎ 01–43–80–30–79, métro Charles de Gaulle-Étoile) has four practice ranges (70 francs per half hour).

Paris itself has no golf courses, but there are a few in the region around the city. **Disneyland Paris** (☎ 01–60–45–68–04, RER Marne-la-Vallée/Chessy) has a course with 27 holes and a great clubhouse (160 francs on weekdays and 290 francs on weekends). The best course near Paris is **Golf de Fontainebleau** (✉ rte. d'Orléans, Fontainebleau, ☎ 01–64–22–22–95). To get there you need a car: Take A6 from Paris, then N152 in the direction of Ury; the course is 1 km (½ mi) before Fontainebleau. It's open Monday and Wednesday through Friday 8 AM–9 PM to nonmembers (350-franc greens fee) and weekends, July and August (500-franc greens free).

Other courses near Paris include the **Golf Régional de St-Quentin-en-Yvelines** (✉ D912, St-Quentin-en-Yvelines, ☎ 01–30–50–86–40), which has a 9-hole and two 18-hole courses and is open from 8 AM to 6 PM during the week (150-franc greens fee) and 8 AM to 7 PM on weekends (250-franc greens fee). **Golf de Mont-Griffon** (✉ D909, Luzarches, ☎ 01–34–68–10–10) has an 18-hole and a 9-hole course and over 300 practice tees. It's open daily 8 AM–6 PM; greens fees are 170 francs weekdays and 310 francs weekends.

Health Clubs

Short-term passes are available from the following health clubs.

Aquaboulevard (⊠ 4 rue Louis-Armand, 15ᵉ, ☏ 01–40–60–10–00, métro Balard), a giant multisports complex, has a gym, swimming pool, Jacuzzi, squash courts, and bowling alley. It's open daily 7 AM–midnight and costs 150 francs per day.

Club Jean de Beauvais (⊠ 5 rue Jean-de-Beauvais, 5ᵉ, ☏ 01–46–33–16–80, métro Maubert-Mutualité) has an entire floor of exercise equipment, and classes. A one-day pass costs 200 francs; a week is 600 francs. It's open Monday, Tuesday, and Thursday 7 AM–10:30 PM, Wednesday and Friday 7 AM–10 PM, Saturday 8:30–7, and Sunday 9:30–5.

Club Quartier Latin (⊠ 19 rue de Pontoise, 5ᵉ, ☏ 01–55–42–77–88, métro Maubert-Mutualité) has a 33-m skylighted pool, squash courts, and exercise equipment. For 70 francs per day you can use the gym and pool (the pool only is 25 francs); add another 75 francs per 40 minutes for squash (15-franc racquet rental). It's open weekdays 9–midnight, and weekends 9:30–7.

Espace Vit'Halles (⊠ Pl. Beaubourg, 48 rue Rambuteau, 3ᵉ, ☏ 01–42–77–21–71, métro Rambuteau) has a broad range of aerobics classes (100 francs per class, 800 francs for 10), exercise machines, sauna, and steam room (100 francs a day, 10-franc towel rental). It's open weekdays 8 AM–10 PM, Saturday 10–7, and Sunday 11–4.

Hotel Health Clubs

The hotels with the best fitness facilities are generally the newer ones on the perimeter of the city center.

Hotel Nikko (⊠ 61 quai de Grenelle, 15ᵉ, ☏ 01–45–75–25–45, métro Bir-Hakeim or Javel) has a 17-m pool, a health club, and a weight room. The facilities are open to the public for 100 francs (50 francs for pool only), Monday–Saturday 10–9.

Ritz Health Club (⊠ Pl. Vendôme, 1ᵉʳ, ☏ 01–43–16–30–60, métro Opéra), as fancy as the hotel, has a swimming pool, sauna, steam room, Jacuzzi, exercise machines, and aerobics classes (all for 600 francs on weekdays, 700 francs on weekends). It's open daily 7 AM–10 PM.

Sofitel Paris Vitatop Club (⊠ 8 rue Louis-Armand, 15ᵉ, ☏ 01–45–54–79–00, métro Balard) has a 15-m pool, a sauna, a steam room, and a Jacuzzi, plus a stunning view of the Paris skyline (200 francs per day and free to hotel guests). It's open Monday and Wednesday through Friday 8 AM–10 PM, Tuesday 8 AM–midnight, Saturday 9–7, and Sunday 9–5.

Ice Skating

Every winter from December through March, weather permitting, a small skating rink is erected on **Place de l'Hôtel de Ville** (the square in front of the Hôtel de Ville); hours are 9 AM–10 PM daily. An RER ride away, **Disneyland Paris's Hotel New York** (Disneyland Paris, Marne-la Vallée, ☏ 01–64–74–30–00, RER Marne-la-Vallée, Chessy) has an outdoor skating rink complete with Disney characters (tickets to the park aren't necessary). It's open daily 2–4, 4:30–6:30, and 7:30–10; admission to each session is 60 francs, including skates. In the suburb of St-Ouen is the **Patinoire de St-Ouen** (⊠ 4 rue Dr. Bauer, St-Ouen, ☏ 01–40–11–43–38, métro Mairie de St-Ouen), an indoor rink, open year-round. Admission ranges from 25 to 45 francs, with skate rental, depending on when you go. It's open Tuesday 11:30–1 and 8:30–11; Wednesday 10–12:30 and 2:30–6; Thursday 11:30–1 and 5–8; Friday 11:30–1, 4:30–6, and 8:30–11, Saturday 2:30–6 and 8:30–11; and Sunday 10–12:30 and 2:30–6.

Jogging

Running through the streets of Paris may sound romantic, but it can be quite unpleasant if you don't go early: There's just too much traffic on the narrow streets. Exceptions are the quai de la Tournelle, along the Seine, and along the Canal St-Martin. The city's parks are better places to run. The **Champ de Mars** (métro École Militaire), next to the Eiffel Tower, measures 2½ km (1½ mi) around the perimeter. Another pleasant, though shorter and more crowded route is the 1½-km (1-mi) loop just inside the fence around the **Jardin du Luxembourg** (métro Odéon, RER Luxembourg). The **Jardin du Tuileries** (métro Concorde or Tuileries) also measures about 1½ km (1 mi) around. The **Bois de Boulogne** has miles of trails through woods, around lakes, and across grassy meadows. The equally bucolic **Bois de Vincennes** has a 14½-km (9-mi) circuit or a 1½-km (1-mi) loop around the Château de Vincennes itself.

Rollerblading

A popular place to go rollerblading is along the **Promenade Plantée,** running along the former viaduct in the 12ᵉ arrondissement. On Sunday, when cars are banned, the **quai de la Tournelle,** along the Seine (from 9 to 6), and the **Canal St-Martin** (from 2 to 6) are ideal. Every Friday night starting at 10, hundreds of rollerbladers gather at **Place de l'Italie** to take a different weekly route through Paris (roads are blocked off); for details, check the website (www.pari-roller.com).

Rollerblades can be rented from **Bike 'n Roller** (⊠ 6 rue St-Julien le Pauvre, 5ᵉ, ☎ 01–44–07–35–89) for 25 francs an hour and 75 francs per day. **Roller Location Nomades** (⊠ 37 bd. Bourdon, 4ᵉ, ☎ 01–44–54–07–44) rents skates for 50–60 francs per day. **Vertical Line** (⊠ 60 av. Raymond Poincaré, 16ᵉ, ☎ 01–47–27–21–21) rents skates for 30 francs for a half day and 60 francs for the whole day.

The rink, **La Main Jaune** (⊠ rue du Caporal-Peugeot, 17ᵉ, ☎ 01–47–63–26–47, métro Porte de Champerret) is the spot for old-fashioned rollerskating. It's open Wednesday, Saturday, and Sunday 2:30–7, and Friday and Saturday from 10 PM on for roller discos; admission is 50 francs with skate rental.

Swimming

Every arrondissement has its own public *piscine* (pool); the Paris Tourist Office's *Le Guide du Sport á Paris* lists addresses. One of the biggest and best is the **Piscine des Halles** (⊠ Pl. de la Rotonde, Forum des Halles, 1ᵉʳ, ☎ 01–42–36–98–44, Châtelet–Les Halles), a 50-m pool inside the shopping mall in the center of Paris. It's open Monday 11:30–8; Wednesday 11:30–7; Tuesday, Thursday, and Friday 11:30–10; and weekends 9–5. Admission is 25 francs and you can stay as long as you like; it does, however, get crowded. The **Piscine St-Germain** (⊠ 12 rue de Lobineau, 6ᵉ, ☎ 01–43–29–08–15, métro Mabillon), one of the nicest pools in Paris, is open 7 AM–8 AM and 11:30 AM–1 PM on weekdays and 7 AM–5:30 PM on weekends; admission is 16 francs.

Aquaboulevard (☞ Health Clubs, *above*), the best place to take kids, has an enormous indoor wave pool with water slides and a simulated outdoor beach in summer. The **Club Quartier Latin** (☞ Health Clubs, *above*) has a very nice, skylighted, 33-m pool that you can use for 25 francs.

Tennis

Paris has a number of municipal courts, but getting to play on them is not so easy. Normally, you must apply for a special card from the local *mairie* (town hall; each arrondissement has one), which takes one month, and then reserve a court in advance. You can, however, take a chance, turn up at the public courts, and if there is one available, play (the best time to go is the middle of the day during the week); the cost is 37 francs an hour per court, which you pay there. The most central, and most crowded, courts are in the **Jardin du Luxembourg.** There are also courts in the **Bois de Vincennes** at the Polygone sports ground; they're a 20-minute walk down route de la Pyramide from Château de Vincennes métro, so you might want to take a taxi. Or try the **Centre Sportif Henry-de-Montherlant** (✉ 30–32 bd. Lannes, 16ᵉ, ☎ 01–40–72–28–33, métro Porte Dauphine) it's open Monday–Saturday 7 AM–10 PM, and Sunday 8 AM–7 PM.

SPECTATOR SPORTS

Paris often hosts major international sporting events; in 1998 it was the site of the Soccer World Cup and is the location for the French Open every May. Information on upcoming events can be found on posters around the city or in the weekly guide *Pariscope.* You can also call the ticket agencies of **FNAC** (☎ 01–49–87–50–50) or **Virgin Megastore** (☎ 08–03–02–30–24).

A wide range of sporting events, including indoor athletics, ice skating, horse shows, gymnastics, and stock car racing take place at the **Palais Omnisports de Paris-Bercy** (✉ 8 bd. de Bercy, 12ᵉ, ☎ 01–44–68–44–68, métro Bercy). **Parc des Princes** (✉ 24 rue du Cdt. Guilbaud, 16ᵉ, ☎ 01–42–88–02–76, métro Porte de St-Cloud) is where the city's soccer team, Paris St-Germain, plays its home matches. **Roland-Garros** (✉ 2 av. Gordon Bennett, 16ᵉ, ☎ 01–47–43–48–00, métro Porte d'Auteuil) is the venue for the French Open tennis tournament. The **Stade de France** (✉ St-Denis, ☎ 01–55–93–00–00, RER La Plaine–Stade de France) was built for the World Cup in 1998 and is now home to the French national soccer and rugby teams.

Cricket

Cricket is played every Saturday and Sunday in the **Bois de Vincennes,** near rond-point de la Pyramide. It's also played most weekends in summer on the delightful grounds of the **Château de Thoiry** in Thoiry (☞ Chapter 7).

Horse Racing

Paris and its suburbs are remarkably well endowed with *hippodromes* (racetracks). Admission is usually between 10 and 50 francs. Details can be found in daily newspapers. The easiest racetrack to get to is the **Hippodrome d'Auteuil** (✉ Bois de Boulogne, 16ᵉ, ☎ 01–40–71–47–47, métro Porte d'Auteuil) in the Bois de Boulogne. Also in the Bois de Boulogne is the city's most beautiful track, the **Hippodrome de Longchamp** (✉ rte. des Tribunes, Bois de Boulogne, 16ᵉ, ☎ 01–44–30–75–00, métro Porte Maillot, then Bus 244), stage for the prestigious (and glamorous) Prix de l'Arc de Triomphe in October. The **Hippodrome Vincennes** (✉ rte. Ferme, Bois de Vincennes, ☎ 01–49–77–17–17, RER Joinville-Le-Pont) is a cinder track used for trotting races. The French Derby (Prix du Jockey-Club) and the very chic French Oaks (Prix de Diane-Hermès) are held at the beginning of June at **Chantilly,** north of Paris; direct trains from the Gare du Nord take about 40 minutes. Other racetracks near Paris are in **Enghien-les-Bains, Évry,** and **St-Cloud.**

Rugby

The Paris Université Club plays Sundays in winter at 3 PM in the **Vélo-drome La Citale** (av. de Gravelle, Bois de Vincennes, 12ᵉ, RER Bois de Vincennes); tickets are 30 francs. For information and game dates, call the club directly (☎ 01–44–16–62–62. France's national rugby team plays at the **Stade de France** (☞ *above*) in St-Denis. Admissions range from 50 to 600 francs; your best bet is to get tickets from FNAC or Virgin Megastore in advance (☞ *above*) or contact the **Fédération Française de Rugby** (☎ 01–53–21–15–15). The Racing Club de France has games Saturday or Sunday afternoons at the **Stade Yves du Manoir** (✉ 12 rue François Faber, Colombes, métro Porte de Champerret, then take Bus 164) in a suburb just north of Paris. For information about games, call the Racing Club de Colombes (☎ 01–47–86–89–43).

Soccer

As in most other European cities, *football* (soccer) is the sport that pulls in the biggest crowds. Paris St-Germain, the city's main club, plays at the **Parc des Princes** (☞ *above*) stadium in southwest Paris. Games are usually on Saturday evenings with an 8 PM kickoff; admission varies from 50 to 450 francs; your best bet is to get tickets from FNAC in advance (☞ *above*).

Tennis

The highlight of the tennis season—in fact the second most important European tennis tournament after Wimbledon—is the **French Open,** held during the last two weeks of May at the Roland-Garros Stadium (☞ *above*). Center-court tickets are difficult to obtain; try your hotel or turn up early in the morning (matches start at 11 AM) and buy a general ground ticket. Tickets range from 100 to 350 francs. The **Bercy Indoor Tournament** in November at the Palais Omnisports de Paris-Bercy (☞ *above*) awards one of the largest prizes in the world and attracts most of the top players; tickets can be purchased at FNAC or Virgin Megastore (☞ *above*), or at the stadium.

6 SHOPPING

Every neighborhood in Paris reflects a unique attitude and style, which adds to the appeal of shopping in this fashion capital. Designer extravagance and haute couture characterize avenue Montaigne and rue Faubourg St-Honoré. Classic sophistication pervades St-Germain. Avant-garde style dresses up the Marais. And a hip feel suffuses the area around Les Halles.

WINDOW-SHOPPING is one of Paris's greatest
spectator sports. Tastefully displayed wares—
luscious cream-filled éclairs, lacy lingerie,
exquisite clothing, and gleaming copper pots—entice the eye and
awaken the imagination. Happily, shopping opportunities in Paris are
endless and geared to every taste. You can price emerald earrings at
Cartier, spend an afternoon browsing through bookstalls along the Seine,
buy one of Hermès's famous *foulards* (scarves), tour the high-gloss department stores, or bargain over prices in the sprawling flea markets
on the outskirts of town.

For many, perfume and designer clothing are perhaps the most coveted Parisian souvenirs. Even on haute couture's home turf, however,
bargains are surprisingly elusive. It's best to know prices before coming, to avoid the slings and arrows of international exchange rates. An
Yves St-Laurent tie or the latest Guerlain perfume may be cheaper at
the mall back home, although it won't be as much fun to buy.

When hunting for bargains, watch for the word *soldes* (sales). The two
main sale seasons are January and July, when the average discount is 30%–
50% off regular prices. Also look for goods marked *dégriffé*—designer
labels, often from last year's collection, for sale at a deep discount.

Good places to look for gifts are the gift shops in Paris's museums: The
best have a superb selection of books, posters, accessories, and jewelry, along with excellent reproductions from the museum's collection.

Credit Cards
Credit cards are widely used in France. Even the corner newsstand or
flea market is likely to honor plastic for purchases over 100 francs.
Visa is the most common and preferred card, followed closely by Mas-
terCard/EuroCard. American Express, Diners Club, and Access are also
accepted in the larger international stores.

Duty-Free Shopping
A value-added tax of 20.6%, known in France as the TVA or *détaxe*,
is imposed on most consumer goods. Non–European Union residents,
ages 15 and over, who stay in France and/or the EU for less than six
months can reclaim part of this tax. To qualify, your purchases in a
single shop must total at least 1,200 francs. The amount of the refund
varies from shop to shop but usually hovers between 13% and 16%.
You may opt to be reimbursed by check, but a refund credited directly
to your credit card is the easiest and fastest way to receive your money.
The major department stores have simplified the process with special
détaxe desks where the *bordereaux* (export sales invoices) are prepared.
Most high-profile shops with international clients have détaxe forms,
but stores are not required to do this paperwork. If the discount is extremely important to you, ask if it is available before making your purchase. There is no refund for food, wine, and tobacco. Invoices and
bordereaux forms must be presented to French customs upon leaving
the country. The items purchased should be available for inspection.

Mailing Purchases Home
Smaller shops are reluctant to mail purchases overseas, though department stores often will. Mailing goods oneself is quite easy—all French
post offices sell self-sealing mailing boxes—although postage is costly.
Remember that if you are claiming a Value Added Tax deduction (☞
above), you must have the goods with you when you leave the country.

Shopping by Neighborhood

Avenue Montaigne and surroundings

This exclusive, elegant boulevard and the area around it is a showcase of international haute-couture houses: **Chanel, Dior, Nina Ricci, Jil Sander, Jean-Louis Scherrer, Emanuel Ungaro, Céline, Valentino, Max-Mara, Genny, Krizia, Escada, Thierry Mugler, Hanae Mori, Calvin Klein, Prada,** and **Dolce & Gabbana.** You'll also find accessories by **S. T. Dupont, Loewe, Salvatore Ferragamo,** and **Louis Vuitton.** Neighboring rue François 1er and avenue George V are also lined with many designer boutiques: **Versace, Yves St-Laurent, Balenciaga,** and **Givenchy.**

Champs-Élysées

Cafés and movie theaters keep the once-chic Champs-Élysées active 24 hours a day, but the invasion of exchange banks, car showrooms, and fast-food chains has lowered the tone. Four glitzy 20th-century arcade malls—**Galerie du Lido, Le Rond-Point, Le Claridge,** and **Élysées 26**—capture most of the retail action, not to mention the **Gap** and the **Disney Store.** The opening of the new Peter Marino–designed **Louis Vuitton** boutique and the cosmetic wonder store **Sephora** have re-added a touch of elegance.

The Faubourg St-Honoré

This chic shopping and residential district along rue Faubourg St-Honoré is exemplified by the presence of the Élysée Palace and the official residences of the American and British ambassadors. The Paris branches of **Sotheby's** and **Christie's,** and renowned antiques galleries such as **Didier Aaron** add artistic flavor. Boutiques include **Hermès, Lanvin, Gucci, Chloé, Guy Laroche,** and **Christian Lacroix.**

Left Bank

After decades of clustering on the Right Bank's venerable shopping avenues, the high-fashion houses have stormed the Rive Gauche. The first to arrive were **Sonia Rykiel** and **Yves St-Laurent** in the late '60s. Some of the more recent arrivals have included **Christian Dior, Giorgio Armani,** and **Louis Vuitton.** Rue des St-Pères and rue de Grenelle are lined with designer names; the latter is especially known for its top-quality shoe shops, such as **Christian Louboutin, Sergio Rossi, Patrick Cox, Stéphane Kélian,** and Michel Perry's less expensive line, **Stephen.**

Les Halles

Most of the narrow pedestrian streets on the former site of Paris's wholesale food market are lined with fast-food joints, sex shops, jeans outlets, and garish souvenir stands. But rue du Jour, featuring **Agnès B., Diapositive,** and **Zadig & Voltaire,** is an attractive exception. Not far away, rue Tiquetonne is a mecca for retro cool. In the middle of the action is the **Forum des Halles,** a multilevel underground shopping mall, which, though it has its share of teens and chain stores, also has begun attracting higher-quality merchants and a clutch of promising designers.

Louvre–Palais-Royal

The elegant and eclectic shops clustered in the 18th-century arcades of the Palais-Royal sell such items as antiques, toy soldiers, cosmetics, jewelry, and vintage designer dresses. The glossy, marble **Carrousel du Louvre** mall, beneath the Louvre Museum, is lit by an immense inverted glass pyramid. Shops, including **Virgin Megastore, The Body Shop,** and **Esprit,** along with a lively international food court, are open on Sunday—still a rare convenience in Paris.

Le Marais

Between the pre-Revolution mansions and tiny kosher food shops that characterize this area are scores of trendy gift and clothing stores. Avant-

Champs-Élysées and Avenue Montaigne Area

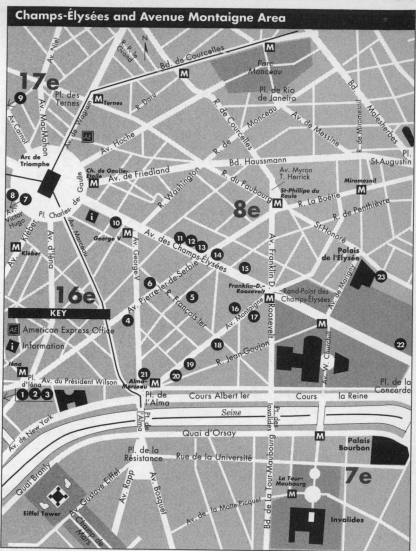

Accessoires à Soie, **9**
Berlutti, **5**
Catherine Baril, **2**
Chanel, **19**
Christian Dior, **18**
Creed, **4**
Façonnable, **22**
Free, **13**
Givenchy, **21**
Guerlain, **11**
Louis Vuitton, **10, 17**
La Maison du Chocolat, **6**

Parfums de Nicolai, **8**
Point à la Ligne, **7**
Porthault, **20**
Réciproque, **1**
Sephora, **12**
Sonia Rykiel, **23**
Souleiado, **3**
Thierry Mugler, **16**
Virgin Megastore, **14**
Zara, **15**

214

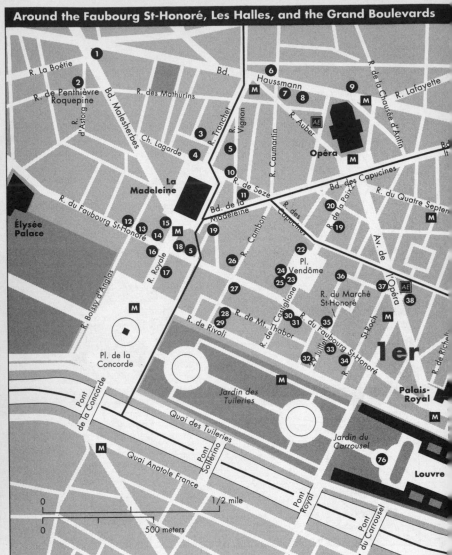

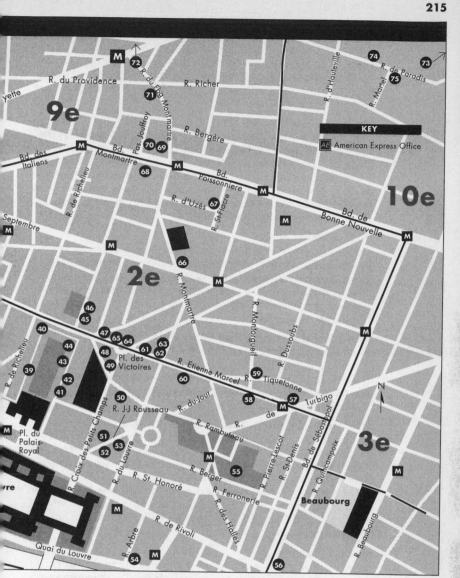

garde designers **Azzedine Alaïa, Lolita Lempicka, Issey Miyake,** and **Atsuro Tayama** have boutiques within a few blocks of the stately Place des Vosges and the Picasso and Carnavalet museums. The Marais is one of the few neighborhoods where nearly all shops are open on Sunday. The streets to the north of the Marais, close to the Arts-et-Métiers métro stop, are historically linked to the cloth trade, and some shops sell garments at wholesale prices.

Opéra to Madeleine

Three major department stores—**Au Printemps, Galeries Lafayette,** and the British **Marks & Spencer**—define boulevard Haussmann, behind Paris's ornate 19th-century Opéra Garnier. Place de la Madeleine is home to two luxurious food stores, **Fauchon** and **Hédiard.** Steps away, on boulevard de la Madeleine, is a classy 75-shop mall, **Les Trois Quartiers. Lalique** and **Baccarat Crystal** also have opulent showrooms near the Église de la Madeleine.

Passy–Victor Hugo

The residential and staid 16ᵉ arrondissement attracts predictably classic and upscale retailers, most of whom are centered on **rue de Passy**—such as **Franck et Fils**—and **Place Victor Hugo.** At a handful of secondhand shops in this wealthy area, exceptionally good deals can be found. **Réciproque,** on rue de la Pompe, for instance, is one of the biggest and best discount haunts in Paris.

Place Vendôme and Rue de la Paix

The magnificent 17th-century Place Vendôme, home of the Ritz Hotel, and rue de la Paix, leading north from Vendôme, are where you can find the world's most elegant jewelers: **Cartier, Boucheron, Buccellati, Van Cleef and Arpels, Répossi, Mauboussin,** and **Mikimoto.** The most exclusive, however, is the discreet **Jar's.**

Place des Victoires and Rue Etienne Marcel

The graceful, circular Place des Victoires, near the Palais-Royal, is the playground of cutting-edge fashion icons such as **Kenzo, Victoire,** and **Thierry Mugler.** Seriously avant-garde designers like **Comme des Garçons, Yohji Yamamoto,** and **Marithé & François Girbaud** line rue Etienne Marcel. In the nearby **Galerie Vivienne** shopping arcade, **Jean-Paul Gaultier** has a shop. And at No. 3 rue d'Argout, one of the hottest clubwear emporiums in the neighborhood, **Le Shop,** rents retail space to hip, up-and-coming designers.

Rue St-Honoré

A fashionable set makes its way to rue St-Honoré to shop at Paris's most trendy boutique, **Colette.** The street is lined with numerous designer names, as well as the delightful vintage jewelry store, **Dary's.** On nearby rue Cambon, you'll find the wonderfully elegant **Maria Luisa** and the main **Chanel** boutique.

Department Stores

Paris's top department stores offer both convenience and style. Most are open Monday through Saturday from about 9:30 AM to 7 PM, and some are open until 10 PM one weekday evening. All six major stores listed below have multilingual guides, international welcome desks, détaxe offices, and restaurants. Most are on the Right Bank, near the Opéra and the Hôtel de Ville; the notable exception is Au Bon Marché on the Left Bank.

Au Bon Marché (⊠ 24 rue de Sèvres, 7ᵉ, ☎ 01–44–39–80–00, métro Sèvres-Babylone), founded in 1852, is an excellent hunting ground on the Left Bank for linens, table settings, and high-quality furniture. The ground-

Around the Marais

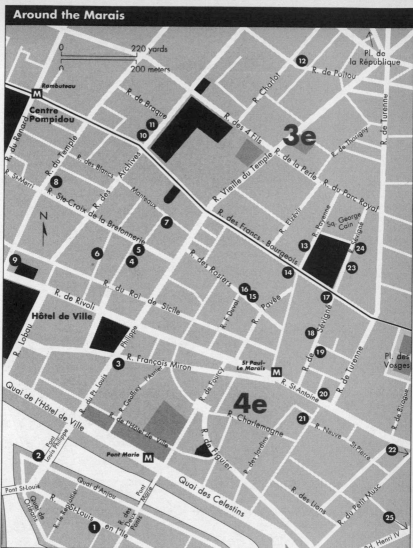

0   220 yards
0   200 meters

Pl. de la République

Rambuteau

Centre Pompidou

R. de Braque

R. du Renard

R. du Temple

R. des Blancs Manteaux

Archives

R. St-Merri

R. Ste-Croix de la Bretonnerie

R. des

R. de Poitou

R. Charlot

R. des 4 Fils

R. Vieille du Temple

R. de la Perle

R. du Parc Royal

R. de Thorigny

R. de Turenne

3e

Elzévir

Payenne

Sq. George Cain

Sévigné

R. des Francs-Bourgeois

R. des Rosiers

R. du Roi de Sicile

R. de Rivoli

Hôtel de Ville

R. Lobau

Philippe

R. François Miron

R. de Fourcy

St Paul–Le Marais

R. St-Antoine

R. de Turenne

Pl. des Vosges

R. F. Duval

Pavée

Sévigné

R. de

Quai de l'Hôtel de Ville

R. du Pl. Louis

R. P. Geoffrey l'Astnier

R. de l'Hôtel de Ville

R. de Figuier

4e

R. Charlemagne

R. Neuve

St-Pierre

R. de Birague

Pont Marie

Pont Louis Philippe

Pont St-Louis

Quai d'Orléans

R. le Regrattier

R. St-Louis en l'Île

Quai d'Anjou

Pont Morîle

R. des Deux Ponts

Quai des Celestins

R. des Jardins

R. des Lions

R. du Petit Musc

Bd. Henri IV

1 2 3 4 5 6 7 8 9 10 11 12 13 14 15 16 17 18 19 20 21 22 23 24 25

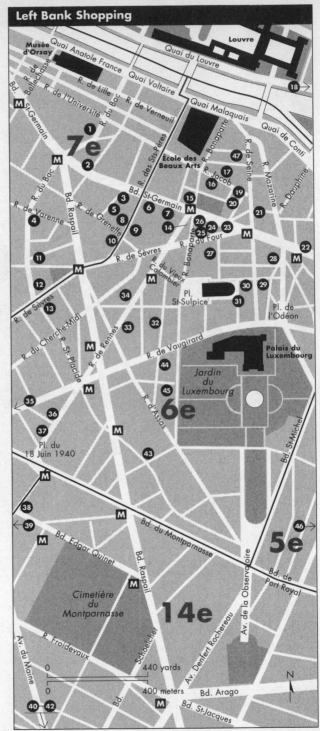

Left Bank Shopping

floor Balthazar men's shop feels like a smart boutique. La Grande
Épicerie (☞ Food and Wine *in* Specialty Shops, *below*) is one of the largest
groceries in Paris and a gourmet's mecca, and the basement is a treasure
trove for books, records, classy stationery, and artsy gifts.

Au Printemps (✉ 64 bd. Haussmann, 9ᵉ, ☎ 01–42–82–50–00, métro
Havre-Caumartin, Opéra, or Auber) has three floors of women's fashion featuring designers like Helmut Lang, Dolce & Gabbana, and
Zara. Free fashion shows are held on Tuesday (all year) and Friday (Apr.–
Oct.) at 10 AM under the cupola on the seventh floor of La Mode, the
building dedicated to women's and children's fashion. (Reservations
can be made in advance by calling ☎ 01–42–82–63–17; tickets can
also be obtained on the day of show at the service desk on the first
floor.) The three-store complex also includes La Maison, for housewares and furniture, and Brummel, a six-floor emporium devoted to
menswear. Flo Prestige, the celebrated Parisian brasserie chain, runs
the in-house restaurant.

Bazar de l'Hôtel de Ville (✉ 52–64 rue de Rivoli, 4ᵉ, ☎ 01–42–74–90–
00, métro Hôtel de Ville), better known as BHV, houses an enormous
basement hardware store that sells everything from doorknobs to cement
mixers. The fashion offerings are minimal, but BHV is noteworthy for
quality household goods, home decor materials, and office supplies.

Galeries Lafayette (✉ 40 bd. Haussmann, 9ᵉ, ☎ 01–42–82–34–56, métro
Chaussée d'Antin, Opéra, or Havre-Caumartin; ✉ Centre Commercial Montparnasse, 15ᵉ, ☎ 01–45–38–52–87, métro Montparnasse-Bienvenüe) carries nearly 80,000 fashion labels under its roof. Free
fashion shows are held every Wednesday at 11 AM (☎ 01–48–74–02–
30 for reservations). Along with the world's largest perfumery, the main
store has the "Espace Lafayette Maison," a huge Yves Taralon–designed
emporium dedicated to the art of living *à la française*. There's also a
gourmet food hall, a separate men's store, and a sports shop.

Marks & Spencer (✉ 35 bd. Haussmann, 9ᵉ, ☎ 01–47–42–42–91, métro
Havre-Caumartin, Auber, or Opéra; ✉ 88 rue de Rivoli, 4ᵉ, ☎ 01–
44–61–08–00, métro Hôtel de Ville) is a British chain chiefly noted for
its moderately priced basics (underwear, socks, sleep- and sportswear)
as well as its popular English grocery store and take-out.

La Samaritaine (✉ 19 rue de la Monnaie, 1ᵉʳ, ☎ 01–40–41–20–20,
métro Pont-Neuf or Châtelet), a sprawling five-store complex, carries
everything from designer fashions to cuckoo clocks but is especially
known for kitchen supplies, housewares, and furniture. Its most famous
asset is the Toupary restaurant in Building 2, from which there's a marvelous view of Notre-Dame and the Left Bank.

Budget

Monoprix and **Prisunic** are French dime stores—with branches throughout the city—that stock inexpensive everyday items like toothpaste, groceries, toys, typing paper, and bath mats—a little of everything. Both
chains carry inexpensive children's clothes of surprisingly fine quality
and are good places to stock up on unexpectedly good wine.

Tati (✉ 140 rue de Rennes, 6ᵉ, ☎ 01–45–48–68–31, métro St-Placide;
2–28 bd. Rochechouart, 18ᵉ, ☎ 01–55–29–50–00, métro Barbès) is
known for its bargain-basement prices and hectic, jumbled sales floors.
Shop carefully, as goods—from clothes to kitchen utensils—vary in quality. The store also sells its own line of trendy fashions, "La Rue Est à
Nous."

Markets

Flea Markets

Le Marché aux Puces St-Ouen (métro Porte de Clignancourt), on Paris's
northern boundary, still attracts the crowds when it opens on week-

ends and Monday, but its once-unbeatable prices are now a feature of the past. This century-old labyrinth of alleyways packed with antiques dealers' booths and junk stalls spreads for over a square mile. Arrive early to pick up the most worthwhile loot (like old prints). But be warned—if there's one place in Paris where you need to know how to bargain, this is it! For lunch, stop for mussels and fries in one of the rough-and-ready cafés.

On the southern and eastern slopes of the city—at **Porte de Montreuil** and **Porte de Vanves**—are other, less-impressive flea markets. Both have an enormous amount of junk to sift through to find any real bargains.

Flower and Bird Markets

Paris's main flower market is in the heart of the city on the Ile de la Cité (métro Cité), between Notre-Dame and the Palais de Justice. It's open every day except Sunday, when a bird market takes its place. Other colorful flower markets are held beside the Madeleine church (métro Madeleine) and on Place des Ternes (métro Ternes), down the road from the Arc de Triomphe. Both are open daily except Monday.

Food Markets

Paris's open-air food markets are among the city's most colorful attractions. Fruits and vegetables are piled high in vibrant pyramids. The variety of cheeses is always astounding. The lively—and somewhat chaotic—atmosphere that reigns in most markets makes them a sight worth seeing, even if you don't want or need to buy anything. Every *quartier* (neighborhood) has at least one, although many are open only a few days each week. Sunday morning, till 1 PM, is usually a good time to go; Monday they are likely to be closed.

Many of the better-known markets are in areas you'd visit for sightseeing: **rue de Buci** (✉ 6ᵉ, métro Odéon, ☺ daily) near St-Germain-des-Prés; **rue Mouffetard** (✉ 5ᵉ, métro Monge, best on weekends) near the Jardin des Plantes; **rue Montorgueuil** (✉ 1ᵉʳ, métro Châtelet–Les Halles, ☺ daily); **rue Lepic** in Montmartre (✉ 18ᵉ, métro Blanche or Abbesses, best on weekends); **rue Lévis** (✉ 17ᵉ, métro Villiers, ☺ daily) near Parc Monceau; **boulevard Richard Lenoir** (✉ 11ᵉ, métro Bastille); and **Bir-Hakeim** (✉ 15ᵉ, métro Bir-Hakeim). The **Marché d'Aligre** (✉ rue d'Aligre, 12ᵉ, métro Ledru-Rollin), open until 1 PM every day except Monday, is a bit farther out, but is the cheapest market in Paris; on weekends a small flea market is also held here.

Stamp Market

Philatelists head for Paris's unique stamp market at the intersection of avenue Marigny and avenue Gabriel (métro Champs-Élysées–Clemenceau) overlooking the gardens at the bottom of the Champs-Élysées. On sale are vintage postcards and stamps from all over the world. It is open Thursday, weekends, and public holidays.

Shopping Arcades

Paris's 19th-century commercial arcades, called *passages*, are the forerunners of the modern shopping mall. Glass roofs, decorative pillars, and inlaid mosaic floors make these spaces delightful. The major arcades are in the 1ᵉʳ and 2ᵉ arrondissements on the Right Bank. Shops range from the avant-garde (Gaultier and Yuki-Torii designs in the luxurious Galerie Vivienne) to the genteel (embroidery supplies and satin ribbons at Le Bonheur des Dames in the Passage Jouffroy). You can find all sorts of dusty curiosity shops tucked into the arcades, with such items as rare stamps, secondhand books, and antique canes.

Galerie Véro-Dodat (⊠ 19 rue Jean-Jacques Rousseau, 1er, métro Les Halles) has painted ceilings and slender copper pillars, and shops selling old-fashioned toys, contemporary art, children's clothing, and jewelry.

Galerie Vivienne (⊠ 4 rue des Petits-Champs, 2e, métro Bourse), between the Stock Exchange (Bourse) and the Palais-Royal, is home to a range of interesting shops, an excellent tearoom, A Priori Thé, and Cave Legrand, a quality wine shop.

Passage Jouffroy (⊠ 12 bd. Montmartre, 9e, métro Montmartre) is full of shops selling toys, postcards, antique canes, perfumes, original cosmetics, and dried flowers: Try Pain d'Epices at No. 29 and Au Bonheur des Dames at No. 39.

Passage des Panoramas (⊠ 11 bd. Montmartre, 2e, métro Montmartre), opened in 1800, is the oldest arcade; it's especially known for its stamp shops.

Passage des Pavillons (⊠ 6 rue de Beaujolais, 1er, métro Palais-Royal), near the Palais-Royal, is an elegant gallery with shops selling gourmet foods, antiquarian books, and fine china.

Passage Verdeau (⊠ 4–6 rue de la Grange Batelière, 9e, métro Montmartre) is across the street from the Passage Jouffroy and has shops carrying antique cameras, comic books, and engravings.

Specialty Shops

Arts and Antiques

Antiques dealers proliferate in the **Carré Rive Gauche** (⊠ between St-Germain-des-Prés and the Musée d'Orsay, 6e, métro St-Germain-des-Prés, Rue du Bac). Several antiques dealers are around the **Drouot** auction house (⊠ corner of rue Rossini and rue Drouot, 9e, métro Richelieu-Drouot) near the Opéra. The **Louvre des Antiquaires** (⊠ Pl. du Palais-Royal, 1er, métro Palais-Royal) is a stylish mall devoted primarily to antiques. Many big-name dealers, such as **Didier Aaron** and **Perrin,** are on rue du Faubourg St-Honoré. The **Viaduc des Arts** (⊠ 9–147 av. Daumensil, 12e, métro Ledru-Rollin) houses dozens of art galleries, artisans' boutiques, and upscale shops under the arches of a stone viaduct that once supported train tracks. **Village St-Paul** (⊠ enter from rue St-Paul, 4e, métro St-Paul) is a clutch of streets with many antique shops. For more art galleries, *see* Galleries *in* Chapter 4.

Bags, Scarves, and Accessories

Alexandre de Paris (⊠ 235 rue St-Honoré, 1er, ☎ 01–42–61–41–34, métro Tuileries) carries a whole array of hair accessories, named after one of the century's most famous hairdressers, whose clients included the Duchess of Windsor, Sophia Loren, Jean Cocteau, and Elizabeth Taylor.

Hermès (⊠ 24 rue du Faubourg St-Honoré, 8e, ☎ 01–40–17–47–17, métro Concorde) was established as a saddlery in 1837 and went on to create the famous, eternally chic Kelly bag, for Grace Kelly. The magnificent silk scarves—truly fashion icons—are legendary for their rich colors and intricate designs, which change yearly. During semiannual sales, in January and July, the astronomical prices are slashed by up to 50%. On the second floor is the Hermès Museum, housing a collection of horse-related objects; visits can be arranged by writing to Bertrand de Courcy at the above address at least a month in advance.

Longchamp (⊠ 390 rue St-Honoré, 1er, ☎ 01–42–60–00–00, métro Concorde) sells bags and leather goods of excellent quality and impeccable taste.

Losco (⊠ 20 rue de Sévigné, 4e, ☎ 01–48–04–39–93, métro St-Paul; ⊠ 5 rue de Sèvres, 6e, ☎ 01–42–22–77–47, métro Sèvres-Babylone) allows customers to design their own high-quality, reasonably priced belts by mixing and matching buckles and straps.

Louis Vuitton (✉ 101 av. des Champs-Élysées, 8ᵉ, ☎ 01–53–27–24–00, métro George V; ✉ 54 av. Montaigne, 8ᵉ, ☎ 01–45–62–47–00, métro Franklin-D.-Roosevelt; ✉ 6 Pl. St-Germain-des-Prés, 6ᵉ, ☎ 01–45–49–62–32, métro St-Germain-des-Prés) is the most famous name in luxury luggage and handbags. In 1998, the house launched a ready-to-wear clothing line, designed by American Marc Jacobs. The postmodern Left Bank boutique was designed by Anouska de Hempel; the new Champs-Élysées store is the work of Peter Marino and takes a more minimalist approach.

Madeleine Gely (✉ 218 bd. St-Germain, 7ᵉ, ☎ 01–42–22–63–35, métro Rue du Bac) is the queen of walking sticks. Late president François Mitterrand used to buy his at this tiny shop also filled with an amazing range of umbrellas.

Maison de Famille (✉ 29 rue St-Sulpice, 6ᵉ, ☎ 01–40–46–97–47, métro Mabillon, St-Sulpice) carries good-quality bags and leather goods.

Souleiado (✉ 78 rue de Seine, 6ᵉ, ☎ 01–43–54–62–25, métro Odéon; ✉ 83 av. Paul Doumer, 16ᵉ, ☎ 01–42–24–99–34, métro La Muette) is *the* name for scarves, quilted bags, and linens in traditional, richly colored Provençal patterns.

DISCOUNT

Accessoires à Soie (✉ 21 rue des Acacias, 17ᵉ, ☎ 01–42–27–78–77, métro Argentine) is where savvy Parisians buy superb silk scarves and ties in all shapes and sizes. The wide selection includes many big-name designers, and everything costs about half of what you'd pay elsewhere.

Books (English-Language)

The scenic open-air bookstalls along the Seine sell secondhand books (mostly in French), prints, and souvenirs. Numerous French-language bookshops—specializing in a wide range of topics including art, film, literature, and philosophy—are found in the scholarly Latin Quarter and the publishing district, St-Germain-des-Prés. For English-language books, try the following.

Brentano's (✉ 37 av. de l'Opéra, 2ᵉ, ☎ 01–42–61–52–50, métro Opéra) is stocked with everything from classics to children's titles.

Comptoir de l'Image (✉ 44 rue de Sévigné, 3ᵉ, ☎ 01–42–72–03–92, métro St-Paul) is where designers John Galliano, Marc Jacobs, and Emanuel Ungaro stock up on old copies of *Vogue, Harper's Bazaar,* and *The Face.* It also sells trendy magazines like *Dutch, Purple,* and *Spoon,* designer catalogues from the past, and rare photo books.

Galignani (✉ 224 rue de Rivoli, 1ᵉʳ, ☎ 01–42–60–76–07, métro Concorde) stocks both French- and English-language books, and is especially known for its extensive range of art books and coffee-table tomes.

Shakespeare & Company (✉ 37 rue de la Bûcherie, 5ᵉ, ☎ no phone, métro St-Michel), the sentimental Left Bank favorite, specializes in expatriate literature. The staff tends to be rather pretentious, but the shelves of secondhand books hold real bargains. Poets often give readings upstairs.

Tea & Tattered Pages (✉ 24 rue Mayet, 6ᵉ, ☎ 01–40–65–94–35, métro Duroc) sells cheap, secondhand paperbacks, plus new books (publishers' overstock) at low prices. Tea and brownies are served, and browsing is encouraged.

Village Voice (✉ 6 rue Princesse, 6ᵉ, ☎ 01–46–33–36–47, métro Mabillon), known for its selection of contemporary authors, hosts regular literary readings.

W. H. Smith (⌧ 248 rue de Rivoli, 1ᵉʳ, ☏ 01–44–77–88–99, métro Concorde) carries an excellent range of travel and language books, cookbooks, and fiction for adults and children.

Clothing (Children's)

Almost all the top designers make minicouture, but you can expect to pay upwards of 1,200 francs for each wee outfit. Following is where mere mortal Parisian parents shop to keep their kids looking chic.

Dipaki (⌧ 18 rue Vignon, 8ᵉ, ☏ 01–42–66–24–74, métro Madeleine) is a mecca for affordably priced infants' and kids' clothing in bold, primary colors.

Du Pareil Au Même (⌧ 15 and 23 rue des Mathurins, 8ᵉ, ☏ 01–42–66–93–80, métro Havre-Caumartin; ⌧ 14 rue St-Placide, 6ᵉ, ☏ 01–40–49–00–33, métro St-Placide) is a moderately priced chain selling well-made, adorable basics in soft, brightly colored jersey and cotton. Sizes and styles range from newborn to young teen.

Pom d'Api (⌧ 28 rue du Four, 6ᵉ, ☏ 01–45–48–39–31, métro St-Germain-des-Prés) stocks quality French and Italian footwear for babies and preteens, as well as miniversions of Doc Martens and Timberlands.

Clothing (Discount)

Rue d'Alésia (métro Alésia), in the 14ᵉ arrondissement, is the main place to find shops selling last season's items at a discount. Mendès, in the 2ᵉ, is a notable exception. Be forewarned: Most of these shops are much more downscale than their elegant sister shops, and dressing rooms are not always provided.

Cacharel Stock (⌧ 114 rue d'Alésia, 14ᵉ, ☏ 01–45–42–53–04) offers impressive savings (up to 40% off) on women's, men's, and children's clothing (plus even bigger markdown sales racks on the second floor).

L'Habilleur (⌧ 44 rue Poitou, 3ᵉ, ☏ 01–48–87–77–12, métro Sébastien-Froissart) carries end-of-line clothing and accessories from designers such as Jean-Paul Gaultier, Dries Van Noten, and Patrick Cox—all sold at half the retail price.

Majestic by Chevignon (⌧ 122 rue d'Alésia, 14ᵉ, ☏ 01–45–43–40–25) discounts Chevignon casual wear for all ages at up to 40% off.

Mendès (⌧ 5 rue d'Uzès, 2ᵉ, ☏ 01–42–36–83–32, métro Grands Boulevards) sells last season's Yves St-Laurent Rive Gauche and Variations lines at half price, as well as fabrics and accessories. Christian Lacroix designs are also sold here at a discount.

SR Store (⌧ 64 rue d'Alésia, 14ᵉ, ☏ 01–43–95–06–13) slices 50% off last year's prices on Sonia Rykiel fashions for men, women, and children and still manages to chop another 20%–30% off during the sales in January and July.

Clothing (Men's)

Brummel (⌧ Au Printemps department store, 61 rue Caumartin, 9ᵉ, ☏ 01–42–82–50–00, métro Havre-Caumartin or Opéra) is Paris's menswear fashion leader: six floors of suits, sportswear, underwear, coats, ties, and accessories in all price ranges.

Charvet (⌧ 28 Pl. Vendôme, 1ᵉʳ, ☏ 01–42–60–30–70, métro Opéra) is the Parisian equivalent of a Savile Row tailor: a conservative, aristocratic institution famed for made-to-measure shirts and exquisite ties and accessories.

Façonnable (⌧ 9 rue du Faubourg St-Honoré, 8ᵉ, ☏ 01–47–42–72–60, métro Concorde) sells fashionable town and weekend clothes for young urbanites.

Flower (⌧ 7 rue Chomel, 7ᵉ, ☏ 01–42–22–11–78, métro Sèvres-Babylones) is the best place to pick up outfits by trendy young designers such as Raf Simons, Alexander McQueen, and Marc Le Bihan. It also stocks women's wear.

Panoplie (✉ 41 rue Coquillière, 1ᵉʳ, ☎ 01–40–28–90–35, métro Les Halles, Louvre) may be small, but it is one of the best addresses in the city for men's designer fashions. It stocks well-known names such as Helmut Lang and Ann Demeulemeester as well as up-and-coming designers like Kostas Murkudis, Xavier Delcour, and Christophe Lemaire.

Clothing (Resale)

Catherine Baril (✉ 14 and 25 rue de la Tour, 16ᵉ, ☎ 01–45–20–95–21, métro Passy) has one-of-a-kind, barely worn haute couture and designer ready-to-wear; the store's specialty is old Chanel. No. 25 is devoted to menswear.

Didier Ludot (✉ Jardins du Palais Royal, 24 galerie Montpensier, 1ᵉʳ, ☎ 01–42–96–06–86, métro Palais-Royal) is the place to buy vintage French couture from the '20s to the '70s—wonderful old Chanel suits, Balenciaga dresses, and Hermès scarves.

Guerrisold (✉ 17 bis bd. Rochechouart, 9ᵉ, ☎ 01–42–80–66–18, métro Barbès-Rochechouart) is a treasure trove of secondhand clothes. Though there's a lot of junk, if you sift through the racks carefully, you can pick up great suits, shirts, and dresses at ridiculously low prices.

Kiliwatch (✉ 64 rue Tiquetonne, 2ᵉ, ☎ 01–42–21–17–37, métro Etienne Marcel) is Paris's hippest hand-me-down shop, with everyone from Carla Bruni to Christian Lacroix stopping by to find the next trend. You'll find racks and racks of fabulous secondhand, vintage, and retro clothing, sexy look-at-me partywear, and hip clubwear from the in-house label.

Réciproque (✉ 88, 89, 92, 95, 101, and 123 rue de la Pompe, 16ᵉ, ☎ 01–47–04–30–28, métro Rue de la Pompe) is Paris's largest and most exclusive swap shop. Savings on designerwear—Hermès, Dior, Chanel, and Louis Vuitton—are significant, but prices are not as cheap as you might expect and there's not much in the way of service or space. The shop at No. 89 specializes in leather goods. The store is closed Sunday and Monday and the end of July through August.

Clothing (Women's)

CHIC AND CASUAL

Chacok (✉ 18 rue de Grenelle, 7ᵉ, ☎ 01–42–22–69–99, métro Sèvres-Babylone) is *the* label for fashion-savvy Parisians, who adore the colorful, sunny, and feminine collection, especially its lightweight muslins and linens, and knits.

Et Vous (✉ 25 rue Royale, 8ᵉ, ☎ 01–47–42–31–00, métro Madeleine) is where hip Parisiennes find their stylish, contemporary womenswear—everything from little zip-up suede dresses to cotton stretch jeans. The marvelous, 1950s-inspired space was designed by Andrée Putman.

Free (✉ 84 av. des Champs-Élysées, 8ᵉ, ☎ 01–43–59–19–59, métro George V; 8–10 rue Montmartre, 1ᵉʳ, ☎ 01–42–33–15–52, métro Châtelet) is packed with sexy, body-hugging clubwear and high-fashion separates at extremely reasonable prices—perfect if you need a fab outfit for a night out on the town.

Tara Jarmon (✉ 18 rue du Four, 6ᵉ, ☎ 01–46–33–26–60, métro Mabillon) is a Canadian designer who has garnered plaudits from Paris's trendwatchers. Her understated, classic knee-length coats are especially popular.

Ventilo (✉ 27 bis rue du Louvre, 2ᵉ, ☎ 01–44–76–83–00, métro Louvre) opened its first Parisian store in 1972 and has since been delighting Parisians with its ethnic-influenced fashions. On the third floor are housewares and a café serving the best chocolate cake in the world.

Zara (✉ 44 av. de Champs-Élysées, 8ᵉ, ☎ 01–45–61–52–80, métro Franklin-D.-Roosevelt; 2 rue Halévy, 9ᵉ, ☎ 01–44–71–90–90, métro

TAKE PICTURES. FURTHER.™

Ever see someone

waiting for the sun to come out

while trying to photograph

a charging rhino?

New!
Kodak Max film:

Now with better color,
Kodak's maximum
versatility film gives
you great pictures in
sunlight, low light,
action or still.

It's all you need
to know about film.

www.kodak.com

Fodor's

Distinctive guides packed with up-to-date expert advice and smart choices for every type of traveler.

Fodor's. For the world of ways you travel.

Opéra) is one of the best places to find the latest trends at reasonable prices.

CLASSIC CHIC

No matter, say the French, that fewer and fewer of their top couture houses are still headed by compatriots. It's the chic elegance, the classic ambience, the *je ne sais quoi,* that remains undeniably Gallic. Most of the high-fashion shops are on avenue Montaigne (☞ Shopping by Neighborhood, *above*), avenue George-V, and rue du Faubourg St-Honoré on the Right Bank, though the St-Germain-des-Prés has also become a stomping ground for renowned designers. Following are just a few of Paris's haute couture highlights.

Chanel (✉ 42 av. Montaigne, 8ᵉ, ☎ 01–47–23–74–12, métro Franklin-D.-Roosevelt; ✉ 31 rue Cambon, 1ᵉʳ, ☎ 01–42–86–28–00, métro Tuileries) is helmed by Karl Lagerfeld, a master at updating Coco's signature look with fresh colors and free-spirited silhouettes.

Christian Dior (✉ 30 av. Montaigne, 8ᵉ, ☎ 01–40–73–56–07, métro Franklin-D.-Roosevelt) installed flamboyant British designer John Galliano as head designer after his triumphant run at Givenchy. His dramatic creations, however, have little to do with the Dior tradition.

Givenchy (✉ 3 av. George-V, 8ᵉ, ☎ 01–44–31–50–00, métro Alma-Marceau) made headlines when it chose another bad boy Briton, Alexander McQueen, to take over where Galliano left off. Across the street at No. 8, Givenchy Boutique presents slightly more affordable versions of the designer's elegant ready-to-wear.

Sonia Rykiel (✉ 175 blvd. St-Germain, 6ᵉ, ☎ 01–49–54–60–60, métro St-Germain-des-Prés; ✉ 70 rue du Faubourg St-Honoré, 8ᵉ, ☎ 01–42–65–20–81, métro Concorde) is the undisputed Queen of French fashion. Since the '60s she has been designing stylish knit separates and has made black her color of predilection.

TRENDSETTERS

A.P.C. (✉ 3 rue de Fleurus, 6ᵉ, ☎ 01–42–22–12–77, métro Rennes), founded in 1987, has become one of the hottest labels for trendy, streetwise fashion. A men's store is opposite at No. 4.

L'Absinthe (✉ 74–76 rue Jean-Jacques Rousseau, 1ᵉʳ, ☎ 01–42–33–54–44, métro Les Halles) is a discreet but magical address where the likes of Peter Gabriel, Lauren Bacall, Tom Cruise, and Catherine Deneuve pick up clothing that is new but looks vintage.

Azzedine Alaïa (✉ 7 rue de Moussy, 4ᵉ, ☎ 01–42–72–19–19, métro Hôtel de Ville) is the undisputed "king of cling." His figure-hugging creations are often so tight that models have to be squeezed into them.

Christophe Lemaire (✉ 36 rue de Sévigné, 3ᵉ, ☎ 01–42–74–51–90, métro St-Paul) is one of France's most talked-about young designers. As well as selling his own collection, he carries CDs and has created a lounge space where you can relax and drink green tea.

Colette (✉ 213 rue St-Honoré, 1ᵉʳ, ☎ 01–55–35–33–90, métro Tuileries) is an enormous minimalist space showcasing all that's trendy in fashion, home design, art, and accessories. The high-tech basement café is a fashionable place to break for coffee or one of a dozen mineral waters.

L'Éclaireur (✉ 3 rue des Rosiers, 4ᵉ, ☎ 01–48–87–10–22, métro St-Paul) has been on the cutting edge of fashion for years. It was the first to introduce Belgian designers like Martin Margiela into France and is still trying to keep one step ahead of the competition; today it stocks names like Prada, Dries Van Noten, and Josephus Thimister as well as hip sportswear and streetwear labels.

L'Epicerie (✉ 30 rue du Temple, 4ᵉ, ☎ 01–42–78–12–39, métro Hôtel de Ville) is a cross between a boutique and art gallery run by three irreverent young guys. They sell their own L'Epicerie label, as well as

Japanese and American streetwear that can't be found elsewhere. Most interesting, they commission the hottest young international designers to create limited-edition pieces for them.

Jean-Paul Gaultier (✉ 6 rue Vivienne, 2ᵉ, ☎ 01–42–86–05–05, métro Bourse or Palais-Royal), who made his name as Madonna's irreverent clothier, continues to create outrageously attention-getting garments for men and women.

Jérôme L'Huillier (✉ Jardins du Palais Royal, 27 rue de Valois, 1ᵉʳ, ☎ 01–49–26–91–61, métro Palais-Royal) is one of France's most talented but underrated designers. His feminine, elegant, and beautifully cut creations have earned him a following amongst young actresses like Chiara Mastroianni and Romane Bohringer.

Lagerfeld Gallery (✉ 40 rue de Seine, 6ᵉ, ☎ 01–55–42–75–51, métro Mabillon) sells Karl's own signature Lagerfeld line, as well as the collection he designs for Italian fur house Fendi. On the first floor are accessories, perfumes, magazines, and exhibitions of Lagerfeld's own photography.

Lance (✉ 9 bis rue des Blancs-Manteaux, 4ᵉ, ☎ 01–42–72–65–58, métro Hôtel de Ville) carries fun, wearable, trendy clothes by young designers that don't cost an arm and a leg. Look out especially for the up-and-coming French designer Isabel Marant.

Lolita Lempicka (✉ 14 rue du Faubourg Saint-Honoré, 8ᵉ, ☎ 01–49–24–94–01, métro Concorde) serves up sharp suits and whimsical silk dresses. Studio Lolita at No. 2 rue des Rosiers in the Marais sells last season's items at a discount.

Maria Luisa (✉ 2 rue Cambon, 1ᵉʳ, ☎ 01–47–03–96–15, métro Concorde) was one of the very first stores to carry Helmut Lang and John Galliano, and now also stocks Martin Margiela, Jean-Paul Gaultier, Ann Demeulemeester, and Martine Sitbon. A men's store is around the corner at No. 38 rue du Mont-Thabor.

Martin Grant (✉ 32 rue des Rosiers, 4ᵉ, ☎ 01–42–71–39–49, métro St-Paul) is a young Australian designer who creates elegant, minimalistic, and beautifully constructed clothes.

Onward (✉ 147 bd. St-Germain, 6ᵉ, ☎ 01–55–42–77–55, métro St-Germain-des-Prés), formerly known as Kashiyama, stocks fashion-forward clothes and accessories by the likes of Ann Demeulemeester, Dolce & Gabanna, Martine Sitbon, and A. F. Vandevorst. It also gives over a space to a guest designer each season; the first two were Jean Colonna and Alexander McQueen.

Raw Essentials (✉ 46 rue Etienne Marcel, 2ᵉ, ☎ 01–42–21–44–33, métro Louvre) is a haven for raw denim jeans. You'll find hot labels like G-Star and Evisu as well as a range of military-inspired clothing.

Ron Orb (✉ 39 rue Etienne Marcel, 1ᵉʳ, ☎ 01–40–28–09–33, métro Etienne-Marcel) creates a line of streetwear that he calls "anatomical": Instead of being straight, the sleeves follow the line of the body and the knees are rounded to allow for more flexibility. He also has a funky line of shoes influenced by athletic wear.

Le Shop (✉ 3 rue d'Argout, 2ᵉ, ☎ 01–40–28–95–94, métro Louvre) is the Parisian address for fans of streetwear and techno. The industrial-style shop carries numerous hip designers as well as skateboards, sports shoes, and flyers for raves and parties.

Victoire (✉ 10 and 12 Pl. des Victoires, 2ᵉ, ☎ 01–42–61–09–02, métro Bourse or Palais-Royal; menswear at ✉ 10–12 rue du Colonel Driant, 1ᵉʳ, ☎ 01–42–97–44–87, métro Palais-Royal) stocks a range of designer labels under one roof, such as Donna Karan, Lawrence Steele, Narciso Rodriguez, and Alessandro dell'Acqua; next door is Victoire's own label. The men's store is just a stone's throw away on rue du Colonel Driant.

Cosmetics

When it comes to *le maquillage* (makeup), Parisian women swear by those two beloved dime stores, **Monoprix** and **Prisunic** (☞ Budget *in* Department Stores, *above*). Both are goldmines for inexpensive, good-quality cosmetics (but the Prisunic branch at ⊠ 109 rue de la Boétie, 8ᵉ, métro St-Philippe-du-Roule, is the best-stocked). Brand names to look for are Bourjois, whose products are made in the Chanel factories, and Arcancil.

Anne Sémonin (⊠ 2 rue des Petits-Champs, 2ᵉ, ☎ 01–42–60–94–66, métro Palais-Royal; ⊠ 108 rue du Faubourg St-Honoré, 8ᵉ, ☎ 01–42–66–24–22, métro Champs-Elysées–Clémenceau) sells cosmetics made out of seaweed and trace elements, as well as essential oils that are popular with the likes of Madonna and model Karen Mulder.

By Terry (⊠ 21 Galerie Véro-Dodat, 1ᵉʳ, ☎ 01–44–76–00–76, métro Louvre, Palais Royal) is the brainchild of Yves St-Laurent's director of makeup, Terry de Gunzberg. It offers her own brand of "ready-to-wear" makeup as well as personalized lipsticks, foundation, blusher, and eye shadow, developed specifically for each client. The service requires a consultation, which should be booked at least two weeks in advance, and costs about 2,500 francs.

Make Up For Ever (⊠ 5 rue de la Boétie, 8ᵉ, ☎ 01–42–66–01–60, métro St-Augustin) is a must-stop for makeup artists, models (Kate Moss is a regular), and actresses (Madonna has dropped in, too). The ultrahip selection spans 100 shades of foundation, 125 eye shadows, 24 glittering powders, and scores of fake eyelashes.

Sephora (⊠ 70 av. de Champs-Elysées, 8ᵉ, ☎ 01–53–93–22–50, métro Franklin-D.-Roosevelt; ⊠ 1 rue Pierre Lescot, in the Forum des Halles, 1ᵉʳ, ☎ 01–40–26–60–68, métro Châtelet–Les Halles), the leading chain of perfume and cosmetics stores in France, sells its own makeup as well as all the big brands. Choose from 365 colors of lipstick, send E-mail for free, or browse through the "Cultural Gallery" at the Champs-Elysées store.

Fabrics

Madura (⊠ 66 rue de Rennes, 6ᵉ, ☎ 01–45–44–71–30, métro St-Sulpice) is full of gorgeous materials and creative ideas for home decorating.

Manuel Canovas (⊠ 7 rue de Fürstenberg, 6ᵉ, ☎ 01–43–25–75–98, métro St-Germain-des-Prés) is one of the most famous names in French fabrics. This store stocks his extremely varied collections, which are remarkable for their wide range of colors.

Marché St-Pierre (⊠ 2 rue Charles Nodier, 18ᵉ, ☎ 01–46–06–92–25, métro Anvers), a five-floor warehouse in Montmartre, supplied designers like Kenzo in his salad days. Its inventory runs the gamut from fine brocades to fake furs, and there are often good specials on cheap end-of-bolt upholstery and fabrics. The market is open Monday through Saturday afternoon.

Métaphores (⊠ 7 Pl. de Fürstenberg, 6ᵉ, ☎ 01–46–33–03–20, métro St-Germain-des-Prés) sells fabrics for home furnishings and is particularly renowned for its silks, taffetas, and original fibers.

Pierre Frey (⊠ 2 rue de Fürstenberg, 6ᵉ, ☎ 01–46–33–73–00, métro St-Germain-des-Prés) carries all sorts of fabrics as well as tablecloths and pillows.

Flowers

Au Nom de la Rose (⊠ 46 rue du Bac, 7ᵉ, ☎ 01–42–22–08–09, métro Rue du Bac; ⊠ 87 rue St-Antoine, 4ᵉ, ☎ 01–42–71–34–24, métro St-Paul), as its name suggests, specializes in roses of all different kinds.

Christian Tortu (✉ 6 carrefour de l'Odéon, 6ᵉ, ☎ 01–43–26–02–52, métro Odéon) is Paris's most fashionable florist; he also sells very elegant zinc vases.

Milles Feuilles (✉ 2 rue Rambuteau, 3ᵉ, ☎ 01–42–78–32–93, métro Rambuteau, Hôtel de Ville) is one of the best addresses for beautiful bouquets. You'll find flowers in divine shades of red, orange, pink, and yellow, as well as vases, pots, picture frames, and lamps.

Food and Wine

À la Mère de Famille (✉ 35 rue du Faubourg-Montmartre, 9ᵉ, ☎ 01–47–70–83–69, métro Cadet) is an enchanting shop well versed in French regional specialties and old-fashioned bonbons, sugar candy, and more.

Le Cave Augé (✉ 116 bd. Haussmann, 8ᵉ, ☎ 01–45–22–16–97, métro St-Augustin), one of the best wine shops in Paris since 1850, is just the ticket whether you're looking for a rare vintage for a oenophile friend or a seductive Bordeaux for a tête-à-tête. English-speaking Marc Sibard is a knowledgeable and affable adviser.

Debauve & Gallais (✉ 30 rue des Sts-Pères, 7ᵉ, ☎ 01–45–48–54–67, métro St-Germain) was founded in 1800 by two former chemists to Louis XVI who decided to start making chocolates. Today, their delectable recipes can still be found here.

L'Épicerie (✉ 51 rue St-Louis-en-L'Ile, 4ᵉ, ☎ 01–43–25–20–14, métro Pont-Marie) sells 90 types of jam (such as figs in port, and red currant with fresh mint), 70 kinds of mustard (including one with chocolate and honey), numerous olive oils, and flavored sugars.

Fauchon (✉ 26 Pl. de la Madeleine, 8ᵉ, ☎ 01–47–42–60–11, métro Madeleine), established in 1886, sells renowned pâté, honey, jelly, and private-label champagne. Hard-to-find foreign foods (U.S. pancake mix, British lemon curd) are also stocked, and delectable pastries and chocolates are served in the café.

La Fontaine au Chocolat (✉ 201 rue St-Honoré, 1ᵉʳ, ☎ 01–42–44–11–66, métro Tuileries) is run by the third generation of a family of chocolate makers; near the entrance is a fountain of liquefied chocolate.

Galeries Lafayette Gourmet (✉ 48 bd. Haussmann, 9ᵉ, ☎ 01–48–74–46–06, métro Chausée-d'Antin, Opéra), with its gold shopping carts and bistro-style snack bar serving caviar and smoked salmon, is as chic as Fauchon and Hédiard, but less intimidating.

La Grande Épicerie (✉ 38 rue de Sèvres, 7ᵉ, ☎ 01–44–39–81–00, métro Sèvres-Babylone), on the ground floor of Au Bon Marché, stocks an extensive array of fine French foodstuffs.

Hédiard (✉ 21 Pl. de la Madeleine, 8ᵉ, ☎ 01–43–12–88–88, métro Madeleine), established in 1854, was famous in the 19th century for its high-quality imported spices. These—along with rare teas and beautifully packaged house brands of jam, mustard, and cookies—are still sold.

La Maison du Chocolat (✉ 56 rue Pierre Charron, 8ᵉ, ☎ 01–47–23–38–25, métro Franklin-D.-Roosevelt; ✉ 8 bd. de la Madeleine, 9ᵉ, ☎ 01–47–42–86–52, métro Madeleine; ✉ 225 rue du Faubourg St-Honoré, 8ᵉ, ☎ 01–42–27–39–44, métro Ternes) is heaven if you love chocolate: Take some home or have a treat in the tea rooms at the store on rue Pierre Charron or Madeleine.

Mariage Frères (✉ 30 rue du Bourg-Tibourg, 4ᵉ, ☎ 01–42–72–28–11, métro Hôtel de Ville) is the place to get tea in Paris: You can choose from over 450 blends from 32 different countries and purchase teapots, tea cups, books about tea, and tea-flavored biscuits and candies.

Hats

Marie Mercié (✉ 23 rue St-Sulpice, 6ᵉ, ☎ 01–43–26–45–83, métro Mabillon, St-Sulpice; ✉ 56 rue Tiquetonne, 2ᵉ, ☎ 01–40–26–60–68, métro Etienne-Marcel) is one of Paris's most fashionable hatmakers.

The Left Bank store is decidedly chic; the Right Bank store carries younger, more casual styles, as well as men's hats designed by her husband, Anthony Peto.

Philippe Model (⊠ 33 Pl. du Marché St-Honoré, 1ᵉʳ, ☎ 01–42–96–89–02, métro Tuileries) started off making hats favored by fashionable society ladies. Now he has added shoes and housewares in two adjacent shops.

Housewares

Argenterie des Francs-Bourgeois (⊠ 17 rue des Francs-Bourgeois, 4ᵉ, ☎ 01–42–72–04–00, métro St-Paul), a dusty secondhand shop, sells old-fashioned silver settings from estates and grand hotels by the kilo. The inexpensive bracelets made of Victorian silver spoons and forks make marvelous gifts.

Catherine Memmi (⊠ 32–34 rue St-Sulpice, 1ᵉʳ, ☎ 01–44–07–22–28, métro Mabillon, St-Sulpice) sells wonderfully chic bed linens, bath products, lamps, table settings, furniture, and cashmere sweaters—all in elegantly neutral colors and minimalist designs.

Christian Liaigre (⊠ 42 rue du Bac, 7ᵉ, ☎ 01–53–63–33–66, métro Rue du Bac) is one of the most fashionable interior decorators at the moment. He designed the Mercer Hotel in New York and the homes of designer Kenzo and French actress Carole Bouquet. His range of fashionably simple furniture is sold in this flagship boutique.

Christofle (⊠ 24 rue de la Paix, 2ᵉ, ☎ 01–42–65–62–43, métro Opéra; ⊠ 9 rue Royale, 8ᵉ, ☎ 01–49–33–43–00, métro Concorde or Madeleine), founded in 1830, is *the* name to know in French silver. Come here for perfectly elegant table settings, vases, cigarette holders, jewelry boxes, and more.

Compagnie Française de l'Orient et de la Chine (⊠ 163 bd. St-Germain, 6ᵉ, ☎ 01–45–48–00–18, métro St-Germain-des-Prés) imports ceramics and furniture from China and Mongolia. On the first floor are vases, teapots, and table settings; in the basement are straw hats, raffia baskets, and bamboo footstools.

The Conran Shop (⊠ 117 rue du Bac, 7ᵉ, ☎ 01–42–84–10–01, métro Sèvres-Babylone; ⊠ 30 bd. des Capucines, 9ᵉ, ☎ 01–53–43–29–00, métro Madeleine) is the brainchild of British entrepreneur Terence Conran. Here you can find expensive contemporary furniture, beautiful bed linens, glassware, kitchen utensils, vases, lamp shades, and bathroom accessories.

Diptyque (⊠ 34 bd. St-Germain, 5ᵉ, ☎ 01–43–26–45–27, métro Maubert-Mutualité) sells scented candles (fashion designer Karl Lagerfeld is a fan) in natural fragrances such as rose, tea, and honeysuckle. It also has lamp oils and perfumes.

D. Porthault (⊠ 18 av. Montaigne, 8ᵉ, ☎ 01–47–20–75–25, métro Franklin-D.-Roosevelt) makes hand-embroidered table linens, luxurious Old World–style sheets, and sumptuous layettes.

Geneviève Lethu (⊠ 28 rue St-Antoine, 4ᵉ, ☎ 01–42–74–21–25, métro St-Paul; ⊠ in the basement of Galeries Lafayette) sells tea services, potpourri mixtures, and table linens for your real or imagined country house.

Gien (⊠ 18 rue de l'Arcade, 8ᵉ, ☎ 01–42–66–52–32, métro Madeleine) has been making fine china since 1821. As well as traditional designs, you'll also find place settings especially designed by contemporary artists.

Lalique (⊠ 11 rue Royale, 8ᵉ, ☎ 01–53–05–12–12, métro Madeleine; ⊠ in the Carrousel du Louvre) produces crystal vases and statuettes prized for their sinuous, romantic forms and delicate design.

La Maison Ivre (⊠ 38 rue Jacob, 6ᵉ, ☎ 01–42–60–01–85, métro St-Germain-des-Prés) carries traditional pottery from all over France, with an emphasis on yellow and green glazed Provençal styles.

Point à la Ligne (✉ 67 av. Victor Hugo, 16ᵉ, ☎ 01–45–00–87–01, métro Victor Hugo; ✉ in the basement of Galeries Lafayette) specializes in modestly priced, beautiful candles and candlesticks.

R & Augousti (✉ 103 rue du Bac, 7ᵉ, ☎ 01–42–22–22–21, métro Sèvres Babylone) are two Paris-based designers who make furniture and objects for the home in materials like coconut, bamboo, fish skin, palm wood, and parchment. Also on sale here are works by other designers, including trendy New York potter Jonathan Adler.

Sentou Galerie (✉ 24 rue du Pont Louis-Philippe, 4ᵉ, ☎ 01–42–71–00–01, métro St-Paul) specializes in contemporary design objects—lamps designed by artists, furniture by up-and-coming designers, and re-editions of seminal chairs and stools. At No. 18 is a store devoted to tableware.

Toulemonde Bochart (✉ 28 rue Madame, 6ᵉ, ☎ 01–42–84–32–22, métro St-Sulpice) was opened by American-born designer Hilton McConnico, who is best known for designing the set for the film *Diva*. He makes baroque-looking objects for the home, often decorated with cacti, and sells the work of other designers, such as former model Inès de la Fressange.

La Tuile à Loup (✉ 35 rue Daubenton, 5ᵉ, ☎ 01–47–07–28–90, métro Censier-Daubenton) is jam-packed with traditional pottery, faience, basketry, and gift items from every region of France.

La Vaissellerie (✉ 85 rue de Rennes, 6ᵉ, ☎ 01–42–22–61–49, métro Rennes; ✉ 92 rue St-Antoine, 4ᵉ, ☎ 01–42–72–76–66, métro St-Paul; ✉ 332 rue St-Honoré, 1ᵉʳ, ☎ 01–42–60–64–50, métro Tuileries) is chockablock with the sort of ingenious kitchen accoutrements that the French do so well, priced below what you would pay for such creativity back home.

DISCOUNT

If you come armed with style numbers, pocket calculators, and comparison prices from home, you may be able to profit from serious savings on fine porcelain in the showrooms on Rue de Paradis (métro Gare de l'Est) in the 10ᵉ arrondissement.

Baccarat Crystal (✉ 30 bis rue de Paradis, 10ᵉ, ☎ 01–47–70–64–30, métro Château-d'Eau or Gare de l'Est) may not have many bargains, but this elegant, red-carpeted showroom with an in-house museum is worth a visit.

La Tisanière (✉ 21 rue de Paradis, 10ᵉ, ☎ 01–47–70–22–80) sells china seconds from prestigious European porcelain makers.

Jewelry

Most of the big names are on or near Place Vendôme. Designer semi-precious and costume jewelry can generally be found in boutiques on avenue Montaigne and rue du Faubourg St-Honoré.

Alexandre Reza (✉ 23 Pl. Vendôme, 1ᵉʳ, ☎ 01–42–96–64–00, métro Opéra), one of Paris's most exclusive jewelers, is first and foremost a gemologist. He travels the world looking for the finest stones and then works them into stunning pieces, many of which are replicas of jewels of historical importance.

Alexis Lahellec (✉ 14 rue Jean-Jacques Rousseau, 1ᵉʳ, ☎ 01–42–33–40–33, métro Châtelet–Les Halles) is a lawyer-turned-designer who makes fun jewelry and objects for the house. Director Pedro Almodovar used Lahellec's teapot-motif jewelry in the film *Women on the Verge of a Nervous Breakdown*.

Arthus-Bertrand (✉ 6 Pl. St-Germain-des-Prés, 6ᵉ, ☎ 01–49–54–72–00, métro St-Germain-des-Prés) dates back to 1803 and is the official purveyor of medals and decorations to the State. It also carries a whole range of designer jewelry and numerous objects to celebrate births.

Au Vase de Delft (⊠ 19 rue Cambon, 1ᵉʳ, ☎ 01–42–60–92–49, métro Concorde) specializes in fine vintage jewelry, ivory sculptures from China and Japan, gold boxes, watches, and Russian-made silverware (some by Fabergé).

Dary's (⊠ 362 rue St-Honoré, 1ᵉʳ, ☎ 01–42–60–95–23, métro Tuileries) is a treasure trove of antique jewelry; it also carries modern secondhand jewelry, paperweights, and porcelain trinkets. Less expensive than Au Vase de Delft, it's a favored haunt of models and fashion stylists.

Matière Première (⊠ 12 rue de Sévigné, 4ᵉ, ☎ 01–42–78–40–87, métro St-Paul) sells everything you need to make your own necklaces and bracelets—thousands of beads, pendants, and wire. If you prefer to buy ready-made items, there's a delightful in-house jewelry collection.

Sic Amour (⊠ 20 rue Pont-Louis-Philippe, 4ᵉ, ☎ 01–42–76–02–37, métro Pont Marie) is a small store highlighting contemporary jewelry designers including rising stars like Stefano Poletti, Hervé van der Straeten, and Zazou.

Siki (⊠ 33–35 rue de Valois, 1ᵉʳ, ☎ 01–42–60–61–10, métro Palais-Royal) sells extraordinary semiprecious costume jewelry that mixes African themes with haute couture classic tradition.

Lingerie

Alice Cadolle (⊠ 14 rue Cambon, 1ᵉʳ, ☎ 01–42–60–94–94, métro Concorde) has been selling the finest lingerie to Parisians since 1889. In the first floor boutique are ready-to-wear bras, corsets, and sleepwear. Upstairs, Mme. Cadolle offers a made-to-measure service, popular with couture clients from nearby Chanel.

Capucine Puerari (⊠ 63 rue des Sts-Pères, 6ᵉ, ☎ 01–42–22–14–09, métro St-Germain-des-Prés) is one of those discreet addresses loved by Parisian women; it's well stocked with lingerie, swimwear, and a stylish collection of clothing.

Sabbia Rosa (⊠ 73 rue des Sts-Pères, 6ᵉ, ☎ 01–45–48–88–37, métro St-Germain-des-Prés) is where supermodels Naomi Campbell and Claudia Schiffer, and actresses Sharon Stone, Catherine Deneuve, and Isabelle Adjani buy lingerie in the finest French silk.

Miscellaneous

Magasin Général (⊠ 45 rue Madame, 6ᵉ, ☎ 01–45–48–72–42, métro Rennes) was set up by the founder of A.P.C., Jean Touitou, in 1996. It stocks A.P.C. jeans and records from Touitou's own label, as well as eclectic objects like magazines, olive oil, and Dr. Bronner's magic soap.

Nature et Découvertes (⊠ in the Carrousel du Louvre, 1ᵉʳ, ☎ 01–47–03–47–43, métro Palais-Royal) has a large selection of children's toys as well as a whole range of objects linked to nature—telescopes, bird seed, gardening equipment, hiking gear, crystals, aromatherapy diffusers, and little zen gardens.

Music

FNAC (⊠ Forum des Halles, 1ᵉʳ, ☎ 01–40–41–40–00, métro Les Halles; ⊠ 26 av. Ternes, 17ᵉ, ☎ 01–44–09–18–00, métro Ternes; ⊠ 136 rue de Rennes, 6ᵉ, ☎ 01–49–54–30–00, métro St-Placide) is a high-profile French chain selling music and books, and photo, TV, and audio equipment at good prices, by French standards.

Virgin Megastore (⊠ 52 av. des Champs-Elysées, 8ᵉ, ☎ 01–49–53–50–00, métro Franklin-D.-Roosevelt; ⊠ in the Carrousel du Louvre, 99 rue de Rivoli, 1ᵉʳ, ☎ 01–49–53–52–90, métro Palais-Royal) has acres of CDs and tapes; the Champs-Élysées store has a large book section and a trendy café upstairs.

Perfumes

Annick Goutal (⊠ 14 rue de Castiglione, 1ᵉʳ, ☎ 01–42–60–52–82, métro Concorde) sells its own exclusive signature perfume line.

L'Artisan Parfumeur (⊠ 32 rue du Bourg Tibourg, 4ᵉ, ☎ 01–48–04–
55–66, métro Hôtel de Ville) sells its own brand of scents for the home
and perfumes with names like Méchant Loup (Naughty Wolf) and Riviera Palace.

Creed (⊠ 38 av. Pierre 1ᵉʳ de Serbie, 8ᵉ, ☎ 01–47–20–58–02, métro
George V) was founded in 1760 and was the official perfume supplier
to Queen Victoria and numerous European courts. Today, it sells a selection of its own scents and makes personalized perfumes.

Guerlain (⊠ 68 av. des Champs-Élysées, 8ᵉ, ☎ 01–45–62–52–37,
métro Franklin-D.-Roosevelt; ⊠ 47 rue Bonaparte, 6ᵉ, ☎ 01–43–26–
71–19, métro Mabillon) boutiques are the only authorized Paris outlets for legendary perfumes like Shalimar, Jicky, Vol de Nuit, Mit-
souko, Chamade, and the latest, Champs-Élysées.

Parfums de Nicolaï (⊠ 69 avenue Raymond Poincaré, 16ᵉ, ☎ 01–47–
55–90–44, métro Victor Hugo) is run by a member of the Guerlain
family, Patricia de Nicolaï. It has a range of children's, women's, and
men's perfumes, as well as sprays for the home and scented candles.
Celebrity clients include Isabelle Adjani and Elton John.

Les Salons du Palais Royal Shiseido (⊠ Jardins du Palais Royal, 142
Galerie de Valois, 25 rue de Valois, 1ᵉʳ, ☎ 01–49–27–09–09, métro
Palais-Royal) is a magical place with marble floors and purple walls.
Every year Shiseido's creative director, Serge Lutens, dreams up two
new scents, which are sold exclusively in this boutique.

DISCOUNT

The airport duty-free shops are your best bet for minor purchases. But
if you're going to spend more than 1,200 francs, it's worthwhile to seek
out the top discounters. Don't forget to claim your détaxe!

Les Halles Montmartre (⊠ 85 rue Montmartre, 2ᵉ, ☎ 01–42–33–11–
13, métro Bourse) routinely discounts its wide range of perfumes and
cosmetics by 30%–40%.

Michel Swiss (⊠ 16 rue de la Paix, 2nd floor, 2ᵉ, ☎ 01–42–61–61–11,
métro Opéra; ⊠ 24 av. de l'Opéra, 1ᵉʳ, ☎ 01–47–03–49–11, métro
Pyramides) offers savings of up to 25% on perfumes, designer jewelry,
and fashion accessories. There's no storefront window; enter the courtyard to take the elevator upstairs.

Shoes

Berluti (⊠ 26 rue Marbeuf, 8ᵉ, ☎ 01–53–93–97–97, métro Franklin-
D.-Roosevelt) has been making exquisite and expensive men's shoes
for over a century. Clients have included the Duke of Windsor, John
F. Kennedy, Fred Astaire, and James Joyce.

Christian Louboutin (⊠ 19 rue Jean-Jacques Rousseau, 1ᵉʳ, ☎ 01–42–
36–05–31, métro Palais Royal; ⊠ 38 rue de Grenelle, 7ᵉ, ☎ 01–42–
22–33–07, métro Sèvres-Babylone) is famous for his wacky but elegant creations and his trademark blood-red soles; Caroline of Monaco,
Catherine Deneuve, and Elizabeth Taylor are some of his clients.

Kabuki (⊠ 13 rue de Turbigo, 2ᵉ, ☎ 01–42–36–44–34, métro Etienne-
Marcel) is a fashionable shoe store where you'll find labels like Miu
Miu, Barbara Bui, and Rodolphe Menudier.

Mare (⊠ 23 rue des Francs-Bourgeois, 4ᵉ, ☎ 01–48–04–74–63, métro
St-Paul; ⊠ 4 rue du Cherche-Midi, 6ᵉ, ☎ 01–45–44–55–33, métro St-
Sulpice) has stylish, trendy shoes made from fine Italian leather.

Michel Perry (⊠ 4 rue des Petits Pères, 2ᵉ, ☎ 01–42–44–10–04, métro
Palais-Royal) is famous for his elegant, slender, high-heeled shoes. Upstairs, the store stocks clothes by a range of hip young designers, including Hussein Chalayan, Colette Dinnigan, and Kostas Murkudis.

Shoe Bizz (⊠ 42 rue Dragon, 6ᵉ, ☎ 01–45–44–91–70, métro St-Germain-des-Prés; ⊠ 25 rue Beaubourg 3ᵉ, ☎ 01–42–74–72–40, métro

Rambuteau) zeroes in on the season's hottest shoe styles and replicates them at prices 30% cheaper than you'll find elsewhere in the city.

Stéphane Kélian (⊠ 23 bd. de la Madeleine, 1er, ☎ 01–42–96–01–84, métro Madeleine; ⊠ 6 Pl. des Victoires, 2e, ☎ 01–42–61–60–74, métro Bourse, Palais-Royal) creates chic, high-style shoes for men and women.

DISCOUNT

Mi-Prix (⊠ 27 bd. Victor, 15e, ☎ 01–48–28–42–48, métro Porte-de-Versailles) is an unruly jumble of end-of-series designer shoes and accessories from the likes of Maud Frizon, Philippe Model, Walter Steiger, Prada, Michel Perry, and Azzedine Alaïa, priced at up to 60% below retail.

Stationery

Cassegrain (⊠ 422 rue St-Honoré, 8e, ☎ 01–42–60–20–08, métro Sèvres-Babylone; ⊠ 81 rue des Sts-Pères, 6e, ☎ 01–42–22–04–76, métro Sèvres-Babylone) is the last word on beautifully engraved cards and elegant French stationery. The desk accessories and inexpensive glass-nib writing pens make great gifts.

Marie Papier (⊠ 26 rue Vavin, 6e, ☎ 01–43–26–46–44, métro Vavin) sells an extraordinary variety of colored, marbled, and Japanese writing paper and notebooks, plus every kind of stylish writing accessory.

Toys

Au Nain Bleu (⊠ 408 rue St-Honoré, 8e, ☎ 01–42–60–39–01, métro Concorde) is a high-priced wonderland of elaborate dollhouses, miniature sports cars, and enchanting hand-carved rocking horses.

C'est Ma Chambre (⊠ 45 rue des Archives, 3e, ☎ 01–48–87–26–67, métro Rambuteau) is the place to spoil your kids; it sells beautiful wooden toys, and gorgeous furniture for kids' rooms.

Marais Plus (⊠ 20 rue des Francs-Bourgeois, 3e, ☎ 01–48–87–01–40, métro St-Paul) is one of the most delightful addresses in the city for children's toys and clothes. Upstairs are dolls, teddy bears, hobby horses, and mobiles; downstairs are very cute clothes made out of recycled materials, and a tea shop.

7 SIDE TRIPS FROM PARIS

The soft light of the region around Paris inspired painters and kings. Corot, Cézanne, and van Gogh took up residence here, as did Louis XIV, who built one of the world's most spectacular châteaux at Versailles. Here, too, Gothic architecture reached a pinnacle in the soaring spires of Chartres and Senlis.

EVEN THOUGH PARIS HAS SO MUCH TO SEE, you might consider taking a short trip outside the city. The region around the capital, known as Ile-de-France, has much to offer and is less frenzied than Paris. Though Ile-de-France is not actually an island (*île*), it is figuratively isolated from the rest of France by three rivers—the Seine, the Oise, and the Marne—that weave majestic, meandering circles around its periphery. Remarkably, this area contains more than 10 million people—almost one-fifth of France's population. This type of statistic conjures up visions of a never-ending suburban sprawl, but nothing could be further from the truth.

Revised and updated by Simon Hewitt

Grand cathedrals and stately châteaux dot the lush, rolling landscape. The kings and clerics who ruled France liked to escape from the capital now and then: Châteaux went up at Versailles, Fontainebleau, Chantilly, and Thoiry; abbeys and cathedrals soared skyward in Chartres, Reims, Senlis, and Laon. The region never lost favor with the powerful, partly because its many forests—large chunks of which still stand—harbored sufficient game to ensure even the most bloated monarch an easy kill. First Fontainebleau, in humane Renaissance proportions, then Versailles, on a minion-crushing, Baroque scale, reflected the royal desire to transform hunting lodges into palatial residences.

Painters from the Barbizon School loved this verdant region for its soft light. Established in the mid-19th century in the village of Barbizon, the school created a naturalistic painting style that inspired the Impressionists. The Impressionists, in turn, influenced van Gogh, who came to Auvers-sur-Oise to paint in the late 19th century.

In 1992 Disney brought its own kind of kingdom to this region: Disneyland Paris. Since then, the park has emerged as France's leading tourist attraction, with 11 million visitors a year. Getting from the capital to the sights in this region is easy: Almost all are within an hour of central Paris and most are easily accessible by train.

AUVERS-SUR-OISE

Cézanne, Pissarro, Corot, Daubigny, and Berthe Morisot all painted in Auvers in the second half of the 19th century. But it is Vincent van Gogh whose memory haunts every nook and cranny of this pretty riverside village. Van Gogh moved here from Arles in 1890 to be with his brother, Theo. Little has changed since the summer of 1890, during the last 10 weeks of van Gogh's life, when he painted no fewer than 70 pictures, then shot himself behind the village château. He is buried next to his brother in a simple, ivy-covered grave in the village cemetery. The whole village is peppered with plaques marking the spots that inspired van Gogh's art; the plaques bear reproductions of his paintings, enabling you to compare his final works with the scenes as they are today. After years of indifference and neglect, van Gogh's last abode has been turned into a shrine. The château is now home to a stunning high-tech exhibit on the Impressionist era. You can also visit the medieval village church, subject of one of van Gogh's most famous paintings, *L'Église d'Auvers,* and admire Osip Zadkine's powerful modern statue of van Gogh in the village park.

The Auberge Ravoux, the inn where van Gogh stayed, was opened to the public as the **Maison de van Gogh** (van Gogh House) in 1993, after painstaking restoration. A dingy staircase leads up to the tiny, spartan, wood-floored attic where van Gogh stored some of modern art's most famous pictures under the bed in which he breathed his last. A

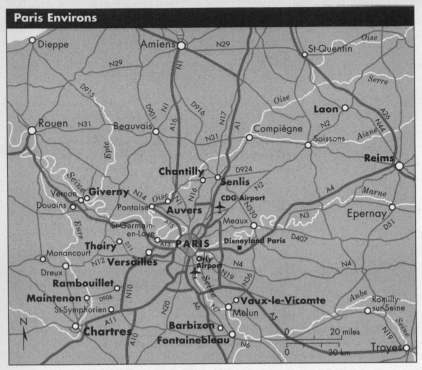

short film retraces van Gogh's time at Auvers, and there is a well-stocked souvenir shop. Stop for a drink or for lunch at the ground-floor restaurant, complete with glasswork, lace curtains, and wall decor carefully modeled on the original designs (☞ Dining, *below*). ⊠ *8 rue de la Sansonne,* ☎ *01–30–36–60–60.* 🎫 *30 frs.* ⊙ *Tues.–Sun. 10–6.*

If you want to see more art, head to the **Musée Daubigny** to admire the drawings, lithographs, and occasional oils by local 19th-century artists. It's opposite the Maison de van Gogh, above the tourist office. ⊠ *Manoir des Colombières, rue de la Sansonne,* ☎ *01–30–36–80–20.* 🎫 *20 frs.* ⊙ *Easter–Sept., Wed.–Sun. 2:30–6:30; Oct.–Easter, Wed.– Sun. 2–5:30.*

The landscapist Charles-François Daubigny, a precursor of the Impressionists, lived in Auvers from 1861 until his death in 1878. On display at his studio, the **Atelier Daubigny,** are a remarkable array of mural and roof paintings by Daubigny and fellow artists Camille Corot and Honoré Daumier. ⊠ *61 rue Daubigny,* ☎ *01–34–48–03–03.* 🎫 *25 frs.* ⊙ *Tues.–Sun. 2–6:30.*

An elegant 17th-century village château, above split-level gardens, is now home of the **Voyage au Temps des Impressionnistes** (Journey Through the Impressionist Era). At this museum devoted to the Impressionists, you get a set of infrared headphones (English available), with commentary that progresses as you walk past various tableaux of Belle Epoque life. Although there are no Impressionist originals— 500 reproductions pop up on screen—some say this is one of France's most imaginative, enjoyable, and innovative museums. Some of the special effects—talking mirrors, computerized cabaret dancers, a train ride past Impressionist landscapes—rival Disney at its best. ⊠ *Rue de Léry,* ☎ *01–34–48–48–48.* 🎫 *60 frs.* ⊙ *May–Oct., Tues.–Sun. 10–7:30; Nov.– Apr., Tues.–Sun. 10–6:30.*

The small **Musée de l'Absinthe** (Absinthe Museum) near the château contains publicity posters and other Belle Epoque artifacts evoking the history of absinthe—a forerunner of today's anise-based aperitifs, like Ricard and Pernod. Before it was banned in 1915 because of its negative effects on the nervous system, absinthe was France's national drink. A famous painting by Edgar Degas shows two absinthe drinkers; van Gogh probably downed a few glasses at the Auberge Ravoux. ⊠ *44 rue Callé,* ☎ *01–30–36–83–26.* ▨ *25 frs.* ☉ *Oct.–May, weekends 11– 6; June–Sept., Wed.–Sun. 11–6.*

Dining

$ ▥ **Auberge Ravoux.** The restaurant where van Gogh used to eat is the obvious choice for lunch. The 185-franc three-course menu changes regularly and usually includes a fish or meat dish. There's also a good-value wine list. But it is the setting and the history that make eating here special. ⊠ *52 rue du Général-de-Gaulle,* ☎ *01–30–36–60–63. Reservations essential. AE, DC, MC, V.*

Auvers-sur-Oise A to Z

Arriving and Departing

BY CAR

Auvers is 38 km (24 mi) northwest of Paris. Take highway A1, then A15 toward Pontoise; then head east along N184 to Méry-sur-Oise and pick up the N328, which crosses the river to Auvers.

BY TRAIN

Two trains depart every hour for Auvers from Paris's Gare du Nord; a change is necessary, usually at St-Ouen-l'Aumône, and the journey time varies from 60 to 90 minutes. A quicker (53 minutes) but more infrequent train leaves from Paris's Gare St-Lazare and involves a change at Pontoise.

Visitor Information

Auvers-sur-Oise Office de Tourisme (⊠ Rue de la Sansonne, opposite the Maison de van Gogh, 95430 Auvers-sur-Oise, ☎ 01–30–36–10–06).

CHANTILLY AND SENLIS

Chantilly, with its forest and château, and nearby Senlis, with its cathedral and old town, are just 30 minutes north of Paris and provide a perfect setting for a day away from the capital. Although separated by just a few miles of forest, the two towns are very different. Senlis has narrow, winding medieval streets and one of the Gothic style's most elegant spires. Chantilly is spacious and aristocratic; its stately moated château is fronted by France's premier racecourse and palatial Baroque stables.

Chantilly

Romantic Chantilly has a host of attractions: a faux Renaissance château, an eye-popping art collection, splendid Baroque stables, a classy racecourse, and a vast (nearly 16,000-acre) forest. Yet it attracts far fewer sightseeing hordes than Versailles or Fontainebleau.

Although the lavish exterior may be overdone—the style is 19th-century Renaissance pastiche—the **Château de Chantilly** is photogenic behind its moat. Housed here is the **Musée Condé,** with its outstanding collection of medieval manuscripts and European paintings, including masterpieces by Raphael, Watteau, and Ingres. The extensive park is a miniature Versailles, complete with grand canal and fairy-tale hamlet. ☎ *03–44–57–08–00.* ▨ *39 frs; park only, 17 frs.* ☉ *Mar.–Oct., Wed.–Mon. 10–6; Nov.–Feb., 10:30–12:45 and 2–5. Orchestra per-*

formance every afternoon during the summer and Christmas holidays, 80 frs.

The majestic 18th-century **Grandes Écuries** (Grand Stables) are still in use as the **Musée Vivant du Cheval** (Living Museum of the Horse), with 30 horses and ponies performing dressage exercises. The stables, next to the racecourse, opposite the château, were designed by architect Jean Aubert to accommodate 240 horses and 500 hounds for stag and boar hunts in the forests nearby. ⊠ *7 rue du Connétable,* ☎ *03–44–57–40–40.* ▨ *50 frs.* ⊘ *Wed.–Mon. 10:30–5:30.*

Dining

$ ✕ **La Capitainerie.** The former château kitchens form a majestic setting for this lunchtime eatery, with a three-course menu available for 95 francs. ⊠ *Château de Chantilly,* ☎ *03–44–57–15–89. MC, V. Closed Tues. and Jan.–Feb. No dinner.*

Senlis

This ancient town has a maze of crooked streets to explore beneath the svelte soaring spire of its Gothic cathedral.

The **Cathédrale Notre-Dame** (⊠ Pl. du Parvis), one of France's oldest (and narrowest) cathedrals, dates from the second half of the 12th century. The superb spire—arguably the most elegant in France—was added around 1240 and has been restored to its original splendor.

The **Musée de la Vénerie** (Hunting Museum) stands on the grounds of the ruined royal castle across from the cathedral. One of France's few full-fledged hunting museums, it displays related artifacts, prints, and paintings, including excellent works by 18th-century animal portraitist Jean-Baptiste Oudry. ⊠ *Château Royal,* ☎ *03–44–53–00–80.* ▨ *14 frs; grounds only, 7 frs.* ⊘ *Mid-Jan.–mid-Dec., Wed. 2–6, Thurs.–Mon. 10–noon and 2–6.*

Dining

$$ ✕ **Le Bourgeois Gentilhomme.** This cozy restaurant in old Senlis serves interesting dishes such as fricassee of burbot with mushrooms. It also has a fine wine list. The 145-franc prix-fixe menu is ideal for a weekday lunch (it's not served on weekends). ⊠ *3 Pl. de la Halle,* ☎ *03–44–53–13–22. MC, V. Closed Mon. and last 3 wks in Aug. No dinner Sun.*

Chantilly and Senlis A to Z

Arriving and Departing

BY CAR

Take highway A1 from Paris (Porte de la Chapelle) to Senlis, 50 km (31 mi) away; Chantilly is 10 km (6 mi) west along pretty D924.

BY TRAIN

Chantilly is about 30 minutes from Paris's Gare du Nord; at least one train departs every hour. A shuttle bus links Chantilly station to Senlis (25 minutes).

Visitor Information

Chantilly Office du Tourisme (⊠ 60 av. Maréchal-Joffre, 60500 Chantilly, ☎ 03–44–57–08–58). **Senlis Office du Tourisme** (⊠ 1 Pl. du Parvis-Notre-Dame, 60300 Senlis, ☎ 03–44–53–06–40).

CHARTRES, MAINTENON, AND RAMBOUILLET

The noble, soaring spires of Chartres are one of the most famous sights in Europe. Try to catch a glimpse of them surging out of the vast, golden grain fields of the Beauce as you approach from the northeast. Maintenon, with its château and ruined aqueduct, and Rambouillet, a stately town whose château has a lake and extensive park land, are within easy reach of Chartres by road or rail.

Chartres

Although you're probably visiting Chartres chiefly for its magnificent Gothic cathedral with world-famous stained-glass windows, the whole town is worth leisurely exploration. It's one of the prettiest in France, with old houses and picturesque streets. Ancient streets tumble down from the cathedral to the Eure River; the view of the rooftops beneath the cathedral from rue du Pont-St-Hilaire is particularly appealing.

Chartres Cathedral is the sixth church to occupy the same spot. It dates mainly from the 12th and 13th centuries; the previous, 11th-century building burned down in 1194. A well-chronicled outburst of religious fervor followed the discovery that the Virgin's relic had miraculously survived unsinged. Reconstruction went ahead at a breathtaking pace. Just 25 years were needed for Chartres cathedral to rise again, and it has remained substantially unchanged ever since.

Worship on the site of the cathedral goes back to before the Gallo-Roman period; the crypt contains a well that was the focus of Druid ceremonies. The original cult of the fertility goddess merged into that of the Virgin Mary with the arrival of Christianity. In the late 9th century, King Charles the Bold presented Chartres with what was believed to be the tunic of the Virgin. This precious relic attracted hordes of pilgrims, and Chartres swiftly became—and has remained—a prime destination for the faithful. Pilgrims trek to Chartres from Paris on foot to this day.

The lower half of the facade is all that survives from the 11th-century Romanesque church. (The Romanesque style is evident in the use of round, rather than pointed, arches.) The main door—the **Portail Royal** (Royal Door)—is richly sculpted with scenes from the life of Christ. The flanking towers are also Romanesque, though the upper part of the taller of the two **spires** (380 ft versus 350 ft) dates from the start of the 16th century, and its fanciful flamboyance contrasts with the stumpy solemnity of its Romanesque counterpart. The **rose window** above the main portal dates from the 13th century. The three windows below it contain some of the finest examples of 12th-century stained glass in France.

The interior is somber, and you'll need time to adjust to the dark. Your reward will be a view of the gemlike richness of the stained glass, dominated by the famous deep "Chartres blue." The oldest window, and perhaps the most stunning, is **Notre Dame de la Belle Verrière** (Our Lady of the Lovely Window), in the south choir. It is well worth taking a pair of binoculars, if you have some, to pick out the details. If you wish to know more about stained-glass techniques and the motifs used, visit the small exhibit in the gallery opposite the north porch. The vast black-and-white medieval pattern on the floor of the nave is one of the few to have survived from the Middle Ages. The faithful were expected to travel along its entire length (some 300 yards) on their knees.

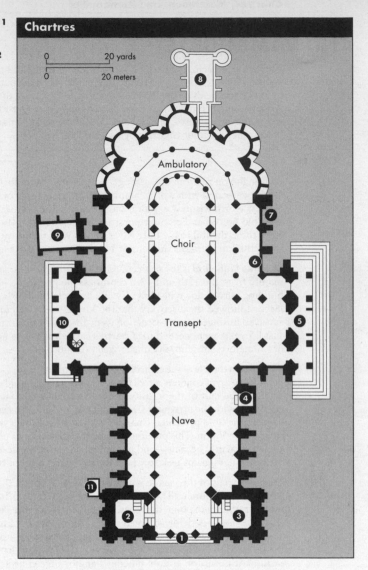

Chartres

Ambulatory

Choir

Transept

Nave

Guided tours of the crypt start from the **Maison de la Crypte** (Crypt House) opposite the south porch. The Romanesque and Gothic chapels running around the crypt have recently been stripped of the 19th-century paintings that used to disfigure them. You will also be shown a 4th-century Gallo-Roman wall and some 12th-century wall paintings. ⊠ *16 cloître Notre-Dame*, ☏ *02–37–21–56–33*. 🎫 *Towers 10 frs; English guided tour 30 frs.* ☺ *Guided tours of crypt: Easter–Oct., daily at 11, 2:15, 3:30, 4:30, 5:15; Nov.–Easter, daily at 11, 4.*

The **Musée des Beaux-Arts** (Fine Arts Museum) is a handsome 18th-century building just behind the cathedral—it used to serve as the bishop's palace. Its varied collection includes Renaissance enamels, a portrait of Erasmus by Holbein, tapestries, armor, and some fine, mainly French paintings of the 17th, 18th, and 19th centuries. There is also a room devoted to the forceful 20th-century works of painter Maurice de Vlaminck, who lived in the region. ⊠ *29 cloître Notre-Dame*, ☏

02–37–36–41–39. ▦ *10 frs (20 frs for special exhibitions).* ☉ *Apr.–Oct., Wed.–Mon. 10–6; Nov.–Mar., Wed.–Mon. 10–noon and 2–5.*

The Gothic **Église St-Pierre** (✉ Rue St-Pierre) near the Eure River has magnificent medieval windows from a period (circa 1300) not represented at the cathedral. The oldest stained glass here, portraying Old Testament worthies, is to the right of the choir and dates from the late 13th century. There is more fine stained glass (17th century) to admire at the **Église St-Aignan** (✉ Rue des Grenets), around the corner from St-Pierre.

Dining

$$$ ✕ **Château d'Esclimont.** This magnificently restored Renaissance château, part of the Relais & Châteaux group, is frequented by high-profile Parisian businesspeople. Lamb with asparagus, hare fricassee (in season), and lobster top the menu. After dining on the rich cuisine, take a stroll through the luxuriant grounds, with lawns and lake. ✉ *2 rue du Château-d'Esclimont, St-Symphorien-le-Château (6 km [4mi] west of Ablis exit on A11 and about 24 km [15 mi] from Chartres and Rambouillet),* ☎ *02–37–31–15–15. Reservations essential. Jacket and tie. AE, DC, MC, V.*

$$ ✕ **La Vieille Maison.** Close to Chartres cathedral, in the same narrow street as Le Buisson Ardent (☞ *below*), this intimate spot with a flower-filled patio has a regularly changing menu. Invariably, however, it includes regional specialties such as truffles and asparagus with chicken. Prices, though justified, can be steep; the 160-franc prix-fixe lunch menu is a good bet. ✉ *5 rue au Lait,* ☎ *02–37–34–10–67. AE, MC, V. Closed Mon. No dinner Sun.*

$–$$ ✕ **Le Buisson Ardent.** This wood-beamed restaurant on a quaint old street near Chartres cathedral has two prix-fixe menus, imaginative food, and attentive service. Some of the excellent dishes include chicken ravioli with leeks and rolled beef with spinach. ✉ *10 rue au Lait,* ☎ *02–37–34–04–66. AE, DC, MC, V. No dinner Sun.*

Maintenon

The town's Renaissance **Château de Maintenon** once belonged to Louis XIV's mistress and morganatic spouse, Madame de Maintenon. Her private apartments are open for viewing. The square, 12th-century **keep** is the sole vestige of a fortress that once occupied this site. The formal gardens stretch behind the château to the ivy-covered arches of the ruined **aqueduct**—one of the Sun King's most outrageous projects. His aim: to provide the ornamental ponds in the gardens of Versailles (48 km/30 mi away) with water from the Eure River. In 1684, some 30,000 men were signed up to construct a three-tier, 5-km (3-mi) aqueduct as part of this project. Many died of fever before the enterprise was called off in 1689. ✉ *Pl. Aristide-Briand,* ☎ *02–37–27–18–09.* ▦ *34 frs.* ☉ *Apr.–Oct., Wed.–Mon. 2–6:30; Nov.–Mar., weekends 2–5:30. Closed Jan.*

Rambouillet

Surrounded by a huge forest, Rambouillet was once the residence of kings and dukes. Today the **Château de Rambouillet** belongs to the French president, although he is seldom in residence. Most of the buildings date from the early 18th century, but the brawny **Tour François I** (Francois I Tower), named for the king who breathed his last here in 1547, was part of the 14th-century fortified castle that first stood on this site. The château backs a lake; you can stroll around it and explore the extensive grounds, which contain a sheepfold and dairy. ▦ *27 frs.* ☉ *Daily 10–11:30 and 2–5:30.*

Chartres, Maintenon, and Rambouillet A to Z

Arriving and Departing

BY CAR

The A10/A11 expressways link Paris to Chartres, 88 km (55 mi) away. Maintenon is 19 km (12 mi) and Rambouillet is 43 km (27 mi) northeast of Chartres via D906. If you are coming from Paris, take A13 toward Versailles, then A12/N10 to Rambouillet (total distance 53 km/33 mi); D906 leads to Maintenon (total distance 77 km/48 mi).

BY TRAIN

Trains depart hourly from Paris's Gare Montparnasse to Chartres (travel time is 50–70 minutes, depending on service). Many of the trains between Paris and Chartres stop at Maintenon (50 minutes) and Rambouillet (35 minutes); some also stop at Versailles. There is also an hourly service between Paris's Gare Montparnasse and Rambouillet.

Guided Tours

Cityrama (⊠ 4 Pl. des Pyramides, Paris, ☎ 01–44–55–61–00) organizes half-day trips to Chartres (275 frs) and combined excursions to Chartres and Versailles (595 frs).

Visitor Information

Chartres (⊠ Pl. de la Cathédrale, 28000 Chartres, ☎ 02–37–21–50–00). **Maintenon** (⊠ 7 Pl. Aristide-Briand, 28130 Maintenon, ☎ 02–37–23–05–04). **Rambouillet** (⊠ 8 Pl. de la Libération, 78120 Rambouillet, ☎ 01–34–83–21–21).

DISNEYLAND PARIS

♻ In April 1992 American pop culture secured a mammoth outpost just 32 km (20 mi) east of Paris in the form of Disneyland Paris. On 1,500 acres in Marne-la-Vallée, Disneyland Paris has a convention center, sports facilities, an entertainment and shopping complex, restaurants, thousands of hotel rooms, and, of course, the theme park itself. The theme park is made up of five "lands": Main Street U.S.A., Frontierland, Adventureland, Fantasyland, and Discoveryland. The central theme of each land is relentlessly echoed in every detail, from attractions to restaurant menus to souvenirs.

Main Street U.S.A. is the scene of the Disney Parades held every afternoon and—during holiday periods—every evening, too.

Top attractions at **Frontierland** are the chilling Phantom Manor, haunted by holographic spooks, and the thrilling runaway mine train of Big Thunder Mountain, a roller coaster that plunges wildly through floods and avalanches in a setting meant to evoke Monument Valley.

Whiffs of Arabia, Africa, and the West Indies give **Adventureland** its exotic cachet; the spicy meals and snacks served here rank among the best food in the theme park. Don't miss the Pirates of the Caribbean, an exciting mise-en-scène populated by eerily human computer-driven figures, or Indiana Jones and the Temple of Doom, a breathtaking ride that relives some of our luckless hero's most exciting moments.

Fantasyland charms the youngest park goers with familiar cartoon characters from such Disney classics as Snow White, Pinocchio, Dumbo, and Peter Pan. The focal point of Fantasyland, and indeed Disneyland Paris, is Le Château de la Belle au Bois Dormant (Sleeping Beauty's Castle), a 140-ft, bubble-gum pink structure topped with 16 blue- and gold-tipped turrets. The castle design was allegedly inspired by illustrations from a medieval Book of Hours. In the dungeon is a scaly, green,

2-ton dragon who rumbles and grumbles in his sleep and occasionally rouses to roar—an impressive feat of engineering that terrifies every tot in the crowd!

Discoveryland is a futuristic setting for high-tech Disney entertainment. Robots on roller skates welcome you to Star Tours, a pitching, plunging, sense-confounding ride through intergalactic space. Space Mountain pretends to catapult you through the Milky Way.

For entertainment outside the theme park, check out **Disney Village,** a vast pleasure mall designed by American architect Frank Gehry. Featured are American-style restaurants (crab shack, diner, deli, steak house), a disco, and a dinner theater where Buffalo Bill stages his Wild West Show twice nightly. An 18-hole golf course is open to the public (☎ 01–60–45–68–04 for information). ✉ *Disneyland Paris (prices vary according to season): 160–210 frs.* ☉ *Mid-June–mid-Sept., daily 9 AM–10 PM; mid-Sept.–mid-June, daily 10–6; weekends, Dec., and spring school holidays, 9–8.*

Dining

$–$$ ✕ **Disneyland Restaurants.** Disneyland Paris is peppered with places to eat, ranging from snack bars and fast-food joints to five full-service restaurants—all with a distinguishing theme. In addition, all Disney hotels and Festival Disney have restaurants that are open to the public. But since these are outside the theme park, you probably don't want to waste time traveling to them for lunch. Wine and beer are served in the theme park's five sit-down restaurants, as well as in the hotels and restaurants outside the park. Eateries serve nonstop as long as the park is open. *AE, DC, MC, V at sit-down restaurants; no credit cards at others.*

Disneyland Paris A to Z

Arriving and Departing

BY BUS

Shuttle buses link Disneyland Paris to Roissy (56 km/35 mi) and Orly (50 km/31 mi) airports. The fare is around 80 frs one-way.

BY CAR

The Strasbourg-bound A4 expressway leads from Paris to Disneyland Paris, at Marne-la-Vallée, a journey of 32 km (20 mi) that in normal traffic takes about 30 minutes. The 4-km (2½-mi) route from the expressway to the entrance of the theme park is clearly marked. Day visitors must head for the *Parking Visiteurs,* which costs 40 frs per car and is 600 yards from the theme-park entrance.

BY TRAIN

Disneyland Paris's suburban train station (Marne-la-Vallée-Chessy) is just 100 yards from the entrance to both the theme park and Festival Disney. Trains run every 10 to 20 minutes from RER-A stations in central Paris: Charles de Gaulle–Étoile, Auber, Châtelet–Les Halles, Gare de Lyon, and Nation. The trip takes about 40 minutes and costs 78 frs round-trip (including the métro to the RER). A TGV station next to the RER station at Disneyland Paris has trains running direct from Lille, Lyon, and Marseille.

Visitor Information

Disneyland Paris S.C.A. (✉ Central Reservations Office, BP 104, 77777 Marne-la-Vallée, Cedex 4, France, ☎ 01–60–30–60–30, ⅎⅩ 01–49–30–71–00). **Walt Disney World Central Reservations** (✉ Box 10,100 Lake Buena Vista, FL 32830–0100, ☎ 407/934–7639).

FONTAINEBLEAU, BARBIZON, AND VAUX-LE-VICOMTE

Fontainebleau, with its historic château, is a favorite place for excursions, especially since a lush forest containing the painters' village of Barbizon and the superb Baroque château of Vaux-le-Vicomte are close by.

Fontainebleau

Numbers in the text correspond to numbers on the Fontainebleau map.

Like Chambord in the Loire Valley or Compiègne to the north of Paris, Fontainebleau earned royal esteem as a hunting base. As at Versailles, a hunting lodge once stood on the site of the current château, along with a chapel built in 1169 and consecrated by exiled (later murdered and canonized) English priest Thomas à Becket.

The **Château de Fontainebleau** you see today dates from the 16th century, although additions were made by various royal incumbents through the next 300 years. The palace was begun under flamboyant Renaissance king François I, the French contemporary of England's Henry VIII.

The king hired Italian artists Il Rosso (a pupil of Michelangelo) and Primaticcio to embellish his château. In fact, they did much more: By introducing the pagan allegories and elegant lines of Mannerism to France, they revolutionized French decorative art. Their extraordinary frescoes and stuccowork can be admired in the **Galerie François-I** ① (Gallery Francis I) and the jewel of the interior, the **Salle de Bal** ②. Here in the ceremonial ballroom, which is nearly 100 ft long, you can admire the dazzling 16th-century frescoes and gilding. Completed under Henri II, François's successor, it is luxuriantly wood-paneled, with a gleaming parquetry floor that reflects the patterns on the ceiling. Like the château as a whole, the room exudes a sense of elegance and style—but on a more intimate, human scale than at Versailles: This is Renaissance, not Baroque.

Napoléon's apartments ③ occupied the first floor. You can see a lock of his hair, his Légion d'Honneur medal, his imperial uniform, the hat he wore on his return from Elba in 1815, and one bed in which he definitely did spend a night (almost every town in France boasts a bed in which the emperor supposedly snoozed). There is also a throne room—Napoléon spurned the one at Versailles, a palace he disliked, establishing his imperial seat in the former King's Bedchamber—and the Queen's Boudoir, known as the Room of the Six Maries (occupants included ill-fated Marie-Antoinette and Napoléon's second wife, Marie-Louise). Highlights of other salons include 17th-century tapestries, marble reliefs by Jacquet de Grenoble, and paintings and frescoes by the versatile Primaticcio.

Although Louis XIV's architectural fancy was concentrated on Versailles, he commissioned Mansart to design new pavilions and had André Lenôtre replant the gardens at Fontainebleau, where he and his court returned faithfully in the fall for the hunting season. However, it was Napoléon who made a Versailles out of Fontainebleau, by spending lavishly to restore it to its former glory. He held Pope Pius VII prisoner here in 1812, signed the second Church-State concordat here in 1813, and, in the cobbled **Cour des Adieux** ④ (Farewell Courtyard), said goodbye to his Old Guard in 1814 as he began his brief exile on the Mediterranean island of Elba. The famous Horseshoe Staircase that dominates the Cour

Cour des
Adieux, **4**

Cour de la
Fontaine, **5**

Galerie
François-I, **1**

Napoléon's
apartments, **3**

Porte
Dauphine, **6**

Salle de Bal, **2**

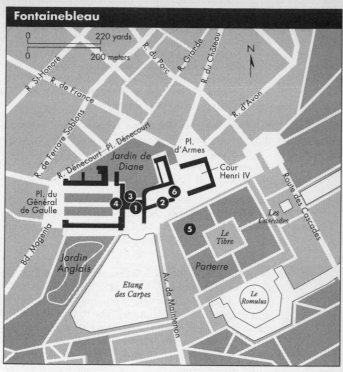

des Adieux, once the Cour du Cheval Blanc (White Horse Courtyard), was built by Androuet du Cerceau for Louis XIII (1610–43).

Another courtyard—the **Cour de la Fontaine** ⑤ (Fountain Court-yard)—was commissioned by Napoléon in 1812 and adjoins the Etang des Carpes (Carp Pond). Ancient carp are alleged to swim here, although Allied soldiers drained the pond in 1915 and ate all the fish, and, in the event they missed some, Hitler's hordes did likewise in 1940.

The **Porte Dauphine** ⑥ is the most beautiful of the various gateways that connect the complex of buildings; its name commemorates the fact that the Dauphin—the heir to the throne, later Louis XIII—was christened under its archway in 1606. ⊠ *Pl. du Gal-de-Gaulle*, ☎ *01–60–71–50–70.* ⌨ *Château 35 frs, gardens free.* ☉ *Château Wed.–Mon. 9:30–12:30 and 2–5, gardens 9–dusk.*

Dining

$$ ✕ **Le Beauharnais.** Opposite the château, in the Aigle Noir hotel, this restaurant serves classic French fare in a grand setting; especially good is the duck with marjoram. Prix-fixe menus are 150, 180, and 450 francs. There's a tranquil garden for alfresco dining in summer. ⊠ *27 Pl. Napoléon-Bonaparte*, ☎ *01–60–74–60–00. Jacket and tie. AE, DC, MC, V. Closed last 2 wks of Dec.*

Barbizon

On the western edge of the 62,000-acre Forest of Fontainebleau is the village of Barbizon, home to a number of mid-19th-century landscape artists, whose innovative outdoor style paved the way for the Impressionists.

Corot, Millet, Théodore Rousseau, Daubigny, and Diaz, among others, all painted here, repairing to the Auberge du Père Ganne after working hours to brush up on their social life. Father Ganne's inn still stands and is now the **Musée de l'École de Barbizon** (Barbizon School Museum). Its two ground-floor rooms have been reconstituted much as they were; a sample of original works is displayed upstairs, and there's a film (in French) as well as information about the village as it was in the 19th century. ✉ *92 Grande-Rue,* ☎ *01–60–66–22–27.* ☜ *25 frs, joint ticket with the Maison-Atelier Théodore Rousseau (☞ below).* ⊙ *Wed.–Mon. 10–12:30 and 2–5.*

The **Maison-Atelier Théodore Rousseau** is the painter's house-cum-studio that now doubles as an exhibition center and tourist office. ✉ *55 Grande-Rue,* ☎ *01–60–66–22–38.* ☜ *25 frs, joint ticket with the Maison-Atelier Théodore Rousseau.* ⊙ *Wed. and Fri.–Mon. 10–12:30 and 2–5.*

Farther along the main street you can soak up the arty mood at Millet's cluttered studio, the **Atelier Jean-François Millet** (if it's not too crowded with tourists). ✉ *27 Grande-Rue,* ☎ *01–60–66–21–55,* ⊙ *Wed.–Mon. 9:30–12:30 and 2–5:30.*

Dining

$ ✕ **Le Relais de Barbizon.** Solid home-cooked meals are served outdoors or in the rustic interior. Among the offerings are duckling with cherries, and lamb with parsley, depending on the season. Expect crowds and brusque service in summer. The four-course, 150-franc weekday menu is an excellent value, but the wine list is expensive and no *pichets* (pitchers) of house wine are served. ✉ *2 av. Charles-de-Gaulle,* ☎ *01–60–66–40–28. MC, V. Closed Wed. No dinner Tues.*

Vaux-le-Vicomte

The majestic **Château de Vaux-le-Vicomte,** started in 1656 by court finance wizard Nicolas Fouquet, is one of the most impressive buildings in Ile-de-France. The construction process was monstrous: Villages were razed, then 18,000 workmen were called in to execute the plans of architect Louis Le Vau, decorator Charles Le Brun, and landscape gardener André Lenôtre. The housewarming party was so lavish that star guest Louis XIV, tetchy at the best of times, threw a jealous fit. He hurled Fouquet into the slammer and promptly began building Versailles to prove just who was boss.

Decoration of the château's landmark feature, the **cupola,** was halted at Fouquet's arrest, and the ceiling of the oval **Grand Salon** beneath remains depressingly blank. Le Brun's major achievement is the ceiling of the **Chambre du Roi** (King's Room) depicting *Time Bearing Truth Heavenwards.* The word "squirrel" in French is *écureuil,* but in local dialect they were known as *fouquets;* they appear here (along the frieze) and throughout the château, a sly visual tribute to the château's hapless founder. Le Brun's other masterwork is the ceiling in the **Salon des Muses** (Salon of the Muses), a brilliant allegorical composition painted in glowing, sensuous colors surpassing anything he achieved at Versailles.

A clever **exhibit,** complete with life-size wax figures, explains the rise and fall of Nicolas Fouquet. Although accused by Louis XIV and subsequent historians of megalomania and shady financial dealings, he was apparently condemned on little evidence by a court eager to please the jealous, irascible monarch. The exhibition continues in the basement, whose cool, dim rooms used to store food and wine and house the château's staff. The **kitchens,** a more cheerful sight with their gleaming copperware and old menus, are also down here.

Lenôtre's stupendous, studiously restored **gardens** contain statues, waterfalls, and fountains. There is also a **Musée des Équipages** (Carriage Museum)—stocked with carriages, saddles, and a smithy—near the entrance. ⊠ *Domaine de Vaux-le-Vicomte, 77950 Maincy,* ☎ *01–64–14–41–90.* ⌨ *56 frs; grounds only, 30 frs.* ⊙ *Château Easter–Nov. 11, daily 10–6. Candlelight visits May–Oct., Sat. 8:30–11 PM (70 frs).*

Dining

$ ✕ **L'Écureuil.** An imposing barn to the right of the château entrance has been transformed into this self-service cafeteria where you can enjoy fine steaks (insist yours is cooked enough), coffee, or a snack beneath the ancient rafters of a wood-beam roof. The restaurant is open daily for lunch and tea, and for dinner during candlelit visits. ⊠ *Château de Vaux-le-Vicomte. Reservations not accepted. MC, V.*

Fontainebleau, Barbizon, and Vaux-le-Vicomte A to Z

Arriving and Departing

BY CAR

From Paris's Porte d'Orléans or Porte d'Italie, take A6, then N7 to Fontainebleau (total distance 72 km/45 mi). Barbizon is 8 km (5 mi) northwest of Fontainebleau. From Fontainebleau take N7; the Barbizon exit is clearly marked. Vaux-le-Vicomte is 21 km (13 mi) north of Fontainebleau. Take N6 to Melun, then N36 northeast (direction Meaux), turning right after 1½ km (1 mi) or so along D215.

BY TRAIN

Fontainebleau is about 50 minutes from Paris's Gare de Lyon; take a bus to complete the 3-km (2-mi) trip from the station (Fontainebleau-Avon) to the château. Vaux-le-Vicomte is a 7-km (4-mi) taxi ride from the nearest station at Melun, served by regular trains from Paris and Fontainebleau. The taxi ride costs about 80–100 francs. Barbizon is not accessible by train.

Guided Tours

Cityrama (☞ Guided Tours *in* Chartres, Maintenon, and Rambouillet A to Z, *above*) and **Paris Vision** (⊠ 214 rue de Rivoli, Paris, ☎ 01–42–60–30–01) run half-day trips to Fontainebleau and Barbizon. The cost is 330 frs and the tours depart Wednesday, Friday, and Sunday at 1:00 or 1:45.

Visitor Information

Barbizon (⊠ 55 Grande Rue, 77630 Barbizon, ☎ 01–60–66–41–87). **Fontainebleau** (⊠ 4 rue Royale, 77300 Fontainebleau, ☎ 01–60–74–99–99).

GIVERNY

The village of Giverny has become a place of pilgrimage for art lovers. It was here that Claude Monet lived for 43 years, until his death in 1926 at the age of 86. After decades of neglect, his pretty pink house with green shutters, the **Maison et Jardin de Claude Monet** (Claude Monet House and Garden), his studios, and his garden with its famous lily pond have been lovingly restored—thanks to gifts from around the world and in particular from the United States. Late spring is perhaps the best time to visit, when the apple trees are in blossom and the garden is a riot of color. Try to avoid summer weekends and afternoons in July and August, when the limited capacity of Monet's home and gardens is pushed to the limit by busloads of tourists.

Monet was brought up in Normandy and, like many of the other Impressionists, was attracted by the soft light of the Seine Valley. After several years at Argenteuil, just north of Paris, he moved downriver to Giverny in 1883 along with his two sons, his mistress Alice Hoschedé (whom he later married), and her six children. By 1890, a prospering Monet was able to buy the house outright. Three years later, he purchased another plot of land across the lane to continue his gardening experiments, diverting the Epte River to make a pond.

Monet's house has a warm family feeling that may come as a welcome break after visiting stately French châteaux. The rooms have been restored to Monet's original designs: the kitchen with its blue tiles, the buttercup-yellow dining room, and Monet's bedroom on the second floor. There are reproductions of his own works, and some of the Japanese prints Monet avidly collected, displayed around the house. His studios are also open for viewing.

The garden, with flowers spilling out across the paths, is as cheerful and natural as the house—quite unlike formal French gardens. The enchanting water garden, with its water lilies, bridges, and rhododendrons, is across the lane that runs to the side of the house and can be reached through a tunnel. The lilies and Japanese bridges became special features of his garden and now help to conjure up an image of a grizzle-bearded Monet dabbing cheerfully at his canvases—capturing changes in light and weather in a way that was to have a major influence on 20th-century art. From Giverny, you may want to continue up the Seine Valley to the site of another of his celebrated painting series: Rouen Cathedral. ⊠ *84 rue Claude-Monet,* ☎ *02–32–51–28–21.* ⊠ *35 frs; gardens only, 25 frs.* ☉ *Apr.–Oct., Tues.–Sun. 10–6.*

The spacious, airy **Musée Américain** (American Museum), endowed by Chicago art patrons Daniel and Judith Terra, displays works by American Impressionists who were influenced by—and often studied with—Claude Monet. ⊠ *99 rue Claude-Monet,* ☎ *02–32–51–94–65.* ⊠ *35 frs.* ☉ *Apr.–Oct., Tues.–Sun. 10–6.*

Dining

$$$ ✕ **Château de Brécourt.** Part of the stylish Relais & Châteaux group, this 17th-century brick château on extensive grounds is outside of Giverny (you'll need a car to get here). The menu, serving creative spins on French cuisine, may include smoked salmon-and-crab cakes, turbot with caviar, and pears in a flaky pastry roasted in honey for dessert. ⊠ *Douains (11 km [7mi] west of Giverny via D181),* ☎ *02–32–52–40–50. AE, DC, MC, V.*

$–$$ ✕ **Les Jardins de Giverny.** This commendable restaurant, a few minutes' walk from Monet's house, has an old-fashioned dining room overlooking a rose garden. On the prix-fixe menus (130, 170, and 230 frs) you may get such inventive dishes as foie gras laced with applejack or seafood terrine with a mild pepper sauce. ⊠ *1 rue Milieu,* ☎ *02–32–21–60–80. AE, V. Closed Mon. and Feb. Dinner Sat. only.*

Giverny A to Z

Arriving and Departing

BY CAR

Take expressway A13 from Paris to the Vernon exit (D181). Cross the Seine in Vernon and follow D5 to Giverny (total distance 84 km/52 mi).

BY TRAIN

Take the train from Paris's Gare St-Lazare to Vernon (50 minutes). Giverny is 5½ km (3½ mi) away by bus or taxi, which you can get at the train station. Call the **Vernon Tourist Office** (☎ 02–32–51–39–60) for information.

Guided Tours

Guided excursions are organized by **American Express** (⊠ 11 rue Scribe, Paris, ☎ 01–47–77–77–37) on either a half-day or full-day basis, combined with trips to Rouen. The **RATP Tourist Office** (⊠ Pl. de la Madeleine, Paris, ☎ 01–40–06–71–45) also arranges tours to Giverny.

REIMS AND LAON

Champagne and cathedrals make a trip to the renowned city of Reims, and the lesser-known hilltop town of Laon, an ideal two-day break northeast of Paris. Both have historic links with royalty: Laon was once capital of France—12 centuries ago—and Reims was the setting for the coronations of the French kings (Charles X's was the last, in 1825).

Reims

Reims is best known as the center of the champagne industry. Several major producers have their headquarters here, and you can visit their chalky, labyrinthine cellars that tunnel beneath the city. Reims cathedral is one of the most historic in France, although restoring it to medieval glory, after its partial destruction during World War I, has taken most of the century. Despite much indifferent postwar rebuilding, Reims is rich with attractions dating from Roman times to the modern era.

The glory of Reims's **Cathédrale Notre-Dame** is its facade. Its proportions are curiously deceptive; the building is actually considerably larger than it appears. Above the north (left) door is the *L'Ange Au Sourire (Smiling Angel)*, a delightful statue whose kindly expression threatens to turn into an acid-rain scowl: Pollution has succeeded war as the ravager of the building. The postcard shops nearby have views of the cathedral after World War I, and on seeing the destruction, you'll understand why restoration here is an ongoing process. The high, solemn nave is at its best in summer, when the lower walls are adorned with 16th-century tapestries relating the Life of the Virgin. The east-end windows were designed by Marc Chagall. With the exception of the 15th-century towers, most of the original building was constructed in the hundred years after 1211. A stroll around the outside gives the impression of harmony and discipline, almost belying all the decorative richness. The east end presents an idyllic vista across well-tended lawns. There are spectacular light shows both inside (40 frs) and outside (free) the cathedral in July and August. ⊠ *Cours Anatole-France.* ☉ *Daily 8–7. Guided tours in English available.*

The **Palais du Tau** (Bishop's Palace), the former archbishop's palace built by Robert de Cotte next to the cathedral in 1690, contains tapestries, coronation robes, and several outstanding statues removed from the cathedral's facade before they fell off. From the upper stories you can get an excellent view of the cathedral. ⊠ *2 Pl. du Cardinal-Luçon,* ☎ *03–26–47–81–79.* ⊡ *32 frs.* ☉ *Apr.–Oct., daily 10–12:30 and 2–6; Nov.–Mar., daily 10–noon and 2–5.*

The **Musée des Beaux-Arts** (Fine Arts Museum) has an outstanding painting collection crowned by 27 Corots and David's celebrated portrait of Revolutionary leader Marat dead in his bath. Nine Boudins and Jongkinds are among the finer Impressionist works here. ⊠ *8 rue Chanzy,* ☎ *03–26–47–28–44.* ⊡ *10 frs.* ☉ *Wed.–Mon. 10–noon and 2–6.*

The 11th-century **Basilique St-Rémi,** devoted to the 5th-century saint who gave his name to the city, is nearly as long as the cathedral; its interior seems to stretch away into the distance. The Gothic choir has retained much of its original 12th-century stained glass. ⊠ *53 rue Simon.* ⊗ *Daily 8–noon and 2–6.*

Several producers run tours of their champagne cellars, combining video presentations with guided walks through their cavernous, chalk-hewn underground warehouses. Few, however, show much generosity when it comes to pouring out samples of bubbly; **Mumm** is an exception. ⊠ *34 rue du Champ-de-Mars,* ☎ *03–26–49–59–69.* ⊗ *Daily 9:30–noon and 2–5; closed weekends Easter–Oct.*

If you don't mind paying for samples, the most spectacular champagne cellars are those of **Taittinger.** ⊠ *34 rue du Champ-de-Mars,* ☎ *03–26–49–59–69.* ⊗ *Daily 9:30–noon and 2–5; closed weekends Easter–Oct.*

The **Chapelle Foujita** opened in 1966 across from the Mumm Cellars. It was decorated by Paris-based Japanese artist Tsuguharu Fujita (1886–1968), a member of the Montparnasse set in the '20s who converted to Catholicism and was baptized in Reims. ⊠ *33 rue du Champ-de-Mars,* ☎ *03–26–40–06–96.* ▣ *10 frs.* ⊗ *Easter–Oct., Thurs.–Tues. 2–6.*

In the well-preserved, map-covered **Salle du 8-mai-1945** (War Room) near the railroad station, Eisenhower established Allied headquarters and the German surrender was signed in May 1945 at the end of World War II. ⊠ *12 rue Franklin-Roosevelt,* ☎ *03–26–47–84–19.* ▣ *10 frs.* ⊗ *Easter–Oct., Wed.–Mon. 10–noon and 2–6.*

The **Porte Mars,** an impressive Roman arch adorned with faded bas-reliefs depicting Jupiter, Romulus, and Remus, looms up just across from the railroad station.

Dining and Lodging

$$$$ ✕ **Boyer.** Gérard Boyer is one of the most highly rated chefs in France; duck, foie gras in pastry, and truffles are among his delicious specialties. The setting, not far from the Basilique St-Rémi, is magnificent, too: a 19th-century château, built for the champagne firm Pommery, surrounded by an extensive, well-tended park. ⊠ *Les Crayères, 64 bd. Henry-Vasnier,* ☎ *03–26–82–80–80. Reservations essential. Jacket and tie. AE, DC, MC, V. Closed Mon. and late Dec.–mid-Jan. No lunch Tues.*

$$–$$$ ▦ **Paix.** A modern, eight-story hotel, 10 minutes' walk from the cathedral, the Paix has stylish rooms with 18th- and 19th-century reproductions, a pretty garden, and a rather incongruous chapel. Its brasserie-style restaurant serves good, though not inexpensive, cuisine (mainly grilled meats and seafood). ⊠ *9 rue Buirette, 51100,* ☎ *03–26–82–80–80,* 𝖥𝖠𝖷 *03–26–47–75–04. 106 rooms. Restaurant, bar, pool. AE, DC, MC, V.*

Laon

The enchanting old town of Laon, known as the Crowned Mountain on account of the many-towered silhouette of its venerable cathedral, is on a spectacular hilltop 40 km (25 mi) northwest of Reims.

The **Cathédrale Notre-Dame** was constructed from 1160 to 1235 and is a superb example of early Gothic architecture. The light interior gives the impression of immense length (120 yards in total). The flat east end—an English-inspired feature—is unusual in France. The second-floor galleries that run around the building are typical early Gothic; you can visit them (and the towers) with a guide from the tourist office on the cathedral square. The airy elegance of the five remaining towers is audacious by any standard and highly unusual: French medieval architects preferred to concentrate on soaring interiors and usually allowed for just two towers at the west end. You don't have to be an architectural scholar to appreciate the sense of movement about Laon's west-end facade compared with the more placid, two-dimensional feel of Notre-Dame in Paris. Look for the stone bulls protruding from the towers, a tribute to the stalwart beasts who carted the blocks of stone from quarries far below.

The medieval **ramparts,** the old fortification walls, lie virtually undisturbed by passing traffic and provide a ready-made route for a tour of old Laon as well as panoramic views of the plains below.

The **Musée de Laon** has a wide array of local and Mediterranean archaeological findings and a variety of pictures and sculpture from the 15th through 19th centuries. The museum grounds contain a notable and well-preserved survivor from medieval times, the **Chapelle des Templiers** (Templars' Chapel)—a small, octagonal 12th-century chapel. ⊠ *32 rue Georges-Ermant,* ☎ *03–23–20–19–87.* ▦ *16 frs.* ☉ *Apr.–Sept., Wed.–Mon. 10–noon and 2–6; Oct.–Mar., Wed.–Mon. 10–noon and 2–5.*

Dining and Lodging

$$ ✕ **La Petite Auberge.** Expect some imaginative nouvelle dishes from chef Willy-Marc Zorn in this 18th-century-style restaurant close to the train station in Laon's *ville basse* (lower town). Pigeon, fillet of plaice with champagne vinegar, and frozen nougat are among the choices. ⊠ *45 bd. Pierre-Brossolette,* ☎ *03–23–23–02–38. AE, MC, V. Closed Aug. No lunch Sat. No dinner Sun.*

$$ ✕▥ **Bannière de France.** In business since 1685, this old-fashioned, uneven-floored hostelry is just five minutes from the cathedral. Madame Lefèvre, the patronne, speaks fluent German and English. Rooms are cozy and quaint. The restaurant's venerable dining room features sturdy cuisine (trout, guinea fowl, lemon sole à la Normande) and good-value, prix-fixe menus. ⊠ *11 rue Franklin-Roosevelt, 02000,* ☎ ℻ *03–23–23–21–44. 18 rooms, 14 with bath or shower. Restaurant. AE, DC, MC, V. Closed late Dec.–early Jan.*

Reims and Laon A to Z

Arriving and Departing

BY CAR

Expressway A4 heads from Paris east to Reims, 144 km (90 mi) away, on its way to Strasbourg. The Belgium-bound N2 links Paris to Laon, 140 km (87 mi) away. The N44 highway links Laon to Reims, a 40-km (25-mi) trip. If you're not in a hurry, leave N44 at Corbény and explore the Chemin des Dames, a hilltop road that played an important frontline role during WWI.

BY TRAIN

Trains run daily between the SNCF stations in Laon and Reims; the trip takes 35–55 minutes. The trip from Paris's Gare de l'Est to Reims takes 90 minutes. The Paris–Laon route (from Gare du Nord, not Gare de l'Est) takes up to 2 hours.

Visitor Information

Laon (⊠ Pl. du Parvis, 02000 Laon, ☎ 03–23–20–28–62). **Reims** (⊠ 2 rue Guillaume-de-Machault, 51100 Reims, ☎ 03–26–77–45–25).

THOIRY

Thoiry, 40 km (25 mi) west of Paris, is an ideal day-trip destination, especially for families with children. It offers a splendid combination of history and culture—chiefly in the form of a superbly furnished 16th-century château with its own archives and gastronomy museum—and outdoor adventure, in the form of a safari park with more than 800 wild animals.

The **Château de Thoiry** was built by Philibert de l'Orme in 1564. Its handsome Renaissance facade is set off by **gardens** landscaped by André Le Nôtre in the disciplined French fashion; in contrast is the less formal **Jardin Anglais** (English garden). Owners Vicomte de La Panouse and his American wife, Annabelle, have restored the château and grounds to their former glory and opened both to the public. Highlights of the interior include the grand staircase; the 18th-century Gobelins tapestry in the dining room, inspired by the adventures of Don Quixote; and the Green and White Salons, with portraits, tapestries, and an old harpsichord.

The distinguished history of the La Panouse family—one member, Comte César, fought in the American Revolution—is retraced in the **Musée des Archives** (Archives Museum), where papal bulls and Napoléonic letters are displayed side by side with missives from Thomas Jefferson and Benjamin Franklin. The château pantries house a **Musée de Gastronomie** (Gastronomy Museum), whose *pièces montées* (banquet showpieces) re-create the designs of the premier 19th-century chef, Antoine Carême (his clients included George IV of England and the emperors of Austria and Russia). One is more than 15 ft high and took eight months to confect. Engravings, old copper pots, and early recipe books are also on display.

You can stroll at leisure around the picturesque grounds, stop off at the Pré Angélique to watch a cricket match (summer weekends) or admire giraffes, wolves, tigers, lions, and elephants in the safari park. There is an exploratory play area for children, featuring giant burrows and cobwebs. For obvious reasons, pedestrians are not allowed into the **Bear Park** or the **African Reserve.** Keep your car windows closed if you want to remain on peaceful terms with marauding lions, rhinos, elephants, and megahorned Watusi cattle. ☎ *01–34–87–52–25.* ⊠ *Château only, 30 frs; château, park, and game reserve, 100 frs.* ☉ *Summer, weekdays 10–6, weekends 10–6:30; winter, daily 10–5.*

Dining

$ ✕ **Commerce.** This bar on Thoiry's main street has an attractive upstairs dining room where locals in the know come for hearty weekday lunches. Start with a first course from the extensive buffet—pâté, salami, and carrot salad are staple favorites—followed by a sturdy main course, such as steak and fries or beef Wellington. ⊠ *Rue de la Porte-St-Martin,* ☎ *01–34–87–40–18. No credit cards. Closed Sat. No dinner.*

$ ✕ **Étoile.** This restaurant, in a dowdy hotel on the main street just 300 yards from the château, has special tourist (which doesn't mean it's bad) and children's menus, as well as a wide selection of à la carte items. Robust, traditional French dishes are served: steak, chicken, fish, and pâté. ⊠ *38 rue de la Porte-St-Martin,* ☎ *01–34–87–40–21. MC, V. Closed Mon.*

Thoiry A to Z

Arriving and Departing

BY CAR
Take highway A13 from Paris; then follow signs for Dreux along A12/ N12. Just past Pontchartrain, D11 heads off right toward Thoiry (total distance from Paris: 44 km/27 mi).

BY TRAIN
Trains run every hour or so from Paris's Gare Montparnasse to Montfort-L'Amaury (the trip takes 35 minutes), which is 8 km (5 mi) from

Thoiry or a 10-minute taxi ride (☎ 01–34–86–01–51 for information). A special shuttle bus operates to and from the château on Sundays in summer (call the château for details).

VERSAILLES

Numbers in the text correspond to numbers on the Versailles map.

Paris in the 17th century was a rowdy, rabble-ridden city. Louis XIV hated it and set about in search of a new power base. He settled on Versailles, 20 km (12 mi) west of Paris, where his father had a small château–hunting lodge.

❶ Today the **Château de Versailles** seems monstrously big, but it wasn't large enough for the army of 20,000 noblemen, servants, and hangers-on who moved in with Louis. A new city—a new capital, in fact—had to be constructed from scratch to accommodate them. Tough-thinking town planners promptly dreamt up vast mansions and avenues broader than the Champs-Élysées—all in bicep-flexing Baroque.

It was hardly surprising that Louis XIV's successors rapidly felt out of sync with their architectural inheritance. The Sun King's successors, Louis XV and Louis XVI, preferred to cower in small retreats in the gardens, well out of the mighty château's shadow. The two most famous of these structures are the Petit Trianon, a model of classical harmony and proportion built by Louis XV; and the Hameau, where Marie-Antoinette could play at being a shepherdess amid the ersatz rusticity of her Potemkin hamlet.

The contrast between the majestic and the domesticated is an important part of Versailles's appeal. But pomp and bombast dominate the mood here, and you won't need reminding that you're in the world's grandest palace—or one of France's most popular tourist attractions. The park outside is the ideal place to get your breath back. Le Nôtre's gardens represent formal landscaping at its most rigid and sophisticated.

The château was built under court architects Le Vau and Mansart between 1662 and 1690; the entrance is through the gilt-and-iron gates from the huge place d'Armes. In the center of the building, across the sprawling cobbled forecourt, are the rooms that belonged to the king and queen. The two wings were occupied by the royal children and princes; attendants were up in the attics.

One of the highlights of the tour is the **Galerie des Glaces** (Hall of Mirrors), fully restored to its original dazzle. It was here that Bismarck proclaimed the unified German Empire in 1871, and the controversial Treaty of Versailles, asserting Germany's responsibility for World War I, was signed in 1919. The **Grands Appartements** (Main Suites) are formal; the **Petits Appartements** (Small Suites), where royal family and friends lived, are on a more human scale. The intimate **Opéra Royal,** the first oval hall in France, was designed for Louis XV. Touch the "marble" loges—they're actually painted wood. The chapel, built by Mansart, is a study in white-and-gold solemnity. In 1997 the former state rooms and the sumptuous debate-chamber of the **Aile du Midi** (South Wing) were opened to the public, with infrared headphone commentary (available in English) explaining Versailles's parliamentary history. ☎ *01–30–84–76–18. ▨ Château 45 frs, parliament exhibition 25 frs extra. ☯ Tues.–Sun. 9–6:30; winter, Tues.–Sun. 9–5:30. Opéra Royal 9:45–3:30 (tours every 15 min).*

❷ The 250-acre **Parc de Versailles** has woods, lawns, flower beds, statues, lakes, and fountains. An extensive tree-replacement scheme—nec-

254

Château, **1**
Grand
Écuries, **5**
Grand
Trianon, **3**
Parc de
Versailles, **2**
Petit
Trianon, **4**

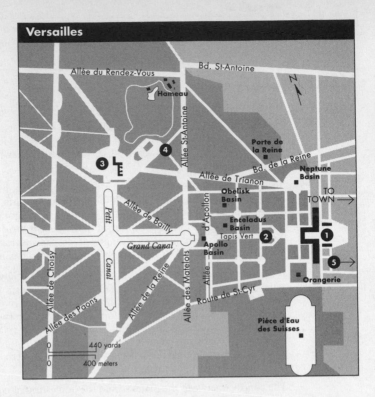

essary once a century (because the trees get too old, big, and un-
wieldy)—was launched at the start of 1998 to recapture the full im-
pact of Le Nôtre's artful vistas. The fountains are turned on Sundays
from May through September, making a fabulous spectacle. ✉ *Free
(25 frs for fountains).* ◷ *Grounds daily 7–dusk.*

③ At one end of the Petit Canal, about 1½ km (1 mi) from the château,
stands the **Grand Trianon**, built by Jules Hardouin-Mansart in the late
1680s. This pink-marble pleasure palace is sometimes used to enter-
tain visiting heads of state; at other times it is open to the public. ✉
25 frs. ◷ *Oct.–Apr., Tues.–Fri. 10–12:30 and 2–5:30; May–Sept.,
Tues.–Sun. 10–6:30.*

④ The **Petit Trianon**, close to the Grand Trianon, is a sumptuously furnished
Neoclassical mansion erected in the 1760s by architect Jacques Gabriel.
Louis XV had a superb botanical garden planted here; some of the trees
from that era survive today. Louis XVI presented the Petit Trianon to
Marie-Antoinette, who spent lavish sums creating an idealized world
nearby, the charming **Hameau**, a hamlet of thatched-roof cottages,
complete with watermill, lake, and pigeon loft. ✉ *15 frs.* ◷ *Oct.–Apr.,
Tues.–Fri. 10–noon and 2–5:30; May–Sept., Tues.–Sun. 10–6:30.*

⑤ Facing the château are the Trojan-sized royal stables, the **Grandes
Écuries** (Great Stables). Nowadays the **Musée des Carosses** is housed
here, with its distinguished array of royal and imperial carriages. ✉ *1
av. de Paris,* ☎ *01-30-21-54-82.* ✉ *20 frs.* ◷ *Weekends 2–6.*

The **town of Versailles** is often overlooked. Although you may be tired
from exploring the palace and park, it's worth strolling along the
town's broad, leafy boulevards. The majestic scale of many buildings
are reminders that this was, after all, the capital of France from 1682
to 1789 (and again from 1871 to 1879). Visible farther to the right,

as you look toward the town from the palace, is the dome of the austere **Cathédrale St-Louis** (⊠ Pl. St-Louis), built from 1743 to 1754; it has a fine organ loft and two-tiered facade.

To the left of Place d'Armes, beyond the elegant, octagonal Place Hoche, is the sturdy Baroque church of **Notre-Dame** (⊠ at rue Hoche and rue de la Paroisse), built from 1684 to 1686 by Jules Hardouin-Mansart as the parish church for Louis XIV's brand-new town. The street in front of Notre-Dame, rue de la Paroisse, leads up to **Place du Marché,** site of a magnificent morning market every Tuesday, Friday, and Sunday. The wide-ranging **Musée Lambinet,** behind Notre-Dame church, is an imposing 18th-century mansion with a maze of cozy rooms furnished with paintings, weapons, fans, and porcelain. ⊠ *54 bd. de la Reine,* ☎ *01–39–50–30–32.* ⊡ *25 frs.* ☉ *Tues.–Sun. 2–6.*

Dining

$$$–$$$$ ✕ **Les Trois Marches.** One of the best-known restaurants in the Paris area, in the Trianon Palace Hotel near an entrance to the château park, serves Chef Gérard Vié's creative dishes such as duckling roasted with vinegar and honey. The prix-fixe (270 frs) weekday lunch is the most affordable option. ⊠ *1 bd. de la Reine,* ☎ *01–39–50–13–21. Reservations essential. Jacket and tie. AE, DC, MC, V. Closed Sun., Mon., and Aug.*

$$–$$$ ✕ **Café Trianon.** In the Trianon Palace Hotel, Chef Benoist Bambaud serves traditional French cuisine: salmon, roast bream, confit de canard, and lamb with rosemary. The prix-fixe menus are your best bet. ⊠ *1 bd. de la Reine,* ☎ *01–30–84–38–47. AE, DC, MC, V.*

$$ ✕ **Quai No. 1.** Barometers, sails, and model boats fill this small seafood restaurant. In summer you can enjoy your meal outside on the terrace. Fish with sauerkraut and home-smoked salmon are specialties; any dish on the two prix-fixe menus is a good value. ⊠ *1 av. de St-Cloud,* ☎ *01–39–50–42–26. MC, V. Closed Mon. No dinner Sun.*

Versailles A to Z

Arriving and Departing

BY CAR

From Paris, head west on highway A13 from Porte d'Auteuil (a total distance of 20 km/12 mi). Allow 15–30 minutes depending on traffic.

BY TRAIN

Three train routes travel between Paris and Versailles (20–30 minutes away). The RER-C to Versailles Rive-Gauche takes you closest to the château (600 yards away via av. de Sceaux). The other trains run from Paris's Gare St-Lazare to Versailles Rive-Droite (closer to the Trianons, but 1 km/¾ mi from the château via rue du Maréchal-Foch and av. de St-Cloud) and from Paris's Gare Montparnasse to Versailles-Chantiers (1 km/¾ mi to the château via rue des États-Généraux and av. de Paris). From Versailles, some trains continue on to Chartres.

Guided Tours

Cityrama (☞ Guided Tours *in* Chartres, Maintenon, and Rambouillet A to Z, *above*) and **Paris Vision** (☞ Guided Tours *in* Fontainebleau, Barbizon, and Vaux-le-Vicomte A to Z, *above*) arrange half- and full-day guided tours of Versailles for 195 or 395 francs.

Visitor Information

Versailles Office du Tourisme (⊠ 7 rue des Reservoirs, 78000 Versailles, ☎ 01–39–50–36–22).

8 BACKGROUND AND ESSENTIALS

Portrait of Paris

Books and Videos

Chronology

Smart Travel Tips A to Z

French Vocabulary

Menu Guide

PARIS À LA PARISIENNE

It is midnight at the neighborhood brasserie. Waiters swathed in starchy white linen glance discreetly at their watches as a family—mother, son, and wife—sip the last of a bottle of Chiroubles and scrape up the remains of their steak tartare on silverware dexterously poised with arched wrists. They are all wearing scarves: The mother's is a classic silk *carré*, tastefully folded at the throat; the wife's is Indian gauze and glitters; the son's is wool and hangs like a prayer shawl over his black turtleneck. Finished, they stir their coffee without looking. They smoke: the mother, Gitanes; the son, Marlboros; the wife rolls her own from a silver case. Alone, they act out their personal theater, uncontrived and unobserved, their Doisneauesque tableau reflected only in the etched-glass mirrors around them, enhanced by the sobriety of their dress and the pallor of their Gallic skin.

Whoever first said that "God found Paris too perfect, so he invented the Parisians," had it wrong. This extraordinary maquette of a city, with its landscape of mansards and chimneys, its low-slung bridges and vast boulevards, is nothing but a rough-sketched stage set that drinks its color from the lifeblood of those infamous Parisians whom everyone claims to hate, but whom everyone loves to emulate.

Mythologized for their arrogance, charm, and savoir faire—as well as their disdain for the foreigners they find genetically incapable of sharing these characteristics—the Parisians continue to mesmerize. For the generations of American and English voyeurs who have ventured curiously, enviously into countless mirrored brasseries, downed numerous bottles of *cuvée maison*, fumbled at nautical knots in newly bought scarves, even suffered squashed berets and unfiltered Gauloises, the Parisian remains inimitable—and infinitely fascinating.

Alternately patronizing and self-effacing, they move through their big-city lives with enviable style and urban grit. They are chronically thin, despite the truckloads of beef stew, pâté, and *tarte Tatin* they consume without blushing. They still make the cigarette look glamorous—and a graceful bit of stage business indispensable to good talk—in spite of the gas-mask levels of smoke they generate. They stride over bridges aloof to the monuments framed in every sweeping perspective, yet they discourse—lightly, charmingly—on Racine, NATO, and the latest ruling of the Académie Française. They are proud, practical, often witty and always chic, from the thrift-shop style of the Sorbonne student to the Chanel suit on the thin shoulders of a well-boned *dame d'un certain âge*.

Ferociously (with some justice) in love with their own culture—theater, literature, film, art, architecture, haute cuisine, and haute couture—Parisians worship France as ardently as New Yorkers dismiss the rest of America. While Manhattanites berate the nonentities west of the Hudson, Parisians romanticize the rest of France, making an art of the weekend foray and the regional vacation: Why should we go *à l'étranger* (abroad) when we have the Dordogne, the Auvergne, and Bretagne?

And for all their vulnerability to what they frame as the "American Assault," for every Disney store, action film, and McDonald's in Paris (not to mention Benetton and Laura Ashley, and France's own Celio, Orcade, and Descamps chains), there is a plethora of unique shops selling all-white blouses, African bracelets, dog jackets, and Art Deco jewelry.

And for every commercial bookstore chain there are five tiny *libraries* selling tooled-leather encyclopedias, collections of out-of-print plays, and yellow paperbacks lovingly pressed in waxed paper. The famous *bouquinistes* hover like squatters along the Seine, their folding metal boxes opening to showcase a treasure trove of old magazines, scholarly journals, and hand-colored botanical prints that flap from clothespins in the wind. Yet they are not nomads, these bouquinistes: Dormant through winter, their metal stands are fixtures as permanent and respectable as those of the medieval merchants that built shops along the Pont Neuf. They are determinedly Parisian—individual, independent, and one-of-a-kind.

But in spite of their fierce individuality, Parisians also demand that certain conformities be followed. And here the gap between native and visitor widens. If Parisians treat tourists a bit like occupying forces—disdainfully selling them Beaujolais-Nouveau in July, seating them by the kitchen doors, refusing to understand honest attempts at French—they have formed their opinions based on bitter experience. The waiter who scorches tourists with flared nostrils and firmly turned back was trained to respect his métier—meaning not pouring Coke with foie gras or bringing the check with dessert. The meal is a sacred ritual here and diverging from the norm is tantamount to disgrace.

Doing as the Parisians do, you can go a long way toward closing the gap of disdain. When dining, for example, give yourself over to the meal. Order a kir as an aperitif, instead of a whiskey or beer. Drink wine or mineral water with your meal. Order coffee *after* dessert, not with it. And accept the fact that diet sodas are rarely available in restaurants.

The wine will come chilled, aired, and ready for tasting with the respect usually reserved for a holy relic. Enjoy each course, sipping, discussing, digesting leisurely; the waiter will not be pressed by hurried tourists. When you're done eating, align your silverware on the plate (a sign for the waiter to clear). Cheese can be the climax of the meal, well worth skipping dessert if necessary, and a magnificent way to finish the wine. Have your coffee after dessert and, without exception, black with sugar; a milky froth will not do on a full stomach. The art of stirring *un express* in Paris rivals the art of scarf-tying.

Ask for *l'addition;* the waiter will not commit the gaffe of bringing the check uninvited. And no matter how deeply you enter into your role as Parisian manqué, avoid saying "Garçon!" (Say "S'il vous plait" instead.) These are rules that apply at the most unassuming corner bistro and the grandest three-star restaurant; following them can thaw the waiterly chill that can render a meal unforgettable—for all the wrong reasons—and can make for meals that are memorable as an evening at the Opéra de la Bastille, complete with sets and choreography.

It is this fixed attention to experience and detail that sets the Parisians apart. Desk-eaters they are not: When they work, they work without a coffee break. When they eat, business still grinds to a halt. Weekends are sacred. And oh, do they vacation, all of them at once, all of them abandoning Paris in August with a fierceness of purpose that mirrors their commitment to food—an all-night drive, a rental booked months in advance.

By matching that Parisian passion for the complete, the correct, the comme il faut, your own experience will be all the more authentic. Having eaten with proper reverence, keep your sightseeing agenda at the same lofty level. If you go to the Louvre, spend the day; do not lope through the wide corridors in search of *La Joconde* (Mona Lisa). You can leave for a three-hour lunch, if you choose, and come back with the same ticket, even avoiding the lines by reentering via the Passage Richelieu. If time won't allow an all-day survey, do as the locals do: Choose an era and immerse yourself. Then take a break and plunge into another.

Eavesdrop on a guided tour. Go back and look at a painting again. And take the time to stare at the ceilings: The architecture alone of this historic monument merits a day's tour.

As you apply yourself to the Parisian experience in spirit, diverge in fact: Walk. The natives may prefer to sit in a café or even hurry straight home by métro (*"métro, boulot, dodo"*— "métro, work, sleep"—as the saying goes). You, as a visitor, are obliged to wander down tortuous medieval streets; up vast boulevards so over-scaled you seem to gain no ground; over bridges that open up broad perspectives on illuminated monuments that outnumber even those in Rome.

They are all there, the clichés of Paris romance: The moon over the Seine reflected in the wake of the Bateaux Mouches; the steps Leslie Caron blushed down in *An American in Paris;* the lovers kissing under the lime tree pollards. But there are surprises, too: a troop of hunting horns striking unearthly sonorities under a resonant bridge; flocks of wild geese flying low over the towers of Notre-Dame; and a ragged expatriate-writer leaving a well-scraped plat du jour on the table as he bolts away from the bill. (*C'est dommage:* He would have been well-fed by Ragueneau, the baker-writer in *Cyrano de Bergerac* who opened his Paris pastry shop to starving poets.)

The more resourceful you are, the more surprises you will unearth in your Paris wanderings. Follow the strains of Lully into a chamber orchestra rehearsal in St-Julien-le-Pauvre; if you're quiet and still, you may not be asked to leave. Brave the smoking lounge at intermission at the Comédie-Française and you'll find the battered leather chair that the young actor Molière sat in as *L'Invalide Imaginaire.* Take the métro to *L'Armée du Salut* (Salvation Army) in the 13e arrondissement, and you'll not only find Art Deco percolators and hand-knit stockings, but you'll also be inside the futuristic curves of a 1933 Le Corbusier masterwork.

Tear yourself away from the big-name museums and you'll discover a world of small galleries. Go in: You don't have to press your nose to the glass. The exhibits are constantly changing and you can always find one relevant to Paris—Frank Horvat's photos of Pigalle or a Christo retrospective, including the Pont Neuf wrappings. It is worth buying one of the weekly guides—*Pariscope, Les Officiels des Spectacles, Figaroscope*—and browsing through it over your *café crème* and croissant.

Resourcefulness, after all, is a sign of enthusiasm and appreciation—for when you are well-informed and acutely tuned in to the nuances of the city, you can approach it as a connoisseur. Then you can peacefully coexist with Parisians, partaking, in their passion for this marvelous old city, from the same plate of cultural riches. Hemingway, as usual, put it succinctly: "It was always pleasant crossing bridges in Paris." Cultural bridges, too.

Bon séjour à Paris.

— Nancy Coons

A frequent contributor to Fodor's, Nancy Coons has written on food and culture for *National Geographic Traveler, Wall Street Journal, Opera News,* and *European Travel & Life.* Based in Luxembourg and France since 1987, she now works out of her 300-year-old farmhouse in Lorraine, which she shares with her husband and two daughters.

WHAT TO READ & WATCH BEFORE YOU GO

Books

For a look at American expatriates in Paris between the wars, read *Sylvia Beach and the Lost Generation* by Noel R. Fitch or *A Moveable Feast* by Ernest Hemingway. Flaubert's *Sentimental Education* includes excellent descriptions of Paris and its environs, as do many Zola novels. Other recommended titles include Charles Dickens's *A Tale of Two Cities,* Henry James's *The Ambassadors,* Colette's *The Complete Claudine,* Hemingway's *The Sun Also Rises,* and Gertrude Stein's *Paris, France.* George Orwell's *Down and Out in Paris and London* gives an account of life on a shoestring in these two European capitals. More essays about Paris are excerpted in *A Place in the World Called Paris.* Yet another anthology of essays on Paris the *Travelers' Tales Guides: Paris.*

Jules Verne's *Paris in the Twentieth Century* provides a view from the past of Paris in the future. A history of Paris from the Revolution to the Belle Epoque is found in Johannes Willms's *Paris: Capital of Europe. A Traveller's History of Paris* by Robert Cole is a good overview. Tyler Stovall's *Paris Noir: African-Americans in the City of Light* is a history of African-Americans in Paris. *Inside Paris* is a photography book of Paris interiors. Two unconventional guides to Paris are Karen Elizabeth Gordon's witty and surreal *Paris Out of Hand* and Lawrence Osborne's unusual *Paris Dreambook.*

Three memoirs by Americans who have lived in Paris are Art Buchwald's *I'll Always Have Paris,* Edmund White's *Our Paris,* and Stanley Karnow's *Paris in the Fifties. Paris Notebooks* by Mavis Gallant is her observations of Paris life. *Between Meals* by A. J. Liebling looks at the art of eating in Paris. *A Corner in the Marais: Memoir of a Paris Neighborhood* is Alex Karmel's history of the neighborhood.

If you're looking for love in Paris, try Henry Miller's *Tropic of Cancer* or *The Diary of Anaïs Nin,* by Miller's lover. For a racy read, take along *Mistral's Daughter* by Judith Krantz. Diane Johnson's *Le Divorce* is a comedy of manners set in Paris. Helen MacInnes's *The Venetian Affair* and Alan Furst's *The World at Night* are spy thrillers that wind through Paris.

Videos

For a glimpse of Paris before you go, rent one of the following films: *A Bout de Souffle* (*Breathless,* 1960; in French), by Jean-Luc Godard, about a car thief who flees with his American girlfriend; *An American in Paris* (1951; in English), a Hollywood musical; *Charade* (1963; in English), a comic thriller starring Cary Grant and Audrey Hepburn; *Diva* (1981; in French), about a singer in Paris who becomes involved in murder and drug smuggling; *La Double Vie de Véronique* (1991; in French), a Krzysztof Kieslowski film about two identical women living in Paris and Poland; *Everyone Says I Love You* (1996; in English), a Woody Allen musical with Paris, New York, and Venice as its backdrop; and *La Femme Nikita* (1990; in French), a noir thriller with Anne Parillaud as a sexy killer.

More films include: *Forget Paris* (1995; in English) with Billy Crystal, and Debra Winger; *French Kiss* (1995; in English), a Lawrence Kasdan comedy with Kevin Kline as a French jewel thief who meets Meg Ryan; *Funny Face* (1957; in English), a Roger Edens musical with Audrey Hepburn and Fred Astaire in Paris; *Last Tango in Paris* (1972; in English), a Bertolucci film starring Marlon Brando; *Ready to Wear* (1994; in English), a Robert Altman film about the fashion industry; *Ronin* (1998; English), an action-thriller directed by John Frankenheimer, with Robert De Niro; *'Round Midnight* (1986; in English and French), a Bertrand Tavernier film about a troubled jazz musician played by Dexter Gordon; *The Tango Lesson* (1997; in English), Sally Potter's film about tango and love in Paris and Buenos Aires; *When the Cat's Away* (1996; in French), Cédric Klapisch's comedy about a woman searching for her cat in Paris; and *Zazie Dans le Métro* (1960; in French), a Louis Malle film about the adventures of a 10-year-old girl in Paris.

PARIS AT A GLANCE

ca. 200 BC The Parisii—Celtic fishermen—live on the Ile de la Cité.

52 Romans establish a colony, Lutetia, on the Ile de la Cité, which soon spreads to both Seine banks. Under the Romans, Paris becomes a major administrative and commercial center, its situation on a low, defensible crossing point on the Seine making it a natural communications nexus.

ca. AD 250 St. Denis, the first bishop of Paris and France's patron saint, is martyred in Christian persecutions.

451 The hordes of Attila the Hun are said to be halted before reaching Paris by the prayers of Ste-Geneviève (died 512); in fact they are halted by an army of Romans and mercenaries. Few traces of the Roman era in Paris remain. Most of those that do are from the late empire, including the catacombs of Montparnasse and the baths that form part of the National Museum of the Middle Ages.

The Merovingian Dynasty (486–751)

507 Clovis, king of the Franks and founder of the Merovingian dynasty, makes Paris his capital. Many churches are built, including the abbey that will become St-Germain-des-Prés. Commerce is active; Jewish and Asian communities are founded along the Seine.

The Carolingian Dynasty (751–987)

Under the Carolingians, Paris ceases to be the capital of France and sinks into political insignificance, but it remains a major administrative, commercial, and ecclesiastical center—and, as a result of the last, one of the foremost centers of culture and learning west of Constantinople.

845–87 Parisians restore the fortifications of the city, which are repeatedly sacked by the Vikings (up to 877).

The Capetian Dynasty (987–1328)

987 Hugh Capet, Count of Paris, becomes king. Paris, once more the capital, grows in importance. The Ile de la Cité is the seat of government, commerce makes its place on the Right Bank, and a university develops on the Left Bank.

1140–63 The Gothic style of architecture appears at St-Denis: Notre-Dame, begun in 1163, sees the style come to maturity. In the late 12th century streets are paved.

1200 Philippe-Auguste charters a university, builds walls around Paris, and constructs a fortress, the first Louvre.

1243–46 The Sainte-Chapelle is built to house the reputed crown of thorns brought by Louis IX (St. Louis) from Constantinople.

1253 The Sorbonne is founded, to become a major theological center.

The Valois Dynasty (1328–1589)

1348–49 The Black Death and the beginning of the Hundred Years' War bring misery and strife to Paris.

1364–80 Charles V works to restore prosperity to Paris. The Bastille is built to defend new city walls. The Louvre is converted into a royal palace.

1420–37 After the battle of Agincourt, Henry V of England enters Paris. Joan of Arc leads an attempt to recapture the city (1429). Charles VII of France drives out the English (1437).

1469 The first printing house in France is established at the Sorbonne.

1515–47 François I imports Italian artists, including Leonardo da Vinci, to work on his new palace at Fontainebleau, bringing the Renaissance to France. François resumes work on the Louvre and builds the Hôtel de Ville in the new style. The Tour St-Jacques (bell tower) is completed (all that now remains of the church of St-Jacques-de-la-Boucherie).

1562–98 In the Wars of Religion, Paris remains a Catholic stronghold. On August 24, 1572, Protestant leaders are killed in the St. Bartholomew's Day Massacre.

The Bourbon Dynasty (1589–1789)

1598–1610 Henri IV begins his reign after converting to Catholicism, declaring "Paris is worth a mass." He embellishes Paris, laying out the Renaissance place des Vosges, first in a new Parisian style of town planning that will last till the 19th century. In 1610, Henri is assassinated. His widow, Marie de' Medici, begins the Luxembourg Palace and Gardens.

1624 Cardinal Richelieu is appointed minister to Louis XIII and concludes the ongoing religious persecution by strictly imposing Catholicism on the country. In 1629 he begins construction of the Palais-Royal.

1635 The Académie Française is founded.

1643–1715 Reign of Louis XIV, the Sun King. Paris rebels against him in the Fronde uprisings (1648–52). During most of his reign, he creates a new palace at Versailles, away from the Paris mobs. It is the largest royal complex in Europe, the symbolic center of a centralized French state. His minister of finance, Colbert, establishes the Gobelins factory-school for tapestries and furniture (1667). André Lenôtre transforms the Jardin de Tuileries (Tuileries Gardens) and lays out the Champs-Élysées (1660s). Louis founds the Hôtel des Invalides (1670).

1715–89 During the reigns of Louis XV and Louis XVI, Paris becomes the European center of culture and style.

1783 New outer walls of Paris are begun, incorporating customs gatehouses to control the flow of commerce into the city. The walls, which include new parks, triple the area of Paris.

The Revolution and the First Empire (1789–1814)

1789–99 The French Revolution begins as the Bastille is stormed on July 14, 1789. The First Republic is established. Louis XVI and his queen, Marie-Antoinette, are guillotined in Place de la Concorde. Almost 2,600 others perish in the same way during the Terror (1793–94). The transformation of Ste-Geneviève's church into the Panthéon is completed.

1799–1814 Napoléon begins to convert Paris into a neoclassical city—the Empire style. The Arc de Triomphe and the first iron bridges across the Seine are built. In 1805 he orders the completion of the Louvre Museum.

1815 The Congress of Vienna ensures the restoration of the Bourbon dynasty following the fall of Napoléon.

1828–42 Urban and political discontent causes riots and demonstrations in the streets. Yet another uprising replaces Charles X with Louis-Philippe's liberal monarchy in 1830. Napoléon's remains are returned to Paris in 1840.

1848 Europe's "Year of Revolutions" brings more turmoil to the Paris streets.

The Second Empire and the Second Republic (1852–70)

1852 In 1852 further additions to the Louvre are made. Under Napoléon III, the Alsatian town planner Baron Haussmann guts large areas of medieval Paris to lay out broad boulevards linking important squares. Railroad stations and the vast covered markets at Les Halles are built.

1862 Victor Hugo's *Les Misérables* is published in Paris while the liberal author remains in exile by order of Napoléon III.

1870–71 Franco-Prussian War; Paris is besieged by Prussian troops; starvation is rampant—each week during the winter, 5,000 people die. The Paris Commune, an attempt by the citizens to take power in 1871, results in bloody suppression and much property damage (the Tuileries Palace is razed). Hugo returns to Paris.

The Third Republic (1875–1944)

1875 The Paris Opéra is inaugurated after 15 years of construction.

1889 The Eiffel Tower is built for the Paris World Exhibition.

1900 The International Exhibition in Paris popularizes the curving forms of Art Nouveau with the entrance for the newly opened Paris métro.

1910 Sacré-Coeur (in Montmartre) is completed.

1914–18 World War I. The Germans come within 9 mi of Paris (so close that Paris taxis are used to carry troops to the front).

1919 The Treaty of Versailles is signed, formally ending World War I.

1925 International Decorative Art exhibition consecrates the restrained, sophisticated design style now known as Art Deco.

1918–39 Between the wars, Paris attracts artists and writers, including Americans Ernest Hemingway and Gertrude Stein.

Paris nourishes Existentialism, a philosophical movement, and major modern art movements—Constructivism, Dadaism, Surrealism.

1939–45 World War II. Paris falls to the Germans in 1940. The French government moves to Vichy and collaborates with the Nazis. The Resistance movement uses Paris as a base. The Free French Army, under Charles de Gaulle, joins with the Allies to liberate Paris after D Day, August 1944.

The Fourth and Fifth Republics (1944–present)

1944–46 De Gaulle moves the provisional government to Paris.

1958–69 De Gaulle is president of the Fifth Republic.

1960s–70s Paris undergoes physical changes: Dirty buildings are cleaned, beltways are built around the city, and expressways are driven through the heart of it. Major new building projects (especially La Défense) are banished to the outskirts.

1962 De Gaulle grants Algeria independence; growing tensions with immigrant workers in Paris and other cities.

1968 Parisian students declare the Sorbonne a commune in riots that lead to de Gaulle's resignation.

1969 Les Halles market is moved and its buildings demolished.

1970s Paris, with other Western capitals, becomes the focus of extreme leftist and Arab terrorist bomb outrages.

1977 The Pompidou Center opens to controversy, marking a high point in modern political intervention in the arts and public architecture.

1981 François Mitterrand (1916–96) is elected president. Embarks on a major building program throughout the city.

1986 Musée d'Orsay opens in the former Gare d'Orsay train station.

1988 President Mitterrand is elected to a second term.

1989 Paris celebrates the bicentennial of the French Revolution. The Grande Arche (La Défense) and the Opéra Bastille are completed. The Louvre's glass pyramid is completed.

1992 Disneyland Paris opens in Marne-la-Vallée near Paris.

1993 After nine years of painstaking renovations by architect I. M. Pei, the Richelieu wing of the Louvre is opened.

1994 Paris–London rail link via Channel Tunnel becomes operational. The Grande Galerie de l'Evolution reopens after 30 years at the Jardin des Plantes. The Champs-Élysées's face-lift is completed.

1995 Mayor Jacques Chirac replaces François Mitterrand as the president of France.

1996 Late President Mitterrand's last large project, the Bibliothèque Nationale François-Mitterrand, the national library, is completed.

1997 President Jacques Chirac calls early elections; a socialist coalition wins the majority, and Lionel Jospin becomes prime minister. The Pompidou Center is closed for two years for renovation.

1998 Amidst scenes of popular fervor not seen since the Liberation in 1944, France hosts and wins the Soccer World Cup. A new museum of Jewish Art and History opens in the Marais. A new métro line links the emerging Bercy sector of east Paris to the heart of the capital.

1999 The Musée des Monuments at Trocadéro and the Conservatoire des Arts et Métiers both reopen after extensive restoration.

2000 Special events mark the new millennium. The Pompidou Center and the Musée Guimet reopen after major renovation.

ESSENTIAL INFORMATION

ADDRESSES

Addresses in Paris are fairly straight-forward: There is the number, the street name and, often, the location in one of Paris's 20 arrondissements (for instance, Paris 75010 or, simply, the last two digits, 10ᵉ, both of which indicate that the address is in the 10th). Due to its large size, the 16th arrondissement has two numbers assigned to it: 75016 and 75116. Occasionally you may see an address with a number plus "bis," for instance, 20 bis rue Vavin: This indicates that 20 bis is the next entrance or door down from 20 rue Vavin.

AIR TRAVEL

BOOKING YOUR FLIGHT

When you book **look for nonstop flights** and **remember that "direct" flights stop at least once.** Try to avoid connecting flights, which require a change of plane.

CARRIERS

➤ MAJOR AIRLINES: **Air France** (☎ 800/237–2747 in the U.S.; 08–02–80–28–02 in France). **American Airlines** (☎ 800/433–7300 in the U.S.; 01–69–32–73–07 in France). **Continental** (☎ 800/231–0856 in the U.S.; 01–42–99–09–09 in France). **Delta** (☎ 800/241–4141 in the U.S.; 01–47–68–92–92 in France). **Northwest** (☎ 800/225–2525 in the U.S., 01–42–66–90–00 in France). **TWA** (☎ 800/892–4141 in the U.S., 08–01–89–28–92 in France). **United** (☎ 800/538–2929 in the U.S.; 08–01–72–72–72 in France). **US Airways** (☎ 800/428–4322 in the U.S.; 01–49–10–29–00 in France).

➤ TRAVEL BETWEEN THE U.K. AND FRANCE: **Air France** (☎ 020/8742–6600 in the U.K.; ☎ 08–02–80–28–02 in France). **Air U.K.** (☎ 0345/666–777 in the U.K.; ☎ 01–44–56–18–08 in France). **British Airways** (☎ 0345/222–111 in the U.K.); ☎ 08–02–80–29–02 in France). **British Midland**

(☎ 020/8754–7321 or 0345/554–554 in the U.K.; ☎ 01–48–62–55–65 in France).

➤ TRAVEL WITHIN FRANCE: **Air France** (☎ 800/237–2747 in the U.S.; 08–02–80–28–02 in France). **Air Liberté** (☎ 08–03–80–58–05)

CHECK-IN & BOARDING

Assuming that not everyone with a ticket will show up, airlines routinely overbook planes. When that happens, airlines ask for volunteers to give up their seats. In return these volunteers usually get a certificate for a free flight and are rebooked on the next flight out. If there are not enough volunteers, the airline must choose who will be denied boarding. The first to get bumped are passengers who checked in late and those flying on discounted tickets, so **get to the gate and check in as early as possible,** especially during peak periods.

Don't forget to **bring your passport**; you will be asked to show it when you check in.

CUTTING COSTS

The least-expensive airfares to Paris must usually be purchased in advance and are non-refundable. It's smart to **call a number of airlines, and when you are quoted a good price, book it on the spot**—the same fare may not be available the next day. Always **check different routings** and look into using different airports. Travel agents, especially low-fare specialists (☞ Discounts & Deals, *below*), are helpful.

Consolidators are another good source. They buy tickets for scheduled international flights at reduced rates from the airlines, then sell them at prices that beat the best fare available directly from the airlines, usually without restrictions. Sometimes you can even get your money back if you need to return the ticket. Carefully read the fine print detailing penalties for changes and cancellations, and **confirm your consolidator reservation with the airline.**

When you **fly as a courier** you trade your checked-luggage space for a ticket deeply subsidized by a courier service. There are restrictions on when you can book and how long you can stay.

You can save on air travel within Europe if you plan on traveling to and from Paris aboard Air France. If you **sign up for Air France's Euro Flyer program,** you can buy between three and nine flight coupons, valid on the airline's flights to more than 100 European cities. At $120 each (April–October) and $99 each (November–March), these coupons are a good deal, and the fine print still allows you plenty of freedom.

➤ CHARTERS: **Tower Air** (☎ 800/348–6937).

➤ CONSOLIDATORS: **Cheap Tickets** (☎ 800/377–1000). **Up & Away Travel** (☎ 212/889–2345). **Discount Airline Ticket Service** (☎ 800/576–1600). **Unitravel** (☎ 800/325–2222). **World Travel Network** (☎ 800/409–6753).

➤ COURIERS: **Air Courier Association** (✉ 15000 W. 6th Ave., Suite 203, Golden, CO 80401, ☎ 800/282–1202, www.aircourier.org). **International Association of Air Travel Couriers** (✉ 220 South Dixie Highway #3, P.O. Box 1349, Lake Worth, FL, 33460, ☎ 561/582–8320, FAX 561/582–1581. www.courier.org). **Now Voyager Travel** (✉ 74 Varick St., Suite 307, New York, NY 10013 ☎ 212/431–1616, FAX 212/219–1753 or 212/334–5243, www.nowvoyagertravel.com).

FLYING TIMES

Flying time to Paris is 7 hours from New York, 9½ hours from Chicago, and 11 hours from Los Angeles. Flying time from the United Kingdom to Paris is 1½ hours.

HOW TO COMPLAIN

If your baggage goes astray or your flight goes awry, complain right away. Most carriers require that you **file a claim immediately.**

➤ AIRLINE COMPLAINTS: U.S. Department of Transportation **Aviation Consumer Protection Division** (✉ C-75, Room 4107, Washington, DC 20590, ☎ 202/366–2220). **Federal Aviation Administration Consumer Hotline** (☎ 800/322–7873).

AIRPORTS & TRANSFERS

Paris's major airports are Charles de Gaulle (also known as Roissy), 26 km (16 mi) northeast of Paris, and Orly, 16 km (10 mi) south of Paris. It doesn't really matter which one you fly into; both are easily accessible to Paris, though Roissy is the only one with a TGV station.

➤ AIRPORT INFORMATION: **Charles de Gaulle/Roissy** (☎ 01–48–62–22–80 in English). **Orly** (☎ 01–49–75–15–15).

TRANSFERS

Charles de Gaulle/Roissy: From the Charles de Gaulle airport, **the least expensive way to get into Paris is on the RER-B line,** the suburban express train, which leaves from beneath Terminal 2 (look for signs for the RER in the airport terminal; you may have to catch the free bus to get to the RER station, which is only a short ride away). Trains to central Paris (Les Halles, St-Michel, Luxembourg) depart every 15 minutes. The fare (including métro connection) is 48 francs, and journey time is about 35 minutes. Note that you have to carry your luggage down to the train tracks, and trains can be crowded if you are traveling during rush hour.

Another way to get into Paris is to **take the Air France bus** between Charles de Gaulle airport and the city (you needn't have flown Air France to use this service). Buses run every 12 minutes between the airport and Montparnasse, as well as between the airport and the Arc de Triomphe, with a stop at the Air France air terminal at Porte Maillot. The fare is 55 francs, and journey time is about 40 minutes. Another option is to **take Roissybus, operated by the Paris Transit Authority,** which runs between Charles de Gaulle and the Opéra every 15 minutes; the cost is 45 francs. Note that you have to hail the bus that you want—it will not stop automatically—and that rush-hour traffic can make the trip slow.

At the airport, **taxis are readily available.** Journey time is around 30 minutes, depending on the traffic, and the average fare is 150–250 francs; ask what the fare will be before getting in the taxi. Expect to pay a 6 franc supplement per piece of luggage. Another option is to **arrange a ride with Paris Airports Service or Airport Shuttle,** which can meet you on arrival in a private car and drive you to your destination (about 120 francs for one person, and 89 francs per additional person).

Orly: From the Orly airport, **the most economical way to get into Paris is to take the RER-C line;** catch the free shuttle bus from the terminal to the train station. Trains to Paris leave every 15 minutes. The fare is 30 francs, and journey time is about 35 minutes. Another option is to **take the monorail service, Orlyval,** which runs between the Antony RER-B station and Orly airport every 7 minutes. The fare to downtown Paris is 57 francs.

You can also **take an Air France bus** from Orly to Les Invalides on the Left Bank; these run every 12 minutes (you need not have flown on Air France to use this service). The fare is 45 francs, and journey time is between 30 and 45 minutes, depending on traffic. The Paris Transit Authority's **Orlybus is yet another option**; buses leave every 15 minutes for the Denfert-Rochereau métro station; the cost is 30 francs.

In light traffic, **taxis take around 25 minutes from Orly to downtown Paris;** the fare will be about 160 francs. Be sure to ask about the fare before getting in the taxi. With advance reservations, **Paris Airports Service or Airport Shuttle can pick you up at Orly** and drive you directly to your destination. If possible make your Airport Shuttle reservations two to three days in advance; MasterCard and Visa are accepted and the operators speak English. Note that prices depend on the total number of people traveling.

➤ TAXIS & SHUTTLES: **Air France Bus** (☎ 01–41–56–89–00 for recorded information in English). **Airport Shuttle** (☎ 01–45–38–55–72, or toll free from the U.S. 888/426–2705). **Paris Airports Service** (☎ 01–49–62–78–78);

BOAT & FERRY TRAVEL

For information about seeing Paris by boat, *see* Sightseeing, *below.*

A number of different ferry and hovercraft routes connect the United Kingdom and France. Driving distances from the French ports to Paris are as follows: from Calais, 290 km (180 mi); from Boulogne, 243 km (151 mi); from Dieppe, 193 km (120 mi); from Dunkerque, 257 km (160 mi). The fastest routes to Paris from each port are via N43, A26, and A1 from Calais and the Channel Tunnel; via N1 from Boulogne; via N15 from Le Havre; via D915 and N1 from Dieppe; and via A25 and A1 from Dunkerque.

➤ DOVER–CALAIS: **Hoverspeed** (✉ International Hoverport, Marine Parade, Dover CT17 9TG, ☎ 01304/240241) operates up to 15 crossings a day by Hovercraft and catamaran. The crossings take 35 minutes (Hovercraft) or 55 minutes (catamaran).

P&O European Ferries (✉ Channel House, Channel View Rd., Dover, Kent CT17 9TJ, ☎ 020/8575–8555) has up to 25 sailings a day; the crossing takes about 75 minutes. **Seafrance** (✉ 23 rue Louis le Grand Paris, France 75002, ☎ 01–44–94–40–40) operates up to 15 sailings a day; the crossing takes about 90 minutes.

➤ FOLKESTONE–BOULOGNE: **Hoverspeed** (☞ Dover–Calais, *above*) is the sole operator on this route, with ten 35-minute crossings a day.

➤ NEWHAVEN–DIEPPE: **Seafrance** (☞ Dover–Calais, *above*) has as many as four sailings a day, and the crossing takes four hours.

➤ PORTSMOUTH–LE HAVRE: **P&O European Ferries** (☞ Dover–Calais, *above*) has up to three sailings a day, and the crossing takes 5½ hours by day, 7½ by night.

BUS TRAVEL TO AND FROM PARIS

It's possible to take a bus (via ferry) to Paris from the U.K.; Eurolines operates a nightly service from London's Victoria Coach Station, via the Dover–Calais ferry, to Paris. France's excellent train service means that long-distance bus service in the country is rare; **regional buses are found mainly where train service is spotty.**

FARES & SCHEDULES

Following are Eurolines bus departures from the U.K. to Paris: departing at 9 AM, arriving at 6 PM; noon, arriving at 9 PM; and 10 PM, arriving at 7 AM. Fares are £60 round-trip (under-25 youth pass £56), £35 one-way. Hoverspeed offers up to four daily departures from Victoria Coach Station. Fares are £60 round-trip, £38 one-way.

➤ BUS COMPANIES: **Eurolines** (⊠ 28 av. Général-de-Gaulle, Bagnolet, ☎ 08–36–69–52–52 in France, 0171/730–3499 in the U.K.). **Hoverspeed** (⊠ International Hoverport, Marine Parade, Dover CT17 9TG, ☎ 01304/240241). **Paris Vision** (⊠ 1 rue d'Auber, 75009 Paris, ☎ 01–47–42–27–40). SNCF (⊠ 88 rue St-Lazare, 75009 Paris, ☎ 08–36–35–35–39 in English).

BUS TRAVEL WITHIN PARIS

Although it's slower than the métro, **traveling by bus is a convenient and scenic way to get around the city.** Paris buses are green and white; route number and destination are marked in front and major stopping-places along the sides. When you want to get off, press the red request button and the *arret demandé* sign will light up. Most routes operate from 7 AM to 8:30 PM; some continue to midnight. Eighteen Noctambus, or night buses, operate hourly (1:30–5:30 AM) between Châtelet and various nearby suburbs; they can be stopped by hailing them at any point on their route.

The brown bus shelters, topped by red and yellow circular signs, contain timetables and route maps. Paris-Visite/Mobilis passes (☞ Métro, *below*) are valid, otherwise it costs 30 francs. Regular buses accept métro tickets, or you can buy a single ticket on board. If you have individual tickets, you should **be prepared to punch one or more tickets in the red and gray machines on board the bus.**

You need to show (but not punch) weekly, monthly, and Paris-Visite/Mobilis tickets to the driver.

The Balabus, a public bus that runs between May and September, gives an interesting tour around the major sights. Terminus: La Défense or Gare de Lyon.

➤ BUS INFORMATION: SNCF (⊠ 88 rue St-Lazare, 75009 Paris, ☎ 08–36–35–35–39 in English).

BUSINESS HOURS

BANKS & OFFICES

During **weekdays, banks are open,** generally 9:30AM–4:30 or 5 PM (note that the Banque de France closes at 3:30) and some banks are also open on Saturday 9–5 as well. In general government offices and businesses are open 9–5. For information about post office hours, *see* Mail Shipping, *below.*

GAS STATIONS

Gas stations in the city are generally open 7:30AM–8PM, though those near the city's *portes* (or principal entranceways) near the *péripherique* (beltway) are open 24 hours a day.

MUSEUMS & SIGHTS

Most **museums close one day a week**—usually either Monday or Tuesday—and on national holidays. Generally, museums and national monuments are open from 10 AM to 5 or 6 PM. A few close for lunch (noon–2) and are open Sunday only in the afternoon. Many of the large museums have one *nocturne* (nighttime) opening per week when they are open until 9:30 or 10 PM.

PHARMACIES

Pharmacies are generally open Monday–Saturday 8:30 AM–8 PM. Those pharmacies that are nearby and open late, 24 hours, or on Sunday are listed on the door. *See* Emergencies, *below,* for information about specific late-night and 24-hour pharmacies.

SHOPS

Generally, **large shops are open from 9:30 or 10 AM to 6 or 7 PM** and don't close at lunchtime. Many of the large department stores stay open until 10 PM on Wednesday or Thursday.

Smaller shops and many supermarkets often open earlier (8 AM) but take a lengthy lunch break (1 PM–3 PM) and generally close around 8 PM; small food shops are often open Sunday mornings, 9 AM–1 PM. Some corner grocery stores stay open until about 10 PM. Most shops close all day Sunday, except some around the Marais, the Bastille, the Latin Quarter, and the Ile de la Cité.

CAMERAS & PHOTOGRAPHY

If you need to get your camera repaired, your best bet is to go to one of the FNAC stores in Paris. Note that it might take some time to have your camera fixed.

➤ CAMERA REPAIR AND PHOTO DEVELOPING: **FNAC** (⊠ 26–30 av. des Ternes, 17ᵉ; in the Forum des Halles, 1–7 rue Pierre Lescot, 1ᵉʳ; 136 rue St-Lazare, 9ᵉ; 157 rue du Faubourg St-Antoine, 11ᵉ).

➤ PHOTO HELP: **Kodak Information Center** (☎ 800/242–2424). *Kodak Guide to Shooting Great Travel Pictures,* available in bookstores or from Fodor's Travel Publications (☎ 800/533–6478; $16.50 plus $4 shipping).

EQUIPMENT PRECAUTIONS

Always **keep your film and tape out of the sun.** Carry an extra supply of batteries, and **be prepared to turn on your camera or camcorder** to prove to security personnel that the device is real. Always **ask for hand inspection of film,** which becomes clouded after successive exposures to airport X-ray machines, and **keep videotapes away from metal detectors.**

FILM & DEVELOPING

The easiest place to get film developed and printed is at one of the various FNAC stores around the city (☞ Cameras & Photography, *above*). Keep in mind that it's expensive to have film developed and printed in Paris—around $20 per 36-exposure roll.

VIDEOS

Video systems are not the same all over the world. The U.S., for instance, uses NTSC and France uses SECAM. Other European countries, including the U.K., use PAL. This means that you probably won't be able to play video tapes from the U.S. in France. You should also **bring extra blank video tapes with you from home** for your camcorder as you may not be able to find compatible tapes in France.

CAR RENTAL

Rates in Paris begin at approximately $70 a day and $200 a week for an economy car with air-conditioning, manual transmission, and unlimited mileage. This does not include tax on car rentals, which is 20.6% or, if you pick it up at the airport, the airport tax. To save money, **make reservations before you go;** you can generally get a much better deal. Note that driving in Paris is best avoided, and parking is very difficult to find. You're better off renting a car only when you want to take excursions out of the city.

➤ MAJOR AGENCIES: **Alamo** (☎ 800/522–9696; 020/8759–6200 in the U.K.). **Avis** (☎ 800/331–1084; 800/879–2847 in Canada; 02/9353–9000 in Australia; 09/525–1982 in New Zealand). **Budget** (☎ 800/527–0700; 0144/227–6266 in the U.K.). **Dollar** (☎ 800/800–6000; 020/8897–0811 in the U.K., where it is known as Eurodollar, 02/9223–1444 in Australia). **Hertz** (☎ 800/654–3001; 800/263–0600 in Canada; 020/8897–2072 in the U.K.; 02/9669–2444 in Australia; 03/358–6777 in New Zealand). **National InterRent** (☎ 800/227–3876; 0345/222525 in the U.K., where it is known as Europcar InterRent).

CUTTING COSTS

To get the best deal **book through a travel agent who will shop around.** Do **look into wholesalers,** companies that do not own fleets but rent in bulk from those that do and often offer better rates than traditional car-rental operations. Payment must be made before you leave home.

➤ WHOLESALERS: **Auto Europe** (☎ 207/842–2000 or 800/223–5555, FAX 800–235–6321). **DER Travel Services** (⊠ 9501 W. Devon Ave., Rosemont, IL 60018, ☎ 800/782–2424, FAX 800/282–7474 for information; 800/860–9944 for brochures). **Europe by Car** (☎ 212/581–3040 or 800/223–1516, FAX 212/246–1458). **Kemwel Holiday Autos** (☎ 914/835–3000 or 800/678–0678, FAX 914/835–5126).

INSURANCE

When driving a rented car you are generally responsible for any damage to or loss of the vehicle. Before you rent see what coverage your personal auto-insurance policy and credit cards already provide.

Collision policies that car-rental companies sell for European rentals usually do not include stolen-vehicle coverage. Before you buy it, check your existing policies—you may already be covered.

REQUIREMENTS & RESTRICTIONS

In France **your own driver's license is acceptable.** An International Driver's Permit is not necessary unless you are planning on a long-term stay; you can get one from the American or Canadian automobile association, and, in the United Kingdom, from the Automobile Association or Royal Automobile Club. You must be 18 years old to drive. To rent a car you must be 21 or older and have a major credit card, though you are charged a 110 franc per day supplement if you're under 25.

➤ AUTO CLUBS: **American Automobile Association** (☎ 800/564–6222). **Automobile Association** (☎ 0990/500–600). **Royal Automobile Club** (☎ 0990/722–722 for membership inquiries, 0345/121345 for insurance).

SURCHARGES

Before you pick up a car in one city and leave it in another **ask about drop-off charges or one-way service fees,** which can be substantial. Note, too, that some rental agencies charge extra if you return the car before the time specified in your contract.

CAR TRAVEL

EMERGENCIES

If your car breaks down on an expressway, **go to a roadside emergency telephone.** If you have a breakdown

anywhere else, find the nearest garage or contact the police.

➤ CONTACTS: **Police** (☎ 17).

FROM THE U.K.

Motorists from the U.K. have a choice of either the Channel Tunnel or the ferry services when traveling to the continent. Reservations are essential at peak times and always a good idea, especially when going via the Chunnel. Cars don't drive in the Chunnel, but are loaded onto trains. ☞ Channel Tunnel, Ferry & Boat Travel, and Train Travel, *below*.

GASOLINE

Gas is expensive and prices vary enormously; anything from 5.80 to 6.80 francs per liter.

PARKING

Finding parking in Paris is very difficult. Meters and ticket machines (pay and display) are common: Make sure you **have a supply of 1-, 2-, 5-, and 10-franc coins.** If you're planning on spending a lot of time in Paris with a car, **it might be a good idea to buy a parking card** (*carte de stationnement*) for 100 francs at any café sporting the red TABAC sign. This card works like a credit card in the parking meters, allowing you to avoid the inconvenience of finding exact change. Note that in August, parking is free in certain residential areas; however, **only parking meters with a dense yellow circle on them indicate free parking in August; if you do not see the circle, pay.** Parking tickets are expensive and there is no shortage of the blue-uniformed parking police. Parking lots, indicated by a blue sign with a white "P" are usually underground and are generally expensive.

ROAD MAPS

France's roads are classified into five types, numbered and prefixed *A* (Autoroute), *N* (Route Nationale), *D* (Route Départementale), *C*, or *V*. Roads marked *A* (Autoroutes) are expressways. There are excellent links between Paris and most French cities. When trying to get around Ile-de-France, it is often difficult to avoid Paris—just **try to steer clear of the rush hours** (7–9:30 AM and 4:30–7:30 PM). A *péage* (toll) must be paid on most expressways: The rate varies but can be steep.

To leave Paris by car, figure out which of the *portes* (gates) correspond to the direction you are going in France. Directions are indicated by major cities and the major highways connect to Paris at these points. For instance, heading north, look for Porte de la Chapelle (direction Lille and Charles de Gaulle Airport); east, for Porte de Bagnolet (direction Metz and Nancy); south, for Porte d'Orléans (diretion Lyon and Bordeaux); and west, for Porte d'Auteuil (direction Rouen and Chartres) or Porte de St-Cloud.

RULES OF THE ROAD

In France, you drive on the right and **yield to drivers coming from streets to the right.** Drive on the right and **yield to drivers coming from streets to the right.** However, this rule does not necessarily apply at roundabouts, where you should watch out for just about everyone. You must **wear your seat belt,** and children under 12 may not travel in the front seat. Speed limits are 130 kph (80 mph) on expressways, 110 kph (70 mph) on divided highways, 90 kph (55 mph) on other roads, 50 kph (30 mph) in towns.

THE CHANNEL TUNNEL

Short of flying, the "Chunnel" is the fastest way to cross the English Channel; only trains travel through it, though cars can be put on trains. For more information, *see* Train Travel, *below.*

CHILDREN IN PARIS

BABY-SITTING

Agencies can provide English-speaking baby-sitters with just a few hours' notice. The hourly rate is approximately $7 (3 hour minimum) plus an agency fee of $10.

➤ AGENCIES: **Ababa** (⊠ 8 av. du Maine, 15ᵉ, ☎ 01–45–49–46–46). **Allo Maman Poule** (⊠ 7 Villa Murat, 16ᵉ, ☎ 01–45–20–96–96). **Baby Sitting Service** (⊠ 18 rue Tronchet, 8ᵉ, ☎ 01–46–37–51–24).

DINING

The best restaurants in Paris do not welcome small children; except for the traditional family Sunday-noon dinner, fine dining is considered an adult pastime. With kids, **you're best off taking them to more casual bistros, brasseries, and cafés**; these also offer the flexible meal times that children often rquire. And if you—or they—get desperate, Paris has its share of McDonald's, Pizza Huts, and other fast-food restaurants.

Many mainstream restaurants have highchairs and serve children's portions *(menu enfant)*, usually spaghetti or the ubiquitous *steak-frites,* a mountain of fries with a thin steak or fat patty of ground beef, usually extremely rare. If you're queasy about this, ask for it *bien cuit* (well done).

If your children go to bed early, opt for your hot meal at noon (there are cheaper prix-fixe menus, too) and consider having a sandwich, quiche, or pizza at a café or brasserie in the early evening; full-service restaurants usually do not serve before 7 PM.

FLYING

If your children are two or older **ask about children's airfares.** As a general rule, infants under two not occupying a seat fly at greatly reduced fares or even for free. When booking **confirm carry-on allowances** if you're traveling with infants. In general, for babies charged 10% of the adult fare, you are allowed one carry-on bag and a collapsible stroller; if the flight is full the stroller may have to be checked or you may be limited to less.

Experts agree that it's a good idea to use safety seats aloft for children weighing less than 40 pounds. Airlines set their own policies: U.S. carriers usually require that the child be ticketed, even if he or she is young enough to ride free, since the seats must be strapped into regular seats. Do **check your airline's policy about using safety seats during takeoff and landing.** And since safety seats are not allowed just everywhere in the plane, get your seat assignments early.

LODGING

Most hotels in Paris allow children under a certain age to stay in their parents' room at no extra charge, but others charge for them as extra adults; be sure to **find out the cutoff**

age for children's discounts. Larger hotels often provide cribs free to guests with young children (this is often not the case in pensions and smaller hotels).

The Novotel chain allows up to two children under 15 to stay free in their parents' room, and many properties have playgrounds. Sofitel hotels offer a free second room for children during July and August and over the Christmas period.

➤ FAMILY-FRIENDLY CHOICES: **Novotel** (☎ 800/221–4542 for international reservations). **Sofitel** (☎ 800/221–4542 for international reservations).

SIGHTS & ATTRACTIONS

Paris has plenty of diversions for the young (noted by a duck icon in the margin throughout this book), and **almost all museums and movie theaters offer discounted rates** to children. *Le Pariscope* and *L'Officiel des Spectacles* are two weekly publications that have sections in English about entertainment for children. The **CIDJ,** the Centre d'Information et de Documentation pour la Jeunesse (Center for Information and Documentation for Young People), also has information about activities and events for youngsters in Paris.

➤ LOCAL INFORMATION: **CIDJ** (✉ 101 quai Branly, 75015 Paris, ☎ 01–44–49–12–00).

SUPPLIES & EQUIPMENT

Supermarkets carry several major brands of diapers (*couches à jeter*), universally referred to as Pampers (pawm-paires). Junior sizes are hard to come by, as the French toilet-train early. There's always plenty of baby food, and pharmacies provide the essentials.

TRANSPORTATION

Getting around **Paris with a stroller can be a challenge,** especially since not all métro stations have escalators. Buses are a better bet in off-peak hours since they are often not as crowded as the métro. Many museums require you to check strollers at the entrance. If you are renting a car don't forget to **arrange for a car seat** when you reserve.

COMPUTERS ON THE ROAD

If you use a major internet provider, getting online in Paris shouldn't be difficult. Call your internet provider to get the local access number in Paris. Many hotels have business services with internet access and even in-room modem lines. You may, however, need an adapter for your computer for the European-style plugs.

➤ ACCESS NUMBERS IN PARIS: **AOL** (☎ 01–41–45–81–00). **Compuserve** (☎ 08–03–00–60–00, 08–03–00–80–00, or 08–03–00–90–00).

➤ INTERNET CAFÉS: **Les Jardins de l'Internet Cybercafé** (✉ 79 rue Bd. St-Michel, 4ᵉ, ☎ 01–44–07–22–20, métro Cluny–La Sorbonne). **Web Bar** (✉ 32 rue de Picardie, 3ᵉ, ☎ 01–42–72–57–47, métro République).

➤ INTERNET PROVIDER IN ENGLISH: **Alma-Net** (✉ 8 rue Dupont des Loges, 2ᵉ, ☎ 01–44–18–70–70, www.alma-net.net).

CONCIERGES

Concierges, found in many hotels, can help you with theater tickets and dinner reservations. You can also turn to your hotel's concierge for help with travel arrangements, sightseeing plans, services ranging from aromatherapy to zipper repair, and emergencies. Always, **always tip** a concierge who has been of assistance (☞ Tipping, *below*).

CONSUMER PROTECTION

Whenever shopping or buying travel services, **pay with a major credit card** so you can cancel payment or get reimbursed if there's a problem. If you're doing business with a particular company for the first time, **contact your local Better Business Bureau and the attorney general's offices** in your state and the company's home state, as well. Have any complaints been filed? Finally, if you're buying a package or tour, always **consider travel insurance** that includes default coverage (☞ Insurance, *below*).

➤ LOCAL BBBs: **Council of Better Business Bureaus** (✉ 4200 Wilson Blvd., Suite 800, Arlington, VA 22203, ☎ 703/276–0100, ℻ 703/525–8277).

COOKING SCHOOLS

Cooking schools in Paris offer half-day to 10-week courses.

➤ COOKING SCHOOLS: **Le Cordon Bleu** (✉ 8 rue Léon Delhomme, 75015 Paris, ☎ 01–53–68–22–50, FAX 01–48–56–03–77, infoparis@cordonbleu.net). **Ritz-Escoffier** (☎ 800/966–5758) in Paris's Ritz hotel.

CUSTOMS & DUTIES

When shopping, **keep receipts** for all purchases. Upon reentering the country, **be ready to show customs officials what you've bought.** If you feel a duty is incorrect or object to the way your clearance was handled, note the inspector's badge number and ask to see a supervisor. If the problem isn't resolved, write to the appropriate authorities, beginning with the port director at your point of entry.

IN AUSTRALIA

Australia residents who are 18 or older may bring home A$400 worth of souvenirs and gifts (including jewelry), 250 cigarettes or 250 grams of tobacco, and 1,125 ml of alcohol (including wine, beer, and spirits). Residents under 18 may bring back A$200 worth of goods. Prohibited items include meat products. Seeds, plants, and fruits need to be declared upon arrival.

➤ INFORMATION: **Australian Customs Service** (Regional Director, ✉ Box 8, Sydney, NSW 2001, ☎ 02/9213–2000, FAX 02/9213–4000).

IN CANADA

Canadian residents who have been out of Canada for at least 7 days may bring home C$500 worth of goods duty-free. If you've been away less than 7 days but more than 48 hours, the duty-free allowance drops to C$200; if your trip lasts 24–48 hours, the allowance is C$50. You may not pool allowances with family members. Goods claimed under the C$500 exemption may follow you by mail; those claimed under the lesser exemptions must accompany you. Alcohol and tobacco products may be included in the 7-day and 48-hour exemptions but not in the 24-hour exemption. If you meet the age requirements of the province or territory through which you reenter Canada, you may bring in, duty-free, 1.14 liters (40 imperial ounces) of wine or liquor *or* 24 12-ounce cans or bottles of beer or ale. If you are 16 or older you may bring in, duty-free, 200 cigarettes and 50 cigars. Check ahead of time with Revenue Canada or the Department of Agriculture for policies regarding meat products, seeds, plants, and fruits.

You may send an unlimited number of gifts worth up to C$60 each duty-free to Canada. Label the package UNSOLICITED GIFT—VALUE UNDER $60. Alcohol and tobacco are excluded.

➤ INFORMATION: **Revenue Canada** (✉ 2265 St. Laurent Blvd. S, Ottawa, Ontario K1G 4K3, ☎ 613/993–0534; 800/461–9999 in Canada).

IN FRANCE

If you're coming from outside the European Union (EU), you may import duty free: (1) 200 cigarettes or 100 cigarillos or 50 cigars or 250 grams of tobacco (twice that if you live outside Europe); (2) 2 liters of wine and, in addition, (a) 1 liter of alcohol over 22% volume (most spirits) or (b) 2 liters of alcohol under 22% volume (fortified or sparkling wine) or (c) 2 more liters of table wine; (3) 50 milliliters of perfume and 250 milliliters of toilet water; (4) 200 grams of coffee, 100 grams of tea; and (5) other goods to the value of 300 francs (100 francs for those under 15).

If you're arriving from an EU country, you may be required to declare all goods and prove that anything over the standard limit is for personal consumption. But there is no limit or customs tariff imposed on goods carried within the EU.

Any amount of French or foreign currency may be brought into France, but foreign currencies converted into francs may be reconverted into a foreign currency only up to the equivalent of 5,000 francs.

➤ INFORMATION: **Direction des Douanes** (✉ 16 rue Yves Toudic, 10ᵉ, ☎ 01–40–40–39–00).

IN NEW ZEALAND

Homeward-bound residents 17 or older may bring back $700 worth of souvenirs and gifts. Your duty-free allowance also includes 4.5 liters of wine or beer; one 1,125-ml bottle of spirits; and either 200 cigarettes, 250 grams of tobacco, 50 cigars, or a combination of the three up to 250 grams. Prohibited items include meat products, seeds, plants, and fruits.

➤ INFORMATION: **New Zealand Customs** (Custom House, ✉ 50 Anzac Ave., Box 29, Auckland, New Zealand, ☎ 09/359–6655, FAX 09/ 359–6732).

IN THE U.K.

If you are a U.K. resident and your journey was wholly within the European Union (EU), you won't have to pass through customs when you return to the United Kingdom. If you plan to bring back large quantities of alcohol or tobacco, check EU limits beforehand.

➤ INFORMATION: **HM Customs and Excise** (✉ Dorset House, Stamford St., Bromley Kent BR1 1XX, ☎ 020/ 7202–4227).

IN THE U.S.

U.S. residents who have been out of the country for at least 48 hours (and who have not used the $400 allowance or any part of it in the past 30 days) may bring home $400 worth of foreign goods duty-free.

U.S. residents 21 and older may bring back 1 liter of alcohol duty-free. In addition, regardless of your age, you are allowed 200 cigarettes and 100 non-Cuban cigars. Antiques, which the U.S. Customs Service define as objects more than 100 years old, enter duty-free, as do original works of art done entirely by hand.

You may also send packages home duty-free: up to $200 worth of goods for personal use, with a limit of one parcel per addressee per day (and no alcohol or tobacco products or perfume worth more than $5); label the package PERSONAL USE and attach a list of its contents and their retail value. Do not label the package UNSOLICITED GIFT or your duty-free exemption will drop to $100. Mailed items do not affect your duty-free allowance on your return.

➤ INFORMATION: **U.S. Customs Service** (inquiries, ✉ 1300 Pennsylvania Ave. NW, Washington, DC 20229, ☎ 202/927–6724; complaints, ✉ Office of Regulations and Rulings, 1300 Pennsylvania Ave. NW, Washington, DC 20229; registration of equipment, ✉ Resource Management, 1300 Pennsylvania Ave. NW, Washington, DC 20229, ☎ 202/927–0540).

DINING

For information on mealtimes, reservations, what to wear, and specific restaurants, *see* Chapter 3. The restaurants we list are the cream of the crop in each price category.

DISABILITIES & ACCESSIBILITY

Although the city of Paris is doing much to ensure that public facilities accommodate people with mobility difficulties, it still has a long way to go. Some sidewalks now have low curbs, and many arrondissements have public rest rooms and telephone boxes that are wheelchair accessible.

➤ LOCAL RESOURCES: **Association des Paralysés de France** (✉ 17 bd. Auguste-Blanqui, 75013 Paris, ☎ 01–40–78–69–00) for a list of Paris hotels. **Comité Nationale Français de Liaison pour la Réadaptation des Handicapés** (✉ 236-B rue de Tolbiac, 75013 Paris, ☎ 01–53–80–66–66).

LODGING

When discussing accessibility with an operator or reservations agent **ask hard questions.** Are there any stairs, inside *or* out? Are there grab bars next to the toilet *and* in the shower/tub? How wide is the doorway to the room? To the bathroom? For the most extensive facilities meeting the latest legal specifications **opt for newer accommodations.** Some hotels, particularly those constructed in the past decade, are equipped with ramps, elevators, and special toilet facilities. It's a good idea, however, to ask about elevators, since many smaller, older hotels do not have them, or if they do, they are tiny.

SIGHTS & ATTRACTIONS

Some monuments and museums, especially those constructed in the past decade, are equipped with ramps, elevators, and special toilet facilities. However, it is best to **ask about access** before you go.

TRANSPORTATION

Not many métro and RER stations are wheelchair accessible, nor are many buses, though the French government is working to change this: in early 1999 work was started to ensure that by the year 2002 all major transportation centers will be accessible. For information about accessibility, **get the RER and métro access guide,** available at most stations and from the Paris Transit Authority. For now, the SNCF has special cars on some trains that have been reserved exclusively for people using wheelchairs and can arrange for those passengers to be escorted on and off trains and assisted in making connections (the latter service must, however, be requested in advance). Taxi drivers are required by law to assist travelers with disabilities in and out of their vehicles.

The Airhop shuttle company runs adapted vehicles to and from the airports; Orly–Paris costs 180F and Charles de Gaulle–Paris costs 250F; this service is available Monday through Friday only. Reservations (in French) must be made in advance. Note that you must pay 15 francs for every 15 minutes there is a delay.

➤ LOCAL RESOURCES: **Airhop** (☎ 01–41–29–01–29). **Paris Transit Authority** (RATP) kiosk (✉ 54 Quai de la Rapée, 75599 Cedex 12, ☎ 08–36–68–77–14).

➤ COMPLAINTS: **Disability Rights Section** (✉ U.S. Department of Justice, Civil Rights Division, Box 66738, Washington, DC 20035-6738, ☎ 202/514–0301; 800/514–0301; 202/514–0301 TTY; 800/514–0301 TTY, FAX 202/307–1198) for general complaints. **Aviation Consumer Protection Division** (☞ Air Travel, *above*) for airline-related problems.

TRAVEL AGENCIES

In the United States, although the Americans with Disabilities Act requires that travel firms serve the needs of all travelers, some agencies specialize in working with people with disabilities.

➤ TRAVELERS WITH MOBILITY PROBLEMS: **Accessible Vans of the Rockies, Activity and Travel Agency** (✉ 2040 W. Hamilton Pl., Sheridan, CO 80110, ☎ 303/806–5047 or 888/837–0065, FAX 303/781–2329). **CareVacations** (✉ 5-5110 50th Ave., Leduc, Alberta T9E 6V4, ☎ 780/986–6404 or 780/986–8332) has group tours and is especially helpful with cruise vacations. **Flying Wheels Travel** (✉ 143 W. Bridge St., Box 382, Owatonna, MN 55060, ☎ 507/451–5005 or 800/535–6790, FAX 507/451–1685). **Hinsdale Travel Service** (✉ 201 E. Ogden Ave., Suite 100, Hinsdale, IL 60521, ☎ 630/325–1335).

➤ TRAVELERS WITH DEVELOPMENTAL DISABILITIES: **Sprout** (✉ 893 Amsterdam Ave., New York, NY 10025, ☎ 212/222–9575 or 888/222–9575, FAX 212/222–9768).

DISCOUNTS & DEALS

Be a smart shopper and **compare all your options** before making decisions. A plane ticket bought with a promotional coupon from travel clubs, coupon books, and direct-mail offers may not be cheaper than the least expensive fare from a discount ticket agency. And always keep in mind that what you get is just as important as what you save.

Paris Tourist Offices, railroad stations, major métro stations, and participating museums sell the *Carte Musées et Monuments* (Museums and Monuments Pass), which offers unlimited access to more than 65 museums and monuments in Paris over a one-, three-, or five- consecutive day period; the cost, respectively, is 80, 160, and 240 francs. Temporary exhibitions are not included in this pass. This pass is beneficial if you are going to visit many museums and monuments in a short amount of time; also, it may allow you access to museums and monuments without having to wait in line. However, if don't plan on seeing that many museums or monuments, you may be better off paying per sight. *See also* Métro *and* Train Travel, *below,* for information on métro and train passes.

DISCOUNT RESERVATIONS

To save money **look into discount-reservations services** with toll-free numbers, which use their buying power to get a better price on hotels, airline tickets, even car rentals. When booking a room, always **call the hotel's local toll-free number** (if one is available) rather than the central reservations number—you'll often get a better price. Always ask about special packages or corporate rates.

When shopping for the best deal on hotels and car rentals **look for guaranteed exchange rates,** which protect you against a falling dollar. With your rate locked in, you won't pay more, even if the price goes up in the local currency.

➤ AIRLINE TICKETS: ☎ 800/FLY–4–LESS. ☎ 800/FLY–ASAP.

➤ HOTEL ROOMS: **Hotel Reservations Network** (☎ 800/964–6835). **International Marketing & Travel Concepts** (☎ 800/790–4682). **Steigenberger Reservation Service** (☎ 800/223–5652). **Travel Interlink** (☎ 800/888–5898).

PACKAGE DEALS

Don't confuse packages and guided tours. When you buy a package, you travel on your own, just as though you had planned the trip yourself. Fly/drive packages, which combine airfare and car rental, can be a good deal. In cities, ask the local visitor's bureau about hotel packages that include tickets to major museum exhibits or other special events. If you **buy a rail/drive pass** you may save on train tickets and car rentals. All Eurail- and Europass holders get a discount on Eurostar fares through the Channel Tunnel.

ELECTRICITY

To use your U.S.-purchased electric-powered equipment **bring a converter and adapter.** The electrical current in France is 220 volts, 50 cycles alternating current (AC); wall outlets take continental-type plugs, with two round prongs.

If your appliances are dual-voltage you'll need only an adapter. Don't use 110-volt outlets, marked FOR SHAVERS ONLY, for high-wattage appliances such as blow-dryers. Most laptops operate equally well on 110 and 220 volts and so require only an adapter.

EMBASSIES

➤ AUSTRALIA: ✉ 4 rue Jean-Rey, Paris, 15ᵉ, ☎ 01–40–59–33–00, métro Bir Hakeim, ☾ weekdays 9:15–12:15.

➤ CANADA: ✉ 35 av. Montaigne, Paris, 8ᵉ, ☎ 01–44–43–29–00, métro Franklin-D.-Roosevelt, ☾ weekdays 8:30–11.

➤ NEW ZEALAND: ✉ 7 ter rue Léonardo da Vinci, Paris, 16ᵉ, métro Victor Hugo ☎ 01–45–00–24–11, ☾ weekdays 9–1.

➤ UNITED KINGDOM: ✉ 35 rue du Faubourg-St-Honoré, Paris, 8ᵉ, ☎ 01–44–51–31–00, ☾ métro Madeleine, ☾ weekdays 9:30–12:30 and 2:30–5.

➤ UNITED STATES: ✉ 2 rue St-Florentin, Paris, 1ᵉʳ, ☎ 01–43–12–22–22 in English or ☎ 01–43–12–23–47 in emergencies, métro Concorde, ☾ weekdays 9–3.

EMERGENCIES

The American Hospital and the Hertford British Hospital both have 24-hour emergency service. Many doctors and dentists will also make house calls. Locals usually call the fire department first in all kinds of emergency situations as it has fully trained paramedics and is very efficient. Locals call the police if there has been a crime or an act of violence. Pharmacies also can be of help; often those in major tourist areas speak some English.

➤ DOCTORS & DENTISTS: **Dentists** (☎ 01–43–37–51–00). **Doctors** (☎ 01–47–07–77–77).

➤ EMERGENCY SERVICES: **Ambulance** (☎ 15 or ☎ 01–45–67–50–50). **Fire Department** (☎ 18). **Police** (☎ 17).

➤ HOSPITALS: **The American Hospital** (✉ 63 bd. Victor Hugo, Neuilly, ☎ 01–46–41–25–25). **The Hertford British Hospital** (✉ 3 rue Barbès, Levallois-Perret, ☎ 01–46–39–22–22).

➤ HOTLINES: **FACTS–Line** I ☎ 01–47–23–80–80, ☾ Mon., Wed., Fri., 6–10PM offers HIV/AIDS support in English. **SOS Help** (☎ 01–47–23–80–80, ☾ 3–11PM) is an English-language crisis line.

➤ LATE-NIGHT AND 24-HOUR PHARMA-CIES: **Dhéry** (✉ Galerie des Champs, 84 av. des Champs-Élysées, 8ᵉ, ☎ 01–45–62–02–41) is open 24 hours. **Pharmacie des Arts** (✉ 106 bd. Montparnasse, 14ᵉ) is open daily until midnight. **Pharmacie Matignon** (✉ rue Jean Mermoz, at the Rond-Point de Champs-Élysées, 8ᵉ) is open daily until 2 AM.

ENGLISH-LANGUAGE MEDIA

BOOKS

For information about bookstores in Paris, *see* Specialty Shops *in* Chapter 6. The American Library in Paris is another resource for English-language books; it's open Tuesday–Saturday 10–7.

➤ LIBRARY: **American Library** (✉ 10 rue du Général Ganou, 7ᵉ, ☎ 01–53–59–12–60).

NEWSPAPERS & MAGAZINES

A number of free magazines in English, with all kinds of listings, including events, bars, restaurants, shops, films, and museums, are available in Paris. Look for *Time Out Paris, FUSAC, The Paris Free Voice,* and *Irish Eyes.* Besides a large variety of French newspapers and magazines, all kinds of English-language newspapers and magazines can be found at newsstands, especially in major tourist areas, including: *The International Herald Tribune, USA Today, The New York Times, The European Financial Times, The Times* of London, *Newsweek, The Economist, Vogue,* and *Elle.*

TELEVISION & RADIO

Turn on the television and you'll notice many American shows dubbed into French (Canal Jimmy, Channel 8, shows American shows in their original, undubbed format). France has both national stations (TF1, France 2, France 3, La Cinq/Arte, and M6) and cable stations (most notably Canal+, France's version of HBO). Every morning at 7:05 AM, ABC News (from the night before) is aired. You can also find CNN, BBC World, and BBC Prime on cable.

Radio in France is an eclectic mix, with more variety of music than you'd expect. Most stations broadcast in French. A number play Top 40 music, including: Cherie FM (91.3), Skyrock (96), NRJ (100.3), Radio Nova (101.5), and Fun Radio (101.9). A variety of music can be found on FIP (105.1); classical on Radio Classique (101.1); '60s–'90s on Nostalgie (90.4); techno on Radio FG (98.2); and the news (in French) on France Info (105.5).

GAY & LESBIAN TRAVEL

In Paris, several gay and lesbian organizations provide information on events, medical care, and counseling. A number of informative newspapers and magazines that cover the Parisian gay/lesbian scene are available at stores and kiosks in the city, including *TETU, Gai Guide, Gai Pied Hebdo,* and *Lesbia.*

➤ GAY- AND LESBIAN-FRIENDLY TRAVEL AGENCIES: **Different Roads Travel** (✉ 8383 Wilshire Blvd., Suite 902, Beverly Hills, CA 90211, ☎ 323/651–5557 or 800/429–8747, FAX 323/651–3678). **Kennedy Travel** (✉ 314 Jericho Turnpike, Floral Park, NY 11001, ☎ 516/352–4888 or 800/237–7433, FAX 516/354–8849). **Now Voyager** (✉ 4406 18th St., San Francisco, CA 94114, ☎ 415/626–1169 or 800/255–6951, FAX 415/626–8626). **Yellowbrick Road** (✉ 1500 W. Balmoral Ave., Chicago, IL 60640, ☎ 773/561–1800 or 800/642–2488, FAX 773/561–4497). **Skylink Travel and Tour** (✉ 1006 Mendocino Ave., Santa Rosa, CA 95401, ☎ 707/546–9888 or 800/225–5759, FAX 707/546–9891), serving lesbian travelers.

➤ ORGANIZATIONS: **Agora** (✉ 33 bd. Picpus, 12ᵉ, ☎ 01–43–42–19–02) provides information on events, meetings, and rallies. **Association des Médecins Gais** (☎ 01–48–05–81–71) and **Ecoute Gaie** (☎ 01–44–93–01–02 after 6 PM) give advice and information over the phone. **Centre Gai et Lesbien** (✉ 3 rue Keller, 11ᵉ, ☎ 01–43–57–21–47).

HEALTH

For information on doctors and hospitals in Paris, *see* Emergencies, *above.*

HOLIDAYS

With 11 national holidays (*jours fériés*) and 5 weeks of paid vacation, the French have their share of repose. In May, there is a holiday nearly every week, so be prepared for stores, banks, and museums to shut their doors for days at a time. But some exchange booths in tourist areas, small grocery stores, restaurants, cafés, and bakeries usually remain open. Bastille Day (July 14) is observed in true French form. Celebrations begin on the evening of the 13th and finish the next day with an annual military parade.

January 1 (New Year's Day); April 3 (Easter Monday); May 1 (Labor Day); May 8 (VE Day); May 13 (Ascension); May 22 (Pentecost Monday); July 14 (Bastille Day); August 15 (Assumption); November 1 (All Saints); November 11 (Armistice); December 25 (Christmas).

INSURANCE

The most useful travel insurance plan is a comprehensive policy that includes coverage for trip cancellation and interruption, default, trip delay, and medical expenses (with a waiver for preexisting conditions).

If you're traveling internationally, a key component of travel insurance is coverage for medical bills incurred if you get sick on the road. Such expenses are not generally covered by Medicare and by some private policies. U.K. residents can buy a travel-insurance policy valid for most vacations taken during the year in which it's purchased (but check preexisting-condition coverage). British and Australian citizens need extra medical coverage when traveling overseas.

Always **buy travel policies directly from the insurance company**; if you buy it from a cruise line, airline, or tour operator that goes out of business you probably will not be covered for the agency or operator's default, a major risk. Before you make any purchase **review your existing health and home-owner's policies** to find what they cover away from home.

➤ TRAVEL INSURERS: In the U.S. **Access America** (✉ 6600 W. Broad St., Richmond, VA 23230, ☎ 804/285–3300 or 800/284–8300), **Travel Guard International** (✉ 1145 Clark St., Stevens Point, WI 54481, ☎ 715/345–0505 or 800/826–1300). In Canada **Voyager Insurance** (✉ 44 Peel Center Dr., Brampton, Ontario L6T 4M8, ☎ 905/791–8700; 800/668–4342 in Canada).

➤ INSURANCE INFORMATION: In the U.K. the **Association of British Insurers** (✉ 51–55 Gresham St., London EC2V 7HQ, ☎ 020/7600–3333, FAX 020/7696–8999). In Australia the **Insurance Council of Australia** (☎ 03/9614–1077, FAX 03/9614–7924).

LANGUAGE

The French may appear prickly at first to English-speaking visitors. But it usually helps if you **make an effort to speak a little French.** A simple, friendly *bonjour* (hello) will do, as will asking if the person you are greeting speaks English (*Parlez-vous anglais?*). Be patient, and speak English slowly. *See* the French Vocabulary and Menu Guide at the back of the book, for more suggestions.

LANGUAGES FOR TRAVELERS

A phrase book and language-tape set can help get you started.

➤ PHRASE BOOKS & LANGUAGE-TAPE SETS: *Fodor's French for Travelers* (☎ 800/733–3000 in the U.S.; 800/668–4247 in Canada; $7 for phrasebook, $16.95 for audio set).

LODGING

The lodgings we list are the cream of the crop in each price category. We always list the facilities that are available—but we don't specify whether they cost extra: When pricing accommodations, always ask what's included and what costs extra.

Assume that hotels operate on the European Plan (EP, with no meals) unless we specify that they use the Continental Plan (CP, with a Continental breakfast daily), Modified American Plan (MAP, with breakfast and dinner daily), or the Full American Plan (FAP, with all meals).

APARTMENT RENTALS

If you want a home base that's roomy enough for a family and comes with cooking facilities **consider a furnished rental.** These can save you money, especially if you're traveling with a group. You might also look in the bimonthly journal *France-USA Contacts* (known as *FUSAC*), which lists rentals as well as apartment exchanges.

➤ INTERNATIONAL AGENTS: **At Home Abroad** (✉ 405 E. 56th St., Suite 6H, New York, NY 10022, ☎ 212/421–9165, FAX 212/752–1591). **At Home in France** (✉ P.O. Box 643, Ashland, OR, 97520, ☎ 541/488–9467, FAX 541/488–9468, www.athomein-france.com). **Drawbridge to Europe** (✉ 5456 Adams Rd., Talent, OR 97540, ☎ 541/512–8927 or 888/268–1148, FAX 541/512–0978). **El Sol** (✉ P.O. Box 329, Wayne, PA 19087, ☎ 610/353–2335, FAX 610/353–7756 **Idyll** (✉ P.O. Box 405, Media, PA 19063, ☎ 888/868–6871, FAX 610/565–5142, www.untours.com). **Interhome** (✉ 1990 N.E. 163rd St., Suite 110, Miami Beach, FL 33162, ☎ 305/940–2299 or 800/882–6864, FAX 305/940–2911). **Orion** (✉ 30 Pl. d'Italie, 75013, ☎ 01–40–78–54–54; 800/546–4777, 212/688–9538 in the U.S., FAX 01–40–78–54–55; 212/688–9467 in the U.S.). **Paris Appartements Services** (✉ 69 rue d'Argout, 75002, ☎ 01–40–28–01–28, FAX 01–40–28–92–01). **Rental Directories International** (✉ 2044 Rittenhouse Sq., Philadelphia, PA 19103, ☎ 215/985–4001, FAX 215/985–0323). **Rent-a-Home International** (✉ 7200 34th Ave. NW, Seattle, WA 98117, ☎ 206/789–9377, FAX 206/789–9379). **Unitour** (✉ Idyll Ltd, P.O. Box 405, Media PA 19063, ☎ 888/868–6871, FAX 610/565–5142). **Vacation Home Rentals Worldwide** (✉ 235 Kensington Ave., Norwood, NJ 07648, ☎ 201/767–9393 or 800/633–3284, FAX 201/767–5510). **Villas and Apartments Abroad** (✉ 420 Madison Ave., Suite 1003, New York, NY 10017, ☎ 212/759–1025 or 800/433–3020, FAX 212/755–8316). **Villas International** (✉ 950 Northgate Dr., Suite 206, San Rafael, CA 94903, ☎ 415/499–9490 or 800/221–2260, FAX 415/499–9491). **Ville et Village** (✉ 2124 Kittredge St., Suite 200 Berkeley, CA, ☎ 510/559–8080; FAX 510/559–8217). **Hideaways International** (✉ 767 Islington St., Portsmouth, NH 03801, ☎ 603/430–4433 or 800/843–4433, FAX 603/430–4444; membership $99).

➤ LOCAL AGENTS: *See* Chapter 3.

➤ RENTAL LISTINGS: **FUSAC** (✉ 326 rue Bénard, Paris 75014, ☎ 01–56–53–54–54; Box 115, Cooper Station, New York, NY, 10276, ☎ 212/929–2929).

B&BS

Bed & Breakfasts are beginning to open in Paris, though they are not as prevalent as in London or elsewhere.

➤ RESERVATION SERVICES: **Paris Bed & Breakfast** (☎ 800/872–2632).

HOME EXCHANGES

If you would like to exchange your home for someone else's **join a home-exchange organization.** It's up to you to make specific arrangements. You can also find listings in FUSAC (☞ Apartment Rentals, *above*).

➤ EXCHANGE CLUBS: **HomeLink International** (✉ Box 650, Key West, FL 33041, ☎ 305/294–7766 or 800/638–3841, FAX 305/294–1448; $88 per year). **Intervac U.S.** (✉ Box 590504, San Francisco, CA 94159, ☎ 800/756–4663, FAX 415/435–7440; $83 per year).

HOSTELS

No matter what your age you can **save on lodging costs by staying at hostels.** Hostelling International (HI), the umbrella group for a number of national youth-hostel associations, offers single-sex, dorm-style beds and, at many hostels, couples rooms and family accommodations. Membership in any HI national hostel association, open to travelers of all ages, allows you to stay in HI-affiliated hostels at member rates (one-year membership in the U.S. $25, in Canada C$26.75, in the U.K. £9.30, in Australia $44, in New Zealand $24; hostels run about $10–$25 per night). Members also have priority if the hostel is full; they're eligible for discounts around the world, even on rail and bus travel in some countries.

➤ ORGANIZATIONS: **Australian Youth Hostel Association** (✉ 10 Mallett St., Camperdown, NSW 2050, ☎ 02/9565–1699, ℻ 02/9565–1325). **Hostelling International—American Youth Hostels** (✉ 733 15th St. NW, Suite 840, Washington, DC 20005, ☎ 202/783–6161, ℻ 202/783–6171). **Hostelling International—Canada** (✉ 400–205 Catherine St., Ottawa, Ontario K2P 1C3, ☎ 613/237–7884, ℻ 613/237–7868). **Paris Youth Hostel Central Booking Office** (✉ 4 Bd. Jules Ferry, Paris 75011, ☎ 01–45–57–55–60). **Youth Hostel Association of England and Wales** (✉ Trevelyan House, 8 St. Stephen's Hill, St. Albans, Hertfordshire AL1 2DY, ☎ 01727/855215 or 01727/845047, ℻ 01727/844126). **Youth Hostels Association of New Zealand** (✉ Box 436, Christchurch, New Zealand, ☎ 03/379–9970, ℻ 03/365–4476).

HOTELS

It's always a good idea to **make hotel reservations in Paris as far in advance as possible,** especially in late spring, summer, and fall. Faxing is the easiest way to contact the hotel (the staff is probably more likely to read English than to understand it over the phone long distance), though calling also works. In your fax (or over the phone), specify the exact dates that you want to stay at the hotel (when you will arrive and when you will check out); the size of the room you want and how many people will be sleeping there; what kind of bed you want (two twins, double, etc.); and what kind of bathroom (private with shower or bath, or both). You might also ask if a deposit (or your credit card number) is required and, if so, what happens if you cancel. Request that the hotel fax you back so that you have a written confirmation of your reservation in hand when you arrive at the hotel.

If you arrive in Paris without a reservation, the tourist offices in major train stations may be able to help you.

You may be able to get a better rate per night if you are staying a week or longer; ask.

Note that the quality of accommodations, particularly older properties and even in luxury hotels, can vary from room to room; **if you don't like the room you're given, ask to see another.**

In addition to smaller properties and luxury hotels, Paris has—but is not dominated by—big chains. Examples in the upper price bracket are Frantel, Hilton, Hyatt, Marriott, and Novotel. The Best Western, Campanile, Climat de France, Holiday Inn, Ibis, and Timhotel chains are more moderate. Typically, chains offer a more consistent standard of modern features (modern bathrooms, TV, etc.), but tend to lack atmosphere.

All hotels listed have private bath unless otherwise noted. For more information, *see* Chapter 3.

➤ DIRECTORIES AND TOLL-FREE NUMBERS: **Best Western** (☎ 800/528–1234 in the U.S.). **Inter-Continental** (☎ 800/327–0200 in the U.S.). **Logis de France** (☎ 01–45–84–70–00, ℻ 01–44–24–08–74). **Marriott** (☎ 800/228–9290 in the U.S.). **Relais & Châteaux** (☎ 01–45–72–96–50 in France; 212/856–0115 or 800/860–4930 in the U.S., ℻ 01–45–72–96–69 in France; 212/856–0193 in the U.S.). **Sheraton** (☎ 800/325–3535 in the U.S.). **Small Luxury Hotels of the World** (☎ 713/522–9512 or 800/525–4800 in the U.S.; 44/01372–361873 in the U.K., ℻ 713/524–7412 in the U.S.; 44/01372–361874 in the U.K.). **Westin Hotels & Resorts** (☎ 800/228–3000 in the U.S.).

MAIL & SHIPPING

Post offices, or PTT, are scattered throughout every arrondissement and are recognizable by a yellow LA POSTE sign. They are usually open weekdays 8 AM–7 PM, Saturday 8 AM–noon.

➤ POST OFFICES: **Main office** (✉ 52 rue du Louvre, 1ᵉʳ), open 24 hours. **Champs-Élysées office** (✉ 10 rue Balzar, 8ᵉ), open until 7 PM.

OVERNIGHT SERVICES

Sending overnight mail from Paris is relatively easy. Besides DHL, Federal Express, and UPS, the French post office has an overnight mail service called Chronopost. All agencies listed can be used as drop-off points and all have information in English.

➤ COMPANIES: **DHL** (✉ 6 rue des Colonnes, 7ᵉ, ☎ 01–55–35–30–30; ✉ 59 rue Iéna, 16ᵉ, ☎ 01–45–01–91–00). **Federal Express** (✉ 63 bd. Haussmann, 8ᵉ, ☎ 01–40–06–90–16, ✉ 2 rue 29 Juillet, 1ᵉʳ, ☎ 01–49–26–04–66, ☎ 08–00–12–38–00 for information in English about pick ups). **UPS** (✉ 34 bd. Malesherbes, 8ᵉ, ✉ 107 rue Réaumur, 2ᵉ, ☎ 08–00–87–78–77 for both).

POSTAL RATES

Airmail letters to the United States and Canada cost 4.40 francs for 20 grams, 8.20 francs for 40 grams, and 13 francs for 60 grams. Letters to the United Kingdom cost 3 francs for up to 20 grams, as they do within France. Postcards cost 3 francs within France and EU countries, and 4.40 francs to the United States and Canada. Stamps can be bought in post offices and cafés sporting a red TABAC sign.

RECEIVING MAIL

If you're uncertain where you'll be staying, have mail sent to American Express (if you're a card member) or to Poste Restante at any post office.

MÉTRO

Métro stations are recognizable either by a large yellow *M* within a circle or by the distinctive curly green Art Nouveau railings and archway bearing the full title (Métropolitain). Taking **the métro is the most efficient way to get around Paris.**

Fourteen métro and two RER (Réseau Express Régional, or the Regional Express Network) lines crisscross Paris and the suburbs, and you are seldom more than 500 yards from the nearest station. The métro network connects at several points in Paris with the RER, the commuter trains that go from the city center to the suburbs. RER trains crossing Paris on their way from suburb to suburb can be great time-savers because they only make a few stops in the city (you can use the same tickets for both the métro and the RER within Paris).

It's essential to **know the name of the last station on the line you take,** as this name appears on all signs. A connection (you can make as many as you like on one ticket) is called a *correspondance.* At junction stations, illuminated orange signs bearing the name of the line terminus appear over the correct corridors for each correspondance. Illuminated blue signs marked *sortie* indicate the station exit. Note that tickets are only valid inside the gates or *limites.*

Métro service starts at 5:30 AM and continues until 1:00 AM, when the last train on each line reaches its terminus. Some lines and stations in the less salubrious parts of Paris are a bit risky at night, in particular Lines 2 and 13. But in general, the métro is relatively safe throughout, providing you **don't walk around with your wallet hanging out of your back pocket or (especially women) travel alone late at night.**

FARES & SCHEDULES

All **métro tickets and passes are valid not only for the métro, but also for all RER and bus travel within Paris.** Métro tickets cost 8 francs each; a *carnet* (10 tickets for 52 francs) is a better value. The best deal is the weekly (*coupon jaune*) or monthly (*carte orange*) ticket, sold according to zone. Zones 1 and 2 cover the entire métro network; tickets cost 80 francs a week or 271 francs a month. If you plan to take suburban trains to visit places in Ile-de-France, consider a four-zone (Versailles, St-Germain-en-Laye; 134 francs a week) or six-zone (Rambouillet, Fontainebleau; 184 francs a week) ticket. For these weekly/monthly tickets, you need a pass (available from rail and major métro stations) and a passport-size photograph (many stations have photo booths).

The advantage of one-day (Mobilis) and three- and five-day (Paris Visite) unlimited travel tickets for the métro, bus, and RER is that, unlike the coupon jaune, which is good from Monday morning to Sunday evening, Mobilis and Paris Visite passes are valid starting any day of the week and also give you discounts on a limited number of museums and tourist attractions. The price is 30 francs (one-day), 80 francs (two-day), 120

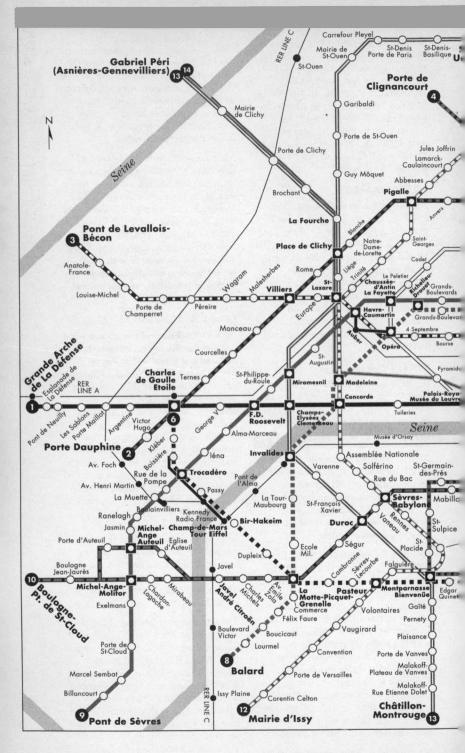

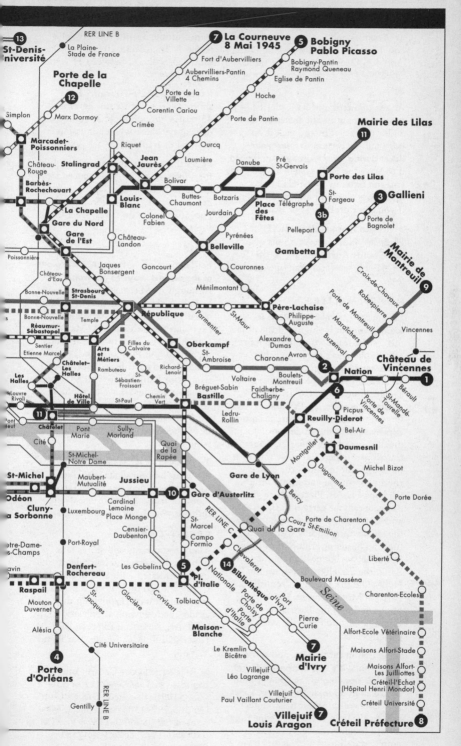

francs (three-day), and 175 francs (five-day) for Paris only. Suburbs such as Versailles and St-Germain-en-Laye cost 175 (one-day). Disneyland Paris costs 155, 225, 280, and 357 francs repectively for a one- to four-day pass.

Access to métro and RER platforms is through an automatic ticket barrier. Slide your ticket in and pick it up as it pops out. Be certain to **keep your ticket during your journey;** you'll need it to leave the RER system and in case you run into any green-clad ticket inspectors who will impose a big fine if you can't produce your ticket.

➤ Métro Information: RATP (✉ Pl. de la Madeleine, 8e; 53 bis quai des Grands-Augustins, 6e, ☎ 08–36–68–41–14, www.ratp.fr); open daily 9–5.

MONEY MATTERS

Like many capital cities, **Paris is expensive.** But if you avoid the obvious tourist traps, you can find more affordable places to eat and shop. Prices tend to reflect the standing of an area in the eyes of Parisians; much sought-after residential arrondissements such as the 7e, 16e, and 17e—of limited tourist interest—are far more expensive than the student-oriented, much-visited Latin Quarter. The tourist area where value for money is most difficult to find is the 8e arrondissement, on and around the Champs-Élysées. Places where you can generally be certain to shop, eat, and stay without overpaying include the streets surrounding Montmartre (not the Butte, or hilltop, itself); the St-Michel/Sorbonne area on the Left Bank; the mazelike streets around Les Halles and the Marais in central Paris; in Montparnasse, south of the boulevard; and the Bastille, République, and Belleville areas of eastern Paris.

Note that in cafés, bars, and some restaurants, **it's less expensive to eat or drink standing at the counter than it is to sit at a table.** Two prices are listed, *au comptoir* (at the counter) and *à salle* (at a table), and sometimes a third for the terrace. A cup of coffee, standing at a bar, costs from 7 francs; if you sit, it will cost from 10–

40 francs. A glass of beer costs from 10 francs standing and from 15–40 francs sitting; a soft drink costs between 10 francs and 20 francs. A ham sandwich will cost between 17 francs and 30 francs.

Expect to pay 20–70 francs for a short taxi ride. Museums entry is 20–45 francs, though there are hours or days of the week when admission is reduced or free.

Prices throughout this guide are given for adults. Substantially reduced fees are almost always available for children, students, and senior citizens. For information on taxes, *see* Taxes, *below*.

ATMS

Fairly common in Paris, **ATMs are one of the easiest ways to get francs.** Although ATM transaction fees may be higher abroad than at home, banks usually offer excellent, wholesale exchange rates through ATMs. You may, however, have to look around for Cirrus and Plus locations; it's a good idea to get a list of locations from your bank before you go. Note, too, that you may have better luck with ATMs if you're using a credit card or a debit card that is also a Visa or MasterCard, rather than just your bank card.

To get cash at ATMs in Paris, **your PIN must be four digits long.** Note, too, that you may be charged by your bank for using ATMs overseas; inquire at your bank about charges.

CREDIT CARDS

Many restaurants and stores take both credit cards and bank debit cards (affiliated with Visa or MasterCard), though there is often a 100-franc minimum. Throughout this guide, the following abbreviations are used: **AE,** American Express; **DC,** Diner's Club; **MC,** Master Card; and **V,** Visa.

➤ Reporting Lost Cards: **American Express** (☎ 336/939–1111 or 336/668–5309) call collect. **Diner's Club** (☎ 303/799–1504) call collect. **Mastercard** (☎ 0800/90–1387). **Visa** (☎ 0800/90–1179; collect: 410/581–9994).

CURRENCY

The units of currency in France are the franc (fr) and the centime. Bills are in denominations of 500, 200, 100, 50, and 20 francs. Coins are 20, 10, 5, 2, and 1 francs and 50, 20, 10, and 5 centimes. Pay close attention to the one hundred and two hundred franc notes as they can be easily confused. At press time (1999), the exchange rate was about 6.1 francs to the U.S. dollar, 4.2 to the Canadian dollar, 10 to the pound sterling, 4 to the Australian dollar, 3.4 to the New Zealand dollar, and 8.3 to the Irish punt.

The euro, or single European currency, was launched on January 1, 1999. One euro equals 6.55 francs. At the moment, the euro functions as an alternative currency, but by 2002 it will replace the national currencies of eleven of the fifteen countries in the European Union. Prices on all items from coffee to cars are now listed in euros as well as francs.

CURRENCY EXCHANGE

These days, **the easiest way to get francs is through ATMs** (☞ *above*); you can find them in airports, train stations, and throughout the city. It's a good idea, however, to bring some francs with you from home and to always have some cash and traveler's checks as back up. For the best deal, **compare rates at banks and booths** and **look for exchange booths that clearly state "no commission."** At exchange booths always confirm the rate with the teller before exchanging money. You won't do as well at exchange booths in airports or rail and bus stations, in hotels, in restaurants, or in stores. Of all the banks in Paris, **Banque de France generally has the best rates.**

➤ EXCHANGE SERVICES: **International Currency Express** (☎ 888/842–0880 on East Coast; 888/278–6628 on West Coast). **Thomas Cook Currency Services** (☎ 800/287–7362 for telephone orders and retail locations).

TRAVELER'S CHECKS

Although you can get francs from ATMs, you may also want to **bring some money in traveler's checks, just in case.** The benefit of traveler's checks is that lost or stolen checks can usually be replaced within 24 hours. To ensure a speedy refund, buy your own traveler's checks—don't let someone else pay for them. Traveler's checks in dollars or other currencies can easily be exchanged at banks or exchange bureaus, though you need your passport to do this.

PACKING

Over the years, **casual dress has become more acceptable in Paris,** although the city is still the world's fashion capital and people dress accordingly. You don't have to wear a jacket and tie at most restaurants (unless specified), and these days jeans are often de rigueur (a jeans-and-sneakers-and-t-shirt outfit, however, may raise eyebrows when going out). More Parisians are wearing sneakers, but you may still stand out as a tourist with them on. Nonetheless, you want to wear sturdy walking shoes for sightseeing: Paris is full of cobblestone streets, and many historic buildings are surrounded by gravel paths.

Summer in Paris can be hot and muggy (though the hot weather doesn't usually last that long) and early spring, late fall, and winter can be cold, damp, and rainy. Even when it's hot, most Parisians don't wear shorts, however. Since it rains all year round, it's a good idea to **bring a raincoat and umbrella.** Also, bring clothes that you can layer.

To protect yourself against purse snatchers and pickpockets, **take a handbag with long straps that you can sling across your body,** bandolier-style, with a zippered compartment for your money and some form of identification—French law requires that you carry identification at all times. It may be best, however, to leave your passport in your hotel safe, and just carry your license or a copy of your passport.

In your carry-on luggage **bring an extra pair of eyeglasses or contact lenses** and **enough of any medication you take** to last the entire trip. You may also want your doctor to write a spare prescription using the drug's generic name, since brand names may vary from country to country. In luggage to be checked, **never pack prescription drugs or valuables.** To avoid customs delays, carry medications in their original packaging. And don't forget to copy down and carry addresses of offices that handle refunds of lost traveler's checks.

CHECKING LUGGAGE

How many carry-on bags you can bring with you is up to the airline. Most allow two, but not always, so make sure that everything you carry aboard will fit under your seat, and get to the gate early. Note that if you have a seat at the back of the plane, you'll probably board first, while the overhead bins are still empty.

On international flights, note that baggage allowances may be determined not by piece but by weight—generally 88 pounds (40 kilograms) in first class, 66 pounds (30 kilograms) in business class, and 44 pounds (20 kilograms) in economy.

Airline liability for baggage is limited to $1,250 per person on flights within the United States. On international flights it amounts to $9.07 per pound or $20 per kilogram for checked baggage (roughly $640 per 70-pound bag) and $400 per passenger for unchecked baggage. You can buy additional coverage at check-in for about $10 per $1,000 of coverage, but it excludes a rather extensive list of items, shown on your airline ticket.

Before departure **itemize your bags' contents** and their worth, and label the bags with your name, address, and phone number. (If you use your home address, cover it so that potential thieves can't see it readily.) Inside each bag **pack a copy of your itinerary.** At check-in **make sure that each bag is correctly tagged** with the destination airport's three-letter code. If your bags arrive damaged or fail to arrive at all, file a written report with the airline before leaving the airport.

PASSPORTS & VISAS

When traveling in France, **you need to have a passport.** It's a good idea to **make two photocopies of your passport's data page** (one for someone at home and another for you, carried separately from your passport), in case you lose it. If you lose your passport promptly call the nearest embassy or consulate and the local police.

ENTERING FRANCE

All citizens of Australia, Canada, New Zealand, the United States, and the United Kingdom, even infants, need only a valid passport to enter France for stays of up to 90 days. If you lose your passport, promptly call the nearest embassy or consulate and the local police.

PASSPORT OFFICES

➤ AUSTRALIAN CITIZENS: **Australian Passport Office** (☎ 131–232).

➤ CANADIAN CITIZENS: **Passport Office** (☎ 819/994–3500 or 800/567–6868).

➤ NEW ZEALAND CITIZENS: **New Zealand Passport Office** (☎ 04/494–0700 for information on how to apply; 04/474–8000 or 0800/225–050 in New Zealand for information on applications already submitted).

➤ U.K. CITIZENS: **London Passport Office** (☎ 0990/210–410) for fees and documentation requirements and to request an emergency passport.

➤ U.S. CITIZENS: **National Passport Information Center** (☎ 900/225–5674; calls are 35¢ per minute for automated service, $1.05 per minute for operator service).

REST ROOMS

All cafés are required by law to let the public use their bathrooms, although this doesn't necessarily mean that they will be pleasant about it (you may also have to pay a few francs to use the toilet). Bathrooms are often located downstairs, are usually unisex, and are often just holes in the ground surrounded by porcelain pads for your feet. Your best bet is fast-food chains or large department stores. You can also find pay-per-use toilet units on the street, which require 2 francs (small children, however, should not use these alone, as the self-sanitizing system works with weight-related sensors that might not detect a child's presence). There are bathrooms in the larger métro stations and in all train stations for a cost of 1–2 francs.

SAFETY

Beware of petty theft—purse snatching, pickpocketing, and pilfering from automobiles. Use common sense: Avoid pulling out a lot of money in public; wear a handbag with long straps that you can sling across your body, bandolier-style, with a zippered compartment for your money and passport; and don't leave your luggage showing in the car.

WOMEN IN PARIS

Overall, statistics show that Paris is relatively safe; however, you should take the same precautions you would in any big city. Avoid walking alone in dark, unknown areas at night and be very careful on the métro late at night. Note that a smile or steady eye contact is often seen as an invitation. If someone is making you uncomfortable, ignore the person and walk quickly into the nearest, busiest, brightest area. Also, be careful when taking money out of ATMs, particularly at night.

SENIOR-CITIZEN TRAVEL

Travelers sixty years or older to Paris can take advantage of many discounts, such as reduced admissions of 20%–50% to museums and movie theaters. For rail travel outside of Paris, the Carte Senior entitles travelers 60 years or older to discounts (☞ Train Travel, *below*).

To qualify for age-related discounts **mention your senior-citizen status up front** when booking hotel reservations (not when checking out) and before you're seated in restaurants (not when paying the bill). When renting a car ask about promotional car-rental discounts, which can be cheaper than senior-citizen rates.

➤ EDUCATIONAL PROGRAMS: **Elderhostel** (✉ 75 Federal St., 3rd fl., Boston, MA 02110, ☎ 877/426–8056, FAX 877/426–2166). **Interhostel** (✉ University of New Hampshire, 6 Garrison Ave., Durham, NH 03824, ☎ 603/862–1147 or 800/733–9753, FAX 603/862–1113).

SIGHTSEEING TOURS

There are many ways to see Paris on a guided tour.

BIKE TOURS

A number of companies organize bike tours around Paris and its environs (Versailles, Chantilly, and Fontainebleau) for about 150–200 francs per person. *See* Chapter 5 for more information about bike tours in Paris.

➤ INFORMATION: **Butterfield & Robinson** (✉ 70 Bond St., Toronto, Canada M5B 1X3, ☎ 416/864–1354 or 800/678–1147). **Paris Bike** (✉ 83 rue Daguerre, 14ᵉ, ☎ 01–45–38–58–58) **Paris à Vélo, C'est Sympa** (✉ 37 bd. Bourdon, 4ᵉ, ☎ 01–48–87–60–01).

BOAT TOURS

Boat trips along the Seine run throughout the day and evening for a cost of 40–100 francs. Many of the tours include lunch or dinner for an average cost of 300 francs–600 francs. Reservations for meals are usually essential and some require jacket and tie.

Bateaux-Mouches boats depart from the Pont de l'Alma (Right Bank) 10–noon, 2–7, and 8:30–10:30. Lunch is served at 1 PM and dinner at 8:30 PM. Bateaux Parisiens-Tour Eiffel boats depart from the Pont d'Iéna (Left Bank) every half hour in summer and every hour in winter, starting at 10 AM. The last boat leaves at 9 PM (11 PM in summer). There are lunch and dinner cruises. Bat-O-Bus's trip along the Seine without commentary gives you the advantage being able to get on and off at any one of five stops along the river, including Trocadero, Musée d'Orsay, the Louvre, Notre-Dame, and Hôtel de Ville. Take it one stop for 20 francs, pay 60 francs for a full-day ticket, or buy a season ticket for 250 francs. Note that it operates from April 15 to October 31 and departs every half hour between 10 and 6. Canauxrama organizes leisurely canal tours in flat-bottom barges along the St-Martin and Ourcq canals in East Paris. Departures from the quai de la Loire are at 9:15 and 2:45, and departures from the Bassin de l'Arsenal (opposite 50 boulevard de la Bastille) are at 9:30 and 2:30. The trip lasts about 2½ hours. Reservations should be made. Paris Canal runs three-hour trips with bilingual commentary between the Musée d'Orsay and the Parc de La Villette, between April and mid-November only. Reservations are essential. Vedettes du Pont Neuf boats depart every half hour from the Square du Vert Galant, 10–noon, 1:30–6:30, and 9–10:30 from March to October. Yachts de Paris organizes 2½-hour "gourmet cruises" (for about 890 francs) year-round.

➤ INFORMATION: **Bateaux-Mouches** (✉ Pont de l'Alma, 8ᵉ, ☎ 01–42–25–96–10). **Bateaux Parisiens-Tour Eiffel** (✉ Pont d'Iéna, 7ᵉ, ☎ 01–44–11–33–44). **Bat-O-Bus** (☎ 01–44–11–33–99). **Canauxrama** (✉ 5 bis quai de la Loire, 19ᵉ; Bassin de l'Arsenal, 12ᵉ; ☎ 01–42–39–15–00). **Paris Canal** (✉ 19 quai de la Loire, 19ᵉ, ☎ 01–42–40–96–97). **Vedettes du Pont Neuf** (✉ Ile de la Cité, 1ᵉʳ, ☎ 01–46–33–98–38). **Yachts de Paris** (✉ Port de Javel, ☎ 01–44–37–10–20)

BUS TOURS

For a two-hour orientation tour by bus, the standard price is about 150 francs. The two largest bus tour operators are Cityrama and Paris Vision; for a more intimate-albeit-expensive-tour of the city, Cityrama also runs several minibus excursions per day. Paris Bus gives tours in a London-syle double-decker bus. You can catch the bus at any of nine pickup points; tickets cost 125 francs and allow you unlimited use for two days. For 135 francs the "Paris Open Tour" gives you two days of freedom to visit Paris in a double-decker bus with an open top. The bilingual tour lasts about two hours but you can get on and off as you please since the bus stops at over 20 spots along a circular route. A copy of the timetables for these tours are available from the main Paris Tourist Office (☞ Visitor Information, *below*). RATP (Paris Transit Authority) also gives guide-accompanied excursions in and around Paris by bus.

➤ INFORMATION: **Air France** (✉ 119 av. des Champs-Élysées, 8ᵉ, ☎ 01–44–08–22–22). **American Express** (✉ 11 rue Scribe, 9ᵉ, ☎ 01–47–77–77–07). **Cityrama** (✉ 4 Pl. des Pyramides, 1ᵉʳ, ☎ 01–44–55–61–00). **Paris Bus** (☎ 01–42–30–55–50). **Paris Vision** (✉ 214 rue de Rivoli, 1ᵉʳ,

☎ 01–42–60–31–25). **RATP** (✉ Pl. de la Madeleine, 8ᵉ; 53 bis quai des Grands-Augustins, 6ᵉ, ☎ 08–36–68–41–14. **Wagons-Lits** (✉ 31 rue Coloniel Pierre Avia, 15ᵉ, ☎ 01–41–33–68–00).

HELICOPTER TOURS

For a spectacular aerial view of Paris, Delta Lima offers a helicopter tour; it takes off from Toussus le Noble (15 minutes from Paris). Tours last 35 minutes and cost 962 francs per person.

➤ INFORMATION: **Delta Lima** (☎ 01–40–68–01–23).

MINIBUS TOURS

Paris Bus and Paris Major Limousine organizes tours of Paris and environs by luxury minibuses (for 4 to 15 passengers) for a minimum of four hours. The price varies from 1,300 to 2,200 francs. Reservations are essential.

➤ INFORMATION: **Paris Bus** (✉ 22 rue de la Prevoyance, Vincennes, ☎ 01–43–65–55–55). **Paris Major Limousine** (✉ 6 Pl. de la Madeleine, 8ᵉ, ☎ 01–42–45–34–14).

WALKING TOURS

There are a number of English-language walking tours of Paris. Walking tours generally last about two hours and cost about 60 francs. Paris Contact arranges walking tours of popular sights such as the Louvre and Versailles and unique theme tours, such as "Jefferson's Paris" and "The Paris of Proust" and can, upon request, do individually organized tours. Paris Walking Tours offers a wide variety of tours, from neighborhood visits to museum tours and theme tours (such as "Hemingway's Paris"). Bohemian Paris organizes a stroll on the left bank, filled with literary discussion, biographical information, and gossipy anecdotes about Paris in the '20s; this tour, led by a university professor and writer, costs 200 francs and lasts two and a half hours. A list of walking tours is also available from the Caisse Nationale des Monuments Historiques, and in the weekly magazines *Pariscope* and *L'Officiel des Spectacles,* which lists walking tours under the heading "conférences" (most are in French, unless otherwise noted).

➤ INFORMATION: **Bohemian Paris** (☎ 01–56–24–36–00). **Butterfield & Robinson** (✉ 70 Bond St., Toronto, Canada M5B 1X3, ☎ 416/864–1354 or 800/678–1147). **Caisse Nationale des Monuments Historiques** (✉ Bureau des Visites/Conférences, Hôtel de Sully, 62 rue St-Antoine, 4ᵉ, ☎ 01–44–61–21–70). **Paris Contact** (☎ 01–42–51–08–40). **Paris Walking Tours** (☎ 01–48–09–21–40).

SMOKING

The French are smokers, there's no way around it. And they're notorious for disregarding the few no-smoking laws that do exist, with little retribution. Even in restaurants, cafés, and train and métro stations that have no-smoking sections, you'll see people smoking. You may ask people to move or not to smoke, but don't expect them to respond or respect your request. Your best bet for finding as smoke-free an environment as possible is to stick to the larger cafés and restaurants where there might be the possibility of having more clearly defined smoking and no-smoking areas.

SNCF trains have cars designated for smoking and no-smoking (specify when you make reservations), and these are among the few places where the laws are respected. Some hotels, too, have designated no-smoking rooms; ask for these when reserving.

STUDENTS IN PARIS

For a detailed listing of deals for students in Paris, ask for the brochure **"Jeunes à Paris"** from the main tourist office (☞ Visitor Information, *below*). **France-USA Contacts** (FUSAC), a twice-monthly publication available free in restaurants and bookstores also has useful information.

➤ STUDENT I.D.s & SERVICES: **Council on International Educational Exchange** (CIEE, ✉ 205 E. 42nd St., 14th fl., New York, NY 10017, ☎ 212/822–2600 or 888/268–6245, FAX 212/822–2699) for mail orders only, in the U.S. **FUSAC** (✉ 3 rue Larochelle, Paris 75014, ☎ 01–45–38–56–57; Box 115, Cooper Station,

New York, NY, 10276, ☎ 212/929–2929). **Travel Cuts** (✉ 187 College St., Toronto, Ontario M5T 1P7, ☎ 416/979–2406 or 800/667–2887) in Canada.

TAXES

All taxes must be included in affixed prices in France. Prices in **restaurants and hotel prices must by law include taxes and service charges:** If these appear as additional items on your bill, you should complain. VAT (value added tax, known in France as TVA), at a standard rate of 20.6% (33% for luxury goods), is included in the price of many goods, but **foreigners are often entitled to a refund.**

VALUE-ADDED TAX (V.A.T.)

Europe Tax-Free Shopping is a V.A.T. refund service that makes getting your money back hassle-free. E.T.S. is Europe-wide and has 90,000 affiliated stores. In participating stores, **ask for the E.T.S. refund form** (called a Shopping Cheque). As is true for all customs forms, when leaving the European Union you get them stamped by the customs official. Then you take them to the E.T.S. counter and they will refund your money right there in cash, by check, or a refund to your credit card. All that convenience will cost you 20%—but then it's done.

➤ VAT REFUNDS: **Europe Tax-Free Shopping** (✉ 233 S. Wacker Dr., Suite 9700, Chicago, IL 60606-6502, ☎ 312/382–1101).

TAXIS

Taxi rates are based on location and time. Daytime rates, A (7 AM–7 PM), within Paris are 3.53 francs per kilometer, and nighttime rates, B, are around 5.83 francs per kilometer. Suburban zones and airports, C, are 7.16 per kilometer. There is a basic hire charge of 13 francs for all rides, a 6-franc supplement per piece of luggage, and a 5-franc supplement if you're picked up at a SNCF station. Waiting time is charged at 130 francs per hour. The easiest way to get a taxi is to **ask your hotel or a restaurant to call a taxi for you or go to the nearest taxi stand** (you can find one every couple of blocks); cabs with their signs lit can be hailed but are annoyingly difficult to spot (and they are not all one, uniform color). Note that taxis seldom take more than three people at a time. Tip the driver about 10%.

TELEPHONES

COUNTRY & AREA CODES

The country code for France is 33. The first two digits of French numbers are a prefix determined by zone: Paris and Ile-de-France, 01; the northwest, 02; the northeast, 03; the southeast, 04; and the southwest, 05. Numbers beginning with 08 can either be toll-free calls or calls that you are charged for (it depends on how the company has set up the number).

Note that **when dialing France from abroad, drop the initial 0 from the telephone number** (all number listed in this book include the initial 0, which is used for calling numbers *in* France). To call a telephone number in Paris from the United States, dial 011–33 plus the phone number minus the initial 0 (phone numbers in this book are listed with the full 10 digits, which you use to make local calls). To call France from the United Kingdom, dial 00–33, then dial the number in France minus the initial 0.

DIRECTORY & OPERATOR INFORMATION

To find a number in France, **dial 12 for information.** For international inquiries, dial 00–33 plus the country code.

Another source of information is the Minitel, an on-line network similar to the Internet. You can use one— they look like small computer terminals—for free in most post offices. To access the on-line phone book, hit the *appel* (call) key, then type the name you are looking for and hit *envoi* (return). It is also useful for tracking down services: tap in *piscine* (swimming pool) under *activité* (activity), for example, and it will give you a list of all the pools in Paris. Go to other lines or pages by hitting the *suite* (next) key. Newer models will connect automatically when you hit the book-icon key. To disconnect, hit *fin* (end).

INTERNATIONAL CALLS

To make a direct international call out of France, dial 00 and wait for the tone, then dial the country code (1 for the United States and Canada, 44 for the United Kingdom, 61 for Australia, and 64 for New Zealand) and the area code (minus any initial 0) and number.

Expect to be overcharged if you make calls from your hotel. Approximate daytime rates, per minute, are 2.25 francs to the United States and Canada (8:00 AM–9:30 PM), and 2.10 francs for the United Kingdom (2:00 PM–8:00 PM); reduced rates at other time intervals, per minute, are 1.80 francs to the United States and Canada and 1.65 francs to the United Kingdom.

To call home with the help of an operator, dial 00–33 plus the country code. There is an automatic 44.5 franc service charge.

Telephone cards (☞ *below*) are sold that enable you to make long-distance and international calls from pay phones.

INTERNATIONAL-CALLING SERVICES

AT&T, MCI, and Sprint access codes make calling long distance relatively convenient, but you may find the local access number blocked in many hotel rooms. First ask the hotel operator to connect you. If the hotel operator balks ask for an international operator, or dial the international operator yourself. If all else fails call from a pay phone.

➤ ACCESS CODES: **AT&T Direct** (☎ 08–00–99–00–11 or 08–00–99–01–11; 800/874–4000 for information). **MCI Call USA** (☎ 08–00–99–00–19; 800/444–4444 for information). **Sprint Express** (☎ 08–00–99–00–87; 800/793–1153 for information).

LOCAL CALLS

When making a local call in Paris or to Ile-de-France, **dial the full 10-digit number, including the intial 0.** A local call costs 74 centimes for every three minutes.

LONG-DISTANCE CALLS

To call from region to region within France, **dial the full 10-digit number, including the initial 0.**

PHONE CARDS

Most **French pay phones are operated by** *télécartes* (phone cards), which you can buy from post offices, tabacs, and métro stations. These phone cards will save you money and hassle, since it's hard to find phones that take change these days. There are two types of cards: the *télécarte international,* which allows you to make local calls and offers greatly reduced rates on international calls (instructions are in English and the cost is 50 francs for 60 units and 100 francs for 120 units); and the simple *télécarte,* which allows you to make calls in France (the cost is 49 francs for 50 units; 97.5 francs for 120 units). You can also use your credit card in much the same way as a télécarte but be careful—its much more expensive.

In a few cafés you may still be able to find pay phones that operate with 1-, 2-, and 5-franc coins (1.5 francs for local calls). Lift the receiver, place your coin(s) in the appropriate slots, and dial.

PUBLIC PHONES

Public **telephone booths can almost always be found in post offices, métro stations, and in many cafés,** as well as on the street.

TIME

The time difference between New York and Paris 6 hours (so when it's 1 PM in New York, it's 7 PM in Paris). The time difference between London and Paris is 1 hour; between Sydney and Paris, 8–9 hours; and between Auckland and Paris, 12 hours.

TIPPING

Bills in bars and restaurants must, by law, include service, but **it is customary to round out your bill with some small change** unless you're dissatisfied. The amount varies—from 50 centimes or 1 franc for a beer to 10 or 15 francs after a meal. In expensive restaurants, it's common to leave an additional 5% of the bill on the table.

Tip taxi drivers and hairdressers about 10% of the bill. Give theater and cinema ushers a couple of francs. In some theaters and hotels, cloakroom attendants may expect nothing (watch for signs that say *pourboire interdit*—tipping forbidden); otherwise, give them 5 francs. Washroom attendants usually get 2 francs, though the sum is often posted.

If you stay more than two or three days in a hotel, it is customary to leave something for the chambermaid—about 10 francs per day. Expect to pay about 10 francs (5 francs in a moderately priced hotel) to the person who carries your bags or who hails you a taxi. In hotels providing room service, give 5 francs to the waiter (this does not apply if breakfast is routinely served in your room). If the chambermaid does some pressing or laundering for you, give her 5–10 francs on top of the bill. If the concierge has been very helpful, it is customary to leave a tip of 50–100 francs, depending on the type of hotel and the level of service.

Service station attendants get nothing for pumping gas or checking oil, but 5 or 10 francs for checking tires. Train and airport porters get a fixed sum (6–10 francs) per bag. Museum guides should get 5–10 francs after a guided tour. It is standard practice to tip bus drivers about 10 francs after an excursion.

TOURS & PACKAGES

On a prepackaged tour or independent vacation everything is prearranged so you'll spend less time planning—and often get it all at a good price.

BOOKING WITH AN AGENT

Travel agents are excellent resources. But it's a good idea to collect brochures from several agencies because some agents' suggestions may be influenced by relationships with tour and package firms that reward them for volume sales. If you have a special interest **find an agent with expertise in that area**; ASTA (☞ Travel Agencies, *below*) has a database of specialists worldwide.

Make sure your travel agent knows the accommodations and other services of the place they're recommending. Ask about the hotel's location, room size, beds, and whether it has a pool, room service, or programs for children, if you care about these. Has your agent been there in person or sent others whom you can contact?

Do some homework on your own, too: Local tourism boards can provide information about lesser-known and small-niche operators, some of which may sell only direct.

BUYER BEWARE

Each year consumers are stranded or lose their money when tour operators—even large ones with excellent reputations—go out of business. So **check out the operator.** Ask several travel agents about its reputation, and try to **book with a company that has a consumer-protection program.** (Look for information in the company's brochure.) In the United States, members of the National Tour Association and United States Tour Operators Association are required to set aside funds to cover your payments and travel arrangements in case the company defaults. It's also a good idea to choose a company that participates in the American Society of Travel Agent's Tour Operator Program (TOP); ASTA will act as mediator in any disputes between you and your tour operator.

Remember that the more your package or tour includes the better you can predict the ultimate cost of your vacation. Make sure you know exactly what is covered, and **beware of hidden costs.** Are taxes, tips, and transfers included? Entertainment and excursions? These can add up.

➤ TOUR-OPERATOR RECOMMENDATIONS: **American Society of Travel Agents** (☞ Travel Agencies, *below*). **National Tour Association** (NTA, ✉ 546 E. Main St., Lexington, KY 40508, ☎ 606/226–4444 or 800/682–8886). **United States Tour Operators Association** (USTOA, ✉ 342 Madison Ave., Suite 1522, New York, NY 10173, ☎ 212/599–6599 or 800/468–7862, FAX 212/599–6744).

TRAIN TRAVEL

The SNCF, France's rail system, is fast, punctual, comfortable, and comprehensive. There are various options: local trains, overnight trains with sleeping accomodations, and the high-speed TGV, or *Trains à Grande Vitesse* (averaging 255 kph/160 mph on the Lyon/southeast line, and 300 kph/190 mph on the Lille and Bordeaux/southwest lines).

The TGV, the fastest way to get around the country, operate between Paris and Lille/Calais, Paris and Lyon/Switzerland/the Riviera, Paris and Angers/Nantes, Paris and Tours/Poitiers/Bordeaux, Paris and Brussels, and Paris and Amsterdam. As with other main-line trains, a small supplement may be assessed at peak hours.

Paris has six international rail stations: Gare du Nord (northern France, northern Europe, and England via Calais or Boulogne); Gare St-Lazare (Normandy, England via Dieppe); Gare de l'Est (Strasbourg, Luxembourg, Basel, and central Europe); Gare de Lyon (Lyon, Marseille, the Riviera, Geneva, Italy); and Gare d'Austerlitz (Loire Valley, southwest France, Spain). Note that Gare Montparnasse has taken over as the main terminus for trains bound for southwest France since the introduction of the new TGV-Atlantique service.

BETWEEN THE U.K. AND FRANCE

Short of flying, the "Chunnel" is the fastest way to cross the English Channel: 3 hours from London's central Waterloo Station to Paris's central Gare du Nord, 35 minutes from Folkestone to Calais, and 60 minutes from motorway to motorway. Round-trip tickets range from 3,400 francs for first class to 690 francs for second class. It's a good idea to **make a reservation if you're traveling with your car on a Chunnel train;** cars without reservations, if they can get on at all, are charged 20 percent extra.

British Rail also has four daily departures from London's Victoria Station, all linking with the Dover-Calais/Boulogne ferry services through to Paris. There is also an overnight service on the Newhaven-Dieppe ferry. Journey time is about eight hours. Credit-card bookings are accepted by phone or in person at a British Rail Travel Centre.

➤ CAR TRANSPORT: Le Shuttle (☎ 0990/353–535 in the U.K., 03–21–00–61–00 in France, www.eurotunnel.co.uk).

➤ PASSENGER SERVICE: BritRail Travel (☎ 800/677–8585 in the U.S., 020/7834–2345 in the U.K.). Eurostar (☎ 0990/186–186 in the U.K., 08–36–35–35–39 in France, www.eurostar.com). InterCity Europe (✉ Victoria Station, London, ☎ 020/7834–2345, 020/7828–0892 or 0990/848–848 for credit-card bookings). Rail Europe (☎ 800/942–4866 in the U.S., www.raileurope.com).

FARES, SCHEDULES, & RESERVATIONS

You can **call for train information or reserve tickets in any Paris station,** irrespective of destination. If you know what station you'll depart from, you can get a free schedule there (while supplies last), or you can access the new multilingual computerized schedule information network at any Paris station. You can also make reservations and buy you ticket while at the computer. Go to the Grandes Lignes counter for travel within France and to the Billets Internationaux desk if you're heading out of the country. Note that calling the SNCF's 08 number (☞ *below*) will cost you money (you're charged per minute), so it's better just to go to the nearest station and make reservations.

Seat reservations are required on TGVs, and are a good idea on trains that may be crowded-particularly in summer and holidays on popular routes. You also need a reservation for sleeping accommodations.

➤ TRAIN INFORMATION: BritRail Travel (☎ 800/677–8585 in the U.S., 020/7834–2345 in the U.K.). Eurostar (☎ 08–36–35–35–39 in France; 0345/881881 in the U.K., www.eurostar.com). InterCity Europe (✉ Victoria Station, London, ☎ 020/7834–2345, 020/7828–0892 or 0990/848–848 for credit-card bookings). Rail Europe (☎ 800/942–4866 in the U.S., www.raileurope.com). SNCF (✉ 88 rue St-Lazare, 75009 Paris, ☎ 08–36–35–35–35, www.sncf.fr).

RAIL PASSES

If you plan to travel outside of Paris by train, **consider purchasing a France Rail Pass,** which allows three days of unlimited train travel in a one-month period. Prices begin at $130 for two adults traveling together in second class and $165 second class for a solo traveler. First-class rates are $156 for two adults and $195 for a solo traveler. Additional days may be added for $30 a day in either class. Other options include the France Rail 'n Drive Pass (combining rail and rental car), France Rail 'n Fly Pass (rail travel and one air travel journey within France), and the France Fly Rail 'n Drive Pass (a rail, air, and rental car program all in one).

France is one of 17 countries in which **you can use EurailPasses,** which provide unlimited first-class rail travel, in all of the participating countries, for the duration of the pass. If you plan to rack up the miles, get a standard pass. These are available for 15 days ($522), 21 days ($678), one month ($838), two months ($1,148), and three months ($1,468). If your plans call for only limited train travel, **look into a Europass,** which costs less money than a EurailPass. Unlike EurailPasses, however, you get a limited number of travel days, in a limited number of countries, during a specified time period. For example, a two-month Europass ($316) allows between 5 and 15 days of rail travel, but costs $200 less than the least expensive EurailPass. Keep in mind, however, that the Europass is good only in France, Germany, Italy, Spain, and Switzerland, and the number of countries you can visit is further limited by the type of pass you buy.

In addition to standard EurailPasses, **ask about special rail-pass plans.** Among these are the Eurail Youthpass (for those under age 26), the Eurail Saverpass (which gives a discount for two or more people traveling together), a Eurail Flexipass (which allows a certain number of travel days within a set period), the Euraildrive Pass and the Europass Drive (train and rental car).

Whichever of the above passes you choose, remember that **you must**

purchase your Eurail and Euro passes at home before leaving for France.

Another option is to **purchase one of the discount rail passes available only for sale in France** from SNCF.

When traveling together, **two people (who don't have to be a couple) can save money with the Prix Découverte à Deux.** You'll get a 25% discount during "périodes bleus" (blue periods: weekdays and not on or near any holidays). Note that you have to be with the person you said you would be traveling with.

You can **get a reduced fare if you're a senior citizen (over 60).** There are two options: For the Prix Découverte Senior, all you have to do is show a valid ID with your age and you're entitled to up to a 25% reduction in fares in first and second class. The second, the Carte Senior, is better if you're planning on spending a lot of time traveling; it costs 285F, is valid for one year, and entitles you to up to a 50% reduction on most trains with a guaranteed minimum reduction of 25%. It also entitles you to a 30% discount on trips outside of France.

With the Carte Enfant Plus, for 350F **children under 12 and up to 4 accompanying adults can get 50% off on most trains for an unlimited number of trips.** This card is perfect if you're planning on spending a lot of time traveling in France with you're children, as it's valid for one year. You can also opt for the Prix Découverte Enfant Plus: When you buy your ticket, simply show a valid ID with your child's age and you can get a significant discount for your child and a 25% reduction for up to four accompanying adults.

If you purchase an individual ticket from SNCF in France and you're under 26, you automatically get a 25% reduction (a valid ID, such as an ISIC card or your passport, is necessary). If you're going to be using the train quite a bit during your stay in France and **if you're under 26, consider buying the Carte 12–25** (270F), which offers unlimited 50% reductions for one year (provided that there's space available at that price,

otherwise you'll just get the standard 25% discount).

If you don't benefit from any of these reductions and **if you plan on traveling at least 200 km minimum roundtrip and don't mind staying over a Saturday night, look into the Prix De(ac)couverte Séjour.** This ticket gives you a 25% reduction.

Don't assume that your rail pass guarantee you a seat on the train you wish to ride. You need to **book seats ahead even if you're using a rail pass.**

TRAVEL AGENCIES

A good travel agent puts your needs first. Look for an agency that has been in business at least five years, emphasizes customer service, and has someone on staff who specializes in your destination. In addition **make sure the agency belongs to a professional trade organization,** such as ASTA in the United States. If your travel agency is also acting as your tour operator *see* Buyer Beware *in* Tours & Packages, *above*.

➤ LOCAL AGENT REFERRALS: American Society of Travel Agents (ASTA, ☎ 800/965–2782 24-hr hot line, FAX 703/684–8319). Association of Canadian Travel Agents (✉ 1729 Bank St., Suite 201, Ottawa, Ontario K1V 7Z5, ☎ 613/521–0474, FAX 613/521–0805). Association of British Travel Agents (✉ 55–57 Newman St., London W1P 4AH, ☎ 020/7637–2444, FAX 020/7637–0713). Australian Federation of Travel Agents (✉ Level 3, 309 Pitt St., Sydney 2000, ☎ 02/9264–3299, FAX 02/9264–1085). Travel Agents' Association of New Zealand (✉ Box 1888, Wellington 10033, ☎ 04/499–0104, FAX 04/499–0786).

➤ PARIS AGENCIES: Access Voyages (6 rue Pierre Lescot, 1ᵉ, métro Châtelet–Les Halles, ☎ 01–44–76–84–50). American Express (✉ 11 rue Scribe, 8ᵉ, ☎ 01–47–77–77–07; ✉ 38 av. de Wagram, 8ᵉ, ☎ 01–42–27–58–80). Nouvelles Frontières (5 ave. de l'Opéra, 1ᵉʳ, métro Pyramides, ☎ 08–03–33–33–33). Soltours (48 rue de Rivoli, 4ᵉ, métro Hôtel-de-Ville, ☎ 01–42–71–24–34).

VISITOR INFORMATION

➤ FRANCE TOURISM OFFICES: **France On-Call** (☎ 410/286–8310 Mon.–Fri. 9–7, www.francetourism.com). **Chicago** (676 N. Michigan Ave., Chicago, IL 60611, fgto@mcs.net). **Los Angeles** (9454 Wilshire Blvd., Suite 715, Beverly Hills, CA 90212, fgto@gte.net).**New York City** (444 Madison Ave., 16th floor, New York, NY 10022, info@francetourism.com). **Canada** (1981 Ave. McGill College, Suite 490, Montréal, Québec H3A 2W9). **U.K.** 178 Piccadilly, London W1V OAL, ☎ 171/6399–3500, ℻ 171/6493–6594.

➤ LOCAL TOURIST INFORMATION: **Espace du Tourisme d'Ile-de-France** (Carrousel du Louvre, 99 rue de Rivoli, 75001 ☎ 08–03–81–80–00 or 01–44–50–19–98). **Office du Tourisme de la Ville de Paris** (Paris Tourist Office, 127 av. des Champs-Élysées, ☎ 01–49–52–53–54 or 01–49–52–53–56 for recorded information in English).

➤ U.S. GOVERNMENT ADVISORIES: **U.S. Department of State** (✉ Overseas Citizens Services Office, Room 4811 N.S., 2201 C St. NW, Washington, DC 20520; ☎ 202/647–5225 for interactive hot line; 301/946–4400 for computer bulletin board; ℻ 202/647–3000 for interactive hot line); enclose a self-addressed, stamped, business-size envelope.

WEB SITES

Eurail (www.eurail.com/). **Eurostar** (www.eurostar.com). **Louvre Museum** (mistral.culture.fr/louvre/louvrea.htm). **French Embassy** (www.france.diplo-matie.fr). **French Government Tourist Office** (www.francetourism.com). **French Ministry of Culture** (www .culture.fr). **Paris Tourist Office** (www.paris.org). **Rail Europe** (www.raileurope.com). **RATP** (www.ratp.fr). **SNCF** (www.sncf.fr).

WHEN TO GO

The major tourist season in France stretches from Easter to mid-September, but **Paris has much to offer in every season.** Paris in the early spring can be disappointingly damp, though it's relatively tourist free; May and June are delightful, with good weather and plenty of cultural and other attractions. July and August can be sultry. Moreover, many theaters and some of the smaller restaurants and shops close for at least four weeks in August. If you're undeterred by the hot weather and the pollution, you'll notice a fairly relaxed atmosphere around the city, as this is the month when most Parisians are on vacation. September is ideal. Cultural life revives after the summer break, and sunny weather often continues through the first half of October. The ballet and theater are in full swing in November, but the weather is part wet and cold, part bright and sunny. December is dominated by the *fêtes de fin d'année* (end-of-year festivities), and a busy theater, ballet, and opera season into January.

➤ FORECASTS: **Weather Channel Connection** (☎ 900/932–8437), 95¢ per minute from a Touch-Tone phone.

CLIMATE

What follow are the average daily maximum and minimum temperatures for Paris.

Climate in Paris

Jan.	43F	6C	May	68F	20C	Sept.	70F	21C
	34	1		49	10		53	12
Feb.	45F	7C	June	73F	23C	Oct.	60F	16C
	34	1		55	13		46	8
Mar.	54F	12C	July	76F	25C	Nov.	50F	10C
	39	4		58	14		40	5
Apr.	60F	16C	Aug.	75F	24C	Dec.	44F	7C
	43	6		58	14		36	2

FESTIVALS AND SEASONAL EVENTS

➤ LATE NOV.: **Salon des Caves Particulières** brings French producers to the exhibition center at Porte de Versailles for a wine-tasting jamboree.

➤ LATE NOV.–LATE DEC.: The festive **Christmas Market** (✉ pl. du 11-Novembre-1918, 10ᵉ, métro Gare de l'Est) features crafts, gifts, and toys from every region of France.

➤ LATE DEC.: **Christmas** is highlighted by illuminations throughout the city, particularly on the Champs-Élysées, avenue Montaigne, and boulevard Haussmann. In the Jardin des Tuileries there's a fair with a Ferris wheel and outside the Hôtel de Ville is a giant **Crèche.**

➤ DEC. 31: For New Year's Eve **L'An 2000** (The Year 2000) big events are planned; contact the French Tourist Office (☞ Visitor Information, *above*) for more information.

➤ FEB.: **Foire à la Feraille de Paris** is an antiques and bric-a-brac fair held in the Bois de Vincennes.

➤ MAR.: **Salon du Livre,** an international book exposition, is held annually at the end of the month.

➤ MAR.–APR.: **Foire du Trône,** an amusement park, is set up in the Bois de Vincennes.

➤ MAR.–APR.: The **Prix du Président de la République** takes place at the Auteuil Racecourse.

➤ LATE APR.: The **International Marathon of Paris** runs through the city and large parks on the outskirts.

➤ EARLY MAY: At the **Foire de Paris** hundreds of booths display everything from crafts to wines.

➤ END OF MAY: The **Course des Garçons de Café** is an entertaining race through the streets of Paris by waiters bearing full trays of drinks; it begins and ends at the Hôtel de Ville.

➤ MAY–LATE SEPT.: **Grandes Eaux Musicales** is a fountain display at the Château de Versailles (Sundays only).

➤ LATE MAY–EARLY JUNE: The **Festival de Jazz de Boulogne-Billancourt** attracts big names and varied styles of jazz in Boulogne-Billancourt, a suburb of Paris.

➤ LATE MAY–EARLY JUNE: The **French Open Tennis Championships** take place at Roland Garros Stadium.

➤ MID-JUNE–MID-JULY: **Festival du Marais** features everything from music to dance to theater in the churches and historic mansions of the Marais (tickets: ✉ 44 rue François-Miron, 4ᵉ, ☎ 01–48–87–60–08, métro St-Paul). A similar celebration takes place at the **Butte Montmartre Festival** (☎ 01–42–62–46–22).

➤ JUNE: **Paris Air Show,** which takes place in odd-numbered years only, is a display of old and new planes at Le Bourget Airport.

➤ MID-JUNE: The **Grand Steeplechase de Paris** is a popular horse race at the Auteuil Racecourse.

➤ JUNE 21: The **Fête de la Musique** celebrates the summer solstice with parades, street theater, and live bands throughout the city.

➤ LAST WEEKEND IN JUNE: The **Fête du Cinéma** allows you to take in as many movies as you can for the price of a single ticket.

➤ LATE JUNE: The **Grand Prix de Paris,** is held on the flat at Longchamp Racecourse.

➤ JULY 13: **Bals des Sapeurs-Pompiers** (Firemen's Balls), held to celebrate the start of Bastille Day the next day, spill into the streets of every arrondissement.

➤ JULY 14: **Bastille Day** celebrates the storming of the Bastille prison in 1789. There's a military parade along the Champs-Élysées in the morning and fireworks at night at Trocadéro.

➤ LATE JULY: The **Tour de France,** the world's leading bicycle race, speeds to a Sunday finish on the Champs-Élysées.

➤ LATE JULY–END AUG.: The **Fête Musique en l'Ile** (☎ 01–45–23–18–25 for details) is a series of concerts held in the picturesque 17th-century Église St-Louis on Ile St-Louis.

➤ MID-JULY–LATE SEPT.: **Festival Estival** (tickets: ✉ 20 rue Geoffroy-l'Asnier, 4ᵉ, ☎ 01–48–04–98–01, métro St-Paul) features classical music concerts in churches, museums, and concert halls throughout the city.

➤ SEPT.: **Fête à Neu-Neu,** an amusement park, is set up in the Bois de Boulogne.

➤ MID–LATE SEPT.: **Biennale des Antiquaires** (even-numbered years only), an antiques fair, takes place at the Carrousel du Louvre.

➤ MID-SEPT.–DEC.: **Fête d'Automne** (tickets: ✉ 156 rue de Rivoli, 1ᵉʳ, ☎ 01–42–96–96–94, métro Louvre-Rivoli) is a series of concerts, plays, dances, and exhibitions throughout Paris.

➤ LATE SEPT.: On the **Journée du Patrimonie,** the third Sunday in September, normally closed historic buildings—such as the state residences of the President and Prime Minister—are open to the public.

➤ EARLY OCT.: **Fêtes des Vendanges,** held the first Saturday of October, marks the grape harvest in the Montmartre vineyard, at the corner of rue des Saules and rue St-Vincent.

➤ EARLY OCT.: **FIAC** (International Fair of Contemporary Art) takes place at Porte de Versailles.

➤ EARLY OCT.: **Prix de l'Arc de Triomphe,** Europe's top flat race, is the first Sunday of the month at Longchamp Racecourse.

➤ OCT.: **Paris Auto Show** (even-numbered years only) takes place at the Porte de Versailles.

➤ MID-OCT.–EARLY NOV.: The **Fête de Jazz de Paris** (☎ 01–47–83–33–58 for information) is a two-week celebration that includes lots of big-name musicians.

➤ OCT.–NOV.: The **Fête d'Art Sacré** (☎ 01–42–77–92–26 for information) is a series concerts and exhibitions held in churches throughout the city.

➤ NOV. 11: **Armistice Day** ceremonies at the Arc de Triomphe include a military parade down the Champs-Élysées.

➤ 3RD THURS. IN NOV.: **Beaujolais Nouveau,** that light, fruity wine from the Beaujolais region of France, is officially released at midnight on Wednesday; its arrival is celebrated on the third Thursday in November in true Dionysian form in cafés and restaurants around the city.

Paris with Arrondissements

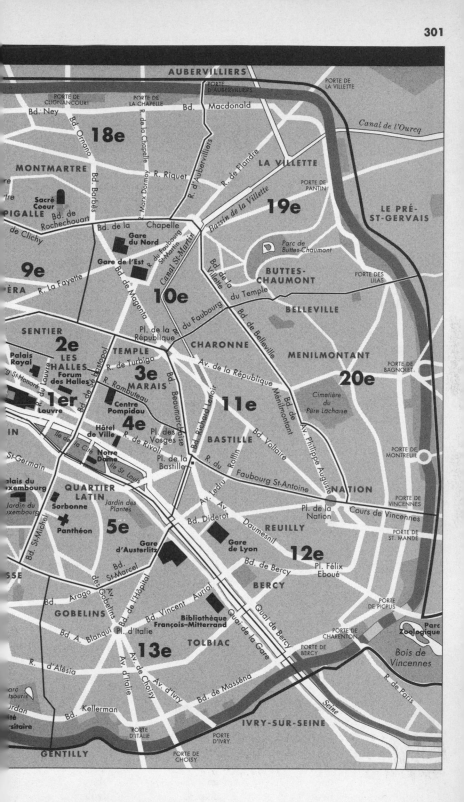

AUBERVILLIERS

PORTE D'AUBERVILLIERS

PORTE DE
LA VILLETTE

PORTE DE
CLIGNANCOURT

PORTE DE
LA CHAPELLE

Bd. Ney

Bd. Macdonald

Canal de l'Ourcq

18e

R. Riquet

R. de Flandre

LA VILLETTE

PORTE DE
PANTIN

Bd. Ornano

Bd. Barbès

R. Marx Dormoy

R. d'Aubervilliers

Bassin de la Villette

19e

LE PRÉ-
ST-GERVAIS

MONTMARTRE

Sacré
Coeur

PIGALLE Bd. de
Rochechouart

de Clichy

Bd. de la Chapelle

Gare
du Nord

Gare de l'Est

Parc de
Buttes-Chaumont

PORTE DES
LILAS

9e

ÉRA R. La Fayette

Bd. de Magenta

Canal St-Martin

R. du Faubourg
St-Martin

Bd. de la
Villette

BUTTES-
CHAUMONT

PORTE DES
LILAS

10e

du Temple

BELLEVILLE

SENTIER

Pl. de la
République

R. du Faubourg

Bd. de Belleville

CHARONNE

MENILMONTANT

PORTE DE
BAGNOLET

2e

LES
HALLES

Forum
des Halles

TEMPLE

R. de Turbigo

R. Réaumur

3e

MARAIS

R. Rambuteau

Av. de la République

Bd. de Ménilmontant

20e

Palais
Royal

R. St-Honoré

Louvre

1er

Centre
Pompidou

R. Beaumarchais

Bd. Richard Lenoir

11e

Cimetière
du
Père Lachaise

Av. Philippe Auguste

PORTE DE
MONTREUIL

Hôtel
de Ville

4e

Notre
Dame

Pl. des
Vosges

R. de Rivoli

BASTILLE

Bd. Voltaire

Île de la Cité

Île St-Louis

Pl. de la
Bastille

St-Germain

QUARTIER
LATIN

R. du
Pontin

Faubourg St-Antoine

NATION

PORTE DE
VINCENNES

alais du
xembourg

Jardin du
xembourg

Sorbonne

Panthéon

Jardin des
Plantes

Av. Ledru

Av.

Bd. Diderot

Pl. de la
Nation

Cours de Vincennes

PORTE DE
ST. MANDÉ

5e

Gare
d'Austerlitz

Daumesnil

REUILLY

12e

SSE

Bd.
Arago

Bd.
St-Marcel

Gare
de Lyon

Bd. de Bercy

Pl. Félix
Eboué

Bd. A. Blanqui

Av. des Gobelins

R. de l'Hôpital

BERCY

PORTE
DE PICPUS

GOBELINS

Pl. d'Italie

R. Vincent

Auriol

Bibliothèque
François-Mitterrand

Quai de Bercy

Quai de la Gare

PORTE DE
CHARENTON

Parc
Zoologique

R. d'Alésia

13e

TOLBIAC

PORTE DE
BERCY

Bois de
Vincennes

arc
tsouris

rdan
ité
sitaire

R.
Kellerman

Av. de Choisy

Av. d'Italie

Av. d'Ivry

Bd. de Masséna

Seine

R. de Paris

GENTILLY

PORTE
D'ITALIE

PORTE
D'IVRY

IVRY-SUR-SEINE

PORTE DE
CHOISY

FRENCH VOCABULARY

One of the trickiest French sounds to pronounce is the nasal final *n* sound (whether or not the *n* is actually the last letter of the word). You should try to pronounce it as a sort of nasal grunt—as in "huh." The vowel that precedes the *n* will govern the vowel sound of the word, and in this list we precede the final *n* with an *h* to remind you to be nasal.

Another problem sound is the ubiquitous but untransliterable *eu*, as in *bleu* (blue) or *deux* (two), and the very similar sound in *je* (I), *ce* (this), and *de* (of). The closest equivalent might be the vowel sound in "put," but rounded.

Words and Phrases

English	French	Pronunciation

Basics

English	French	Pronunciation
Yes/no	Oui/non	wee/nohn
Please	S'il vous plaît	seel voo play
Thank you	Merci	mair-**see**
You're welcome	De rien	deh ree-**ehn**
That's all right	Il n'y a pas de quoi	eel nee ah pah de kwah
Excuse me, sorry	Pardon	pahr-**dohn**
Sorry!	Désolé(e)	day-zoh-**lay**
Good morning/ afternoon	Bonjour	bohn-**zhoor**
Good evening	Bonsoir	bohn-**swahr**
Goodbye	Au revoir	o ruh-**vwahr**
Mr. (Sir)	Monsieur	muh-**syuh**
Mrs. (Ma'am)	Madame	ma-**dam**
Miss	Mademoiselle	mad-mwa-**zel**
Pleased to meet you	Enchanté(e)	ohn-shahn-**tay**
How are you?	Comment allez-vous?	kuh-mahn-tahl-ay **voo**
Very well, thanks	Très bien, merci	tray bee-ehn, mair-**see**
And you?	Et vous?	ay voo?

Numbers

one	un	uhn
two	deux	deuh
three	trois	twah
four	quatre	**kaht**-ruh

five	cinq	sank
six	six	seess
seven	sept	set
eight	huit	wheat
nine	neuf	nuf
ten	dix	deess
eleven	onze	ohnz
twelve	douze	dooz
thirteen	treize	trehz
fourteen	quatorze	kah-torz
fifteen	quinze	kanz
sixteen	seize	sez
seventeen	dix-sept	deez-**set**
eighteen	dix-huit	deez-**wheat**
nineteen	dix-neuf	deez-**nuf**
twenty	vingt	vehn
twenty-one	vingt-et-un	vehnt-ay-**uhn**
thirty	trente	trahnt
forty	quarante	ka-**rahnt**
fifty	cinquante	sang-**kahnt**
sixty	soixante	swa-**sahnt**
seventy	soixante-dix	swa-sahnt-**deess**
eighty	quatre-vingts	kaht-ruh-**vehn**
ninety	quatre-vingt-dix	kaht-ruh-vehn-**deess**
one hundred	cent	sahn
one thousand	mille	meel

Colors

black	noir	nwahr
blue	bleu	bleuh
brown	brun/marron	bruhn/mar-**rohn**
green	vert	vair
orange	orange	o-**rahnj**
pink	rose	rose
red	rouge	rouge
violet	violette	vee-o-**let**
white	blanc	blahnk
yellow	jaune	zhone

Days of the Week

Sunday	dimanche	dee-**mahnsh**
Monday	lundi	luhn-**dee**
Tuesday	mardi	mahr-**dee**
Wednesday	mercredi	mair-kruh-**dee**
Thursday	jeudi	zhuh-**dee**
Friday	vendredi	vawn-druh-**dee**
Saturday	samedi	sahm-**dee**

French Vocabulary

Months

January	janvier	zhahn-vee-**ay**
February	février	feh-vree-**ay**
March	mars	marce
April	avril	a-**vreel**
May	mai	meh
June	juin	zhwehn
July	juillet	zhwee-**ay**
August	août	ah-**oo**
September	septembre	sep-**tahm**-bruh
October	octobre	awk-**to**-bruh
November	novembre	no-**vahm**-bruh
December	décembre	day-**sahm**-bruh

Useful Phrases

Do you speak English?	Parlez-vous anglais?	par-lay **voo** **ahn**-glay
I don't speak . . . French	Je ne parle pas . . . français	zhuh nuh parl pah frahn-**say**
I don't understand	Je ne comprends pas	zhuh nuh kohm-**prahn** pah
I understand	Je comprends	zhuh kohm-**prahn**
I don't know	Je ne sais pas	zhuh nuh say **pah**
I'm American/ British	Je suis américain/ anglais	zhuh sweez a-may-ree-**kehn**/ahn-**glay**
What's your name?	Comment vous appelez-vous?	ko-mahn voo za-pell-ay-**voo**
My name is . . .	Je m'appelle . . .	zhuh ma-**pell** . . .
What time is it?	Quelle heure est-il?	kel air eh-**teel**
How?	Comment?	ko-**mahn**
When?	Quand?	kahn
Yesterday	Hier	yair
Today	Aujourd'hui	o-zhoor-**dwee**
Tomorrow	Demain	duh-**mehn**
This morning/ afternoon	Ce matin/cet après-midi	suh ma-**tehn**/ set ah-pray-mee-**dee**
Tonight	Ce soir	suh **swahr**
What?	Quoi?	kwah
What is it?	Qu'est-ce que c'est?	kess-kuh-**say**
Why?	Pourquoi?	**poor**-kwa

Who?	Qui?	kee
Where is . . .	Où est . . .	oo ay
the train station?	la gare?	la gar
the subway station?	la station de métro?	la sta-**syon** duh may-**tro**
the bus stop?	l'arrêt de bus?	la-**ray** duh **booss**
the terminal (airport)?	l'aérogare?	lay-ro-**gar**
the post office?	la poste?	la post
the bank?	la banque?	la bahnk
the . . . hotel?	l'hôtel . . .?	lo-**tel**
the store?	le magasin?	luh ma-ga-**zehn**
the cashier?	la caisse?	la **kess**
the . . . museum?	le musée . . .?	luh mew-**zay**
the hospital?	l'hôpital?	lo-pee-**tahl**
the elevator?	l'ascenseur?	la-sahn-**seuhr**
the telephone?	le téléphone?	luh tay-lay-**phone**
Where are the restrooms?	Où sont les toilettes?	oo sohn lay twah-**let**
Here/there	Ici/là	ee-**see**/la
Left/right	A gauche/à droite	a goash/a draht
Straight ahead	Tout droit	too drwah
Is it near/far?	C'est près/loin?	say pray/ lwehn
I'd like . . .	Je voudrais . . .	zhuh voo-**dray**
a room	une chambre	ewn **shahm**-bruh
the key	la clé	la clay
a newspaper	un journal	uhn zhoor-**nahl**
a stamp	un timbre	uhn **tam**-bruh
I'd like to buy . . .	Je voudrais acheter . . .	zhuh voo-**dray ahsh**-tay
a cigar	un cigare	uhn see-**gar**
cigarettes	des cigarettes	day see-ga-**ret**
matches	des allumettes	days a-loo-**met**
dictionary	un dictionnaire	uhn deek-see-oh-**nare**
soap	du savon	dew sah-**vohn**
city map	un plan de ville	uhn plahn de **veel**
road map	une carte routière	ewn cart roo-tee-**air**
magazine	une revue	ewn reh-**vu**
envelopes	des enveloppes	dayz ahn-veh-**lope**
writing paper	du papier à lettres	dew pa-pee-**ay** a **let**-ruh
postcard	une carte postale	ewn cart pos-**tal**

How much is it?	C'est combien?	say comb-bee-**ehn**
It's expensive/cheap	C'est cher/pas cher	say share/pa share
A little/a lot	Un peu/beaucoup	uhn peuh/bo-**koo**
More/less	Plus/moins	plu/mwehn
Enough/too (much)	Assez/trop	a-say/tro
I am ill/sick	Je suis malade	zhuh swee ma-**lahd**
Call a . . . doctor	Appelez un . . . docteur	a-play uhn dohk-**tehr**
Help!	Au secours!	o suh-**koor**
Stop!	Arrêtez!	a-reh-**tay**
Fire!	Au feu!	o fuh
Caution!/Look out!	Attention!	a-tahn-see-**ohn**

Dining Out

A bottle of . . .	une bouteille de . . .	ewn boo-**tay** duh
A cup of . . .	une tasse de . . .	ewn tass duh
A glass of . . .	un verre de . . .	uhn vair duh
Ashtray	un cendrier	uhn sahn-dree-**ay**
Bill/check	l'addition	la-dee-see-**ohn**
Bread	du pain	dew pan
Breakfast	le petit-déjeuner	luh puh-**tee** day-zhuh-**nay**
Butter	du beurre	dew burr
Cheers!	A votre santé!	ah vo-truh sahn-**tay**
Cocktail/aperitif	un apéritif	uhn ah-pay-ree-**teef**
Dinner	le dîner	luh dee-**nay**
Dish of the day	le plat du jour	luh plah dew **zhoor**
Enjoy!	Bon appétit!	bohn a-pay-**tee**
Fixed-price menu	le menu	luh may-**new**
Fork	une fourchette	ewn four-**shet**
I am diabetic	Je suis diabétique	zhuh swee dee-ah-bay-**teek**
I am on a diet	Je suis au régime	zhuh sweez oray-**jeem**
I am vegetarian	Je suis végé-tarien(ne)	zhuh swee vay-zhay-ta-ree-**en**

I cannot eat . . .	Je ne peux pas manger de . . .	zhuh nuh **puh** pah mahn-**jay** deh
I'd like to order	Je voudrais commander	zhuh voo-**dray** ko-mahn-**day**
I'm hungry/thirsty	J'ai faim/soif	zhay fahm/swahf
Is service/the tip included?	Est-ce que le service est compris?	ess kuh luh sair-**veess** ay comb-**pree**
It's good/bad	C'est bon/mauvais	say bohn/mo-**vay**
It's hot/cold	C'est chaud/froid	say sho/frwah
Knife	un couteau	uhn koo-**toe**
Lunch	le déjeuner	luh day-zhuh-**nay**
Menu	la carte	la cart
Napkin	une serviette	ewn sair-vee-**et**
Pepper	du poivre	dew **pwah**-vruh
Plate	une assiette	ewn a-see-**et**
Please give me . . .	Donnez-moi . . .	doe-nay-**mwah**
Salt	du sel	dew sell
Spoon	une cuillère	ewn kwee-**air**
Sugar	du sucre	dew **sook**-ruh
Waiter!/Waitress!	Monsieur!/ Mademoiselle!	muh-**syuh**/ mad-mwa-**zel**
Wine list	la carte des vins	la cart day an

MENU GUIDE

French	English
General Dining	
Entrée	Appetizer/Starter
Garniture au choix	Choice of vegetable side
Plat du jour	Dish of the day
Selon arrivage	When available
Supplément/En sus	Extra charge
Sur commande	Made to order
Petit Déjeuner (Breakfast)	
Confiture	Jam
Miel	Honey
Oeuf à la coque	Boiled egg
Oeufs sur le plat	Fried eggs
Oeufs brouillés	Scrambled eggs
Tartine	Bread with butter
Soupes/Potages (Soups)	
Bisque	Seafood stew
Bouillabaisse	Fish and seafood stew
Potage parmentier	Potato soup
Pot-au-feu	Stew of meat and vegetables
Ragoût	Stew
Soupe à l'oignon gratinée	French onion soup
Soupe au pistou	Provençal vegetable soup
Velouté de . . .	Cream of . . .
Vichyssoise	Cold leek and potato cream soup
Poissons/Fruits de Mer (Fish/Seafood)	
Anchois	Anchovies
Bar	Bass
Brandade de morue	Creamed salt cod
Brochet	Pike
Cabillaud/Morue	Fresh cod
Calmar	Squid
Coquilles St-Jacques	Scallops
Crevettes	Shrimp
Cuisses de grenouilles	Frogs' legs
Daurade	Sea bream
Ecrevisses	Prawns/Crayfish
Harengs	Herring
Homard	Lobster
Huîtres	Oysters
Langoustine	Prawn/Lobster
Lotte	Monkfish

Maquereau	Mackerel
Moules	Mussels
Palourdes	Clams
Raie	Skate
Rouget	Red mullet
Saumon	Salmon
Thon	Tuna
Truite	Trout

Viande (Meat)

Agneau	Lamb
Boeuf	Beef
Boudin	Sausage
Boulettes de viande	Meatballs
Brochettes	Kabobs
Cassoulet	Casserole of white beans, meat
Cervelle	Brains
Chateaubriand	Double fillet steak
Choucroute garnie	Sausages with sauerkraut
Côtelettes	Chops
Côte/Côte de boeuf	Rib/T-bone steak
Cuisses de grenouilles	Frogs' legs
Entrecôte	Rib or rib-eye steak
Épaule	Shoulder
Escalope	Cutlet
Foie	Liver
Gigot	Leg
Langue	Tongue
Médaillon	Tenderloin steak
Pieds de cochon	Pig's feet
Porc	Pork
Ris de veau	Veal sweetbreads
Rognons	Kidneys
Saucisses	Sausages
Selle	Saddle
Tournedos	Tenderloin of T-bone steak
Veau	Veal

Methods of Preparation

A point	Medium
A l'étouffée	Stewed
Au four	Baked
Ballotine	Boned, stuffed, and rolled
Bien cuit	Well-done
Bleu	Very rare
Bouilli	Boiled
Braisé	Braised
Frit	Fried
Grillé	Grilled
Rôti	Roast
Saignant	Rare
Sauté/Poêlée	Sautéed

Volailles/Gibier (Poultry/Game)

Blanc de volaille	Chicken breast
Caille	Quail
Canard/Caneton	Duck/Duckling
Cerf/Chevreuil	Venison (red/roe)
Coq au vin	Chicken stewed in red wine
Dinde/Dindonneau	Turkey/Young turkey
Faisan	Pheasant
Lapin/Lièvre	Rabbit/Wild hare
Oie	Goose
Pintade/Pintadeau	Guinea fowl/Young guinea fowl
Poulet/Poussin	Chicken/Spring chicken

Légumes (Vegetables)

Artichaut	Artichoke
Asperge	Asparagus
Aubergine	Eggplant
Carottes	Carrots
Champignons	Mushrooms
Chou-fleur	Cauliflower
Chou (rouge)	Cabbage (red)
Choux de Bruxelles	Brussels sprouts
Courgette	Zucchini
Cresson	Watercress
Epinard	Spinach
Haricots blancs/verts	White kidney/French beans
Laitue	Lettuce
Lentilles	Lentils
Oignons	Onions
Petits pois	Peas
Poireaux	Leeks
Poivrons	Peppers
Pomme de terre	Potato
Tomates	Tomatoes

Sauces and Preparations

Béarnaise	Vinegar, egg yolks, white wine, shallots, tarragon
Béchamel	White sauce
Bordelaise	Mushrooms, red wine, shallots, beef marrow
Bourguignon	Red wine, herbs
Chasseur	Wine, mushrooms, onions, shallots
Diable	Hot pepper
Forestière	Mushrooms
Hollandaise	Egg yolks, butter, vinegar
Marinière	White wine, mussel broth, egg yolks

Meunière	Brown butter, parsley, lemon juice
Périgueux	With goose or duck liver purée and truffles
Poivrade	Pepper sauce
Provençale	Onions, tomatoes, garlic

Fruits/Noix (Fruits/Nuts)

Abricot	Apricot
Amandes	Almonds
Ananas	Pineapple
Banane	Banana
Cacahouètes	Peanuts
Cassis	Blackcurrants
Cerises	Cherries
Citron/Citron vert	Lemon/Lime
Fraises	Strawberries
Framboises	Raspberries
Groseilles	Red currants
Marrons	Chestnuts
Mûres	Blackberries
Noisettes	Hazelnuts
Noix de coco	Coconut
Noix	Walnuts
Pamplemousse	Grapefruit
Pêche	Peach
Poire	Pear
Pomme	Apple
Prunes/Pruneaux	Plums/Prunes
Raisins/Raisins secs	Grapes/Raisins

Desserts

Coupe (glacée)	Sundae
Crème Chantilly	Whipped cream
Gâteau au chocolat	Chocolate cake
Glace	Ice cream
Sabayon	Egg-and-wine-based custard
Tarte tatin	Caramelized apple tart
Tourte	Layer cake

Drinks

A l'eau	With water
Avec des glaçons	On the rocks
Kir	White wine with black-currant syrup
Bière	Beer
Blonde/brune	Light/dark
Café noir/crème	Black coffee/with steamed milk
Décaféiné	*Caffeine-free*
Chocolat chaud	Hot chocolate
Eau-de-vie	Brandy
Eau minérale	Mineral water

Menu Guide

gazeuse/non gazeuse	*carbonated/still*
Jus de . . .	. . . juice
Lait	Milk
Sec	Straight or dry
Thé	Tea
au lait/au citron	*with milk/lemon*
Tisane	Herb tea
Vin	Wine
blanc	*white*
doux	*sweet*
léger	*light*
brut	*very dry*
mousseux	*sparkling*
rouge	*red*

INDEX

Icons and Symbols

★ Our special recommendations

✕ Restaurant

▦ Lodging establishment

✕▦ Lodging establishment whose restaurant warrants a special trip

🐤 Good for kids (rubber duck)

☞ Sends you to another section of the guide for more information

✉ Address

☎ Telephone number

🕐 Opening and closing times

🎟 Admission prices

Numbers in white and black circles ③ ❸ that appear on the maps, in the margins, and within the tours correspond to one another.

L@@king

@ FOR A
great place to go?

We know just the place. In fact, it attracts more
than 125,000 visitors a day, making it one of
the world's most popular travel destinations. It's
previewtravel.com, the Web's comprehensive
resource for travelers. It gives you access to
over 500 airlines, 25,000 hotels, rental cars,
cruises, vacation packages and support from
travel experts 24 hours a day. Plus great
information from Fodor's travel guides and
travelers just like you. All of which makes
previewtravel.com quite a find.

**Preview Travel has everything you
need to plan & book your next trip.**

**air, car & hotel
reservations**

**vacation packages
& cruises**

**destination planning
& travel tips**

**24-hour
customer service**

previewtravel.com

**preview
travel** ℠

aol keyword: previewtravel
www.previewtravel.com

FODOR'S PARIS 2000

EDITOR: Natasha Lesser

Editorial Contributors: Megan Beardsley, Stephen Brewer, Melisse Gelula, Simon Hewitt, Nicola Keegan, Alexander Lobrano, Christopher Mooney, Lauren Myers, Ian Phillips

Editorial Production: Tom Holton

Maps: David Lindroth, *cartographer*; Bob Blake, *map editor*

Design: Fabrizio La Rocca, *creative director*; Guido Caroti, *art director*

Picture Editor: Jolie Novak; *photo researcher:* Melanie Marin

Production/Manufacturing: Rebecca Zeiler

COPYRIGHT

Copyright © 1999 by Fodor's Travel Publications, Inc.

Fodor's is a registered trademark of Random House, Inc. All rights reserved under International and Pan-American Copyright Conventions. Published in the United States by Fodor's Travel Publications, Inc., a division of Random House, Inc., New York, and simultaneously in Canada by Random House of Canada Limited, Toronto. Distributed by Random House, Inc., New York.

No maps, illustrations, or other portions of this book may be reproduced in any form without written permission from the publisher.

ISBN 0-679-00322-3

ISSN 0149-1288

SPECIAL SALES

Fodor's Travel Publications are available at special discounts for bulk purchases for sales promotions or premiums. Special editions, including personalized covers, excerpts of existing guides, and corporate imprints, can be created in large quantities for special needs. For more information, contact your local bookseller or write to Special Markets, Fodor's Travel Publications, 201 East 50th Street, New York, NY 10022. Inquiries from Canada should be directed to your local Canadian bookseller or sent to Random House of Canada, Ltd., Marketing Department, 2775 Matheson Boulevard East, Mississauga, Ontario L4W 4P7. Inquiries from the United Kingdom should be sent to Fodor's Travel Publications, 20 Vauxhall Bridge Road, London SW1V 2SA, England.

PRINTED IN THE UNITED STATES OF AMERICA

10 9 8 7 6 5 4 3 2 1

IMPORTANT TIP

Although all prices, opening times, and other details in this book are based on information supplied to us at press time, changes occur all the time in the travel world, and Fodor's cannot accept responsibility for facts that become outdated or for inadvertent errors or omissions. So **always confirm information when it matters,** especially if you're making a detour to visit a specific place.

PHOTOGRAPHY

Cover Design: *Pentagram.*

Corbis: *Philip Gould, cover (Place des Vosges).*

Corbis Images, *3 top left, 3 top right, 3 bottom left, 8F, 26 top, 26 bottom, 27, 28 top, 28 center, 29, 30A, 30F, 30H.*

Philippe Detourbe, *30G.*

DIAF: *Jean Gabanou, 12A, 15E. G. Guittot, 19C. Rosine Mazin, 18B, 20A, 24A, 24B. Giovanni Simeone, 4–5. Daniel Thierry, 9 center, 12B, 19E.*

Christian Dior, *15F.*

Alain Ducasse: *16A. P. Hussenot, 2 top right.*

Familia Hôtel, *30B.*

Emmanuel Ferrand, *25F.*

Owen Franken, *7D, 10A, 10 bottom right, 10B, 11D, 14A, 16 top, 16 bottom, 17B, 17C, 21C, 22A, 22 bottom, 23D, 25E.*

Galeries Lafayette, *14B, 14C.*

Hôtel Caron de Beaumarchais, *30J.*

Hôtel Ritz Paris, *2 bottom center.*

Hôtel de Vendôme, *30E.*

The Image Bank: *Daniel Barbier, 6C. Alain Choisnet, 6A. Greg Christensen, 30C. Antony Edwards, 11E. Herb Hartmann, 25C. F. Hidalgo, 9H. Mahaux Photography, 18A. Marvin E. Newman, 7E, 13C, 13D, 14D, 19D, 21D, 22B. Pascal Perret, 1. Andrea Pistolesi, 11C, 32. Bernard Roussel, 9G. Harald Sund, 21E. Matthew Weinreb, 13F. Hans Wolf, 30I.*

Catherine Karnow, *13E, 17 center, 20B, 23C.*

La Tuile à Loupe, *3 bottom right.*

James Lemass, *6B, 25D.*

Le Relais Saint Germain, *30D.*

Paris Convention and Visitors Bureau: *Frédéric Buxin, 2 bottom right.*

Sonia Rykiel, *2 bottom left.*

Sebastian Sousser, *2 top left.*

ABOUT OUR WRITERS

Every Y2K trip is a significant trip. So if there was ever a time you needed excellent travel information, it's now. Acutely aware of that fact, we've pulled out all stops in preparing *Fodor's Paris*. To help you zero in on what to see in Paris, we've gathered some great color photos of key sights. To show you how to put it all together, we've created great itineraries and neighborhood walks. And to direct you to the places that are truly worth your time and money in this important year, we've rallied the team of endearingly picky know-it-alls we're pleased to call our writers. Having seen all corners of Paris, they're real experts on the subjects they cover for us. If you knew them, you'd poll them for tips yourself.

Simon Hewitt, our expert on what to see and do in Paris and environs, headed to Paris straight from studying French and art history at Oxford. It was a return to base: His grandmother was French, as are his wife and daughter. He moved to Versailles in 1996 to gain a different perspective on life in and around the French capital. When not contemplating the Sun King's bicep-flexing Baroque, he captains the French national cricket team.

Nicola Keegan was born in Ireland and raised in Iowa. But after spending one year at the Sorbonne university, she knew Paris was going to be her home forever. Now she has been there 10 years and has become an expert at finding her way around Paris. In Smart Travel Tips A to Z, she provides helpful advice to make your trip to the French capital easier.

Though **Natasha Lesser,** editor of *Paris 2000,* lived in Paris, she always finds something new and surprising no matter how many times she returns to the boulevards and back rues of this inexhaustible city. Her advice: Take time to soak in the city's atmosphere, whether that means basking in the sun on the green chairs of the Luxembourg Gardens or enjoying a glass of red wine at an outdoor café.

Alexander Lobrano has lived in Paris for 13 years, after eating his way through Boston, New York, and London. He writes a weekly dining column for *Paris Time Out,* is editor of the *Zagat Survey of Paris,* and has reported on French food and restaurants for many British and American publications, including *Departures, Food & Wine, Bon Appetit,* and *Condé Nast Traveler.* His most recent best meal in Paris? At Guy Savoy.

Christopher Mooney came to Paris to study French philosophy, smoke Gîtanes cigarettes, and hang out in cafés. Nine years later he's still there, but his taste for Gallic thought and tobacco has given way to an unslakable thirst for French wine. A born-again Epicurean, he herein devotes his efforts to finding the best accomodations in Paris.

Ian Phillips originally moved from Britain to Paris by mistake. He had applied for a job in the Mediterranean, following his dream of sailing yachts, but ended up taking Bateaux Mouches down the Seine instead. Still, he very swiftly found his way around the French capital—in his first three years there he lived in 13 different apartments. Finally he found his footing as a freelance journalist, writing on culture and fashion for publications in Paris, London, and New York.

Don't Forget to Write

We love feedback—positive and negative—and follow up on all suggestions. So contact the Paris editor at editors@ fodors.com or c/o Fodor's, 201 East 50th Street, New York, New York 10022. Have a wonderful trip!

Karen Cure

Karen Cure
Editorial Director